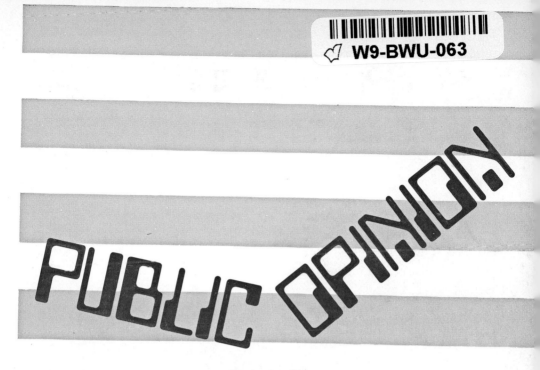

PUBLIC OPINION

ITS FORMATION, MEASUREMENT, AND IMPACT

Edited by

SUSAN WELCH
and
JOHN COMER

The University of Nebraska

Mayfield Publishing Company

Copyright © 1975 by Susan Welch and John Comer
First edition 1975

All rights reserved. No portion of this book may be reproduced in any form or by any means without written permission of the publisher.

Library of Congress Catalog Card Number: 74-33580
International Standard Book Number: 0-87484-295-6

Manufactured in the United States of America
Mayfield Publishing Company
285 Hamilton Avenue, Palo Alto, California 94301

This book was set in Times Roman by Typographic Service Company and was printed and bound by the George Banta Company. Sponsoring editor was Alden C. Paine, Carole Norton supervised editing, and Fiorella Ljunggren was manuscript editor. Michelle Hogan supervised production, the book was designed by Nancy Sears, and Jim M'Guinness designed the cover.

CONTENTS

PREFACE

The study of public opinion encompasses a constellation of incredibly diverse topics, as all who have been faced with designing a course on this subject well know. This range of topics can lead the student of public opinion from analyzing the psychological factors behind individual attitudes to identifying the sociological antecedents of mass opinion; from determining the impact of opinion on policy making to investigating the influence of political culture; from studying sampling theory and measures of mass opinion to defining the characteristics of the responsible, rational voter.

This book attempts to gather together these diverse topics within a comprehensive reader. The selections presented have been grouped in six sections, each section treating a major aspect of public opinion study: (1) the nature and scope of public opinion; (2) some salient characteristics of public opinion in the United States; (3) the psychological and sociological factors that underlie opinion; (4) the influence of society, the media, and the government on public opinion; (5) the techniques and validity of opinion measurement; (6) the impact of public opinion on policy making—what it is, what it is not, both in theory and practice.

That questions will arise concerning the choice of the selections included is inevitable. Our primary criterion for choosing the readings was that they represented a thought-provoking selection of diverse approaches and viewpoints as well as a balanced offering of "classic" statements and current research findings. The introduction to each section provides an overview of the major relevant literature, rather than a summary of the readings. We have particularly attempted to highlight the main issues and findings relevant to each topic and point out those areas where current knowledge is scanty or absent. We hope that this approach will not only help the reader fit each of the selections into the context of the overall subject matter of each section, but also provide him with a summary review of the pertinent, available research.

The editors would like to express their thanks to the authors and publishers of the selections herein and to Alden Paine of Mayfield Publishing Company for his continuing assistance in putting this book together. We would also like to thank the Department of Political Science, University of Nebraska at Lincoln, for all their clerical assistance, with a special note of gratitude to Mrs. Gladys Oakley. Alan Booth provided many helpful comments on our introductory material. Finally, as is traditional, the editors would like to blame each other for all errors and omissions found within.

PART 1

DEFINING PUBLIC OPINION

PART 1 AN OVERVIEW

Defining the term "public opinion" has been a popular and elusive pastime of political scientists for decades. The deceptive simplicity of the term dissolves upon close examination. As V.O. Key states in the first selection of this section (*see pp. 13–27*), "[t]o speak with precision of public opinion is a task not unlike coming to grips with the Holy Ghost."

The main objective of this first section is to define public opinion and to describe some of its essential characteristics. It is not facetious to assert that perhaps the major problem in trying to define the term "public opinion" is to determine what is meant by "public" and what is meant by "opinion." Let us first examine the term "public."

"PUBLIC"

When we say the President is trying to follow public opinion on a particular issue, what do we mean by "public"? The term has different meanings to different users. Certainly, as Lowell (1913) and others have suggested, unanimity is not a prerequisite for calling an opinion "public." Nor does an opinion even have to be held by a majority of the public in order to qualify as "public" opinion, for on many issues there is no majority opinion. This was the case, for example, of opinion on Vietnam. Many times members of the public were asked about which strategy they favored in Vietnam. Results often looked like this:

Table 1

Percent Preferring	*Strategy*
21%	Withdraw all troops from Vietnam immediately
25%	Withdraw all troops from Vietnam by end of 18 months
38%	Withdraw all troops from Vietnam but take as many years to do this as are needed to turn the war over to the South Vietnamese
7%	Send more troops to Vietnam and step up the fighting
9%	No opinion

SOURCE: March, 1970 poll printed in Gallup Opinion Index, Issue Number 58. Reprinted from Mueller (1973, p. 95).

Can any one of these options be said to reflect "public" opinion? The largest group (38 percent) favored holding on as long as needed; but, together, the two groups favoring withdrawal represented an even larger segment of the public (46 percent)—though they didn't agree on when to withdraw. Complicating a reading of "public opinion" on that issue were seemingly contradictory results from other polls. In April, 1970—only a month after the opinion poll reprinted in Table 1—56 percent of Americans said they favored withdrawing from Vietnam at the current pace, even if the South Vietnamese government collapsed, and only 27 percent disapproved of that course of action (Mueller, 1973, p. 95). This pair of polls is only one example of lack of majority opinion for one course of action or policy proposal, a situation that occurs frequently. Thus, if public opinion were to be interpreted as majority opinion, on many issues there would be no opinion that could be called public.

Sometimes, as Key points out, the term public opinion is used as if the "public" had a life of its own, as if it were an organized entity that had systematically reached a collective opinion (*p. 18*). Few examples in real life fit this notion. The above examples of opinion on Vietnam indicate that no collective opinion existed even on an issue which had received widespread attention over a number of years.

Students of public opinion often make a distinction between special publics and the general public. Most issues do not concern the public as a whole—the general public. But on almost all issues there are special publics: people who have a particular interest in the topic being discussed. Safety regulations in asbestos manufacturing concerns may not be of particular import to the general public, but to asbestos workers and manufacturers it is of keen interest whether the government chooses to enforce safety standards. The asbestos workers and manufacturers can be said to be members of special publics on that issue. Obviously, the composition of the general and special publics shifts from issue to issue, as different questions become salient to different sets of people. A Midwest corn and soybean grower may be part of the general public on the issue of auto emission regulation, but very much a member of a special public when the issue is farm support.

"Special publics" are themselves further subdivided. For example, on an issue concerning regulation of automobile exhaust to reduce air pollutants, there may be a number of "publics," each with a different opinion on the matter: the car manufacturers; the United Auto Workers Union leaders, members, and their families; organized environmental groups and their supporters; bureaucrats in the Environmental Control Agency and in state and local environment protection agencies, and so on.

Sometimes the term public opinion is also used to differentiate the opinion of the general public, or laymen, from opinions of elite groups—those who, by virtue of training or position, or both, may have special competence concerning an issue.[1]

These few examples illustrate that the term "public" in public opinion is used in many different ways—among them, to refer to the majority opinion, or to the opinions of different groups within the general population concerned with specific issues, or to the opinion of the mass as contrasted with the elite. None of these definitions seems both realistic and precise. In an attempt to move away from "the formation of a theoretical representation of an eerie entity called 'public opinion'," Key provides what he calls a working definition of public opinion. He states that public opinion "may be simply taken to mean those opinions held by private persons which governments find it prudent to heed," (*p. 23*). We might note that even Key's rather broad view of public opinion may be too circumscribed: are opinions 

which governments do not find it prudent to heed not public opinion? Often, in democracies as well as dictatorships, substantial segments of the public go unheeded for long periods of time; yet these opinions are certainly part of the "public" opinion.[2] We might broaden Key's definition further by simply saying that an opinion may be considered to be public when it relates to an issue or event of public concern. In this sense, the number of people holding such opinion is irrelevant. Though, clearly, if the number of people holding the opinion is trivial, the opinion is generally not subject to extensive analysis.

"Opinion"

Some social psychologists have spent a good deal of time differentiating opinions from attitudes.[3] While some feel that this distinction makes little practical difference, many draw a distinction beween attitudes, opinions and beliefs. We shall briefly analyze this question before turning to a more specific discussion of the characteristics of opinion.

Beliefs have been described as propositions or expectations about how the world behaves (Best, 1973, p. 7). To say, for example, that someone believes that the Democratic party is the best party is to say that the person believes in a certain relationship (Democratic party = best), regardless of the "truth" of such relationship (Bem, 1970). The believer needs no evidence. Belief is at the basis of attitudes and opinions, the very foundation upon which attitudes and opinions develop.

Opinions are sometimes seen as expressions of attitudes, of what Katz calls "the predisposition of the individual to evaluate some symbol or object or aspect of his world in a favorable or unfavorable manner" (1960, p. 169). Thus, some define attitudes as relatively stable in contrast to the more changeable opinions (Rosenberg, 1960). Just as often, however, the words "attitude" and "opinion" are used interchangeably.

Opinions, such as those measured in surveys, are only reflections of deeper beliefs.[4] Opinions are much more subject to change than are attitudes and beliefs. Nevertheless, when we are trying to find out what the public believes, we have largely opinions to work with.

Several characteristics of opinions are basic to an understanding of the term public opinion. These include the direction, informational content, stability, and intensity of opinion. Let us briefly describe each of these characteristics.

Direction

Direction has a rather simple meaning: on which side of an issue does an individual stand? Is his opinion in favor of the President on Watergate or opposed? An individual's opinion on any issue, then, can be characterized and compared to others in terms of direction. When we say that 22 percent of the American public feels that racial integration is going too slow and 44 percent feel that it is going too fast, with the rest having no opinion or feeling that it is "about right," we have distinguished three segments of American public by virtue of the direction (or lack of direction) of their opinions.

Informational content

Another characteristic of an individual's opinion is the extent to which the opinion is based on factual knowledge or information. Lippmann (1922) was one of the first to point out the relative lack of informational content in most opinions. People have "pictures in their heads" that are rarely challenged by first-hand exposure. Many Americans, for example, pay very little or no attention at all to news about politics. Nineteen percent of the people questioned during a national survey responded that they never follow accounts of political and governmental affairs,[5] and only about 25 percent said they followed the news regularly (Almond and Verba, 1965).

There are other indicators of this relative lack of interest in politics. When asked to name their hopes and fears, most Americans do not put political events at the top of their list. Concern with the family, health, and economic problems are those most often mentioned (Free and Cantril, 1968; Cantril and Roll, 1971). Concerns with political problems or issues such as crime, pollution, or corruption are rarely mentioned. The one exception are fear of war and hope for peace, both ranking third in order or priority (Erskine, 1973a).

This lack of interest is reflected in the low level of knowledge that Americans show about a whole variety of political issues and events, both national and international. For example, in 1964—fifteen years after the Communists had taken over—only 72 percent of the American public knew that China had a Communist government (University of Michigan, Survey Research Center, 1964), and by 1968 the informed group had risen only to 76 percent (Survey Research Center). Only one-third of Americans can name the United States senators from their state, but most of the public know the capital city of the United States, the President, the presidential term, and the governor of their state.[6] In other words, most Americans, though not completely ignorant of politics and government, are not knowledgeable about the specifics of issues and events.[7]

Another, and predictable, result of the lack of interest in public issues displayed by most Americans is the remarkably large number of people who hold no opinions at all on such issues. At the height of the ABM debate, 41 percent had no opinion about ABM; 40 percent of the public in 1964 were without opinions as to whether China should be admitted to the

United Nations, years after the question first became a matter of public debate. Even on several controversial questions relating to domestic issues that affect directly the lives of the people, such as racial integration, government job guarantees, and health care, about 20 percent of the public has no opinion (Erickson and Luttbeg, 1973, pp. 26–28).

Stability

We have noted above that attitudes and beliefs are more stable than opinions. But the expressions that we label "opinions" range widely in terms of stability, some showing remarkable stability over time, others subject to great fluctuation. Expressions of one's party preference change very little over time (Converse, 1964): they are among the most stable of "opinions."[38] Further, research on presidential election campaigns reveals that only a minority change their presidential preference during a campaign (Campbell, et al., 1964, p. 91). In spite of vast attempts through the media and personal campaigning to sway opinion, between 65 and 75 percent of the voters apparently have their minds made up before the conventions are over, while only around 10 percent decide in the last weeks of the campaign.

Other types of stable opinion are those dealing with major issues in American politics that persist over long periods of time. Opinions concerning government-provided health care, government aid to education, foreign aid, regulations against discrimination in public accommodations, are a few examples of highly stable issues. However, public opinion is measured by polls, and polls can only indicate the stability of aggregate opinions. They reveal nothing about whether individual opinion fluctuates over time since in most public opinion polls different people are queried for each poll. There is therefore no way to know if *individual* opinions remained constant. However, in 1956, 1958, and 1960, the University of Michigan's Survey Research Center conducted surveys in which the *same* people were interviewed at each time period. These researchers found that on any given issue only about a 65 percent majority would express the same opinion in 1958 as they did in 1956 (Converse, 1964; 1970).[9] This shift in individual opinion might have meant that voters were learning about the issues and rationally changing their minds. However, Converse found that almost half of those people who responded in favor of foreign aid in 1956, but against it in 1958, changed their mind again in 1960. This would seem to indicate that a large number of people have very unstable opinions. Instead of being converted to a new opinion in 1958 (and thus presumably sticking with it in 1960), they simply wobbled back and forth. This, of course, is partly an outcome of limited information and interest on the part of many who responded. Converse (1964; 1970) estimates that only about 20 percent of the public have meaningful, and therefore presumably stable, opinions on abstract issues, such as government involvement in the economy. Other findings tend to support the notion that on fundamental opinions about whether the government is trustworthy, responsive to the average person, overly complex, and so forth, most individuals have no stable opinion (Welch and Clark, 1974).

Of course, some opinion trends show real (as contrasted with random) change over time. The third article of this section (*pp. 49–62*) represents a specific and concrete illustration of some of these changes. Greeley and Sheatsley discuss how attitudes toward racial integration have changed dramatically over the last three decades, with positions that formerly had only minority support now no longer at issue (blacks eating at same restaurants as whites, for example). Overall support for integration has increased steadily over this time period.[10] Support for admitting China to the United Nations and support for abolishing capital punishment are other examples of real change (increases in this case) in public attitudes over time (Erskine, 1970; 1971).

On the whole, then, individual opinion on political events and objects is stable over time only in a small range of instances (political party affiliation and on some major long-term social issues). Individual public opinion on many ordinary and sometimes major political issues seem to be weakly held and subject to fluctuation.

Intensity

Another basic characteristic of opinion, intensity, is simply a measure of the individual's involvement in an issue. Some people feel very strongly about a particular issue, while others may not really care much one way or another. In the first instance, we say that an opinion is characterized by high intensity; in the second, by low intensity.

There are many reasons why a person might feel intensely about a public issue. One is that the issue affects the person directly, or affects groups of which he is a member or with which he identifies. For example, one would expect that college students would hold more intense opinions about issues of coed dormitory visitation or government scholarships than would the general public. Naturally, if an issue affecting a person directly or closely is also a threat, the intensity of that person's opinion will be higher in proportion to the degree of threat. This factor explains in part the different levels of intensity in the feelings about racial matters, particularly with regard to housing, education, and jobs in different segments of the population (*see Greeley and Sheatsley* and also Key, 1961, pp. 225–226).

Another factor that may produce high intensity of opinion relates to issues about which the individual is well informed. Finally, and of particular importance here, a high level of interest and involvement in politics is generally accompanied by high-intensity opinion. Key (1961, p. 226) illustrates this point by showing that those with high concern about politics in general tend to express intense opinions on a wide variety of specific issues, from school integration to aid to neutrals. Further, people who participate in politics generally have higher intensity of opinion levels than those who do not participate (Key, 1961, p. 230).

An interesting and perhaps significant characteristic of intense opinions is that they tend to be extreme opinions. It is to this characteristic and to patterns of intensity in public opinion that Lane and Sears address themselves in the second selection of this section (*see pp. 28–48*). They are concerned with what kinds of distributions of intensity and direction are conducive to democracy. They, as well as others, have come to the conclusion that the uninvolved and the apathetic contribute to democratic stability by providing a setting in which extreme points of view can be compromised because most people don't care much one way or another. However, apathy and noninvolvement cannot extend too far. A population characterized by apathy and indifference as the modal orientation toward politics may not long remain a democracy, for in that situation leaders are under little constraint to act in accordance with popular wishes.[11] The linkage between public opinion and policy making will be covered in much greater detail in Section VI of this book.

ENDNOTES

1. Students of public opinion have long been interested in the effect education and certain marks of status or responsibility have on an individual's opinion (see Bryce, 1900). Recent researchers have found significant differences between the opinions of the elites and those of the general public (McClosky, 1964; Stouffer, 1955).

2. One can also argue that opinions governments don't heed at one point in time, may be later heeded or may have some subtle impact on government policy. For example, the early "dovish" opinion on Vietnam was not heeded in 1964, but certainly had an impact on later events. This, of course, does not negate the fact that there are indeed some opinions that government does not heed.

3. Readers who would like to explore this topic, should consult Katz, 1960; Rosenberg, 1960; and Bem, 1970.

4. See Section V for an analysis of some of the problems related to measuring opinions.

5. There is some evidence, though, that Americans pay more attention to political issues and news than the citizens of many other nations (Almond and Verba, 1965; Converse and Dupeux, 1962, p. 6). For example, a survey revealed that 32 percent of the British, 25 percent of the Germans, 4 percent of the Mexicans, and 62 percent of the Italians never follow accounts of political affairs (Almond and Verba, 1965).

6. Erickson and Luttbeg, 1973, present an excellent up-to-date picture of the information levels of the United States population.

7. Surveys researchers who are trying to measure public opinion take pains to filter out the completely uninformed, in an attempt to get a fairly accurate picture of public sentiment on a given issue. Since some people, perhaps in an effort to be polite or to appear knowledgeable, will offer an opinion on a topic about which they have not even heard, surveyors will often ask "filter" questions. In the early years of the Vietnam war, one such question was, "Have you been paying attention to what is going on in Vietnam?" Recently, another example of a filter question was, "Have you read or heard about the Watergate crisis?" Only after an affirmative response to the filter question or questions, would the interviewers go ahead with the substantive questions, such as, "What should we do in Vietnam?" or "What is your opinion about the Watergate hearings?"

8. Party identification represents a relatively constant orienting force toward a wide variety of other political issues.

9. About one-half would express the same opinion simply by chance.

10. Attitudes toward interracial marriage and dating, though, have not changed much (Erskine, 1973b).

11. On the other hand, apathy and noninvolvement do not always go hand in hand. Key (1961) found, for example, that many people combined high levels of intensity about politics with lack of active involvement, and wondered what this portended for democratic stability. More recent research has revealed the coexistence of high-intensity opinions with feelings of helplessness in ghettos and other underprivileged sectors of the population (Zurcher, 1970; Parenti, 1970).

REFERENCES AND FURTHER READING

Almond, Gabriel A., and Verba, Sidney. *The Civic Culture: Political Attitudes and Democracy in Five Nations.* Boston: Little, Brown & Co., 1965.

Bem, Daryl J. *Beliefs, Attitudes, and Human Affairs.* Monterey, Ca.: Brooks/Cole, 1970.

Best, James. *Public Opinion.* Homewood, Ill.: Dorsey Press, 1973.

Bryce, James. *The American Commonwealth.* New York: 1900.

Campbell, Angus, et al. *The American Voter.* New York: John Wiley & Sons, 1964.

Cantril, Albert H., and Roll, Charles W. *The Hopes and Fears of the American People.* New York: Universe Books, 1971.

Converse, Philip E. "The Nature of Belief Systems in Mass Publics." In *Ideology and Discontent,* edited by David E. Apter. New York: Free Press, 1964.

Converse, Philip E. "Attitudes and Non-Attitudes: Continuation of a Dialogue." In *Quantitative Analysis of Social Problems,* edited by Edward R. Tufte. Reading, Mass.: Addison-Wesley, 1970.

Converse, Philip E., and Dupeux, George. "The Politicization of the Electorate in France and the U.S." *Public Opinion Quarterly* 26 (1962): 1–23.

Erickson, Robert, and Luttbeg, Norman. *American Public Opinion: Its Origins, Content and Impact.* New York: John Wiley & Sons, 1973.

Erskine, Hazel. "The Polls: Capital Punishment." *Public Opinion Quarterly* 34 (1970): 291–296.

Erskine, Hazel. "The Polls: Red China and the U.N." *Public Opinion Quarterly* 35 (1971): 125–137.

Erskine, Hazel. "The Polls: Hopes, Fears, Regrets." *Public Opinion Quarterly* 37 (1973a): 132–245.

Erskine, Hazel. "The Polls: Interracial Socializing." *Public Opinion Quarterly* 37 (1973b): 283–294.

Free, Lloyd A., and Cantril, Hadley. *The Political Beliefs of Americans: A Study of Public Opinion*. New York: Simon & Schuster, 1968.

Greeley, Andrew M., and Sheatsley, Paul B. "Attitudes toward Racial Integration." *Scientific American* 225 (December 1971): 13–19.

Katz, Daniel. "The Functional Approach to the Study of Attitudes." *Public Opinion Quarterly* 24 (1960): 163–204.

Key, V. O., Jr. *Public Opinion and American Democracy*. New York: Alfred A. Knopf, 1961.

Lane, Robert E., and Sears, David O. *Public Opinion*. Englewood Cliffs, N.J.: Prentice-Hall, 1964.

Lippmann, Walter. *Public Opinion*. New York: Macmillan, 1922.

Lowell, A. Lawrence. *Public Opinion and Popular Government*. New York: Longmans, Green, 1913.

McClosky, Herbert. "Consensus and Ideology in American Politics." *American Political Science Review* 58 (1964): 361–382.

Mueller, John E. *War, Presidents and Public Opinion*. New York: John Wiley & Sons, 1973.

Parenti, Michael. "Power and Pluralism: A View from the Bottom." *Journal of Politics* 32 (1970): 501–530.

Rokeach, Milton. *Beliefs, Attitudes, and Values: A Theory of Organization and Change*. San Francisco: Jossey-Bass, 1970.

Rosenberg, Milton., et al. *Attitude Organization and Change: An Analysis of Consistency among Attitude Components*. New Haven: Yale University Press, 1960.

Stouffer, Samuel A. *Communism, Conformity and Civil Liberties*. New York: John Wiley & Sons, 1955.

Welch, Susan, and Clark, Cal. "Political Efficacy as an Underlying Political Orientation: The Problem of Attitudinal Instability." Paper delivered at the Midwest Political Science Association Meeting, Chicago, Illinois, 1974.

Zurcher, Louis A., Jr. "The Poverty Board: Some Consequences of Maximum Feasible Participation." *Journal of Social Issues* 26 (1970): 85–107.

From *Public Opinion and American Democracy,* by V. O. Key, Jr. Copyright © 1961 by V. O. Key, Jr. Reprinted by permission of Alfred A. Knopf, Inc.

An Introduction to *Public Opinion and American Democracy*

V. O. KEY, JR.

Governments must concern themselves with the opinions of their citizens, if only to provide a basis for repression of disaffection. The persistent curiosity, and anxiety, of rulers about what their subjects say of them and of their actions are chronicled in the histories of secret police. Measures to satisfy such curiosity by soundings of opinion are often only an aspect of political persecution; they may also guide policies of persuasion calculated to convert discontent into cheerful acquiescence. And even in the least democratic regime opinion may influence the direction or tempo of substantive policy. Although a government may be erected on tyranny, to endure it needs the ungrudging support of substantial numbers of its people. If that support does not arise spontaneously, measures will be taken to stimulate it by tactical concessions to public opinion, by the management of opinions, or by both.[1]

POWER AND PUBLIC OPINION

The incubation and gradual spread of the ideas of democracy radically altered expectations about the relations between the views of the citizenry and the acts of its rulers. In early times governments found legitimacy for their authority in various sources—from divine right on down—but rarely did they place much store on the consent of the governed. The citizen's duty was to obey. Gradually over several centuries, from small beginnings in medieval towns to the American and French Revolutions, these rationalizations of authority were revised to ground the right to govern in the consent of the governed. The percolation of this idea into the mind of man generated an ethical imperative that gave a new color to the relations of governors and governed. The dynasties of Europe learned from Napoleon that they had to take into account the wishes of the governed in order to maintain their power, but the democratic doctrine assumed this to be a condition of governing rightly. In the nineteenth century the struggles for suffrage expansion and for parliamentary government led to the establishment of institutions appropriate to the belief that the mass of the people should in some way participate in the great decisions of state and thereby govern themselves. The bundle of ideas, beliefs, and emotions connected with this view had an appeal so universal and so powerful that modern dictatorships took over much of the symbolism, ritual, and semantics of democracy.

Progressivism and the efflorescence of faith in the public

The ethical imperative that government heed the opinion of the public has its origins, thus, in democratic ideology as well as in the practical necessity that governments obtain the support of influential elements in society. The notion of government by public opinion, nourished on memories of government as exploitation of the mass of men by a few men, stirred millennial hopes of a lasting popular emancipation. By the enthronement of public opinion, governors could be brought to heel and the supposedly idealistic hopes of all men could be realized. Through the history of American political thought these ideas have flowed—at times thinly, as disillusionment set in; at times in flood, as democratic idealism flourished. Democratic hopes and expectations reached a great peak in the United States in the years before World War I, when the doughty Progressives fought their battles against privilege and preached the righteousness of the popular will. To see that the popular will prevailed, they contrived no end of means to involve the people in the process of government. Not only were officials to be elected; they were to be subject to recall by the voters. Legislators, long subservient to special interests, were to find themselves subject to a popular veto through a referendum on their acts. Or the people were to be free to take matters into their own hands and to initiate legislative action through the new instruments of direct democracy. The courts, regarded as the sturdiest bastion of the special interests, were to be subjected to the humiliation of a popular review of their constitutional decisions.

Disenchantment: Mr. Lippmann and the straw man

This heightened faith in the people proved to be a momentary exaltation, and it was dimmed, if not snuffed out, as Wilsonian idealism declined in the aftermath of World War I. In 1922 Walter Lippmann published his *Public Opinion,* in which he reappraised the function of public opinion in the democratic process. The years of Harding and Coolidge were not times to inspire high hopes in the future of the human race, and in 1925 Mr. Lippmann issued *The Phantom Public,* a volume whose title put more bluntly than did its argument a thesis severely deflating the role of the public.

What Mr. Lippmann did was to destroy a straw man. He did it thoroughly nonetheless. He refuted the more extravagant beliefs about the role of the average man in self-governance by citation of a few cold, hard facts. Whether these beliefs had ever been held save in the autointoxication of political oratory directed to the average man may be doubted. Yet Mr. Lippmann demolished whatever illusion existed that "the public" could be regarded as an omnicompetent and omniscient collectivity equipped to decide the affairs of state. The average person, Mr. Lippmann made clear, had little time for the affairs of state. He exhausted his energies earning a livelihood, and, once home from work, he was likely to take off his shoes and indulge his feet as he looked at the comics rather than to attempt to inform himself on the intricate pros and cons of the weighty matters currently confounding Washington. Even if he were willing to devote his spare time to the study of public issues, the information available to him was both inadequate and unenlightening. The newspapers of that day were no more dedicated to the clarification of public issues than are those of the present. Nor was the amorphous public, even if informed, capable of taking the initiative in any public action.[2]

The new Machiavellians: Barnums and cabals

Blows from other sources also battered the idyllic vision of the guidance of affairs by the opinions of a virtuous public. In the decades after World War I belief in the ability of propagandists to manipulate public attitudes grew apace. New theories of psychology brought new conceptions of the nature of man, conceptions that made him a nonrational creature of subconscious urges and external suggestion. During World War I itself the propagandists took great strides in the development of their art. The belief that the people could readily be manipulated by the mass media became even more widely held later as radio and television attracted vast audiences. Propagandists and advertising men encouraged the acceptance of the most exaggerated estimates of their powers. Given enough money, they could sell soap, cigarettes, policies, presidential candidates, even monstrous and nonfunctional automobiles. As a group at bottom professionally dedicated to the dissemination of falsehood (we need not think so obvious a fact), the advertising fraternity had few inhibitions against the propagation of myths that inflated its own capabilities. Eventually the image of public opinion as an irresistible giant yielded to the image of the all-powerful opinion manipulators, engineers of consent and molders of mass opinion.

Obviously no conception of American politics that placed at the apex of power advertising men and public-relations counselors—insecure, ulcer-ridden hucksters—could satisfy for long. A more elegant theory of politics was needed. Mr. C. Wright Mills brought the theoretical evolution full circle in the 1950's as he expounded the role and function of the "power elite." Behind all the constitutional trappings and the self-important activities of most politicians and other front men, he thought he perceived a clique of the big rich, the corporate bosses, the military brass, and a few key politicians. By their consultations and maneuvers this group, if we may caricature Mr. Mills—and he invites caricature—fixes the principal lines of national policy. Behind them trail the lesser men: the press, the radio and TV, and the minor politicians. Then in due course the public tags along.[3]

New situational limits to public opinion

Without doubt the conditions affecting the relations between government and public opinion have been radically altered during the past half-century. The means for informing and influencing the public have undergone a transformation. With the concentration in large corporations, in labor unions, and in other organizations of the powers of private decision formerly widely dispersed has come a parallel concentration of the power of autonomous political decision into relatively fewer hands. With the growth in range of governmental functions and the increase in their complexity, the average man is, or at least is said to be, more and more bewildered, or repelled, by questions of public policy. With the movement of decision to Washington and with the growth in salience of foreign policy questions, matters of public policy are less and less intimately relevant to the experience and knowledge of most people. With the extension of the curtain of secrecy over wider areas, the public is denied information and thereby the opportunity for meaningful criticism of public policy.

Despite all these developments, it is too early to conclude that governments can ignore public opinion or that democratic government amounts only to a hoax, a ritual whose performance serves only to delude the people and thereby to convert them into willing subjects of the powers that be. The most superficial comparison of American public policy in 1900 and in 1960 indicates that there have been changes of no little consequence for the average man. Not all these policy innovations have been willed by a power elite of 100 or 200 persons; nor have they been entirely unconnected with mass sentiment. Unless mass views have some place in the shaping of policy, all the talk about democracy is nonsense. As Lasswell has said, the "open interplay of opinion and policy is the distinguishing mark of popular rule."[4] Yet the sharp definition of the role of public opinion as it affects different kinds of policies under different types of situations presents an analytical problem of extraordinary difficulty. That problem, however, should not lead us to ignore, or to deny, the phenomenon of the conduct of enormous governmental operations in a manner that by and large wins the support of a citizenry of millions and is in the main in accord with their preferences. Given control of the apparatus of authority, to govern is easy; but to govern without heavy reliance on the machinery of coercion is a high art.

CONCEPTIONS AND DISTINCTIONS

Among philosophers, publicists, and spare-time commentators on public affairs, the discussion of public opinion is conducted with style. Aphorisms, epigrams, axioms, and figures embellish the verbal display. One can, with Pascal, christen public opinion the "Queen of the World." One can observe, with the authors of *The Federalist*, that "all government rests on opinion" or, with Hume, that it is "on opinion only that government is founded." One can assert that governments derive their powers from the "consent of the governed" or can picture public opinion as "a giant who is fickle and ignorant yet still has a giant's strength, and may use it with frightful effect."[5]

Such metaphors serve principally to ornament prose rather than to enlighten the reader about the nature of public opinion. Yet the discussion of public opinion becomes murky when meticulous scholars try to define their conceptions and to form distinctions that enable them to make statements that seem to fit the observable realities of the interaction of public opinion and government. This murkiness by no means flows solely from the incomprehensibility of men of learning. To speak with precision of public opinion is a task not unlike coming to grips with the Holy Ghost. Public opinion, Leiserson notes, "has come to refer to a sort of secular idol, and is a 'god-term' to which citizens, scientists, and office-holders alike pay allegiance, partly as an act of faith, partly as a matter of observation, partly as a condition of sanity."[6] Nevertheless, a brief review of some of the conceptions and distinctions that have been developed by scholars in their discussions of the topic should be of value as an aid in orientation.

Public as organic entity

Some speculators on public opinion have imagined the public to be a semi-organized entity that in some way or another could move through stages of initiation and debate and reach a recognizable collective decision on an issue. The images of the city-state and of the New England town meeting often color such attempts to form a conception of the reality of public opinion in the modern state. The intricate structure of the nation-state cannot easily be grasped, and some students seek in the processes of opinion formation the equivalent of the citizenry gathered in the town hall or in the market place to discuss, debate, and settle public issues. In its simplest form this analogous thinking personifies the public: "The public expects"; "The public demands"; "Public opinion swept away all opposition."[7] Perhaps a comparable conception is concealed in the assertion that public opinion "is a deeply persuasive organic force," which "articulates and formulates not only the deliberative judgments of the rational elements within the collectivity but the evanescent common will, which somehow integrates and momentarily crystallizes the sporadic sentiments and loyalties of the masses of the population."[8]

Some observers, in their search for a conception to encompass the public opinion process as a whole, produce statements more complex than the town-meeting analogy but not fundamentally different in kind. An image emerges of a rudimentary organism consisting of individuals and groups linked together by mass communications, which centers its attention on an issue, discusses and deliberates, and in some mysterious way proceeds to a decision. A public becomes a social entity, different from a mob and not the same as a mass. Thus, Young notes that "in terms of stability and degree of institutionalization, . . . a public is a transitory, amorphous, and relatively unstructured association of individuals with certain interests in common."[9] From the conception of the "public" as a social entity it is but a short step to the attempt to identify some pattern of actions or behavior through which the entity travels to reach decision or to form public opinion on an issue. Analysis in such terms is called the study of the dynamics of opinion formation, in contrast with the study of opinion as static (or at a moment in time). On occasion the process is likened to individual action in response to a problem. "Public opinion then becomes a form of group thinking, and the process bears more than an analogous relation to the individual's complete act of thought."[10] Or a sequence of steps is suggested as a standard pattern through which the public moves in the formation of opinion—for example, the rise of an issue, discussion and deliberation, and arrival at a decision.[11]

More is lost than is gained in understanding by the organismic view of the public. Occasionally, in relatively small communities, citizen concern and involvement over an issue may be widespread and community consideration may move in close articulation with the mechanisms of authority to a decision that can realistically be said to be a decision by public opinion. At far rarer intervals great national populations may be swept by a common concern about a momentous issue with a similar result. Yet ordinarily a decision is made not by the public but by officials after greater or a lesser consideration of the opinion of the public or of parts of the public.

Special publics and the general public

While the organismic conceptions of the public and of the opinion process may be of more poetic than practical utility, other distinctions developed by students of public opinion serve as handy aids to thought on the subject. There is, for example, the distinction between special publics and the general public. At one time it was the custom to speak of "the public." In due course it became evident that on only a few questions did the entire citizenry have an opinion. The notion of special publics was contrived to describe those segments of the public with views about particular issues, problems, or other questions of public concern. In actual politics one issue engages the attention of one subdivision of the population, while another arouses the interest of another group, and a third question involves still another special public. This distinction between general and special publics does, of course, do violence to the basic idea that "the" public shall prevail; it also warps the meaning of the term "public." Yet the usage mirrors the facts of political life and, incidentally, creates a problem for the public opinion theorist. He sometimes copes with the difficulty by the assertion that when the concern of a small special public prevails, it does so with the tacit consent of the general public.

Blumer deals in a different way with the problem created by the existence of special publics. He remarks that public opinion may be "different from the opinion of any of the groups in the public. It can be thought of, perhaps, as a composite opinion formed out of the several opinions that are held in the public; or better, as the central tendency set by the striving of these separate opinions and, consequently, as being shaped by the relative strength and play of opposition among them."[12] Blumer thus brings together the opinions of the special publics into something of a weighted average that takes into account both the numbers holding different kinds of opinions (or no opinion) and the strength of the holders of opinion. Whether this notion has validity, the question of who has what kind of opinion is of basic significance in a consideration of interactions between public and government.

Public and private opinion

There are opinions and opinions; their number is as numerous as the kinds of objects about which men have preferences and beliefs. On what range of topics may opinion be considered to be public? Not all opinions of the public, even when widely held within the population, are to be properly regarded as public opinion. It may be assumed that opinions about the desirability of tailfins on Chevrolets are not public opinions, or that preferences for striped or solid white toothpaste fall outside the concern of the student of public opinion. On the other hand, opinion about the length of automobile tailfins may become public opinion if the question becomes one of whether the length of nonfunctional automobile ornamentation has become a public nuisance by its pressure on the available parking acreage. Goldhamer suggests that an opinion is public "if it attaches to an object of public concern."[13] The content of the phrase, "object of public concern," may vary from time to time with the changing scope of governmental action, or it may differ from society to society.

Many American students of public opinion have limited themselves to a narrow range of public opinion; they have tended to regard public opinion as concerned with substantive issues of public policy. That focus results from the basic tenet that public opinion should determine public policy, but it excludes a range of opinions of undoubted political relevance. Opinions about candidates, views about political parties, attitudes about the performance of governments, basic assumptions about what is right and proper in public affairs, and general beliefs and expectations about the place of government in society are also opinions of political relevance, as would be such opinions or states of mind as are embraced by the term "national morale."

Characteristics of public opinion

The differentiation between opinions about public objects and about private objects crudely defines the outer limits of the opinion sphere that may be regarded as public. It leaves untouched the question of the characteristics of public opinion. In recent decades considerable scholarly effort has been devoted, principally by social psychologists, to ascertaining the characteristics of public opinion. In an earlier day the practice was to treat the direction of opinion in simple pro and con categories. The majority could be described as for or against, as voting yes or no. The psychometricians have made it clear that a pro-and-con categorization of opinion often conceals wide gradations in opinion. They have contrived scales to measure opinion in its dimension of direction. For example, a division of people who support and oppose government ownership of industry does not provide a useful indication of the nature of public opinion on the question of government policy toward economic activity. Views on economic policy may be arranged along a scale from the extreme left to the extreme right. The opinion of an individual may be located at any one of many points along such a scale. One person may favor governmental ownership of all the means of production; another may be satisfied with a large dose of governmental regulation; still another may prefer only the most limited control of the economy; and others may wish to abolish whatever controls exist. The determination of the distribution of the population along such scales measuring the direction of opinion makes possible a more informed estimate of the nature of public opinion, in its dimension of direction, than did earlier and cruder conceptions.

Closely related to the conception of direction of opinion are ideas about the qualities or properties of opinion. Intensity of opinion is one of these qualities. A person may be an extreme conservative or radical on the scale of direction of opinion, but he may care a great deal, a little, or scarcely at all about that opinion; that is, opinions may vary in the intensity with which they are held. Obviously the incidence of opinion intensity within the electorate about an issue or problem is of basic importance for politics. An issue that arouses only opinion of low intensity may receive only the slightest attention, while one that stirs opinions of high intensity among even relatively small numbers of people may be placed high on the governmental agenda. Another quality of opinion of some importance is its stability. An individual, for example, may have a view, expressed on the basis of little or no information, which may readily be changed. On the other hand, an opinion may be so firmly held that it is not easily altered. Issues that relate to opinions of high stability widely held within the population present radically different problems for government than do those matters on which opinion is unstable.

Students of public opinion often differentiate between opinion and custom. Utilizing this distinction, public opinion concerns those issues whose solution is not more or less automatically provided by custom or by the expectations shared predominantly by members of the group. Public opinion, then, concerns live issues. Park said that public opinion emerges when action is in process; it is opinion "before it has been capitalized and, so to speak, funded in the form of dogma, doctrine, or law."[14] The exclusion from public opinion of the settled attitudes of the community unduly narrows the meaning of the term. Governments must pay heed to the mores, the customs, the "funded" or the "standing" opinions quite as much as to the effervescence of today's popular discussion. The distinction between opinion and custom really amounts to a differentiation between qualities of opinions.

Prerequisites for the existence of public opinion

Students of public opinion have also sought to identify those broad conditions under which public opinion could sensibly be said to exist as a force in government. Democratic theorists that they were, they specified democratic conditions as a prerequisite for even the existence of public opinion. Freedom of speech and discussion, for example, are said to be prerequisites, since it is by public discussion that opinion is formed. Closely associated with this condition is that of the free availability of information about public issues and public questions; those problems handled by government in secrecy can scarcely be a subject of informed public debate.

Opinion theorists almost uniformly place emphasis on the importance of the existence of a consensus on fundamentals as a basis for the settlement of the differences involved in the development of a prevailing opinion on transient issues. Otherwise, government cannot be founded upon public opinion. "There is," says MacIver, "no public opinion unless an area of common ground lies underneath and supports the differences of opinion, finding expression in the traditions and conventions and behavior patterns characteristic of the folk."[15] Similarly, Park argued that there needs to be within a public "a general understanding and a community of interest among all parties sufficient to make discussion possible."[16]

In keeping with this general vein of thought, Lowell sharply restricted the content of the term "public opinion." In his system the views of people generally on public questions of all sorts did not constitute public opinion. For a "real" public opinion to exist, it had to be a community opinion. Thus, when two highwaymen meet a traveler on a dark road and propose to relieve him of his wallet, it would be incorrect to say that a public opinion existed favorable to a redistribution of property. Public opinion, Lowell thought, need not be a unanimous opinion, but it should create an "obligation moral or political on the part of the minority," an obligation, at least under certain conditions, to submit. He laid great stress on the grounds of consensus as a basis for public opinion. "A body of men are politically capable of a public opinion only so far as they are agreed upon the ends and aims of government and upon the principles by which those ends shall be attained." No public opinion could exist in nations with large minorities unwilling to abide by majority decision. Moreover, public opinion could exist only when "the bulk of the people are in a position to determine of their own knowledge or by weighing a substantial part of the facts required for a rational decision," or when the question involves an issue of "apparent harmony or contradiction with settled convictions."[17]

It seems clear that consensus does not have to prevail for opinions to exist to which governments must accord weight. Yet the emphasis on consensus identifies special problems in governments that accord deference to public opinion. If the public is to project its opinions into public policy, some sectors of the public must be prepared to accept actions distasteful to them. The limits of the general consensus may fix the limits within which widespread participation in public affairs may lead to decisions distasteful yet acceptable to those whose opinions do not prevail.

A WORKING VIEW OF PUBLIC OPINION

For purposes of political analysis one need not strain painfully toward the formation of a theoretical representation of an eerie entity called "public opinion." One need not seek to find "the" public embodied in some kind of amorphous social structure that goes through recurring patterns of action as it reaches a decision. "Public opinion" in this discussion may simply be taken to mean those opinions held by private persons which governments find it prudent to heed. Governments may be compelled toward action or inaction by such opinion; in other instances they may ignore it, perhaps at their peril; they may attempt to alter it; or they may divert or pacify it. So defined, opinion may be shared by many or by few people. It may be the veriest whim, or it may be a settled conviction. The opinion may represent a general agreement formed after the widest discussion; it may be far less firmly founded. It may even be contingent opinion—that is, estimates by decision makers of probable responses to actions they consider taking. Whatever the character or distribution of opinion, governments may need to estimate its nature as an incident to many of their actions."[18] Probably any regime needs to heed at least some opinions outside the government; yet the range of opinions that enter into the calculations of governors obviously varies among societies with their political norms and customs.

This view of public opinion resembles the conceptions of several other commentators. Speier defines, for the purposes of historical analysis, "public opinion" as "opinions on matters of concern to the nation freely and publicly expressed by men outside the government who claim a right that their opinions should influence or determine the actions, personnel, or structure of their government."[19] Wirth observed that the "decisive part of public opinion, then, is the organization of views on issues that exercise an impact upon those who are in a position to make decisions."[20] In the context of a criticism of those pollsters who regard all the responses obtained by their interviewers as public opinion, Blumer remarks that "the character of public opinion in terms of meaningful operation must be sought in the array of views and positions which enter into the consideration of those who have to take action on public opinion."[21]

Virtues and consequences of a broad view of opinion

The adoption of a broad, and somewhat vague, conception of public opinion has consequences for a general survey of the field. While it permits an avoidance of some analytical problems, it also brings within the range of the discussion an extremely wide variety of phenomena. When public opinion is regarded as those opinions that may influence government, it is unnecessary to assume that the "public" exists as any particular sort of loosely structured association or other ghostly sociological entity. On a given question the operative public may consist of a highly structured association, while on another matter opinions may be diffused through a wide public that lacks any special organization. The form of the public concerned about subsidies to maritime shipping could plausibly be expected to differ radically from that of the public concerned about honesty in public office. On one issue the public may consist of one sector of the population; on another, of a quite different sector. Not much overlap would be expected between those deeply interested in policy toward upland game and those concerned about practices in the licensing of plumbers. Or publics may be differentiated by the nature of their involvement in public questions. Almond speaks of the "mass public" and the "attentive public." The mass public, informed by the mass media, pays heed to the tone of discussion of issues and responds by moods of apprehension or complacency. The attentive public, a far smaller group, follows public issues in an analytical manner, is relatively well informed, and constitutes a critical audience for the discussion of public affairs.[22]

To emphasize, in the definition of opinion, relevance for government is to bring opinions with widely varying properties or qualities within our range of concern. Lowell limited opinion to "the acceptance of one among two or more inconsistent views which are capable of being accepted by a rational mind as true."[23] By "opinion" Young means "a belief or conviction more verifiable and stronger in intensity than a mere hunch or impression but less strong than truly verifiable or positive knowledge."[24] Under the present conception no such restricted view of opinion is necessary. Lightly held views and transient anxieties, prejudices, preferences, demands, and convictions all have their relevance for governmental action. Nor need the common distinction between opinion and the mores exclude a set of attitudes from our range of interest. Some students of public opinion conclude that they need to concern themselves only with those contentious issues about which opinion is in process of formation and that settled matters—the mores, the enduring attitudes, the customs—are beyond their purview. Although these distinctions between types of citizen outlook are analytically useful, governments must take both kinds of views into account. The prescriptions of custom may control particular actions; particular actions may aim to modify custom, an objective best undertaken after reflection about the probable public response.

These comments on the qualities of "opinion" bring within the limits of that term a considerable range of views—from whim to conviction to custom—but the term acquires an even broader connotation by mention of the objects about which opinion may be considered "public." The most common assumption is that public opinion concerns issues of substantive policy; yet our emphasis on opinions to which governments need to pay heed requires attention to opinions about many objects other than issues. Indeed, a contented—or discontented—people may have opinions that are most relevant politically but in the main about matters other than concrete issues. They may be exercised about economic conditions; they may have anxieties about the threat of war. In either case their views may not be, at least for most people, centered sharply on well-defined policy issues. Or people may have images of institutions or expectations about institutional performance of evaluations of public personnel—all questions of the most direct relevance for governmental actions though not formulated as policy issues.

Although all regimes must pay heed to the opinions of their peoples, obviously in democratic orders opinion plays a different role than in dictatorial states. When the doctrine prevails that citizens have a right to be heard and governments have a duty to hear, private opinion may have an impact on most major public actions. For the maximum participation of the public (or the publics) a practice of disclosure or notice of prospective actions and of announcement of the considerations underlying actions must be followed. Freedom of association and freedom of expression of opinion on public matters need also to exist. For these reasons, public opinion is sometimes regarded as that opinion communicated to the government. Yet, in practice, governments may (and often do) give weight to latent opinion; in advance of action, they need to estimate the kinds of opinions that may be expressed if a given course is followed or proposed. Hence, communication of views to the government is not essential to transform opinion into public opinion, although communication may be the general rule.

ENDNOTES

1. See Alex Inkeles: *Public Opinion in Soviet Russia* (Cambridge: Harvard University Press; 1950).

2. It should be remembered that Mr. Lippmann's *Public Opinion* had sprinkled through it a goodly number of insights that the public opinion specialists of a quarter of a century later stumbled on independently and proclaimed as new discoveries.

3. C. Wright Mills: *The Power Elite* (New York: Oxford University Press; 1956).

4. Harold D. Lasswell: *Democracy Through Public Opinion* (Menasha, Wis.: Banta; 1941), p. 15.

5. Thomas A. Bailey: *The Man in the Street* (New York: Macmillan; 1948), p. 1.

6. Avery Leiserson: "Notes on the Theory of Opinion Formation," *American Political Review*, XLVII (1953), 171.

7. For a discussion of such fictions and fallacies, see F. H. Allport: "Toward a Science of Public Opinion," *Public Opinion Quarterly*, 1 (January, 1937), 7–23.

8. Wilhelm Bauer: "Public Opinion," in *Encyclopaedia of the Social Sciences* (New York: Macmillan; 1935), XII, 669–74.

9. Kimball Young: "Comments on the Nature of 'Public' and 'Public Opinion,'" *International Journal of Opinion and Attitude Research*, II (1948), 385.

10. Carroll D. Clark: "Concept of the Public," *Southwestern Social Science Quarterly*, XIII (1932–3), 311–20.

11. See W. Phillips Davison: "The Public Opinion Process," *Public Opinion Quarterly*, XXII (1952), 91–106.

12. Herbert Blumer: "The Mass, the Public, and Public Opinion," in Bernard Berelson and Morris Janowitz: *Reader in Public Opinion and Communication*, enlarged ed. (Glencoe: Free Press; 1953), p. 46–8.

13. Herbert Goldhamer: "Public Opinion and Personality," *American Journal of Sociology*, LV (1949–50), 346.

14. Robert E. Park: "News and the Power of the Press," *American Journal of Sociology*, XLVII (1941), 1–11.

15. R. M. MacIver: *Academic Freedom in Our Time* (New York: Columbia University Press, 1955), p. 23. See also Bernard Berelson: "Democratic Theory and Public Opinion," *Public Opinion Quarterly*, XVI (1952), 313–30.

16. Park: loc. cit., 6.

17. A. Lawrence Lowell: *Public Opinion and Popular Government* (New York: Longmans, Green; 1913), chs. 1, 2.

18. The conception of public opinion advanced here, it is cheerfully conceded, is difficult to apply in research. If one is to know what opinions governments heed, one must know the inner thoughts of presidents, congressmen, and other officials. It is even more difficult to know what opinions prudent governments should heed for the sake of the success of their policies or even for their survival.

19. Hans Speier: "Historical Development of Public Opinion," *American Journal of Sociology*, LV (1949–50), 376.

20. Louis Wirth: "Consensus and Mass Communication," *American Sociological Review*, XIII (1948), 1–15.

21. Herbert Blumer: "Public Opinion and Public Opinion Polling," *American Sociological Review*, XIII (1948), 545.

22. Gabriel Almond: "Public Opinion and National Security Policy," *Public Opinion Quarterly*, XX (1956), 371–8.

23. A. Lawrence Lowell: *Public Opinion in War and Peace* (Cambridge: Harvard University Press; 1923), p. 12.

24. Young: loc. cit., 387.

PART 1 SELECTION 2

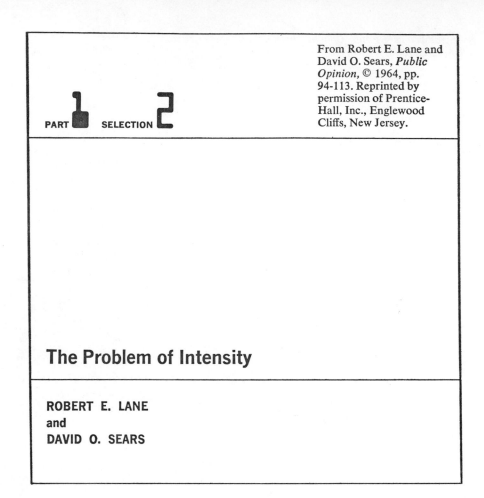

From Robert E. Lane and David O. Sears, *Public Opinion,* © 1964, pp. 94-113. Reprinted by permission of Prentice-Hall, Inc., Englewood Cliffs, New Jersey.

The Problem of Intensity

ROBERT E. LANE
and
DAVID O. SEARS

The agency of change in society is very often the social movement—religious, nationalist, communist, racist, and activist. Each has had its currency. Sometimes even in the absence of a mass movement, the zealot, the fanatic with a single value and a single cause, stimulates the society to change. The men of the mass movements and the fanatics with a cause are, in Hoffer's terms, "True Believers," men with missions framed in some more or less embracing ideology, seeking to redeem their lives and themselves through their apostolic actions.[1]

In distinction to the True Believer with his intense commitment, there is the Concerned Citizen, the man who is likely to register in the American surveys of public opinion as "very interested" in public affairs, who "personally cares a good deal about the outcome of elections," and who "agrees strongly" or "disagrees strongly" with various proposed policies. Like the

True Believer, he has an "intense commitment' to certain opinions and groups, is active, gives a portion of his life to his beliefs.

History has required the zealot and the mass movement to break the bonds of tradition. Hoffer says "Christianity was a civilizing and modernizing influence among the savage tribes of Europe. The Crusades and the Reformation both were crucial factors in shaking the Western world from the stagnation of the Middle Ages. In modern times, the mass movements involved in the realization of vast and rapid change are revolutionary and nationalist. . . . The phenomenal modernization of Japan would probably not have been possible without the revivalist spirit of Japanese nationalism."[2] Such movements embody ideologies and utopian hopes, but says Daniel Bell, there is now "an end to chiliastic hopes, to millenarianism, to apocalyptic thinking—and to ideology. For ideology, which once was a road to action, has come to a dead end."[3] In America, the Populist, the socialist, the Social Darwinist, the Liberty Leaguer, even the technocrat, the union militant, the Black Legionnaire, the Ham and Egger, the Townsendite all are dead or dying. Granted the Black Muslim, granted the southern racist, the John Birchers—they represent in scores what once was a field populated by thousands. And in their place, as monitors of society and agents of social change, there stand the Concerned Citizens.

If this is true, we must know more about this situation, for several reasons, one of which is the possibility that along with some members of the British Commonwealth and the Scandinavian nations, we are developing a political style and a variety of mass opinion appropriate to a new and different phase of history. Our interest here lies with the emotional commitment of the Concerned Citizens in this transitional phase. First, then, it behooves us to examine the nature of this emotional commitment, to see what a Concerned Citizen is concerned about. Second, we shall briefly review some of the more immediate sources of this concern. Third, we must examine the deeper social and psychological factors which might account for both the absence of fanaticism and the presence of concern—a two-edged problem. And fourth, we will look at a special aspect of this distribution of intensity, the problem raised by an intense minority confronted by an indifferent majority.

THE NATURE OF AN EMOTIONAL COMMITMENT

O'Hara, the Eastport maintenance man*. . . feels strongly about the way President Eisenhower "allowed the recession to come along."[4] Examining his

*In the first chapter of the book from which this article is reprinted, the authors introduce O'Hara as a "sprightly little mechanic" who has very vague ideas about politics. He thinks that certain groups control his city's political machinery, but is not sure who they are.—ED.

discussion of the way he feels, we find that he was (1) interested in the problem; (2) concerned about it; he (3) feels strongly that the government should give out more defense contracts in his area; he is (4) partisan in his opposition to Republicans in general and to President Eisenhower in particular; and he is (5) certain (has conviction) that the Republicans could do something about it if they wanted to. Let us take these in order.

Interest is "a sense that giving attention to some phenomenon is rewarding,"[5] and by this index there are many concerned citizens in America. Asked "Would you say that you have been very much interested, somewhat interested, or not much interested in following the political campaign so far this year (1952)" 71 per cent of the American public said they were either very much or somewhat interested.[6] Compared with the French, Americans report themselves much more interested in their elections: "three to four times as many Americans say during Presidential elections, that they are 'very' interested" and this difference, while smaller, is still marked when we look at attitudes during congressional elections in non-presidential years.[7] In both countries, of course, interest in public affairs, or special areas of public affairs such as foreign policy, tends to fall off rather markedly compared with the interest in elections.

Concern. A man may be interested without being concerned, and indeed some small fraction of the American public say they are interested in elections but report that they "don't personally care very much which party wins" and even more people don't think the election outcome makes much difference to the country one way or the other.[8] Concern implies that there is some value at stake in a situation, some gain in a preferred outcome; it is future-oriented, while an interest may apply only to the pleasures of the moment. It is central to our Concerned Citizen.

Opinion strength. When a Concerned man makes up his mind (he may be ambivalent for a while; he may be uncertain), he develops opinions which matter to him because they reflect this concern. He will agree or disagree strongly; that is, his opinions will have strength. In general this kind of intensity is measured by a Likert scale, a form of question asking about some stated position whether the respondents "agree strongly, not very strongly, not sure, disagree but not very strongly, or disagree strongly." In 1956 the Survey Research Center asked this kind of question on a wide range of issues; the outcome gives us a picture of the areas of more intense concern in the public-opinion firmament. In examining these data the late V. O. Key presents information on the "per cent of total sample with strong opinions"—both agree and disagree, from which we can compile a list of areas of intense feeling.

Table 1 *Issues in 1956 with High and Low Degrees of Intensity*

Selected Issues	*Percentage of Total Sample with Strong Opinions*
High intensity issues	
Integration	64%
Job guarantees	60
Acting tough toward Russia & China	59
Isolationism	58
Federal aid to education	57
Due process in firing communist suspects	57
Low intensity issues	
Influence of big business	46
Public power and housing	45
Tax cuts	44
Economic aid to foreign nations	37
Aid to neutrals	33

Source: V. O. Key, *Public Opinion and American Democracy* (New York: Knopf, 1961), pp. 213–18.

Partisanship. Not every issue is characterized by conflict; for example, during and just after the war some 96 per cent of the American public stated a belief that there is a God (whereas about 80 per cent of the Czechoslovakian public believed this) (AIPO 11/15/44, CZIPO July, 1946). But where there is a conflict, and therefore parties to the conflict, we may say that an opinion strongly favoring one side is *partisan.* In an election situation, partisanship often follows interest, for an interest tends to "develop" a person's group loyalties and latent predispositions as the chemical developer reveals the picture in the photographic negative.[9] Once a salient partisan loyalty is enlisted, often other opinions "fall into line"; in Norway and much of Europe, class identification is the salient partisan crystallizer of opinion; in the United States it is party loyalty.[10]

Consonance. Partisanship is one emotion; when partisan attitudes are consonant with one another that emotion is intensified. From a variety of sources, it appears to be the case that lack of inner opinion conflict leads to greater emotional commitment and the kinds of behavior which this implies.[11] Conflict-free commitment is a quality as well as a source of intensity. In an election situation, the more a person's issue, candidate, and party preferences line up on one side the more intensely partisan he becomes, the more he cares about the outcome, the more likely he is to participate.[12] The same thing is true of intensity of belief on other issues.

Conviction. As V. O. Key pointed out, intensity of opinion "may be simply an assurance founded on knowledge."[13] It is generally true that the better-educated hold their opinions more strongly than do the less well-educated; it is as though they felt they had a better right to their opinions. Intensity and certainty go together. Moreover, there is a circularity of emotional commitments: interest leads to knowledge, "knowledge leads to concern, while concern leads to a receptivity to information."[14]

O'Hara is a modestly Concerned Citizen: he is no True Believer. How does he differ therefrom? In the first place, he is interested in his work, family, coaching a boys' baseball team—indeed his interests are more varied than a True Believer's. One might almost say of him that his work in the Little League was his "true belief." Politics and public affairs occupy a much smaller part of his attention span. He has not one, but multiple interests. Second, his level of concern is relative, not total; for the True Believer, everything rides on the succss or failure of the "Movement," but for O'Hara, when the Republicans won, he shrugged and said "Well, the Democrats make mistakes, too. Eisenhower may be a good man." Third, he does not use his political, religious, or ethnic opinions to serve as the sole criterion for including or excluding others: he has friends among all groups. This is a matter of principle with him. He is not, in Rokeach's sense, opinionated.[15] His partisanship is more limited. Fourth, he has convictions: there are certain things he thinks he knows but he reports that on all matters it is better to hear two sides than one; his knowledge is not absolute and for all time. He even questions part of his own church's doctrine, although he thinks of himself as a good church member. The True Believer is future-oriented, but O'Hara lives partly for pleasure in the present; he enjoys his family, sports—life now. And yet, he is active in his union, supports the urban redevelopment in his town, votes and talks politics at the shop, cares what happens. He is good for a stable society; but he could never crack the cake of custom or change the social order. That must be done by others.

To appraise, control, understand these varieties of emotional commitments we need to know something of their causes. We turn now to this inquiry.

SOME SOURCES OF INTENSITY

We have two problems: (1) What kinds of situations produce intense opinions in the opinion market today? (2) How shall we account for a political style which seems, with some exceptions, to generate a capacity for interest, concern, partisanship without fanaticism, true-belief, total commitment? On the first of these, Key offers some interesting information and some sage advice. First, he says, pure self-interest leads to more intense opinions; for example, students feel much more strongly about compulsory chapel in college than do adults who don't have to go to it. Second, group identification leads to more intense feeling on an issue: union members who feel close to their unions have more intense opinions on unions in politics than do those members who have not this sense of close union-identification. Third, general social values, such as the importance of education, generate a pattern of intensity which is not dependent on special advantages and self-interest and may even conflict with them. This is reflected by the lack of relationship between intensity of support for education and having children of school age in the family. Fourth, a special kind of "self-interest," contained in a sense of threat implied by some proposed policy, may affect intensity but not direction of opinion. Thus, although the per cent agreeing to questions on government's responsibility for protecting Negroes does not vary with the proportion of Negroes in a community, the intensity of support declines with an increase in the proportion of Negroes living in the white respondent's community. Finally, intensity of opinion seems to be part of a general pattern of political involvement and concern; each issue borrows significance and probably partisan implications from a more general interest and partisanship. These data lead Key to say, "Intensity of opinion seems by and large to develop when persons are confronted by issues or circumstances that might be expected . . . to arouse their concern most deeply."[16]

We might ask, as Smith, Bruner, and White do, "Of what use to a man are his opinions?" If we knew the answer to that, we would know the sources of interest, concern, partisanship, and conviction of O'Hara's views. Smith and his associates answer their own question by saying that a man's opinions serve (1) to orient him in an instrumental way in the world—that is, to help him get what he wants; (2) they serve to help him adjust to his associates; and (3) they help him to externalize and express his inner conflicts.[17] In the broadest sense, these functions of an opinion help a person to relate to nature and the impersonal world, to other people, and to himself. These seem to be exhaustive, and other functions, such as the immediate gratification involved in expressive acts, and the reinforcement of moral control mechanisms in the self and others,[18] come within their scope. As these functions serve intensely felt needs, so opinions will be intense and a man's emotional commitment suitably greater.

But Key's framework is too narrow and Smith and associates' answers too general to explain our national pattern of controlled intensity. Why does this intensity not spill over into fanaticism? Why, in the end, is it compatible with adjustment to frustration and defeat?

INTENSITY WITHOUT FANATICISM

Historical epoch. In the first place, looking at the problem with the sweep of history in perspective, we can see that the United States has now passed through a set of "standard" crises which seem to stir the emotions of men to a feverish intensity whenever, in the course of national development, they may occur. We achieved our independence through a war which "stirred men's souls." Our establishment of a constitution was more easily agreed upon than might have been expected; but then it was foreshadowed by the institutions we had lived under during our colonial period. The problem of unification brought about one of the bloodiest civil wars of history, and is not yet forgotten among the defeated citizens of the South. We have never had religious wars, though we have had theocracy and much religious persecution, and the problems of the relations of church and state still evoke some intensity. Even so, these issues are still not so evocative here as in some other nations, where clericalism and anticlericalism frame one of the main unresolved issues. The question of the distribution of income and property was eased by a great historic prosperity, but the Greenbackers, the Populists, the socialists, and the heritage and unfinished business of the New Deal show a record and a persistence of intense feeling. Today, beyond all others, the race problem stirs men to violent emotion—but in its most intense form only in the South.

The first and most important answer to the question of whence the controlled intensity and partisanship of American politics spring is to be found in this review of history. We have been through some stirring crises; we may have others in store, but at the moment, as the first of the "new nations" we have won through to a period of respite—with the important exception of the race issue. Latent True Believers must await history's call.

Social cleavage. Issues that evoke intense feelings imply social cleavages; social groups with strong identities and loyalties imply divisive issues. The other side of the question of the great historic issues is, then, the question of hostile social groups, and three of the most important of these are class, religion, and race.

(1) *Class.* About one-third of the people in the nation have indicated that they never think of themselves as belonging to a social class (even though they would name "their" class when pressed), and for this group class identification is largely unrelated to political choice. Social class is not a political reference group, even an unconscious one, for this third of a nation. For the others, those who sometimes think of themselves in class terms, the relationship between class identification and political choice declined continuously from 1948 to 1956. Moreover, the importance of class identification for orienting people on certain ideological issues, such as

the proper role of the welfare state, also declined steadily over this period.[19] As noted above, compared with Norway (and presumably other European countries), social class in the United States is not a reference group upon which intense partisan feeling can be built.[20]

(2) *Religion.* There is a Catholic-Protestant tension in the United States;[21] the assimilation process has not so reduced the differential association as to obliterate differences in political loyalties;[22] there are persistent substantive issues which divide Catholics from Protestants. Given this state of affairs, the apparent historic *change* of divisive attitudes relevant to this form of cleavage is as important as the current state of conflict. For the Catholic, the idea that a Catholic communicant could not be President has been an important symbolic issue since 1928; today this has been removed and with it a shriveling of certain religious political differences. The relative religious-political alignment has changed recently in such a way as to imply a rapprochement. This is revealed in Table 2 and 3. The "difference" figures themselves do not measure religious-political cleavages, since they mask class and urbanism factors as well. Moreover, the candidates are not the same in

Table 2 *Would You Vote for a Catholic for President?*

Year	*Yes*	*No*	*Undecided*
1940	62%	31%	7%
1958	68	25	7
1959	69	20	11
1960	71	20	9
1961	82	13	5
1963	84	13	3

Source: AIPO 10/4/63.

Table 3 *Catholic and Protestant Support for Democratic Party Ticket, 1956, 1960, 1963*

Year	*Catholic Support for Democratic Ticket; % of Two-Party Vote*	*Protestant Support for Democratic Ticket; % of Two-Party Vote*	*Difference*
1956	51	37	14
1960	78	38	40
1963* (April)	86	58	28

* Kennedy *vs.* Rockefeller
Source: AIPO 10/30/60, 4/7/63.

Note: In the 1968 election, 26% of the Protestants and 56% of the Catholics supported the Democratic ticket, while 66% of the Protestants and 39% of the Catholics supported the Republicans. The remainder were supporters of George Wallace (SRC election data).—ED.

each case. However, compared with one another they suggest important changes over time; the 1960–1963 comparison involves, in each year, a Catholic running against a Protestant. It suggests, tentatively at least, the declining impact of religion on political choice; the difference has moved about halfway toward the 1956 situation, which, incidentally, was one in which Catholic-Protestant differences were historically low. This view is supported by the finding in Elmira in 1948 that the sons of Catholics were more Republican than their fathers and the sons of Protestants were more Democratic than their fathers.[23]

Nor is this (rather modest) rapprochement limited to strictly electoral issues. In recent times the issue of public aid to Catholic schools has been divisive, but differences between religious groups have declined:

Table 4 *Percentage Approving Federal Aid to Catholic and Other Private Schools, 1961, 1963, by Religion*

Group	*1963*	*1961*
Protestants	42%	29%
Catholics	71	66
Difference	29	37

Source: AIPO 2/10/63.

(3) *Race.* There is reason to believe that in some quarters the intensity of opinions on racial matters is growing, and as we reported, it is the issue on which there was the highest ratio of "strong" to "not so strong" opinions on each side of the segregation issue in 1960. Yet there is some evidence of a set of opposing forces working to de-intensify the group partisanship—and this in the South, as well. Among these forces are the influence of the national media, the changed attitudes that come with increased urbanization, and the demands of the Negroes themselves.

The dramatic increase in the per cent of the Southern public anticipating the success of the integration movement may be ephemeral (the Birmingham riots later in 1963 had a marked effect on public opinion), but together with the long-term increase in Southern white support for desegregation they suggest one reason why the True Believers of the Ku Klux Klan and the Black Muslims have not been in possession of the field of battle.

Permanence of issues. Intensity of loyalty to a party or a union or even a class or religion seems to be a product of the span of years a person has experienced that loyalty.[24] The same may be true of an opinion about other matters: the longer an opinion is held the more intense the feeling associated

Table 5 *White Southern Views on Race Relations in 1942 and 1956*

White South Only	*1942*	*1956*
Approve school integration	2%	14%
Approve integration of transportation	4	27
Do not object to residential proximity	12	38

Source: Herbert H. Hyman and Paul B. Sheatsley, "Attitudes Toward Desegregation," *Scientific American*, Vol. 195 (1956, pp. 36–37).

Note: For information on more up-to-date attitudes of Northerners and Southerners toward a variety of issues in racial integration, see the following selection by Greeley and Sheatsley (pp. 49-62).—ED.

with it. But in a modern society, and particularly in the United States, issues come and go with a bewildering rapidity. Whereas, for example, the issue of socialism is an old story in Europe and men have grown up with their socialist or anti-socialist beliefs, the American equivalent, the welfare state, is an issue which dates back in its broad modern form only to the New Deal, and in that guise is hardly controversial any more. In a society where issues tend to emerge as ad hoc responses to specific problems, and the mental set of the people is such as to encourage their perception as such, devoid of an ideological superstructure,[25] issues rarely acquire this enduring quality. Hence they rarely acquire that intensity of feeling which comes with long acquaintance and partisanship.

Table 6 *Changing Southern Estimates of Race Relations, 1957–1963*

"Do you think the day will ever come in the South when whites and Negroes will be going to the same schools, eating in the same restaurants, and generally sharing the same public accommodations?"

Date	*Yes*	*No*	*Uncertain*
August 1957	45%	33%	22%
October 1958	53	31	16
January 1961	76	19	5
July 1963	83	13	4

Source: AIPO 7/19/63.

Frustration. Fanaticism thrives on frustration with the old order and an abandonment of hope that it will offer relief. "For men to plunge headlong into an undertaking of vast change, they must be intensely discontented";[26] they must feel that their homes and farms are in jeopardy, their religious practices threatened, their national identity impugned. But a comparison of attitudes in eight modern Western nations and Mexico shows that Americans rank fairly high, generally third or fourth, in their satisfaction with "how they are getting on" in life, with the Australians and the Norwegians, generally ahead of them, and the British and the Dutch generally about the same. Moreover, in the United States, compared with other nations, the levels of satisfaction[27] were most nearly equalized among the various status and occupational groups; there was a kind of equality of satisfaction embracing owners and workers alike. Although there is no evidence that Americans are psychologically healthier than others, it does seem that a sense of political frustration and alienation does not develop because, in general, American men feel that their lives are more or less satisfying. There is no need for "a desperate clinging to something which might give worth and meaning to our futile, spoiled lives,"[28] because men did not see their lives as futile or spoiled. And in the United States, as in England and Norway, there is no need to hate a scapegoated group or love a charismatic leader who promises radical change—two of the great sources of fanatical emotion in politics.

Public and private spheres. What we are talking about is the intensity of opinion on public and primarily political matters, matters which usually come to a focus in government action. If it should be the case that politics in the United States occupied a smaller sphere of the attention orbit than is the case in other countries, another reason for the lack of intense emotional investment in political questions would come into view. The matter is not easy to decide. In addition, it must be observed that Americans hold more elections for more offices than any other nation; they employ the initiative and referendum more than any other country (with the possible exception of Switzerland); they tend to join political organizations to about the same extent as the French and attend only slightly fewer political rallies than they do. On the other hand, Americans attempt to influence others politically rather more than the French. (The relatively lower voting turnout seems to be a product of more stringent registration requirements, rather than lower interest.)[29] Americans are not apolitical. On the other hand, observers have often commented on the lower American level of political partisanship. For example, Bernard Barber refers to certain kinds of political apathy as being the product of "the pre-eminence of occupational and kinship-role obligations in American society" and their divorce from political life.[30]

The problem, we think, is partially resolved by considering the special style of political and social involvement in the United States. Compared with others, Americans seem to regard public affairs as an equally important but more limited sphere of life. And in a cross-cultural comparison of values, Charles Morris finds that compared with students in India, Japan, China, and Norway, students in the United States "seem to wish most of all to be flexible and many-sided. They show less restraint than the Indian students and *less commitment to social causes than do the Chinese or Indian students.* But [the data also] very much show that they do not want to be socially irresponsible."[31] As reported above, McClelland found that American students, compared with German students, participate more in voluntary groups, yet they have a smaller sense of obligation to society and a greater sense of obligation to develop themselves.[32] This pattern of social and political participation, combined with a relatively higher focus on self-advancement, self-indulgence and self-development, may contribute to our understanding of the sources of involvement without fanaticism, of commitment with a capacity for adjustment. The sphere of government and politics is, so to speak, balanced off against a weightier private sphere.

Extremity. One of the best established patterns of public opinion is the U-shaped relationship between extremity on some substantive issue (such as the degree of Negro integration desired, or the degree of regulation desired for industry) and intensity of feeling. The more extreme the stand, the more intensely do people feel about it. In the above illustration, the most integrationist position and the most segregationist position would be held most intensely; and those in the middle, the moderates, would be relatively less emotionally committed.[33] This is so well established, in fact, that in searching for a "zero" position on an issue scale, researchers will choose the position on which people feel least strongly, "folding" as they say, the scale at that point.[34] Speculation on this relationship has produced a number of ideas: Allport and Hartman suggest that extremists are usually taking a more selective view of a situation and must devote energy (emotional intensity) to screening out opposing considerations. Lying behind this selectivity, they say, there are often repressed emotional drives; the intensity and assertion of their opinions are employed to help in this repression.[35] On a more common-sense level, Cantril argues that those who are on the defensive because of their extreme views must either develop an intensity of feeling or else succumb to community pressures to moderate their views. Thus those who remain extremists represent what is left over after those who might adopt an extreme position, for a variety of reasons, have been winnowed and the less intense partisans and the emotionally less active has been culled from the group.[36]

But there are other grounds as well. One way of being moderate is to believe that "there is something to be said on both sides." In a study of attitudes toward the teachers' oath in California, Wilner and Fearing found that those who answered *both* of the following questions in either a pro-oath or an anti-oath position tend to report themselves as being more "certain" of their stand, more "interested" in the problem, and having a better "understanding" of it:

> Are you in favor of requiring all faculty members on this campus to sign a loyalty oath which includes a declaration that the individual is not a member of the Communist Party?
>
> Do you favor dismissing from the university, faculty members who refuse to sign such a loyalty oath?

But about an eighth of the sample answered the first question "yes" and the second question "no," and this group of "fence-straddlers" had a lower sense of conviction and were less interested in the issue, two measures of emotional intensity.[37] Moderation can imply conflict, or dissonance, and conflict and dissonance often tend to be handled psychologically by a withdrawal of emotion. As we said earlier, consonance is an important ingredient in intense partisanship. Because of their geographic and social mobility, Americans may tend to be placed more often than other nationals in such conflict positions, where there is more dissonance than consonance.

Finally, there is something congenial between extremity and intensity which suggests a mutual support. For example, among democratic (non-authoritarian) samples, there is a tendency for those who are most extreme in their equalitarianism to be most militant in the advocacy of their position.[38] The forces nourishing extremity seem also to nourish the intensity.

It might be the case that a people had a general preference for extremist views, preferring to distinguish themselves in exotic ways, or voting "far left" without a commitment to a leftist program because it represents an extreme, or preferring splinter parties which differentiate one's position from the great middle. But in America it seems not to be that way. This is apparent not only in the voting patterns, but also in studies of opinions on a range of issues. Cantril shows that on attitudes on government policy toward business, the middle position (with the lowest intensity) is the most frequently chosen; although usually on an extremity (Thurstone) scale there is not a normal curve, with the most popular choices in the middle, there is a tendency for the extremes to be less chosen than some more moderate position. Extremity is, then, associated with *deviance*, and all of the forces of conformity and "other-directedness" discussed above are mobilized to bring Americans away from the wings and toward the center. This moves them at once away from the areas of intense feeling to the area of more moderate and manageable emotion.

Socialization. One source of intensity in politics is a socialization (maturation) process which somehow invests this area of life with special emotional significance. One could imagine that this would come about in two different ways: (1) parents themselves moralize political choices and these are internalized by the growing child, or (2) children rebel against their parents and employ political difference as a vehicle of rebellion. On the first point, it appears from Greenstein's work that politics is little talked about in the American home, that the children absorb a party identification without many supporting attitudes or much information, and that children's earliest disposition is to think of government in terms of a "benevolent leader" who looks after his people.[39] This not the material out of which fanaticism, or even marked deviance, is developed. Lane's material on the memories of politics in the home possessed by working-class men supports this view.[40] On the second point, the political rebellion of American adolescents, the findings of a recent study by Middleton and Putney show that although there is considerable (but, still, easily contained) generalized adolescent rebellion, this has almost nothing to do with political deviance from parental political positions. On the other hand, those who do not "feel close" to their parents are more likely to rebel politically, but this turns out to be important only if the parents were seen as interested in politics, thus making political rebellion "worthwhile." Yet, on the whole, the authors of this study agree with Hyman in that "political attitudes in America are not in general generated by adolescent rebellion" and the role of other factors seem to them to be more important.[41] Moreover, students tend to feel closer to parents who are seen as interested in politics (because the socially involved adult is a better parent or because parents who communicate an interest to their children create this kind of closeness?)—an unexpected finding which suggests that the awakening of political interests is more likely to be done in a beneficent home environment where parental ties are strong. It seems this sheds light on an important influence shaping the involved but unfanatical participant in political life.

Daniel Bell, who, as we noted above, claims the end of ideology is here, concludes that the politics of our era has changed, there has been an exhaustion of new political ideas, a decline of social movements, a tendency no longer for ideas to serve as levers for action. "What gives ideology its force," he says, "is its passion" and this is spent.[42] Bell is disappointed and believes that the intellectuals of the West are both disappointed and angry because the springs of ideology have run dry and questions of technique have come to the fore in their place. But what this suggests for the United States and other Western nations is that the "True Believer," the mass man in a mass government, is (temporarily?) dead as well. What we have been exploring here are the wellsprings of that other source of interest and action, controlled and patient emotion, disciplined by experience, surely in the modern nations a better foundation for a better society.

THE POLITICAL CONSEQUENCES OF THE INTENSITY PATTERN

We have been discussing these things as though there were only one important matter—namely, the control and rationalization of intensely felt opinions in the political game. But the social distribution of these emotions is important as well. On this point Berelson says:

> How could a mass democracy work if all the people were deeply involved in politics? . . . Extreme interest goes with extreme partisanship and might culminate in rigid fanaticism that could destroy the democratic process if generalized throughout the community. . . . Low interest provides maneuvering room for political shifts necessary for a complex society in a period of rapid change. . . . Hence, an important balance between action motivated by strong sentiments and action with little passion behind it is obtained by heterogeneity within the electorate.[43]

But he does not say where the balance should lie and it is important.

One of the aspects of this problem is most cogently raised by Robert Dahl in his discussion of the relation of democratic theory to the social distribution of intense opinions.[44] He postulates several circumstances, which are best understood by a series of figures. The first of these is a strong consensus marked by strong preferences, as shown in Fig. 1. Here most people strongly prefer one alternative policy and there is no conflict between majority rule and minority intensity. Neither is there in a situation where most people rather weakly prefer one alternative, as shown in Fig. 2. Figure 3 shows a situation where opinion is about evenly divided but the intensity of opinion is low and the "injustice" in a decision for either group is not great; nor would there be much sense of grievance if the distribution of opinion were tilted one way or the other. Now we come to a situation in which there is a strong and intense feeling on each side, and the sides are about the same in size, as shown in Fig. 4. Relatively few people are indifferent, and those who care a great deal about some policy decision are about equally divided. This is the situation which Dahl thinks characterized public opinion just before the Civil War. And if the issue is crucial, as it seemed to be in that case, it may presage the breakdown of democratic government. Finally, there is the situation which poses the most difficult problem of equity, the indifferent majority and the intense minority, shown in Fig. 5. Relating this to the problem of minority rights, Dahl finds that most of the devices designed to protect minorities do so without regard as to whether or not the majority has equally intense preferences and, in any event, tend to protect rich and powerful minorities at the expense of weak minorities, such as Negroes and sharecroppers. Dahl believes that most controversies in a stable democracy are best described by variations of the situations portrayed in Figs. 1, 2, and 3; but the problems of the intense minority bothers him as it did Madison.

Looking at V. O. Key's calculations of "intensity ratios" on a range of issues (measured by a ratio between "strongly agree" and "agree not so strongly" = intensity of agreement, and "strongly disagree" and "disagree not so strongly" = intensity of disagreement) let us see how intense opinions fit into Dahl's several models.[45] From these data we learn several things. In the first place, in only three out of 32 instances are there more people with moderate "agree" or "disagree" opinions than intense ones. This means that in almost every case the situations tend to resemble Dahl's explosive model as represented by Fig. 4, except that instead of U-shaped, they

Figure 1 *Strong Consensus with Strong Preferences*

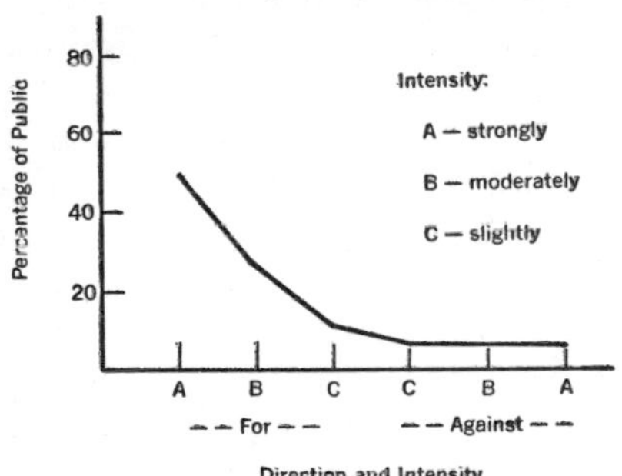

Source: Robert A. Dahl, *A Preface to Democratic Theory* (Chicago: Phoenix Publications, University of Chicago, 1963), pp. 93, 94.

Figure 2 *Strong Consensus with Weak Preferences*

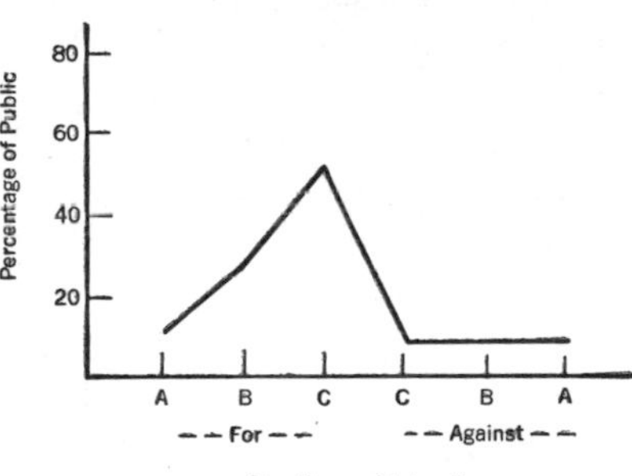

Source: Dahl, *op. cit.*, pp. 93, 94.

Figure 3 *Opinion about Evenly Divided; Weak Preferences*

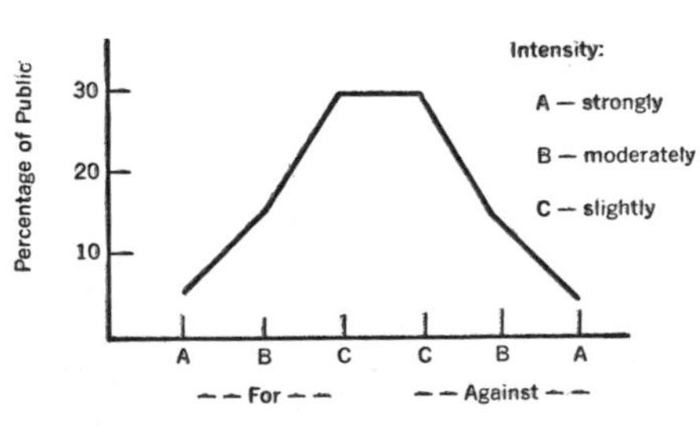

Source: Dahl, *op. cit.*, pp. 93, 94.

Figure 4 *Opinion about Evenly Divided; Strong Preferences*

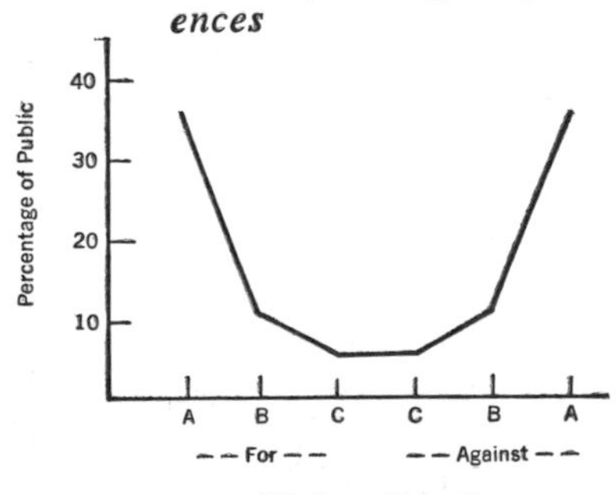

Source: Dahl, *op. cit.*, pp. 98, 99.

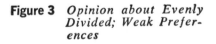

tend to be J-shaped, because there are more intense opinions on one side than the other. Yet, when we look, not at the intensity of reported feeling but at the substance of the questions, only one question seems to reflect an explosive situation: "The government in Washington should stay out of the question of whether white and colored children go to the same school." We must remind ourselves, as Key does on several occasions, that "intensity" of opinion has many meanings. Specifically it is not the same as *cruciality,* which might be defined as an opinion for which a person is likely to sacrifice his ordinary support of law and order.

The second point is that among the 16 issues on which we have data, there are *no* instances of the problem which bothered Dahl: an indifferent majority and an intense minority, although there are two instances of the reverse: an intense majority and a relatively indifferent minority, each dealing with aspects of foreign policy on which there were relatively high numbers of no opinion responses. But is it true that the problem of an indifferent majority and an intense minority disappears for want of cases in the real world? So far the evidence is not conclusive because of the general tendency to choose the more intense "strongly agree (disagree)" option. Taking into account the tendency of people to agree and disagree "strongly," discounting for this, we can look for situations where there is a higher intensity ratio in the minority than in the majority, making for a *relatively* more intense minority than majority. Examining the sixteen issues we find only one instance where this is the case ("The United States should give economic help to the poorer countries of the world even if they can't pay for it," agree 43%, no opinion 17%, disagree 40%; agree intensity ratio: .99; disagree intensity ratio 1.67). It is an issue on which feeling runs low and on which the two sides are almost evenly divided. Our conclusion must be that even taking *relative* intensity into account, on political issues with a broad public, there are very few cases where there is an indifferent majority and an intense minority. On more highly specialized issues (the wool tariff, an airport in New Haven) of course, there will often be intense minorities; this is indeed the world of the special interests: but in their world they very often win.

But the problem of the intense minority and the apathetic majority does not disappear. For perhaps it is the case that political parties exhibit this characteristic; that is, perhaps it is the case that Republicans, although in a minority, tend to be intense partisans, whereas Democrats with almost twice as many "members" in the national public, tend to be more apathetic. But this is not the case, either. By a few percentage points there are more "weak" Democrats than "strong" ones (at least there were in 1952 and 1953) and there are almost exactly the same number of weak as strong Republicans.[46] Little injustice can be read into this picture of the distribution of intense party loyalties.

Finally, we come to the question of intensity of support for political leaders. In the 1952 election, the candidate partisanship scores of the Survey Research Center gives us a measure of partisan support (though this may reflect only roughly how strongly people feel about their man). But here again the majority seems more intense. The Eisenhower supporters were more "partisan" than the Stevenson supporters (5% of the population were *strong* Stevenson partisans on this measure; 20% were *strong* Eisenhower partisans).[47] Yet the situation Dahl had in mind does occur with respect to political leaders, as a 1953 survey of attitudes toward McCarthy shows. The AIPO asked a national sample about McCarthy (June 24, 1953), using a special card to show intensity. The interviewers handed the respondents these cards saying: "You notice that the 10 boxes on this card go from the HIGHEST position of plus 5—or something you like very much—to the LOWEST position of minus 5—or something you dislike very much. Will you put your finger on any one of the 10 boxes which best represents your opinion of Senator Joseph E. McCarthy?" The results follow (see also Fig. 6).

Here, at last, we have a clear-cut case of an intense minority and a relatively indifferent majority—but the differences in size and intensity are still not very great. Nevertheless, something of the quality of the political conflict surrounding the Senator may have come from this complexion of support and opposition: a defensive majority ("I like his goals but don't approve of his methods.") and the cornered bitter opposition of

Figure 5 *Majority with Weak Preferences; Minority with Strong Preferences*

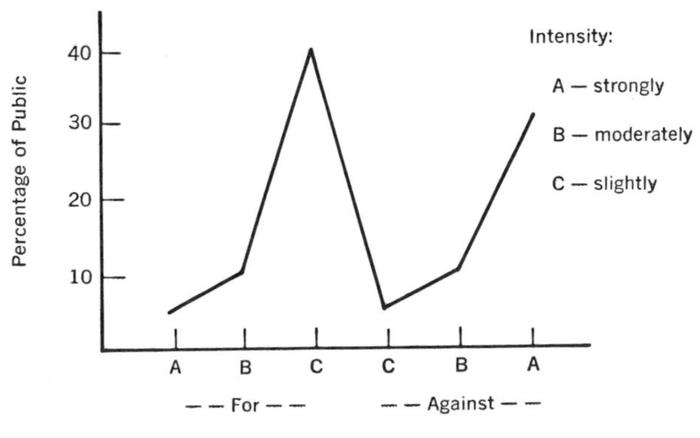

Source: Dahl, *op. cit.*, 98, 99.

Figure 6 *Intensity of Support and Opposition to Senator McCarthy*

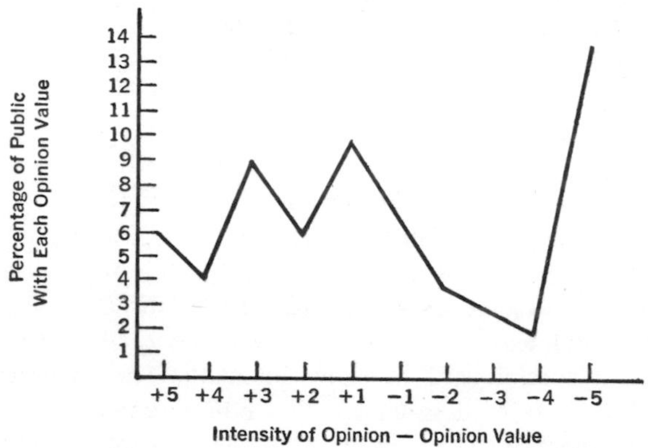

Source: AIPO 6/24/53.

his opponents who feel frustrated and angry about their political position. The minority did feel a certain unfairness in the political process which produced this situation, as Dahl said they would. The problem of the relatively indifferent majority and the intense minority is a real one, but in perspective, and on the broad canvas of national issues, parties, and candidates, not a frequent one.

Table 7 *Intensity of Support and Opposition to Senator McCarthy, 1953*

Value	*Percentage at Each Value*	*Majority and Minority Totals*	*Average Intensity Score for Majority and Minority*
5	6		
4	4	Majority pro-McCarthy = 35%	2.7 majority
3	9		
2	6		
1	10		
−1	7		
−2	4	Minority anti-McCarthy = 30%	3.4 minority
−3	3		
−4	2		
−5	14		
No opinion	35	35	
Total	100	100	

Source: AIPO July 24, 1953.

ENDNOTES

1. See Eric Hoffer, *The True Believer* (New York: Mentor, 1958).

2. *Ibid.*, pp. 14–15.

3. Daniel Bell, *The End of Ideology* (New York: The Free Press of Glencoe, 1960), p. 370.

4. O'Hara is one of the men in Lane's *Political Ideology: Why the American Common Man Believes What He Does* (New York: The Free Press of Glencoe, 1962).

5. Robert E. Lane, *Political Life: Why People Get Involved in Politics* (New York: The Free Press of Glencoe, 1959), p. 133.

6. Angus Campbell, Gerald Gurin, Warren E. Miller, *The Voter Decides* (Evanston, Ill.: Row, Peterson, 1954), p. 34. Apparently this degree of interest was about the same in 1956. See Angus Campbell, Philip E. Converse, Warren E. Miller, and Donald E. Stokes, *The American Voter* (New York: Wiley, 1960), p. 103.

7. Philip E. Converse and Georges Dupeux, "Politicization of the Electorate in France and the United States," *Public Opinion Quarterly*, Vol. 26 (1962), p. 4.

8. Campbell, Gurin, and Miller, *op. cit.*, pp. 36, 38.

9. Paul F. Lazarsfeld, Bernard Berelson, and Hazel Gaudet, *The People's Choice* (New York: Columbia University Press, 1948), pp. 71–86.

10. Angus Campbell and Henry Valen, "Party Identification in Norway and the United States," *Public Opinion Quarterly*, Vol. 25 (1961), pp. 505–525.

11. See, for example, Lazarsfeld, Berelson, and Gaudet, *op. cit.*, pp. 52–64.

12. Campbell, Converse, Hiller, and Stokes, *op. cit.*, pp. 64–97.

13. V. O. Key, *Public Opinion and American Democracy* (New York: Knopf, 1961), p. 227.

14. M. Brewster Smith, "The Personal Setting of Public Opinions: A Study of Attitudes Toward Russia," *Public Opinion Quarterly*, Vol. 11 (1947–48), p. 515.

15. See Milton Rokeach, *The Open and Closed Mind* (New York: Basic Books, 1960), pp. 80–87.

16. Key, *op. cit.*, pp. 219–227. The quotation is from p. 227.

17. M. Brewster Smith, Jerome S. Bruner, and Robert W. White, *Opinions and Personality* (New York: Wiley, 1956), pp. 1, 39–44.

18. For example, Talcott Parsons distinguishes the expressive, the instrumental, and the moral gratifications in his *The Social System* (New York: The Free Press of Glencoe, 1951), p. 59.

19. Campbell, Converse, Miller, and Stokes, *op cit.*, pp. 343–349.

20. Campbell and Valen, *op. cit.*

21. John L. Kane, "Protestant-Catholic Tensions," *American Sociological Review*, Vol. 16 (1951), pp. 663–672.

22. Scott Greer, "Catholic Voters and the Democratic Party," *Public Opinion Quarterly*, Vol. 25 (1961), pp. 611–625

23. Bernard R. Berelson, Paul F. Lazarsfeld, and William N. McPhee, *Voting* (Chicago: University of Chicago Press, 1954), p. 70.

24. Campbell, Converse, Miller, and Stokes, *op. cit.*, pp. 323–327.

25. See Lane, *Political Ideology*, pp. 346–363.

26. Hoffer, *op cit.*, p. 20

27. Alex Inkeles, "Industrial Man: The Relation of Status to Experience, Perception, and Value," *American Journal of Sociology*, Vol. 66 (1960), pp. 1–31.

28. Hoffer, *op. cit.*, p. 24.

29. Converse and Dupeux, *op. cit.*, pp. 4–9.

30. Bernard Barber, "Participation and Mass Apathy in Associations," in Alvin W. Gouldner (ed.), *Studies in Leadership* (New York: Harper, 1950), p. 478.

31. Charles Morris, *Varieties of Human Value* (Chicago: University of Chicago Press, 1956), p. 50.

32. David C. McClelland, *The Achieving Society* (Princeton: Van Nostrand, 1961), p. 198.

33. Hadley Cantril, "The Intensity of an Attitude," *Journal of Abnormal and Social Psychology*, Vol. 41 (1946), pp. 129–135.

34. Edward A. Suchman, "The Intensity Component in Attitude and Opinion Research," in Samuel A. Stouffer and others (eds.), "Measurement and Prediction," Vol. 4 of *Studies in Social Psychology in World War II* (Princeton: Princeton University Press, 1950), pp. 213–276.

35. Floyd H. Allport and D. A. Hartman, "Measurement and Motivation of Atypical Opinions in a Certain Group," *American Political Science Review*, Vol. 19 (1925), pp. 735–760.

36. Cantril, *op. cit.*

37. Daniel M. Wilner and Franklin Fearing, "The Structure of Opinion: A 'Loyalty Oath' Poll," *Public Opinion Quarterly*, Vol. 14 (1950–51), p. 742.

38. Lawrence A. Dombrose and Daniel J. Levinson, "Ideological 'Militancy' and 'Pacifism' in Democratic Individuals," *Journal of Social Psychology*, Vol. 32 (1950), pp. 101–113.

39. Fred I. Greenstein, "The Benevolent Leader: Children's Images of Political Authority," *American Political Science Review*, Vol. 54 (1960), pp. 934–943.

40. Robert E. Lane, "Fathers and Sons: Foundations of Political Belief," *American Sociological Review*, Vol. 24 (1959), pp. 502–511.

41. Russell Middleton and Snell Putney, "Political Expression of Adolescent Rebellion," *American Journal of Sociology*, Vol. 68 (1963), pp. 527–535; quotation on p. 534. See also Herbert Hyman, *Political Socialization* (New York: The Free Press of Glencoe, 1959).

42. Bell, *op. cit.*, p. 371.

43. Berelson, Lazarsfeld, and McPhee, *op. cit.*, pp. 314–315.

44. Robert A. Dahl, *A Preface to Democratic Theory* (Chicago: University of Chicago Press, 1956), pp. 90–119.

45. Key, *op. cit.*, pp. 212–218.

46. Campbell, Gurin, and Miller, *op. cit.*, p. 94.

47. *Ibid.*, p. 140

Reprinted with permission. Copyright © 1971 by Scientific American, Inc. All rights reserved.

Attitudes toward Racial Integration

ANDREW M. GREELEY
and
PAUL B. SHEATSLEY

We present herewith the third report in these pages on the findings of the National Opinion Research Center concerning the attitudes of white Americans toward the position black Americans should occupy in American society.* Together the reports cover a period of almost 30 years, which

*The second of the three reports, which appeared in 1964, disclosed that support for integration among both Southern and Northern whites had risen steadily since 1956 despite the racial conflicts that had occurred during that period. Most of the increased integration support was due to conversion of segregationists—rather than to changes among persons previously undecided about the issue—and to dramatic changes in basic attitudes of whites toward the inherent capacities of blacks. In the first report (Herbert H. Hyman and Paul B. Sheatsley, "Attitudes on Integration," *Scientific American,* December 1956, pp. 35–39) the authors found that while a majority of Northern whites favored racial integration in the public schools and public transportation, a majority of Southern whites opposed this integration. Even between 1942 and 1956, however, public sentiment in both North and South had moved increasingly toward the acceptance of integration.—ED.

is the length of time the Center has been sampling these attitudes. In that time the trend has been distinctly and strongly toward increasing approval of integration. For the most part the trend has not been slowed by the racial turmoil of the past eight years. We believe these findings have significant political implications.

Our sample usually consists of about 1,500 people, chosen to represent a spectrum of the population of adults in the U.S. About 1,250 of the people in the sample are white, and it is with the attitudes of whites that this article is concerned. With a sample of this size we are able to test for opinion by age, region, income, occupation, education, religion and ethnic origin.

Since the last report [see "Attitudes toward Desegregation," by Herbert H. Hyman and Paul B. Sheatsley; *Scientific American*, July, 1964] the U.S. has experienced what is probably the most acute crisis in race relations since the end of the Civil War. City after city suffered racial violence, with Watts, Detroit and Newark only the most conspicuous among them. Martin Luther King, the apostle of nonviolence, was assassinated and another spasm of riots shook the nation. King was replaced on the television screen by a far more militant brand of black leader. Stokely Carmichael, H. Rap Brown, Eldridge Cleaver, Bobby Seale and LeRoi Jones became nationally known. Newspapers carried accounts of blacks arming for guerrilla warfare. The Black Panthers appeared on the scene, and in several cities there were gunfights between the police and the Panthers. Columnists, editorial writers and political analysts worried publicly about the "backlash." George Wallace did well in several primaries, and in the presidential election of 1968 he made the most successful third-party showing in many decades.

Concurrently with these dramatic events the attitudes of white Americans toward desegregation continued to change almost as though nothing was happening. The data do offer a certain amount of evidence of a negative reaction to black militancy; we shall return to this point. Even so, the negative reaction has not impeded the steady increase in the proportion of white Americans willing to endorse integration.

Two questions have been asked throughout the period covered by the National Opinion Research Center's surveys, which were conducted in 1942, 1956, 1963 and 1970. One question is: "Generally speaking, do you think there should be separate sections for Negroes in streetcars and buses?" The other question is: "Do you think white students and Negroes should go to the same schools or separate schools?"

In 1942 some 44 percent of the white population was willing to endorse integrated transportation [*see Figure 1*]. By 1970 the proportion had doubled, reaching 60 percent in 1956 and 88 percent in 1970. In the South the change has been even more pronounced. Only 4 percent of

Figure 1

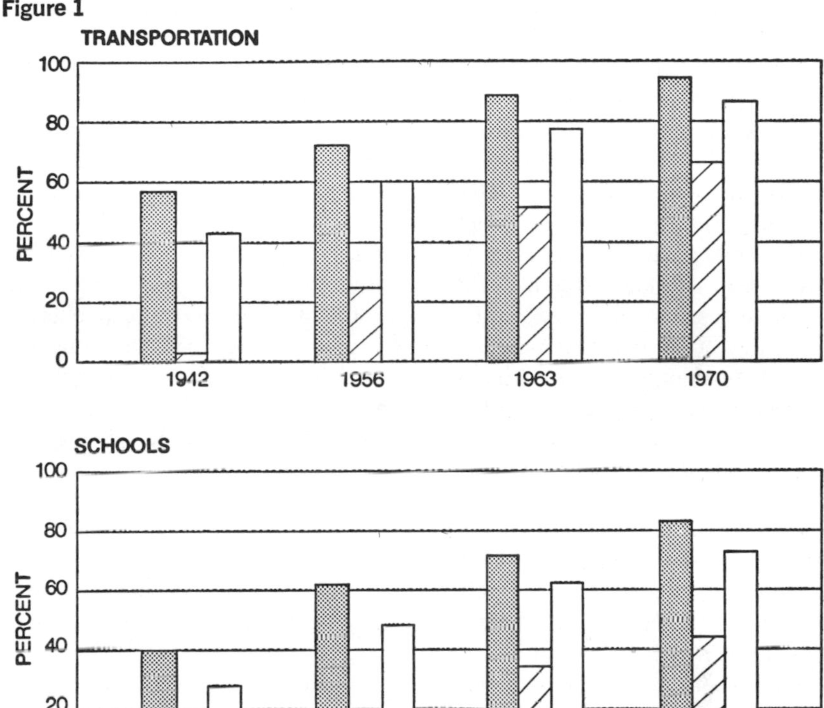

TREND OF WHITE OPINION on integration of transportation and schools is traced for 28 years in surveys by the National Opinion Research Center. For each of the four surveys cited the percentage of people giving an integrationist response is shown for the North (*gray*), South (*hatched line*) and nation (*white*). Questions were identical in each survey.

white Southerners accepted integrated transportation in 1942; by 1970 the proportion was 67 percent.

Integrating transportation, then, is no longer a significant issue. In retrospect it may well be said that the right of blacks to sit where they wish in public vehicles is not a very important right, since obtaining it does not notably improve the welfare of black people. From the perspective of 1971 such an assertion is certainly correct, but when one recalls what the attitudes were in 1942 or even in 1956, the change is striking. In less than 15 years—since Martin Luther King's historic boycott in Montgomery, Ala.—integrated transportation has virtually disappeared as an issue.

The integration of schools, however, is still an issue, even though in the North the idea is now endorsed by eight of every 10 respondents. In 1942, 2 percent of whites in the South favored school integration. By 1956 the proportion had increased to only 14 percent Since 1956—two years after the U.S. Supreme Court's decision in *Brown* v. *Board of Education*—the proportion of Southern whites accepting school integration has increased sharply. Now almost half of them favor it. Nationally the support of whites for integrated schools is 75 percent.

An interesting pattern emerging in the successive surveys is that the proportion of the Northern white population supporting integration at one point in time is quite close to the proportion of the total white population accepting it at the next point in time. If the trend continues, one can expect a majority of the white population in every region to accept integrated schooling by 1977. Perhaps 60 percent of Southern whites will be willing to accept it. One could then say that desegregating schools had ceased to be a significant issue.

In 1963 the National Opinion Research Center employed in its survey a "Guttman scale" prepared by Donald Treiman of the Center's staff. The properties of a Guttman scale (named for Louis Guttman, now of the Israeli Institute of Public Opinion, who devised it) are such that if a respondent rejects one item on the scale, the chances are at least 90 percent that he will also reject all the items below it [*see Figure 2*]. We used a similar scale in 1970. It has seven questions, relating successively to integrated transportation; integrated parks, restaurants and hotels; integrated schools; having a member of the family bring a black friend home for dinner; integrated neighborhoods; mixed marriages, and blacks intruding where they are not wanted.

The first six items on the scale show a consistent increase in support of integration between 1963 and 1970. Indeed, on transportation, public facilities, schools and having a black guest to dinner a large majority of whites respond favorably. Only neighborhood integration and mixed marriages still divide white Americans about equally. If present trends persist, it seems likely that both neighborhood integration and racial intermarriage will be accepted by 60 percent of the white population at the time of the next report by the National Opinion Research Center in about seven years.

Only on the last item of the Guttman scale does one find any evidence of a backlash response to events of the period from 1963 to 1970. In 1963 about 25 percent of the white population rejected the idea that "Negroes shouldn't push themselves where they're not wanted." By 1970 the proportion taking an integrationist stand on this issue had dropped to 16 percent. One can surmise that this change is a response to black militancy, but even if that is

Figure 2

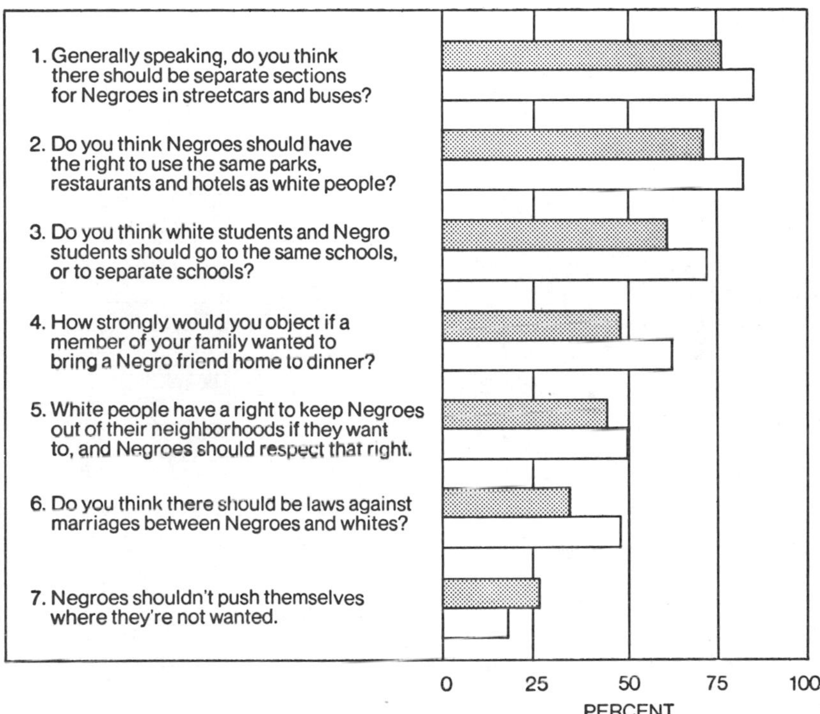
1. Generally speaking, do you think there should be separate sections for Negroes in streetcars and buses?
2. Do you think Negroes should have the right to use the same parks, restaurants and hotels as white people?
3. Do you think white students and Negro students should go to the same schools, or to separate schools?
4. How strongly would you object if a member of your family wanted to bring a Negro friend home to dinner?
5. White people have a right to keep Negroes out of their neighborhoods if they want to, and Negroes should respect that right.
6. Do you think there should be laws against marriages between Negroes and whites?
7. Negroes shouldn't push themselves where they're not wanted.
0
25
50
75
100
PERCENT

SCALED QUESTIONS were employed in 1963 and 1970 to test white opinion. The property of the scale is such that if a respondent has rejected one item, the likelihood is that he also rejected all the succeeding items. The bars at right reflect the percentage of integrationist responses elicited by each question in 1963 (*gray*) and seven years later (*white*).

so, the change has not interfered with increasing support for specific aspects of racial integration.

The seven items of the Guttman scale comprise a "pro-integration scale" on which each respondent can be assigned a score ranging from 0 to 7 depending on the number of pro-integration responses he gave: 0 if he gave none and 7 if he favored integration in all his responses. From there it is a small step to compute mean scores for various population groups to see where the strongest integrationist and anti-integrationist positions are. The mean score for all white Americans in 1970 was 4.2, indicating that the typical American accepts at least four of the seven integrationist attitudes. The mean score in 1963 was 3.57 [*see Figure 3*]. Another way of putting

Figure 3

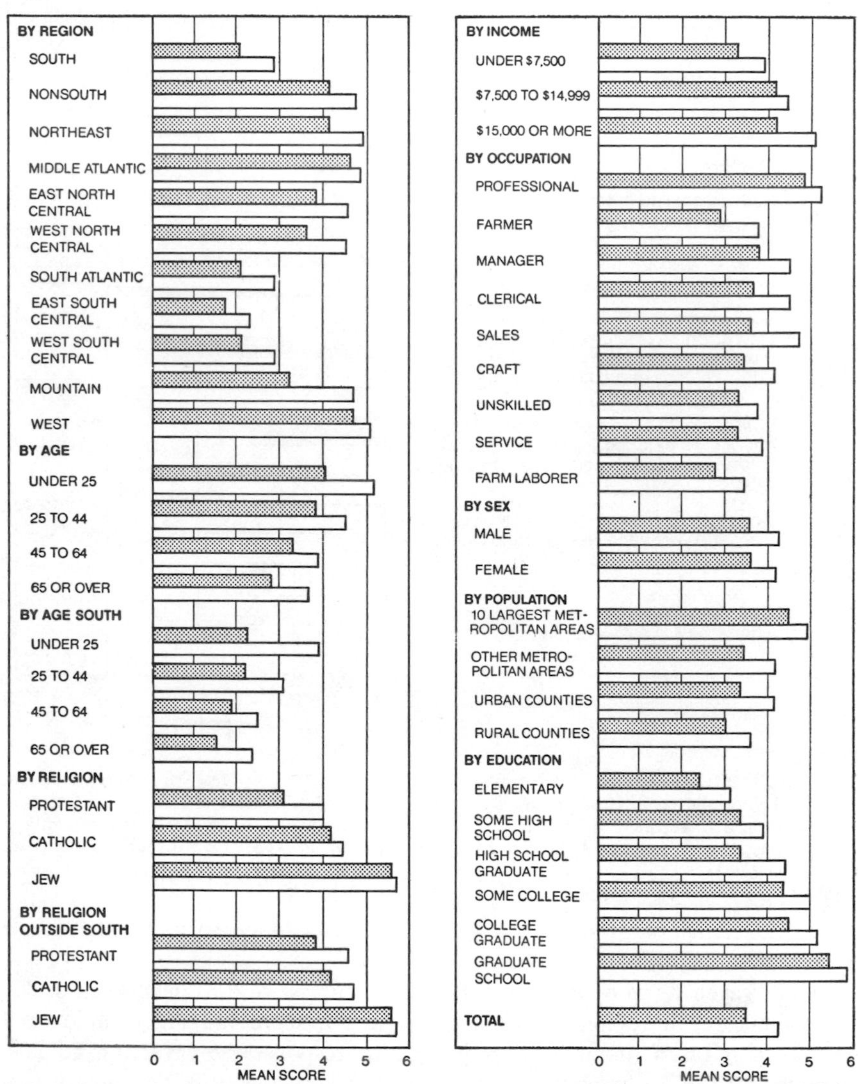

CHANGING SCORES on the pro-integration scale are depicted by various groupings for 1963 (*gray*) and 1970 (*white*). The range of scores is obtained by assigning each respondent a rating of 0 to 7 depending on the number of pro-integration responses he gave to the scaled questions. His score was 0 if he gave no pro-integration replies and 7 if he took an integrationist position on all the questions. The individual scores were used to compute the mean scores shown here for the various regions and groups and for the nation.

it is that the average white American in 1963 could live with integrated transportation, integrated education and integrated parks, restaurants and hotels; he could accept, although just barely, a black dinner guest. In 1970 he was no longer concerned about having a black dinner guest and was no longer ready to totally reject the possibility of integrated neighborhoods.

As one might expect, the greatest differences are regional. The typical Southerner accepts completely only the first two items on the scale, although he leans toward the third. The typical Northerner accepts the first four items and is strongly disposed toward the idea of accepting neighborhood integration. The net change of mean score, however, has been somewhat larger in the South than in the North: .77 compared with .6.

Also as one might expect, the highest pro-integration scores are among people aged 25 and under, both in 1963 and in 1970. As one might not have expected, the most dramatic increase in any age group is among the young: the mean score for people under 25 has increased by 1.08. It is even more striking that young Southerners manifest the largest net rise in integrationist scores: from 2.35 to 3.87. In other words, Southerners under 25 were as likely to be integrationist in 1970 as Northerners aged 45 to 64, whereas in 1963 young Southerners were less likely to be integrationist than Northerners over 65. Moreover, Southerners at each of the three older age levels had higher pro-integration scores than the people at the next-younger age level had had in 1963. Thus one can say that the changing attitudes in the South entail not only the influx of a new generation but also an actual change of position by many older white Southerners.

The mean scores of the various groups can be summarized by saying that there is an increase in integrationist sympathies in all segments of the white population, with the most notable changes at present taking place among people whose scores in the past were the lowest. The net result is that groups at the extremes seem to be moving toward a more central position. For example, the Jewish score is still higher than the Protestant score, but the Protestant score is catching up. People who have been to graduate school still score higher than people who went no further than grammar school, but the difference between the two groups is narrowing. Similarly, whites in large cities continue to be more likely than whites in rural areas to endorse integration, but again the difference is declining. Finally, unskilled workers and service workers now have scores closer to the scores of professionals.

To a certain extent this catching up is a statistical artifact. People with high scores in 1963 did not have much room for improving the scores by 1970. Nonetheless, the diminishing differences indicate that the turbulence of the past few years has not interfered with increasing sympathy for integration, even among people who were least likely to have been sympathetic in the early 1960's. Their scores on the integration scale can increase more rapidly than the scores of people who sympathized with integration in 1963 because there is more room for improvement in their scores. It is not a statistical artifact that the scores continue to increase. That phenomenon reflects changing attitudes in the midst of turmoil and conflict.

Popular mythology would lead one to believe that if there is a backlash, it would be most likely to appear among the "white ethnic" groups, because they are less securely established in American society and also are the people most likely to be in direct conflict with newly militant blacks over such issues as jobs, education and housing. No ethnic-background question was asked in 1963, so that we are unable to compare the attitudes of white ethnics in 1963 and 1970. The 1970 scores alone, however, provide little evidence for the existence of a white backlash [*see Figure 4*]. When the ethnics are compared with white Protestants in the North (the only comparison that is valid since most ethnics live in the North), it turns out that Irish Catholics and German Catholics have a higher average score on the integration scale than the typical white Protestant Northerner does. Catholics of southern European origin (mostly Italian) and Catholics of Slavic origin (mostly Polish) scored only slightly below Anglo-Saxon Protestants. Whatever direct confrontations there may be between blacks and Catholics of southern European and eastern European origin, they have had only a marginal effect on the integrationist sympathies of these two groups. It is also interesting to note that Irish Catholics are second only to Jews in their support of integration.

Considering the integrationist sentiments of ethnic groups by educational background, one finds that insofar as there is a white ethnic backlash it seems to be limited to people who have not finished high school [*see Figure 5*]. (The sample here is small, so that the finding is at best suggestive.) Among people who have graduated from high school, only Slavic Catholics have scores lower than the white Protestant mean (and not much lower). Irish Catholics, German Catholics and southern European Catholics have scores that are higher than the Anglo-Saxon Protestant mean.

One of the most sensitive issues in Northern urban politics is open-occupancy legislation, which forbids racial discrimination in housing. An item measuring attitudes on this subject was included in the 1970 survey [*see Figure 6*]. Three of the four ethnic groups—the Irish, the Germans and the largely Italian southern Europeans—are slightly more likely than Northern Anglo-Saxon Protestants to support such legislation. Only among the Slavic Catholics is there less inclination to be in favor of open-housing laws.

The question of the relation between blacks and white ethnics is a complicated one, lying largely beyond the scope of this article. On the basis of the data available to us, however, there seems to be no evidence of racism among white ethnics except in the Slavic Catholic group. To the

Figure 4

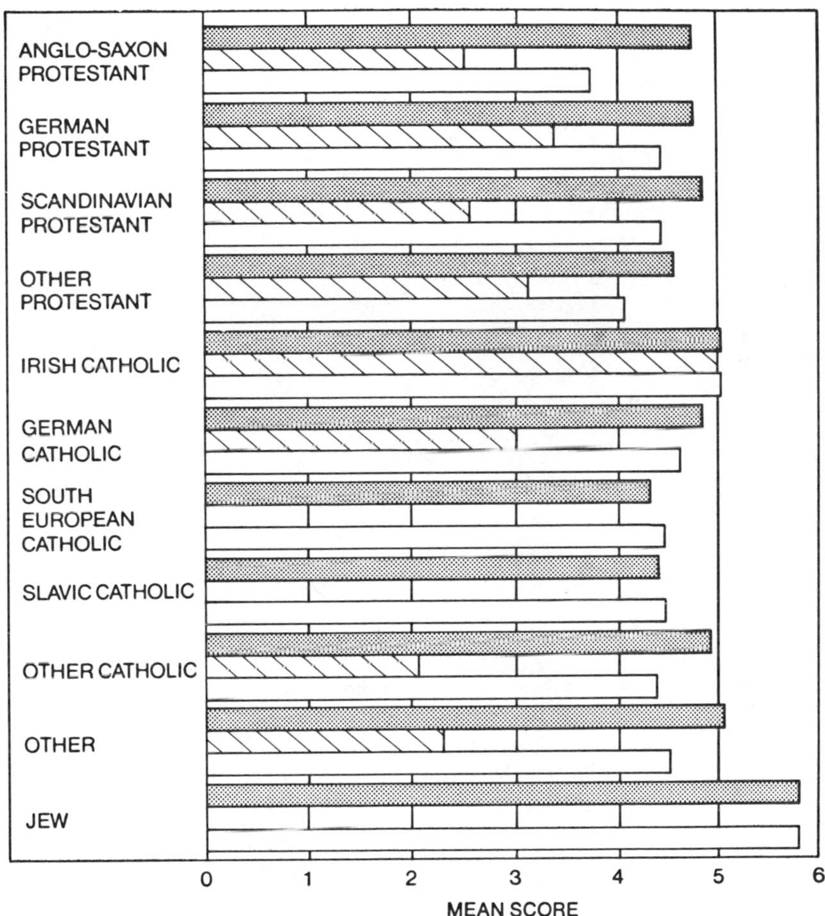

RELIGIOUS DISTRIBUTION of integrationist responses to the scaled questions is depicted by region for the questions asked in 1970. The distribution also reflects certain ethnic groupings. In each case the mean scores are shown for the North (*gray*), the South (*hatched*) and the entire country (*white*). Three groups had little representation in the South.

extent that a backlash exists even in that group, it seems to be concentrated among the less educated people. The other three Catholic ethnic groups are, if anything, even more integrationist than the typical Northern Protestant white—although less so than the typical Northern Jew.

Why, then, is the popular image of the "hard hat" ethnic racist so powerful? Our colleague Norman Nie has suggested that the reason may well be

Figure 5

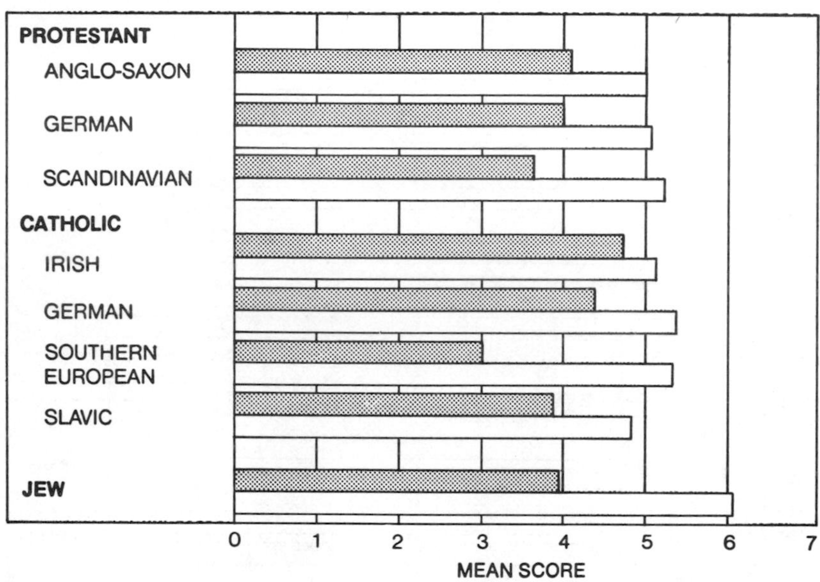

EDUCATIONAL BACKGROUND of Northern whites responding to the scaled questions is shown by religious and ethnic groupings. Mean scores are shown according to whether the respondents had less than a high school education (*gray*) or had at least been graduated from high school (*white*). Many respondents in the second group went beyond high school.

that the ethnics, particularly those from southern and eastern Europe, are "next up the ladder" from blacks and are most likely to be in competition with them for jobs and housing. We were able to put this hypothesis to a crude test by dividing the respondents to our survey into two groups, one comprising people who live in places where fewer than .5 percent of the residents are black and one comprising people who live in places with a higher proportion of blacks. Our supposition was that ethnics would be more likely to be in the latter group and that scores on the integration scale would be lower in that group.

Although the number of respondents is small, the findings indicate confirmation of Nie's suggestion [*see Figure 7*]. Every ethnic group in an integrated area had a lower integration score than members of the same ethnic group in nonintegrated areas except the Irish Catholics, the German Catholics and the Jews. The differences between Anglo-Saxon Protestants and southern Europeans were slight when the comparison was made among

Figure 6

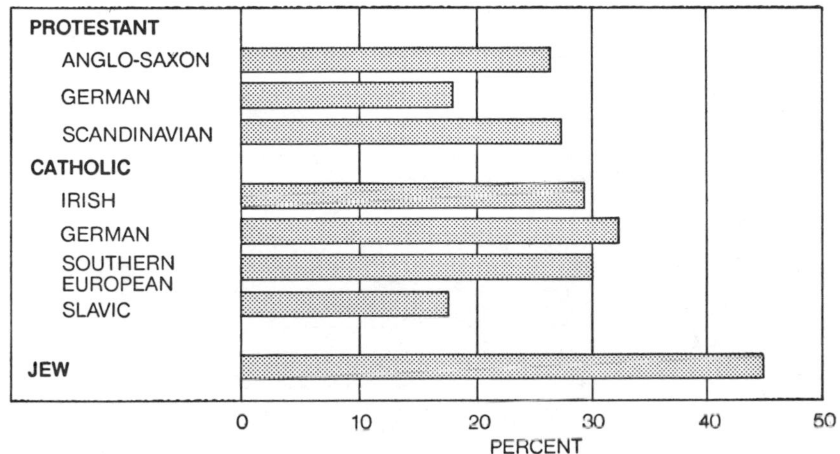

ATTITUDES ON HOUSING appear in the percentages of Northern whites who gave integrationist responses to the question, "Would you favor or oppose making it against the law to refuse to sell or rent houses and apartments to Negroes?" Eight groups are shown.

people living in nonintegrated areas. Thus there does seem to be a correlation between lower scores and feeling "threatened." It is interesting to note that living close to blacks raises the level of Jewish support for integration. German support rises slightly with propinquity, but the Irish score is unaffected.

In the light of our various findings one inevitably asks: Where is the backlash? It could be said to appear in the responses to the item on blacks intruding where they are not wanted. The decline between 1963 and 1970 in the proportion of whites willing to reject the item is, however, fairly evenly distributed in the white population, although it is somewhat less likely to be observed among the young and among the better educated [*see Figure 8*]. It is also somewhat less likely to be observed among Catholics than among Jews and Protestants. (Here is further evidence against the validity of the notion that there is a "white ethnic racist backlash.") In short, if the extent to which whites are now somewhat more likely to say that blacks should not intrude where they are not wanted is a measure of negative response to black militance, the response is fairly evenly distributed among the Northern white population.

Two important observations are in order. First, attitudes are not necessarily predictive of behavior. A man may be a staunch integrationist and still flee when his neighborhood is "threatened." A man with segregationist

Figure 7

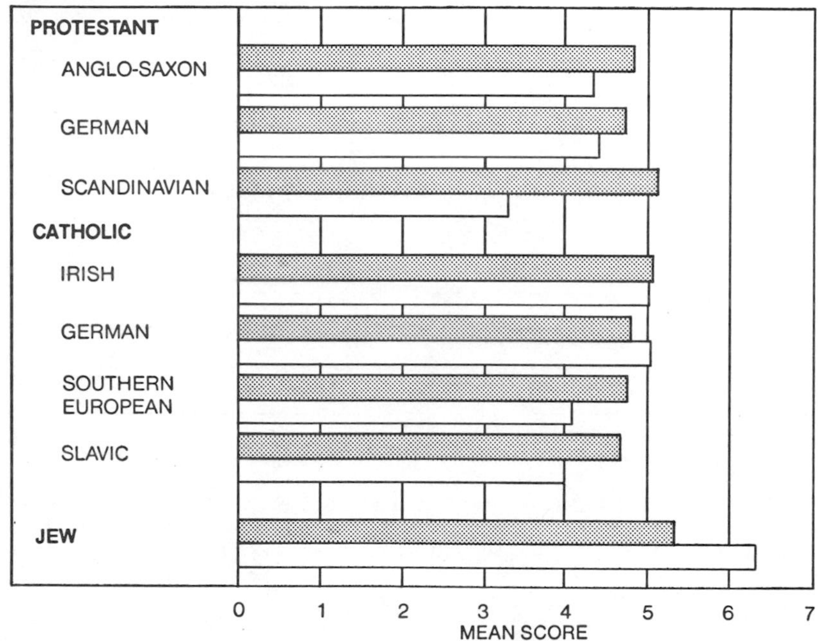

ETHNIC VIEWS are portrayed according to the residential situation of the respondents. The bars show the mean scores on the list of scaled questions of Northerners living in neighborhoods with a black population of less than .5 percent (*gray*) and people in more integrated areas (*white*). The analysis was made to test the assumption that proximity to blacks might lower the scores of ethnics who are in competition with blacks for housing and jobs.

views may vote for an integrationist candidate if the key issues of the election are nonracial.

Second, responses to the interviewers from the National Opinion Research Center may reflect what the white American thinks he ought to say rather than what he believes. Nonetheless, even a change in what one thinks one ought to say is significant. In any case, no one can measure another person's inner feelings with full confidence. If someone asserts that notwithstanding our evidence white ethnics are racists, it seems to us that a

---

EVIDENCE OF BACKLASH appears in a uniform decline between 1963 (*gray*) and 1970 (*white*) in rejection by Northern whites of the proposition that blacks should not intrude where they are not wanted. Even this change of attitude, however, did not alter the prolonged trend toward greater acceptance of integration by whites on more specific issues.

Figure 8

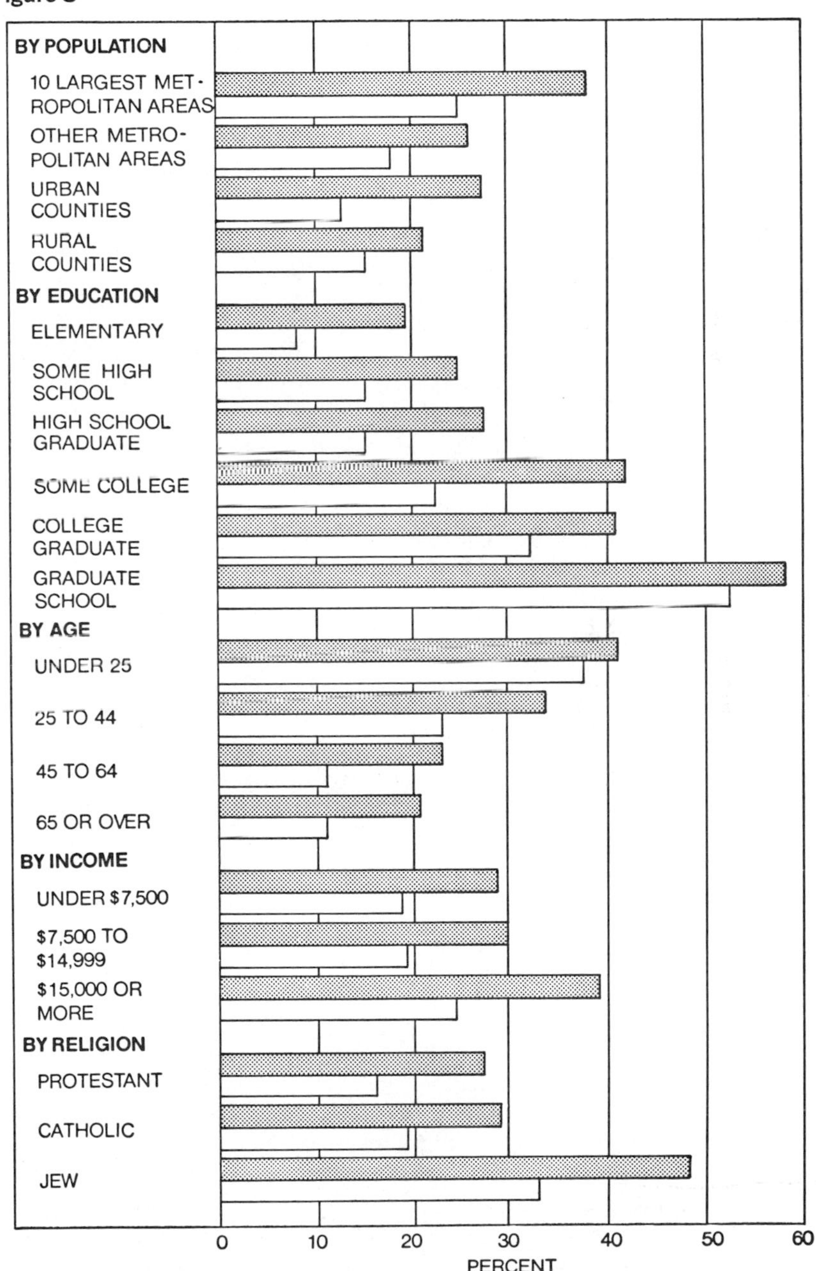
BY POPULATION
10 LARGEST METROPOLITAN AREAS
OTHER METROPOLITAN AREAS
URBAN COUNTIES
RURAL COUNTIES
BY EDUCATION
ELEMENTARY
SOME HIGH SCHOOL
HIGH SCHOOL GRADUATE
SOME COLLEGE
COLLEGE GRADUATE
GRADUATE SCHOOL
BY AGE
UNDER 25
25 TO 44
45 TO 64
65 OR OVER
BY INCOME
UNDER $7,500
$7,500 TO $14,999
$15,000 OR MORE
BY RELIGION
PROTESTANT
CATHOLIC
JEW
0
10
20
30
40
50
60
PERCENT

claim is being made to some kind of special revelation about what the white ethnic really thinks.

Although a change of attitude does not necessarily predict a change in behavior, it does create a context in which behavioral change becomes possible. Increasing support for school integration, for example, makes it somewhat easier for official policies of school integration to be pursued. The increase in support for integrated neighborhoods may facilitate at least tentative solutions to the vexing problem of changing neighborhoods in Northern cities. In sum, changing attitudes—even the dramatic ones monitored by our group over the past 30 years—do not by themselves represent effective social reform, but one can see them as a sign of progress and as creating an environment for effective social reform.

It is not our intention to argue that the data point to a need for more militant or less militant action by blacks. The appropriate strategy for blacks is also beyond the scope of this article. To note that American attitudes have changed is not to suggest that all is well in American society; it is merely to note that there has been change. Presumably no one will argue that the fact of change should go unrecorded because it will diminish the motive to work for further change.

It has been argued recently that American politics are politics of the center, albeit a floating center. We do not want to deny the utility of such a model, but we would point out that at least on the matter of racial integration the center has floated consistently to the left since 1942. We would also note that the shift has not been impeded (or accelerated either) by the racial turmoil of recent years.

The political significance of these conclusions is twofold. On the one hand, the political leader who adjusts his style to an anti-integration backlash is, on the basis of our data, adjusting to something that does not exist. On the other hand, the leader who thinks social conditions are suitable for leading the center even further to the left on the subject of racial integration would find strong support for his strategy in the findings made by the National Opinion Research Center.

We cannot say with measurable precision that sustained pressure by the national leadership is the reason for the increasing support for integration since 1942. It does seem reasonable to argue, however, that if every president since Franklin D. Roosevelt had not endorsed an integrationist position, the change of attitude monitored by our surveys might not be anywhere near as impressive as it is. By the same token it is reasonable to argue that if the present Administration and future ones put forward the case for integration more forcefully, they will find basic attitudinal support among the nation's white people.

PART 2

DESCRIBING PUBLIC OPINION

PART 2 AN OVERVIEW

By now it should be clear that public opinion, as we define it, is a very wide-ranging, eclectic term. It may be a highly stable opinion remaining unchanged for decades; it may be the most ephemeral viewpoint concerning a current, transient issue. The subject matter of public opinion may range from the issue of fluoridation in a small community to questions about the nation's political system and institutions. Thus, in describing public opinion—the subject matter of this section—we shall be referring to a broad spectrum of "publics" and of issues, from the very parochial to those of national import. In selecting material for this section, however, we have focused on those aspects of public opinion that are fairly stable over time; those that are reasonably widespread in that they concern a significant portion of the population; and those that are generally considered to have important consequences for this country's political system. These aspects of public opinion are sometimes labeled political culture—a term that deserves some definition at this point.

Political culture is a system of beliefs about politics, namely, political actors, political institutions, and oneself as a political actor (Almond, 1956; Almond and Verba, 1965; Verba, 1965). Political culture represents the subjective aspect of politics—both the knowledge of (cognitive response) and the feeling about (emotional response) the political system, the roles played in the system, the incumbents who play the roles, the inputs and outputs. This subjective aspect of politics involves having knowledge and opinions about the nation's history and traditions; an awareness and evaluation of the political institutions, structures, office holders, and the policies and programs of the political system. It also involves a critical understanding and appreciation of the means of influencing the system—voting, petitioning, and generally assuming a political role. Finally, it includes recognition of one's obligations and duties as a citizen and some understanding of one's competence to satisfy the requirements of citizenship.

As an introduction to this section, we shall be examining certain aspects of political culture. In such examination we are interested in how citizens feel about the rules that govern political decision making. We are interested in how citizens feel about the institutional structure of government. We are concerned with the factors that enter into the decisions citizens are called on to make, and, finally, we are interested in the extent to which citizens participate in politics.

CONSENSUS IN SUPPORT FOR DEMOCRATIC VALUES

One area of concern in political science has been the study of the conditions surrounding the creation and continuation of liberal democratic government. This interest grows out of the normative concern that implies that democracy is a superior form of government and that people should be concerned with establishing democracy where it does not exist and ensuring its continuation where it does. The interest among contemporary political scientists in the creation and contribution of the democratic state has its origins in the post-World War II period, when it had become clear that democracy was not the inevitable outcome of efforts of humans to govern themselves. Events in Germany, Italy, and Japan made it apparent that under certain conditions nations turn to dictatorship to resolve social and economic problems. Political scholars focused their attention on those factors that seem to be essential to the existence of democracy, and the literature of public opinion reflects this concern with the identification of the characteristics and attributes of the "public" that are conducive to democratic regimes.

It is generally believed that a necessary condition for democracy to be maintained is that the mass of citizens support democratic values or so-called democratic rules of the game, such as freedom of speech, religion, assembly, etc. However, even in the United States, popular support for democratic values is somewhat qualified, as Prothro and Grigg demonstrate in their lucid challenge to the "theory of consensus" *(see pp. 76–91).* We can safely anticipate that this is true in many other countries, particularly where there are conflicting cultural and ethnic patterns. Americans are nearly unanimous in their support for democracy in the abstract, that is, they agree with statements such as "everybody should have the right to vote" and "democracy is the best form of government." They are however somewhat less likely to endorse specific applications of democratic values. For example, many Americans are unwilling to allow blacks, socialists, communists, and other minority groups the same basic freedoms they endorse in the abstract (Stouffer, 1955); Prothro and Grigg, 1960; McClosky, 1964). While elites (decision makers) are reported to be more supportive of minority rights than mass publics (Stouffer, 1955; McClosky, 1964; for evidence to the contrary, see Jackman, 1972), even here, a sizeable number are unwilling to extend the protections of the Bill of Rights to members of minority groups.

What we have, then, is support for the basic tenets of democracy in theory but not always in practice. Whether this antidemocratic attitude is widespread enough to pose a threat to the continuation of democracy in the United States is difficult to say. Probably, it is not. In addition to mass support and the support of elites, there are many other factors contributing to democracy, including the nation's historical tradition, culture, and economic system. The absence of any one of these conditions is probably not a sufficient cause for concern. However, the willingness of some to deprive certain groups and individuals of their constitutional rights is fertile ground for antidemocratic movements such as McCarthyism in the early fifties. Another interesting question to which this section addresses itself is what are the conditions that give rise to a display of antidemocratic sentiment.

SUPPORT FOR THE POLITICAL SYSTEM

Political scientists have also been particularly concerned with the issue of mass support for political systems and political institutions. When the focus is support for *democratic* political systems, this aspect of political culture overlaps that discussed above—support for democratic values. However, citizen support is a problem totalitarian regimes face as well. We can conceive of system support ranging from blind loyalty, where the citizens unquestioningly accept the system and its every act, to the opposite condition where public support is almost totally lacking, and the survival of the system is no longer assured, or even possible (Patterson, Boynton, and Hedlund, 1969). The healthiest situation probably exists when support is less than unanimous, but considerably above the 50 percent level. This guarantees that the system can function without fear of being overthrown, but at the same time makes possible a healthy measure of criticism on the part of the citizens.

While there are differences among subgroups in their society, Americans, in general, support their political system and its institutions. One factor contributing to this support is pride in government and politics. Almond and Verba note that Americans, as compared with citizens in Great Britain, West Germany, Italy, and Mexico, are quite proud of their nation's political system (1965). Germans find the German people a source of pride; Italians are proud of the physical attributes of their country and of its contributions to the arts. Of particular interest here is that few people in either country point to the political system as a source of pride. This may be in part due to the relative newness of the current political systems and political institutions in these countries. Institutions need some time to develop support among the citizenry, and the current system in West Germany and Italy are barely thirty years old. In sharp contrast are the United States and Great Britain, where the systems have been operating for several generations.

In spite of the very positive responses of Americans toward this nation's political system in general, there is some evidence of late that they may have become less positive toward government and politics. The feeling that the individual can influence government and political decision making has been declining steadily since 1960 (Converse, 1972). Trust in government has also declined (Miller, Brown, and Raine, 1973). It is unclear whether this is a transient phenomenon related to the nature of politics of the period, or whether it represents a more profound and therefore more durable change. For some time Americans have been showing a distinction between political structures, which they hold in high esteem, and political leaders, toward whom they are less positive. The changes in attitudes we are witnessing may be directed toward political incumbents and not toward the still highly regarded institutional structure.

IDEOLOGY AND POLITICAL BEHAVIOR

The term ideology in the context of public opinion refers to the political values and belief structure of an individual. A typical ideological designation, and one that is discussed frequently in American politics, although not often defined, is liberal-conservative. The presence of this ideology in America can be inferred from the bases on which people evaluate political objects. The authors of *The American Voter* discuss the extent to which voters in presidential elections employ ideological frames of reference (Campbell, et al., 1964). They suggest four levels of conceptualization.

At the highest conceptual level, an individual is able to place the parties and candidates on a liberal-conservative continuum. Few people are able to do this. Those that can are referred to as ideologues.[1] In 1956, less than 4 percent of those who voted could be classified as ideologues. Also included in the group with the highest level of conceptualization are those who show some appreciation for liberal-conservative differences between the parties, but who lack a complete understanding of the terms. This category contains three types of individuals, all referred to as near-ideologues. First, there is the individual who recognizes liberal and conservative as terms which characterize political parties, but shows little appreciation of the fact that the terms represent poles of a continuum and that political parties can be placed on the continuum and shift their positions along this continuum over time. This group also includes those who use the same level of conceptualization in discussing political parties, but use labels other than liberal and conservative. A second group of near-ideologues are those who employ a liberal-conservative label but fail to effectively relate these designations to the behavior and policies of the parties. Finally, a third group are those who appear to show some understanding of the performance of the parties, but fail to employ the liberal-conservative distinction. Combining the near-ideologues with the ideologues, only 15 percent of the voters in 1956 fell into this group.

A second and lower level of conceptualization is characterized by those who identify the parties and candidates as representatives of group interests. The frequent association of labor with the Democratic Party and business with the Republican Party is an example of the way persons operating at this level evaluate parties and candidates. Nearly one-half of the voters in 1956 were included in this group. The distinguishing characteristics of individuals at a third conceptual level is their overriding concern with a single issue or policy. The economy is the most common single issue concern. About one-fourth of the voters in 1956 were included here. Those at the fourth and lowest level show a complete absence of issue content in their response to the parties and candidates.

Philip Converse too *(see pp. 92–106)* uses a multileveled scale of conceptualization in analyzing the "ideological dimensions of judgment" of the American electorate. But he approaches the definition of conceptual levels in a somewhat different manner by probing whether persons can identify one of the major parties as more liberal or conservative than the other, and what the labels liberal and conservative in general stand for. He finds that about 17 percent of the American electorate recognize and fully understand the distinction; 37 percent are completely vague. The remaining 46 percent fall into two groups; one demonstrates considerable uncertainty and guesswork in its responses, while the other understands the distinction, but has little understanding of the implications of this distinction. For this group, the spend-save dichotomy plays the biggest role in differentiating the parties in liberal-conservative terms. Converse also notes that there are very few consistent liberals and conservatives, with most people taking a liberal position on some issues and a conservative position on others.

The above evidence suggests that ideology plays a minor role in American politics, at least at the level of mass publics. This is not too surprising given the nature of American parties. The need to build a large coalition of voters requires that parties blur differences between themselves and the opposition. As a result, citizens often lack coherent frames of reference and are unable to place parties on a liberal-conservative continuum. American parties are simply not very distinguishable in liberal-conservative terms. There is some evidence to support the proposition that a more ideological party system might result in a more ideologically oriented electorate. A larger proportion of the electorate responded to the candidates in ideological terms in 1964 than in 1960 or 1956, as Pierce remarks in the following selection (*see pp. 107–116*. See also Field and Anderson, 1969). The candidacy and campaign of Barry Goldwater may have resulted in more people responding to the parties in ideological terms. The difference may reflect, however, a more general change. There is evidence to suggest that the capacity of the electorate to distinguish the parties in ideological terms has increased substantially since 1956 (Pomper, 1972), and Pierce sees party identification as a potential source of ideological conflict in this country *(p. 107)*.

Today a number of political scientists are challenging the traditional view of an uninformed and uninterested mass public, almost incapable of an intellectual grasp of politics. Bennett's selection *(see pp. 117–131)* represents an expression of this new critical look. "Questions are being raised," Bennett says, "as to whether the negative attributions assigned to democratic mass publics may be simply the artifacts of poorly defined and tested theory and hastily drawn empirical inference."

PARTY IDENTIFICATION AND POLITICAL BEHAVIOR

Party identification is a psychological tie to a political party and is extremely important in accounting for certain kinds of political behavior.[2] Party identification is measured by asking people to identify with either the Republicans, Democrats, or independents, and to indicate their strength of attachment.

The result is placement of the adult population on a seven-point scale ranging from strong Republican to strong Democrat.

Party identification, for most people, begins very early in life and shows a remarkable degree of stability. Most inherit their party identification from their parents and retain this identification throughout life. There are, however, exceptions. A shift of social milieu or economic status, for example, may very well cause a person to change his party identification. Such changes are always taking place, but are not likely to benefit either party over the longer run. More important are the massive short-term shifts that occur toward a single partisan direction. Such changes occur in connection with an election or a series of elections. These realigning elections cause a shift in the distribution of party identification that influences electoral politics for years. To date, it is believed that there have been three such elections: in 1860, in 1896, and in 1932. Prior to the election in 1932, the Republicans were the majority party in terms of party identification. Following the election, the Democrats became the majority, and this alignment is still influencing American electoral politics.[3] It is apparent that realignments only occur in conjunction with very dramatic circumstances like the Great Depression of the thirties.

As Stokes points out in the following selection *(see pp. 132–142)*, party identification can be conceptualized at two levels. At the individual level, it can be used to explain individual political attitudes and voting behavior. At the aggregate level, party identification can be used to explain the outcome of elections and estimate the probability of deviating elections. Party identification at the individual level exerts a strong influence on voting behavior, both directly and indirectly. Indirectly, it influences the individual's reaction to the candidates and the issues, which in turn influence his vote. These factors combine to determine vote choice. At the aggregate level, the influence of party identification on political behavior has been described as a long-term influence that reflects the distribution of party loyalty in the electorate. Party identification at the aggregate level is constant over all elections, save a realigning election.[4]

For convenience, we call short-term influence all influences on voters except party identification—in particular, the influence of the candidates—their personalities, political styles, and issue positions. The short-term influence causes fluctuations around the baseline or "normal vote" that in any particular election can benefit either party. The short-term influence changes from one election to another, and reflects circumstances unique to that particular political campaign.

The division of more than two-thirds of the electorate into Democrats and Republicans adds a high degree of stability and predictability to

American electoral politics. The parties have a core of voters that they can count on at all times, which explains the very close elections that characterize American politics. Rarely does a candidate for the presidency receive more than 60 percent of the vote. Two exceptions to this rule in the recent years—the elections of 1964 and 1972—suggest the very potent impact that the short-term influence had in these two occasions. This division of such an overwhelming portion of the American electorate into the Democratic and Republican camps not only explains the stability of the country's two-party system, but also explains the difficulty of any third parties gaining a foothold.

PARTICIPATION IN POLITICS

Another important aspect of American political culture is the degree to which citizens participate in politics. Verba and Nie (1972) suggest that participation in politics is important for three reasons. First, it is considered one of the defining characteristics of democracy. The greater the number of participants involved in political decision making, the more democratic the system. Second, participation in politics represents the mechanism for communicating the needs and interests of the citizens to the government and for helping it determine goals, priorities, and the appropriate utilization of the nation's resources. Third, it enables the citizen to develop himself. Participation is an educational device. In the course of participating, citizens learn what is expected of them in the way of civic responsibilities. They also develop a sense of responsibility for their own lives by participating in decisions that directly affect their lives.

Participation can be conceptualized in a variety of ways. An important distinction is that between legitimate (sanctioned by law) and illegitimate modes of political participation. We conceive of legitimate participation as ranging from holding a public or party office to merely exposing oneself to political stimuli, such as following current events on television, in newspapers, etc. (Milbrath, 1965). While what we have called legitimate political participation is more widespread in the United States than in other democracies, it is by most other standards quite low. Few people hold political offices, and very few ever run for political office. In the selection that follows (*see pp. 143–60*), Burnham analyzes the drop-off in voter turnout that has represented one of the most striking aspects of the "changing American political universe" over the past century. Today, rarely does voter turnout reach levels higher than 75 percent of the eligible electorate, and even this occurs only in high-stimulus presidential elections. In state and local elections and in primary elections, the figure ranges from 20 to 40 percent. Beyond voting, participation drops still further. For example, less than 10 percent of the electorate reported ever belonging to a political club, working for a political party, or attending a political rally during the 1968 presidential election campaign.

Quite obviously, many more participate legitimately in politics by following current events on television and in newspapers. Watching television and reading a newspaper requires far less time and energy than working for a political party. But even here, participation is not particularly high. Three-fourths reported reading about political campaigns in newspapers during the 1968 presidential election campaign. Less than 50 percent reported following the campaigns on radio or in magazines. Low exposure to political campaigns contributes to low levels of political information regarding the parties and candidates. In the 1956 presidential campaign, anywhere from 10 to 20 percent, depending on the issue, were unable to offer an opinion on the more salient issues. Ten to 40 percent had an opinion about a particular issue, but had no knowledge of the current government policy with regard to that issue (Campbell, et. al., 1960).

What we have called "illegitimate participation" became widespread, relatively speaking, during the mid- to late sixties, when many of the nation's large cities were plagued with riots confined almost exclusively to black neighborhoods. A survey conducted for the National Advisory Commission on Civil Disorders (Campbell and Schuman, 1968) revealed that while only 2 percent of the black population in fifteen of the largest cities reported taking part in a riot, as many as 15 percent approved of the riots and saw violence as a strategy for achieving Negro rights. Moreover, about 5 percent of the whites interviewed showed propensity to violence as a response to the black riots. While the percentages are relatively small, the actual number of persons willing to engage in acts of violence is substantial. The seventies have been witnessing a decline in black riots. At the same time, however, other minorities are becoming more vocal, for example, Mexican Americans and American Indians. The decline of black protest, or at least in its more violent forms, may reflect a net improvement in the conditions of black people, recognition among blacks that violence is not an effective way to achieve their objectives, or fear of reprisals.

Low levels of legitimate participation suggest more generally that politics is relatively unimportant for most Americans; they are more concerned with earning a living and taking care of their families. The consequences of this attitude are difficult to assess. Some suggest that this situation combines the necessary attributes required for a democratic political system—involvement and indifference, stability and flexibility, consensus and cleavage (Berelson, Lazarsfeld, and McPhee, 1954). Others take a less positive view (Schattschneider, 1960). The issue is related, in part, to the factors that contribute to such low levels of legitimate participation. One of the goals of the next section is to explain these low levels of participation as well as the other patterns of political culture we have discussed above.

ENDNOTES

1. The term is generally reserved for persons who exhibit a high degree of consistency and organization in their attitudes.

2. Most of this discussion is drawn from Cambell et al., 1960, 1964.

3. Since the early thirties, the Democrats (strong and weak) have outnumbered the Republicans by about two to one.

4. The Survey Research Center calculates that in a presidential election governed exclusively by the long-term influence (a theoretical possibility only), the Democrats would win with about 54 percent of the vote.

REFERENCES AND FURTHER READING

Almond, Gabriel A. "Comparative Political Systems." *Journal of Politics* 18 (1956): 391–409.

Almond, Gabriel A., and Verba, Sidney. *The Civic Culture: Political Attitudes and Democracy in Five Nations.* Boston: Little, Brown & Co., 1965.

Bennett, Lance. "Public Opinion: Problems of Description and Inference." Unpublished paper.

Berelson, Bernard R., Lazarsfeld, Paul F., and McPhee, William N. *Voting: A Study of Opinion Formation in a Presidential Campaign.* Chicago: University of Chicago Press, 1954.

Burnham, Walter D. "The Changing Shape of the American Political Universe." *American Political Science Review* 59 (1965): 7–28.

Campbell, Angus. "The Passive Citizen." *Acta Sociologica* 6 (1962): 9–21.

Campbell, Angus, et al. *Elections and the Political Order.* New York: John Wiley & Sons, 1960.

Campbell, Angus, et al. *The American Voter.* New York: John Wiley & Sons, 1964.

Campbell, Angus, and Schuman, Howard. "Racial Attitudes in Fifteen American Studies." In *Supplemental Studies for the National Advisory Commission on Civil Disorders.* Washington, D.C.: U.S. Government Printing Office, 1968.

Converse, Philip E. "The Nature of Belief Systems in Mass Publics." In *Ideology and Discontent,* edited by David E. Apter. New York: Free Press, 1964.

Converse, Philip E. "Change in the American Electorate." In *The Human Meaning of Social Change,* edited by Angus Campbell and Philip E. Converse. New York: Russell Sage Foundation, 1972.

Devine, Donald J. *The Political Culture of the United States: The Influence of Member Values on Regime Maintenance.* Boston: Little, Brown & Co., 1972.

Field, John O., and Anderson, Ronald E. "Ideology in the Public's Conception of the 1964 Election." *Public Opinion Quarterly* 33 (1969): 380–398.

Flanigan, William H. *Political Behavior of the American Electorate.* 2nd ed. Boston: Allyn & Bacon, 1972.

Free, Lloyd A., and Cantril, Hadley. *The Political Beliefs of Americans: A Study of Public Opinion.* New York: Simon & Schuster, 1968.

Jackman, Robert W. "Political Elites, Publics and Support for Democratic Principles." *Journal of Politics* 34 (1972): 753–773.

McClosky, Herbert. "Consensus and Ideology in American Politics." *American Political Science Review* 58 (1964): 361–382.

Milbrath, Lester W. *Political Participation: How and Why Do People Get Involved in Politics.* Chicago: Rand McNally, 1965.

Miller, Arthur H., Brown, Thad A., and Raine, Alden S. "Social Conflict and Political Estrangement." Paper presented at the Midwest Political Science Association Meeting, Chicago, Illinois, May 3–5, 1973.

Patterson, Samuel C., Boynton, G. R., and Hedlund, Ronald D. "Perceptions and Expectations of the Legislature and Support for It." *American Journal of Sociology* 75 (1969): 62–76.

Pierce, John C. "Party Identification and the Changing Role of Ideology." *Midwest Journal of Political Science* 14 (1970): 25–42.

Pomper, Gerald M. "From Confusion to Clarity: Issues and American Voters, 1956–1968." *American Political Science Review* 66 (1972): 450–458.

Prothro, James W., and Grigg, Charles M. "Fundamental Principles of Democracy: Bases of Agreement and Disagreement." *Journal of Politics* 22 (1960): 276–294.

Schattschneider, E. E. *Semisovereign People: A Realist's View of Democracy in America.* New York: Holt, Rinehart and Winston: 1960:

Stokes, Donald E. "Party Loyalty and the Likelihood of Deviating Elections." In *Elections and the Political Order,* edited by Angus Campbell et al. New York: John Wiley & Sons, 1960.

Stouffer, Samuel A. *Communism, Conformity and Civil Liberties.* New York: John Wiley & Sons, 1955.

Verba, Sidney. "Comparative Political Culture." In *Political Culture and Political Development,* edited by Lucian W. Pye and Sidney Verba. Princeton, N.J.: Princeton University Press, 1965.

Verba, Sidney, and Nie, Norman H. *Participation in America: Political Democracy and Social Equality.* New York: Harper & Row, 1972.

Reprinted with permission from *Journal of Politics*, 22 (1960), 276-294.

Fundamental Principles of Democracy: Bases of Agreement and Disagreement

JAMES W. PROTHRO
and
CHARLES M. GRIGG

The idea that consensus on fundamental principles is essential to democracy is a recurrent proposition in political theory. Perhaps, because of its general acceptance, the proposition has never been formulated in very precise terms. When authoritative sources state, for example, that "a successful democracy requires the existence of a large measure of consensus in society," exactly what is meant? We assume that the term "successful democracy," although far from precise, carries a widely shared meaning among political scientists. But we are not told in this typical assertion on what *issues* or *problems* consensus must exist. Presumably they are the basic issues about how political power should be won. Nor are we told what degree of agreement democracy requires. Since the word "consensus" is used to refer to "general agreement or concord," however, a "large measure of consensus" presumably falls somewhere close to 100 per cent.[1] For the purpose of examining the proposition as it is generally formulated, then, we interpret it as asserting: a necessary condition for the existence of a democratic government is widespread agreement (approaching 100 per cent) among the adult members of society on at least the basic questions about how political power is won. Specifically, we propose to submit this proposition to empirical examination in an effort to give it more precise meaning and to discover bases of agreement and/or disagreement on fundamental principles.

A recent symposium by three leading political theorists illustrates both the widespread assumption that consensus is necessary and the lack of precision with which the concept of consensus is discussed. In considering the cultural prerequisites of democracy, they all assume the necessity of agreement on basic values, differing only as to the underlying sources of "the attitudes we regard as cultural prerequisites."[2] Ernest S. Griffith supplies an initial list of "the necessary attitudes to sustain democratic institutions," but he is not clear on whether an actual consensus is necessary: ". . . I believe that they must be sufficiently widespread to be accepted as *norms* of desirable conduct, so that deviations therefrom are subject to questioning and usually social disapproval."[3]

John Plamenatz emphasizes individualism as "the sentiment which must be widespread and strong if democracy is to endure," and adds that individualism "has a less general, a less abstract side to it" than the vague "right of every man to order his life as he pleases provided he admits the same right in others." Here the requisite attitudes must be *strong* as well as *widespread*, but when Plamenatz shifts to the specific side he refers to "the faith of the *true* democrat," a somewhat less inclusive reference.[4]

J. Roland Pennock says, "We are in agreement that certain attitudes are essential to democracy," and his initial quantitative requirements are similar to the "widespread" and "strong" criteria: "Unless *the bulk of the society* is committed to a high valuation of these ideals [liberty and equality] it can hardly be expected that institutions predicated upon them will work successfully or long endure."[5] But when he turns to the idea of consensus as such, he withdraws all precision from the phrase "the bulk of the society": "Of course democracy, like other forms of government but to a greater extent, must rest upon a measure of consensus. . . . But can we say with any precision what must be the nature or extent of this consensus, what matters are so fundamental that they must be the subject of general agreement? I doubt it."[6] Here consensus appears necessary as a matter "of course," but we cannot say on what matters it must exist (Pennock cites two opposing views—the necessity of agreement on the substance of policy versus the necessity of agreement on procedures for determining policy); nor need consensus have a great "extent," which presumably means that it can vary from the "great bulk" to even greater portions of society.[7]

Other theorists take similar positions. William Ebenstein, for example, submits that "the *common agreement on fundamentals* is a . . . condition indispensable to . . . political democracy."[8] Bernard R. Berelson asserts, "For political democracy to survive . . . a basic consensus must bind together the contending parties."[9] The same assumption is implicit in Harry V. Jaffa's more specific formulation of the content of consensus: "To be dedicated to this proposition [that 'all men are created equal'], whether by the preservation of equal rights already achieved, or by the preservation of the hope of an equality yet to be achieved, was the 'value' which was the *absolutely necessary condition* of the democratic process."[10]

All of these theorists thus assume the necessity of consensus on some principles but without giving the term any precise meaning.[11] In specifying the principles on which agreement must exist, some differences appear. Although, as Pennock notes, some have gone so far as to argue the need for agreement on the substance of policy, the general position is that consensus is required only on the procedures for winning political power. At the broadest level Ebenstein says that "the most important agreement . . . is the common desire to operate a democratic system."[12] and Pennock begins his list with "a widespread desire to be self-governing."[13] In addition to this highly general commitment, most theorists speak of consensus on the general values of liberty, equality, individualism, compromise, and acceptance of procedures necessary to majority rule and minority rights. For most of these general principles, the existence (and therefore perhaps the necessity) of consensus is supported by "common sense" observation, by logic, and by opinion survey results. Consensus certainly seems to exist among the American people on the desirability of operating "a democratic system" and on such abstract principles as the idea that "all men are created equal."[14]

But for some of the principles on which agreement is said (without empirical support) to be necessary, the certainty of consensus cannot so easily be taken for granted. Ernest S. Griffith, in maintaining that the essential attitudes of democracy stem from the Christian and Hebrew religions, submits: "Moreover, it would appear that it is these faiths, and especially the Christian faith, that perhaps alone can *cloak such attitudes with the character of 'absolutes'*—a character which is not inly *desirable*, but perhaps even *necessary* to democratic survival."[15] Rather than taking absolutist attitudes as desirable or necessary for democracy, Ebenstein asserts that an opposite consensus is necessary: "The dogmatic, totalitarian viewpoint holds that there is only one Truth. The democratic viewpoint holds that different men perceive different aspects of truth . . . and that there will be at least two sides to any major question."[16] At least one of these positions must be incorrect. Does democracy in fact require rejection or acceptance of the "one Truth" idea? In the survey reported in this paper, neither position appears correct: both Midwestern and Southern Americans were found to be closer to a complete absence of consensus than to common agreement in either accepting or rejecting the "one Truth" idea.[17]

Not only do political theorists speak of consensus on abstract principles where none exists, but they also suggest the need for consensus on more specific principles without empirical support. Griffith, for example, insists that the individualistic "view of the nature of individual personality leads straight to true equality of opportunity and treatment as well as to liberty."[18] And this "true equality" must include dedication not only to the old inalienable rights such as freedom of speech, but also to "the right of each one to be treated with dignity as befits a free person—without regard to sex or creed or race or class."[19] As we shall see, the findings below do not support the assumption of general agreement on "true equality" even in such spheres as freedom of speech. And the same is true of the specific proposition that Pennock uses to illustrate the values on which "the bulk of the society" must be agreed—"The proposition that each vote should count for one and none for more than one is doubtless sufficiently implied by the word 'equality'."[20] "True believers" in democracy may be able to make an unimpeachable case for this proposition, but it is not accepted by the bulk of the society.

The discovery that consensus on democratic principles is restricted to a few general and vague formulations might come as a surprise to a person whose only acquaintance with democracy was through the literature of political theory; it will hardly surprise those who have lived in a democracy. Every village cynic knows that the local church-goer who sings the creed with greatest fervor often abandons the same ideas when they are put in less lyrical form. Political scientists are certainly not so naive as to expect much greater consistency in the secular sphere. The theorists who argue the necessity of consensus on such matters as the existence or absence of multifaceted truth, true equality in the right of free speech, and dedication to an equal vote for every citizen are no doubt as aware of these human frailties as the village cynic.[21] But we tend to regard that which seems a *logically necessary* belief in the light of democratic processes as being *empirically necessary* to the existence of those processes. We assume, in a two-step translation, that what people *should* (logically) believe is what they *must believe* (this being a democracy), and that what they *must* believe is what they *do* believe!

In undertaking to discover what kind of consensus actually exists, we assumed that we would find the anticipated agreement on the basic principles of democracy when they were put in a highly abstract form, but that consensus would not be found on more concrete questions involving the application of these principles. We further assumed that regional and class-related variations would be found on the specific formulation of democratic principles. In pinning down these assumptions, we are no doubt demonstrating the obvious—but such a demonstration appears necessary if the obvious is to be incorporated into the logic of political theory. With empirical support for these two assumptions, we can put the proposition about consensus in more precise form and test the following hypothesis: *consensus in a meaningful sense (at both the abstract and specific levels) exists among some segment(s) of the population (which can be called the "carriers of the creed").* Should our findings support this hypothesis, we could reformulate the proposition about democratic consensus with reference to a smaller group than the total population, whereupon it could be tested more fully, both in the United States and in other democracies for further refinement.

PROCEDURE

Our research design was based upon the major assumption that the United States is a democracy. Taking this point for granted, we prepared an interviewing schedule around the presumably basic principles of democracy and interviewed samples of voters in two American cities to elicit their attitudes toward these principles.

While the general research design was thus quite simple, the preparation of a questionnaire including the basic points on which agreement is thought to be necessary was a difficult and critical step. From the literature on consensus cited above and from general literature on democracy, however, we conclude that the principles regarded as most essential to democracy are majority rule and minority rights (or freedom to dissent). At the abstract level, then, our interviewers asked for expressions of agreement or disagreement on the following statements:

Principle of Democracy Itself
Democracy is the best form of government.

Principle of Majority Rule
Public officials should be chosen by majority vote.
Every citizen should have an equal chance to influence government policy.

Principle of Minority Rights
The minority should be free to criticize majority decisions.
People in the minority should be free to try to win majority support for their opinions.

From the general statements, specific embodiments of the principles of democracy were derived.

Principle of Majority Rule in Specific Terms

1. In a city referendum, only people who are well informed about the problem being voted on should be allowed to vote.
2. In a city referendum deciding on tax-supported undertakings, only tax-payers should be allowed to vote.
3. If a Negro were legally elected mayor of this city, the white people should not allow him to take office.
4. If a Communist were legally elected mayor of this city, the people should not allow him to take office.
5. A professional organization like the AMA (the American Medical Association) has a right to try to increase the influence of doctors by getting them to vote as a bloc in elections.

Principle of Minority Rights in Specific Terms

6. If a person wanted to make a speech in this city against churches and religion, he should be allowed to speak.
7. If a person wanted to make a speech in this city favoring government ownership of all the railroads and big industries, he should be allowed to speak.
8. If an admitted Communist wanted to make a speech in this city favoring Communism, he should be allowed to speak.
9. A Negro should not be allowed to run for mayor in this city.
10. A Communist should not be allowed to run for mayor in this city.

These specific propositions are designed to embody the principles of majority rule and minority rights in such a clear fashion that a "correct" or "democratic" response can be deduced from endorsement of the general principles. The democratic responses to statements 1 and 2 are negative, for example, since a restriction of the franchise to the well-informed or to tax-payers would violate the principle that "Every citizen should have an equal chance to influence government policy."[22] The same general principle requires an affirmative answer to the fifth statement, which applies the right of people to "influence government policy" to the election efforts of a specific professional group. The correct responses to statements 3 and 4 are negative because denial of an office to any person "legally elected" would violate the principle that "public officials should be chosen by majority vote."

Of the five statements derived from the broad principle of minority rights, 6, 7, and 8 put the right of "the minority . . . to criticize majority decisions" and "to try to win majority support for their opinions" in terms of specific minority spokesmen; agreement is therefore the correct or democratic answer. Disagreement is the correct response to statements 9 and 10, since denial of the right to seek office to members of minority ethnic or ideological groups directly violates their right "to try to win majority support for their opinions."

Since the proposition being tested asserts the existence of consensus, the interviewing sample could logically have been drawn from any group of Americans. Because we assume regional and class differences, however, we could not rely on the most available respondents, our own college students. The registered voters of two academic communities, Ann Arbor, Michigan, and Tallahassee, Florida, were selected as the sampling population, primarily because they fitted the needs of the hypothesis, and partly because of their accessibility. Although a nationwide survey was ruled out simply on the ground of costs, these atypical communities offer certain advantages for our problem. First, they do permit at least a limited regional comparison of attitudes on democratic fundamentals. Second, they skew the sample by over-representing the more highly educated, thus permitting detailed comparison of the highly educated with the poorly educated, a comparison that could hardly be made with samples from more typical communities.

The over-representation of the highly educated also served to "stack the cards" in favor of the proposition on concensus. Since our hypothesis holds that consensus is limited, we further stacked the cards against the hypothesis by choosing the sample from registered voters rather than from all residents of the two communities. Although the necessity of consensus is stated in terms of the society as a whole, a line of regression is available in the argument that it need exist only among those who take part in politics. Hence our restriction of the sample to a population of registered voters.

In each city the sample was drawn by the system of random numbers from the official lists of registered voters. The sample represents one per cent of the registered voters from the current registration list in each of the two communities. In a few cases the addresses given were incorrect, but if a person selected could be located in the community, he was included in the sample. A few questions on a limited number of individuals were not recorded in usable form, which accounts for a slight variation in the totals in the tables presented in the paper.

FINDINGS: THE CONSENSUS PROBLEM

In the two communities from which our samples were drawn, consensus can be said to exist among the voters on the basic principles of democracy when they are put in abstract terms. The degree of agreement on these principles ranges from 94.7 to 98.0 per cent, which appears to represent consensus in a truly meaningful sense and to support the first of our preliminary assumptions. On the generalized principles, then, we need not look for "bases of disagreement"—the agreement transcends community, educational, economic, age, sex, party, and other common bases of differences in opinion.[23] We may stop with the conclusion that opinions on these abstract principles have a cultural base.

When these broad principles are translated into more specific propositions, however, consensus breaks down completely. As Table 1 indicates, agree-

Table 1 *Percentage of "Democratic" Responses to Basic Principles of Democracy Among Selected Population Groups*

	Total	Education† High	Education† Low	Ann Arbor	Tallahassee	Income‡ High	Income‡ Low
	N=244	N=137	N=106	N=144	N=100	N=136	N=99
Majority Rule							
1. Only informed vote*	49.0	61.7	34.7	56.3	38.4	56.6	40.8
2. Only tax-payers vote*	21.0	22.7	18.6	20.8	21.2	20.7	21.0
3. Bar Negro from office*	80.6	89.7	68.6	88.5	66.7	83.2	77.8
4. Bar Communist from office*	46.3	56.1	34.0	46.9	45.5	48.9	43.0
5. AMA right to bloc voting**	45.0	49.6	39.2	44.8	45.5	45.5	44.4
Minority Rights							
6. Allow anti-religious speech**	63.0	77.4	46.5	67.4	56.6	72.8	52.1
7. Allow socialist speech**	79.4	90.2	65.7	81.3	76.8	83.8	73.7
8. Allow Communist speech**	44.0	62.9	23.5	51.4	33.3	52.2	36.7
9. Bar Negro from candidacy*	75.5	86.5	60.2	85.6	58.0	78.6	71.1
10. Bar Communist from candidacy*	41.7	48.1	30.3	44.1	38.2	44.8	34.4

* For these statements, disagreement is recorded as the "democratic" response.
** For these statements, agreement is recorded as the "democratic" response.
† "High education" means more than 12 years of schooling; "low education," 12 years or less.
‡ "High income" means an annual family income of $6,000 or more; "low income," less than $6,000.

ment does not reach 90 per cent on any of the ten propositions, either from the two samples combined or from the communities considered separately. Indeed, respondents in both communities are closer to perfect discord than to perfect consensus on over half the statements. If we keep in mind that a 50–50 division represents a total absence of consensus, then degrees of agreement ranging from 25 to 75 per cent can be understood as closer to the total absence of consensus (50 per cent agreement) than to its perfect realization (100 per cent agreement). Responses from voters in both communities fall in this "discord" range on six of the statements (1, 4, 5, 6, 8, and 10); voters in the Southern community approach maximum discord on two additional statements (3 and 9), both of which put democratic principles in terms of Negro participation in public office. These findings strongly support the second of our preliminary assumptions, that consensus does not exist on more concrete questions involving the application of democratic principles.

Three of the statements that evoke more discord than consensus deal with the extension of democratic principles to Communists, a highly unpopular group in the United States. But it should be noted that these statements are put in terms of generally approved behaviors (speaking and seeking public office), not conspiratorial or other reprehensible activities. And the other statements on which discord exceeds consensus refer to groups (as well as activities) that are not in opposition to the American form of government: the right of all citizens to vote, the right of a professional group to maximize its voting strength, and the right to criticize churches and religion.

The extent to which consensus breaks down on the specific formulation of democratic principles is even greater than suggested by our discussion of the range of discord. To this point we have ignored the content of the opinions on these principles, which would permit an overwhelming *rejection* of a democratic principle to be accepted as consensus. Specifically, responses to statement 2 were not counted as falling in the "discord" category, but the approach to consensus in this case lies in rejection of the democratic principle of the "majority vote" with an "equal chance" for "every citizen." But the proposition about consensus holds, of course, that the consensus is in favor of democratic principles. On four statements (2, 4, 5, and 10) a majority of the voters in Ann Arbor express "undemocratic" opinions; and on six statements (1, 2, 4, 5, 8, and 10) a majority of the voters in Tallahassee express "undemocratic" opinions.

However the reactions to our specific statements are approached, they run counter to the idea of extended consensus. On none of them is there the real consensus that we found on the abstract form of the principles; responses to over half of the statements are closer to perfect discord than perfect consensus; and the responses to about half of the statements express the "wrong" answers. Unlike the general statements, then, the specific propositions call for an appraisal of bases of agreement and disagreement.

FINDINGS: BASES OF AGREEMENT AND DISAGREEMENT

The report of findings on the consensus problem has already suggested that regional subcultures are one basis of differences in opinions on democratic principles. Table 1 also shows differences along educational and income lines. Not included are other possible bases of disagreement that were found to have only a negligible effect, *e.g.*, age, sex and party.

Community, education and income all have an effect on opinions about democratic principles. More "correct" responses came from the Midwestern than from the Southern community, from those with high education than from those with less education, and from those with high income than from those with low income. The systematic nature of these differences supports the assumption that regional and class-related factors affect attitudes toward democratic principles when they are put in specific terms.

Which of these variables has the greatest effect on attitudes toward basic principles of democracy? Table 1 suggests that education is most important on two counts: (1) for every statement, the greatest difference in opinions is found in the high education-low education dichotomy; (2) for every statement, the grouping with the most "correct" or "democratic" responses is the high education category. Before education can be accepted as the independent variable in relation to democratic attitudes, however, the relationship must be examined for true independence. Since more Ann Arbor than Tallahassee respondents fall in the high education category, and since more high income than low income respondents have high education, the education variable might prove to be spurious—with the concealed community and income factors accounting for its apparent effect. Tables 2 and 3 show that when we control for community and income, differences between the high and low education respondents remain. When we control for education, on the other hand, the smaller differences reported in Table 1 by community and income tend to disappear.[24]

Since educational differences hold up consistently when other factors are "partialled out," education may be accepted as the most consequential basis

Table 2 *Percentage of "Democratic" Responses to Basic Principles of Democracy by Education, With Income Controlled*

Statement	High — Low Education Differences N = 134 N = 101	Low Income: High Education N = 42	Low Income: Low Education N = 58	Low Income: Difference	High Income: High Education N = 92	High Income: Low Education N = 43	High Income: Difference
1	27.0	67.5	22.4	45.1	59.1	51.2	7.9
2	4.1	20.0	22.0	−2.0	23.9	14.0	9.9
3	21.1	94.4	64.4	30.0	87.8	73.2	14.6
4	22.1	55.0	35.0	20.0	56.5	32.6	23.9
5	10.4	52.5	39.0	13.5	48.4	39.5	8.9
6	30.9	67.5	41.1	26.4	81.7	53.5	28.2
7	24.5	87.5	64.4	23.1	91.4	67.4	24.0
8	39.4	59.0	22.0	37.0	64.5	25.6	38.9
9	26.3	86.1	59.6	26.5	86.7	61.0	25.7
10	17.8	41.0	39.8	1.2	51.1	31.0	20.1

Table 3 *Percentage of "Democratic" Responses to Basic Principles of Democracy by Education, with Community Controlled*

Statement	High — Low Education Differences N = 137 N = 106	Ann Arbor High Education N = 92	Ann Arbor Low Education N = 52	Ann Arbor Difference	Tallahassee High Education N = 45	Tallahassee Low Education N = 54	Tallahassee Difference
1	27.0	63.7	42.3	21.4	57.1	26.5	30.6
2	4.1	24.2	15.4	8.8	19.5	22.0	−2.5
3	21.1	94.4	77.6	16.8	78.4	56.8	21.6
4	22.1	56.7	28.8	27.9	54.8	39.2	15.6
5	10.4	48.4	38.5	9.9	53.3	38.9	14.4
6	30.9	80.2	47.1	33.1	71.4	45.8	25.6
7	24.5	92.3	61.5	30.8	85.7	70.0	15.7
8	39.4	67.0	23.1	43.9	53.7	24.5	29.2
9	26.3	96.6	65.3	31.3	62.2	53.8	8.4
10	17.8	48.9	34.6	14.3	46.4	25.5	20.9

of opinions on basic democratic principles.[25] Regardless of their other group identifications, people with high education accept democratic principles more than any other grouping. While the highly educated thus come closest to qualifying as the carriers of the democratic creed, the data do not support our hypothesis; consensus in a meaningful sense (on both the abstract and the specific principles) is not found even among those with high education. On only three of the ten specific statements (3, 7, and 9) does agreement among those with high education reach 90 per cent in Ann Arbor, and in Tallahassee it fails to reach 90 per cent on any of the statements. On the proposition that the vote should be restricted to taxpayers in referenda deciding on tax-supported undertakings, 75.8 per cent of the highly educated in Ann Arbor and 81.5 per cent in Tallahassee reject the democratic principle of an equal vote for every citizen. And on five statements (1, 4, 5, 8, and 10) the highly educated in both communities are closer to perfect discord than to perfect harmony. Even when the necessity of consensus is reformulated in terms of the group most in accord with democratic principles, then, consensus cannot be said to exist.

SUMMARY AND CONCLUSIONS

The attitudes of voters in selected Midwestern and Southern communities offer no support for the hypothesis that democracy requires a large measure of consensus among the carriers of the creed, *i.e.*, those most consistently in accord with democratic principles. As expected, general consensus was found on the idea of democracy itself and on the broad principles of majority rule and minority rights, but it disappeared when these principles were put in more specific form. Indeed, the voters in both communities were closer to complete discord than to complete consensus; they did not reach consensus on any of the ten specific statements incorporating the principles of majority rule and minority rights; and majorities expressed the "undemocratic" attitude on about half of the statements.

In trying to identify the carriers of the creed, the excepted regional and class-related variations were found in attitudes toward democratic principles in specific form, with education having the most marked effect. While attitudes on democratic fundamentals were not found to vary appreciably according to age, sex or party affiliation, they did vary according to education, community, and income. The greatest difference on every statement was between the high-education group and the low-education group, and the high-education group gave the most democratic response to every question, whether compared with other educational, community or income groupings. Education, but not community or income, held up consistently as a basis of disagreement when other factors were controlled. We accordingly conclude that endorsement of democratic principles is not a function of class as such (of which income is also a criterion), but of greater acquaintance with the logical implications of the broad democratic principles. Note, for example, that the highly educated renounce in much greater degree than any other group the restriction of the vote to the well-informed, a restriction that would presumably affect them least of all.

Although high education was the primary basis of agreement on democratic principles, actual consensus was not found even among this segment of the voting population. The approach to consensus is closer among the highly educated in Ann Arbor, where greater agreement exists on the extension of democratic rights to Negroes, but in both communities the highly educated are closer to discord than consensus on half of the statements. On the basis of these findings, our hypothesis appears to be invalid.

Our failure to find a more extended consensus may, of course, be attributed to the possibility that the statements we formulated do not incorporate the particular "fundamentals" that are actually necessary to democracy.[26] When the approach to consensus is in the "undemocratic" direction—as in the question about restricting the vote to taxpayers—two possible objections to our interviewing schedule are suggested. First, perhaps the question is not a logical derivation from the basic principles with which we began. Second, perhaps the respondents are not interpreting the questions in any uniform way.

On the first point, the logical connection of the specific proposition with the general proposition is virtually self-evident. In syllogistic terms, we have:

major premise—every citizen should have an equal chance to influence government policy; minor premise—non-taxpayers are citizens; conclusion—non-taxpayers should be allowed to vote in a city referendum deciding on tax-supported undertakings. Since decisions on tax-supported undertakings are clearly matters of government policy, rejection of the conclusion is inconsistent with acceptance of the major premise. As a matter of policy, perhaps the vote should be restricted—as it often is—under the circumstances indicated. We simply note that such a position is inconsistent with the unqualified major premise.

As to the second apparent difficulty, varying interpretations of the questions undoubtedly influenced the results. As our pre-test of the questionnaire indicated, the wordings finally chosen conveyed common meanings but tapped different attitudes embedded in different frames of reference. In surveys, as in real political situations, citizens are confronted with the need for making decisions about questions to which they attribute varying implications. We can infer, for example, that the respondents who repudiate free speech for Communists are responding in terms of anti-Communist rather than anti-free speech sentiments, especially since they endorse the idea of free speech in general. Conversely, those who endorse free speech for Communists are presumably reflecting a more consistent dedication to free speech rather than pro-Communist sentiments. But our concern in this study is with the opinions themselves rather than with the varying functions that a given opinion may perform for different individuals.[27] The significant fact is that the opinions (and presumably the frames of reference that produce them) vary systematically from group to group, not randomly or on a meaninglessly idiosyncratic basis.

Assuming that the United States is a democracy, we cannot say without qualification that consensus on fundamental principles is a necessary condition for the existence of democracy. Nor does it appear valid to say that, although consensus need not pervade the entire voting population, it must exist at least among the highly educated, who are the carriers of the creed. Our data are not inconsistent, of course, with the qualified proposition that consensus on fundamental principles in a highly abstract form is a necessary condition for the existence of democracy. But the implication of political theory that consensus includes more specific principles is empirically invalid. Our findings accordingly suggest that the intuitive insights and logical inferences of political theorists need to be subjected more consistently to empirical validation.

Discussions of consensus tend to overlook the functional nature of apathy for the democratic system. No one is surprised to hear that what people *say* they *believe* and what they *actually do* are not necessarily the same. We usually assume that verbal positions represent a higher level—a more "democratic" stance—than non-verbal behavior. But something close to the opposite may also be true: many people express undemocratic principles in response to questioning but are too apathetic to act on their undemocratic opinions in concrete situations. And in most cases, fortunately for the democratic system, those with the most undemocratic principles are also those who are least likely to act. A sizeable number (42.0 per cent) of our Southern respondents said, for example, that "a Negro should not be allowed to run for mayor of this city," but a few months before the survey a Negro actually did conduct an active campaign for that office without any efforts being made by the "white" people to obstruct his candidacy.

In this case, the behavior was more democratic than the verbal expressions. If the leadership elements—the carriers of the creed—had encouraged undemocratic action, it might have materialized (as it did in Little Rock in the school desegregation crisis). But, in fact, people with basically undemocratic opinions either abstained from acting or acted in a perfectly democratic fashion. "The successful working of the system is not deliberately aimed at by those who work it," John Plamenatz says, "but is the result of their behaving as they do."[28] As J. Roland Pennock puts it, democracy can tolerate less conscious agreement on principles if people are willing to compromise and to follow set rules and procedures.[29] Loose talk of consensus as a self-evident requirement of democracy should have no place beside such insightful observations as these. Carl J. Friedrich appears to have been correct in asserting, eighteen years ago, that democracy depends on habitual patterns of behavior rather than on conscious agreement on democratic "principles."[30] His argument has been largely ignored because, like the position from which he dissented, it was advanced without the support of directly relevant research findings. Our results are offered as a step toward settling the question on empirical grounds.

ENDNOTES

1. The consensus of Quaker meetings seems to mean unanimity; although no formal vote is recorded, discussion continues until a position emerges on which no dissent is expressed. Similarly, the literature on the family refers to "family consensus" in a way that suggests unanimity; in a family of three or four people, even one dissenter would make it impossible to speak of consensus. At a different extreme, some students of collective behavior employ a functional definition of consensus, taking it to mean that amount of agreement in a group which is necessary for the group to act. Political scientists clearly do not have such limited agreement in mind when they speak of consensus as necessary to democracy. Majorities as large as three-fourths are required by the Constitution (in ratifying amendments), but such a large majority is no more thought of as consensus than a majority of 50 per cent plus one. Our purpose here is not to develop a general definition of consensus. We interpret the

vague usage of the term to suggest agreement approaching unanimity. And, since our study actually found agreement as great as 98 per cent on some questions, we regard any degree of agreement that falls significantly below this figure to be less than consensus.

2. Ernest S. Griffith, John Plamenatz and J. Roland Pennock. "Cultural Prerequisites to a Successfully Functioning Democracy: A Symposium," *The American Political Science Review*, L (March, 1956), 101.

3. *Ibid.*, pp. 103–104. Italics are his.

4. *Ibid.*, p. 118. Italics are added.

5. *Ibid.*, pp. 129–131. Italics are added.

6. *Ibid.*, p. 132.

7. If the term consensus has any meaning, it is in a great extent of agreement; Pennock's reference to the varying "extent" of consensus must accordingly mean variations from large to even larger majorities.

8. *Today's Isms* (Englewood Cliffs, 1954), p. 99. Italics are his.

9. Bernard R. Berelson, Paul F. Lazarsfeld and William N. McPhee, *Voting: A Study of Opinion Formation in a Presidential Election* (Chicago, 1954), p. 313. Although not a political theorist, Berelson was speaking here on the "theoretical" aspects of "Democratic Practice and Democratic Theory."

10. " 'Value Consensus' in Democracy: The Issue in the Lincoln-Douglas Debates," *The American Political Science Review*, LII (September, 1958), 753. Italics are added. Among the other theorists who have offered similar conclusions is Norman L. Stamps: "Democracy is a delicate form of government which rests upon conditions which are rather precarious. . . . It is impossible to overestimate the extent to which the success of parliamentary government is dependent upon a considerable measure of agreement on fundamentals." *Why Democracies Fail: A Critical Evaluation of the Causes of Modern Dictatorship* (Notre Dame, Indiana, 1957), pp. 41–42. Walter Lippmann, in explaining "the decline of the West," cites "the disappearance of the public philosophy—and of a consensus on the first and last things. . . ." *Essays in the Public Philosophy* (Boston, 1955), p. 100. Joseph A. Schumpeter submits: ". . . democratic government will work to full advantage only if all the interests that matter are practically unanimous not only in their allegiance to the country but also in their allegiance to the structural principles of the existing society." *Capitalism, Socialism, and Democracy* (3rd ed., New York, 1950), p. 296.

11. In Pennock's case, the lack of precision is deliberate, reflecting a well-defined position that the necessary amount of consensus on fundamentals varies according to the strength of two other prerequisites of democracy—"willingness to compromise" and "respect for rules and set procedures." *Op. cit.*, p. 132.

12. *Op. cit.*, p. 99.

13. *Op. cit.*, p. 129.

14. For findings of overwhelming endorsement of the general idea of democracy, see Herbert H. Hyman and Paul B. Sheatsley, "The Current Status of American Public Opinion," in Daniel Katz *et al.* (eds.), *Public Opinion and Propaganda* (New

York, 1954, pp. 33–48, reprinted from the *National Council for Social Studies Yearbook*, 1950, Vol. XXI, pp. 11–34.

15. *Op. cit.*, p. 103. Italics are added.

16. *Op. cit.*, p. 101.

17. This item is not included in the results below because we report only on those propositions that relate directly to the question of how political power is gained. The recognition of "different aspects of truth" logically underlies the ideas of majority rule and minority rights, but it is not as directly connected with them as the propositions on which we report.

18. *Op. cit.*, p. 105.

19. *Ibid.*

20. *Op. cit.*, 131.

21. That the awareness is so consistently forgotten attests to the need of uniting research in political theory with research in public opinion.

22. We are not arguing, of course, that these propositions are incorrect in any absolute sense. Good arguments can no doubt be advanced in support of each of the positions we label as "incorrect." Our point is simply that they are incorrect *in the sense* of being undemocratic, *i.e.*, inconsistent with general principles of democracy.

23. See Angus Campbell and Homer C. Cooper, *Group Differences in Attitudes and Votes* (Ann Arbor, 1956).

24. Those statements with particular salience for one of the regional subcultures (Southern anti-Negro sentiment) constitute an exception.

25. For a discussion of this approach to controlling qualitative data, see Herbert Hyman, *Survey Design and Analysis* (Glencoe, 1955), Ch. 7.

26. The lack of extended consensus cannot, however, be attributed to the possibility that the responses classified as "correct" are actually "incorrect," for we found consensus neither in acceptance nor in rejection of the statements.

27. The latter approach is, of course, a fruitful type of investigation, but it is not called for by our problem. For a functional analysis of opinions, see M. Brewster Smith, Jerome S. Bruner and Robert W. White, *Opinions and Personality*, New York, 1956).

28. *Op. cit.*, p. 123.

29. *Op. cit.*, p. 132.

30. *The New Belief in the Common Man* (Boston, 1942).

Reprinted with permission of Macmillan Publishing Co., Inc. from *Ideology and Discontent* by David Apter. Copyright © 1964 by The Free Press, a Division of Macmillan Publishing Co., Inc.

PART 2 SELECTION 2

The Nature of Belief Systems in Mass Publics

PHILIP E. CONVERSE

RECOGNITION OF IDEOLOGICAL DIMENSIONS OF JUDGMENT

Dimensions like the liberal-conservative continuum . . . are extremely efficient frames for the organization of many political observations. Furthermore, they are used a great deal in the more ambitious treatments of politics in the mass media, so that a person with a limited understanding of their meaning must find such discussions more obscure than enlightening. Aside from active cognitive use, therefore, the simple status of public comprehension of these terms is a matter of some interest.

It is a commonplace in psychology that recognition, recall, and habitual use of cognized objects or concepts are rather different. We are capable of *recognizing* many more objects (or concepts) if they are directly presented to us than we could readily *recall* on the basis of more indirect cues; and we are capable of recalling on the basis of such hints many more objects (or concepts) than might be *active* or *salient* for us in a given context without special prompting. In coding the levels of conceptualization from free-answer material, our interest had been entirely focused upon concepts with the last status (activation or salience). It had been our assumption that such activation would be apparent in the responses of any person with a belief system in which these organizing dimensions had high centrality. Nevertheless, we could be sure at the same time that if we presented the terms "liberal" and "conservative" directly to our respondents, a much larger number would recognize them and be able to attribute to them some kind of meaning. We are interested both in the proportions of a normal sample who would show some recognition and also in the meaning that might be supplied for the terms.

In a 1960 reinterview of the original sample whose 1956 responses had been assigned to our levels of conceptualization,* we therefore asked in the context of the differences in "what the parties stand for," "Would you say that either one of the parties is more *conservative* or more *liberal* than the other?" (It was the first time we had ever introduced these terms in our interviewing of this sample.) If the answer was affirmative, we asked which party seemed the more conservative and then, "What do you have in mind when you say that the Republicans (Democrats) are more conservative than the Democrats (Republicans)?" When the respondent said that he did not see differences of this kind between the two parties, we were anxious to distinguish between those who were actually cynical about meaningful party differences and those who took this route to avoid admitting that they did not know what the terms signified. We therefore went on to ask this group, "Do you think that people generally consider the Democrats or the Republicans more conservative, or wouldn't you want to guess about that?" At this point, we were willing to assume that if a person had no idea of the rather standard assumptions, he probably had no idea of what the terms meant; and indeed, those who did try to guess which party other people thought more conservative made a very poor showing when we went on to ask them (paralleling our "meaning" question for the first group), "What do people have in mind when they say that the Republicans (Democrats) are more conservative than the Democrats (Republicans)?" In responding to the

*The author refers to an inquiry he conducted in 1956 to assess the "evaluative dimensions of policy significance" that seemed to be employed by the masses in lieu of the liberal-conservative continuum. A system of several levels of conceptualization was devised, and the respondents were placed in the various levels on the basis of the conceptual grasp of the political system they seemed to have.—ED.

"meaning" questions, both groups were urged to answer as fully and clearly as possible, and their comments were transcribed.

The responses were classified in a code inspired by the original work on levels of conceptualization, although it was considerably more detailed. Within this code, top priority was given to explanations that called upon broad philosophical differences. These explanations included mentions of such things as *posture toward change* (acceptance of or resistance to new ideas, speed or caution in responding to new problems, protection of or challenge to the *status quo*, aggressive posture towards problems *vs.* a *laissez-faire* approach, orientation toward the future or lack of it, and so forth); *posture toward the welfare state, socialism, free enterprise, or capitalism* (including mention of differential sensitivity to social problems, approaches to social-welfare programs, governmental interference with private enterprise, and so forth); *posture toward the expanding power of federal government* (issues of centralization, states' rights, local autonomy, and paternalism); and *relationship of the government to the individual* (questions of individual dignity, initiative, needs, rights, and so forth). While any mention of comparably broad philosophical differences associated with the liberal-conservative distinction was categorized in this top level, these four were the most frequent types of reference. . . .

Then, in turn, references to differences in attitude toward various interest groupings in the population; toward spending or saving and fiscal policy more generally, as well as to economic prosperity; toward various highly specific issues like unemployment compensation, highway-building, and tariffs; and toward postures in the sphere of foreign policy were arrayed in a descending order of priority, much as they had been for the classification into levels of conceptualization. Since respondents had been given the opportunity to mention as many conservative-liberal distinctions as they wished, coding priority was given to the more "elevated" responses, and all the data that we shall subsequently cite rests on the "best answer" given by each respondent.[1]

The simple distributional results were as follows. Roughly three respondents in eight (37%) could supply no meaning for the liberal-conservative distinction, including 8% who attempted to say which party was the more conservative but who gave up on the part of the sequence dealing with meaning. . . . Between those who could supply no meaning for the terms and those who clearly did, there was naturally an intermediate group that answered all the questions but showed varying degrees of uncertainty or confusion. The situation required that one of two polar labels (conservative or liberal) be properly associated with one of two polar clusters of connotations and with one of two parties. Once the respondent had decided to explain what "more conservative" or "more liberal" signified, there were four possible patterns by which the other two dichotomies might be associated with the first. Of course, all four were represented in at least some interviews. For example, a respondent might indicate that the Democrats were the more conservative because they stood up for the working man against big business. In such a case, there seemed to be a simple error consisting in reversal of the ideological labels. Or a respondent might say that the Republicans were more liberal because they were pushing new and progressive social legislation. Here the match between label and meaning seems proper, but the party perception is, by normal standards, erroneous.

The distribution of these error types within the portion of the sample that attempted to give "meaning" answers (slightly more than 60%) is shown in Table 1. The 83% entered for the "proper" patterns is artificially increased

Table 1 *Association of Ideological Label with Party and Meaning*

Ideological Label	*Meaning*	*Party*	*Proportion of Those Giving Some Answer*
Conservative	Conservative	Republican	83%
Liberal	Liberal	Democrat	
Conservative	Liberal	Republican	
Liberal	Conservative	Democrat	5
Conservative	Conservative	Democrat*	
Liberal	Liberal	Republican	6
Conservative	Liberal	Democrat	
Liberal	Conservative	Republican	6
			100%

*While this pattern may appear entirely legitimate for the southern respondent reacting to the southern wing of the Democratic Party rather than to the national party, it showed almost no tendency to occur with greater frequency in the South than elsewhere (and errors as well as lacunae occurred more frequently in general in the less well educated South). Data from a very different context indicate that southerners who discriminate between the southern wing and the national Democratic Party take the national party as the assumed object in our interviews, if the precise object is not specified.

to an unknown degree by the inclusion of all respondents whose connotations for liberalism-conservatism were sufficiently impoverished so that little judgment could be made about whether or not they were making proper associations (for example, those respondents whose best explanations of the distinction involved orientations toward defense spending). The error types thus represent only those that could be unequivocally considered "errors." While Table 1 does not in itself constitute proof that the error types resulted from pure guesswork, the configuration does resemble the probable results if 20–25% of the respondents had been making random guesses about how the two labels, the two polar meanings, and the two parties should be sorted out. People making these confused responses might or might not *feel* confused in making their assessments. Even if they knew that they were confused, it is unlikely that they would be less confused in encountering such terms in reading or listening to political communications, which is the important point where transmission of information is concerned. If, on the other hand, they were wrong without realizing it, then they would be capable of hearing that Senator Goldwater, for example, was an extreme conservative and believing that it meant that he was for increased federal spending (or whatever other more specific meaning they might bring to the term). In either case, it seems reasonable to distinguish between the people who belong in this confused group at the border of understanding and those who demonstrate greater clarity about the terms. And after the confused group is set aside (stratum III in Table 2), we are left with a proportion of the sample that is slightly more than 50%. This figure can be taken as a maximum estimate of reasonable recognition.

We say "maximum" because, once within this "sophisticated" half of the electorate, it is reasonable to consider the quality of the meanings put forth to explain the liberal-conservative distinction. These meanings varied greatly in adequacy, from those "best answers" that did indeed qualify for coding under the "broad philosophy" heading (the most accurate responses, as defined above) to those that explained the distinction in narrow or nearly irrelevant terms (like Prohibition or foreign-policy measures). In all, 17% of the total sample gave "best answers" that we considered to qualify as "broad philosophy."[2] This group was defined as stratum I, and the remainder, who gave narrower definitions, became stratum II.

Perhaps the most striking aspect of the liberal-conservative definitions supplied was the extreme frequency of those hinging on a simple "spend-save" dimension *vis-à-vis* government finances. Very close to a majority of all "best" responses (and two-thirds to three-quarters of all such responses in stratum II) indicated in essence that the Democratic Party was liberal because it spent public money freely and that the Republican Party was more conservative because it stood for economy in government or pinched pennies. In our earlier coding of the levels of conceptualization, we had already noted that this simple dimension seemed often to be what was at stake when "ideological" terms were used. Frequently there was reason to believe that the term "conservative" drew its primary meaning from the cognate "conservation." In one rather clear example, a respondent indicated that he considered the Republicans to be more conservative in the sense that they were "... more saving with money and our *natural resources.* Less apt to slap on a tax for some non-essential. More conservative in promises that can't be kept." (Italics ours.)

Of course, the question of the proportion of national wealth that is to be spent privately or channeled through government for public spending has been one of the key disputes between conservatives and liberal "ideologies" for several decades. From this point of view, the great multitude of "spend-save" references can be considered essentially as accurate matching of terms. On the other hand, it goes without saying that the conservative-liberal dialogue does not exhaust itself on this narrow question alone, and our view of these responses as an understanding of the differences depends in no small measure on whether the individual sees this point as a self-contained distinction or understands the link between it and a number of other broad questions. On rare occasions, one encounters a respondent for whom the "spend-save" dimension is intimately bound up with other problem areas. For example, one respondent feels that the Republicans are more conservative because "... they are too interested in getting the budget balanced—they should spend more to get more jobs for our people." More frequently when further links are suggested, they are connected with policy but go no further:

> [Republicans more conservative because] "Well, they don't spend as much money." [What do you have in mind?] "Well, a lot of them holler when they try to establish a higher interest rate but that's to get back a little when they do loan out and make it so people are not so free with it."

Generally, however, the belief system involved when "liberal-conservative" is equated with "spend-save" seems to be an entirely narrow one. There follow a number of examples of comments, which taken with the preceding citations, form a random drawing from the large group of "spend-save" comments:

> [Democrats more conservative because] "they will do more for the people at home before they go out to help foreign countries. They are truthful and not liars."
>
> [Republicans more liberal judging] "by the money they have spent in this last administration. They spent more than ever before in a peace time. And got less for it as far as I can see."
>
> [Republicans more conservative because] "Well, they vote against the wild spending spree the Democrats get on."
>
> [Republicans more conservative because] "they pay as you go."
>
> [Democrats more conservative because] "I don't believe the Democrats will spend as much money as the Republicans."
>
> [Republicans more conservative because] "it seems as if the Republicans try to hold down the spending of government money." [Do you remember how?] "Yes," [by having] "no wars."

From this representation of the "spend-save" references, the reader may see quite clearly why we consider them to be rather "narrow" readings of the liberal-conservative distinction as applied to the current partisan scene. In short, our portrait of the population, where recognition of a key ideological dimension is concerned, suggests that about 17% of the public (stratum I) have an understanding of the distinction that captures much of its breadth. About 37% (strata IV and V) are entirely vague as to its meaning. For the 46% between, there are two strata, one of which demonstrates considerable uncertainty and guesswork in assigning meaning to the terms (stratum III) and the other of which has the terms rather well under control but appears to have a fairly limited set of connotations for them (stratum II). The great majority of the latter groups equate liberalism-conservatism rather directly with a "spend-save" dimension. In such cases, when the sensed connotations are limited, it is not surprising that there is little active use of the continuum as an organizing dimension. Why should one bother to say that a party is conservative if one can convey the same information by saying that it is against spending?

Since the 1960 materials on liberal-conservative meanings were drawn from the same sample as the coding of the active use of such frames of reference in 1956, it is possible to consider how well the two codings match. For a variety of reasons, we would not expect a perfect fit, even aside from coding error. The earlier coding had not been limited to the liberal-conservative dimension, and, although empirical instances were rare, a person could qualify as an "ideologue" if he assessed politics with the aid of some other highly abstract organizing dimension. Similarly, among those who did employ the liberal-conservative distinction, there were no requirements that the terms be defined. It was necessary therefore to depend upon appearances, and the classification was intentionally lenient. Furthermore, since a larger portion of the population would show recognition than showed active use, we could expect substantial numbers of people in the lower levels of conceptualization to show reasonable recognition of the terms. At any rate, we assumed that the two measures would show a high correlation, as they in fact did (Table 2).

Of course, very strong differences in education underlie the data shown in Table 2. The 2% of the sample that occupy the upper left-hand cell have a mean education close to seven years greater than that of the 11% that occupy the lower right-hand cell. Sixty-two per cent of this lower cell have had less formal education than the least educated person in the upper corner.... Although women have a higher mean education than men, there is some sex bias to the table, for women are disproportionately represented in the lower right-hand quadrant of the table. Furthermore, although age is negatively correlated with education there is also rather clear evidence that the sort of political sophistication represented by the measures can accumulate with age. Undoubtedly even sporadic observation of politics over long enough periods

Table 2 *Levels of Conceptualization (1956) by Recognition and Understanding of Terms "Conservatism" and "Liberalism" (1960)*

	Stratum	*Levels of Conceptualization* *Ideologue*	*Near Ideologue*	*Group Interest*	*Nature of the Times*	*No Issue Content*
	I	51%	29%	13%	16%	10%
Recognition and understanding*	II	43	46	42	40	22
	III	2	10	14	7	7
	IV	2	5	6	7	12
	V	2	10	25	30	49
		100%	100%	100%	100%	100%
Number of cases		(45)	(122)	(580)	(288)	(290)

*The definitions of the strata are: I. recognition and proper matching of label, meaning, and party and a broad understanding of the terms "conservative" and "liberal"; II. recognition and proper matching but a narrow definition of terms (like "spend-save"); III. recognition but some error in matching; IV. recognition and an attempt at matching but inability to give any meaning for terms: V. no apparent recognition of terms (does not know if parties differ in liberal-conservative terms and does not know if anybody else sees them as differing).

of time serves to nurture some broader view of basic liberal-conservative differences, although of course the same sophistication is achieved much more rapidly and in a more striking way by those who progress greater distances through the educational system.

CONSTRAINTS AMONG IDEA-ELEMENTS

In our estimation, the use of such basic dimensions of judgment as the liberal-conservative continuum betokens a contextual grasp of politics that permits a wide range of more specific idea-elements to be organized into more tightly constrained wholes. We feel, furthermore, that there are many crucial consequences of such organization: With it, for example, new political events have more meaning, retention of political information from the past is far more adequate, and political behavior increasingly approximates that of sophisticated "rational" models, which assume relatively full information.

It is often argued, however, that abstract dimensions like the liberal-conservative continuum are superficial if not meaningless indicators: All that they show is that poorly educated people are inarticulate and have difficulty expressing verbally the more abstract lines along which their specific political beliefs are organized. To expect these people to be able to express what they know and feel, the critic goes on, is comparable to the fallacy of assuming that people can say in an accurate way why they behave as they do. When it comes down to specific attitudes and behaviors, the organization is there nonetheless, and it it this organization that matters, not the capacity for discourse in sophisticated language.

If it were true that such organization does exist for most people, apart from their capacities to be articulate about it, we would agree out of hand that the question of articulation is quite trivial. As a cold empirical matter, however, this claim does not seem to be valid. Indeed, it is for this reason that we have cast the argument in terms of constraint,* for constraint and organization are very nearly the same thing. Therefore when we hypothesize that constraint among political idea-elements begins to lose its range very rapidly once we move from the most sophisticated few toward the "grass roots," we are contending that the organization of more specific attitudes into wideranging belief systems is absent as well.

Table 3 *Constraint between Specific Issue Beliefs for an Elite Sample and a Cross-Section Sample, 1958**

	Domestic					*Foreign*		
	Employment	*Education*	*Housing*	*F.E.P.C.*	*Economic*	*Military*†	*Isolationism*	*Party Preference*
Congressional candidates								
Employment	...	.62	.59	.35	.26	.06	.17	.68
Aid to education		...	.61	.53	.50	.06	.35	.55
Federal housing			...	.47	.41	−.03	.30	.68
F.E.P.C.				...	.47	.11	.23	.34
Economic aid					...	.19	.59	.25
Military aid						...	.32	−.18
Isolationism							...	.05
Party preference								...
Cross-Section Sample								
Employment	...	.45	.08	.34	−.04	.10	−.22	.20
Aid to education		...	.12	.29	.06	.14	−.17	.16
Federal housing			...	.08	−.06	.02	.07	.18
F.E.P.C.				...	.24	.13	.01	−.04
Economic aid					...	.16	.33	−.07
Soldiers abroad†						...	.21	.12
Isolationism							...	−.03
Party preference								...

*Entries are tau-gamma coefficients, a statistic proposed by Leo A. Goodman and William H. Kruskal in "Measures of Association for Cross Classification," *Journal of the American Statistical Association*, 49 (Dec. 1954), No. 268, 749. The coefficient was chosen because of its sensitivity to constraint of the scalar as well as the correlational type.

†For this category, the cross-section sample was asked a question about keeping American soldiers abroad, rather than about military aid in general.

*Constraint, or functional interdependence, refers to the assumption that certain attitudes and ideas tend to be interrelated and tightly organized, so that if a person's attitude on one issue is known, his attitudes on other (interrelated) issues can be reliably predicted.—ED.

Table 3 gives us an opportunity to see the differences in levels of constraint among beliefs on a range of specific issues in an elite population and in a mass population. The elite population happens to be candidates for the United States Congress in the off-year elections of 1958, and the cross-section sample represents the national electorate in the same year. The assortment of issues represented is simply a purposive sampling of some of the more salient political controversies at the time of the study, covering both domestic and foreign policy. The questions posed to the two samples were quite comparable, apart from adjustments necessary in view of the backgrounds of the two populations involved.[3]

For more purposes, however, the specific elite sampled and the specific beliefs tested are rather beside the point. We would expect the same general contrast to appear if the elite had been a set of newspaper editors, political writers or any other group that takes an interest in politics. Similarly, we would expect the same results from any other broad sampling of political issues or, for that matter, any sampling of beliefs from other domains: A set of questions on matters of religious controversy should show the same pattern between an elite population like the clergy and the church members who form their mass "public." What is generically important in comparing the two-types of population is the difference in levels of constraint among belief-elements.

Where constraint is concerned, the absolute value of the coefficients in Table 3 (rather than their algebraic value) is the significant datum. The first thing the table conveys is the fact that, for both populations, there is some falling off of constraint *between* the domains of domestic and foreign policy, relative to the high level of constraint *within* each domain. This result is to be expected: Such lowered values signify boundaries between belief systems that are relatively independent. If we take averages of appropriate sets of coefficients entered in Table 3 however, we see that the strongest constraint *within* a domain for the mass public is less than that *between* domestic and foreign domains for the elite sample. Furthermore, for the public, in sharp contrast to the elite, party preference seems by and large to be set off in a belief system of its own, relatively unconnected to issue positions (Table 4).[4]

It should be remembered throughout, of course, that the *mass* sample of Tables 3 and 4 does not exclude college-educated people, ideologues, or the politically sophisticated. These people, with their higher levels of constraint, are represented in appropriate numbers, and certainly contribute to such vestige of organization as the mass matrix evinces. But they are grossly outnumbered, as they are in the active electorate. The general point is that the

Table 4 *Summary of Differences in Level of Constraint within and between Domains, Public and Elite (based on Table 3)*

	Average Coefficients			
	Within Domestic Issues	*Between Domestic and Foreign*	*Within Foreign Issues*	*Between Issues and Party*
Elite	.53	.25	.37	.39
Mass	.23	.11	.23	.11

matrix of correlations for the elite sample is of the sort that would be appropriate for factor analysis, the statistical technique designed to reduce a number of correlated variables to a more limited set of organizing dimensions. The matrix representing the mass public, however, despite its realistic complement of ideologies, is exactly the type that textbooks advise against using for factor analysis on the simple grounds that through inspection it is clear that there is virtually nothing in the way of organization to be discovered. Of course, it is the type of broad organizing dimension to be suggested by factor analysis of specific items that is usually presumed when observers discuss "ideological postures" of one sort or another.

Although the beliefs registered in Table 3 are related to topics of controversy or political cleavage, McClosky has described comparable differences in levels of constraint among beliefs for an elite sample (delegates to national party conventions) and a cross-section sample when the items deal with propositions about democracy and freedom—topics on which fundamental consensus among Americans is presumed.[5] Similarly, Prothro and Grigg, among others, have shown that, while there is widespread support for statements of culturally familiar principles of freedom, democracy, and tolerance in a cross-section sample, this support becomes rapidly obscured when questions turn to specific cases that elites would see as the most direct applications of these principles.[6] In our estimation, such findings are less a demonstration of cynical lip service than of the fact that, while both of two inconsistent opinions are honestly held, the individual lacks the contextual grasp to understand that the specific case and the general principle belong in the same belief system: In the absence of such understanding, he maintains psychologically independent beliefs about both. This is another important instance of the decline in constraint among beliefs with declining information.

While an assessment of relative constraint between the matrices rests only on comparisons of absolute values, the comparative algebraic values have some interest as well. This interest arises from the sophisticated observer's almost automatic assumption that whatever beliefs "go together" in the visible political world (as judged from the attitudes of elites and the more articulate spectators) must naturally go together in the same way among mass public. Table 3 makes clear that this assumption is a very dangerous one, aside from the question of degree of constraint. For example, the politician who favors federal aid to education could be predicted to be more, rather than less, favorable to an internationalist posture in foreign affairs, for these two positions in the 1950s were generally associated with "liberalism" in American politics. As we see from Table 3, we would be accurate in this judgment considerably more often than chance alone would permit. On the other hand, were we to apply the same assumption of constraint to the American public in the same era, not only would we have been wrong, but we would actually have come closer to reality by assuming no connection at all.

All the correlations in the elite sample except those that do not depart significantly from zero exhibit signs that anybody following politics in the newspapers during this period could have predicted without hesitation. That is, one need only have known that Democrats tended to favor expansion of government welfare activities and tended to be internationalists in foregn affairs, to have anticipated all the signs except one. This exception, the -.18 that links advocacy of military aid abroad with the Republican Party, would hold no surprises either, for the one kind of international involvement that Republicans came to accept in this period limited foreign aid to the military variety, a view that stood in opposition to "soft" liberal interests in international economic welfare. If these algebraic signs in the elite matrix are taken as the culturally defined "proper" signs—the sophisticated observer's assumption of what beliefs go with what other beliefs—then the algebraic differences between comparable entries in the two matrices provide an estimate of how inaccurate we would be in generalizing our elite-based assumptions about "natural" belief combinations to the mass public as a whole. A scanning of the two matrices with these differences in mind enhances our sense of high discrepancy between the two populations.

To recapitulate, then, we have argued that the unfamiliarity of broader and more abstract ideological frames of reference among the less sophisticated is more than a problem in mere articulation. Parallel to ignorance and confusion over these ideological dimensions among the less informed is a general decline in constraint among specific belief elements that such dimensions help to organize. It cannot therefore be claimed that the mass public shares ideological patterns of belief with relevant elites at a specific level any more than it shares the abstract conceptual frames of reference.

CONCLUSION

We have long been intrigued, in dealing with attitudinal and behavioral materials drawn from cross-section publics, at the frequency with which the following sequence of events occurs. An hypothesis is formed that seems reasonable to the analyst, having to do with one or another set of systematic differences in perceptions, attitudes, or behavior patterns. The hypothesis is tested on materials from the general population but shows at best some rather uninteresting trace findings. Then the sample is further subdivided by formal education, which isolates among other groups the 10% of the American population with college degrees or the 20% with some college education. It frequently turns out that the hypothesis is then very clearly confirmed for the most educated, with results rapidly shading off to zero within the less educated majority of the population.

We do not claim that such an analytic approach always produces findings of this sort. From time to time, of course, the hypothesis in question can be more broadly rejected for all groups, and, on rare occasions, a relationship turns out to be sharper among the less educated than among the well-educated. Nevertheless, there is a strikingly large class of cases in which confirmation occurs only, or most sharply, among the well educated. Usually it is easy to see, after the fact if not before, the degree to which the dynamics of the processes assumed by the hypothesis rest upon the kinds of broad or abstract contextual information about currents of ideas, people, or society that educated people come to take for granted as initial ingredients of thought but that the most cursory studies will demonstrate are not widely shared. As experiences of this sort accumulate, we become increasingly sensitive to these basic problems of information and begin to predict their results in advance.

This awareness means that we come to expect hypotheses about wide-ranging yet highly integrated belief systems and their behavioral consequences to show results among relative elites but to be largely disconfirmed below them. It is our impression, for example, that even some of the more elaborate "ideological" patterns associated with the authoritarian personality syndrome follow this rule. Some recent results that have accumulated in connection with the Protestant-ethic hypothesis of Weber seem to hint at something of the same pattern as well.

In this paper, we have attempted to make some systematic comments on this kind of phenomenon that seem crucial to any understanding of elite and mass belief systems. We have tried to show the character of this "continental shelf" between elites and masses and to locate the sources of differences in their belief systems in some simple characteristics of information and its social transmission.

The broad contours of elite decisions over time can depend in a vital way upon currents in what is loosely called "the history of ideas." These decisions in turn have effects upon the mass of more common citizens. But, of any direct participation in this history of ideas and the behavior it shapes, the mass is remarkably innocent. We do not disclaim the existence of entities that might best be called "folk ideologies," nor do we deny for a moment that strong differentiations in a variety of narrower values may be found within subcultures of less educated people. Yet for the familiar belief systems that, in view of their historical importance, tend most to attract the sophisticated observer, it is likely that an adequate mapping of a society (or, for that matter, the world) would provide a jumbled cluster of pyramids or a mountain range, with sharp delineation and differentiation in beliefs from elite apex to elite apex but with the mass bases of the pyramids overlapping in such profusion that it would be impossible to decide where one pyramid ended and another began.

ENDNOTES

1. Some modest internal support for the validity of the distinction between those who spoke in terms of broad philosophy and those who offered narrower explanations may be seen in the fact that only 5% of the former category had previously judged the Democrats to be more conservative than the Republicans. Among those giving less elevated "best answers," 14% deemed the Democrats the more conservative party. And, to give some sense of the "continental shelf" being explored here, among those who had responded that a certain party was more conservative than the other but who subsequently confessed that they did not know what the distinction implied, 35% had chosen the Democrats as the more conservative, a figure that is beginning to approach the 50-50 assignment of sheer guesswork.

2. In all candor, it should probably be mentioned that a teacher grading papers would be unlikely to give passing marks to more than 20% of the attempted definitions (or to 10% of the total sample). We made an effort, however, to be as generous as possible in our assignment.

3. This cell is laden, of course, with people who are apathetic and apolitical, although more than half of them vote in major elections. Flanigan, working with the total sample, set aside those who never vote as politically inconsequential and then set about comparing the remainder of self-styled independents with strong partisans. Some of the customary findings relating political independence with low involvement and low information then became blurred or in some cases reversed themselves altogether. Our highly sophisticated independents contribute to this phenomenon. See William H. Flanigan, "Partisanship and Campaign Participation" (Unpublished doctoral dissertation, Yale University, 1961).

4. As a general rule, questions broad enough for the mass public to understand tend to be too simple for highly sophisticated people to feel comfortable answering

without elaborate qualification. The pairing of questions, with those for the mass public given first, are as follows:

Employment. "The government in Washington ought to see to it that everybody who wants to work can find a job." "Do you think the federal government ought to sponsor programs such as large public works in order to maintain full employment, or do you think that problems of economic readjustment ought to be left more to private industry or state and local government?"

Aid to Education. "If cities and towns around the country need help to build more schools, the government in Washington ought to give them the money they need." "Do you think the government should provide grants to the states for the construction and operation of public schools, or do you think the support of public education should be left entirely to the state and local government?"

Federal Housing. "The government should leave things like electric power and housing for private businessmen to handle." "Do you approve the use of federal funds for public housing, or do you generally feel that housing can be taken care of better by private effort?"

F.E.P.C. "If Negroes are not getting fair treatment in jobs and housing, the government should see to it that they do." "Do you think the federal government should establish a fair employment practices commission to prevent discrimination in employment?"

Economic Aid. "The United States should give economic help to the poorer countries of the world even if those countries can't pay for it." "First, on the foreign economic aid program, would you generally favor expanding the program, reducing it, or maintaining it about the way it is?"

Military Aid. "The United States should keep soldiers overseas where they can help countries that are against Communism." "How about the foreign military aid program? Should this be expanded, reduced, or maintained about as it is?"

Isolationism. "This country would be better off if we just stayed home and did not concern ourselves with problems in other parts of the world." "Speaking very generally, do you think that in the years ahead the United States should maintain or reduce its commitments around the world?"

5. We are aware that drawing an average of these coefficients has little interpretation from a statistical point of view. The averages are presented merely as a crude way of capturing the flavor of the larger table in summary form. More generally, it could be argued that the coefficients might be squared in any event, an operation that would do no more than heighten the intuitive sense of contrast between the two publics.

6. Herbert McClosky, "Consensus and Ideology in American Politics," *American Political Science Review,* 58 (June, 1964), No. 2.

7. James W. Prothro and C. W. Grigg, "Fundamental Principles of Democracy: Bases of Agreement and Disagreement," *Journal of Politics,* 22 (May, 1960), No. 2, 276–94.

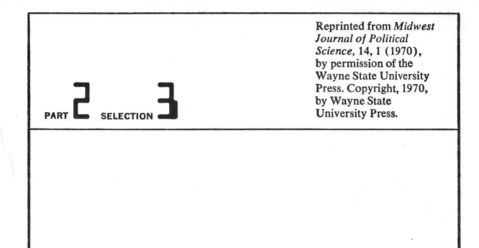

Reprinted from *Midwest Journal of Political Science,* 14, 1 (1970), by permission of the Wayne State University Press. Copyright, 1970, by Wayne State University Press.

Party Identification and the Changing Role of Ideology in American Politics

JOHN C. PIERCE

The findings reported in this paper stem from an analysis of data collected in three national surveys of the American electorate conducted by the Survey Research Center of the University of Michigan in 1956, 1960, and 1964. These data are distributed through the Inter-University Consortium for Political Research. Between 1,500 and 2,000 respondents are included in each survey. The two variables whose measurement needs explanation at this time are partisanship and ideological influence manifestation. The partisanship of the voters is measured in the conventional manner. Each individual is asked to identify himself as one of the following: Strong Democrat, Weak Democrat, Independent Democrat, Independent, Independent Republican, Weak Republican, or Strong Republican. Some respondents refuse to classify themselves on this dimension when claiming no orientation at all to these parties or claiming to be a partisan of some other minor party. However, those particular respondents comprise a very small proportion of the electorate. So, later in the [selection] when the reference is to Strong Democrats the basis of that classification is the strength of the verbalized psychological identification of the individual with the Democratic party.

The manifestation of ideological influence in a voter is measured in three ways:[1] a conceptual measure, an informational measure, and an affective measure. Those who manifest the influence of ideology in any one of these three ways are "ideologues," while those who manifest no influence of ideology by any measure are "non-ideologues." An individual may be identified as an ideologue on more than one of the measures or he may be classified as an ideologue on none of them.

The conceptual measure of ideological influence manifestation is a content analysis of the responses of individuals to questions about what they dislike and like about American parties and candidates, in particular the Republican and Democratic parties and their particular presidential candidates. The basis for the application of the measure is the way in which individuals conceptualize politics through their analysis of the parties and candidates.[2] Individuals who use ideological terms and concepts to evaluate these political objects are classified as "ideologues." In its scope, this ideological conceptualization is considered to be the most sophisticated and broad-sweeping of conceptualizations. Moving away from ideological conceptualization there are the following levels: group interest, the nature of the times, and no issue content at all in the responses. An example of the ideological conceptualization would be: "I don't like the Democrats because they are too liberal. They want the government to do too much." An example of group interest conceptualization: "The Republicans are good for business," or, "The Republicans are tough on the working man." An example of the nature of the times conceptualization: "Times are good when the Democrats are in power." Moreover, within the ideological level of conceptualization one can distinguish between full ideologues and near-ideologues. The near-ideologues employ ideological terms and concepts but do not seem to back them up with reference to substantive policies. So, the conceptual measure has the following levels: ideologue, near-ideologue, group interest, nature of the times, and no issue content. However, for this study the ideologue and near-ideologue categories are collapsed together into one "ideologue" group.

The informational ideologues are determined through a measure called the "strata of knowledge and understanding."[3] Respondents are asked to identify the "conservative" party when comparing the Republicans and the Democrats in American politics. They are also asked to give a definition of conservatism. Those individuals who give a broad accurate definition of conservatism and identify the Republicans as the more conservative are defined as informational ideologues.[4] Other points on the measure evidence less generality and accuracy in the ideological definition and knowledge to a point where the bottom stratum contains those individuals with no idea of what comprises conservatism and no idea of which party is the more conservative.

The affective measure of ideological influence manifestation involves responses of individuals to a question asking them to place their feelings towards liberals and conservatives on a thermometric dimension running from very hot to very cold. Those individuals who are very hot (quite favorable) in their affect towards one group and quite cold toward the other are designated as affective ideologues. This measure taps an individual's psychological orientations to the dominant ideologies and ideological grouping in American politics.

The conceptual, informational and affective constructs of the manifestation of ideological influence in individuals measure three basically different orientations to political objects. The conceptual orientation is essentially a "functional" one. Ideological terms and concepts perform an evaluative function for the individual in that they provide a basis by which to evaluate or judge political objects.[5] Ideology, or an ideological term, therefore may be economical for the individual to use when coping with his political environment. The informational measure assesses the substantive cognitive mass about ideological objects which the individual brings to politics.[6] Presumably, the individual who has a greater mass of information about ideological objects is able to consider ideological phenomena in a manner different from one who has no such mass. The affective measure examines the extremity of one's psychological orientation to ideological symbols, but this orientation need not necessarily rely on either information or the functional use of the symbols.

These three distinct orientations are useful in comparing the ideological basis of partisanship and the response of individuals to an ideological object in the campaign rhetoric of an election. The camparisons are somewhat limited by the fact that the conceptual measure is available only for the 1956 and 1964 survey results, the informational is available only for the 1960 and 1964 survey, and the affective only for the 1964 study. However, these measures enable one to undertake the basic tasks of this study: 1) to find out if the presence of an ideological candidate increases the number of ideologues in an electorate and if the increase is related to partisanship and 2) if the ideological candidate seems to influence political behavior or psychological political orientations among ideologues.

THE FINDINGS

Concentrations of "ideologues" within partisan organizations of a political system may have several consequences for that system. Ideology as a basis for political parties (as perhaps a type of mass movement) is said to contribute to the intensity of political conflict and consequently the likelihood of radicalization or ideological polarization in a political system.[7] It is consequently important to determine if the potential for ideological party conflict, as measured by the number of ideologues, seems to vary from year to year along with the ideological character of the actors involved in the political arena. If so, it may be possible for political parties and candidates to stimulate ideological conflict within the electorate. Moreover, one may find that one particular party is more likely to be subject to the appeals of an ideological candidate. Additionally, if one finds a substantial number of ideologues who are psychologically identified with neither of the two major parties, i.e., Independents, there is the potential for ideologically generated conflict which is not bounded or constrained by traditional party politics in America. That is, the Independent ideologues would not have the psychological tie of party identification to mediate between the ideological call and any subsequent political behavior.

Republicans and Democrats differ significantly in the proportion of ideologues.[8] As Table 1 shows, in 1964 almost twice as many Strong Republicans are ideologues as are Strong Democrats. Moreover, more Independents than Democrats are ideologues. So, at least in the number of individuals who manifest the influence of ideology the direction of partisanship seems to play a fairly important role. One might also conclude from this that the Republican sector of the electorate would be more likely to respond to political phenomena presented in ideological terms. Even among the Democrats, however, there are enough ideologues for that party to become a vehicle for ideological conflict.

The campaigns for president in 1956 and 1960 can be safely described as non-ideological. Neither the candidates nor the issues were essentially ideological in nature. However, the successful bid of Senator Barry Goldwater for the Republican presidential nomination in 1964 enabled a self-proclaimed conservative[9] to become the focus of national attention. This ideological stimulus in the political arena seems to have been associated with an increase in the number of conceptual ideologues, but not with an increase in the number of informational ideologues. As Table 2 shows, in every category of partisanship the proportion of conceptual ideologues in 1964 more than doubled the proportion found in 1956. The absolute increases from 1956 to 1964 are much greater for the Republicans than for the Democrats. Consequently, not only did the Republicans have a greater

Table 1 *Ideological Influence Manifestation and Party Identification, 1964*

A. *Ideologues Collapsed* *

	Party Identification				
	Strong Dem.	Weak Dem.	Ind.	Weak Rep.	Strong Rep.
Proportion Ideologues	.33	.30	.40	.45	.65
N	(377)	(355)	(306)	(190)	(157)

B. *Ideologues Separated* *

Proportion Ideologue Type	Party Identification				
	Strong Dem.	Weak Dem.	Ind.	Weak Rep.	Strong Rep.
Conceptual	.22	.19	.28	.35	.41
Informational	.16	.13	.14	.13	.31
Affective	.05	.04	.06	.07	.16
N	(377)	(355)	(306)	(190)	(157)

* Part A of the table collapses all of the ideologue types together, while part B keeps them separate. Because individual respondents may be identified as more than one type of ideologue, the total within a partisanship category in part B does not equal the total number of ideologues in part A for that same category.

reservoir of conceptual ideologues with which to work (.19 to .10) but the increase in ideologues evidenced by them was also much greater than that of the Democrats (+.22 to +.12). So, the conclusion that there is a greater ideological basis to the Republican following than to the Democratic following seems to be reinforced. However, the greater increase in ideological sensitivity among the Republicans may be a function of the party of the candidate, i.e., also Republican. For more adequate substantiations of this explanation one needs data from an election with a Democratic ideological candidate.

Although a significant increase in the number of conceptual ideologues was evidenced in 1964, no such increase in the proportion of informational ideologues is found in any of the partisanship categories. One might ask the reason for this and the explanation is probably found in the divergent character of the phenomena examined by the two measures. That is, it would

Table 2 *Changes in Proportion of Ideologues in Partisanship Categories*

A. *Conceptual Manifestation: 1956-1964.*

Proportion Ideologues	Party Identification				
	Strong Demo.	Weak Demo.	Ind.	Weak Rep.	Strong Rep.
1956	.10	.09	.13	.16	.19
1964	.22	.19	.28	.35	.41
Change	+.12	+.10	+.15	+.19	+.22
Ratio *	2.22	2.11	2.17	2.18	2.16

B. *Informational Manifestation: 1960-1964.*

Proportion Ideologues	Party Identification				
	Strong Demo.	Weak Demo.	Ind.	Weak Rep.	Strong Rep.
1960	.14	.14	.20	.21	.31
1964	.16	.13	.19	.23	.31
Change	+.02	−.01	−.01	+.02	.00
Ratio **	1.14	.93	.95	1.10	0.00

* The ratio is the proportion of ideologues in 1964 over the proportion of ideologues in 1956.

** The ratio is the proportion of ideologues in 1964 over the proportion of ideologues in 1960.

take much less psychological effort for an individual to merely reflect campaign rhetoric emphasizing the ideological character of political agents (the conceptual measure) than for him to increase the mass of information he holds. In fact, the reflection of the ideological content of campaign rhetoric in one's evaluation of relevant political objects without a concurrent increase in the mass of information held by him should save the individual a great deal of psychological effort.[10]

Even if it is psychologically easy for one to reflect campaign rhetoric, it does not necessarily follow that the increase in conceptual ideologues stemmed from the influx of unsophisticated voters. Table 3 presents the percentages of individuals at each level of conceptual manifestation within each of the partisanship categories for 1956 and 1964. As that table shows, the increase in the ideologues seems to have come at the benefit of the "group interest" categorization. That is, the decrease in the percentage on the group interest level is very similar to the increases in the ideologue level.[11] So, it appears that many individuals merely moved up from one level to the next in their conceptualization of political phenomena. Conclusive proof of this assertion would demand panel studies of the same respondents in 1964 as in 1956. Unfortunately, these data are not available.

Table 3 *Percentage of Levels of Conceptual Manifestation within Partisan Categories, 1956–1964*

	Party Identification				
Conceptual Level	Strong Demo.	Weak Demo.	Ind.	Weak Rep.	Strong Rep.
1956					
Ideologue	10%	9%	13%	16%	19%
Group Interest	65	50	38	31	29
Nature of Times	16	20	24	28	39
No Issue Content	9	21	25	25	21
Total	100%	100%	100%	100%	100%
N	(363)	(401)	(412)	(247)	(261)
1964					
Ideologue	22%	19%	28%	35%	41%
Group Interest	42	33	21	13	10
Nature of Times	20	20	22	20	16
No Issue Content	16	18	30	33	32
Total	100%	100%	101%	100%	100%
N	(417)	(384)	(353)	(209)	(201)

To this point the following conclusions can be made. The proportion of ideologues among Republican identifiers is greater than the proportion of ideologues among Democratic identifiers. The proportion of ideologues among self-identified Independents is large enough for an ideological movement to develop outside of the traditional two party system. Increases in the number of ideologues in 1964 appear for the conceptual measure but not for the informational. Although the Republicans had more conceptual ideologues to begin with they also demonstrated the greatest increase in 1964 in the number of those ideologues—presumably because of the party of the ideological candidate.[12]

SUMMARY AND CONCLUSIONS

The results of this study suggest that political party followings are a potential source of ideological conflict in the United States. Three measures of "ideologues" assessed the scope of ideological sensitivity in the American electorate. Using three distinct measures increased the number of individuals encompassed by the "ideologue" concept. By employing only one measure the number of ideologues would have been greatly reduced; and, the differences between ideologues and non-ideologues would have been diminished because of the inclusion in the non-ideologue category of many identified as ideologues by another measure. . . .

The number of ideologues is the greatest in the Republican party ranks, providing a substantial base for such ideological candidates as Barry Goldwater. The entrance of an ideological candidate such as Goldwater into the political arena increased the salience of ideological concerns among the entire electorate, but most significantly among members of his own party. Moreover, the data for 1964 indicate a sufficient number of ideologues to support future ideologically based movements and candidates both within the Democratic party and outside of the two major parties. Indeed, the 1968 election campaign experienced both of these. The ideological appeals of McCarthy, McGovern, and Kennedy accumulated a great amount of support among Democrats. Likewise, the George Wallace movement drew disproportionately well among the Independents and his appeal was at least in part ideological.[13] Obviously, neither Wallace nor one of the ideological Democrats became president in 1968 but to say that they had no influence on political outcomes would be difficult. Wallace's appeals were certainly echoed in the campaign statements of both Humphrey and Nixon, and many credit McCarthy with stimulating the withdrawal of the incumbent President, Lyndon Johnson.

As well as stimulating an increase in the number of ideologues in 1964, the apparent ideological rhetoric of the campaign stimulated an increase in the participation and psychological involvement of ideologues, and consequently compounded the influence of ideological factors on the electoral outcome. These phenomena, plus the current ideological and social conflict in the United States, suggest several things. Ideology is not dead in the United States. While a majority of the electorate does not seem to be ideologically motivated, it is obvious that such a majority is not needed to profoundly influence political events. The potential consequences of ideological politics for a political system are rather severe and push deep into the foundations of such a system. As Sorauf notes, ideological politics breed rigidity,[14] and rigidity often leads to intense and violent conflict. Such politics even threaten a system whose political life has been based on compromise[15] and a commitment to institutions at the expense of ideologies.

Politics in the present American environment (particularly, but not solely, within the University) certainly appears to be shifting to an emphasis on ideology at the expense of the institutions. Consequently, what makes the sensitivity of individuals to ideological forces important to the political scientist is its systemic consequences. Ideologies or ideological concerns may float in and out of political rhetoric, but they have no real impact unless they move individuals—either leaders or the mass—to act in a significant direction. As noted above, such action may result in an intensification and rigidity of political conflict and, in the end, may substantially change the entire political system.

ENDNOTES

1. That there is a belief system basis for these manifestations is demonstrated in my unpublished paper "The Structural Bases of Orientations to Ideological Symbols."

2. This measure was first employed by Angus Campbell, *et al.* in *The American Voter* (New York: John Wiley and Sons, Inc., 1960), Chapter 10.

3. This measure was first developed by Philip E. Converse, and reported in Converse, "The Nature of Belief Systems in Mass Publics," in *Ideology and Discontent,* edited by David Apter (New York: The Free Press, 1964).

4. Accurate, broad definitions accepted included such things as "posture toward change," the protection of the status quo, positions toward the welfare state, socialism, free enterprise, or capitalism, the expanding power of the government and the relationship of the government to the individual. For a justification of these criteria see Converse, *Ibid.*

5. As David Minar demonstrates, this functional use of ideology is recognized by many scholars. In fact, many definitions of ideology are functionally based. See, David W. Minar, "Ideology and Political Behavior," *Midwest Journal of Political Science,* 5 (November, 1961), No. 4, 317–31.

6. For a discussion and implementation of information mass as a conceptual tool see Philip E. Converse, "Information Flow and the Stability of Partisan Attitudes," *Public Opinion Quarterly,* 26 (Winter 1962), 578–99.

7. Frank J. Sorauf, *Political Parties in the American System* (Boston: Little Brown and Company, 1964), 78–79.

8. Much of Barry Goldwater's campaign strategy was based on the assumption that in the electorate there existed a large reservoir of ideological voters just waiting for a "true" conservative candidate. These voters, presumably, had not found their candidate in any previous election and they consequently would be new voters in the 1964 election. In one sense, Goldwater had an accurate perception of the electorate. Of the ideologues who did not vote in 1960, 64 percent voted in 1964, while only 36 percent of the non-ideologues who failed to vote in 1960 did so in

1964. Consequently, Goldwater did seem to stimulate the ideologues to greater participation. However, there were only 105 ideologues who were non-voters in 1960, compared to 261 non-ideologues not voting in 1960.

Of non-voters in 1960, ideologues were more likely to vote than non-ideologues. This part of Goldwater's thesis seems to be correct. However, to make the outcome of his strategy one of victory, these new voting ideologues should have supported Goldwater overwhelmingly. However, both the ideologue and the non-ideologue voters who did not vote in 1960 voted more than three to one for Johnson in 1964. It is true that a slightly lower percentage (69) of ideologues voted for Johnson than did the non-ideologues (80), (both percentages taken of those who did not vote in 1960), but even among the ideologues stimulated to vote in 1964 Goldwater was clearly a decisive loser.

9. See Barry Goldwater, *Conscience of a Conservative* (Shepardsville, Kentucky: Victor Publishing Co., 1960).

10. Anthony Downs, *An Economic Theory of Democracy* (New York: Harper and Row, 1957).

11. In fact, when separating the ideologues from the near-ideologues, it appears that the movement from the group-interest level was primarily into the near-ideologue level. This would support the contentions that the voters who moved upward in the levels of conceptualization moved the shortest possible distance and the one that would require the least amount of effort to support. It probably would require as much increased effort to reach the full-ideologue level as it would to likewise demonstrate an increase in ideological information.

12. Controls for level of education of respondents (which are generally associated with being Republicans and also with the ability to conceptualize) do not appreciably affect any of these conclusions. They are not reported here in order to preserve space and maintain the continuity of the argument.

13. See *The 1968 Elections,* The Republican National Committee, Washington, D.C., Ray C. Bliss, Chairman, 1969, p. 231.

14. Sorauf, *op. cit.*

15. That much of American politics has been based on compromise is a common conclusion reached by scholars. For example, see Lewis Froman, Jr., *People and Politics* (Englewood Cliffs: Prentice-Hall, Inc., 1962), pp. 56–57.

Public Opinion: Problems of Description and Inference

LANCE BENNETT

The issue of "what the public thinks" has been a central concern of both normative and empirical political theory for some time. Traditional democratic theorists have long argued that democracy is possible only if people recognize the issues that face the state and have attitudes or opinions about these issues. A common complaint throughout history has been that the general public neither knows enough nor cares enough to adequately manage its political destiny.

In the decade of the 1960s, a great deal of empirical evidence was offered in support of such claims about the ignorance and indifference of the average democratic citizen. Important studies by Prothro and Grigg, McClosky, Almond and Verba, Converse, Campbell, Stokes, Miller, and others, all pointed to the same conclusion. It appeared that in America, and elsewhere, citizens in democracies were painfully uninformed, uninterested, and often "undemocratic" in their political outlooks.

A number of political scientists are just beginning to take a critical look at these claims, and the theoretical and methodological underpinnings of the above-mentioned body of survey research are being given a well-deserved examination. Questions are being raised as to whether the negative attributions assigned to democratic mass publics may be simply the artifacts of poorly defined and tested theory and hastily drawn empirical inference.

Though some of the criticisms of this research may be somewhat extreme, the reader should be aware that there are alternative models which should be considered before accepting the popular notion that the average citizen has a poorly articulated grasp of the political world. This article explores some alternatives to this popular, pejorative, and possibly erroneous view of the nature of public opinion in America.

THE POLITICAL STATE OF MIND: FACT OR ARTIFACT?

As suggested above, the problem of what the political world means to the average American citizen has been fairly well resolved in the minds of many political scientists. The consensus seems to be that the average person doesn't have a coherent or stable perspective on political events; or, to put it in simple words, political issues and events do not make much sense to most people. Let's test the foundation of this claim by looking at a few of the general assumptions upon which the claim rests.

First, there is the matter of the relationship between time, people, and the meaning people assign to political events. The problem here is simple. What conclusions can be drawn if you ask someone for his or her attitude on an issue today, and return two years hence to discover that the attitude has changed direction? One possibility is that the social and political conditions that produced the original issue have changed over time, and the person sees the issue in a different light. Another possibility is that the person has been gradually exposed to new information and ways of thinking about the matter and may have modified his or her opinion accordingly. Finally, it is possible that the individual did not find the issue meaningful in the first place. One would have to make assumptions like the last one and reject the first two in order to support the empirical inference that the person has unstable and meaningless attitudes.

A second set of assumptions has to do with the ways in which beliefs and attitudes can be meaningfully related to one another. For example, what do we make of a person who professes a belief in the principle of free speech, yet argues that a Communist should not be allowed to speak in public?

We might consider the possibility that the person has worked out a private, but no less meaningful, perspective on the politics of public speech based on his or her personal experiences with the issues of communism and freedom. The "logic" of this privately developed perspective could allow the coexistence of the two beliefs.[1] On the other hand, we might claim that the only meaningful political perspectives in a democracy are organized in terms of some sort of universal "democratic logic." Under such an assumption, we might infer that since free speech is known to apply to everyone in this country, the above individual does not have a coherent political perspective.[2] Here, again, one must accept the latter assumption and reject the former in order to argue that the mass public is inconsistent in its political beliefs.

A third assumption is a bit more subtle. What if a person seems to have stable attitudes over time (see the first assumption) but only on issues that are of high personal or group interest? One interpretation might be that politics—as people construe it—is an instrumental game which mainly requires attending to one's own concerns. Another interpretation might be that since political attitudes can be organized in terms of some universally known logic (see the second assumption), all political issues are interrelated. Therefore, concentration on *sui generis* issues of personal concern shows a lack of meaningful political perspective. If one accepts the second interpretation over the first, it follows that the person who operates primarily on the basis of personal or group interest may possess an incoherent or inadequate sense of politics.

Despite the existence of such possible alternative assumptions, the above-mentioned claims about the nature of attitudes in the mass public have been among the least debated points in contemporary political theory. These claims have been further dignified by the many theoretical fortifications that have been erected around them. The law-like status of these claims about the American public is typified by Merelman's brief reference near the beginning of an important paper:

> It is by now commonplace that the mass of Americans do not have a sophisticated conceptual organization by which politics may be understood. Perhaps the aptest description of this situation is contained in Philip E. Converse's "The Nature of Belief Systems in Mass Publics."[3]

Indeed, Converse's work has been taken by many as the definitive account of the problem. This is by no means a claim that he is the only one to reach the conclusion that members of the general public are inconsistent, unstable or inarticulate in their orientations toward politics.[4] However, his presentation of data and outline of theory are impressive, and they have provided a focus for the findings and arguments of many other investigators. Let's examine the basis for his claim that "... a mass public contains significant proportions of people who, for lack of information about a particular dimension of controversy, offer meaningless opinions that vary randomly in direction during repeated trials over time."[5]

Converse showed that attitude correlations (stability coefficients) over time were rather low on *each* of a number of political issues presented to a national sample. Subjects were requested to indicate their agreement with certain positions on issues such as school desegregation, fair employment practices, foreign aid, and the regulation of housing and utilities. The correlations on these issues over a two year period ranged from a high near .5 to a low of .3. Converse measured the attitudes of this sample on a third occasion and could again find no consistent pattern or explanation to account for the attitude changes of the group as a whole. Apparently Converse rejects the possibility that individual members of a group may change their attitudes *at different rates* and *for different reasons* based on personal experiences; in other words, that individual members of a sample may change their attitudes with different frequency, in different directions, and to different degrees. These attitudes might be logical from the individual's point of view, but the pattern of the entire sample could appear to be random. Neglecting this possibility of significant, but diverse, individual changes within the group, Converse simply concludes that: "... there is no single meaningful process of change shared by all respondents that would generate this configuration of data."[6]

The important point to keep in mind here is that data do not interpret themselves. The researcher must rely on the kinds of assumptions mentioned above. Converse seems to rely heavily on the assumption that beliefs and attitudes can be organized in terms of some universal logic. His conclusion is therefore based on the belief that meaningful attitudes must be organized and changed according to some *universally shared* set of rules or system of logic. It is important to critically evaluate such assumptions because our "factual" knowledge of public opinion rests heavily upon them. The next section of this article explores the different descriptions of public opinion that would result from different assumptions about how attitudes are organized.

MODELS OF ATTITUDE ORGANIZATION AND THE DESCRIPTION OF PUBLIC OPINION

Converse and others claim that belief systems are socially organized and constrained. The idea of constraint implies the binding together, or "functional interdependence," of beliefs and attitudes within a belief system. Beliefs and attitudes, in short, are constrained if holding one implies holding another, or if changing one implies changing another.[7] There are a number of theories about the sources of constraint in people's belief systems. The most popular theory of mass attitude organization deals with the way in which political elites shape the opinions of the mass public.

This theory argues that elites in the political arena formulate logically constrained issue clusters and positions. The elites are able to do so because their experience with and information about politics gives them a contextual grasp of the larger historical, political, social, and economic settings in which issues and events are played out. The issue clusters then "trickle down" to the general public via the media, organizations, interaction networks and other means of diffusion. As they drift down the political ladder, many of the linkages that hold issues within a logically constrained structure become blurred and the average citizen lacks the contextual grasp to put the structure back together again.[8]

The idea that social constraint operates on a "trickle down" principle hinges on a number of assumptions. First, we must assume that there are no competing (e.g., grassroots) perspective channels in society. Secondly, we must assume that people down the political ladder have no beliefs and outlooks of their own that they use to interpret and reconstruct the flow from media, opinion leaders, and politicians. Finally, we must accept the premise that some universal sociopolitical "logic" exists in society. Such a "logic" would have to: 1) postulate the existence of certain connections among belief elements that are meaningful for elites, and 2) exclude the possibility of alternative connections (or patterns) among belief elements that would be meaningful for the mass.

This latter point merits some expansion. It is often assumed that beliefs and attitudes are organized socially along one or a few general dimensions. A popular example is the liberal-conservative continuum. Serious questions exist as to how, or even whether, such dimensions function in society. We have very little evidence, for example, on the question of whether such ideological dimensions are actually *used* by members of the polity *to organize* beliefs. Belief organization may hinge on a complex set of social and psychological factors. Such factors may include personality needs, the individual's style of thinking and reasoning, the opinions of respected persons and reference groups, and immediate environmental pressures to conform to certain views. It is not clear how important ideology is in comparison to these and the many other factors that can influence belief organization. What does it mean to say that elites have ideology and members of the mass don't? In this context, we might want to take a different view of Converse's statement that the liberal conservative continuum is "... a rather elegant high order abstraction, and such abstractions are not typically conceptual tools for the 'man in the street'."[9]

The most serious problem with a concept like liberal-conservative continuum is that it does not reveal its own logic. The analyst must discover the "logic," or the principle of constraint, which operates within it. It appears to this author that many political scientists have elevated their own notions of the "logic" of liberal democracy to the status of being *the* way of organizing political perceptions in this culture. In the early 1960s, a number of researchers found a large gap among the general public between agreement on general democratic principles and agreement on the application of these principles to specific issues. For example, McClosky found that nearly universal agreement existed on the general principles of free speech and procedural rights. However, there was relatively little agreement that these principles should be applied in sensitive matters involving "foreign ideas," "communism," "treason," and the like.[10] What do we make of these data? McClosky concluded (rightly, I suspect) that the majority of the public are "innocent of ideology" *if* ". . . ideology is defined as that cluster of axioms, values, and beliefs which have given form and substance to American democracy and the Constitution."[11]

A matter of concern here is the possibility that the inference that the public is "innocent of ideology" may have been generalized out of this qualified context. If the analyst assumes that this democratic ideology is the most, or the only, meaningful way to organize beliefs in the society, then he is perfectly justified in dropping the qualification of context. It is just such an assumption that I wish to call in question, however. How much do our assumptions about liberal democracy affect our ability to see other things going on in the society? Are we justified in concluding, as McClosky does, that the "non-ideologues" who comprise the general population have "misguided opinions or non-opinions"?[12]

In an earlier study with similar empirical results, Prothro and Grigg clearly stated that their definition of ideology stemmed from normative concerns about how beliefs ought to be organized in a democracy.[13] They acknowledged that the low order of agreement on specific applications of general democratic principles might be explained by the presence of other, possibly conflicting belief systems in society. For example, beliefs about Communists may compete with beliefs about democracy. Beliefs about minority groups may conflict with beliefs about civil liberties. This important distinction between empirical and normative concerns has been lost in the course of successive studies (beginning with the above-mentioned McClosky study).

As a result of the gradually growing confusion of empirical and normative assumptions, the finding that most people do not always endorse "democratic" principles when they are put in specific terms is often taken as evidence that the average person doesn't know "what goes with what" politically. Converse, for example, voices the following popular *post mortem* on the McClosky and Prothro and Grigg studies:

> . . . the individual lacks the contextual grasp to understand that the specific case and the general principle belong in the same belief system. In the absence of such understanding he maintains psychologically independent beliefs about both. This is another important instance of the decline of constraint among beliefs.[14]

While it is clear that support for democratic values by the mass public is qualified, it is difficult to locate evidence (empirical or otherwise) that the "democratic ideology" is *the* ideology to which political beliefs naturally belong. It is even more difficult to justify leaping from this point to the conclusion that members of the public exhibit little attitudinal coherence or constraint in their belief systems.

ALTERNATIVE MODELS OF ATTITUDE ORGANIZATION

Perhaps some of the traditional notions of political sense and nonsense would change if we looked at social constraint as a more social and less logical phenomenon. In the real world we often encounter people who, for example, defend free speech yet advocate the arrest of Communists or the censorship of the media. While we may *disagree* with them, we can still make *sense* of their positions.

In fact, the utterance of such "inconsistent" opinions may provide us with a great deal of information about the politics of an individual. Often we do not need to hear more than a few opinions before we assign membership status to someone in one of many broad sociopolitical categories. A few salient utterances may constitute grounds for being labelled a Communist, a Fascist, a liberal, a conservative, a hawk, a dove, a hardhat, a patriot, or an effete snob. Such labels often represent important sources of constraint among beliefs.[15] On the basis of a few utterances and a label, we can fairly well predict other beliefs and attitudes that a given individual may hold. A "hawk" on the Viet Nam War might have been expected to hold certain attitudes about political dissent, free speech, defense spending, private enterprise, welfare, and so on. The sources of the connections in this attitude cluster may have little to do with the logic of democracy or with ideology. The dominant source of constraint here may be the person's involvement in social conflicts about issues, or *the social attribution of labels which define membership in groups which claim particular stands on a range of issues.* In this sense, people may incorporate certain attitudes into their political perspective because they strive for consistency within their sociopolitical environment or because they react against the attitudes of those who belong to what they view as undesirable political categories.

Although this model of social constraint in belief systems has not been adequately investigated, there are studies that encourage us to explore it further. Rokeach[16] obtained students' ratings on a number of social and political values. He also elicited their views on equal rights and civil rights demonstrations. He then showed the students that, on the average, they ranked freedom much higher than equality (freedom was ranked first, equality sixth). Rokeach also showed them that those who were unsympathetic to civil rights demonstrations tended to give equality a very low ranking. The students were given time to process this information and were invited to rerank their values and restate their attitudes three weeks later and, again, several months later. Rokeach found, among other things, that students who initially favored civil rights demonstrations but ranked equality low, subsequently raised their ranking of equality significantly. This suggests the possibility that people associate beliefs with particular public identities, and that constraint may simply involve learning the appropriate belief repertoire for the desired identity.[17]

In another interesting study, Brooks[18] rated individuals according to the degree to which *they* identified with certain social institutions. He then tapped their liberal or conservative political outlook by examining their attitudinal responses to contemporary political issues. He found that conservative political perspectives were strongly associated with a high degree of identification with social institutions such as family, church, occupation, state, etc. Brooks concludes that the nature of a person's social identity strongly influences both the type of political beliefs that the person forms and the way in which these beliefs are linked or organized to form the person's political perspective.

In both of these studies the source of constraint among political beliefs involves processes of social membership and identity. Constraint, in short, hinges on the person's knowledge of what goes with what in his or her immediately relevant social environment. The search for the universal organizing principle or the *logic* of belief connections in this context may be a misleading preoccupation. We might more profitably spend our time searching for the mechanisms and social processes that give rise to belief clusters in particular social contexts. Let's further explore this social process approach to see how it compares with models of "democratic logic" and "trickle-down opinion flow" in terms of explaining opinion organization in elite groups.

In many ways, American sociopolitical history can be viewed as an ongoing series of disputes—among the elite—over specific applications of general democratic principles. Serious and recurring disagreement has existed around specific applications of the general principles of free speech, due process, unlawful search and seizure, sedition, privileged communication, equal opportunity, minority rights, and so on. Furthermore, dramatic shifts have characterized the policies of the times regarding these issues. How does this square with the assumption that there is a coherent guiding logic in the principles of democracy and in the Constitution?

Perhaps the "logic" of the Constitution is, in part, dependent on the sociological knowings of those who *use* the Constitution in particular contexts. This factor may be as important as having a contextual grasp of history, being able to discover the intent of the drafter, or understanding the logic of the law. Some of the most serious disputes in the judicial arena involve cases where general democratic principles become associated with specific legal or political issues. The judicial resolution of such disputes typically involves the selective interpretation of narrow judicial and broader social customs.[19]

In this sense, the "logic" of the Constitution is the result of a process of negotiation based in part on members' (judges) social analyses. If democracy or the Constitution contain a set of rules and axioms, the rules or, rather, the metarules that govern their application derive from social usage. Generally, the process of negotiation involves working out and applying the general principles associated with legislated law.[20] The meaning of legislated law is deeply rooted in social usage. Cardozo, for example, suggests that when the Court seeks the meaning of legislated rules it should look ". . . manifestly at their source; that is to say, in the experiences of social life. There resides the strongest probability of discovering the sense of law."[21]

If we are to assume that there is a coherent, guiding logic to liberal democracy, we must close our eyes to numerous illiberal decisions and inconsistent judgments handed down by the highest courts in the land. Are we to consider Supreme Court justices inarticulate or unconstrained when they uphold the conviction of Communists on grounds that the limits of free speech have been violated? Would anyone, for example, accuse Holmes or Brandeis of not having the contextual grasp to recognize that the "specific case and the general principle belong in the same belief system"?

Perhaps the argument hinges on whether members of the elite have worked out a clear and sophisticated logic of free speech. As evidence that such a logic exists, we may point to the axiom that it is unreasonable to shout "fire" in a crowded theater. Unfortunately, the judicial theory surrounding free speech is not as clear as it might seem in this simple application to an hypothetical case. In his landmark opinion in Schenck v. U.S. (249 U.S. 47, 1919), Holmes wrote:

> The question in every case is whether the words are used in such circumstances and are of such a nature as to create a clear and present danger that they will bring about substantive evils that Congress has a right to prevent.

While the "substantive evils" may be clearly defined by law, the concept of "clear and present danger" is a bit of a bother. The determination of clear and present danger requires sociological analysis on the part of the judiciary. In short, an operational definition of the limits of free speech does exist, but the definition contains such social reference that the judiciary must play sociologist and examine the social ramifications, political climate, and perceived intent of the defendant in each free speech case. To expect or detect ideological coherence in such practice (over time) is somewhat myopic.[22]

One suspects that the degree of coherence surrounding the principle and practice of free speech in this society may be more attributable to the socially reinforced practice of self-censorship than to the logic of the underlying ideology. In his dissent in the Scales case, Douglas echoed this sentiment with the words of Mark Twain: "It is by the goodness of God that in our country we have those three unspeakably precious things: freedom of speech, freedom of conscience, and the prudence never to practice either of them."[23]

The point here is not an attack on the politics of the Court. Rather, it is to suggest that if we wish to believe that a "clear and present" democratic ideology exists in practice, we must ignore myriad inconsistencies on the part of some of the most prominent members of the political elite.[24] One begins to suspect that specific attitudes on general democratic principles are constrained to a significant degree by the politics of the times, the pressures of membership, and the lay analysis of contemporary social usage and meaning. And this may be true even for the elite.

Therefore, if we are to understand the nature of public opinion we must exercise caution in interpreting studies which "show" that (ideological) constraint exists in the belief systems of the elite. The problem with most such studies is that little evidence exists as to what the source of the constraint is, and even less evidence that constraint is absent or different in the mass. If beliefs are organized on the basis of social processes in one's immediate social environment, we may be more likely to detect constraint among the opinions of an elite sample than among the opinions of a mass sample simply because with the elite we have tapped a narrow and rather homogeneous set of life experiences. Elite studies often focus on businessmen, elected officials, bureaucrats, judges, and so on. The slice of social life is likely to be more homogeneous in such samples than in broad clusters of persons who comprise a "mass sample."

To illustrate this point, let's explore the possibility that the beliefs of elected officials may be organized more on the basis of occupational contingencies than through ideological coherence. Converse proposes that if we looked at the roll call votes of congressmen we would probably find that they are highly stable on similar legislative issues over time. He "deduces" that eighteen out of twenty congressmen would be likely to take the same position on similar legislative issues over time.[25] I am willing to grant that this is a fair estimate. What does it mean, however, to compare this factor to the finding that only thirteen out of twenty members of the mass public maintain the same position about an issue over a two-year period?

Perhaps we are once again faced with the possibility that the social sources of elite constraint have little to do with ideological considerations and far more to do with social processes and the person's implicit analysis of a fairly well bounded slice of society (i.e., the job of being a congressman). One thing that we have been told about congressmen is that once they enter office, they "... quickly make a public record, and it is often unwise to alter it drastically."[26] Matthews goes on to say that "a Senator's initial 'mandate,' therefore, may be a major influence on his voting many years after it was received."[27]

Other studies suggest that social convention, mandate, and the individual's analysis of his or her best strategy for professional success exert more influence on voting record and public pronouncement than do the dictates of ideology.[28] Cnudde and McCrone show that, on salient issues, congressmen vote the attitudes of their constituency "... [as they perceive them] with a mind to the next election."[29] In place of a "logical" constraint model which would suggest that attitudes shape perceptions, their finding suggests that perceptions of social pressure shape attitudes. Earlier studies present similar findings.[30]

However, Converse does offer "evidence" that attitudes among the elite are more organized and coherent than attitudes among the mass. He shows that the attitude correlations over a group of eight political issues were notably higher for congressional candidates than for a sample of the general electorate.[31] Is this due to some sort of common elite ideology or to pressures similar to those that individual members of Congress experience in their occupational settings? Converse suggests that a factor analysis would reveal whether a single dominant dimension organizes or structures the attitudes of the two groups. He properly notes that the "mass" matrix "... is exactly the type that textbooks advise against using for factor analysis on the simple grounds that through inspection it is clear that there is virtually nothing in the way of organization to be discovered."[32] Inexplicably, he does not present any test of the underlying structure in the elite matrix.

As is often the case, someone else has taken up this challenge. Luttbeg administered a "public policy" issue set to a sample of 1,226 "citizens" and 117 "community leaders" in two moderate sized Northwest communities.[33] He factor analyzed the attitude correlation matrices for both groups. His startling finding was that *each* group produced five important factors. The variance was distributed similarly for both groups across the range of factors. In simple terms, this means that the political issues were not organized by the elites along a single ideological dimension. Although the constraining belief dimensions were different for the elite than for the mass, the important point is that the elite and the mass used the same number of dimensions to organize their beliefs. This finding becomes even more striking in light of the fact that the community leaders undoubtedly share a more homogeneous set of socially and politically "constraining" experiences than do the followers. Luttbeg concludes that:

> The data offer very little support for Converse's hypothesis. The leaders and the public differ in the content of their beliefs, but the leaders do not place the ten issues studied on a single unifying dimension. Indeed, their belief systems show a complexity much in contrast to the simplicity suggested by a liberalism-conservatism distinction.[34]

CONCLUSION

The suggestion in the preceding argument has been that stable and constrained beliefs and attitudes may exist among members of the mass public. We have outlined an alternative model that provides a rather unconventional description of public opinion. As mentioned earlier, this model demands methods of measurement that depart considerably from the Converse, Prothro and Grigg, McClosky, Campbell, Stokes, and Almond and Verba approaches to measuring public opinion. If we are to detect the nature of social constraint among beliefs in the public or in the elite, we must search for more complex perspectives and more sensitive methods. We may also wish to develop other models of opinion flow in the society. Finally, it would be useful to explore further the nature of group processes in order to construct theories of opinion organization based on social usage, labelling, and membership references. The examination of "opinion constraint" as a context-specific *process* of political negotiation may be a rich source of information about beliefs at all levels of social life.

ENDNOTES

1. If we asked the person to defend the coexistence of these beliefs, he might respond that while he values free speech, he knows that the communists want to

take it away. Consequently, it doesn't make sense to extend freedoms to those who would deny freedom of speech to others. Any number of similar "logical" positions could be offered for such seemingly inconsistent attitudes.

2. The logic of this argument holds up better when we try to describe survey data than when we try to make sense of the real world. Outside the realm of the survey finding, the logic of democracy is seldom the product of revelation. Rather, democratic "logic" seems to arise through the abuses of human usage, debate, and negotiation in arenas ranging from the local pub to congressional committees to the Supreme Court.

3. Richard M. Merelman, "The Development of Political Ideology: A Framework for the Analysis of Political Socialization," *American Political Science Review,* Vol. 68, No. 3, 1969, p. 750.

4. See, for example, Herbert McClosky, "Consensus and Ideology in American Politics," *American Political Science Review,* Vol. 58, No. 2, 1964, pp. 361–82; and James W. Prothro and C. W. Grigg, "Fundamental Principles of Democracy: Bases of Agreement and Disagreement," *Journal of Politics,* Vol. 22, No. 2, 1960, pp. 276–94. The perspectives of these and others will be discussed later.

5. Philip E. Converse, "The Nature of Belief Systems in Mass Publics," in David E. Apter, ed., *Ideology and Discontent,* New York: The Free Press, 1964, p. 243.

6. *Ibid,* p. 242.

7. As Converse notes, this is a fairly standard translation of the term "constraint" from cognitive psychology. Garner's definition of "constraint" involves "... the amount of interrelatedness of structure of a system of variables," Wendell R. Garner, *Uncertainty and Structure as Psychological Concepts,* New York: Wiley, 1962, p. 142.

8. See Converse, *op cit.,* p. 212. For more elaborate versions of this model, see: E. Katz, "The Two-Step Flow of Communication: An Up-to-Date Report on an Hypothesis," *Public Opinion Quarterly,* Vol. 21, 1957; Paul F. Lazarsfeld, Bernard Berelson, and Hazel Gaudet, *The People's Choice,* New York: Columbia University Press, 1948; E. Katz and P. F. Lazarsfeld, *Personal Influence: The Part Played by People in the Flow of Mass Communication,* Glencoe, Ill.: The Free Press, 1955; and B. Berelson, P. F. Lazarsfeld, and W. N. McPhee, *Voting: A Study of Opinion Formation in a Presidential Campaign,* Chicago: Univ. of Chicago Press, 1954.

9. Converse, *op. cit.,* p. 215.

10. McClosky, *op. cit.,* pp. 361–82.

11. *Ibid.,* p. 58.

12. *Ibid.,* p. 63.

13. J. W. Prothro and C. M. Grigg, "Fundamental Principles of Democracy: Bases of Agreement and Disagreement," *Journal of Politics,* Vol. 22, No. 2, 1960, pp. 276–94.

14. Converse, *op. cit.,* p. 230.

15. For a review of the labelling perspective in sociology, see: Howard Becker, *The Outsiders,* New York: The Free Press, 1963, ch. 1; E. Rubington and M. S. Weinberg, eds., *Deviance: The Interactionist Perspective,* New York: MacMillan, 1968; and, E. M. Schur, *Labelling Deviant Behavior,* New York: Harper and Row, 1971.

16. Milton Rokeach, *Beliefs, Attitudes and Values,* San Francisco: Jossey-Bass, 1968.

17. Rokeach used these data in the service of a model of psychological consistency. However, data need not be indentured to a particular perspective if they serve others equally well.

18. Richard S. Brooks, "The Self and Political Role: A Symbolic Interactionist Approach to Political Ideology," *The Sociological Quarterly,* Vol. 10, 1969, pp. 22–31.

19. See, for example, Benjamin N. Cardozo, *The Nature of the Judicial Process,* New Haven: Yale University Press, 1921, pp. 60–65.

20. Cardozo notes that constitutions are easier to draft than are ordinary statutes: "Constitutions are more likely to enunciate general principles, which must be worked out and applied thereafter to particular conditions," *Ibid.,* p. 71.

21. *Ibid.,* p. 122.

22. In the Schenck case, where Holmes wrote his famous majority opinion, clear and present danger was detected by the court. The decision was based on the Court's *perception* of Schenck's *intent* to disrupt military recruitment by mailing antiwar propaganda under the auspices of the Socialist Party. A similar situation existed in the more controverial Debs case (Debs v. U.S. 249 U.S. 211, 1919). Holmes wrote the unanimous opinion of the Court that the speech that Debs delivered in Canton, Ohio (dealing with socialism, social change, and objections to war), had the *intent* of disrupting military recruitment. In both cases, the disruption of military recruitment was an evil that Congress was empowered to prevent. However, the determination that certain acts may have intentionally and effectively constituted such an evil was based on the lay analysis of the Court.

The history of the interpretation of free speech by members of the elite in this country is filled with similar cases. The use of the Smith Act facilitated even broader alteration of the free speech principle than did the Espionage Act (under which the Schenck and Debs indictments were upheld). The Smith Act states that it is illegal to "teach, advocate or encourage" the overthrow or destruction of the government of the United States. During the 1950s the Court expanded the notion of clear and present danger to encompass the realm of "clear and probable" danger. In other words, if the evil that Congress is trying to prevent is sufficiently important, the government's case did not have to prove present or immediate danger. (See Dennis v. U.S., 341 U.S. 494, 1951.)

23. From Howard Zinn, *Disobedience and Democracy,* New York: Random House, 1968, p. 75. The decision of the Court in the Scales case in 1961 stretched the logic of free speech into an amorphous notion of "probably intended future danger." The dissent of Justice Douglas in this case argued that the crime com-

mitted involved nothing more than the holding of certain *beliefs* (Scales vs. U.S., 367 U.S. 203, 1961).

24. Inconsistencies which, on the face of it, appear to be failures to recognize that the specific case and the general rule belong in the same belief system.

25. Converse, *op. cit.*, p. 239. It is not clear why Converse spent so little effort in measuring the stability level of an elite sample. If his argument is to have merit, it hinges on showing that the mass is less stable in aggregate terms than some comparison group. If, as he claims, he can place people along a scale ranging from ideologue to inarticulate, he might have partitioned his national sample this way and compared the upper portion with the bottom portion. In any event, we are forced to take it on faith that a broad elite sample would be more stable than a broad mass sample.

26. Donald R. Matthews, *U.S. Senators and Their World*, New York: Vintage Books, 1960, p. 234.

27. *Ibid.*, p. 235.

28. Barber proposes the interesting theory that a leader's first independent political success exerts a dominant influence on his future political style, strategy, and decisions. See James David Barber, *The Presidential Character*, Englewood Cliffs, New Jersey, Prentice-Hall, 1972.

29. Charles F. Cnudde and Donald J. McCrone, "Constituency Attitudes and Congressional Voting: A Causal Model," E. C. Dreyer and W. A. Rosenbaum, *Political Opinion and Electoral Behavior*, Belmont, California: Wadsworth, 1966, p. 408.

30. See, for example, Warren E. Miller and Donald E. Stokes, "Constituency Influence in Congress," *American Political Science Review*, Vol. 57, 1963, pp. 45–63.

31. Converse, *op. cit.*, p. 228.

32. *Ibid.*, p. 230.

33. Norman R. Luttbeg, "The Structure of Beliefs among Leaders and the Public," *Public Opinion Quarterly*, Vol. 32, No. 3, 1968.

34. *Ibid.*, p. 406.

PART 2 SELECTION 5

Reprinted with permission from *Journal of Politics,* 24 (1962), 689-702.

Party Loyalty and the Likelihood of Deviating Elections

DONALD E. STOKES

In voting research, as any branch of inquiry, knowledge is advanced as much by seeing new problems as by solving old ones. Contemporary voting studies have answered many questions that could only be guessed at a few years ago. Yet any such cumulation of findings brings to the fore a number of "second-generation" problems that could hardly be stated except in terms of the theoretical ideas evolving out of current work. This has especially been true in the voting studies as interest has extended from the population of voters to a population of elections; concepts that could explain a good deal about individual choice inevitably spawned additional questions about elections as total social or political events. This [selection] states such a "new" question or problem and draws from historical evidence a preliminary answer, although a sure answer waits for evidence that is not at hand.

The problem can be described briefly as follows. By measuring a limited set of political orientations (among which party loyalty is preeminently important) we are able to state with increasing confidence what the behavior of the American electorate would be in any given election if the vote were to express only the influence of these basic dispositions. But . . . the election returns also reflect the public's reaction to more recent and transitory influences that deflect the vote from what it would have been had these short-term factors not intruded on the nation's decision. Therefore, we think of any national election as an interplay of basic dispositions and short-run influences. Yet the freedom of these "disturbing" influences to modify the effects of long-term dispositions is not well understood. Their capacity to do so is not of trivial importance; there have been few presidential elections in the last hundred years that we could not imagine having gone to the loser, had the right combination of short-term factors appeared in time. And yet each election is not merely tossing the coin again; like all strong prejudices, the electorate's basic dispositions have a tremendous capacity to keep people behaving in accustomed ways. The freedom of short-run influences to deflect the vote has an obvious bearing on how well long-standing party loyalties are able to explain a total election outcome. Plainly a closer estimate of the ease with which short-term electoral tides may run to one party or the other would tell a good deal about the importance of party identification in a predictive theory of elections.

THE ROLE OF BASIC PARTISAN DISPOSITIONS

No element of the political lives of Americans is more impressive than their party loyalties. Our research has amply demonstrated how early partisan identifications take root and how widely they are found in the adult population. Despite the grip of political independence on our civics texts, most Americans freely call themselves Democrats or Republicans when asked, and most of those who say at first that they are Independents will concede some degree of party loyalty under the gentlest urging. If we think of the electorate as spread out along a dimension extending from strong Democrat through Independent to strong Republican, not more than a tenth of the public sees itself at the point of full independence.

In view of the fact that very few Americans have any deep interest in politics, it is a mild paradox that party loyalties should be so widespread. A partial key to this puzzle is that these identifications perform for the citizen an exceedingly useful evaluative function. To the average person the affairs of government are remote and complex, and yet the average citizen is asked periodically to formulate opinions about those affairs. At the very least, he has to decide how he will vote, what choice he will make between candidates offering different programs and very different versions of contemporary political events. In this dilemma, having the party symbol stamped on certain candidates, certain issue positions, certain interpretations of political reality is of great psychological convenience.

Because of this evaluative function, party identification should not be regarded as a simple disposition to vote out of habit for one party or the other. To be sure, there *is* some totally unadorned persistence voting. But for most people the tie between party identification and voting behavior involves subtle processes of perceptual adjustment by which the individual assembles an image of current politics consistent with his partisan allegiance. With normal luck, the partisan voter will carry to the polls attitudes toward the newer elements of politics that support his long-standing bias.

Undoubtedly this perceptual process is seen most melodramatically in popular response to the personal qualities of the presidential candidates. For the millions of Americans identified with a particular party, the candidate bearing the party symbol tends to become more of a lion, his opponent more of a wolf. To take an example that will not excite modern passions, we may suppose that anyone judging the candidates according to the dominant values of American culture, rather than in purely partisan terms, would have found Grover Cleveland a more estimable man than James G. Blaine in the campaign of 1884. Yet we can be sure that the public's actual response to these new presidential personalities was colored almost completely by its prior partisan loyalties, as the small vote swing from 1880 to 1884 suggests.

Therefore, the capacity of party identification to color perceptions holds the key to understanding why the unfolding of new events, the emergence of new issues, the appearance of new political figures fails to produce wider swings of party fortune. To a remarkable extent these swings are damped by processes of selective perception. Because the public so easily finds in new elements of politics the old partisan vices and virtues, our electoral history, as so much else, shows that *plus ça change, plus c'est la même chose.*

And yet the nation's response to a changing political world is not wholly governed by fixed party loyalties. Some elements of political reality not agreeing with these loyalties will get through the perceptual screen raised in the partisan voter. A war, a sharp recession, a rash of scandal will leave their mark on all shades of partisans, though the mark will not be deep enough to change the votes of more than some. What is more, . . . other identifications will at times lead the voter to perceive political objects in a way that contradicts his partisan bias. As they become relevant to politics, identifications of a racial or national or religious or class nature may counter the perceptual effects of long-term partisan loyalties in large segments of the electorate.

This interplay of basic orientations and transient factors underlies the voters' decisions on election day. What is the relative weight of these influences in determining the total vote? What is the freedom of short-term forces to modify the influence of basic dispositions? Current measurements of partisan dispositions indicate that the Republicans could expect about 46 per cent of the vote if the nation expressed only its fixed party loyalties at the polls. Yet as a minority party the Republicans won popular majorities in 1952 and 1956. How probable were these deviating elections in view of the country's underlying partisanship? Given the distribution of party identification found today—or any other distribution of party loyalties—what is the likelihood that the minority party will win?

THE PROBABILITY OF DEVIATING ELECTIONS

Putting the question this way inevitably implies some sort of probability model, and one will be made explicit here in terms of an idealized conception of electoral history. Under this conception the electoral process will be regarded as repeatedly sampling a universe of short-term forces. At each election a sample of such forces is drawn, and the two-party division of the vote deflected according to the strength and partisan direction of the forces that have fallen in the sample.[1] The sum of the forces in the samples drawn in 1956 and 1960 favored the Republicans, although not all the terms contributing to these sums were pro-Republican, especially in the latter year. Each of the samples that might possibly be drawn would deflect the two-party division of the vote by some given amount in a given direction; hence, over all the possible samples that might be drawn (that is, over all possible configurations of short-term influences)these deflections define a sampling *distribution*. We would naturally take the mean or expected value of this distribution to be zero, if its values are to be mapped into percentages of the two-party vote, we would associate this mean with the division of the vote expected from party identification. To do anything else would be to assume that over all possible configurations of short-term factors the electoral process will deal more kindly with one party than the other.[2] The more difficult problem, the one that holds the key to the probability of a deviating election, is to reach an estimate of the *variance* of this sampling distribution.

The connection between the variance of such a distribution and the probability of a deviating election can be brought out by a simple figure. Figure 1 shows three such idealized distributions, drawn over a scale representing the

Republican percentage of the two-party vote for President. Each distribution has the same mean—46 per cent, in accord with our empirical estimate of the expected Republican vote in the present era. And each distribution has the form of a normal probability function.[3] These three hypothetical distributions differ only as to their variances: the variance of *A* is of intermediate size whereas the variance of *B* is small and of *C* large. As is true for any continuous probability function, the probabilities associated with these distributions are interpreted by areas under the curve. Thus for a given distribution the probability of the Republican Party winning a majority of votes is represented by the shaded area under the curve that is to the right of the point of equal division. Because of the differences in the variances, the size of this area (and the probability of the Republicans winning) is very different for the three distributions. In the case of distribution *A*, roughly a third

Figure 1 *Relation of Variance of Theoretical Distribution to Probability of a Deviating Election*

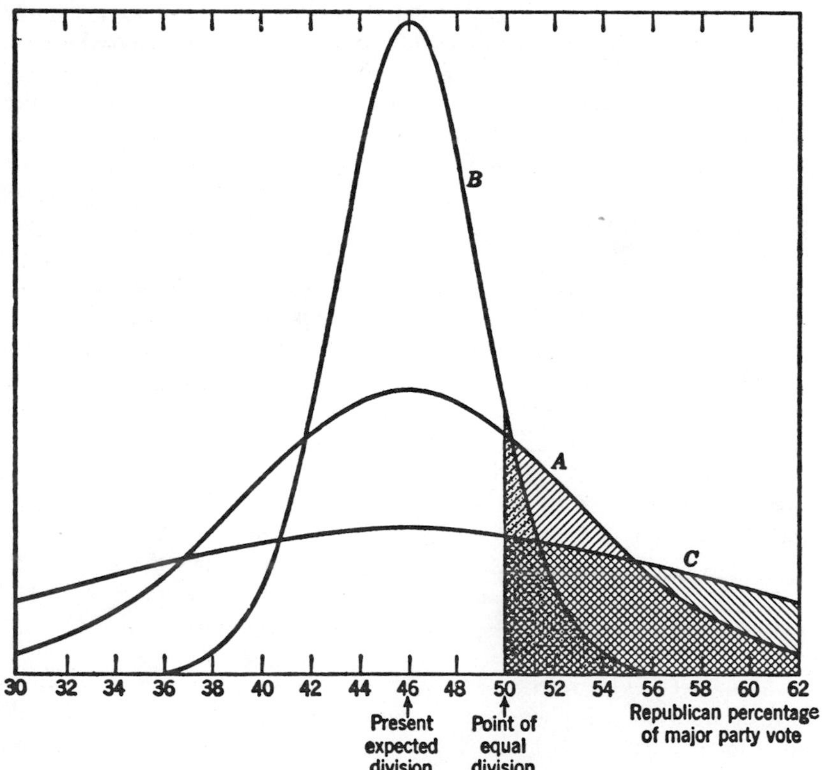

of the total area under the curve lies to the right of 50 per cent; in the case of *B* about a tenth; of *C* not much less than half. Interpreting these areas as probabilities, we would say that the chance of a deviating election under *A* is about .3; under *B* about .1; and under *C* almost .5. Therefore, the meaning of the 4 per cent difference between the expected Republican share of the vote and an equal division would be grossly different according to which of these distributions has the closest fit with the real world. Undoubtedly *B* and *C* are extremes. The electoral process does not give the minority party a trifling chance of winning; neither does it treat each election as a fair toss of a coin. Reality lies somewhere between.

Just where is a question on which the historical record is not moot. To be sure, exact estimates cannot be made because here, as so often is true, significant measurement is hampered by the extreme niggardliness with which history has furnished cases of an event that involves a whole political system, as the choice of an American President does. Nevertheless, the evidence of history can be used to fix an upper bound for the variance of our theoretical distribution and, hence, for the probability of a deviating election.

Seen in terms of our model, past deviations of the vote about some central value are deflections of the party division by successive samples of short-term forces. The central value we would use for any given election if past measurements of basic dispositions were available would, of course, be the division of the vote expected on the basis of the distribution of party loyalties at that time. But with these measurements forever lost, a conservative alternative is to take the mean value of the party division in the period, say, from 1892 to 1960 and to attribute *all* the variation of the vote about this central value to the work of short-run factors.[4] This procedure is conservative in the sense that it tends to inflate the variance estimate we seek and, with it, our estimate of the probability of a deviating election.

The details of this procedure are suggested by Figure 2*a*, in which the Republican proportion of the two-party vote in the elections from 1892 to 1960 is distributed along a percentage scale.[5] The mean of this distribution is roughly 51 per cent, and its variance is obtained by calculating the deviation of the party division from this central value in each election year. The division in 1928, for example, was about 8 per cent more Republican than the mean. The theoretical normal probability distribution we have fitted to this empirical distribution is drawn above the scale.

Calculating deviations about the mean *for the whole period* tends to exaggerate the magnitude of short-term influences on the vote. If we had for each election an expected value based on the distribution of party loyalties at the time, the average deviation would be somewhat reduced. For example, the expected Republican share of the vote in the late 1920's undoubtedly was higher than 51 per cent and the deflection due to transient factors in

1928 less than 8 per cent. Of course we cannot recover the true expected values with any precision, but our estimates can be improved by assuming that the realignment of party loyalties brought on by the Great Depression divides the whole period into an era of Republican dominance, extending from 1892 to 1928, and an era of Democratic dominance from 1932 to 1960. This assumption leads naturally to the use of a separate mean for

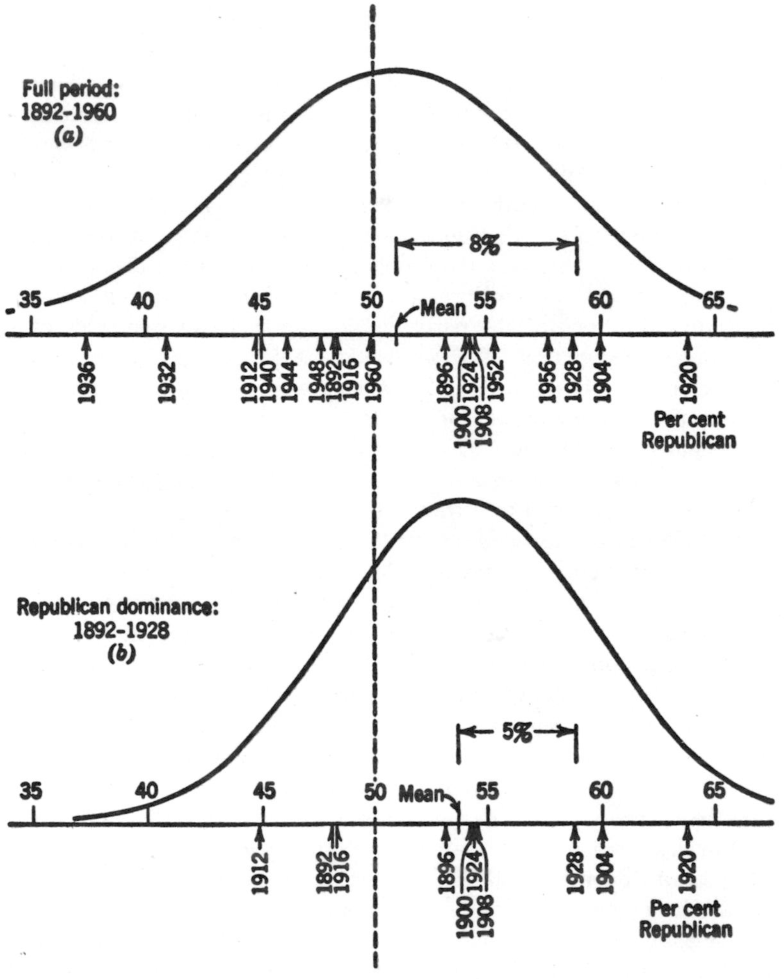

Figure 2 *Historical Estimation of the Variance of the Two-party Vote for President*

each era and the measurement of deviations from these more historically realistic central values.

The consequence of this change is suggested by Figure 2*b*, which shows the empirical distribution for the period of Republican dominance. The central value from which deviations are measured is now about 54 per cent rather than 51 per cent. The magnitude of the deviations is, on the average, reduced. In 1928, for example, it is reduced from 8 per cent to about 5 per cent. Because of this average reduction, the effect of breaking the whole period in two is to lessen the variance of the vote attributed to short-term factors and, with it, the estimated probability of a deviating election. As a result, this refinement—or any other that is faithful to historical realities—leaves undisturbed the upper bound for the probability of a deviating election obtained by the original procedure. It will indeed be clear presently that this refinement has little effect on our probability estimates.

When the variance of our theoretical sampling distribution is estimated from these historical data, it turns out not to look very different from the first of the three hypothetical distributions drawn in Figure 1. The accompanying estimate of the probability of a deviating election is about .28 if deflections of the vote are measured in terms of the mean of the whole period and slightly less if they are measured in terms of the separate means for the eras of Republican and Democratic dominance. Therefore, under the assumptions of the model, the probability is less than three in ten that a minority party, faced at a given election with an expected deficit of 4 per cent, can poll a majority of votes; the chance of a deviating election occurring under the present division of party loyalties is very much less than even.[6]

However, the uses of this simple apparatus extend beyond existing conditions. Having fixed the variance of our theoretical sampling distribution, we may use the model to estimate the probability of a deviating election if the expected division of the vote were other than that derived from the distribution of party loyalties found in the 1950's and early 1960's. These estimates under other assumptions about the departure of the expected division of the vote from 50 per cent are given in Table 1. The table presents estimates based on both procedures for establishing the variance of the sampling distribution, although the two sets of estimates diverge very little.

A word should be said about the Electoral College. A popular majority is not the same as a majority of Electors, and if a deviating election is defined as one in which the minority party captures the White House, we need to consider the impact of the Electoral College. It should frankly be said that the relation between popular and electoral votes introduces some additional uncertainty into our problem. Any close examination of this relation in the modern period of party competition shows that it has been somewhat variable.[7] On the other hand, such an examination gives little

Table 1 *Estimated Probabilities of a Deviating Election*

Difference between expected vote and 50 per cent	0	1	2	3	↓ Present 4	5	6	7	8
Estimates using mean for whole period	.50	.44	.39	.33	.28	.24	.20	.16	.13
Estimates using separate means for eras of party dominance	.50	.44	.38	.32	.27	.23	.18	.13	.10

support to the idea that the Democrats have to win more than a popular majority to capture the Presidency, despite the familiar lore on this point. If anything, the reverse is true, although the points of discrimination in the popular and electoral vote are very close. How nearly these points coincide can be seen by ignoring all extreme values and confining our attention to the five closest elections in the past seventy years, those of 1892, 1896, 1916, 1948, and 1960. When this is done the Republican proportion of the popular vote associated with 50 per cent of the electoral vote is found to be 50.4 per cent. A fair judgment of the historical evidence is that the variability of the relation between popular and electoral votes gives our estimate of the probability of a deviation election a limited additional degree of error without biasing the estimate either for or against the Republicans.

CONCLUSION

If the supporting argument runs true, the estimated likelihood of a deviating election bears out the importance of partisan dispositions in a predictive theory of elections. At the state or local level party loyalties are so frequently all-important in deciding whether a Democrat or Republican will win that they can hardly be overlooked. Most lesser political units of the American commonwealth are one-party or modified one-party areas. But at the national level, especially in presidential elections, party allegiance is sometimes felt to be a limited tool of analysis. The view of some observers is that everything depends on the sample of short-term forces drawn in a particular election, and that nothing of real value is to be learned by measuring the electorate's long-term partisan dispositions. From this it is only a short step to the idea that party allegiance is a purely nominal attachment of slight motivational significance to the voter, at least in choosing a President.

No one who has taken a careful look at the data of voting research can still believe that party identification is of slight significance for *individual* behavior. But voting in presidential elections is not completely determined by party allegiance, and so long as it is not we may ask how likely the electorate is to give a majority of votes to the minority party. If the likelihood proved high, party identification would lose a good deal of its efficacy for the prediction or explanation of a total election outcome, even though it remained a variable of great power for predicting or explaining individual voting choice. Therefore, the probability estimate given here is implicitly a judgment about the appropriate framework for analyzing the national election decision, a judgment confirming the importance of party identification in carrying one candidate to the White House and returning the other to some lesser office or private life.

ENDNOTES

1. Presumably successive samples are not drawn entirely independently, since some short-run influences carry over from one election to the next, as Eisenhower's appeal carried over from 1952 to 1956. The lack of full independence does not bias the estimates we will obtain below, although it does have the interesting consequence of making the *conditional* probability of a deviating election, given the immediate electoral past, somewhat different from the unconditional probabilities we seek.

2. Some may think such an assumption warranted. In view of the maintenance of effective two-party competition since the Civil War, can we not say that the electoral process has been unexpectedly kind to the minority party? Two points should be made in this connection. First, because our attention here is fixed on deviating elections we have excluded those rare elections in which the strength of the minority party is restored by a change in the underlying distribution of party identifications, as it was not in the Eisenhower or Kennedy elections. Second, our computation of an expected division of the vote has already discounted the majority party's strength in certain respects. In particular we have allowed for the fact that the historical circumstances that give a party a majority of party identifiers usually attracts to it a number of people who are only marginally interested in politics and relatively unlikely to vote. Certainly the wave of new recruits to the Democratic Party during the Great Depression and the Roosevelt New Deal included many people of this type who are infrequent voters today. Our method of computing expected strength at the polls has already applied this penalty to the Democrats.

3. The assumption of normality is not gratuitous but is well supported by the form of the empirical distributions to be examined below. The test of normality applied to these distributions is described in M. G. Kendall, *Advanced Theory of Statistics* (London: Charles Griffin, 1948, Vol. 2), p. 105.

4. The choice of 1892 as a starting point was prompted by the fact that the variability and cyclical pattern of the vote in the first generation following the Civil War differed a good deal from what they have been since.

5. Corrected figures are used for the two-party division of the vote in 1912 and 1924 to take account of the fact that a third party in each of these years cut deeply into the strength of the losing major party.

6. This conclusion depends, of course, on the assumption that the average fluctuation of the party division will not differ substantially from what it has been from 1892 to 1960.

7. These comments on the Electoral College are based on the regression of the electoral vote on the popular vote in the period from 1892 to 1960.

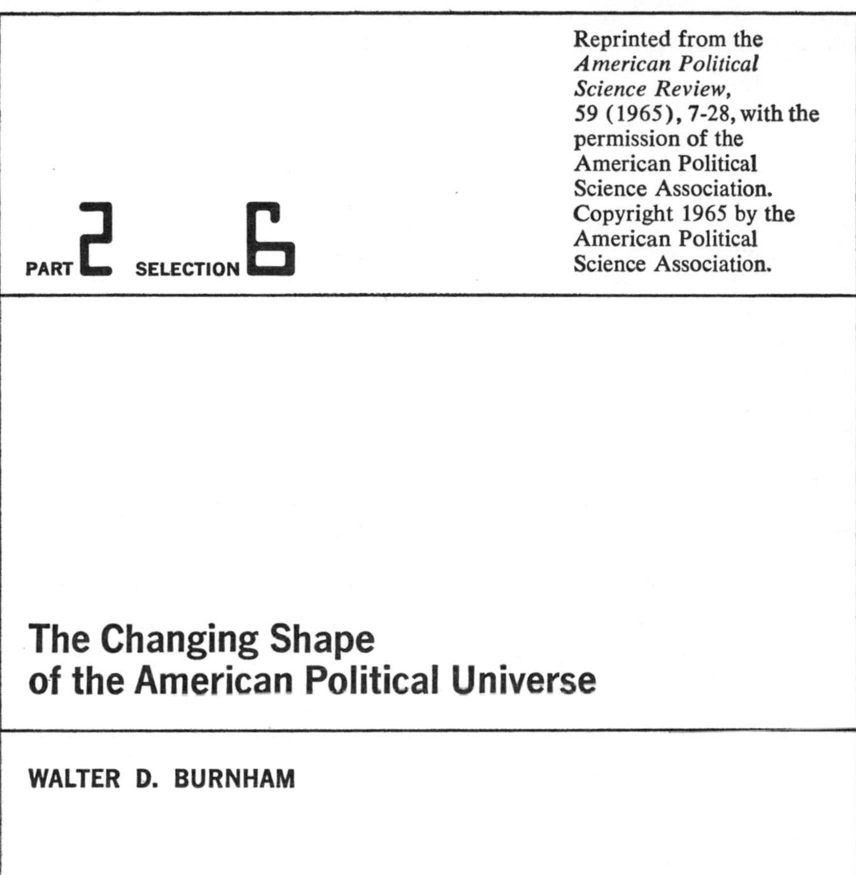

Reprinted from the *American Political Science Review*, 59 (1965), 7-28, with the permission of the American Political Science Association.
Copyright 1965 by the American Political Science Association.

PART 2 SELECTION 6

The Changing Shape of the American Political Universe

WALTER D. BURNHAM

Even the crudest form of statistical analysis makes it abundantly clear that the changes which have occurred in the relative size and shape of the active electorate in this country have not only been quantitatively enormous but have followed a directional course which seems to be unique in the contemporary universe of democratic polities. In the United States these transformations over the past century have involved devolution, a dissociation from politics as such among a growing segment of the eligible electorate and an apparent deterioration of the bonds of party linkage between electorate and government. More precisely, these trends were overwhelmingly prominent between about 1900 and 1930, were only very moderately reversed following the political realignment of 1928–1936, and now seem to be increasing once again along several dimensions of analysis. Such a pattern of development is pronouncedly retrograde compared with those which have obtained almost everywhere else in the Western world during the past century.

Probably the best-known aspect of the changing American political universe has been the long-term trend in national voter turnout: a steep decline from 1900 to about 1930, followed by a moderate resurgence since that time.[1] As the figures in Table 1 indicate, nationwide turnout down through 1900 was quite high by contemporary standards—comparing favorably in presidential years with recent levels of participation in Western Europe—and was also marked by very low levels of drop-off. A good deal of the precipitate decline in turnout after 1896 can, of course, be attributed to the disfranchisement of Negroes in the South and the consolidation of its one-party regime. But as Table 2 and Fig. 1 both reveal, non-Southern states not only shared this decline but also have current turnout rates which remain substantially below 19th-century levels.[2]

Table 1 *Decline and Partial Resurgence: Mean Levels of National Turnout and Drop-off by Periods, 1848–1962**

Period (Presidential Years)	Mean Estimated Turnout	Period (Off-Years)	Mean Estimated Turnout	Mean Drop-Off
	(%)		(%)	(%)
1848–1872	75.1	1850–1874	65.2	7.0
1876–1896	78.5	1878–1898	62.8	15.2
1900–1916	64.8	1902–1918	47.9	22.4
1920–1928	51.7	1922–1930	35.2	28.7
1932–1944	59.1	1934–1946	41.0	27.8
1948–1960	60.3	1950–1962	44.1	24.9

* Off-year turnout data based on total vote for congressional candidates in off years.

The persistence of mediocre rates of American voting turnout into the present political era is scarcely news. It forms so obvious and continuing a problem of our democracy that a special presidential commission has recently given it intensive study.[3] Two additional aspects of the problem, however, emerge from a perusal of the foregoing data. In the first place, it is quite apparent that the political realignment of the 1930s, while it restored two-party competition to many states outside the South, did not stimulate turnout to return in most areas to 19th-century levels. Even if

Figure 1 *Patterns of Turnout: United States, 1860–1964, by Region, and Selected Western European Nations, 1948–1961*

the mere existence of competitiveness precludes such low levels of turnout as are found in the South today, or as once prevailed in the northern industrial states, it falls far short of compelling a substantially full turnout under present-day conditions. Second, drop-off on the national level has shown

Table 2 *Sectionalism and Participation: Mean Turnout in Southern and Non-Southern States in Presidential Elections, 1868–1960*

Period	Mean Turnout: 11 Southern States	Period	Mean Turnout: Non-Southern States
	(%)		(%)
1868–1880	69.4	1868–1880	82.6
1884–1896	61.1	1884–1896	85.4
1900 (transition)	43.4	1900	84.1
1904–1916	29.8	1904–1916	73.6
1920–1948	24.7	1920–1932	60.6
1952–1960	38.8	1936–1960	68.0

markedly little tendency to recede in the face of increases in presidential-year turnout over the last thirty years. The component of peripheral voters in the active electorate has apparently undergone a permanent expansion from about one-sixth in the late 19th century to more than one-quarter in recent decades. If, as seems more than likely, the political regime established after 1896 was largely responsible for the marked relative decline in the active voting universe and the marked increase in peripherality among those who still occasionally voted, it is all the more remarkable that the dramatic political realignment of the 1930s has had such little effect in reversing these trends.

At least two major features of our contemporary polity, to be sure, are obviously related to the presently apparent ceiling on turnout. First, the American electoral system creates a major "double hurdle" for prospective voters which does not exist in Western Europe: the requirements associated with residence and registration, usually entailing periodic registration at frequent intervals, and the fact that elections are held on a normal working day in this employee society rather than on Sundays or holidays.[4] Second, it is very probably true that 19th-century elections were major sources of entertainment in an age unblessed by modern mass communications, so that it is more difficult for politicians to gain and keep public attention today than it was then.[5] Yet if American voters labor under the most cumbersome sets of procedural requirements in the Western world, this in itself is a datum which tends to support Schattschneider's thesis that the struggle for democracy is still being waged in the United States and that there are profound resistances within the political system itself to the adoption of needed procedural reforms.[6] Moreover, there are certain areas—such as all of Ohio outside the metropolitan counties and cities of at least 15,000 population—where no registration procedures have ever been established, but where no significant deviation from the patterns outlined here appears to exist. Finally, while it may well be true that the partial displacement by TV and other means of entertainment has inhibited expansion of the active voting universe during the past generation, it is equally true that the structure of the American voting universe—*i.e.*, the adult population—as it exists today was substantially formed in the period 1900–1920, *prior* to the development of such major media as the movies, radio and television.

I

As we move below the gross national level, the voting patterns discussed above stand out with far greater clarity and detail. Their divergences suggest something of the individual differences which distinguish each state subsystem from its fellows, as their uniformities indicate the universality of the broader secular trends. Five states have been selected for analysis here.* During the latter part of the 19th century two of these, Michigan and Pennsylvania, were originally competitive states which tended to favor the Republican Party. They developed solidly one-party regimes after the realignment of 1896. These regimes were overthrown in their turn and vigorous party competition was restored in the wake of the New Deal realignment. In two other states, Ohio and New York, the 1896 alignment had no such dire consequences for two-party competition on the state level. These states have also shown a somewhat different pattern of development since the 1930s than Michigan and Pennsylvania. . . .

Michigan politics was marked from 1894 through 1930 by the virtual eclipse of a state Democratic Party which had formerly contested elections on nearly equal terms with the Republicans. The inverse relationships developing between this emergent one-partyism on the one hand, and both the relative size of the active voting universe and the strength of party linkage on the other, stand out in especially bold relief.

A decisive shift away from the stable and substantially fully mobilized voting patterns of the 19th century occurred in Michigan after the realignment of 1896, with a lag of about a decade between that election and the onset of disruption in those patterns. The first major breakthrough of

Table 3 *Michigan, 1854–1962: Decay and Resurgence?*

Period	Mean turnout		Mean drop-off	Mean roll-off	Mean split-ticket voting	Mean partisan swing	Mean % D of 2-party vote
	Pres. years	Off-years					
	(%)	(%)	(%)	(%)	(%)	(%)	
1854–1872	84.8	78.1	7.8	0.9	0.8	3.2	43.9
1878–1892	84.9	74.9	10.7	0.8	1.6	2.2	48.0
1894–1908	84.8	68.2	22.3	1.5	5.9	4.7	39.6
1910–1918	71.4	53.0	27.2	3.0	9.8	4.1	40.4*
1920–1930	55.0	31.5	42.9	6.0	10.0	7.3	29.8
1932–1946	63.6	47.3	25.9	6.7	6.0	7.4	47.9
1948–1962	66.9	53.6	19.1	4.1	5.8	4.9	51.0

* Democratic percentage of three-party vote in 1912 and 1914.

characteristics associated with 20th-century American electorates occurred in the presidential year 1904, when the mean percentage Democratic for all statewide offices reached an unprecedented low of 35.6 and the rate of

*Eds. Note: Discussion of New York and Oklahoma has been deleted here for reasons of space.

split-ticket voting jumped from almost zero to 17.1 per cent. A steady progression of decline in turnout and party competition, accompanied by heavy increases in the other criteria of peripherality, continued down through 1930.

The scope of this transformation was virtually revolutionary. During the civil-war era scarcely 15 per cent of Michigan's potential electorate appears to have been altogether outside the voting universe. About 7 per cent could be classified as peripheral voters by Campbell's definition, and the remainder—more than three-quarters of the total—were core voters. Moreover, as the extremely low 19th-century level of split-ticket voting indicates, these active voters overwhelmingly cast party-line ballots. By the 1920s, less than one-third of the potential electorate were still core voters, while nearly one-quarter were peripheral and nearly one-half remained outside the political system altogether. Drop-off and roll-off increased six-fold during this period, while the amplitude of partisan swing approximately doubled and the split-ticket-voting rate increased by a factor of approximately eight to twelve.

For the most part these trends underwent a sharp reversal as party competition in Michigan was abruptly restored during the 1930s and organized in its contemporary mode in 1948. As the mean Democratic percentage of the two-party vote increased and turnout—especially in off-year elections—showed a marked relative upswing, such characteristics of marginality as drop-off, roll-off, split-ticket voting and partisan swing declined in magnitude. Yet, as the means for the 1948–1962 period demonstrate, a large gap remains to be closed before anything like the *status quo ante* can be restored. Our criteria—except, of course, for the mean percentage Democratic of the two-party vote—have returned only to the levels of the transitional period 1900–1918. As is well known, exceptionally disciplined and issue-oriented party organizations have emerged in Michigan since 1948, and elections have been intensely competitive throughout this period.[7] In view of this, the failure of turnout in recent years to return to something approaching 19th-century levels is all the more impressive, as is the continuing persistence of fairly high levels of drop-off, roll-off and split-ticket voting.[8]

The Michigan data have still more suggestive implications. Campbell's discussion of surge and decline in the modern context points to a cyclical process in which peripheral voters, drawn into the active voting universe only under unusual short-term stimuli, withdraw from it again when the stimuli are removed. It follows that declines in turnout are accompanied by a marked relative increase in the component of core voters in the electorate and by a closer approximation in off years to a "normal" partisan division of the vote.[9] This presumably includes a reduction in the level of split-ticket voting as well. But the precise opposite occurred as a secular process—not only in Michigan but, it would seem, universally—during the

1900–1930 era. Declines in turnout were accompanied by substantial, continuous increases in the indices of party and voter peripherality among those elements of the adult population which remained in the political universe at all. The lower the turnout during this period, the fewer of the voters still remaining who bothered to vote for the entire slate of officers in any given election. The lower the turnout in presidential years, the greater was the drop-off gap between the total vote cast in presidential and succeeding off-year elections. The lower the turnout, the greater were the incidence of split-ticket voting and the amplitude of partisan swing. Under the enormous impact of the forces which produced these declines in turnout and party competitiveness after 1896, the component of highly involved and party-oriented core voters in the active electorate fell off at a rate which more than kept pace with the progressive shrinking of that electorate's relative size. These developments necessarily imply a limitation upon the usefulness of the surge-decline model as it relates to secular movements prior to about 1934. They suggest, moreover, that the effects of the forces at work after 1896 to depress voter participation and to dislocate party linkage between voters and government were even more crushingly severe than a superficial perusal of the data would indicate.

Pennsylvania provides us with variations on the same theme. As in Michigan, the political realignment centering on 1896 eventually converted an industrializing state with a relatively slight but usually decisive Republican bias into a solidly one-party G.O.P. bastion. To a much greater extent than in Michigan, this disintegration of the state Democratic Party was accompanied by periodic outbursts of third-party ventures and plural party nominations of major candidates, down to the First World War. Thereafter, as in Michigan, the real contest between competing candidates and political tendencies passed into the Republican primary, where it usually remained

Table 4 *Voting Patterns in Pennsylvania, 1876–1962: Decline and Resurgence?*

Period	Mean turnout: Pres. years	Mean turnout: Off-years	Mean drop-off	Mean roll-off	Mean split-ticket voting	Mean partisan swing	Mean % D of 2-party vote
	(%)	(%)	(%)	(%)	(%)	(%)	
1876–1892	78.5	69.3	9.4	0.6	0.6	1.4	47.7
1894–1908	75.7	64.7	12.2	5.2	1.3	6.3	38.5
1910–1918	64.0	51.4	20.0	4.3	4.7	5.8	43.6*
1920–1930	50.4	39.5	28.0	5.2	8.9	7.1	32.8
1932–1948	61.5	51.9	14.9	2.2	1.4	6.1	49.0
1950–1962	67.5	56.3	12.2	1.8	3.1	3.3	49.3

* Combined major anti-Republican vote (Democrat, Keystone, Lincoln, Washington).

until the advent of the New Deal. In both states relatively extreme declines in the rate of turnout were associated with the disappearance of effective two-party competition, and in both states these declines were closely paralleled by sharp increases in the indices of peripherality.

As Table 4 demonstrates, the parallel behavior of the Michigan and Pennsylvania electorates has also extended into the present; the now-familiar pattern of increasing turnout and party competition accompanied by marked declines in our other indices has been quite visible in the Keystone State since the advent of the New Deal. On the whole, indeed, a better approximation to the *status quo ante* has been reached in Pennsylvania than in Michigan or perhaps in most other states. But despite the intense competitiveness of its present party system, this restoration remains far from complete.

A more detailed examination of turnout and variability in turnout below the statewide level raises some questions about the direct role of immigration and woman suffrage in depressing voter participation. It also uncovers a significant transposition of relative voter involvement in rural areas and urban centers since about 1930.

It is frequently argued that declines in participation after the turn of the century were largely the product of massive immigration from Europe and of the advent of woman suffrage, both of which added very large and initially poorly socialized elements to the potential electorate.[10] There is no question that these were influential factors. The data in Table 5 indicate, for example, that down until the Great Depression turnout was consistently higher and much less subject to variation in rural counties with relatively

Table 5 *Differentials in Aggregate Turnout and Variation of Turnout in Selected Pennsylvania Counties: Presidential Elections, 1876–1960**

County and Type	N	% Foreign stock, 1920	1876–1896		1900–1916		1920–1932		1936–1960	
			Mean turnout	Coef. var.	Mean turnout	Coef. var.	Mean turnout	Coef. var.	Mean turnout	Coef. var.
		(%)	(%)		(%)		(%)		(%)	
Urban:										
Allegheny	1	56.6	71.8	6.75	56.7	2.45	43.8	10.11	68.9	5.82
Philadelphia	1	54.3	85.2	4.61	72.9	6.42	50.5	12.57	68.8	4.40
Industrial-Mining:	4	49.0	88.1	4.48	72.8	4.41	54.2	11.63	64.7	10.88
Rural:	8	13.5	88.5	3.12	76.4	3.63	56.0	8.09	65.2	13.20

* The coefficient of variability is a standard statistical measure; see V. O. Key, Jr., *A Primer of Statistics for Political Scientists* (New York, 1954), pp. 44–52. Since secular trends, where present, had to be taken into account, this coefficient appears abnormally low in the period 1900–1916. During this period many counties registered a straight-line decline in turnout from one election to the next.

insignificant foreign-stock populations than in either the industrial-mining or metropolitan counties.

Yet two other aspects of these data should also be noted. First, the pattern of turnout decline from the 1876–1896 period to the 1900–1916 period was quite uniform among all categories of counties, though the rank order of their turnouts remained largely unchanged. It can be inferred from this that, while immigration probably played a major role in the evolution of Pennsylvania's political system as a whole, it had no visible direct effect upon the secular decline in rural voting participation. Broader systemic factors, including but transcending the factor of immigration, seem clearly to have been at work. Second, a very substantial fraction of the total decline in turnout from the 1870s to the 1920s—in some rural native-stock counties more than half—occurred *before* women were given the vote. Moreover, post-1950 turnout levels in Pennsylvania, and apparently in most other non-Southern states, have been at least as high as in the decade immediately preceding the general enfranchisement of women. If even today a higher percentage of American than European women fail to come to the polls, the same can also be said of such population groups as the poorly educated, farmers, the lower-income classes, Negroes and other deprived elements in the potential electorate.[11] In such a context woman suffrage, as important a variable as it certainly has been in our recent political history, seems to raise more analytical problems than it solves.

Table 6 *Urban-Rural Differences in Stability of Political Involvement: 1936–60 Mean Turnout and Variability of Turnout as Percentages of 1876–96 Mean Turnout and Variability of Turnout, Pennsylvania*

County and Type	N	1936–60 Turnout / 1876–96 Turnout	1936–60 Variability / 1876–96 Variability
Urban:		(%)	(%)
Allegheny	1	95.9	86.2
Philadelphia	1	80.8	95.4
Industrial-Mining:	4	73.4	249.6
Rural:	8	73.7	447.4

Particularly suggestive for our hypothesis of basic changes in the nature of American voting behavior over time is the quite recent transposition of aggregate turnout and variations in turnout as between our rural sample and the two metropolitan centers. In sharp contrast to the situation prevailing before 1900, turnout in these rural counties has tended during the past generation not only to be slightly lower than in the large cities but also subject to far wider oscillations from election to election. In Bedford County, for example, turnout stood at 82.5 per cent in 1936, but sagged to an all-time low of 41.2 per cent in 1948. The comparable figures in Philadelphia were 74.3 and 64.8 per cent, and in Allegheny County 72.5 per cent (in 1940) and 60.6 per cent.

A major finding revealed by survey research is that the "farm vote" is currently one of the most unstable and poorly articulated elements in the American electorate.[12] It is said that since rural voters lack the solid network of group identifications and easy access to mass-communication media enjoyed by their city cousins, they tend to be both unusually apathetic and exceptionally volatile in their partisan commitments. As rural voting turnout was abnormally low in 1948, its rate of increase from 1948 to 1952 was exceptionally large and—fully consistent with Campbell's surge-decline model—was associated with a one-sided surge toward Eisenhower. A restatement of the data in Table 5 lends strong support to this evaluation of the relative position of the rural vote as a description of the *current* American voting universe.

But the data strongly imply that virtually the opposite of present conditions prevailed during the 19th century. Such variables as education level, communications and non-family-group interaction were probably much more poorly developed in rural areas before 1900 than they are today. Not only did this leave no visible mark on agrarian turnout; it seems extremely likely that the 19th-century farmer was at least as well integrated into the political system of that day as any other element in the American electorate. The awesome rates of turnout which can be found in states like Indiana, Iowa and Kentucky prior to 1900 indicate that this extremely high level of rural political involvement was not limited to Pennsylvania.[13] As a recent study of Indiana politics demonstrates, the primarily rural "traditional vote" in that state was marked prior to 1900 by an overwhelming partisan stability as well.[14]

Perhaps, following the arguments of C. Wright Mills and others, we can regard this extraordinary change in rural voting behavior as a function of the conversion of a cracker-barrel society into a subodinate element in a larger mass society.[15] In any event, this rural movement toward relatively low and widely fluctuating levels of turnout may well be indicative of an emergent political alienation in such areas. It is suggestive that these movements have been accompanied generally in Pennsylvania as in states like West Virginia by a strongly positive Republican trend in these agrarian bailiwicks during the last thirty years.[16] The impression arises that the political realignment of the 1930s, which only imperfectly mobilized and integrated urban populations into the political system, had not even these limited positive effects in more isolated communities.

The behavior of the Ohio electorate down to about 1930 closely paralleled the patterns displayed in its neighbor states, Michigan and Pennsylvania. Since then a marked divergence has been manifest.

Two-party competition here was far less seriously affected by the sectional political alignment of 1896–1932 than in most other northern industrial states. Of the eighteen gubernatorial elections held in Ohio from 1895 to 1930, for example, Democrats won ten. But here as elsewhere are to be found the same patterns of decline in turnout and sharp increases in indices of voter peripherality after 1900. Indeed, while turnout bottomed out during the 1920s at a point considerably higher than in Michigan or Pennsylvania, it had also been considerably higher than in either of them during the 19th century. Here too such variables as woman suffrage seem to have played a smaller role as causal agents—at least so far as they affected the growing tendencies toward peripherality among active voters—than is commonly supposed. Drop-off from presidential to off-year elections began to assume its modern shape in Ohio between 1898 and 1910. As Figure 2 shows, roll-off—an especially prominent feature in contemporary Ohio voting behavior—emerged in modern form in the election of 1914.

Ohio, unlike either Michigan or Pennsylvania, has demonstrated only an extremely limited resurgence since the realignment of the 1930s. Presidential-year voting turnout in the period 1948–60 actually declined from the mean level of 1932–44, and was not appreciably higher than it had been in the trough of the 1920s. If mean drop-off has declined somewhat in recent

Figure 2 *Increases in Roll-Off: The Case of Ohio, 1872–1962*

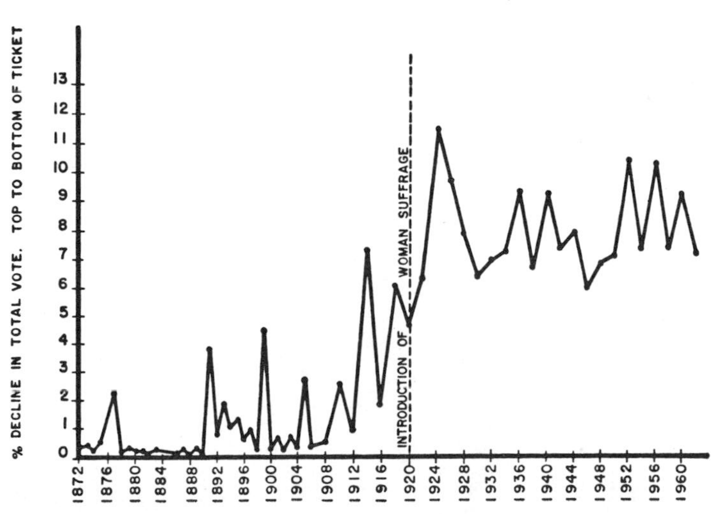

Table 7 *Patterns of Voter Participation in Ohio, 1857–1962; Decline Without Resurgence?*

Period	Mean turnout		Mean drop-off	Mean roll-off	Mean split-ticket voting
	Pres. years	Off-years			
	(%)	(%)			
1857–1879	89.0	78.4	9.7	0.6	0.5
1880–1903	92.2	80.5	11.2	0.8	0.6
1904–1918	80.4	71.2	9.2	2.5	3.3
1920–1930	62.4	45.8	24.1	7.9	9.9
1932–1946	69.9	49.1	27.2	7.6	6.5
1948–1962	66.5	53.3	19.0	8.2	11.1

years, it still stands at a level twice as high as in any period before 1920. Moreover, roll-off and the rate of split-ticket voting have actually increased to unprecedented highs since 1948. By 1962 the latter ratio touched an all-time high of 21.3% (except for the three-party election of 1924), suggesting that Ohio politics may be becoming an "every-man-for-himself" affair. This pattern of behavior stands in the sharpest possible contrast to 19th-century norms. In that period turnout had reached substantially full proportions, drop-off was minimal and well over 99 per cent of the voters cast both

Figure 3 *Increases in Split-Ticket Voting: The Case of Ohio, 1872–1962*

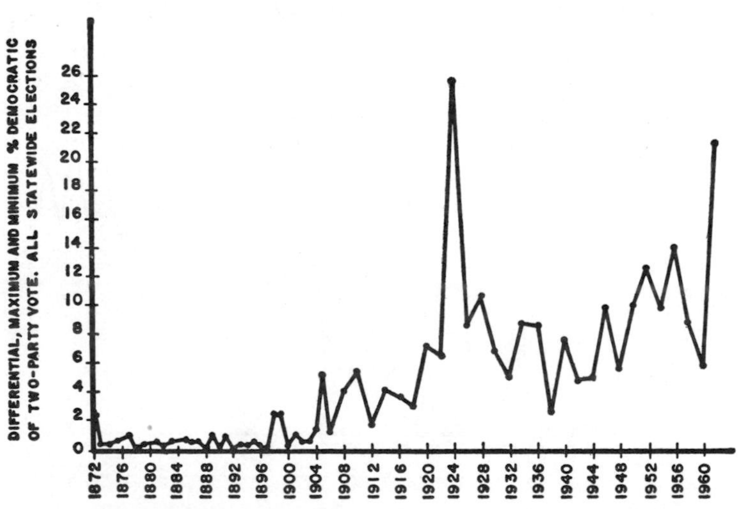

complete ballots and straight party tickets—an achievement that may have been partly an artifact of the party ballots then in use.[17] The political reintegration which the New Deal realignment brought in its wake elsewhere has scarcely become visible in Ohio.

Two recent discussions of Ohio politics may shed some light upon these characteristics. Thomas A. Flinn, examining changes over the past century in the partisan alignments of Ohio counties, concludes that until the first decade of the 20th century the state had a set of political alignments based largely on sectionalism within Ohio—a product of the diverse regional backgrounds of its settlers and their descendants. This older political system broke down under the impact of industrialization and a national class-ethnic partisan realignment, but no new political order of similar coherence or partisan stability has yet emerged to take its place.[18] Finn's findings and the conclusions which Lee Benson has drawn from his study of New York voting behavior in the 1840s are remarkably similar.[19] In this earlier voting universe the durability of partisan commitment and the extremely high levels of turnout appear to have had their roots in a cohesive and persistent set of positive and negative group referents. These, as Flinn notes, provided "no clear-cut class basis for statewide party following from the time of Jackson to that of Wilson.[20]

John H. Fenton, discussing the 1962 gubernatorial campaign, carries the argument one step further.[21] Basic to Ohio's social structure, he argues, is an unusually wide diffusion of its working-class population among a large number of middle-sized cities and even smaller towns. The weakness of the labor unions and the chaotic disorganization of the state Democratic Party seem to rest upon this diffusion. Ohio also lacks agencies which report on the activities of politicians from a working-class point of view, such as have been set up by the United Automobile Workers in Detroit or the United Mine Workers in Pennsylvania or West Virginia. The result of this is that to a much greater extent than in other industrial states, potential recruits for a cohesive and reasonably well-organized Democratic Party in Ohio live in an isolated, atomized social milieu. Consequently they tend to vote in a heavily personalist, issueless way, as the middle and upper classes do not. Such a state of affairs may provide clues not only for the relative failure of voter turnout to increase during the past generation, but for the persistent and growing indications of voter peripherality in Ohio's active electorate as well. . . .

II

The conclusions which arise directly out of this survey of aggregate data and indices of participation seem clear enough. On both the national and state levels they point to the existence and eventual collapse of an earlier political universe in the United States—a universe in many ways so sharply different from the one we all take for granted today that many of our contemporary frames of analytical reference seem irrelevant or misleading in studying it. The late 19th-century voting universe was marked by a more complete and intensely party-oriented voting participation among the American electorate than ever before or since. Approximately two-thirds of the potential national electorate were then "core" voters, one-tenth fell into the peripheral category, and about one-quarter remained outside. In the . . . northern states examined in this survey the component of core elements in the potential electorate was even larger: about three-quarters core voters, one-tenth peripherals and about 15 per cent non-voters.

In other ways too this 19th-century system differed markedly from its successors. Class antagonisms as such appear to have had extremely low salience by comparison with today's voting behavior. Perhaps differentials in the level of formal education among various groups in the population contributed to differentials in 19th-century turnout as they clearly do now. But the unquestionably far lower *general* level of formal education in America during the last century did not preclude a much more intense and uniform mass political participation than any which has prevailed in recent decades. Though the evidence is still scanty, it strongly implies that the influence of rurality upon the intensity and uniformity of voting participation appears to have been precisely the opposite of what survey-research findings hold it to be today. This was essentially a pre-industrial democratic system, resting heavily upon a rural and small-town base. Apparently, it was quite adequate, both in partisan organization and dissemination of political information, to the task of mobilizing voters on a scale which compares favorably with recent European levels of participation.

There is little doubt that the model of surge and decline discussed above casts significant light upon the behavior of today's American electorate as it responds to the stimuli of successive elections. But the model depends for its validity upon the demonstrated existence of very large numbers both of peripheral voters and of core voters whose attachment to party is relatively feeble. Since these were not pronounced characteristics of the 19th-century voting universe, it might be expected that abnormal increases in the percentage of the vote won by either party would be associated with very different kinds of movements in the electorate, and that such increases would be relatively unusual by present-day standards.

Even a cursory inspection of the partisan dimensions of voting behavior in the 19th century tends to confirm this expectation. Not only did the amplitude of partisan swing generally tend to be much smaller then than now,[22] but nationwide landslides of the 20th-century type were almost nonexistent.[23] Moreover, when one party did win an unusually heavy majority, this increase was usually associated with a pronounced and one-sided *decline* in turnout. Comparison of the 1848 and 1852 elections in Georgia and of the October gubernatorial and November presidential elections of 1872 in Pennsylvania, for example, makes it clear that the "landslides" won by one of the presidential contenders in 1852 and 1872 were the direct consequence of mass abstentions by voters who normally supported the other party.[24] Under 19th-century conditions, marked as they were by substantially full mobilization of the eligible electorate, the only play in the system which could provide extraordinary majorities had to come from a reversal of the modern pattern of surge and decline—a depression in turnout which was overwhelmingly confined to adherents of one of the parties.[25]

This earlier political order, as we have seen, was eroded away very rapidly after 1900. Turnout fell precipitately from 19th-century levels even before the advent of woman suffrage, and even in areas where immigrant elements in the electorates were almost nonexistent. As turnout declined, a larger and larger component of the still-active electorate moved from a core to a peripheral position, and the hold of the parties over their mass base appreciably deteriorated. This revolutionary contraction in the size and diffusion in the shape of the voting universe was almost certainly the fruit of the heavily sectional party realignment which was inaugurated in 1896. This "system of 1896," as Schattschneider calls it,[26] led to the destruction of party competition throughout much of the United States, and thus paved the way for the rise of the direct primary. It also gave immense impetus to the strains of anti-partisan and anti-majoritarian theory and practice which have always been significant elements in the American political tradition. By the decade of the 1920s this new regime and business control over public policy in this country were consolidated. During that decade hardly more than one-third of the eligible adults were still core voters. Another one-sixth were peripheral voters and fully one-half remained outside the active voting universe altogether. It is difficult to avoid the impression that while all the forms of political democracy were more or less scrupulously preserved, the functional result of the "system of 1896" was the conversion of a fairly democratic regime into a rather broadly based oligarchy.

The present shape and size of the American voting universe are, of course, largely the product of the 1928–1936 political realignment. Survey-research findings most closely approximate political reality as they relate to this next broad phase of American political evolution. But the characteristics of the present voting universe suggest rather forcefully that the New Deal realignment has been both incomplete and transitional. At present, about 44 per cent of the national electorate are core voters, another 16 or so are peripheral, and about 40 per cent are still outside the political system altogether. By 19th-century standards, indices of voter peripherality stand at very high levels. Party organizations remain at best only indifferently successful at mobilizing a stable, predictable mass base of support.

ENDNOTES

1. See, *e.g.*, Robert E. Lane, *Political Life* (Glencoe, Ill., 1959), pp. 18–26.

2. There are, of course, very wide divergences in turnout rates even among non-Southern states. Some of them, like Idaho, New Hampshire and Utah, have presidential-year turnouts which compare very favorably with European levels of participation. A detailed analysis of these differences remains to be made. It should prove of the utmost importance in casting light upon the relevance of current forms of political organization and partisan alignments to differing kinds of electorates and political subsystems in the United States.

3. *Report of the President's Commission on Registration and Voting Participation* (Washington, 1963), esp. pp. 5–9. Hereafter cited as *Report.*

4. *Ibid.*, pp. 11–14, 31–42.

5. See, *e.g.*, Stanley Kelley, "Elections and the Mass Media," *Law and Contemporary Problems*, Vol. 27, pp. 307–26 (1962).

6. E. E. Schattschneider, *The Semi-Sovereign People* (New York: 1960), pp. 102–3.

7. Joseph La Palombara, *Guide to Michigan Politics* (East Lansing, Mich., Michigan State University Press, 1960), pp. 22–35.

8. This recalls Robinson and Standing's conclusion that voter partcipation in Indiana does not necessarily increase with increasing party competition. Of the eight Michigan gubernatorial elections from 1948 to 1962 only one was decided by a margin of 55% or more, while three were decided by margins of less than 51.5% of the two-party vote. Despite this intensely competitive situation, turnout—while of course much higher than in the 1920s—remains significantly below normal pre-1920 levels.

9. Angus Campbell, "Surge and Decline: A Study of Electoral Change," *Public Opinion Quarterly*, Vol. 24, pp. 397–418 (1960).

10. Herbert Tingsten, *Political Behavior* (Stockholm, Stockholm Economic Studies, No. 7, 1937), pp. 10–36. See also Charles E. Merriam and Harold F. Gosnell, *Non-Voting* (Chicago, University of Chicago Press, 1924), pp. 26, 109–22, for a useful discussion of the effect of woman suffrage on turnout in a metropolitan area immediately following the general enfranchisement of 1920.

11. Survey-research estimates place current turnout among American women at 10% below male turnout. Angus Campbell *et al.*, *The American Voter* (New York, 1960), pp. 484–85. This sex-related difference in participation is apparently universal, but is significantly smaller in European countries which provide election data by sex, despite the far higher European level of participation by both sexes. The postwar differential has been 5.8% in Norway (1945–57 mean), 3.3% in Sweden

(1948–60 mean), and 1.9% in Finland (1962 general election). While in 1956 only about 55% of American women went to the polls, the mean turnout among women in postwar elections was 76.1% in Norway and 79.4% in Sweden.

12. *Ibid.*, pp. 402–40.

13. The estimated rates of turnout in presidential elections from 1876 through 1896, mean turnout in the period 1936–60 and estimated turnout in 1964 were as follows in these states:

State	1876	1880	1884	1888	1892	1896	1936/60 (Mean)	1964 (Prelim.)
Indiana	94.6	94.4	92.2	93.3	89.0	95.1	75.0	73.3
Iowa	89.6	91.5	90.0	87.9	88.5	96.2	71.7	72.0
Kentucky	76.1	71.0	68.0	79.1	72.6	88.0	57.6	52.6

14. V. O. Key, Jr., and Frank Munger, "Social Determinism and Electoral Decision: The Case of Indiana," in Eugene Burdick and Arthur J. Brodbeck, eds., *American Voting Behavior* (Glencoe, Ill., 1959), pp. 282–88.

15. C. Wright Mills, *The Power Elite* (New York, Oxford University Press, 1956), pp. 298–324. See also Arthur J. Vidich and Joseph Bensman, *Small Town in Mass Society* (New York, 1960), pp. 5–15, 202–27, 297–320.

16. John H. Fenton, *Politics in the Border States* (New Orleans, Hauser Press, 1957), pp. 117–20.

17. However, Ohio's modern pattern of split-ticket voting, formed several decades ago, seems to have been little (if at all) affected by the 1950 change from party-column to office-block ballot forms. See Figure 3.

18. Thomas A. Flinn, "Continuity and Change in Ohio Politics," *Journal of Politics*, Vol. 24, pp. 521–44 (1962).

19. Lee Benson, *The Concept of Jacksonian Democracy* (Princeton, Princeton University Press, 1961), pp. 123–207, 288–328.

20. Flinn, *op. cit.*, p. 542.

21. John H. Fenton, "Ohio's Unpredictable Voters," *Harper's Magazine*, Vol. 225, pp. 61–65 (1962).

22. Mean national partisan swings in presidential elections since 1872 have been as follows: 1872–92, 2.3%; 1896–1916, 5.0%; 1920–32, 10.3%; 1936–64, 5.4%.

23. If a presidential landslide is arbitrarily defined as a contest in which the winning candidate received 55% or more of the two-party vote, only the election of 1872 would qualify among the 16 presidential elections held from 1836 to 1896. Of 17 presidential elections held from 1900 through 1964, at least eight were landslide elections by this definition, and a ninth—the 1924 election, in which the Republican candidate received 54.3% and the Democratic candidate 29.0% of a three-party total—could plausibly be included.

24. The total vote in Georgia declined from 92,203 in 1848 to 62,333 in 1852. Estimated turnout declined from about 88% to about 55% of the eligible electorate, while the Democratic share of the two-party vote increased from 48.5% in 1848 to

64.8% in 1852. The pattern of participation in the Pennsylvania gubernatorial and presidential elections of 1872 is also revealing:

Raw Vote	Governor, Oct. 1872	President, Nov. 1872	Absolute Decline
Total	671,147	562,276	−108,871
Democratic	317,760	213,027	−104,733
Republican	353,387	349,249	− 4,138

Estimated turnout in October was 82.0%, in November 68.6%. The Democratic percentage of the two-party vote was 47.3% in October and 37.9% in November.

25. The only apparent exception to this generalization in the 19th century was the election of 1840. But this was the first election in which substantially full mobilization of the eligible electorate occurred. The rate of increase in the total vote from 1836 to 1860 was 60.0%, the largest in American history. Estimated turnout increased from about 58% in 1836 to about 80% in 1840. This election, with its relatively one-sided mobilization of hitherto apolitical elements in the potential electorate, not unnaturally bears some resemblance to the elections of the 1950s. But the increase in the Whig share of the two-party vote from 49.2% in 1836 to only 53.0% in 1840 suggests that that surge was considerably smaller than those of the 1950s.

26. *The Semi-Sovereign People*, *op. cit.*, p. 81.

My reasons for decline in TN + party strength after 1890s.
1. Australian ballot
2. New one-party regions - eg NE, South
3. New issues - Pop, Prog
4. anti-party prop

PART 3

EXPLAINING PUBLIC OPINION

PART 3 AN OVERVIEW

In describing public opinion, the preceding section showed that within the framework of this country's political culture there are widely differing opinions about fundamental principles of government, varying levels of support for governmental institutions and democratic values, and differing degrees of interest in politics and comprehension of political ideas. This section will examine whether these differences can be related to other measurable differences among people, such as their social, biological, and psychological characteristics. It will also analyze how people learn about politics and come to form some of their political opinions.

In reporting public opinion on topics of current interest, pollsters believe it useful to categorize people by social types. The categories of public opinion groups most often used relate to a variety of social or economic classifications—urban and rural; over 55 or under 30; Westerners, Southerners, and Easterners; income of more $10,000 or under $10,000; Protestant, Catholic, and Jew; and so on. Dividing people by social or socioeconomic characteristics largely illustrates only one kind of classification that might be made. Such classification says nothing about how people of various personalities or psychological predispositions might be expected to differ in their political opinions, or how various biological characteristics (except perhaps for race and sex, which are both social and biological attributes) influence people's opinions.

Thus, in addition to social characteristics, we see that there are a variety of other personal characteristics that could potentially influence an individual's opinion. But how do we know which of these personal characteristics are most important in determining public opinion in general? How do we know which influences are going to be most important for any one particular issue? Intuition might tell us, for example, that age could have an important effect on opinions about the draft, drug usage, or Medicare. But would age have an equally important impact on attitudes toward minimum-wage laws or foreign aid or revenue sharing? It seems likely that it would not. But why not? Likewise, blacks have different attitudes about black power than whites (Aberback and Walker, 1970). But do these racial differences carry over to attitudes about foreign policy and fiscal measures? Again, probably not. When considering foreign or fiscal policy, social and psychological characteristics completely divorced from racial differences might be far more important.

In order to go beyond simple speculation about the relationship between social, psychological, biological, or other characteristics and various kinds of political opinion, we need a scheme that can help us understand the interrelationship of these aspects in the individual and the comparative importance of the various factors in any given situation. This is a big order, and one that has not been completely filled by public opinion researchers. Nevertheless, a start has been made.

To examine the combined impact of the various factors on an opinion, we may borrow Smith's "map," which he used to analyze the relationship between social and psychological factors and political behavior (Smith, 1968).[1]

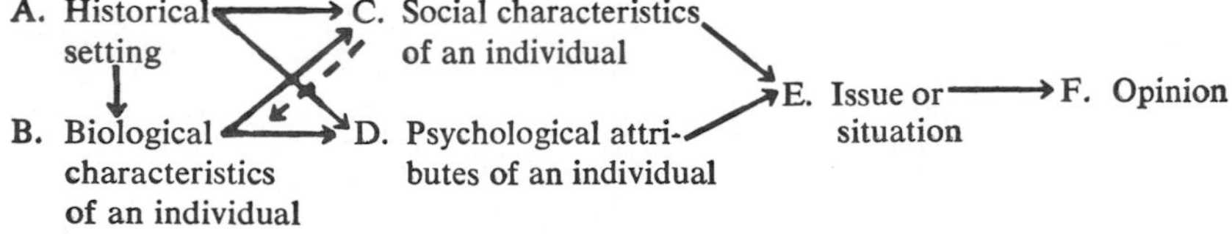

Let us examine each of these factors and their interrelationship.

HISTORICAL SETTING

The historical setting, or what Smith calls "distal" social antecedents, concerns nonimmediate antecedents of opinion. An excellent example of the importance of historical setting on opinions is seen in the long-differing views held by Northerners and Southerners concerning the role of the black in this country's political, social, and legal structure. Here a complex interplay of geographic, historical, economic, and social factors has resulted in totally different political and social traditions in the North and South concerning black-white relationships.[2] Key and Munger (1959) have shown how differences springing out of the respective historical traditions of the North and the South have also influenced the intrastate politics of Ohio, Illinois, and Indiana where, even today, part of the political cleavages stems from different patterns of immigration from the North and South to various parts of the state. There are other regional patterns and traditions that are a part of the salient historical settings influencing current public opinion. The Midwest, for example, has a tradition of isolationism not found in other areas; likewise, some states in the Midwest have a strong heritage of Progressive or Populist traditions that may influence current opinion (Key, 1961). Urban and rural traditions are another kind of distal social antecedent that may affect opinion (Key, 1961). Lipset and Bendix's work on class mobility (1967) indicates that a person's current political behavior is influenced not only by his own class attachment, but by those of his forebears. This too is an example of how current opinion is formed in an historical setting.

The historical setting usually does not influence opinions directly but through other, more immediate factors such as the social and psychological characteristics of the individual himself. For example, whether an individual is born into an era of prosperity or depression influences the probability of his being prosperous or poverty stricken, and this in turn may influence a variety of his opinions. Other factors such as peace or war abroad, domestic tranquility or turmoil, economic stagnation or dramatic growth—all historical settings (distal social antecedents)—may influence an individual's immediate social position. Further, the historical setting may also influence the psychological makeup of an individual. A person who grew up during the Depression may be much less carefree and much more inhibited in economic matters, for example, than someone who has grown up knowing only prosperity. Likewise, a child growing up during a time of war or domestic conflict may form predispositions of hostility and aggression that are retained though no immediate conflict exists.

Finally, as Smith's "map" indicates, the historical setting may have an influence on the biological characteristics of individuals. Malnourishment, resulting from the economic impact of a depression or wartime deprivation, may produce low IQs or physical handicaps, thus influencing the social position and psychological well-being of those affected.

BIOLOGICAL CHARACTERISTICS

The biological characteristics of individuals and their relationships to political attitudes and behavior have barely been explored. Nevertheless, findings thus far suggest that there may indeed be a link between biological characteristics and political opinions. Jaros (1972) finds that an individual's attitudes toward political leaders can be altered by the administration of drugs. Harvey and Harvey (1970) report that intelligence levels of adolescents have an effect on their political attitudes independent of SES characteristics. Welch and Booth (1974) find that crowded living conditions seem to influence people's propensity toward violent political activities.

Part of the problem in dealing with biological influences on opinion is that in some respects they are difficult to separate from social influences. Sex and race, for example, while clearly biological characteristics, seem to be influential in politics largely through their social definition and impact. The relative biological and social impact of intelligence is still disputed among educational psychologists and others, for another example. However, we are arguing here that biological characteristics, like historical settings, operate on opinion indirectly through social and psychological attributes and are not a direct cause of any particular opinion.

Clearly one's biological characteristics may influence one's social position and one's psychological state: a person who is mentally retarded, for example, does not have the same opportunity to earn a high income or have a liberal education (both of which may influence various kinds of opinion) as a person with an average intelligence. Persons born black or female may be barred from some positions in the social, economic or political hierarchies, and this may in turn influence their opinions about significant social and political issues. Biological changes in an individual brought about by exposure to constant stress may produce certain psychological states that may find a political expression. Thus, while the impact of biological condition on political opinions and behavior has not been fully explored, there is evidence to suggest that this impact is potentially great.

SOCIAL CHARACTERISTICS

Unlike the preceding relationships, the link between social characteristics and public opinion has been widely explored by social scientists. This research is so extensive that it cannot be adequately summarized in a few paragraphs or a few pages.[3]

Some general outlines of a part of the literature, however, may be drawn. It has been shown, for example, that people of higher status (education, income, occupational level) tend to be more supportive of democratic values than those of lower status. This includes greater toleration for minority races and points of view, and support for due process (Stouffer, 1955; McClosky, 1964). Those of lower status, in the terms just referred to, seem to be more prone to favor "liberal" socioeconomic policies than people of upper status. That is, people of lower status may be more inclined to support government programs in the health, welfare, employment or similar areas. Alienation from government and the feeling of a lack of individual power or influence over the political system also tend to characterize people of lower socioeconomic status (Finifter, 1970; Nie et al., 1969). Campbell et al., in the selection that follows *(see pp. 176–83)*, discuss how membership in social grouping affects voting behavior and party choice. Free and Cantril's selection *(see pp. 196–202)* deals with the relationship between a number of demographic indicators and attitudes of liberalism and conservatism.

Ethnicity and its relation to political opinion and behavior have been a popular topic in recent years. In two studies, Wilson and Banfield (1964, 1971) show that members of some ethnic groups—WASPs and Jews, for example—are more prone to favor public expenditures for a variety of public services such as schools, hospitals, and so on, while members of other groups—Italians, Poles, and other Southern or Eastern Europeans—tend to favor expenditures for individual benefits such as pensions, welfare payments, and veteran's bonuses. Another study (Parenti, 1967) confronts the question of why members of various ethnic groups retain distinctive political patterns even after they have entered the larger society in terms of education, income, and adoption of many of the values of that society.

A few studies have investigated black-white differences in political attitudes and behavior. Marvick and Finifter have found differences in expectations of treatment by government officials on the part of blacks and whites (Marvick, 1965; Finifter, 1970). Others have found a lesser degree of political efficacy among blacks, more hostility to local government, and different attitudes on various public policies. Little has been done in terms of systematically analyzing the attitudes and behavior of other non-European minority groups in the United States, but there is some slight evidence to indicate that they may hold views similar in some respects to the views of blacks.

An interesting question arises when an individual's social traits or psychological dispositions are in conflict with one another. For example, an individual's occupational associates may push him toward taking positions typical of a conservative Republican, while his family background and parental influence push him in the opposite direction. What happens then? The authors of *Voting* found that under these conditions in an election situation, the potential voter often stays home, not able to choose among the "cross pressures" (Berelson, Lazarsfeld, and McPhee, 1954). On a more general level, those who are subject to status conflicts are likely to be withdrawn from political life and apathetic about it (Lenski, 1954).

PSYCHOLOGICAL CHARACTERISTICS

The influence of psychological attributes on opinion is disputed. Greenstein, in the selection that follows *(see pp. 206–24)*, attempts to clear away the existing objections to the usefulness of research on the impact of personality on politics. Many political scientists, in fact, challenge the usefulness of using psychological variables in analyzing public opinion and believe that social characteristics are more helpful in explaining opinion. On the other hand, few of those who stress the importance of psychological characteristics believe that social variables are unimportant. Rather, they deny that the two are mutually exclusive and tend to view opinions and attitudes as resulting from the interplay of psychological and social variables. Thus, the issue centers on which of the two variables—the social or the psychological—has the greater value in explaining opinion.

Probably the most important single investigation of the impact of psychological variables on an individual's political attitudes was done by Adorno, Frenkel-Brunswick, Levinson, and Sanford in the late 1940s. In a massive work called *The Authoritarian Personality* (1950), they presented evidence that prejudice, propensity toward antidemocratic values, and anti-semitism were linked together in a personality type characterized by (among other things) submissiveness to authority, aggression against subordinates, and intolerance for unconventional beliefs and behavior. According to the findings of *The Authoritarian Personality*, then, one can expect that a person who is prejudiced against blacks, for example, will also be prejudiced toward other "outgroups," and that his attitudes toward authority may be different from those of an unprejudiced person. Many volumes have been written seeking to cast doubt on the findings of this book (Christie and Jahoda, 1954; Shils, 1954); but, while much of the research procedure used by Adorno and his associates has been successfully challenged, thus far the substantive findings have not been contradicted.[4]

Since the publication of *The Authoritarian Personality*, much research has been done on the relationship of personality and psychological characteristics to politics. A portion of this research has attempted to analyze in depth the behavior of individual political leaders (George and George,

1956; Tucker, 1965), while others have investigated the relationship between personality and opinion on the mass level. For instance, personality has been linked to internationalism and isolationism (McClosky, 1958), to conservatism and liberalism (McClosky, 1958), and to a wide variety of measures of political interest, knowledge, and attitudes (Rosenberg, 1962).

While this extensive research has opened up interesting and fruitful areas for further analysis, many problems remain to be solved. How to conceptualize psychological variables without resorting to tautological reasoning, and the development of useful measures of psychological and personality characteristics that are applicable to mass surveys are just two of these problems.

POLITICAL SOCIALIZATION

Because one is born a Southerner or black or into a high-income family obviously does not mean that one automatically inherits a certain set of political attitudes characteristic of that particular group. The process by which the child, and later the adult, acquires and modifies his political beliefs is called "political socialization." Political socialization is a complex process. It can take place directly—for example, through deliberate political education and indoctrination, or by mimicking parental attitudes—or indirectly, when children learn certain societal values while participating in organized or unorganized groups (Boy Scouts, 4-H, neighborhood play groups, and the like).

It has long been thought that most childhood political learning is transmitted by parents, peer groups, and the school; and that the mass media have been primary socialization agents only for adults. Recently, researchers have begun to take a new look at the effects of mass communications media on the political socialization of children as well (see e.g., Kraus, 1973). This section's first article on the subject of political learning, by Easton and Dennis *(pp. 229–49)*, investigates some of the initial points of contact between the child and the system, the child's view of government and political authority figures, and describes how this view changes as the child learns more about the political world.

Sometimes political socialization received through one primary group may be inconsistent with that received from another. For example, socialization received from peers may conflict with that received from one's family. This is bound to happen in any complex society, but seems especially likely when substantial political changes have occurred (such as Germany's transition from a democratic regime to a Nazi regime back to a democratic regime in the period from 1930 to 1950), or when the society is crosscut with major ethnic, religious, or cultural cleavages. The outcome of contradictory socialization experiences has not been widely explored, but Greenberg in the selection that follows *(see pp. 251–70)* discusses one outcome of inconsistencies in political socialization—differences in attitudes toward the political system on the part of black and white children in the United States.

It is through political socialization that a child becomes aware of his social and biological characteristics and is exposed to the traditional modes of thought and behavior characteristic of his environment as defined, among other things, by historical factors. A black child growing up in a slum, for example, learns the implications of being black in a white-dominated world. In general, the political learning he experiences will be very different from that experienced by the son of a professor growing up in Ann Arbor, Michigan, or the daughter of a judge in Birmingham, Alabama, Each, through socialization, learns explicitly or implicitly about some of his characteristics that will affect his future political role. Being black, being a woman, being a Southerner, being a member of a high-status, well-off family—each of these characteristics has implications for attitudes formed about the political system and one's role in it.

Another important part of political socialization relates to the development of cognitive skills. Such skills are needed to understand political events and to judge and evaluate political issues. Cognitive skills include the ability to reason from cause to effect, to think logically, and to recognize that political events are the products of individual and social forces that are largely controllable (Merelman, 1969). Some people can conceptualize political events in a sophisticated manner, seeing multiple causes and effects, recognizing the importance of social institutions and norms to political patterns, and so on. Others have very limited ways of explaining political questions, since they view political outcomes largely as the result of whimsy, personalities, or other factors beyond control.

The development of moral bases of judgment about politics is another important part of political socialization.[5] Some people, for example, judge political events from a universalistic perspective, basing their political preferences on a concern for "fair" treatment of all or most people. Others, instead, are only concerned with the impact of political events on their own fortunes and form their opinions accordingly.

How these different styles of political thought are learned is not clear. It seems, however, that biological, social, and psychological characteristics all affect these developments (Merelman, 1971; see also Kohlberg, 1963; Haan, Smith, and Block, 1968).

In sum, political socialization is an important mechanism that helps define which characteristics of an individual will be important in shaping his opinions about the political world and the way he thinks about political events.

ENDNOTES

1. A similar chain of causality can be found in *The American Voter* (Campbell et al., 1964).

2. Key has documented the influence that these historical patterns have had on politics in the traditional South (1949).

3. The interested reader should see Lane (1959) for a thorough, although now somewhat dated, summary of this research.

4. One of the frequent criticisms of *The Authoritarian Personality* research has been that the indicators of this kind of personality measured only authoritarianism of the right. Milton Rokeach (1960), on the other hand, has presented a typology of belief systems—open and closed—which he believes captures both the left-wing and the right-wing authoritarian.

5. Styles of "moral reasoning" refer to justification for one's own preferences (Merelman, 1971).

REFERENCES AND FURTHER READING

Aberback, Joel D. and Walker, Jack L. "The Meanings of Black Power: A Comparison of White and Black Interpretation of a Political Slogan." *American Political Science Review* 64(1970): 367-388.

Adorno, T. W., et al. *The Authoritarian Personality*. New York: W.W. Norton, 1950. Norton, 1950.

Berelson, Bernard, Lazarsfeld, Paul F., McPhee, William, N. *Voting*. Chicago: University of Chicago Press, 1954.

Campbell, Angus, et al. *The American Voter*. New York: John Wiley & Sons, 1960.

Christie, Richard, and Jahoda, Marie. *Studies in Scope and Method of the Authoritarian Personality*. New York: Free Press, 1954.

Easton, David, and Dennis, Jack. "The Child's Image of Government." *Annals of the American Academy of Political and Social Science* 361 (1965): 40–57.

Finifter, Ada W. "Dimensions of Political Alienation." *American Political Science Review* 64 (1970): 389–410.

Free, Lloyd, and Cantril, Hadley. *The Political Beliefs of Americans: A Study of Public Opinion*. New Brunswick, N.J.: Rutgers University Press, 1968.

George, Alexander L., and George, Juliette L. *Woodrow Wilson and Colonel House: A Personality Study*. New York: John Day, 1956.

Greenberg, Edward S. "Children and Government: A Comparison Across Racial Lines," *Midwest Journal of Political Science* 14 (1970): 249–275.

Greenstein, Fred I. "The Impact of Personality on Politics: An Attempt to Clear Away Underbrush." *American Political Science Review* 61 (1967): 629–641.

Haan, Norma; Smith, M. Brewster; and Block, Jeanne. "Moral Reasoning of Young Adults: Political-Social Behavior, Family Background and Personality Correlates." *Journal of Personality and Social Psychology* 10 (1968): 183–201.

Harvey, S. K., and Harvey, T. G. "Adolescent Political Outlooks: The Effects of Intelligence as an Independent Variable." *Midwest Journal of Political Science* 14 (1970): 565–595.

Hyman, H. and Sheatsley, P. "The Authoritarian Personality—A Methodological Critique." In *Studies in Scope and Method of the Authoritarian Personality*, by Richard Christie and Marie Jahoda. New York: Free Press, 1954.

Jaros, Dean. "Biochemical Desocialization: Depressants and Political Behavior." *Midwest Journal of Political Science* 16 (1972): 1–28.

Jaros, Dean; Hirsh, Herbert; and Fleron, Frederic J. "The Malevolent Leader: Political Socialization in an American Subculture." *American Political Science Review* 62 (1968): 564–575.

Jennings, M. Kent, and Niemi, Richard G. "The Transmission of Political Values from Parent to Child." *American Political Science Review* 62 (1968): 169–184.

Key, V. O., Jr. *Southern Politics in State and Nation*. New York: Alfred A. Knopf, 1949.

Key, V. O., Jr., "Structural Dimensions of Opinion Expression." In *Public Opinion and American Democracy* by V. O. Key, Jr. New York: Alfred A. Knopf, 1961.

Key, V. O., Jr., and Munger, Frank. "Social Determination and Electoral Decision: The Case of Indiana." In *American Voting Behavior*, edited by Eugene Burdick and Arthur J. Brodbeck. Glencoe, Ill.: Free Press, 1959.

Kohlberg, Lawrence. "The Development of Children's Orientations toward a Moral Order: I. Sequence in the Development of Moral Thought." *Vita Humana* 6 (1963): 11–33.

Kraus, Sidney. "Mass Communication and Political Socialization: A Re-assessment of Two Decades of Research." *Quarterly Journal of Speech* 59 (1973): 390–400.

Lane, Robert E. *Political Life*. New York: Free Press, 1959.

Lenski, Gerhard. "Status Crystallization: A Non-Vertical Dimension of Social Status." *American Sociological Review* 19 (1954): 405–413.

Lipset, Seymour M., and Bendix, Reinhard. *Social Mobility in Industrial Society: A Study of Political Sociology*. Berkeley: University of California Press, 1967.

McClosky, Herbert. "Conservatism and Personality." *American Political Science Review* 52 (1958): 27–45.

McClosky, Herbert: "Consensus and Ideology in American Politics." *American Political Science Review* 59 (1964): 361–382.

Marvick, Duane. "The Political Socialization of the American Negro." *Annals of the American Academy of Political and Social Science* 361 (1965): 112–122.

Merelman, Richard. "The Development of Political Ideology: A Framework for the Analysis of Political Socialization." *American Political Science Review* 63 (1969): 750–767.

Merelman, Richard. "The Development of Political Thinking in Adolescence." *American Political Science Review* 65 (1971): 1033–1047.

Nie, Norman; Powell, G. Bingham; and Prewitt, Kenneth. "Social Structure and Political Participation: Developmental Relationships," Parts I and II. *American Political Science Review* 63 (1969): 361–378 and 808–832.

Parenti, Michael. "Ethnic Politics and the Persistence of Ethnic Identification." *American Political Science Review* 61 (1967): 717–726.

Rokeach, Milton. *The Open and Closed Mind.* New York: Basic Books, 1960.

Rosenberg, Morris. "Self-Esteem and Concern with Public Affairs." *Public Opinion Quarterly* 26 (1962): 201–211.

Shils, Edward A. "Authoritarianism Right and Left" in *Studies in the Scope and Method of the Authoritarian Personality*, by Richard Christie and Marie Jahoda. New York: Free Press, 1954.

Smith, M. Brewster. "A Map for the Analysis of Personality and Politics." *Journal of Social Issues* 24 (1968): 15–28.

Stouffer, Samuel A. *Communism, Conformity and Civil Liberties.* New York: John Wiley & Sons, 1955.

Tucker, Robert C. "The Dictator and Totalitarianism." *World Politics* 17 (1965): 555–583.

Welch, Susan, and Booth, Alan. "Crowding and Political Aggression: Theoretical Aspects and an Analysis of Some Cross-National Data." *Social Science Information* 13 (1974):

Wilson, James Q., and Banfield, Edward C. "Public-Regardingness as a Value Premise in Voting Behavior." *American Political Science Review* 58 (1964): 876–887.

Wilson, James Q., and Banfield, Edward C. "Political Ethos Revised." *American Political Science Review* 65 (1971): 1048–1062.

PART 3 SELECTION 1

The American Voter: An Abridgment, by Angus Campbell *et al.*, Copyright © 1964 by John Wiley & Sons, Inc. Reprinted by permission of John Wiley & Sons, Inc.

Membership in Social Groupings

ANGUS CAMPBELL, PHILIP E. CONVERSE, WARREN E. MILLER, and DONALD E. STOKES

During each political campaign we hear comment about the "Catholic vote," the "Negro vote," the "labor vote," and so on. Unlike the political parties, these groups stand at one remove from the political order. Their reason for existence is not expressly political. The labor union exists to force management to provide more liberally for the worker; the Catholic church exists for religious worship. But members of these groups appear to think and behave politically in distinctive ways. We assume that these distinctive patterns are produced, in one fashion or another, by influence from the group.

THE ELEMENTS OF THE MODEL

A model for group influence [in politics] should perform two distinct services:

1. Increase our understanding of deviation from group political standards by individual members. If the group exerts influence on its membership, and these individuals are members, how and why do they resist?

2. Increase our understanding of the waxing and waning of distinctive political behavior on the part of certain social groupings in the population. What specific conditions govern this variation in group political "strength"?

The same system of variables can handle both problems, for the problems are closely related. If we can specify the conditions under which an individual fails to be influenced by his group, then it is likely that the decline of group potency in politics will result from the extension of these conditions to an increasing proportion of the membership.

At the simplest level, there is a triangle of elements involved in the situation: (1) the individual, (2) the group, and (3) the world of political objects. This triangle suggests three different relationships among these elements: (*a*) the relationship of the individual to the group; (*b*) the relationship of the group to the political world; and (*c*) the relationship of the individual to the political world. These three relationships determine the types of variables that we take into account. A full model will call for measurements that adequately capture the important dimensions of each relationship, if we are to understand the way in which the individual will respond to politics *given the presence of a group that is real in the sense that it can exert a greater or lesser influence on his behavior.*

The relationship of the individual to the world of politics represents a combination of group and nongroup forces. The group forces in the field are predictable as a function of two "background" terms; the relationship of the individual to the group and the relationship of the group to the world of politics. The nongroup forces are, of course, independent of either of these terms. An analysis of the social origins of political motives therefore involves (1) the manner in which the two background terms interact to produce group forces; and (2) the manner in which group forces interact with other forces in the immediate field of political attitudes.

Two important implications are suggested by a logical exercise of this sort. On one hand, we must arrive at some means of sorting the group forces in which we are interested from nongroup forces, within the total field that characterizes the relationship of the individual to the world of politics. But if we pay little systematic attention to the total relationship of the individual to the political world in elaborating this portion of the model, we must not forget that these nongroup forces exist. In fact, this is a first-level answer to the problem of member deviation from group political standards. Group members do not make political decisions in a psychological field limited to group forces, any more than nonmembers make decisions in a vacuum. The current objects of orientation in the political world are available to everybody and, if perceived, have characteristics that can be distorted only within limits.

Our immediate concern lies with the strength of group-generated forces. We wish to understand the conditions under which that strength varies, over time, from individual to individual and from group to group. For this task we can conceptually ignore other forces in the field, which derive from the relation of the individual to politics, *group considerations aside*. But we must remember that these forces exist and contribute to the final attitudes and behavior.

THE RELATIONSHIP OF THE INDIVIDUAL TO THE GROUP

The first variables to be considered must define the way in which the individual relates himself to the group. We would like to measure aspects of the individual-group relationship that are meaningful for the relationship of *any* individual to *any* group, whether or not that group ever expends effort in political affairs.

Let us think of the group as a psychological reality that exerts greater or lesser attractive force upon its members. Whatever the nominal membership status of the individual, there is room for a great deal of variation in the degree of psychological membership that characterizes the relationship. Just as party identification measures the sense of personal attachment to a political party, so a measure of group identification will indicate the closeness of "*we* feeling" that an individual senses with regard to his membership group.

We have measured group identification by asking members of various politically significant groups the following questions:

Would you say that you feel pretty close to (e.g.) Negroes in general or that you don't feel much closer to them than you do to other kinds of people?

How much interest would you say you have in how (e.g.) Negroes as a whole are getting along in this country? Do you have a good deal of interest in it, some interest, or not much interest at all?

From responses to these items an index of group identification was prepared. The first hypothesis that the model suggests is as follows: *the higher the identification of the individual with the group, the higher the probability that he will think and behave in ways which distinguish members of his group from nonmembers.*

Actually hypotheses much like this have found supporting evidence in other empirical work on voting behavior. Therefore, we are not surprised to find that if we take all members of groups that vote distinctively Democratic, the people who are highly identified with these groups vote even more distinctively Democratic than members who are less highly identified. The least identified third voted 43 per cent Democratic, a figure not very different from the vote proportion in the population as a whole. Medium identifiers, however, voted 56 per cent Democratic; and those most highly identified with these groups voted 69 per cent Democratic. In general, then, the hypothesis receives clear support, and strength of group identification deserves a place as a variable in our model.

Secondary groups that are not primarily political take little interest in some issues, and in these cases group members do not hold attitudes that differ significantly from those of nonmember control groups nor do high identifiers differ from more peripheral members. But as a general rule, whenever a group holds distinctive beliefs about some issue, then within the group a differentiation appears between members according to the strength of their group identification.

This combination of facts argues most conclusively that we are dealing here with a true group-influence phenomenon. To ascertain that influence exists is but a first step, however. We are also interested in assessing the relative strength of influence exerted by various groups and the conditions under which this strength increases or decreases. We find considerable variation in the degree of disparity in presidential vote between strong and weak identifiers within various groups. Table 1 summarizes this variation. . . . Vote distinctiveness *within the group* bears some relation to distinctiveness between the group and a control group matched for life situation, as we would expect if both were taken to reflect strength of group political influence. . . . Most Negroes are highly identified with their group; therefore the total group is more clearly Democratic than it might appear if the proportion of high and low identifiers within the Negro group was closer to that found within the union group. But part of the discrepancy results from other factors to be added to the model shortly.

Group identifications help to answer the two primary questions with which a theory of group influence must deal. At the individual level, we may sort out a set of nominal members who are most likely to deviate from the group position under nongroup forces. They are the people who do not strongly identify with the group, who are psychologically peripheral to it.

A similar proposition can be formulated at the group level. Some groups boast memberships intensely loyal to group purposes and interests. Others have trouble maintaining member identifications. We shall call a group enjoying high member identification a *cohesive group*.[1] Group cohesiveness

Table 1 *Vote Division Within Four Test Groups, According to Strength of Group Identification, 1956*[a]

	Highly Identi-fied	Weakly Identi-fied	Discrepancy
Members of union households	64	36	+28
Catholics	51	39	+11
Negroes			
Non-South	72	63	+9
South	...[b]	...[b]	...[b]
Jews	83	55	+28

[a] The entries in the first two columns represent the per cent Democratic of the two-party vote division. The final column summarizes the differences between percentages in the first two, a plus indicating that high identifiers in the group voted more strongly Democratic.

[b] Southern Negro voters in the sample are too few for further subdivision.

is one determinant of the influence which a group can wield over its membership.

If a group has generated distinctive political attitudes and behavior among its members, this distinctiveness will fade if group cohesiveness is destroyed. Cohesiveness itself must depend on a number of factors according to the type of group and the setting involved. Within the large and far-flung social groupings under discussion in this chapter, a prime determinant may simply be the degree to which group members feel set apart from other people by virtue of social barriers. If we set up a mean identification score as a simple index of cohesiveness for each group, the resulting array (see Table 2) seems to support this hypothesis.

THE RELATIONSHIP OF THE GROUP TO THE WORLD OF POLITICS

If the relationship between individual and group is summarized by the concept of identification, attempts to deal with the relationship of the group to the world of politics focus upon a vaguer concept of *proximity*. All of our secondary membership groups except the political party have their basic existence outside of the political order. At this point it becomes important to specify this distance from the world of politics more precisely.

If we analyze our intuitions concerning proximity, we find that they depend upon the frequency with which we have seen the group *qua* group associated intimately with objects that are clearly political—issues, candi-

Table 2 *Relation of Group Cohesiveness to Group Identification, 1956*

Cohesiveness	Mean Identification Score[a]	Group
High	2.5	Southern Negro
	2.2	Non-Southern Negro
	2.2	Jewish
Low	1.8	Union member
	1.6	Catholic
	1.6	Member, union household

[a] The response to the two identification questions (see p. 168) are scored such that a maximum value on the index is 3.0, when the most positive response is made to both items. The corresponding minimum value is 0.0, when the most negative response is made to both items. About 61 per cent of Southern Negroes responded positively toward the group on both items; the corresponding proportion among Catholics was 28 per cent.

dates, and parties. We would think, for example, of lobbying activity, political pronouncements, and candidates who publicize the fact of membership in that group. We would consider what we know of the primary goals of the group, and their apparent relevance to politics. The perceived relationship between the group and the world of politics has substantial grounding in objective events, constituted largely by the actions of group leaders. But we could not expect that all individuals, or even all group members, would perceive the relationship of the group to politics in precisely the same manner. Thus we shall think of proximity as a subjective dimension, a tendency to associate group and politics at a psychological level.

Where proximity has partisan significance we would hypothesize that: *as proximity between the group and the world of politics increases, the political distinctiveness of the group will increase.*

Or, at the individual level: *as perception of proximity between the group and the world of politics becomes clearer, the susceptibility of the individual member to group influence in political affairs increases.*

The concept of proximity will have to undergo further refinement before these hypotheses have full meaning. We must specify a good deal more precisely the dimensions that are involved in our general sense of proximity, and attempt to measure them more objectively.

We have suggested that perceptions of proximity between one's group and the world of politics rest upon associations that have been built up between the group and the political objects. How do these links become established? In some cases, the associations are directly given, as when the political candidate is a highly visible member of the group. The link is, so to speak, "built into" the object of orientation itself. We shall discuss phenomena of this sort under the general heading of *group salience* in politics. More often, however, the establishment of associations between the group and politics depends on conscious effort by elements within the group to propagate certain standards of member behavior. This *transmission of standards* is a communication process, and its effectiveness depends on the clarity with which the standard it transmitted and the insistence that accompanies it.

But the perceived proximity of the group to the world of politics depends on more than the perception of a group standard at a point in time. While the successful transmission of a group standard in a particular situation may increase the member's sense of proximity, we would propose that the effect of any particular standard, once received, will vary according to the individual's generalized, preexisting sense of proximity between group and politics. In part, then, proximity is dependent upon reception of past standards; in part, too, it is dependent on the individual's sense of the *fitness* of group activity in politics. Underlying values that deny the group a legitimate role in the political world act as barriers to reduce the sense of proximity, however clearly standards may be received.

What we have roughly labeled proximity, then, has a number of dimensions that demand independent treatment, and we shall discuss several of these. Throughout, we encounter evidence that the perceived relationship of the group to politics, like the relationship of the individual to the group, bears directly upon the strength of group forces in the field at the time of political decision.

The transmission of group political standards

Whatever the process of communication that alerts the member to a partisan group standard, we can think of group norms as forces, having a given direction and varying degrees of strength. The standard prescribes support of one party, candidate, or issue position, and forbids support of the other. And these prescriptions are propagated with varying amounts of urgency or intensity.

There are two conditions in which group standards may lack sufficient clarity to permit influence. The end result of each is the same—a lack of distinctiveness in the aggregate group vote—but the diffierences are of considerable theoretical interest. In one case, the usual channel for communication of such norms is silent as to a particular standard, or emits it very weakly. For example, within international unions where standards were most clear according to the content analysis of preelection editions of official journals, the vote division among members in our sample was 67 per cent Democratic. This fell to 55 per cent, then to 51 per cent, and finally to 44 per cent where standards were least clear. These differences occurred even though the proportion of high identifiers from category to category varied over a range of only 3 per cent, so that we cannot explain the variation in vote by differences in group cohesiveness.

In the other case, conflicting standards are conveyed to the membership. When standards conflict, there are several possible outcomes. At one extreme, we might find that no single member became aware of the conflict in standards, but that various sets of members felt pressures in opposing directions. Here is the point at which analysis of influence at the individual level becomes more accurate than that at a group level. For in such a situation, even if every member responded to influence, the aggregate outcome might lead the observer to believe that no influence had occurred at all.

At the other extreme, all members may be aware of a conflict in standards. To some degree, the group force is cancelled out: even if the member is concerned with respectability in the eyes of the group, he can pick the standard that would best suit his desires independent of group considerations and act accordingly without feeling guilt. If, however, the situation is ripe for influence—if the individual is motivated to conform to the group—it is unlikely that events will work out in just this way. A conflict in group standards usually occurs as a result of decentralization of leadership. Few large and far-flung groups can long maintain a leadership with monolithic control over group standards. Among the secondary membership groups this is especially true. But if an unwieldy group tends to develop its subgroups with their conflicting standards, the general model still applies. Although awareness of different standards among other elements of the total group may relax group pressures to some degree, the individual is likely to feel most strongly the forces from the subgroup with which he is most strongly identified.

The political salience of the group

In some situations, the need for active propagation of group standards is at a minimum, because the standard is self-evident. This is the case when important political objects of orientation embody group cues, so that the course of behavior characteristic of a "good" group member cannot be held in doubt. Fundamentally, this situation is no more than a special case of the transmission of clear and strong standards. But it deserves separate treatment because it implies a simpler and less fallible communication process and because it involves a stratagem dear to the hearts of political tacticians. This dimension is one component of the model that is especially subject to short-term variation, since salience usually depends on the most transient objects of political orientation: the candidates and the issues.

Political salience of the group is high, for example, when a candidate for the election is recognized as a member of the group. Attracting the votes of members of a particular group by nominating a candidate who is a group member is, of course, a time-worn strategy in the art of political maneuver. Frequent executive appointment of group members to high posts is of the same order, although perhaps less potent in creating salience. It is our thesis that the success of the maneuver among group members depends upon the values of other variables in the total model. High salience alone does not create a unanimous group response.

The political salience of the group can also be increased by a coincidence between group goals and current political issues. The degree of salience that accrues with regard to issues in any particular situation is some joint function of the importance of the issue in the campaign and the importance of the goal to the group. One of the central issues of the 1948 campaign was the Taft-Hartley Act, which union leadership felt threatened vital aspects of the movement. To the degree that these elements communicated to the rank and file, the labor union ought to have been particularly salient for members voting in the election. Since that time, civil right controversies have tended to increase the political salience of Negro membership.

The legitimacy of group political activity

However strong the group identification, and however firm the association between group and political objects, the member may resist the intrusion of "nonpolitical" groups upon the political scene. There are cultural values bound up with beliefs about democracy and the individual that inveigh against such activity. The sophisticated view of democracy as a competition between interest groups does not have great popular currency. Voting, whether at the mass or the legislative level, is morally a matter of individual judgment and conscience; recognition of group obligation and interests is thoroughly taboo to some Americans.

We asked members of various groups whether they felt it was "all right" for organizations representing the group to support legislative proposals and candidates for office. The responses to these questions showed a fairly strong relationship with the group identification variable. The more highly identified a group member, the more likely he was to grant the group a right to engage in political activity. Within each level of group identification, however, members of the two religious groups—Catholics and Jews—show much greater reluctance to accept the legitimacy statements than either of the two more secular groupings—Negroes and union members. Also, with identification controlled, there is somewhat less readiness to grant legitimacy among older people. This fact would conform with the impressions that popular values opposing frank interest-group politics represent an older America.

The backgrounds of group identifications

We have indicated some of the sources of feelings about legitimacy. It is natural to inquire as well concerning the roots of group identification. Why do some group members identify with the group, whereas others fail to?

This is a difficult problem, and our evidence to date is fragmentary. But we can draw a few general conclusions about major determinants of identification. There are numerous groups, of course, that are created for the purpose of political and ideological persuasion, such as the National Economic Council or the American Civil Liberties Union. Members are recruited and come to identify with the group on the basis of pre-existing beliefs and sympathies. Here the case for influence is much less clear, except as group activity serves to reinforce and guide member efforts. But in most groups formed along occupational, ethnic, or religious lines membership is more likely to determine attitudes than are attitudes to determine membership.

There is little doubt of this fact in the groups we have watched most closely. Except in some semiorganized areas of the South, even membership in the labor union is effectively involuntary. If labor union members vote distinctively, we cannot say that only workers with certain attitudes join the union; rather, we must concede that influence exists. But if membership is involuntary, identification is not. How can we be sure that high union identification plays a formative role in the development of political attitudes?

There is a clear and substantial relationship between strength of union identification and length of membership in the union. The longer an individual has belonged to the union, the more likely he is to identify strongly with it, and we can find no other causative factors that begin to approach this relationship in strength. A relationship between age and union identification has been observed before, but it was never clear whether the relationship existed because of simple contact with the union over time, or because the unusual "barricades" generation of the 1930's would currently constitute the bulk of older union members. Our data show clearly that older men who have recently joined the union have weak identification with it, whereas younger men aged 25 and 30 who have belonged to the union for longer periods show stronger identifications with it. In fact, if we control length of union membership, we find that the relationship between age and union identification is somewhat negative. The later in life a person joins a union, the less completely he will be identified with it given any particular length of membership. His identification will still increase with length of membership, but the level will not be quite as strong as it would be for a person who had joined when younger.

This cluster of findings is of considerable theoretical significance. In the first place, it makes it difficult to maintain that identification with the union results as a rule from existing political attitudes similar to those represented by the union. Instead, we get a sense of an acculturation process—slow and cumulative influence over a period of time, with identification as the key intervening factor. It appears that a potent force in the growth of group identifications is simple contact and familiarity, just as an immigrant comes to identify with the new country and accepts its customs as time passes. Furthermore, like the immigrant, identifications never become as strongly rooted if the initiate is no longer young.

These findings are important from another point of view as well. For the pattern of relationships between age, length of membership, and strength of identification is precisely the same as we found where the group involved is the political party. That is, party identification appears to grow stronger with age; but the critical variable, instead of being age, is length of psychological membership in the party. With length of membership controlled, age is negatively related to party identification, just as it is in the union case.

Those few persons who have been union members for long periods of time yet who have remained unidentified are less likely to vote Democratic than any of the other union subgroups isolated. Not only are they much more Republican in their vote than union members generally; they are even more Republican than the control group matched with union members on aspects of life situation (33 per cent Democratic vote among those who have been members 15 years or more, as opposed to 36 per cent for the control group). Thus lack of identification among long-standing members of the union may have actively negative implications not present among new members who are not yet strongly identified.

We find no such clear relation between age and group identification among Catholics, Negroes, or Jews. Age, in these groups, logically coincides with "length of membership." There is some faint increase in identification among older Catholics, and an equally faint decrease in identification among older Negroes. We would expect these differences to appear if Catholic cohesiveness is waning and if the current civil rights ferment is beginning to sharpen cohesiveness among Negroes. But these tendencies are very weak, and there is no trend visible at all in the Jewish situation. We must conclude that no reliable relationship is present.

The contrast in the development of identification between these groups and the union or party is sharp. We are led to consider differences in the characteristics of the several groups that might account for such variation. It is obvious that the individual takes on serious membership in a union or in the psychological group represented by a political party later in life than is the case with the other groups. The individual grows up within the atmosphere of a religious or ethnic group in a much more inclusive sense than with either the party or the union.

Thus, different patterns of identification may be traced to basic differences in types of groups. But it is possible to suggest a more general proposition to cover all cases: instead of considering age or even the absolute length of time of group membership as the proper independent variable, let us employ the *proportion of the individual's life* spent as a member. Recast in this fashion, the presence of the strong positive relationship between length of membership and identification, the negative relationship between age and identification with length of membership constant, and the fact that certain ascribed groups show no variation with age would all be predicted by a single independent variable. If there is no relationship between "length of membership" and identification among Catholics, Jews, and Negroes, it is because members of these groups have held membership for 100 per cent of their lives, and variation in their identification must be explained with other factors. We arrive at the general proposition that one fundamental determinant of group identifications is the proportion of one's life spent in close (psychological) contact with the group.

SECONDARY GROUPS, THE POLITICAL PARTY, AND THE INFLUENCE PROCESS

If the political party, and psychological membership in it, fit a more general model for social memberships and political influence, it is equally clear that the party has a peculiar location in the space that the model encompasses. We have laid out with some care what seem to be the components of the relationship between any group and the world of politics. This effort was necessary because the secondary groups with which we dealt were not at base political, and this fact turns out to be a crucial limitation in the political influence they can wield. Now if we were to fill in the values that the scheme requires for prediction, we would find that in the case of the party, proximity is at an upper limit, for the party has a central position in the world of politics. In all major elections, its salience is absolutely high: one candidate is always a group member, the prime group goal is political victory, and all controversial issues represent subordinate goals that the group has assumed. The legitimacy of its activity in politics goes without question, for the major parties at least, and the communication of their standards is perfect. Therefore, we would expect that the political influence of psychological membership in a party would be extremely potent, relative to other secondary memberships. If we take distinctiveness of political attitudes and behavior as a criterion, this proposition cannot be questioned.

We are most directly interested, at this point, in suggesting the processes by which nonpolitical membership groups come to have a certain amount of political influence. Thus far we have paid little attention to the fact that these processes have duration over time. The political influence of secondary memberships, as witnessed in the distinctiveness of a group vote, is not necessarily a product of the immediate situation. The labor union need not indoctrinate its membership anew at each election. If the labor vote was distinctive in 1956, there is no need to presume that this distinctiveness represents only the political action of the union during the 1956 campaign. Influence, when successful, has enduring effects, and in this sense the distinctiveness of a group vote at any point in time represents cumulative influence. We hypothesize that the political party plays a crucial role in the durability of this influence.

When a political candidate is a member of one's group, or when the issues of politics bear directly upon goals important to the group, membership in that group becomes salient in the individual's orientation to politics. In these instances, the need for political translation, for communication of specific standards regarding proper group behavior, is slight. But under normal circumstances, when salience is not high, the group, if it is to have influence, must lend the observed world political meaning in terms relevant to the group.

Now issues and candidates are transient political objects; the entity that endures is the party. If group influence leads the identified member to take on identification with the party, then little renewal of influence is needed. The individual has, as it were, acceded to a self-steering mechanism, that will keep him politically "safe" from the point of view of group standards. He will respond to new stimuli as a party member and code them properly. As time passes, his identification with the party will increase of its own accord, because the individual will find that event after event demonstrates—in nongroup matters as well as group matters now—the rectitude of his own party and the obnoxiousness of its opponent.

If there were no parties, but only a flux of candidates and issues, it does not follow that there would be no political influence exerted by other membership groups. The psychological economy of the individual demands parties as an organizing principle, and if bereft of this, there might be much more straightforward dependence on other groups for guidance. In situations of this sort, secondary groups with quite apolitical origins have in fact come to function as political parites.[2] But where parties exist, influence from nonpolitical secondary groups is likely to have a good deal of continuity.

Given the flux of objects like candidates and issues, group influence is likely to be most effective when meaningful contact is established between the group and the party, for parties subsume candidates and issues and, more important, endure over time. However, this proposition is true only if we define influence in a very particular way, that is, as cumulative over time. An individual led to a Democratic orientation by a group membership in 1930 may still be registering a manifestation of that influence in 1956.

But for the practical politician who wants to know how many votes a group leader can "deliver" to one party or the other in a specific election, influence may have a rather different meaning. Here we encounter a paradox. If party identification is a trustworthy bridge from group identification to "proper" political behavior, it is also a structure which, once laid down, is not readily moved. Thus the mechanisms that are best calculated to build a reliably distinctive group vote are at the same time mechanisms that tend to undermine the maneuverability of the group in politics.

When political events cause a group leadership to switch official support to the opposing party, the strong party loyalties that it has helped to create and reinforce may be reversed only with great difficulty.[3] We can imagine these loyalties, even when direct creations of group influence, gain some functional autonomy as they grow stronger. They come to have a force of their own, rather than remaining dependent on forces from the nonpolitical secondary group. And, since the political party can exert unusually intense influence on political motives, this force may turn out to be stronger than any counter-force that the nonpolitical group can bring to bear *in politics* at a later date. It would follow from the general outlines of our theory that when such reversals of group standards occur, the new influence will have most effect among the youngest group members.

The political party may be treated, then, as a special case of a more general group-influence phenomenon. The party may be located within our model, and values on appropriate dimensions may be calculated for the party member at any point in time. The nature of the group, so located, ensures the power of its influence within the world of politics. But of great significance also is the role of the party as a bridge between other social groupings and that political world. The influence of other secondary groups in politics comes to have more enduring effects as loyalties directed toward them may be transferred to abiding political loyalties.

ENDNOTES

1. Dorwin P. Cartwright and Alvin Zander, *Group Dynamics: Research and Theory* (Row, Peterson and Co., Evanston, Ill., 1953), Part II, pp. 71–134.

2. As an example, see Key's treatment of factionalism in the South. Secondary groups constitute one type of nucleus for the factions that compete for political

power in a one-party system. V. O. Key, *Southern Politics in State and Nation* (Alfred Knopf, New York, 1950), pp. 52–57.

3. It is interesting to note that for large-scale, secondary groups at the national level, these switches are rare and tend to be limited to rebellious factions. Many aspects of political process seem to converge toward maintenance of these continuities. Factors such as the dependence of the party on group support and the loyalties and interpersonal commitments built up between group leaders and the party enhance the temptation to work for reform within the chosen party when things go awry. These facts make treatment of influence in its cumulative sense the more meaningful.

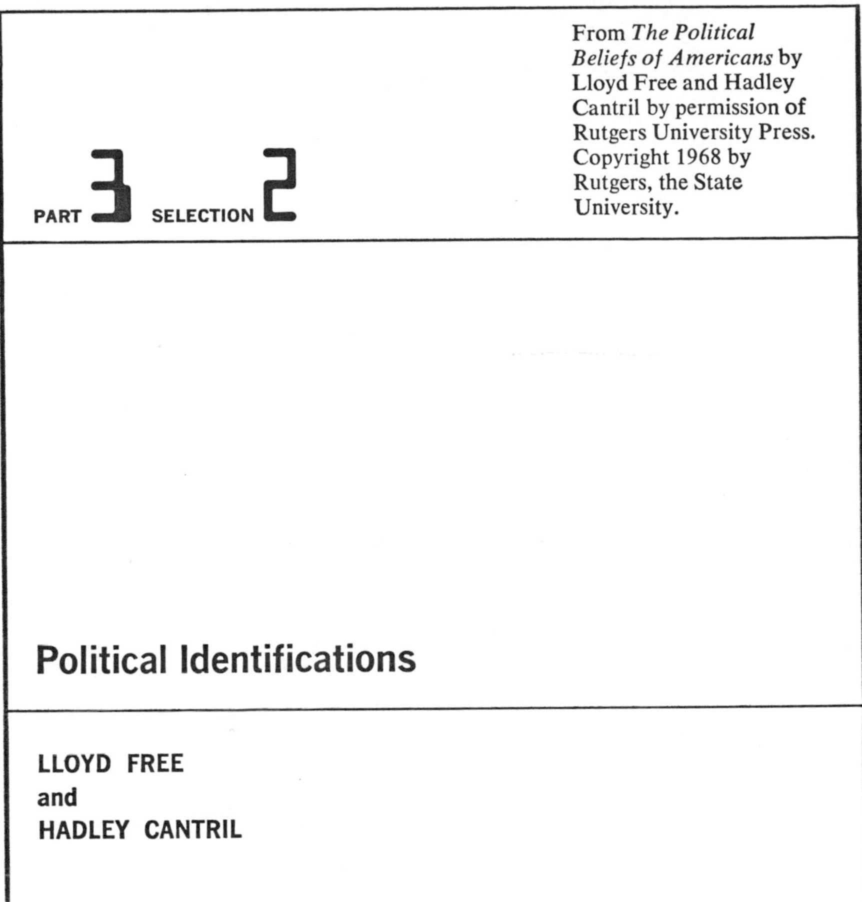

From *The Political Beliefs of Americans* by Lloyd Free and Hadley Cantril by permission of Rutgers University Press. Copyright 1968 by Rutgers, the State University.

PART 3 SELECTION 2

Political Identifications

LLOYD FREE
and
HADLEY CANTRIL

PROPORTION OF REPUBLICANS, DEMOCRATS, AND INDEPENDENTS

At the time of the 1964 elections . . . the then-current Gallup surveys showed that when samples of the national adult population were asked, "In politics as of today, do you consider yourself a Republican, Democrat, or Independent?" about one-half identified themselves as Democrats, about one-fourth as Republicans, and about one-fourth as Independents, with only very small percentages naming other parties or saying they didn't know. Since that time, in the wake of the 1966 elections, the proportion of Democrats has dropped by four percentage points and the percentage of Republicans has risen by two, so that the figures at the present writing are: Democrats 44 per cent; Republicans 29 per cent; Independents 27 per cent

(Gallup: December 21, 1966). Despite this shift, it is obvious that Democrats still greatly outnumber Republicans, while one out of every four respondents refuses to associate himself with either party.

As would be expected, Independents tend much more than Democrats or Republicans to be "swing voters." They also show a proclivity toward ticket-splitting. For example, a majority of Independents voted Democratic in the 1958 Congressional elections, while in the succeeding elections in 1962, a majority opted for the Republican side (Gallup: July 31, 1966). Similarly, in 1964, 56 per cent of the Independents cast their votes for President Johnson, but in 1966 exactly the same percentage indicated they were going to vote for Republican congressmen (Gallup: November 2, 1966). In some elections, as many as 75 per cent of the Independents split their tickets (Gallup: July 31, 1966).

The most significant aspect of these figures is not that one-fourth of the public consider themselves "Independents," but that three-fourths identify themselves psychologically with one or the other of the two major parties —an identification which seems to have real meaning for them. At the practical level of political behavior, many split their tickets, or vote—occasionally or even frequently—for candidates of the opposition party. (Gallup Poll figures show, for example, that as many as 23 per cent of the Democrats indicated an intention to vote for Republican Eisenhower in 1952 and as many as 20 per cent of the Republicans for Johnson in 1964.) Nevertheless, party allegiances tend to remain relatively stable and enduring: if a person once identifies himself in his own mind as a Democrat or a Republican, he is more likely than not to continue doing so throughout his political life,[1] although there are of course many individual exceptions.

Party allegiances tend to be transmitted from one generation to the next to a considerable extent.[2] . . . For example, 56 per cent of those whose father or mother habitually voted Republican also classified themselves as Republicans; and 66 per cent of those whose father or mother voted Democratic labelled themselves Democrats. Democratic-voting parents exceeded Republican-voting parents by about two to one; and at the same time more offspring of Democrats than of Republicans adopted their parents' allegiances—a not-too-promising prospect for the Republican Party.

PARTY DIFFERENCES

One sometimes hears it said that there is little difference between our two major parties. Compared with the range of disagreement existing in countries where the political spectrum runs from parties of the extreme right to parties of the extreme left, this is no doubt correct. But it is true only up to a point. The differences that do exist between Republicans and Democrats have become obscured by the fact that, until the 1964 election when the Republican candidate did, indeed, offer "a choice, not an echo," in recent times the Presidential candidates of both parties have tended to be "moderates," both seeking votes from middle-of-the-road voters and Independents. Thus, the distinctions between what they advocated have appeared to be more of emphasis than of substance. If we examine the attitudes of people who habitually identify themselves with each of the two parties, however, differences do exist, some slight, others marked.

. . . Republicans by and large tended to be less internationalists than Democrats. Correspondingly, a much larger proportion of Republicans were in favor of reducing or terminating foreign aid. Republicans also leaned a great deal more toward the "hawk" side, favoring stronger measures against Cuba and escalation of the war in Vietnam. More of them were also of the opinion that the United States should take a firmer stand against Russia. A plurality of Republicans, but not of Democrats, were opposed to the United States' establishing diplomatic relations with Communist China. The proportion agreeing that the United States should maintain its dominant position in the world, even going to the brink of war if necessary, was higher among Republicans than among Democrats. In all respects, Republicans were inclined to be less internationalist and more nationalist than Democrats and to choose oftener the "hard line."

LIBERALISM AND CONSERVATISM

The greatest difference between rank-and-file Republicans and Democrats, however, is in their domestic outlook, as reflected in our measurements of liberalism and conservatism. Table 1 gives the results on the basis of the

Table 1 *Operational Spectrum by Party*

	Republicans		Independents		Democrats	
Operational Spectrum						
Completely liberal	21%	41%	35%	59%	58%	79%
Predominantly liberal	20		24		21	
Middle of the road	30	30	24	24	16	16
Predominantly conservative	14	29	10	17	3	5
Completely conservative	15		7		2	
	100%		100%		100%	

Operational Spectrum.* Only half as many Republicans as Democrats qualified as operational liberals, the Independents being almost exactly in between. Similarly, almost half of the Republicans felt the Government had too much power, while three-fourths of the Democrats were of the opinion that it has about the right amount of power or should use its powers even more vigorously. Again, the Independents took a mid-way position on this question. Far more Democrats than Republicans favored the Government using its power and resources to accomplish social objectives, with Independents leaning toward the same view but by no means so strongly.

As Table 2 shows, differences were equally marked on the Ideological Spectrum. Thus, a majority of Republicans are middle of the road or conservative at the operational level of Government programs while a very large majority of Democrats are liberal. At the ideological level, a huge majority of Republicans are conservative while two-thirds of the Democrats are either middle of the road or liberal.

It is evident that at the rank-and-file level there are fundamental differences in outlook and orientation between Democrats and Republicans. The

---

*The authors, in the book from which this selection is drawn, classify people as liberal or conservative in three different ways. First, they asked people whether government should sponsor programs in the areas of education, medical care, housing, and unemployment. Those who thought the government should intervene in these areas were called liberal according to the Operational Spectrum. In other words, they were liberals in terms of what they concretely wanted the government to do. Those who felt the government should not intervene were called conservatives according to the Operational Spectrum. Finally, those who believed the government should be involved in some areas but not in others were "middle of the road" on the Operational Spectrum.

The authors also constructed an Ideological Spectrum from questions tapping abstract individual attitudes about the role of government (for example, "Do you believe that in general the government should stay out of business?" and so forth).

Those who abstractly believed that governmental power was too great and its intrusion into private matters too extensive were termed ideological conservatives. Surprisingly, perhaps, Free and Cantril found that large numbers of people were liberal on the Operational Spectrum but conservative on the Ideological Spectrum. That is, even though they believed that government should be active in a number of specific areas, in the abstract they believed that government should not attempt to regulate the free-enterprise system.

As a third measure of liberalism, the authors simply asked the individual if he considered himself a liberal or a conservative. Most people (65 percent) were liberals on the Operational Spectrum, but only 16 percent were liberals on the Ideological Spectrum, and 29 percent on the Self-Identification question. Conversely, only 14 percent were conservatives on the Operational Spectrum, 50 percent were ideological conservatives, and 33 percent identified themselves as conservatives. The remainder in each classification were middle-of-the-roaders.—ED.

Table 2 *Ideological Spectrum by Party*

	Republicans	Independents	Democrats
Ideological Spectrum			
Completely or predominantly liberal	6%	16%	22%
Middle of the road	22	29	42
Predominantly conservative	23 } 72%	20 } 55%	17 } 36%
Completely conservative	49	35	19
	100%	100%	100%

Independents were a special case: a majority of them were operational liberals, but, at the same time, a majority were also ideological conservatives. This may help explain the ambivalence of the Independents' political behavior: they are pulled in different directions by conflicting orientations which increases their tendency toward vote-switching and ticket-splitting.

PARENTAL INFLUENCE

We have noted that there is a certain amount of transference of party allegiance from one generation to the next. Parental influence also seems to have a bearing on the liberal or conservative outlook of their offspring. To trace this more precisely, respondents were asked to place their father as well as themselves on [a] liberal-conservative scale. . . . The relation between self-identification and father-identification is given in Table 3. The interesting fact here is that, for the most part, the offspring tend to be one step more conservative than their fathers except that the offspring of "very conservative" parents shift heavily over to the liberal side. Apparently the child rebels against what he considers the extreme conservatism of his father.

Both the influence of the father on the liberal-conservative outlook at the practical level and the rebellion against the very conservative parent showed up on the Operational Spectrum as well, as shown in Table 4. A large majority of those whose fathers were "very liberal" proved to be operational liberals. From there, the percentage of liberals tends to drop until one reaches those whose fathers were "very conservative," among whom the "completely liberal" figure on the Operational Spectrum is as high as among those whose fathers were "very liberal." . . .

Table 3 *Father as Liberal or Conservative by Offspring's Identification*

	Father Identified As				
	Very Lib.	Mod. Lib.	Middle of Road	Mod. Cons.	Very Cons.
Offspring Is					
Very liberal	6%	2%	2%	2%	45%
Moderately liberal	58	14	15	12	21
Middle of road	22	69	25	24	19
Moderately conservative	13	13	53	35	10
Very conservative	1	2	5	27	5
	100%	100%	100%	100%	100%

Table 4 *Father as Liberal or Conservative by Offspring's Rating on Operational Spectrum*

	Father Identified As									
	Very Lib.		Mod. Lib.		Middle of Road		Mod. Cons.		Very Cons.	
Offspring Qualified on Operational Spectrum As										
Completely liberal	51%	76%	43%	63%	34%	52%	29%	53%	51%	74%
Predominantly liberal	25		20		18		24		23	
Middle of road	16		25		27		25		19	
Predominantly conservative	5	8	7	12	11	21	9	22	3	7
Completely conservative	3		5		10		13		4	
	100%		100%		100%		100%		100%	

CLASS IDENTIFICATIONS

Marked differences . . . appeared in the way Republicans, Democrats, and Independents identify their interests with the propertied class, the middle class, or the working class, as seen in Table 5. Republicans tended to associate their own interests with those of either the propertied or the middle classes, while the Democrats identified predominantly with the working class. Independents were split down the middle.

Table 5 *Class Identification by Party*

	Republicans		Independents		Democrats	
Identify Interests with						
Propertied class	11%	61%	5%	46%	2%	31%
Middle class	50		41		29	
Working class	35		46		65	
Don't know	4		8		4	
	100%		100%		100%	

Both on the score of liberalism-conservatism and of subjective class identifications, it is no wonder that a majority of Americans have an image of the Democratic Party as the party of "labor, the common man, all the people," and of the Republican Party as the party of "the moneyed interests and the privileged few" (Gallup: February 3, 1954). An Iowa painter expressed this notion in highly exaggerated fashion: "The Republicans represent aristocrats and millionaires; the Democrats represent the will of the working class of people." A survey conducted by the Opinion Research Corporation shortly before the 1964 elections confirmed these images. When asked which party is on the workingman's side, 45 per cent named the Democratic Party and only 7 per cent the Republican, the rest replying either "both" or "neither" or saying they had no opinion. At the same time, 37 per cent said the Republican Party favored big business too much, as compared with only 8 per cent who felt this way about the Democratic Party. To show how pervasive this part of the image is, 25 per cent of those identifying themselves as Republicans agreed that their own party favored big business too much. No wonder, then, that when Gallup polled GOP county chairmen across the nation, 59 per cent of them agreed with President Eisenhower that the Republican Party had a "bad image" (January 22, 1965).

As a result, in 1963 at least, when asked "which political party—the Republican or Democratic—do you think best serves the interest of people like yourself?" twice as many Americans named the Democratic Party as named the Republican (Gallup: May 12, 1963). Later (February 28, 1965), Gallup asked this same question of representative samples of persons in families from major occupational groups. The results are given in Table 6, where only the percentages for the Republican Party and the Democratic Party are listed; the percentages of those who said there was no difference between the two parties in this respect or who had no opinion are omitted.

Table 6 *Party Best for Self*

	Republican	Democratic
Professional and business people	56%	22%
White collar workers	27	39
Farmers	20	52
Skilled workers	15	59
Unskilled workers	8	62

It will be seen that only the professional and business people think the Republican Party serves the interests of their own group best.

DEMOGRAPHIC DIFFERENCES

The general outline of the respective strengths and weaknesses of the Republican and Democratic parties among subgroups of the population is well known to all students of politics. Our study showed that while less numerous than the Democrats, the Republicans had a proportionately greater following among those fifty years of age or older, in the professional and business group, among Protestants, among people living in the Midwest, and among those residing in places of under 50,000 population or in rural areas than they did in other population groups. In only two related groups did those who identified themselves as Republicans outnumber those who identified themselves as Democrats: the college-educated and those with an annual income of $10,000 or more. Democrats, on the other hand, were even more numerous among those with less than a college education, among blue-collar workers, among those with incomes of less than $10,000, among people living in the East and in the South, among those in cities of over

50,000 population, and particularly among Negroes, than they were in other groups.

...As Table 7 shows, there is a close correspondence...between the percentages in each group who qualified as "completely liberal" on the Operational Spectrum and the proportion who identified themselves as Democrats. In brief, the larger the proportion of operational liberals in

Table 7 *Per cent Complete Liberals on Operational Spectrum and Per cent Democrats*

	Compl. Liberals	Democrats
Education		
Grade school	54%	58%
High school	42	50
College	32	34
Income		
Under $5,000	52	55
$5,000–$9,999	41	50
$10,000 and over	32	34
Occupation		
Professional and business	33	37
White-collar workers	39	45
Farmers	34	44
Blue-collar workers	51	57
Nonlabor	44	51
Race		
White	40	45
Negro	79	87
City Size		
500,000 and over	55	54
50,000–499,999	43	56
2,500–49,999	31	41
Under 2,500 and rural	36	44

general, and of those "completely liberal" in particular, the higher the percentage in each group who considered themselves Democrats. The converse is of course also true: the lower the proportion of liberals, the higher the percentage of Republicans. The same tendencies appeared on the Ideological Spectrum.

Nor is this any wonder. Despite the presence in Congress of many conservative Democrats, especially Southerners, who frequently have great power as committee chairmen, the image the public has of the Democratic Party is a liberal one, imparted by a series of Democratic Chief Executives operating in the tradition of the New Deal, Fair Deal, New Frontier, and Great Society. It is only natural that those favoring use of Government power and resources to accomplish social objectives should gravitate toward that party. On the other hand, in recent history, the Republican Party's image has been determined primarily by Republicans in Congress, the majority of whom were conservatives who have, initially at least, opposed most major extensions of Federal power as a matter of principle.

RELIGIOUS DIFFERENCES

Up to this point, the patterns revealed by the polls are what would be expected and seem to make sense. Quite understandably, the Democratic Party attracts liberals, people who tend to be less advantaged and more preoccupied with problems and needs which in their eyes can be alleviated by the kinds of Governmental programs which Democratic administrations have advocated and inaugurated, starting with the New Deal. But our figures show a phenomenon which is difficult to explain in these terms: 63 per cent of the Roman Catholics and 65 per cent of the Jews identified themselves as Democrats, compared with only 45 per cent of the Protestants. Yet our study showed that Jews enjoy a much higher socioeconomic status than Protestants and that even Catholics have now more than caught up with Protestants in this area. It is simply no longer true that Catholics are less well off and less well educated than Protestants. The relative status of the three religious groups is of such importance in the social fabric of the United States today that we give a comparative analysis of their education, income, and occupations in Table 8.

On the basis of socioeconomic status alone, Catholics should be no more Democratic than Protestants and Jews much less so. Yet the reverse is the case. This study can go only a short way in trying to explain this phenomenon. Fundamentally, Catholics and Jews are much more Democratic than Protestants because, despite their socioeconomic status, they are much more liberal in their orientations. Table 9 reveals this in terms of the Operational Spectrum.

Table 8 *Education, Income, and Occupation by Religion*

	Protestant	Catholic	Jewish
Education			
College	18%	18%	33%
High school	47	55	45
Grade school	35	27	22
	100%	100%	100%
Income			
$10,000 and over	15%	18%	29%
$5,000–$9,999	38	46	55
Under $5,000	47	36	16
	100%	100%	100%
Occupation			
Professional and business	20%	23%	46%
White-collar workers	9	12	25
Farmers	8	3	—
Blue-collar workers	43	51	18
Non-labor	19	10	9
Undesignated	1	1	2
	100%	100%	100%

Table 9 *Operational Spectrum by Religion*

	Protestant		Catholic		Jewish	
Operational Spectrum						
Completely liberal	38%	60%	55%	77%	69%	90%
Predominantly liberal	22		22		21	
Middle of the road	22		17		7	
Predominantly conservative	9		3		*	
Completely conservative	9		3		3	
	100%		100%		100%	

* Less than one-half of one per cent

The same tendency was evident on the Ideological Spectrum as Table 10 shows. The Jews represent the only population subgroup in our study among whom ideological liberals actually constituted a plurality; Negroes were the only group approaching them in this respect. While the idea of Jewish liberalism sounds neither new nor strange, as recently as the fall of 1965 an associate editor of a leading Catholic publication wrote: "Politically, the American Catholic has tended to be conservative, suspicious of central government."[2] Assuming this may once have been the case, we can only say that it is no longer so: 77 per cent of American Catholics qualified as liberal on our Operational Spectrum, only 13 per cent thought the Federal Government had too much power, and 38 per cent felt the Government should use its powers even more vigorously.

Table 10 *Ideological Spectrum by Religion*

	Protestant	Catholic	Jewish
Ideological Spectrum			
Completely or predominantly liberal	14%	17%	44%
Middle of the road	28	48	39
Predominantly conservative	21 } 58%	18 } 35%	10 } 17%
Completely conservative	37 }	17 }	7 }
	100%	100%	100%

The data offer only partial evidence for the following speculations about the reasons for Catholic and Jewish liberalism. To start on solid ground, we have found that urban living makes for liberal orientations, and both of these groups are much more highly urbanized than Protestants. Seventy-nine per cent of the Catholics in this country live in cities of over 50,000 population, compared with 46 per cent of the Protestants; and no less than 85 per cent of the Jews reside in metropolitan areas of over 500,000 population.

Secondly, both of these groups are in large part descendants of people who came to America in the more recent waves of immigration. When their ancestors arrived in the United States, they were, indeed, disadvantaged minority groups. It is our belief that, despite their spectacular socioeconomic progress since, the habit of perceiving themselves as members of disadvantaged minority groups still persists to some extent—a habit which encourages a liberal outlook.

More concretely, for a variety of reasons applicable to most recent immigrant groups, a majority of Catholics and Jews early developed the habit of considering themselves Democrats. This was chiefly because the Democratic Party, much more than the Republican, assumed the role of champion of disadvantaged minorities and worked to win their allegiance. Witness, for example, the aid and comfort furnished newly arrived immigrants by Tammany Hall and other Democratic political machines in the big cities, ranging from locating jobs for them to supplying food, coal, clothing, and money in time of need. Later, the equalitarian orientation of the New Deal and subsequent Democratic administrations undoubtedly strengthened this Democratic appeal. It is our guess, in short, that the allegiance to the Democratic Party as an institution, initially created at an early date, had a reinforcing effect in developing and perpetuating liberal outlooks among Catholics and Jews as the Party, beginning especially with Franklin D. Roosevelt, followed the path of increasing liberalism.

ETHNIC GROUPS

A phenomenon roughly similar to that posed by the Democratic leanings of Catholics and Jews is presented by the descendants of those who came to America in the more recent waves of immigration. To analyze this, we classified our white respondents (Negro Americans were excluded as constituting a separate ethnic group) in two categories: (1) those with no grandparents born in the United States (many of them of Italian, East European, or Central European origin), and (2) those with some or all grandparents born in this country. As it turned out, all four grandparents of the great majority of the second group were born in the United States. Thus, there was a fairly sharp distinction between the descendants of recent immigrants and the descendants of earlier immigrants. It is a commentary on the composition of our population that no less than one-third of our sample did not have a single grandparent born in the United States. Yet, like the Catholics, these people have all but caught up in socioeconomic status with the descendants of earlier immigrants. They are somewhat deficient still by way of education, but are on a par in terms of income and occupation. Yet, despite the similarity in socioeconomic status, 52 per cent of them consider themselves as Democrats, compared with only 42 per cent of those respondents some or all of whose grandparents were born in the United States.

There are several things that can be said about these figures. In the first place, most of what has been written above about Catholics applies to the descendants of more recent immigrants in general. In fact, they tend to be much more heavily Catholic (41 per cent) than the offspring of the older stock (14 per cent), which reinforces their allegiance to the Democratic Party. Secondly, a far higher proportion of those with no grandparents born in the United States live in the East (45 per cent) and in the great metropolitan centers (47 per cent) than do the descendants of the earlier settlers (19 per cent and 24 per cent, respectively). With this kind of configuration, religious, geographic, and urban, it is not surprising that the descendants of the more recent immigrants are decidedly more liberal than the older stock on the Operational Spectrum and on the question regarding Governmental power, and less conservative on the Ideological Spectrum. . . .

. . . Marked differences in degrees of liberalism and conservatism [are also shown] between those of Irish (Catholic), Italian, and East European or Central European origins, the majority of whom are descendants of more recent immigrants, and those the descendants of earlier immigrants of English, German, or Scandinavian stock. To illustrate the variations involved, here are the percentages of different ethnic groups which qualified as "completely liberal" on the Operational Spectrum:

English	30%
German	34
Scandinavian	39
Irish (Catholic)	54
Eastern or Central European	54
Italian	57

The contention sometimes made that ethnic origins are no longer a significant factor in American politics is obviously not well taken, at least as of the mid-1960's. The special ethnic interests of particular groups may no longer govern their voting behavior: Poles may no longer react primarily to the Polish question or the Irish primarily to the Irish question. But there are very basic differences in outlook between the descendants of more recent immigrants and the descendants of older stock.

"PROFILES" OF THE TWO PARTIES

The strengths and weaknesses of the two major political parties have been discussed in terms of the population groups that compose them. But there remains the question of the relative importance of each of these groups as a potential source of votes for the Democratic and Republican parties. Table 11 shows the composition of the total adult population in our sample of a cross section of potential voters and the corresponding composition of the adherents of the two parties. In short, the table gives "profiles" of the total population, on the one hand, and of Democrats and Republicans, on the other. In studying these figures, we must remember that those who identified themselves as Democrats outnumbered Republicans two to one. Consequently, if the table shows that a given percentage of Democrats belongs to a certain subgroup and the same percentage of Republicans belongs to that group, in absolute terms the number of Democrats involved is twice the number of Republicans.

Table 11 *Parties by Demographic Composition*

	Total Sample	Republicans	Democrats
Age			
21–29	16%	12%	15%
30–49	44	36	46
50 & over	40	52	39
	100%	100%	100%
Education			
Grade school	33%	27%	38%
High school	48	43	48
College	19	30	14
	100%	100%	100%
Income			
Under $5,000	43%	38%	49%
$5,000–$9,999	40	36	40
$10,000 & over	17	26	11
	100%	100%	100%
Occupation			
Professional and business	23%	32%	17%
White-collar workers	10	11	9
Farmers	6	7	6
Blue-collar workers	44	31	51
Nonlabor	17	19	17
	100%	100%	100%
Union Member			
Yes	25%	15%	30%
No	75	85	70
	100%	100%	100%

Table 11 *(Continued)*

	Total Sample	Republicans	Democrats
Religion			
Protestant	71%	85%	64%
Catholic	21	11	27
Jewish	4	1	5
Other or none	4	3	4
	100%	100%	100%
City Size			
500,000 & over	34%	28%	38%
50,000–499,999	22	18	24
2,500–49,999	16	22	13
Under 2,500 & rural	28	32	25
	100%	100%	100%
Region			
East	28%	30%	30%
South	27	17	30
Midwest	29	35	25
West	16	18	15
	100%	100%	100%
Grandparents			
None born in U.S.	32%	27%	36%
Some born in U.S.	68	73	64
	100%	100%	100%
Race			
White	90%	98%	82%
Negro	10	2	18
	100%	100%	100%

The Democratic Party as shown by the make-up of its adherents is clearly a party of the "people," broadly based in terms of all segments of the population, especially Negro Americans and the descendants of more recent immigrant groups. One-half of all Democrats are blue-collar workers; one-half have annual incomes of less than $5,000; one-half have only a high school education. Two-fifths live in large metropolitan centers, where population growth has been most pronounced. In general, the Democratic Party is strongest among exactly those elements of the population which, potentially at least, have the most votes.

In contrast, the Republican Party consists almost entirely of whites, and 85 per cent of its members are Protestants. The startling fact also emerges that 52 per cent of the Republicans are fifty years of age or over. Similarly, one-half of Republican strength is located in smaller cities, towns, and rural areas, which have increasingly been losing their population to the larger centers. The party is strongest among the professional and business class, which also means among the college-educated and the well-to-do. But the professional and business people make up only one-fourth of potential voters and the college-educated and well-to-do less than one-fifth.

Against this background, it is understandable why the number of Americans who identify themselves as Republicans has declined from 38 per cent in 1940 to 29 per cent at the end of 1966 (Gallup: December 21, 1966). The Republican Party has held the Presidency for only eight out of the past thirty-four years. During that time, it has won only two Congressional elections—one in 1946 when Truman was at his low point; and, again, with Eisenhower in 1952, but then only by a one-seat majority in the Senate and a five-seat majority in the House. Despite the current euphoria in Republican ranks over the results of the 1966 elections, although the Party did much better than in 1964 and most other election years, 1966 cannot be considered a year of unqualified victory. The Republicans won the governorships of half the states, but they attracted only a minority (48.3 per cent) of the Congressional vote (as compared with the Democrats' 51.7 per cent), and ended up with only 40 per cent of the seats in the state legislatures.

Given the rather grim history of the last three and a half decades, what about the future of the Republican Party? The 1966 election showed, at least, that the Republicans still have a good deal of vim and vigor, and, under certain conditions, voter appeal. But is the Republican Party doomed to permanent minority status, so that to win nationally it must attract the votes of most of the Independents and some of the Democrats, as well as practically all of the Republicans? As has been the case since the days of the New Deal, will a Republican victory at the national level continue to be the exception?

ENDNOTES

1. Campbell *et al.* review their findings in this connection on page 147 of *The American Voter*.

2. "The American Catholic is Changing" by John Leo, formerly editor of *Commonweal*, writing in the *New York Times Sunday Magazine*, November 14, 1965.

Reprinted from the *American Political Science Review*, 61 (1967), 629-642, with the permission of the American Political Science Association.
Copyright 1967 by the American Political Science Association.

PART 3 SELECTION 3

The Impact of Personality on Politics: An Attempt to Clear Away Underbrush

FRED I. GREENSTEIN

There is a great deal of political activity which can be explained adequately only by taking account of the personal characteristics of the actors involved. The more intimate the vantage, the more detailed the perspective, the greater the likelihood that political actors will loom as full-blown individuals influenced by all of the peculiar strengths and weaknesses to which the species *homo sapiens* is subject, in addition to being role-players, creatures of situation, members of a culture, and possessors of social characteristics such as occupation, class, sex, and age.

To a non-social scientist the observation that individuals are important in politics would seem trite. Undergraduates, until they have been trained to think in terms of impersonal categories of explanation, readily make assertions about the psychology of political actors in their explanations of politics. So do journalists. Why is it that most political scientists are reluctant to deal explicitly with psychological matters (apart from using a variety of rather impersonal psychological constructs such as "party identification," "sense of political efficacy," and the like)? Why is political psychology not a systematically developed subdivision of political science, occupying the skill and energy of a substantial number of scholars?

A partial answer can be found in the formidably tangled and controversial status of the existing scholarly literature on the topic. I am referring to the disparate research that is commonly grouped under the heading "personality and politics": e.g., psychological biographies; questionnaire studies of "authoritarianism," "dogmatism," or "misanthropy"; discussions of "national character"; and attempts to explain international "tensions" by reference to individual insecurities. The interpretations made in psychological biographies often have seemed arbitrary and "subjective"; questionnaire studies have encountered formidable methodological difficulties; attempts to explain large-scale social processes in personality terms have been open to criticism on grounds of "reductionism." And beyond the specific shortcomings of the existing "personality and politics" research, a variety of arguments have been mounted suggesting that there are *inherent* shortcomings in research strategies that attempt to analyze the impact of "personality" on politics. It is not surprising that most political scientists choose to ignore this seeming mare's nest.

If progress is to be made toward developing a more systematic and solidly grounded body of knowledge about personality and politics, there will have to be considerable clarification of standards of evidence and inference in this area.[1] My present remarks are merely a prolegomenon to methodological clarification of "personality and politics" research. It will not be worthwhile to invest in explicating this gnarled literature with a view to laying out standards unless there is a basis for believing that the research itself is promising. Therefore I shall attempt to clear away what seem to be the main reasons for arguing that there are inherent objections—objections in principle—to the study of personality and politics.

Clearing away the formal objections to this *genre* can serve to liberate energy and channel debate into inquiry. More important, several of the objections may be rephrased in ways that are substantively interesting—ways that move us from the vague question "Does personality have an important impact on politics?" to conditional questions about the circumstances under which diverse psychological factors have varying political consequences. As will be evident, the several objections are based on a number of different implicit definitions of "personality." This is not surprising, since psychologists have never come close to arriving at a single, agreed-upon meaning of the term.[2]

OBJECTIONS TO THE STUDY OF PERSONALITY AND POLITICS

A bewildering variety of criticisms have been leveled at this heterogeneous literature. The criticism has been so profuse that there is considerable accuracy to the sardonic observation of David Riesman and Nathan Glazer that the field of culture-and-personality research (within which many of the past accounts of personality and politics fall) has "more critics than practitioners."[3]

The more intellectually challenging of the various objections asserting that *in principle* personality and politics research is not promising (even if one avoids the methodological pitfalls) seems to fall under five headings. In each case the objection is one that can be generalized to the study of how personality relates to any social phenomenon. Listed rather elliptically the five objections are that:

1. Personality characteristics tend to be randomly distributed in institutional roles. Personality therefore "cancels out" and can be ignored by analysts of political and other social phenomena.

2. Personality characteristics of individuals are less important than their social characteristics in influencing behavior. This makes it unpromising to concentrate research energies on studying the impact of personality.

3. Personality is not of interest to political and other social analysts, because individual actors (personalities) are severely limited in the impact they can have on events.

4. Personality is not an important determinant of behavior because individuals with varying personal characteristics will tend to behave similarly when placed in common situations. And it is not useful to study personal variation, if the ways in which people vary do not affect their behavior.

5. Finally, there is a class of objections deprecating the relevance of personality to political analysis in which "personality" is equated with particular aspects of individual psychological functioning. We shall be concerned with one of the objections falling under this heading—*viz.*, the assertion that so-called "deep" psychological needs (of the sort that sometimes are summarized by the term "ego-defensive") do not have an important impact on behavior, and that therefore "personality" in this sense of the term need not be studied by the student of politics.

The first two objections seem to be based on fundamental misconceptions. Nevertheless they do point to interesting problems for the student of political psychology. The final three objections are partially well taken. These are the objections that need to be rephrased in conditional form as "Under what circumstances?" questions. Let me now expand upon these assertions.

TWO ERRONEOUS OBJECTIONS

The thesis that personality "cancels out"

The assumption underlying the first objection seems, as Alex Inkeles points out, to be that "in 'real' groups and situations, the accidents of life history and factors other than personality which are responsible for recruitment [into institutional roles] will 'randomize' personality distribution in the major social statuses sufficiently so that taking systematic account of the influence of personality composition is unnecessary." But, as Inkeles easily shows, this assumption is false on two grounds.

First, "even if the personality composition of any group is randomly determined, random assortment would not in fact guarantee the *same* personality composition in the membership of all institutions of a given type. On the contrary, the very fact of randomness implies that the outcome would approximate a normal distribution. Consequently, some of the groups would by chance have a personality composition profoundly different from others, with possibly marked effects on the functioning of the institutions involved." Secondly,

> there is no convincing evidence that randomness does consistently describe the assignment of personality types to major social statuses. On the contrary, there is a great deal of evidence to indicate that particular statuses often attract, or recruit preponderantly for, one or another personality characteristic and that fact has a substantial effect on individual adjustment to roles and the general quality of institutional functioning.[4]

The objection turns out therefore to be based on unwarranted empirical assumptions. It proves not to be an obstacle to research, but rather—once it is examined—an opening gambit for identifying a crucial topic of investigation for the political psychologist: How are personality types distributed in social roles and with what consequences?

The thesis that social characteristics are more important than personality characteristics

The second objection—asserting that individuals' social characteristics are "more important" than their personality characteristics—seems to result from a conceptual rather than empirical error. It appears to be an objection posing a pseudo-problem that needs to be dissolved conceptually rather than resolved empirically.

Let us consider what the referents are of "social characteristic" and "personality characteristic." By the latter we refer to some inner predisposition of the individual. The term "characteristic" applies to a state of the organism. And, using the familiar paradigm of "stimulus→organism→response," or "environment→predispositions→response," we operate on the assumption that the environmental stimuli (or "situations") that elicit behavior are mediated through the individual's psychological predispositions.[5]

But we also, of course, presume that the individual's psychological predispositions are themselves to a considerable extent environmentally determined, largely by his prior social experiences. And it is these prior environmental states (which may occur at any stage of the life cycle and which may or may not persist into the present) that we commonly refer to when we speak of "social characteristics." Social "characteristics," then, are not states of the organism, but of its environment. (This is made particularly clear by the common usage "*objective* social characteristics.")

It follows that social and psychological characteristics are in no way mutually exclusive. They do not compete as candidates for explanation of social behavior, but rather are complementary. Social "characteristics" can cause psychological "characteristics"; they are not substitutes for psychological characteristics. The erroneous assumption that social characteristics could even in principle be more important than psychological characteristics probably arises in part from the misleading impression of identity fostered by the usage of "characteristics" in the two expressions.[6]

This confusion also very probably is contributed to by the standard techniques used by social scientists to eliminate spurious correlations, namely, controlling for "third factors" and calculating partial correlations. Control procedures, when used indiscriminately and without references to the theoretical standing of the variables that are being analyzed, can lead to the failure to recognize what Herbert Hyman, in the heading of an important section of his *Survey Design and Analysis*, describes as "The Distinction Between Developmental Sequences or Configurations and Problems of Spuriousness."[7]

For an example of how this problem arises, we can consider the very interesting research report by Urie Bronfenbrenner entitled "Personality and Participation: The Case of the Vanishing Variable."[8] Bronfenbrenner reports a study in which it was found that measures of personality were associated with participation in community affairs. However, as he notes, "It is a well-established fact that extent of participation varies with social class, with the lower classes participating the least." Therefore, he proceeds to establish the relationship between personality and participation controlling for social class (and certain other factors). The result: "Most of the earlier . . . significant relationships between personality measures and participation now disappear, leaving only two significant correlations, both of them quite low."

One common interpretation of such a finding would be that Bronfenbrenner had shown the irrelevance of personality to participation. But his finding should not be so interpreted. Hyman's remarks, since they place the problem of relating social background data to psychological data in its more general context, are worth quoting at some length.

> . . . the concept of spuriousness cannot *logically* be intended to apply to antecedent conditions which are associated with the particular independent variable as part of a developmental sequence. Implicity, the notion of an uncontrolled factor which was operating so as to produce a spurious finding involves the image of something *extrinsic* to the . . . apparent cause. Developmental sequences, by contrast, involve the image of a series of entities which are *intrinsically* united or substituted for one another. All of them constitute a unity and merely involve different ways of stating the same variable as it changes over time. . . . Consequently, to institute procedures of control is to remove so-to-speak some of the very cause one wishes to study. . . . How shall the analyst know what antecedent conditions are intrinsic parts of a developmental sequence? . . . One guide, for example, can be noted: instances where the "control" factor and the apparent explanation involve *levels of description from two different systems* are likely to be developmental sequences. For instance, an explanatory factor that was a personality trait and a control factor that was biological such as physique or glandular functions can be conceived as levels of description from different systems. Similarly, an explanatory factor that is *psychological* and a control factor that is *sociological* can be conceived as two different levels of description, i.e., one might regard an attitude as derivative of objective position or status or an objective position in society as leading to psychological processes such as attitudes. Thus, the concept of spuriousness would not be appropriate.[9]

In the Bronfenbrenner example, then, an individual's "objective" socioeconomic background (as opposed to such subjective concomitants as his sense of class consciousness) needs to be analyzed as a possible social determinant of the psychological correlates of participation, taking account of the fact that, as Allport puts it, "background factors never directly cause behavior; they cause attitudes [and other mental sets]" and the latter "in turn determine behavior."[10] A more general lesson for the student of psychology and politics emerges from our examination of the second objection. We can see that investigators in this realm will often find it necessary to lay out schemes of explanation that are developmental—schemes that place social and psychological factors in the sequence in which they seem to have impinged upon one another.

THREE PARTIALLY CORRECT OBJECTIONS

The three remaining objections bear on (a) the question of how much impact individual actors can have on political outcomes, (b) the question of whether the situations political actors find themselves in impose uniform behavior on individuals of varying personal characteristics, making it unprofitable for the political analyst to study variations in the actors' personal characteristics, and (c) the numerous questions that can be raised about the impact on behavior of particular classes of personal characteristics—including the class of characteristics I shall be discussing, the so-called "ego-defensive" personality dispositions. In the remainder of this essay, I shall expand upon each of these three questions, rephrase them in conditional form, and lay out a number of general propositions stating the circumstances under which the objection is or is not likely to hold. As will be evident, the propositions are not hypotheses stated with sufficient precision to be testable. Rather, they are quite general indications of the circumstances under which political analysts are and are not likely to find it desirable to study "personality" in the several senses of the term implicit in the objections.

When do individual actors affect events ("action dispensability")?

The objection to studies of personality and politics that emphasize the limited capacity of single actors to shape events does not differ in its essentials from the nineteenth and early twentieth century debates over social determinism—that is, over the role of individual actors (Great Men or otherwise) in history. In statements of this objection emphasis is placed on the need for the times to be ripe in order for the historical actor to make his contribution. Questions are asked such as, "What impact could Napoleon have had on history if he had been born in the Middle Ages?" Possibly because of the parlor game aura of the issues that arise in connection with it, the problem of the impact of individuals on events has not had as much disciplined attention in recent decades as the two remaining issues I shall be dealing with. Nevertheless, at one time or another this question has received the attention of Tolstoy, Carlyle, Spencer, William James, Plekhanov, and Trotsky (in his *History of the Russian Revolution*). The main attempt at a balanced general discussion seems to be Sidney Hook's vigorous, but unsystematic, 1943 essay *The Hero in History*.[11]

Since the degree to which actions are likely to have significant impacts is clearly variable, I would propose to begin clarification by asking: *What are the circumstances under which the actions of single individuals are likely to have a greater or lesser effect on the course of events?* For shorthand purposes this might be called the question of *action dispensability*. We can conceive of arranging the actions performed in the political arena along a continuum, ranging from those which are indispensable for outcomes that concern us through those which are utterly dispensable. And we can make certain general observations about the circumstances which are likely to surround dispensable and indispensable action. In so reconstructing this particular objection to personality explanations of politics we make it clear that what is at stake is not a psychological issue, but rather one bearing on social processes on decision-making. The question is about the impact of action, not about its determinants.

It is difficult to be precise in stipulating circumstances under which an individual's actions are likely to be a link in further events, since a great deal depends upon the interests of the investigator and the specific context of investigation (the kinds of actions being studied; the kinds of effects that are of interest). Therefore, the following three propositions are necessarily quite abstract.

The impact of an individual's actions varies with (1) the degree to which the actions take place in an environment which admits of restructuring, (2) the location of the actor in that environment, and (3) the actor's peculiar strengths or weaknesses.

1. *The likelihood of personal impact increases to the degree that the environment admits of restructuring.* Technically speaking we might describe situations or sequences of events in which modest interventions can produce disproportionately large results as "unstable." They are in a precarious equilibrium. The physical analogies are massive rock formations at the side of a mountain which can be dislodged by the motion of a single keystone, or highly explosive compounds such as nitroglycerine. Instability in this sense is by no means synonymous with what is loosely known as political instability, the phrase we typically employ to refer to a variety of "fluid" phenomena —political systems in which governments rise and fall with some frequency, systems in which violence is common, etc. Many of the situations commonly referred to as unstable do not at all admit of restructuring. In the politics of many of the "unstable" Latin American nations, for example, most conceivable substitutions of actors and actions would lead to little change in outcomes (or at least in "larger" outcomes). Thus, to continue the physical analogy, an avalanche in motion down a mountainside is for the moment in stable equilibrium, since it cannot be influenced by modest interventions.

The situation (or chain of events) which does not admit readily of restructuring usually is one in which a variety of factors conspire to produce the same outcome.[12] Hook, in *The Hero in History*, offers the outbreak of World War I and of the February Revolution as instances of historical sequences which, if not "inevitable," probably could not have been averted by the actions of any single individual. In the first case the vast admixture of multiple conflicting interests and inter-twined alliances and in the second the powerful groundswell of discontent were such as to make us feel that no intervention by any single individual (excluding the more far-fetched hypothetical instances that invariably can be imagined) would have averted the outcome. On the other hand, Hook attempts to show in detail that without the specific actions of Lenin the October Revolution might well not have occurred. By implication he suggests that Lenin was operating in an especially manipulable environment. A similar conclusion might be argued about the manipulability of the political environment of Europe prior to the outbreak of World War II, on the basis of the various accounts at our disposal of the sequence of events that culminated with the invasion of Poland in 1939.[13]

2. *The likelihood of personal impact varies with the actor's location in the environment.* To shape events, an action must be performed not only in an unstable environment, but also by an actor who is strategically placed in that environment. It is, for example, a commonplace that actors in the middle and lower ranks of many bureaucracies are unable to accomplish much singly, since they are restrained or inhibited by other actors. Robert C. Tucker points out what may almost be a limiting case on the other end of the continuum in an essay on the lack of restraint on Russian policy-makers, both under the Czars and since the Revolution. He quotes with approval Nikolai Turgenev's mid-nineteenth century statement that "In all countries ruled by an unlimited power there has always been and is some class, estate, some traditional institutions which in certain instances compel the sovereign to act in a certain way and set limits to his caprice; nothing of the sort exists in Russia."[14] Elsewhere, Tucker points to the tendency in totalitarian states for the political machinery to become "a conduit of the dictatoral psychology"[15]—that is for there to be a relatively unimpeded conversion of whims of the dictator into governmental action as a consequence of his authoritarian control of the bureaucratic apparatus.

3. *The likelihood of personal impact varies with the personal strengths or weaknesses of the actor.* My two previous observations can be recapitulated with an analogy from the poolroom. In the game of pocket billiards the aim of the player is to clear as many balls as possible from the table. The initial distribution of balls parallels my first observation about the manipulability of the environment. With some arrays a good many shots are possible; perhaps the table can even be cleared. With other arrays no successful shots are likely. The analogy to point two—the strategic location of the actor—is, of course, the location of the cue ball. As a final point, we may note the political actor's peculiar strengths or weaknesses. In the poolroom these are paralleled by the player's skill or lack of skill. The greater the actor's skill, the less his initial need for a favorable position or a manipulable environment, and the greater the likelihood that he will himself subsequently contribute to making his position favorable and his environment manipulable.[16]

The variable of skill is emphasized in Hook's detailed examination of Lenin's contribution to the events leading up to the October Revolution. Hook concludes that Lenin's vigorous, persistent, imaginative participation in that sequence was a necessary (though certainly not sufficient) condition for the outcome. Hook's interest, of course, is in lending precision to the notion of the Great Man. Therefore he is concerned with the individual who, because of especially great talents, is able to alter the course of events. But for our purposes, the Great Failure is equally significant: an actor's capabilities may be relevant to an outcome in a negative as well as a positive sense.

When does personal variability affect behavior ("actor dispensability")?

Often it may be acknowledged that a particular action of an individual is a crucial node in a process of decision-making, but it may be argued that this action is one that might have been performed by any actor placed in a comparable situation, or by anyone filling a comparable role. If actors with differing personal characteristics perform identically when exposed to common stimuli, we quite clearly can dispense with study of the actor's personal differences, since a variable cannot explain a uniformity. This objection to personality explanations of political behavior—and here "personality" means personal variability—is illustrated by Easton with the example of political party leaders who differ in their personality characteristics and who are "confronted with the existence of powerful groups making demands upon their parties." Their "decisions and actions," he suggests, will tend "to converge."[17]

The task of rephrasing this objection conditionally and advancing propositions about the circumstances under which it obtains is not overly burdensome, since the objection is rarely stated categorically. Exponents of the view that situational pressures eliminate or sharply reduce the effects of personality usually acknowledge that this is not always the case. Similarly, proponents of the view that personality *is* an important determinant of political behavior also often qualify their position and note circumstances that dampen the effects of personal variability. These qualifications point to an obvious reconstruction of the question. *Under what circumstances*, we may ask, *do different actors (placed in common situations) vary in their behavior and under what circumstances is behavior uniform?* We might call this the question of *actor dispensability*.[18]

The question of under what circumstances the variations in actor's personal characteristics are significant for their behavior has received a good bit of intermittent attention in recent years. The several propositions I shall set forth are assembled, and to some extent reorganized, from a variety of observations made by Herbert Goldhamer, Robert E. Lane, Daniel Levinson, Edward Shils, and Sidney Verba, among others.[19] But before proceeding to lay out these propositions, it will be instructive to consider a possible objection to the notion of actor dispensability.

The circumstances of actor dispensability are those in which, as Shils puts it, "persons of quite different dispositions" are found to "behave in a more or less uniform manner."[20] A personality-oriented social analyst might attempt to deny the premise that behavior *ever* is uniform (and indeed, Shils says "behave in a *more or less* uniform manner.") The objection is, of course, correct in the trivial, definitional sense: every different act is different. The objection is also empirically correct in that, if we inspect actions with sufficient care, we can always detect differences between them—even such heavily "situation-determined" actions as "the way in which a man, when crossing a street, dodges the cars which move on it"[21] vary from individual to individual. Nevertheless, the objection—if it is meant to invalidate Shils' assertion—is not well taken, since it denies the principle (necessary for analytic purposes) that we can classify disparate phenomena, treating them as uniform for certain purposes. Furthermore, a significant sociological poposition follows from Shils' point: "To a large extent, large enough indeed to enable great organizations to operate in a quite predictable manner, . . . [different individuals] will conform [i.e., behave uniformly] despite the conflicting urges of their personalities."[22]

Yet the objection leads to an important observation. What we mean by uniform behavior depends upon our principle of classification, which in turn depends upon the purposes of our investigation. If our interests are sufficiently microscopic, we are likely to find variability where others see uniformity. Nor, it should be added, is there anything intrinsically unworthy about being interested in microscopic phenomena—in nuances and "small" variations.

Even if one *is* interested in the macroscopic (major institutions, "important" events), the irrelevance of microscopic variations introduced by actors' personal characteristics cannot be assumed, since action dispensability and actor dispensability are independent of each other. Small actor variations may lead to actions with large consequences. Thus, for example, there might be relatively little room for personal variation in the ways that American Presidents would be likely to respond to the warning system that signals the advent of a missile attack, but the consequences of the President's action are so great that even the slightest variations between one or another incumbent in a comparable situation would be of profound interest.

In noting the conditions under which actors' personal characteristics tend to be dispensable and those under which they tend to be indispensable, we may examine conditions that arise from the *environmental situations* within which actions occur, from the *predispositions* of the actors themselves, and from the *kinds of acts* (responses) that are performed—that is, from all three elements of the familiar paradigm of E→P→R (or S→O→R). The propositions I shall list under these headings are neither exhaustive nor fully exclusive of each other, but they do serve to pull together and organize crudely most of the diverse observations that have been made on the circumstances that foster the expression of personal variability.

1. *There is greater room for personal variability in the "peripheral" aspects of actions than in their "central" aspects.* Examples of "peripheral" aspects of action include evidences of the personal *style* of an actor (for example, his mannerisms), the *zealousness* of his performance, and the *imagery* that accompanies his behavior at the preparatory and consummatory phases of action (for example, fantasies about alternative courses of action).

By "central" I refer to the gross aspects of the action—for example, the very fact that an individual votes, writes a letter to a Congressman, etc.

Lane suggests that "the idiosyncratic features of personality" are likely to be revealed in the "images" political actors hold "of other participants." There also is "scope for the expressions of personal differences," Lane points out, in "the grounds" one selects "for rationalizing a political act," and in one's style "of personal interaction in a political group."[23]

Shils, after arguing that "persons of quite different dispositions" often "will behave in a more or less uniform manner," then adds: "Naturally not all of them will be equally zealous or enthusiastic . . ."[24]

Riesman and Glazer point out that although "different kinds of character" can "be used for the same kind of work within an institution," a "price" is paid by "the character types that [fit] badly, as against the release of energy provided by the congruence of character and task."[25]

2. *The more demanding the political act—the more it is not merely a conventionally expected performance—the greater the likelihood that it will vary with the personal characteristics of the actor.*

Lane suggests that there is little personal variation in "the more conventional items, such as voting, expressing patriotic opinions and accepting election results as final." On the other hand, his list of actions which "reveal . . . personality" includes "selecting types of political behavior over and above voting":[26] writing public officials, volunteering to work for a political party, seeking nomination for public office, etc.

3. *Variations in personal characteristics are more likely to be exhibited to the degree that behavior is spontaneous—that is, to the degree that it proceeds from personal impulse, without effort or premeditation.*

Goldhamer refers to "a person's . . . casual ruminations while walking along the street, sudden but perhaps transient convictions inspired by some immediate experience, speculations while reading the newspaper or listening to a broadcast, remarks struck off in the course of an argument. . . . If we have any theoretical reason for supposing that a person's opinions are influenced by his personality structure, it is surely in these forms of spontaneous behavior that we should expect to find the evidence of this relationship."[27]

We may now consider two propositions about actor dispensability that relate to the environment in which actions take place.

4. *Ambiguous situations leave room for personal variability to manifest itself.* As Sherif puts it, "the contribution of internal factors increases as the external-stimulus situation becomes more unstructured."[28] (A classically unstructured environmental stimulus, leaving almost infinite room for personal variation in response, is the Rorschach ink blot.)

Budner[29] distinguishes three types of ambiguous situations. Each relates to instances which have been given by various writers of actor dispensability or indispensability. Budner's three types of situations include:

(a) *a "completely new situation in which there are no familiar cues."*

Shils comments that in new situations "no framework of action [has been] set for the newcomer by the expectations of those on the scene. A new political party, a newly formed religious sect will thus be more amenable to the expressive behavior of the personalities of those who make them up than an ongoing government or private business office or university department with its traditions of scientific work."[30]

Goldhamer argues that the public opinion process moves from unstructured conditions admitting of great personal variability to more structured conditions that restrain individual differences. Immediate reactions to public events, he argues, reflect personal idiosyncrasies. But gradually the individual is constrained by his awareness that the event has become a matter of public discussion. "There is reason to believe that, as the individual becomes aware of the range and intensity of group preoccupation with the object, his orientation to it becomes less individualized, less intimately bound to an individual perception and judgment of the object . . . [H]e is drawn imperceptibly to view this object anew, no longer now as an individual percipient, but as one who selects (unconsciously, perhaps) an 'appropriate' position in an imagined range of public reactions . . . a limitation is thus placed on the degree to which the full uniqueness of the individual may be expected to influence his perceptions and opinions."[31]

The second type of ambiguity referred to by Budner is (b) *"a complex situation in which there are a great number of cues to take into account."*

Levinson suggests that the availability of "a wide range of . . . socially provided . . . alternatives" increases "the importance of intrapersonal determinants" of political participation. "The greater the number of opportunities for participation, the more the person can choose on the basis of personal congeniality. Or, in more general terms, the greater the richness and complexity of the stimulus field, the more will internal organizing forces determine individual adaptation. This condition obtains in a relatively unstructured social field, and, as well, in a pluralistic society that provides numerous structured alternatives."[32]

Finally, Budner refers to (c) *"a contradictory situation in which different elements suggest different structures."*

Several of Lane's examples fall under this heading: "Situations, where reference groups have politically conflicting points of view. . . . Situations at the focus of conflicting propaganda. . . . Current situations which for an individual are in conflict with previous experience."[33]

5. *The impact of personal differences on behavior is increased to the degree that sanctions are not attached to certain of the alternative possible courses of behavior.*

"The option of refusing to sign a loyalty oath," Levinson comments, "is in a sense 'available' to any member of an institution that requires such an oath, but the sanctions operating are usually so strong that non-signing is an almost 'unavailable' option to many who would otherwise choose it."[34]

The foregoing environmental determinants of actor dispensability suggest several aspects of actors' predispositions which will affect the likelihood that any of the ways in which they differ from each other will manifest themselves in behavior.

6. *The opportunities for personal variation are increased to the degree that political actors lack mental sets which might lead them to structure their perceptions and resolve ambiguities.* The sets they may use to help reduce ambiguity include cognitive capacities (intelligence, information) that provide a basis of organizing perceptions, and pre-conceptions that foster stereotyping.

Verba, in an essay on "Assumptions of Rationality and Non-Rationality in Models of the International System," comments that "the more information an individual has about international affairs, the less likely it is that his behavior will be based upon non-logical influences. In the absence of information about an event, decisions have to be made on the basis of other criteria. A rich informational content, on the other hand, focuses attention on the international event itself. . . ."[35]

Wildavsky, in an account of adversary groups in the Dixon-Yates controversy, points to ways in which the preconceptions of members of factions lead them to respond in predictable fashions that are likely to be quite independent of their personal differences. "The public versus private power issue . . . has been fought out hundreds of times at the city, state, county, and national levels of our politics in the past sixty years. A fifty year old private or public power executive, or a political figure who has become identified with one or another position, may well be able to look back to twenty-five years of personal involvement in this controversy . . . The participants on each side have long since developed a fairly complete set of attitudes on this issue which have crystallized through years of dispute. . . . They have in reserve a number of prepared responses ready to be activated in the direction indicated by their set of attitudes whenever the occasion demands. . . ."[36]

7. *If the degree to which certain of the alternative courses of action are sanctioned reduces the likelihood that personal characteristics will produce variation in behavior, then any intense dispositions on the part of actors in a contrary direction to the sanctions increase that likelihood.*

"Personality structure . . . will be more determinant of political activity when the impulses and the defenses of the actors are extremely intense"—for example, "when the compulsive elements are powerful and rigid or when the aggressiveness is very strong."[37]

8. *If, however, the disposition that is strong is to take one's cues from others, the effects of personal variation on behavior will be reduced.* Personality may dispose some individuals to adopt uncritically the political views in their environment, but as a result, Goldhamer comments, the view adopted will "have a somewhat fortuitous character in relation to the personality and be dependent largely on attendant situational factors."[38] (Dispositions toward conformity are, of course, a key variable for students of political psychology. The point here is merely that these dispositions reduce the impact of the individual's other psychological characteristics on his behavior.)

9. *A situational factor working with individual tendencies to adopt the views of others to reduce personal variations is the degree to which the individual is placed in a group context in which "the individual's decision or attitude is visible to others."*[39]

Another predispositional determinant:

10. *The more emotionally involved a person is in politics, the greater the likelihood that his personal characteristics will affect his political behavior.*

Goldhamer comments that "the bearing of personality on political opinion is conditioned and limited by the fact that for large masses of persons the objects of political life are insulated from the deeper concerns of the personality." [But, he adds in a footnote], "this should not be interpreted to mean that personality characteristics are irrelevant to an understanding of the opinions and acts of political personages. In such cases political roles are so central to the entire life organization that a close connection between personality structure and political action is to be expected."[40]

Levinson argues that "[t]he more politics 'matters,' the more likely it is that political behavior will express enduring inner values and dispositions. Conversely, the less salient the issues involved, the more likely is one to respond on the basis of immediate external pressures. When a personally congenial mode of participation is not readily available, and the person cannot create one for himself, he may nominally accept an uncongenial role but without strong commitment or involvement. In this case, however, the person is likely . . . to have a strong potential for change toward a new and psychologically more functional role."[41]

The final proposition has reference to political roles and does not fit neatly into any of the three elements of the Environmental→Predispositions→Response formula.

11. *Personality variations will be more evident to the degree that the individual occupies a position "free from elaborate expectations of fixed content."*[42] Typically these are leadership positions. We have already seen that such positions figure in the conditions of action indispensability; their importance for the student of personality and politics is evident *a fortiori* when we note that the leader's characteristics also are likely to be reflected in his behavior, thus meeting the requirement of actor indispensability.

The military leader, it has been said, may have an especially great impact. "Even those who view history as fashioned by vast impersonal forces must recognize that in war personality plays a particularly crucial part. Substitute Gates for Washington, and what would have happened to the American cause? Substitute Marlborough or Wellington for Howe or Clinton, and what would have happened? These are perhaps idle questions, but they illustrate the fact that the course of a war can depend as much upon the strengths and failings of a commander-in-chief as upon the interaction of geography and economics and social system."[43]

Under what circumstances are ego-defensive needs likely to manifest themselves in political behavior?

The final objection to explanations of politics in terms of personality is one in which the term "personality" denotes not the impact of individuals on social processes (action dispensability), or the mere fact of individual variability (actor dispensability), but rather the specific ways in which "personalities" vary. Once we have found it necessary to explain political behavior by referring to the ways in which political actors vary, objections can be made to whatever specific personality variables we choose to employ. (Objections falling into this final category might be summarized under the heading "actor characteristics.")

Some choices of variables are particularly controversial, especially the variables based on "depth" psychology that have so commonly been drawn upon in such works as Lasswell's *Psychopathology and Politics,* Fromm's *Escape from Freedom,* and *The Authoritarian Personality.*[44] It is the deep motivational variables that many commentators have in mind when they argue that "personality" does not have an important impact on politics. It is sometimes said, for example, that such personality factors do not have much bearing on politics, because the psychic forces evident in the pathological behavior of disturbed individuals do not come into play in the daily behavior of normal people. Rephrasing this assertion conditionally, then, we arrive at the question: *Under what circumstances are ego-defensive*[45] *needs likely to manifest themselves in behavior?* It should be emphasized that my selection of this particular question about actor characteristics carries no implication that "personality" should be conceived of in psychodynamic terms, or that it should be equated with the unconscious, the irrational, and the emotional. It simply is convenient to consider this class of personality characteristics, because psychoanalytic notions have guided so much of the personality and politics literature and have antagonized so many of the literature's critics.

Much of what I have said about actor dispensability also applies to the present question. Wherever the circumstances of political behavior leave room for individuality, the possibility exists for ego-defensive aspects of personality to assert themselves. These circumstances include "unstructured" political situations; settings in which sanctions are weak or conflicting, so that individuals of diverse inclinations are not coerced into acting uniformly; and the various other considerations discussed under the previous heading. These circumstances make it *possible* for ego-defensive personality needs to come to the fore. They do not, of course, make it necessary—or even highly likely—that behavior will have a significant basis in ego defense.

Given the foregoing circumstances, which make ego-defensive behavior possible, what, then, makes it likely (or at least adds to the likelihood) that deeper psychodynamic processes will be at work? We may briefly note these three classes of factors, locating them conveniently in terms of environment, predispositions, and response.

1. *Certain types of environmental stimuli undoubtedly have a greater "resonance" with the deeper layers of the personality than do others.* These are the stimuli which evoke "disproportionately" emotional responses—people seem to be "over-sensitive" to them. They are stimuli which politicians learn to be wary of—for example, such issues as capital punishment,

cruelty to animals, and, in recent years, fluoridation of drinking water. Often their stimulus value may be to only a rather small segment of the electorate, but their capacity to arouse fervid response may be such that a Congressman would prefer to confront his constituents on such knotty matters as revision of the tariff affecting the district's principal industry than on, in the phrase of the authors of *Voting*, a "style issue"[46] such as humane slaughtering.

One element in these sensitive issues, Lane and Sears suggest, is that they touch upon "topics dealing with material commonly repressed by individuals. . . . Obvious examples are war or criminal punishment (both dealing with aggression) and birth control or obscenity legislation (both dealing with sexuality). Socially 'dangerous' topics, such as communism and religion, also draw a host of irrational defensive maneuvers. The social 'dangers' that they represent frequently parallel unconscious intra-psychic 'dangers.' For example, an individual with a strong unconscious hatred for all authority may see in Soviet communism a system which threatens intrusion of authoritarian demands into every area of his life. His anti-communism may thus stem more from a residual hatred for his father than for any rational assessment of its likely effects on his life."

Lane and Sears also suggest that, "Opinions dealing with people (such as political candidates) or social groups (such as 'bureaucrats,' 'blue bloods,' or the various ethnic groups) are more likely to invite irrational thought than opinions dealing with most domestic economic issues. Few people can give as clear an account of why they like a man as why they like an economic policy; the 'warm'—'cold' dimension seems crucial in many 'person perception' studies, but the grounds for 'warm' or 'cold' feelings are usually obscure. Studies of ethnic prejudice and social distance reveal the inaccessibility of many such opinions to new evidence; they are often compartmentalized, and usually rationalized; that is, covered by plausible explanation which an impartial student of the opinion is inclined to discount."[47]

2. *The likelihood that ego-defensive needs will affect political behavior also is related to the degree to which actors "have" ego-defensive needs.* This assertion is not quite the truism it appears to be. We still have very little satisfactory evidence of various patterns of psychopathology in society[48] and even less evidence about the degree to which emotional disturbance tends to become channeled into political action.

Although it is not a truism, the proposition *is* excessively general. It needs to be expanded upon and elaborated into a series of more specific hypotheses about types of ego-defensive needs and their corresponding adaptations as they relate to political behavior. For example, one of the more convincing findings of the prejudice studies of a decade ago was an observation made what neglected *Anti-Semitism and Emotional Disorder* by Ackerman and Jahoda.[49] Personality disorders which manifested themselves in depressive behavior, it was noted, were not accompanied by anti-semitism. But anti-semitism was likely if the individual's typical means of protecting himself from intra-psychic conflict was extra-punitive—that is, if he was disposed to reduce internal tension by such mechanisms as projection. There is no reason to believe that this hypothesis is relevant only to the restricted sphere of anti-semitism.

3. *Finally, certain types of response undoubtedly provide greater occasion for deep personality needs to find outlet than do others*—for example, such responses as affirmations of loyalty in connection with the rallying activities of mass movements led by charismatic leaders and the various other types of response deliberately designed to channel affect into politics. Both in politics and in other spheres of life it should be possible to rank the various classes of typical action in terms of the degree to which the participants take it as a norm that affective expression is appropriate.

SUMMARY AND CONCLUSIONS

My purpose has been to consider a topic that too often has been dealt with in a rather off-hand (and sometimes polemical) fashion: "Is personality important as a determinant of political behavior?" Five of the more intellectually challenging assertions about the lack of relevance of "personality" to the endeavors of the student of politics have been considered. Two of these seem to be based on misconceptions, albeit interesting ones. The three additional objections can be rephrased so that they no longer are objections, but rather provide the occasion for advancing propositions about how and under what circumstances "personality" affects political behavior.

In rephrasing these objections we see three of the many ways in which the term "personality" has been used in statements about politics: to refer to the impact of individual political actions, to designate the fact that individual actors vary in their personal characteristics, and to indicate the specific content of individual variation (and, particularly, "deeper," ego-defensive, psychological processes). It therefore becomes clear that the general question "How important is personality?" is not susceptible to a general answer. It must be broken down into the variety of sub-questions implied in it, and these—when pursued—lead not to simple answers but rather to an extensive examination of the terrain of politics in terms of the diverse ways in which "the human element" comes into play.

ENDNOTES

1. In my own efforts to do this I find that much of the existing research can be considered under three broad headings: psychological studies of single political actors, such as political biographies; studies which classify political actors into types, such as the literature on authoritarianism; and aggregative accounts, in which the collective efforts of personality are examined in institutional contexts—ranging from small aggregates such as face-to-face groups all the way through national and international political processes. Needless to say, it is one thing to suggest that clarification of such diverse endeavors is possible and another thing actually to make some progress along these lines.

2. A standard discussion by Allport notes a full fifty *types* of definition of the term (apart from colloquial usages): Gordon Allport, *Personality* (New York: Holt, 1937), 24–54.

3. David Riesman and Nathan Glazer, "The Lonely Crowd: A Reconsideration in 1960," in Seymour M. Lipset and Leo Lowenthal (eds.), *Culture and Social Character* (New York: The Free Press of Glencoe, 1961), p. 437. For examples of discussions that are in varying degrees critical of personality and politics writings see the essays by Shils and Verba cited in note 17, Reinhard Bendix, "Compliant Behavior and Individual Personality," *American Journal of Sociology*, 58 (1952), 292–303, and David Spitz, "Power and Personality: The Appeal to the 'Right Man' in Democratic States," this REVIEW, 52 (1958), 84–97.

4. Alex Inkeles, "Sociology and Psychology," in Sigmund Koch (ed.), *Psychology: A Study of A Science*, VI (New York: McGraw-Hill, 1963), p. 354.

5. It is a matter of convenience whether the terms "personality" and "psychological" are treated as synonymous (as in the present passage), or whether the first is defined as some subset of the second (as in my discussion of the fifth objection). Given the diversity of uses to which all of the terms in this area are put, the best one can do is to be clear about one's usage in specific contexts.

6. My criticism of the second objection would of course not stand in any instance where some acquired inner characteristic (such as a sense of class consciousness) was being defined as a social characteristic, and it was being argued that this "social" characteristic was "more important" than a "personality" characteristic. In terms of my usage this would imply an empirical assertion about the relative influence of two types of psychological, or "personality" variables. My remarks in the text on the meaning of terms are simply short-hand approaches to clarifying the underlying issue. They are not canonical efforts to establish "correct" usage.

7. Herbert Hyman, *Survey Design and Analysis* (Glencoe, Ill.: The Free Press, 1955), 254–257.

8. Urie Bronfenbrenner, "Personality and Participation: The Case of the Vanishing Variables," *Journal of Social Issues*, 16 (1960), 54–63.

9. Herbert Hyman, *Survey of Design and Analysis* (Glencoe, Ill.: The Free Press, 1955), 254–257. Italics in the original. Also see Hubert Blalock, "Controlling for Background Factors: Spuriousness Versus Developmental Sequences," *Sociological Inquiry*, Vol. 34 (1964), pp. 28–39, for a discussion of the rather complex implications of this distinction for data analysis.

10. Gordon Allport, review of *The American Soldier, Journal of Abnormal and Social Psychology,* 45 (1950), p. 173. Nothing in this discussion is intended to gainsay the use of controls. "I am not, of course, arguing against the use of breakdowns or matched groups," Allport adds. "They should, however, be used to show where attitudes come from, and not to imply that social causation acts automatically apart from attitudes." Often a control, by suggesting the source of a psychological state, helps explain its dynamics and functions. A good example can be found in Hyman and Sheatsley's well-known critique of *The Authoritarian Personality.* The critique shows that certain attitudes and ways of viewing the world which the authors of *The Authoritarian Personality* explained in terms of a complex process of personal pathology are in fact typical of the thought processes and vocabulary of people of lower socio-economic status. Hyman and Sheatsley are therefore able to suggest that such attitudes may be a learned part of the respondents' *cognitions* rather than a psychodynamic manifestation serving ego-defensive functions. It should be clear from what I have said in the text, however, that Hyman and Sheatsley's thesis cannot legitimately be phrased as an argument that such attitudes are social (or cultural) rather than psychological: Herbert Hyman and Paul B. Sheatsley, "The Authoritarian Personality—A Methodological Critique," in Richard Christie and Marie Jahoda (eds.), *Studies in the Scope and Method of "The Authoritarian Personality"* (Glencoe: The Free Press, 1954), 50–122.

11. Sidney Hook, *The Hero in History* (Boston: Beacon Press, 1943).

12. Compare Wassily Leontief's interesting essay "When Should History be Written Backwards?" *The Economic History Review,* 16, (1963), 1–8.

13. For an account of European politics in the 1930's that is consistent with this assertion see Alan Bullock, *Hitler: A Study in Tyranny* (New York: Harper, rev. ed., 1962). Needless to say, any attempt to seek operational indicators of environments that "admit of restructuring" in order to restate the present proposition in testable form could not take the circular route of simply showing that the environment *had* been manipulated by a single actor.

14. Robert C. Tucker, *The Soviet Political Mind* (New York: Praeger, 1963), 145–65; quotation from Turgenev at p. 147.

15. Robert C. Tucker, "The Dictator and Totalitarianism," *World Politics,* Vol. 17 (1965), p. 583.

16. In other words, the skill of the actor may feed back into the environment, contributing to its instability or stability. To the degree that we take environmental conditions as given (i.e., considering them statically at a single point in time), we underestimate the impact of individuals on politics. For examples of political actors shaping their own roles and environments see Hans Gerth and C. Wright Mills, *Character and Social Structure* (London: Routledge and Kegan Paul, 1953), Chapter 14.

17. David Easton, *The Political System* (New York: Knopf, 1953), p. 196.

18. Strictly speaking, it is not the actor who is dispensable in this formulation, but rather his personal characteristics. In an earlier draft I referred to "actor substitutability," but the antonym, "non-substitutability," is less successful than "indis-

pensability" as a way of indicating the circumstances under which an explanation of action demands an account of the actor. On the other hand, "substitutability" is a very handy criterion for rough and ready reasoning about the degree to which the contribution of any historical actor is uniquely personal, since one may easily perform the mental exercise of imagining how other available actors would have performed under comparable circumstances.

19. Robert E. Lane, *Political Life* (Glencoe, Ill.: The Free Press, 1959), pp. 99–100; Edward A. Shils, "Authoritarianism: 'Right' and 'Left'," in Richard Christie and Marie Jahoda, (eds.), *op. cit.*, pp. 24–49; Herbert Goldhamer, "Public Opinion and Personality" *American Journal of Sociology*, 55 (1950), 346–354; Daniel J. Levinson, "The Relevance of Personality for Political Participation," *Public Opinion Quarterly*, 22 (1958), 3–10; Sidney Verba, "Assumptions of Rationality and Non-Rationality in Models of the International System," *World Politics*, 14 (1961), 93–117.

20. Shils, *op. cit.*, p. 43.

21. This is a quotation from a well-known passage in Karl Popper's *The Open Society and Its Enemies* (New York: Harper Torchbook edition, 1963), II, p. 97, arguing that sociology is an "autonomous" discipline because psychological evidence is so often of limited relevance—compared with situational evidence—to explanations of behavior. For a critique of Popper's analysis see Richard Lichtman, "Karl Popper's Defense of the Autonomy of Sociology," *Social Research*, 32 (1965), 1–25.

22. Shils, *op. cit.*, p. 44.

23. Lane, *op. cit.*, p. 100.

24. Shils, *op. cit.*, p. 43.

25. Riesman and Glazer, *op. cit.*, pp. 438–439.

26. Lane, *op. cit.*, p. 100.

27. Goldhamer, *op. cit.*, p. 349.

28. Muzafer Sherif, "The Concept of Reference Groups in Human Relations," in Muzafer Sherif and M. O. Wilson (eds.), *Group Relations at the Crossroads* (New York: Harper, 1953), p. 30.

29. Stanley Budner, "Intolerance of Ambiguity as a Personality Variable," *Journal of Personality*, 30 (1960), p. 30.

30. Shils, *op. cit.*, 44–45.

31. Goldhamer, *op. cit.*, 346–347.

32. Levinson, *op. cit.*, p. 9.

33. Lane, *op. cit.*, p. 99.

34. Levinson, *op. cit.*, p. 10.

35. Verba, *op. cit.*, p. 100. By "non-logical" Verba means influences resulting from ego-defensive personality needs, but his point applies generally to personal variability.

36. Aaron Wildavsky, "The Analysis of Issue-Contexts in the Study of Decision-Making," *Journal of Politics*, 24 (1962), 717–732.

37. Shils, *op. cit.*, p. 45.

38. Goldhamer, *op. cit.*, p. 353.

39. Verba, *op. cit.*, p. 103.

40. Goldhamer, *op. cit.*, p. 349.

41. Levinson, *op. cit.*, p. 10.

42. Shils, *op. cit.*, p. 45. The term "role" is commonly used so as to have both an environmental referent (the prevailing expectations about his duties in a role incumbent's environment) and a predispositional referent (the incumbent's own expectations). For a valuable discussion see Daniel Levinson, "Role, Personality, and Social Structure in the Organizational Setting," *Journal of Abnormal and Social Psychology,* 58 (1959), 170–180.

43. Henry Wilcox, *Portrait of a General* (New York: Knopf, 1964), ix-x.

44. Harold D. Lasswell, *Psychopathology and Politics*, originally published in 1930, reprinted in *The Political Writings of Harold D. Lasswell* (Glencoe, Ill.: The Free Press, 1951); Erich Fromm, *Escape From Freedom* (New York: Rinehart, 1941); T. W. Adorno, et al., *The Authoritarian Personality* (New York: Harper, 1950).

45. For the present purpose a detailed conceptual side-trip into the meaning of "ego-defensive needs" will not be necessary. In general, I am referring to the kind of seemingly inexplicable, "pathological" behavior that classical, pre-ego psychology psychoanalysis was preoccupied with. A rough synonym would be needs resulting from "internally induced anxieties," a phrase that appears in Daniel Katz's remarks on ego-defense. "The Functional Approach to the Study of Attitudes," *Public Opinion Quarterly*, 24 (1960), 163–204. Also see Fred I. Greenstein, "Personality and Political Socialization: The Theories of Authoritarian and Democratic Character," *Annals*, 361 (1965), 81–95.

46. Bernard Berelson, et al., *Voting* (Chicago: University of Chicago Press, 1954), p. 184.

47. The quotations are from Robert E. Lane and David O. Sears, *Public Opinion* (Englewood Cliffs, New Jersey: Prentice-Hall, 1964), p. 76. Also see Heinz Hartmann, "The Application of Psychoanalytic Concepts to Social Science," in his *Essays on Ego Psychology* (New York: International Universities Press, 1964), p. 90f. Lane and Sears also suggest that "irrational" opinion formation is fostered where the "referents of an opinion" are "vague," where the issue is "remote" and it is "difficult to assess its action consequences," and where the "terms of debate" are "abstract." These are points which, in terms of the present discussion, apply generally to the possibility that personal variability will affect behavior (actor dispensability), as well as more specifically to the possibility that ego-defense will come to the fore.

48. But see Leo Srole et al., *Mental Health in the Metropolis,* (New York: McGraw-Hill, 1962).

49. Nathan W. Ackerman and Marie Jahoda, *Anti-Semitism and Emotional Disorder* (New York: Harper, 1950).

Reprinted from "The Child's Image of Government" by David Easton and Jack Dennis in volume no. 361 of *The Annals* of The American Academy of Political and Social Science. © 1965, by The American Academy of Political and Social Science.

PART 3 SELECTION 4

The Child's Image of Government

DAVID EASTON
and
JACK DENNIS

Political socialization refers to the way in which a society transmits political orientations—knowledge, attitudes or norms, and values—from generation to generation. Without such socialization across the generations, each new member of the system, whether a child newly born into it or an immigrant newly arrived, would have to seek an entirely fresh adjustment in the political sphere. But for the fact that each new generation is able to learn a body of political orientations from its predecessors, no given political system would be able to persist. Fundamentally, the theoretical significance of the study of socializing processes in political life resides in its contribution to our understanding of the way in which political systems are able to persist,[1] even as they change, for more than one generation.

THE THEORETICAL SETTING

A society transmits many political orientations across the generations, from the most trivial to the most profound. One of the major tasks of research is to formulate criteria by which we may distinguish the significant from the less important. Once we posit the relationship between socialization and system persistence, this compels us to recognize that among many theoretical issues thereby raised, a critical one pertains to the way in which a society manages or fails to arouse support for any political system, generation after generation. In part, it may, of course, rely on force or perception of self-interest. But no political system has been able to persist on these bases alone. In all cases, as children in society mature, they learn through a series of complicated processes to address themselves more or less favorably to the existence of some kind of political life.

But socialization of support for a political system is far too undifferentiated a concept for fruitful analysis. As has been shown elsewhere,[2] it is helpful to view the major objects towards which support might be directed, as the political community, the regime, and the authorities (or loosely, the government). The general assumption is that failure to arouse sufficient support for any one of these objects in a political system must lead to its complete extinction.

This paper seeks to illuminate one of the numerous ways in which the processes of socialization in a single political system, that of the United States, manages to generate support for limited aspects of two political objects: the regime and the government (authorities). Ultimately, comparable studies in other systems should enable us to generalize about the processes through which members learn to become attached to or disillusioned with all the basic objects of a system.

Within this broad theoretical context our specific problems for this paper can be simply stated: How does each generation born into the American political system come to accept (or reject) the authorities and regime? As the child matures from infancy, at what stage does he begin to acquire the political knowledge and attitudes related to this question? Do important changes take place even during childhood, a time when folklore has it that a person is innocent of things political? If so, can these changes be described in a systematic way?

GOVERNMENT AS A LINKAGE POINT

In turning to the political socialization of the child, we are confronted with a fortunate situation. The area that the theoretical considerations of a systems analysis dictates as central and prior—that of the bond between each generation of children and such political objects as the authorities and regime —happens to coincide with what research reveals as part of the very earliest experiences of the child. As it turns out empirically, children just do not develop an attachment to their political system, in the United States, in some random and unpatterned way. Rather, there is evidence to suggest that the persistence of this system hinges in some degree on the presence of some readily identifiable points of contact between the child and the system. From this we have been led to generalize that in one way or another every system will have to offer its maturing members objects that they can initially identify as symbolic or representative of the system and toward which they feel able to develop sentiments and attitudes deemed appropriate in the system. If a system is to persist, it will probably have to provide each new age cohort with some readily identifiable points of contact with the system. But for this, it would scarcely be likely that children could relate in any meaningful way to the various basic objects in a system.

In this respect our point of departure diverges markedly from the few past studies in the area of political socialization. In these it has been customary to take for granted the object towards which the child does, in fact, become socialized. Thus, following the pattern of adult studies, efforts have been made to discover how the child acquires his party identification, his attitudes towards specific issues, or his general political orientations on a liberal-conservative or left-right axis. But such research has adopted as an assumption what we choose to consider problematic. How, in fact, does a child establish contact with the broad and amorphous political world in which he must later take his place as an adult? What kind of political objects do, in fact, first cross his political horizon? Which of these does he first cathect?

For the American democratic system, preliminary interviewing led us to conclude that there are two kinds of initial points of contact between the child and the political system in its broadest sense. One of these is quite specific. The child shows a capacity, with increasing age, to identify and hold opinions about such well-defined and concrete units among the political authorities as the President, policeman, Congress, and Supreme Court. But we also found that simultaneously another and much more general and amorphous point of contact is available. This consists of the conglomeration of institutions, practices, and outcomes that adults generically symbolize in the concept "government." Through the idea of government itself the child seems able to reach out at a very early age to establish contact both with the authorities and with certain aspects of the regime. In a mass society where the personnel among the authorities changes and often remains obscure for the average person, the utility of so generalized and ill-defined a term as "the government" can be readily appreciated. The very richness and variability of its meaning converts it into a useful point of contact between the child and the system.

But the discovery of the idea of "government" as an empirically interesting point of reference for the child brings with it numerous complications for purposes of research. In the first place, any awareness of government as a whole is complicated by the necessary diffuseness of the idea; it applies to a broad and relatively undifferentiated spectrum of disparate events, people, structures, and processes. Government speaks with a cacophony of voices. It takes innumerable actions both large and small, visible and virtually invisible; and these locate themselves at the national as well as the local level, with many strata in between. Furthermore, the usual child is not likely to place *res publica* very high among his daily concerns.

Thus, the child's marginal interest in things political combined with the complexities of the object itself discourages a clear perception of the overall nature of government. This enormously complicates the task of isolating the specific image and attitudes that children do acquire. However, the points of contact between maturing members of the system and its basic parts are not so numerous that we could allow these obvious difficulties to discourage a serious effort to explore the nature of this connection and the part it may play in the growth of supportive or negative attitudes towards the authorities and regime.

OUR DATA

The children whom we have surveyed concerning what they think and feel about government, as well as about a number of other political orientations (which we will report elsewhere), are for the most part children in large metropolitan areas of the United States. They are, with few exceptions, white, public school children, in grades two through eight, and were selected from both middle-class and working-class neighborhoods. We have conducted many individual interviews and administered a series of pencil-and-paper questionnaires. The latter we read out to the children in their regular classrooms while they individually marked their answers.

The data to be reported below are some fairly uncomplicated examples of these responses; we use them to illustrate the kinds of developments of greatest interest about orientations towards "the government." In some we are attempting to discern the pattern of cognitive development about government as a whole; in others there is some mixture of cognitive and affective elements; and in a third type, the affective or supportive aspects dominate.

PREVIEW OF FINDINGS

The findings which grew out of this analysis will, perhaps, surprise those readers who are accustomed to think of children as innocent of political thought. For not only does the child quite early begin to orient himself to the rather remote and mystical world of politics, but he even forms notions about its most abstract parts—such as government in general. Our data at least suggest this. The political marks on the *tabula rasa* are entered early and are continually refurbished thereafter.

We will, perhaps, disappoint as well those readers who are accustomed to think of the American as one who is brought up on the raw meat of rugged individualism, which supposedly nourishes our national frame. We find that the small child sees a vision of holiness when he chances to glance in the direction of government—a sanctity and rightness of the demigoddess who dispenses the milk of human kindness. The government protects us, helps us, is good, and cares for us when we are in need, answers the child.

When the child emerges from his state of nature, therefore, he finds himself a part of a going political concern which he ordinarily adopts immediately as a source of nurturance and protection. His early experience of government is therefore, analogous to his early experience of the family in that it involves an initial context of highly acceptable dependency. Against this strongly positive affective background the child devises and revises his cognitive image of government. Let us first turn to some empirical evidence bearing upon this cognition.

THE CHILD'S EARLY RECOGNITION OF GOVERNMENT

In earlier studies of the child's growing awareness of political objects and relationships, it was found that the President of the United States and the policeman were among the first figures of political authority that the child recognized.[3] In part, at least, we would expect that attitudes towards political authority would begin to take shape in relationship to these objects. They are clearly the first contact points in the child's perception of wider external authority. In general, data collected since the early exploratory studies have supported these findings. . . .

We can, however, now raise a question which takes us beyond these findings. Does the child also establish some early perceptual contact with the more amorphous, intangible abstraction of government itself, that is, with the more general category of political authority among whose instances are counted presidents and policemen? Is the child's cognitive development such that he is likely to work immediately from a few instances to the general class of objects? This would then put him in a position to apply his concept to new instances, as well as to refurbish it as the experiences of its instances grow. If this is so, we can anticipate that, in addition to such points of contact as the policeman and the President, in the American political system the child will also be able to orient himself to political life through perceptions of and attitudes towards the more generalized and diffuse object that we call "the government."

The crystallization of the concept

When do our respondents first begin to recognize the general category of things labeled "government"? One simple way of exploring this is to see whether the child himself thinks he knows what the word "government" means, even if no verbalization of his understanding is called for. On this simple test we would contend that even the seven- or eight-year-old child is likely to feel that he has attained some rudimentary grasp of this general concept. This test is met in a question we asked on our final questionnaire which read as follows: "Some of you may not be sure what the word *government* means. If you are not sure what government means, put an X in the box below." The changing pattern of response to this question over the grades is shown in Table 1.

What we find from these simple data is that 27 percent of the second-grade children feel some uncertainty about the concept. This proportion declines rather regularly over the grades, however, so that for the eighth-grade children, less than 10 percent express this uncertainty. In general, these data suggest that a considerable portion of the youngest children had already crystalized some concept of government prior to our testing, and with each higher grade level the likelihood that they had not formed some concept decreases. With these data—and similar data from other protocols—as a background, it is plausible for us to proceed to a more detailed consideration of the content of the child's understanding of government.

Symbolic associations of the concept "government"

Since it appears that the child is rather likely to develop some working conception of government in these early years, we can move on to ask: Is there any specific content to this concept, especially of a kind that is political in character? We might well expect that because of the inherent ambiguity and generally of the term, even for adults, considerable differences and disjunctiveness would characterize this concept for aggregates of children. Our findings do, in part, support this expectation. Yet there are clear patterns of "dominance" in these collective conceptions, and these patterns vary to a large degree with the age and grade level of the children.

One way we have devised for getting fairly directly at which patterns are dominant in this period and at how these patterns change involves a pictorial presentation of ten symbols of government. These are symbols which appeared strongly in our extensive pretest data when children were asked either to define government or to "free associate" with a list of words, one of which was government.

What we asked in our final instrument was the following: "Here are some pictures that show what our government is. Pick the *two* pictures that show best what our government is." This instruction was then followed for the balance of the page by ten pictures plus a blank box for "I don't know." Each of the ten pictures represented a salient symbol of the United States government and was accompanied by its printed title underneath the picture. The options in order were: (1) Policeman; (2) George Washington; (3) Uncle Sam; (4) Voting; (5) Supreme Court; (6) Capitol; (7) Congress. (8) Flag; (9) Statue of Liberty; (10) President (Kennedy); (11) I Don't Know. The pattern of response to these ten symbols of government is shown in Table 2.

Several interesting facts emerge from this table. If we take 20 percent as a rough guide to what we might expect purely by chance as a maximum level of response to each of the ten symbol options (for two-answer format), we see that only four of these pictures were chosen with a frequency greater than chance. These four are George Washington, Voting, Congress, and President Kennedy. These four are considerably more dominant than any of the others, but this dominance varies by grade level. For the youngest children, the two most popular options are the two Presidents, Washington and Kennedy. But these choices drop in the later grades. In Figure 1, the developmental curves for the four dominant options are plotted over the grade span in order to interpret more easily the major changes that are taking place.

It would appear that, in terms of these symbols, the youngest child's perception of government is quite likely to be framed by the few personal figures of high governmental authority that cross his cognitive horizon, probably both in the school (where the portraits of presidents are often prominently displayed) and outside. The young child focuses most directly upon personal or perhaps "charismatic" aspects of political authority for his interpretation of what government is. But as he moves into the middle years, there is a greater likelihood that his attention will be turned to rather different, prominent aspects of the authorities.

First, he revises his notions to include the Congress and drop George Washington—who suffers a precipitous decline after his initial showing. Undoubtedly, the growing adoption of Congress reflects an awareness of several things, and these are supported by various other data. First, the older children become more aware of the group character of government rather than simply identifying it with single persons. Second, the more frequent choice of Congress probably also reflects a greater awareness of governmen-

Table 1 *Development of a Sense of Confidence in Understanding the Concept of Government (Responses of Children by Grade Level)*[a]

Grade	%	N
2	27.29	1,655
3	19.01	1,678
4	17.61	1,749
5	11.15	1,803
6	12.41	1,749
7	8.36	1,723
8	9.79	1,695

[a]The questionnaire which contained this item was administered to a purposively selected group of 12,052 white, public school children in regular classrooms in eight large metropolitan areas (100,000 and over) in four major geographic regions (South, Northeast, Midwest, and Far West) in late 1961 and early 1962. The children were in grades two through eight and from both middle- and working-class areas. We will refer to this questionnaire hereinafter as simply "CA-9," which is our code name for Citizenship Attitude Questionnaire #9. This question is item #55, page 12. [Page number refers to original article.]

Table 2
Development of a Cognitive Image of Government: Symbolic Associations (Percent of Children and Teachers Responding)[a]

GRADE	Policeman	George Washington	Uncle Sam	Voting	Supreme Court	Capitol	Congress	Flag	Statue of Liberty	President Kennedy	I Don't Know	N Responding	N Not Responding
2	8.15	39.47	15.63	4.32	4.51	13.65	5.93	15.75	12.11	46.26	15.69	1,619	36
3	4.09	26.77	19.01	8.36	6.38	16.13	12.94	16.49	14.26	46.81	12.94	1,662	16
4	5.74	14.19	18.02	10.83	10.25	16.57	28.97	13.33	12.92	37.25	13.15	1,726	23
5	2.74	6.93	19.40	19.23	16.77	11.57	49.08	11.57	11.18	38.51	4.86	1,789	14
6	2.36	4.94	16.78	27.99	16.84	9.94	49.66	11.38	17.07	30.52	4.66	1,740	9
7	3.03	3.44	18.26	39.44	13.54	9.39	44.22	12.84	18.61	27.89	2.98	1,714	9
8	1.66	1.72	16.40	46.77	15.87	6.93	49.14	11.78	19.60	22.91	1.54	1,689	6
TEACHERS	1.00	1.00	5.00	72.00	13.00	5.00	71.00	6.00	8.00	15.00	1.00	390	1

[a](1) Percentages should add to 200 due to the two-answer format, but do not, because of the failure of some children to make two choices. This is especially the case for those answering "I don't know." (2) 113 children failed to respond to this question. Thus the N at each grade are those responding and the percentages are of that number. (3) We have added, at the bottom, the responses of the teachers of these children, for the sake of comparison. The teachers were given a similar questionnaire at the time of administration of the children's questionnaire.

Figure 1 *Development of a Cognitive Image of Government: The Four Dominant Symbolic Associations (the Number of Children Responding at Each Grade Level Varies from 1,619 to 1,789)*

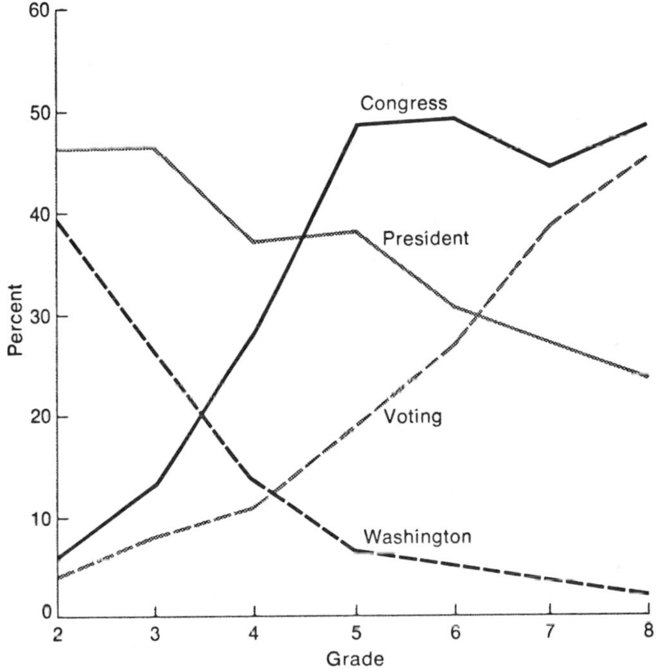

tal institutions—particularly the ongoing organizations engaged in *law-making* (as suggested undoubtedly in the beginning social studies, history, or civic texts). Children move, in a sense, from a very personalized conception of governmental authority to one better characterized as "legal-rational," institutionalized, or impersonal political authority, to continue the Weberian parallel.

Third, children appear to reflect a greater awareness of the representative character of these institutions. Impersonalization of authority is coincident with some growth in the recognition of regime norms, in this case of the rules of behavior that contribute to representation. This conclusion is borne out to some degree by the third marked shift which occurs—that concerning the older child's greater tendency to pick "voting" as the best picture of our government. Thus, by grade eight nearly half the children choose voting. This suggests some beginning awareness of the regime rules associated with popular democracy and the role of ordinary people in it.

The child's conception of government is, therefore, brought in stages from far to near, from one small set of persons to many people, from a personalistic to an impersonalized form of authority, and toward an awareness of the institutionalization in our system of such regime norms as are embodied in the idea of a representative, popular democracy. There are obviously a number of further tests we would wish to make on these hypotheses. We would also wish to keep in mind that by no means all of these children appear to be going through these stages of cognitive development. But the patterns which emerge seem to us at least very striking, and they are supported in various ways from our other data.[4]

Generally, therefore, in these data about the cognitive development of this rather abstract category of the individual's political thought, we detect more than a mere glimmering of a concept. Furthermore, the emergent conception in this instance seemingly reflects some fairly wide and regularly changing comprehension for aggregates of children.

This suggests that considerable societal efforts are probably being made to transmit a concept deemed appropriate in the American political system. If we compare children with their teachers, for example, we find that the latter most roundly endorse the two options dominant for the eighth-grade children. The propositions are even higher for the teachers, however, so that in terms of the statistical norms, they stand perhaps closer to the end-state suggested by the direction of movement of the children. Thus the teachers—who are highly salient agents of the child's political and general conceptual development—have a concept that is quite in line with the child's apparent maturational tendencies. One could hypothesize, therefore, that a part of society's efforts to inform the child is reflected in the teacher's responses.

The concept of government and the law-making function

A supporting piece of evidence which is connected to the above, but supplements it from the standpoint of governmental functions (rather than from the structural aspects of the concept alone), has to do with the child's changing awareness of the chief law-makers in our system of government. One thing we find is the fact that, of the various kinds of political or other functions that the child most readily associates with government, the making of laws is very prominent. That is, when the child is asked, "What does the government do?" he is quite likely to answer that he, it, or they make the laws.

A questionnaire item that we presented in this connection reads as follows: "Who makes the laws? Put an X next to the *one* who does the most to make the laws." The options were: (1) Congress, (2) President, (3) Supreme Court, (4) I Don't Know. The same pictures as before were used. In Table 3 we see the patterns of change over the grade span for this aspect of the child's understanding.

Table 3 *Development of an Awareness of the Chief Law-maker (Percent of Children and Teachers Responding)*[a]

GRADE	*Congress*	*President*	*Supreme Court*	*I Don't Know*	*N Responding*	*N Not Responding*
2	4.79	75.55	11.49	8.17	1,627	28
3	11.41	66.14	16.93	5.52	1,648	30
4	27.51	44.11	21.07	7.31	1,723	26
5	57.39	19.35	19.85	3.40	1,793	10
6	65.06	13.25	18.30	3.38	1,743	6
7	72.14	8.88	16.41	2.57	1,712	11
8	85.33	5.44	7.87	1.36	1,690	5
TEACHERS	96.00	1.00	3.00	0.00	339	5

[a] CA-9, item 33.

Here the President's early dominance is apparent, but Congress gradually supplants him by grade five. Thus, by the middle grades the child is both increasingly prone to identify Congress as the chief source of law-making as well as a more representatives symbol of our government than the President.

If this trend should continue into adulthood, we would expect great support for Congress as the primary institution of government vis-à-vis the President. We would expect that, of the opposing observations of Max Lerner and Robert Lane, for example, those of Lane would be given support. Lerner observed (as cited by Lane) that "when the American thinks of his government, he thinks first of the President as its symbol."[5] If "first" means while he is a second or third grader, then Lerner is correct. But this does not appear to be the sense in which he is using the word.

In light of the developmental trends we see in our data, our respondents seem to resemble more closely the "common men" in Lane's Eastport study. Lane found that his respondents were more likely to perceive government in terms of its legislative functions than its administrative or judicial ones.[6] As far as the common men in Eastport were concerned, Congress was the most important focus of their concept of government. Lane also found that government (and Congress) are thought of in terms of their products, namely, the laws they make.[7] His subjects consider government and Congress as benign, helpful, and responsive—an organization "working for the people, not merely restraining them."[8]

All of these findings converge with our data as far as the developmental trends are concerned. The oldest children in our test group are those who most resemble the common men of Eastport. One can therefore interpret what we find as an indication that this image of government is one not confined to the period of Lane's study but seems to have more general application. Our respondents tend over the grades toward the adoption of a vision of government which puts great emphasis upon Congress as the center of government, upon law as its most visible product, and upon benign, helpful, protective, and responsive qualities as those most appropriately describing its manner of operation. The latter, more affective image will be discussed shortly after we present some further findings concerning cognitive development.

Differentiation of the public sector

Even though the children tested assert a growing awareness of government as an idea and object, are they, in fact, able to distinguish it as a sphere separate from other areas of social life? If attitudes towards the authorities as an object are to have relevance for later ties to the system, we need some evidence indicating that even in their earliest years children are, in fact, able to recognize some minimal difference between that which is governmental and that which is not. Only under such conditions could we infer that attitudes towards government—to which we shall turn in a moment—refer to distinctively political bonds.

To discover whether the child's declared knowledge of what government means includes a capacity to discriminate governmental from nongovernmental objects, we chose to test his awareness of the difference between what we normally view as the public and private sectors of life. A variety of contexts could be used to test for this differentiation—activities of various kinds, organizations, symbols, or personnel. We have chosen for our test the last because we found that the formulation, "people who do various jobs to help the community," is a rather familiar context for the child who has been exposed to the beginning social studies texts. The child learns that a variety of "community helpers" exist, ranging from doctors and nurses to firemen and street sweepers.

What we asked was very simple. Taking various occupations—milkman, policeman, soldier, judge, postman, and teacher—we said: "Here are some people. Which ones work for the government?" Then followed six questions with an appropriate picture for each such as: "Does the MILKMAN work for the government?" The options were: (1) Yes. (2) No. What we found is shown in Table 4.

Only the first of these people was considered by us be clearly outside the governmental system as determined by his occupation.[9] Of the rest two were more directly local government workers—the policeman and the teacher; two were clearly national government workers—the soldier and the postman; and one was intermediate as among levels—the judge.

Several things are apparent from the table. Of these workers, the milkman is the one (as we would expect) who is least often identified as a member of

Table 4 *Development of an Awareness of the Public and Private Sectors (Percent of Children and Teachers Responding)*[a]

GRADE	*Milkman*	*Policeman*	*Soldier*	*Judge*	*Postman*	*Teacher*	*N Responding (varies by item)*
2	29.12	86.04	68.33	86.42	56.87	48.01	1,601–1,626
3	30.77	89.11	79.16	88.35	62.74	54.95	1,627–1,656
4	28.03	90.98	83.17	88.70	71.35	58.29	1,702–1,730
5	20.54	88.99	90.18	90.45	80.02	62.65	1,778–1,792
6	16.24	87.84	93.28	91.70	85.53	64.48	1,730–1,747
7	12.85	82.47	95.52	94.16	89.02	64.03	1,697–1,718
8	8.38	80.95	98.11	93.72	93.20	59.31	1,681–1,692
TEACHERS	1.00	77.00	100.00	91.00	99.00	45.00	330–341

[a]CA-9, items 49-54.

the public sector. Around 70 percent of the youngest children were able to make an accurate assessment of his nongovernmental status. From grade four on, this proportion steadily increased so that by grade eight, less than 10 per cent were in error.

For the rest, the policeman and the judge are most easily recognized as belonging in the governmental system by the youngest children. Then come the soldier, postman, and teacher in that order. Both the soldier and the postman—the more nearly exclusively national government workers—increase in the proportions of children endorsing them at successively higher grade levels, until, by grade eight, they are the ones who, with the judge, get the greatest governmental identification.

The teacher, on the other hand, does not really make any major gains over the grades, but remains somewhat ambiguous with respect to her governmental status. And this effect holds for the teacher respondents as well. Somehow the status of the teacher is a more complex one.

That something else is probably at work is seen when we compare with the others the perception over the grades of the teacher and the policeman—both local-governmental status. Both, over the grades, suffer some net decline in the proportions of children endorsing their governmental status while the other government workers show gains. Possibly the older child is more likely to direct his attention to the national level for his image of government, and, therefore, his differentiation is conflicted for local government workers. This would fit, at least, other somewhat similar findings about the child's greater awareness of the national than of the lower levels of government.[10] It also explains the markedly lower percentage of teachers who identify policemen and teachers as working for the government.

In general, the child in his elementary years attains the capacity to differentiate the governmental system of behavior from nongovernmental systems. This does not mean that he is able to do so in every conceivable way. Our data suggest only that he is increasingly able to do this for the personnel of government. His concept of government, therefore, does become a differentiated one, at least in these terms. Again, this suggests a development beyond that of only a rudimentary grasp of this complex object in these early years of political awareness.

There is thus sufficient content in the child's perception of government for us to have some confidence that when we now come to talk about his attitudes toward this object, it will reflect affect towards a genuinely political (that is, public) authority. It will also prove significant for our interpretation that there is even a tendency to think of government at the national rather than at the local level.

Summary of findings on the child's developing cognitive image of government

As a possible object toward which affect might be directed, the idea of government undergoes far-reaching changes in the cognitive development of the child as represented in our test group. As he passes through grades two to eight, he begins with a rudimentary notion in which government is personal in character, represented by a few high-ranking and visible leaders. But as he grows older, the child sees government in less personal terms. He becomes increasingly aware of its group character and its major institutions; he learns something about the norms (voting) of a representative and popular democracy. In addition, it is crucial that the child proves increasingly able to identify government as something that is different from the private sector of life, however the latter may be defined in different epochs of society. All of these things suggest that, aside from any feelings that may be associated with government, the efforts by society to convey an adequate representation of this abstract object are by no means in vain.

THE CHILD'S AFFECTIVE RESPONSE TO GOVERNMENT

Although analytically we are able to separate the cognitive aspects of the image of government from accompanying feelings towards it, empirically they go hand in hand. For an understanding of the way in which the American political system stimulates diffuse support for the political authorities, it is critical to appreciate the fact that from the very beginning of his awareness

—at its conceptually most rudimentary stage—the child interprets government as something provided to further his welfare and that of the people around him. The benevolent, protective, helpful, and otherwise good qualities of government constitute the first and continuing overall context of evaluation. Even at the end of this period—when the child is thirteen or fourteen years of age, and government and individual authorities, such as the President and the policeman, are beginning to be seen more realistically and less ideally—the child still regards them as great blessings, if slightly mixed ones.

The child thus continues to endorse government even though what he understands it to be is changing. Having started off his evaluation in highly positive terms, he seems reluctant to give it up. In this we see, perhaps, the early formation of a bond that is hard to loosen. It is a bond that entails future diffuse support for the governmental system.[11]

The child's approval of government's role

In our pilot data, we found such a uniformly favorable affective image of government, from the earliest grades onward, that we felt no special large-scale effort was necessary to deal with this in our final instrument. Yet we do have some data from our eight cities which bear upon the question. First, however, we shall present a few examples of our considerable body of pilot data in order to show how highly consensual our young children's approval of government is over the whole grade range.

In an instrument administered to children in the Chicago area, we proposed that the children either agree or disagree with statements such as these:

1. The government is getting too big for America.
2. The government meddles too much in our private lives.
3. The government has too much power.
4. The United States government usually knows what is best for the people.
5. The government ought to give money and food to people out of work.
6. The government should have more power over the people.[12]

We attempted as far as possible to retain the original wording of statements of children in our pretest interviews—but reversing the items in several cases. The patterns of response to these statements are shown in Table 5.

What we see is that children at all of these grade levels roundly approve of government. They reject, at a fairly high level of agreement (75 per cent or more), the first three statements about the scope of government becoming too large. Statements four and five, on the other hand, reflect approval of the

Table 5 *Attitudes Toward the Role of Government*

	1. "The government is getting too big for America."		2. "The government meddles too much in our private lives."		3. "The government has too much power."		4. "The government usually knows what is best for the people."		5. "The government ought to give money and food to people out of work."		6. "The government should have more power over the people."	
GRADE	% *Agree*	*N*	% *Agree*	*N*	% *Agree*	*N*	% *Agree*	*N*	% *Agree*	*N*	% *Agree*	*N*
3	16	113	28	108	36	116	80	69	70	69	22	69
4	14	125	21	118	19	122	77	119	84	119	33	120
5	10	118	17	116	22	118	87	117	80	117	24	117
6	7	146	19	145	10	146	84	145	78	143	13	145
7	13	143	19	139	12	139	91	139	71	139	20	138
8	11	149	14	148	15	147	84	147	77	145	19	145

role of government in guiding and caring for the people, and these statements elicit a high level of agreement. Only for the last statement do we see any impetus toward restricting the role of government; that is, the children like it the way it is.

The overall response is one which is better characterized as collectivist endorsement than individualistic disapproval of government. In spite of the great myth of rugged individualism which is supposed to pervade the American consciousness, these children, at least, seem to be inclined toward the opposite kind of feeling about government. Thus the child begins as something of a natural collectivist, and whatever individualistic tendencies he may exhibit are developed later on.

The sixth item suggests, moreover, that the child is likely to be a "conservative collectivist" in that he is not much in favor of extending the scope of government beyond its present limits. He is rather happy with government as it stands and would not give it "more power over the people." Thus, the child's early contentment with government is fairly complete, and it is one which exhibits the characteristics of a high acceptance of government as a given, necessary part of the natural environment. If the child is to develop discontent and a desire for change, it is undoubtedly yet to be learned. It thus will be overlaid upon an early base of high regard for the government.

The child's rating of government's qualities

The early positive regard for the government is shown, as well, over a larger group of respondents in some ratings of the government in our final "eight cities" questionnaire. Using five role attributes and qualities of government as descriptions, we asked the child to "think of the Government as it really is." The items (CA–9, items 32–36) read as follows:

Think of the *Government* as it really is . . . (Circle the number of your choice)

1	*2*	*3*	*4*	*5*	*6*
Almost never makes mistakes	Rarely makes mistakes	Sometimes makes mistakes	Often makes mistakes	Usually makes mistakes	Almost always makes mistakes

1	*2*	*3*	*4*	*5*	*6*
Would always want to help me if I needed it	Would almost always want to help me if I needed it	Would usually want to help me if I needed it	Would sometimes want to help me if I needed it	Would seldom want to help me if I needed it	Would not usually want to help me if I needed it

1	*2*	*3*	*4*	*5*	*6*
Makes important decisions all the time	Makes important decisions a lot of the time	Makes important decisions sometimes	Makes important decisions seldom	Almost never makes important decisions	Never makes important decisions

1	*2*	*3*	*4*	*5*	*6*
Can punish anyone	Can punish almost anyone	Can punish many people	Can punish some people	Can punish a few people	Can punish no one

1	*2*	*3*	*4*	*5*	*6*
Knows more than anyone	Knows more than most people	Knows more than many people	Knows less than many people	Knows less than most people	Knows less than anyone

We asked for these ratings at grades four to eight. The results are shown in Table 6.

Over-all on these five ratings approval of government is high across the grades. There is some decline for two of three ratings, however, and an increase on three. The most apparently affectively loaded item, "would want to help me if I needed it," for example, shows a greater tendency for the older child to rate the government's willingness to help him "almost always" or "usually" rather than "always." And the same is true for the somewhat affectively loaded item "makes mistakes." The more cognitively directed role-relevant items show steady increases in the more positive categories, although the perception of government's capacity to punish is seemingly never as high as the other two—"makes important decisions" and "knows more than other people."

Perhaps the most interesting observation is that the most directly affective item, "would want to help me if I needed it," elicits a high regard for government over the whole span of grades, with a small drop of this support for the older children.

Table 6 *Ratings of the Qualities of Government (Percent of Children Responding)*

1. "Makes mistakes"

GRADE	1. Almost Never	2. Rarely	3. Some-times	4. Often	5. Usually	6. Almost Always	Mean Rating	N Responding	N Not Responding
4	29.75	42.70	25.02	1.13	.87	.53	2.02	1,499	250
5	23.95	45.72	27.87	1.90	.39	.17	2.10	1,787	16
6	22.18	47.93	27.18	1.67	.40	.63	2.12	1,740	9
7	16.78	48.89	31.59	2.21	.12	.41	2.21	1,716	7
8	13.44	45.51	38.25	2.26	.18	.36	2.31	1,681	14

2. "Would want to help me if I needed it"

GRADE	1. Always	2. Almost Always	3. Usually	4. Some-times	5. Seldom	6. Not Usually	Mean Rating	N Responding	N Not Responding
4	25.27	31.72	23.92	11.63	5.17	2.28	2.47	1,488	261
5	16.60	31.01	27.80	16.26	5.29	2.98	2.72	1,777	26
6	16.60	31.12	28.36	16.43	4.50	3.00	2.70	1,735	14
7	15.64	29.00	30.92	15.99	5.72	2.74	2.75	1,714	9
8	13.66	28.82	32.34	15.93	6.26	2.98	2.81	1,676	19

3. "Makes important decisions"

GRADE	1. All the Time	2. A Lot of the Time	3. Some-times	4. Seldom	5. Almost Never	6. Never	Mean Rating	N Responding	N Not Responding
4	35.01	47.93	13.92	2.21	.54	.40	1.87	1,494	255
5	38.75	46.89	12.00	1.63	.45	.28	1.79	1,783	20
6	47.70	40.39	9.78	1.32	.35	.46	1.68	1,738	11
7	54.32	35.06	8.75	1.46	.06	.35	1.59	1,714	9
8	57.81	35.16	5.72	.83	.18	.30	1.51	1,678	17

4. "Can punish"

GRADE	1. Anyone	2. Almost Anyone	3. Many People	4. Some People	5. A Few People	6. No One	Mean Rating	N Responding	N Not Responding
4	13.90	29.28	24.11	19.01	9.13	4.57	2.94	1,489	260
5	13.68	33.67	25.45	16.61	6.53	4.05	2.81	1,776	27
6	19.83	31.82	23.29	14.47	6.22	4.38	2.69	1,735	14
7	22.46	31.79	23.75	13.43	5.34	3.23	2.57	1,705	18
8	26.44	30.58	21.28	12.83	5.52	3.36	2.50	1,668	27

5. "Knows"

GRADE	1. More Than Anyone	2. More Than Most People	3. More Than Many People	4. Less Than Many People	5. Less Than Most	6. Less Than Anyone	Mean Rating	N Responding	N Not Responding
4	13.68	44.67	36.35	2.88	1.41	1.01	2.37	1,491	258
5	11.35	52.11	33.56	1.46	.79	.73	2.30	1,779	24
6	14.02	52.05	29.95	2.25	.75	.98	2.27	1,733	16
7	16.05	54.09	27.34	1.65	.53	.35	2.18	1,701	22
8	15.34	58.24	23.83	1.56	.60	.42	2.15	1,662	33

Summary of the child's affective response to government

The child's affect in this context begins high but diminishes somewhat as he learns more about the political world. He begins with deep sympathy for government, and this early aura of approval is likely to remain at the base of his acceptance of the government, whatever later modifications and limitations he puts on his trust and approval. These limited data, at least, suggest that he certainly begins with highly supportive feelings.

CONCLUSION

To maintain a social construct as varied, extensive, and demanding of social resources as government, a broad panoply of forces need to be set in motion to provide the requisite support. The political socialization of new members is one of the most far-reaching and most consequential of these forces. The political system must somehow provide a flow of information about and continuously create deep feelings of loyalty and obedience for its basic forms. One of these is its government or authorities. Government is a primary focus for the generation of politically supportive or disaffective orientations. Our data suggest that in the United States a supportive image of government is being widely and regularly reproduced for young new members. The average grade school child of our test group appears to experience some rather basic changes in his conception of government—changes which move him toward a cognitive image that conforms to the requirements of a democratic political system.

He begins, as a "political primitive," with a vision of government as the embodiment of a man or a small set of men who constitute a yet dimly recognized form of external authority. This authority applies to the immediate environment of the child in a rather abstract way as well as to the wider world beyond. Probably the first recognizable shadow that flickers across the wall of the cave of the child's uniformed political mind is that of the President. He forms the initial visible object of the political world, and, from him, the child builds down, gradually incorporating more and more objects below him until the image becomes rounded and complex.

The child, moving down toward a plural, complex, and functional conception of government . . . runs upon representative and popular institutions. He raises Congress and voting in his mind's eyes to positions of dominance as symbolic associations and thus elicits democracy in his interpretation of what our government is. At the same time, he is beginning to sharpen his knowledge about the boundaries of government by sorting what is outside the realm of government from what is within it.

This finally adds up to a picture supportive of a democratic interpretation and evaluation, a picture that becomes rapidly and forcefully exhibited in these years, as other data, not reported as yet, confirm. The child is initiated into a supportive stance by what is probably high exposure to cues and messages about government, even while he is essentially unconcerned with such matters and too young to do much about them even if he wished. He learns to like the government before he really knows what it is. And as he learns what it is, he finds that it involves popular participation (voting) and that this is a valuable part of its countenance. It is further reason for liking it; and liking it is what the child continues to do. The child has somehow formed a deep sympathy for government even before he knows that he is in some way potentially part of it.

We know of course that such a process of changing understanding and feeling must go beyond these early years. And later experiences may upset these earlier formed images. Yet we know as well, from what little evidence there is directly about support for government *per se*, that adult Americans are also highly supportive of their government, whatever exaggerations may exist about their belief in limited government.[13] In these exploratory data that we have presented, we think we see growing the deep roots of this supportive sentiment.

Furthermore, our data enable us to link up our discussion of the cognitive and affective aspects of the child's image of government, at least in a speculative way. Two things stand out in our data. First, the child begins with a view of government as composed of palpable, visible persons—such as the President or a past President, Washington. Second, as he makes his initial contact with government, it becomes a symbol of orientation to political life that is charged with positive feelings. If we now make the plausible assumption that a child of seven or eight is not likely to develop such feelings about *impersonal* organizations or institutions, we can appreciate the significance of the fact that his first glimpse of government is in the form of the President. It permits the child to express toward a figure of political authority sentiments that he is already accustomed to displaying to other human beings in his environment.

From this we would draw the hypothesis that the personalizing of the initial orientation to political authority has important implications for the input of support to a political system as the child continues through his early years into adolescence. As he fills in his picture of government, adding, to leading figures, such institutions as Congress and such regime rules as voting, we would suggest that the affect originally stimulated by his personalized view of government subtly spills over to embrace other aspects of government and the regime itself.

But for this process it is difficult to see how impersonal, remote, and complex organizations such as Congress or practices such as voting could possibly catch the imagination of a child and win his affection. Yet our data do show that positive sentiment towards government, even after the child has begun to see it in impersonal terms, is so high as to approach a consensual level. When we add to this the fact that children tend to view government as national rather than local in its scope, we can appreciate the unifying force that this image must have in a system such as the United States.

This interpretation carries us far beyond its immediate significance for socialization into the American political system. In effect, we may have encountered here a central mechanism available to many political systems in building up diffuse support in each wave of children as they enter a political system through birth into it. In many ways a child born into a system is like an immigrant into it. But where he differs is in the fact that he has never been socialized to any other kind of system. That is to say, he is being socialized politically for the first time rather than resocialized as for an immigrant. The fact that the new member is a child rather than an adult with a pre-existing set of attitudes towards political life, creates a need for special devices to build support for the regime and authorities. Each system will, of course, have its own specific mode of personalization. It may take the form of a monarch, a paramount chief, a renowned elder or ancestor, a charismatic leader, or a forceful dictator. But the pattern of making government a warm and palpable object through its initial symbolization as a person, the high affect that this permits for a child, and the possible subsequent overflow of this feeling to cold and impersonal institutions and norms may form a complex but widespread mechanism for attaching to the system those members who are new to it by virtue of their birth in it.

ENDNOTES

1. For the idea that persistence includes change, see D. Easton, *A Framework for Political Analysis* (Englewood Cliffs, N.J.: Prentice-Hall, 1965) and *A Systems Analysis of Political Life* (New York: John Wiley & Sons, 1965).

2. See Easton, *A Framework for Political Analysis and A Systems Analysis of Political Life.*

3. David Easton, with R. D. Hess, "The Child's Changing Image of the President," 24 *Public Opinion Quarterly*, pp. 632–644; "Youth and the Political System," *Culture and Social Character,* ed. S. M. Lipset and L. Lowenthal (New York: Free Press, 1961); and "The Child's Political World," 6 *Midwest Journal of Political Science* (1962), pp. 229–246.

4. Some of these supporting data will be presented below.

5. Max Lerner, *America as a Civilization* (New York: Simon and Schuster, 1957), p. 377.

6. Robert Lane, *Political Ideology* (New York:Free Press, 1962), p. 146.

7. Lane, pp. 147–148.

8. Lane, pp. 145, 149.

9. Pretesting had indicated that "the milkman" was a good an indicator as numerous other private roles.

10. See Fred Greenstein, *Children and Politics* (New Haven: Yale University Press, 1965), pp. 60–61.

11. For the concept "diffuse support," see D. Easton, *A Systems Analysis of Political Life.*

12. These questions are from our pilot questionnaire "In My Opinion—# III" items 50, 125, 169, 170, and 151, respectively.

13. See V. O. Key, Jr., *Public Opinion and American Democracy* (New York: Knopf, 1961), pp. 28–32; M. Janowitz, D. Wright, and W. Delancey, *Public Administration and the Public: Perspectives toward Government in a Metropolitan Community* (Ann Arbor: Bureau of Government, University of Michigan, 1958), pp. 31–35; and Donald E. Stokes, "Popular Evaluation of Government: An Empirical Assessment," *Ethics and Bigness,* ed. Harlan Cleveland and Harold D. Lasswell (New York: Harper & Row, 1962), pp. 61–72.

Reprinted from *Midwest Journal of Political Science*, 14, 2 (1970), by permission of Wayne State University Press. Copyright, 1970, by Wayne State University Press.

Children and Government: A Comparison Across Racial Lines

EDWARD S. GREENBERG

People relate to government in a variety of ways. The manner in which they do determines, to a large extent, the direction and form of their participation in the political life of their community. Many people who, for instance, feel hostile toward governmental institutions become apathetic and withdraw from the political arena. Others frequently opt for the politics of violence and revolution. In American politics, it seems to be the case that the hostile leave the political field for the nonhostile, politically efficacious. Research suggests that it is precisely those people who feel most positive toward government institutions and officials who are most likely to be active participants in the political process.[1]

There is evidence that in the political arena black people behave somewhat differently than other Americans.[2] It would be interesting and instructive to determine the degree to which this difference in political behavior is grounded in divergent perceptions and evaluations of government.

This paper explores the socialization of black and white children to governmental orientations. To be more specific, the focus is upon children's evaluation of government and judgments as to their own relationship to it.

Political socialization is selected as the framework for analysis because it is now apparent that the nature of a person's basic attachment to government is determined before he leaves elementary school.[3] In order to gain insight into the nature and process of a citizen's link to a system of government, as well as to gain some predictive power relative to future behavior, an examination of childhood socialization is an important research task.[4]

Black children will receive most of the attention in this paper. This is so for two primary reasons, one practical, the other theoretical. First, the racial situation in America is at the crisis stage, and it is the opinion of a growing number of people that it is incumbent upon scholars to turn their attention to the edification of both public and private policy decisions relative to that crisis.[5] It is important, for instance, to gain insight into the extent to which the present racial conflict is based on a conflict over values within an accepted system of rules and expectations, or contrariwise whether that conflict is grounded in a profound divergence of political world view. If disparate world views are indeed evident, it is important to determine the sources and strength of such cleavages.

Second, it can hardly be denied that political science has largely ignored black children in socialization research.[6] Indeed, the discipline has been remiss with other ethnic and cultural minorities as well.[7] Major attention has been paid to white, urban children (middle class ones, at that) and this has quite naturally resulted in the painting of a relatively homogeneous, consensual portrait of the political socialization process in America. This portrait hardly squares with the recurring urban violence, political assassination and campus disorder conveyed by the TV screen. Hopefully, this paper will help rectify these lucunae in the literature as we turn to the examination of children's perceptions and evaluations of government, and of their personal posture towards it.

METHODOLOGY

Previous research has demonstrated the importance of the elementary school years in the political socialization of the child. Therefore it was deemed important that all children in the elementary school with the ability to understand a paper and pencil test be included. Pretesting suggested that the effective lower range of such abilities was the third grade.

Given the high probability that the political socialization of black children changes as they become older and gain new life experiences, older children were also included in the sample. However, given the high dropout rate of black youth during the high school years, it was felt that the ninth grade would be the effective upper limit. Sampling from grades above the ninth would have meant drawing respondents from an atypical population. Moreover, since time and resource limitations prevented a longitudinal design, a cross-sectional approach was utilized.

Because of the nature of the research problem, a purposive sample was drawn and not a cross-sectional probability sample.[8] The study was interested in making comparisons across race and class lines. Therefore, schools were selected that were relatively homogeneous with respect to race and class. Thus, an elementary and junior high school were selected with each of the following characteristics: black lower class; black middle class; white lower class; and white middle class.

Matching social class groups across race lines, however, presents problems. One of the most widely used indicators in the social sciences for the assignment of respondents to a social class has been occupation. However, in a society with unequal opportunities for economic and social advancement, the occupational structures of the black and white communities are not congruent. Black people tend to concentrate at the bottom of the occupational structure, whereas whites dominate the middle ranges.[9] Consequently, occupation does not have the same meaning in the black community as it does in the larger society. Thus, occupations such as clerk, mailman, or redcap may be seen by the white community as distinctly lower class yet afford the perquisites for a middle class life style within the segregated community.[10] Objective occupational data, therefore, are inadequate for assignment of black respondents to social class. Such data do not adequately reflect the possible middle class life style and aspirations of the respondents.

Because of this noncomparability across race lines using occupational data, and given the inability of younger children to report accurately the income of their parents, neighborhood was selected as the basic indicator of social class. This was done with full appreciation of the limitations of the method, no alternative procedure being available. It remains the case that within the segregated black community, neighborhoods differ sharply with respect to quality of housing, schools and city services. In short, the ghetto community, like the remainder of society, is differentiated along class lines.

Thus, the city was divided into relatively homogeneous race and class districts (based on home valuations, opinions of school officials, etc.). One elementary school was randomly selected within each district type, and the allied junior high school was added. Two classes were randomly selected at each grade level used in the study. Children were assigned to the modal social class of their school, unless the occupation of the father was clearly atypical of the neighborhood (e.g., such as a doctor or lawyer in the "core" ghetto area).

The sampling procedure appears to have quite successfully distinguished between social class neighborhoods within each racial group. The evidence appears below. Since access to school records was denied, data were drawn from the census tracts that school officials estimate most closely correspond to areas feeding children into each school.

The study was conducted in Philadelphia in the spring of 1968, utilizing 980 children. Since we shall make statements of the type, "black children think so and so . . . ," and "white children think so and so . . . ," it was necessary to weight the black lower class sample.[11]

Table 1 *Census Tract Approximations of School District Boundaries: Selected Demographic Characteristics*

	Black			
	Lower Class		Middle Class	
	Elem. School	Jr. High School	Elem. School	Jr. High School
% of Housing Deteriorating	5.5	5.1	0.9	0.5
Ave. Value of Dwelling	$6,000	$5,750	$9,750	$8,500
	White			
	Lower Class		Middle Class	
	Elem. School	Jr. High School	Elem. School	Jr. High School
% of Housing Deteriorating	2.2	3.2	0.2	0.03
Ave. Value of Dwelling	$6,750	$6,350	$11,500	$14,500

The questionnaires were self-administered for children in junior high school (grades seven and nine). Questionnaires were read to the younger children item by item by trained interviewers of the same race as the children in the elementary grades (grades three and five).

The items in the questionnaire related to children's orientations toward government were subjected to McQuitty's "elementary factor analysis," a crude but effective method for isolating highly interrelated items.[12] The analysis was done separately for white and black children, and similar clusters were apparent in the seventh and ninth grades. For younger children, factors are not in evidence; all of the items merge into one or two clusters. The movement thus appears to be from diffuseness to distinctiveness; a movement from confusion to a more sharply defined and sophisticated perspective.

Each cluster of questions is formed into an index by giving one point for every positive response.[13] Thus, the highest score for both perceptions of government paternalism-benevolence and a sense of goodwill towards government would be three and the lowest would be zero; with respect to role performance, high and low scores would equal two and zero.[14]

GOODWILL

The first index is related to children's general sense of goodwill toward government; the extent to which they see it as friendly, not to be feared and competent.

Consistent with the major work in the field of political socialization, it seems that most young children hold highly positive attitudes toward political institutions, a perspective which declines with age. This pattern of gradually declining goodwill does not diverge appreciably by race. In one sense this decline is quite functional and healthy for a democracy. Democratic political arrangements require debate and dissent, a state of affairs manifestly impossible in a context of youthful adulation of government. This decline of adulation opens a space, however small, for critical thought and action.

Despite aggregate similarities, there may be differentiations within the black sample that are both interesting and important. Communities are, for instance, stratified along a number of dimensions, including, but not confined to, social status and wealth.[15] One of these dimensions is political information and accuracy of perception.[16] We measure such a dimension in this paper by determining whether black children held accurate (Item: black people and white people are not treated equally in this country) or inaccurate (Item: black people and white people are treated equally in this country) perceptions of American race relations.[17] While the measure is admittedly crude, it reveals some interesting results on this (Figure 2) and subsequent indices. Notice that with respect to goodwill, those children with the more accurate perceptions of race relations experience a slight reversal in trend between the seventh and ninth grades. This is a phenomenon that we will wish to keep in mind as we return to the other indices.

Figure 1[a] *Index of Goodwill Towards Government: Percent Scoring High (2 or 3) on The Index by Race and Grade*

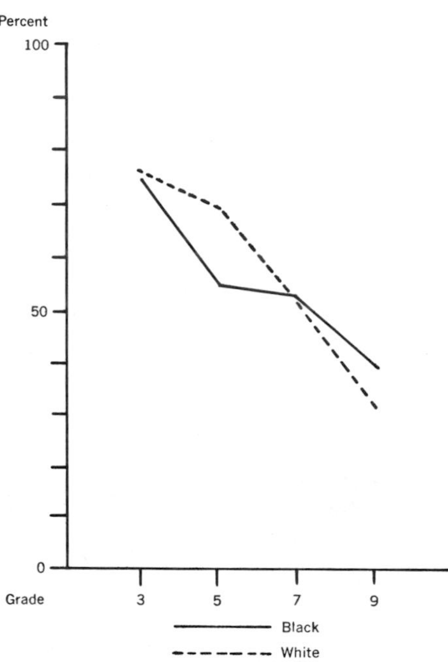

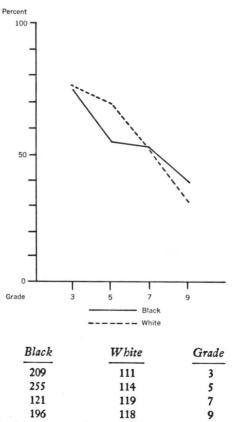

Black	*White*	*Grade*
209	111	3
255	114	5
121	119	7
196	118	9

[a] In this and all subsequent graphs and tables, percentages are based on the total number of children sampled (that is, don't know responses are included). This decision was based on a consideration of the scope and direction of the inquiry. The focus is on the development of positive support for various aspects of government. Both negative and don't know responses are interpreted in this context as non-positive.

ROLE PERFORMANCE

The elementary factor analysis isolated two items related to children's judgments about the competence of government in dealing with the burdens citizens demand of it (Figure 3).

Contrariwise to the goodwill index, it seems that most children are likely to judge government as competent to its assigned tasks, and that this judg-

Figure 2 *Index of Goodwill Towards Government: Percent of Black Children by Grade Scoring High, Controlling for Accuracy of Perception of Race Relations*

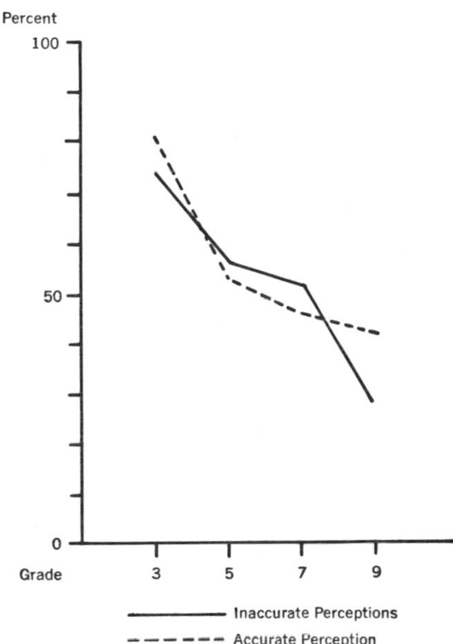

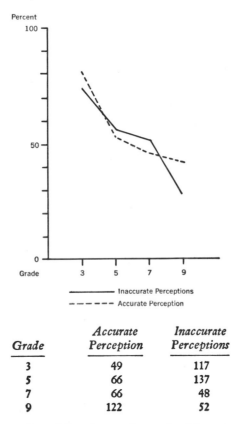

Grade	*Accurate Perception*	*Inaccurate Perceptions*
3	49	117
5	66	137
7	66	48
9	122	52

ment is relatively unaffected by changes in grade. Of most central concern to this paper is the great similarity between children of the two races.[18]

Accuracy of perception of American race relations continues to be a powerful predictor of orientations toward government among black children (Figure 4). It seems that the more perceptive black children are more aware and appreciative of governmental talents. What's more, the developmental patterns proceed in opposite directions.

PATERNALISM-BENEVOLENCE

Unlike the goodwill and role performance dimensions, black and white children diverge significantly with respect to their judgments as to govern-

Figure 3[a] *Index of Government Role Performance: Percent Scoring High on Index (2) by Race and Grade*

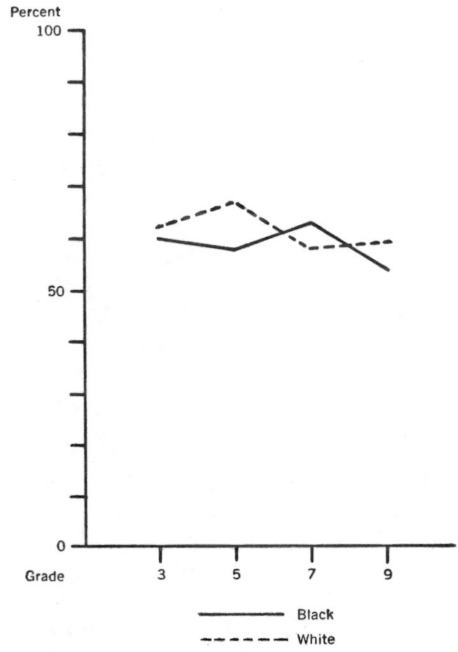

[a] N same as in Figure 1.

ment's benevolence and protection (Figure 5). Young children of both races see government as protective and nurturant but lose this sense as they get older. This is especially marked with respect to black children who experience a rapid and serious erosion of this vision of government. As they grow older they see government as less helpful and caring and less to be trusted. Thus black and white children come to hold sharply divergent orientations toward government. Of some interest is the slight reversal of the pattern for black children in the ninth grade, consistent with prior findings. Apparently, children in the seventh to ninth grade span come to see the possibility that government is helpful in many ways.[19] It should be noted that it is within this grade span that children are first seriously exposed to civics and American history, and black children probably learn for the first time about the major civil rights activities by the federal government. What may be operative here is the redundancy effect first reported by Langton

Figure 4[a] *Index of Government Role Performance: Percent of Black Children by Grade Scoring High, Controlling for Accuracy of Perception of Race Relations*

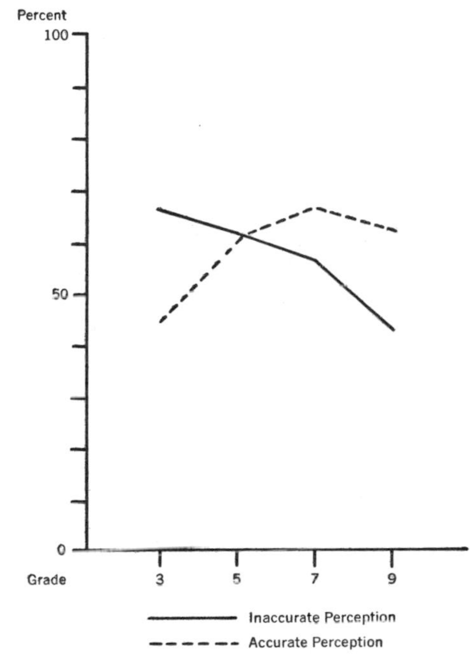

[a]N same as in Figure 2.

and Jennings.[20] That is, school history and civics courses seem to play a greater role for black children than for white children, because the classroom material tends to be new and nonredundant for the former.

Accuracy of perception of race relations again is a powerful predictor of orientations (Figure 6). Note that the most perceptive children account for most of the serious decline and subsequent recovery.

THE LEVEL OF GOVERNMENT QUESTION

Does the black child direct his renewed confidence in government towards all jurisdictions? Do black children make any distinctions in their images between national, state and local government? There is evidence pointing to marked hostility among black adults toward local government but continued faith in the national government.[21] Are analogous orientations found

Figure 5[a] *Index of Government Paternalism-Benevolence: Percent Scoring High (3) by Race and Grade*

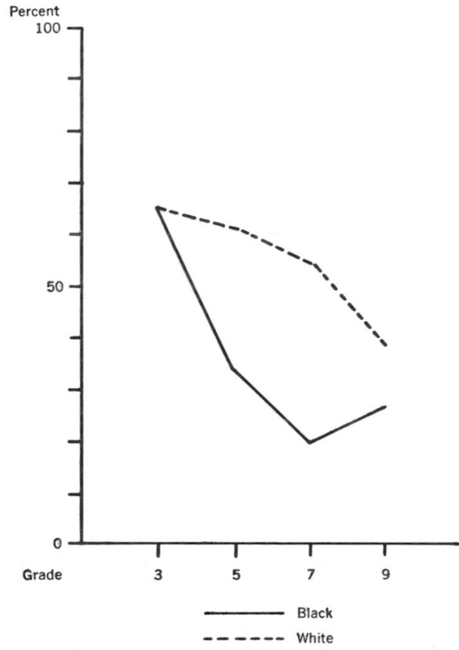

[a] N same as in Figure 1.

in young children? The following three questions were asked to help provide some answers.

1. Does the United States government
2. Does the government of Pennsylvania
3. Does the government of Philadelphia

} Make things better for most people? / Make things worse for most people? / Make no difference?

Several things are immediately apparent in the children's response patterns (Figure 7).[22] For all levels of government and in all grades except the ninth, white children are more likely to judge government favorably than are black children. Black children manifest serious declines for all levels of government, and the rebound effect between the seventh and ninth grades

Figure 6[a] *Index of Government Paternalism-Benevolence: Percent of Black Children by Grade Scoring High, Controlling for Accuracy of Perception of Race Relations*

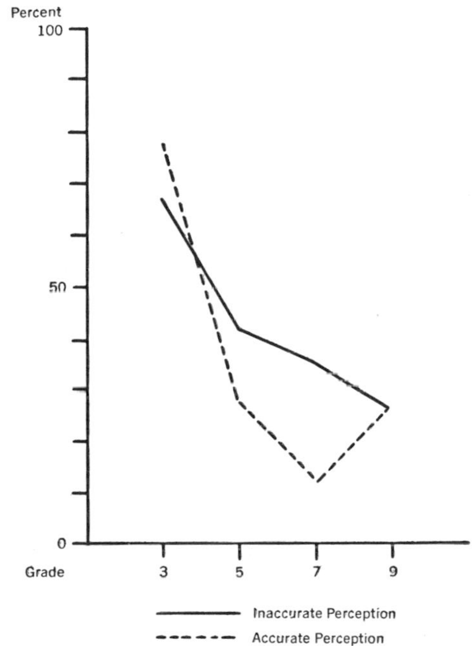

[a] N same as in Figure 2.

recurs in all cases. The variations within this general pattern, however, are most revealing and instructive.

Turning our attention solely to the black sample, we may begin to better understand how these children evaluate the different levels of government. Consistent with adult black orientations, children show most of their renewed confidence in the national government and least for local government.

It is clear, for instance, that black students in the third grade manifest their highest confidence in local government and their lowest in the national government, yet the situation is completely reversed by the ninth grade. The data are summarized in Table 2. Local government suffers the worst erosion while the original confidence in the national government is recovered by the ninth grade.

I have repeatedly asserted that black children experience a seventh to ninth grade recovery in affect for all levels of government. However, it

Figure 7[a] *Children's Evaluations of the Impact of Government (by Race and Grade)*

Percent Affirming that "The Government of the United States makes things better for most people"

Percent Affirming that "The Government of Pennsylvania makes things better for most people"

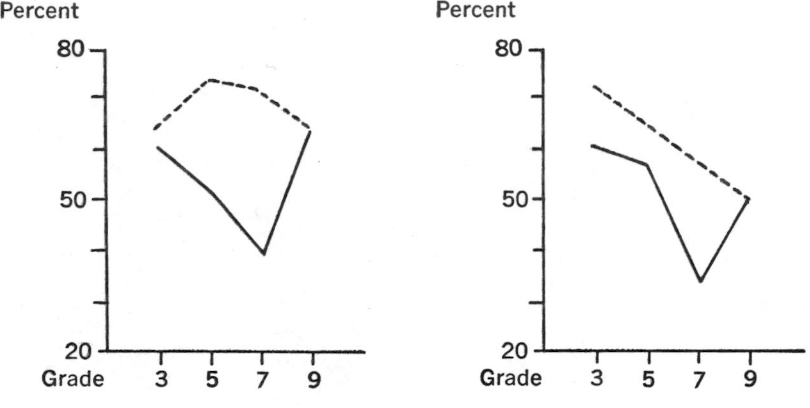

Percent Affirming that "The Government of Philadelphia makes things better for most people"

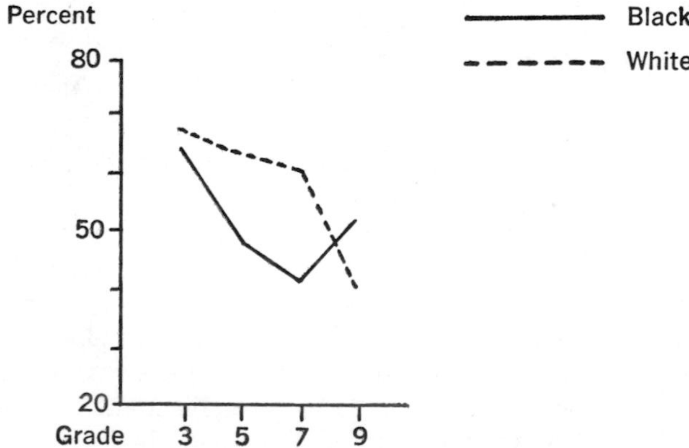

[a] N same as in Figure 1.

seems to be the case that the national government enjoys the greatest recovery and local government the least. Percentages recovered between the seventh and ninth grades are as follows: national, 24%; state 17%; and local, 11%.

Table 2 *Black Children's Perceptions of Whether Government "Makes Things Better for People" by Level of Jurisdiction (Percent Agreeing)*

	Third Grade	Ninth Grade	Change
National Government	60	64	+4
State Government	60	50	−10
Local Government	65	53	−12

Of added significance is the fact that the most marked rally to the national government is manifested by those black students who perceive unequal treatment for whites and blacks in America.

The general pattern of decline and recovery and its accentuation among the most perceptive black children suggests an exchange interpretation of

Figure 8[a] *Percent of Black Children by Grade, Affirming that "The United States Government Makes Things Better for Most People," Controlling for Accuracy of Perception of Race Relations*

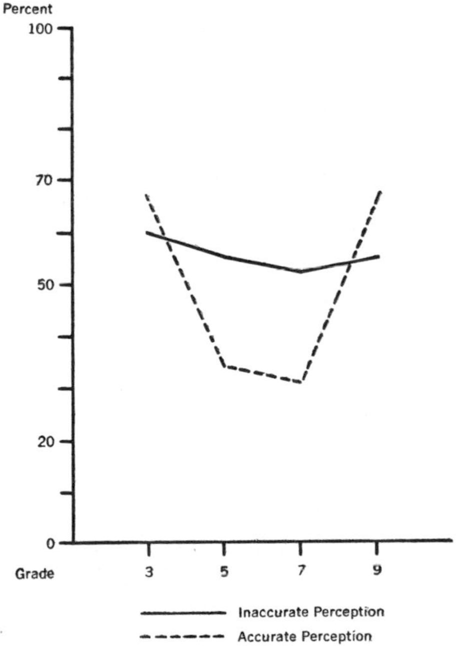

[a] N same as in Figure 1.

the development of political orientations. In a simple exchange theory one returns some sentiment *y* in exchange for some value *x*. Within this framework a child would return attitudes favorable towards government when he is aware that something of value is or is likely to be forthcoming from government.

Thus, between the third and seventh grades there seems to be a growing awareness among black children of the poverty and deprivation which surrounds them, and this observation is seemingly transferred to social institutions, including the political. The radical reversal during the junior high school years seems to indicate that significant numbers of black children perceive that whatever progress has been made in the past or will be made in the future is based at the national level of political life. Children do not seem to become aware of this until they engage in historical and political materials in junior high school. Such an interpretation ties in nicely with the redundancy effect discovered by Langton and Jennings mentioned above.[23]

We can easily combine the exchange and nonredundancy interpretations. That is, attitudes favorable towards the national level of government by older children appear only when they become aware of the activities of that government beneficial to black people. In short, children respond when they become aware of the terms of the exchange.

"SUBJECT" OR "PARTICIPANT" ORIENTATION?

In summary, relatively few racial or social class differences are evident in either the "role performance" or "goodwill" dimensions. Trends toward rather sharp racial differences appear, however, with respect to the paternalism-benevolence dimension, trends which are unaffected by social class controls but which are accentuated by controls for accuracy of perception.

The sudden reversal on the paternalism-benevolence index, this growing tendency for older black children to see government in paternalistic terms, suggests a "subject" orientation to political life. Almond and Verba define the "subject" orientation as the existence of

> . . . a high frequency of orientations toward a differentiated political system and toward the output aspects of the system, but orientations toward specifically input objects, and toward the self as an active participant approach 0 . . . the relationship is toward the system on the general level, and toward the output, administrative, or "downward flow" side of the political system; it is essentially a passive relationship. . . .[24]

To inquire further into the styles of orientation among black children, two questions were asked in order to tap their conceptions of the role of the average citizen.

The children were first asked "How do we pick our leaders?" Three alternatives were offered: "whoever the most people want"; "whoever is smartest"; and finally "whoever is strongest." A strong "participant" would no doubt select the option reflecting popular participation in governance. The data show that black students lag behind white students in the realization that people select their own leaders (Figure 9). Indeed, black students do not reach white levels even by the time they reach the upper grades. Relative to white students, therefore, Negroes lag in their development of the participant orientation.

Controlling for social class reveals, however, that most of the lag (but not all) is accounted for by lower class black children, although middle class children also lag behind their white counterparts (Table 3). A glance at the white lower class figures suggests that the question of subject-participant orientation is greatly affected by social class (although race remains a factor).

Figure 9[a] *"How Do We Pick Our Leaders in This Country?" Percent (by Race and Grade) Selecting "Whoever The Most People Want"*

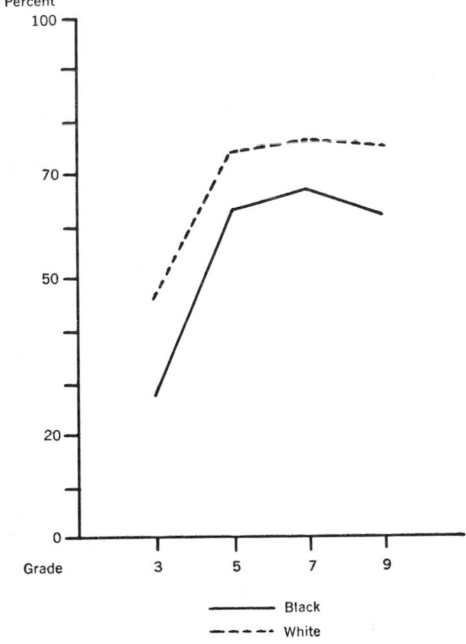

[a] N same as in Figure 1.

Table 3 [a] *Children's Conceptions of How We Pick Our Leaders*

Grade	N	Whoever is Strongest Middle Class	Whoever is Strongest Lower Class	Whoever is Smartest Middle Class	Whoever is Smartest Lower Class	Whoever the Most People Want Middle Class	Whoever the Most People Want Lower Class	Don't Know Middle Class	Don't Know Lower Class
				Black Children					
3	52	4		35		58		4	
	56		14		48		20		18
5	53	0		15		72		13	
	72		7		25		58		10
7	40	5		28		60		8	
	29		0		24		69		7
9	43	2		16		72		9	
	64		6		22		57		15
				White Children					
3	55	0		36		56		7	
	6		9		38		39		14
5	70	0		21		76		3	
	44		5		23		66		7
7	85	0		20		77		4	
	34		0		27		62		12
9	81	1		16		82		1	
	36		3		19		47		31

[a] Again, percentages are based on the total sample. "Don't know" responses are included because we are concerned primarily with how many children select the participant option ("whoever the most people want"). Either selection of an alternative option or "Don't Know" is considered a negative or non-participant oriented response.

The children were then asked to select out of a series of sentences "which sentence tells best what democracy is?" Relative to whites, black children showed a stronger tendency to select "where leaders do what they think is best for people," and a weaker inclination to select "where government does what the most people want." Black children, therefore, are less likely to see government leaders as responsive to the demands of people. Controlling for social class does not wash out this generalization. Black middle class children are no more likely to see the impact of ordinary people than lower class children, and they trail far behind white students of equal social status (Table 4).[25]

The evidence for interpreting black children's stance toward government as "subject" is very strong. They are less likely than white children to see government and its leaders as responsive to common people, and are slightly more likely by the ninth grade to see government as paternalistic and benevolent.

Many have suggested that the major problem suffered by black people is not poverty and discrimination per se, but powerlessness.[26] I would suggest that the "subject" stance toward government is but another facet of this phenomenon. Life in the black community serves generally to convey to people that they have no control over their lives, surroundings or destinies.

Figure 10 *Black Children's Choice (by Grade) of Best Description of Democracy*

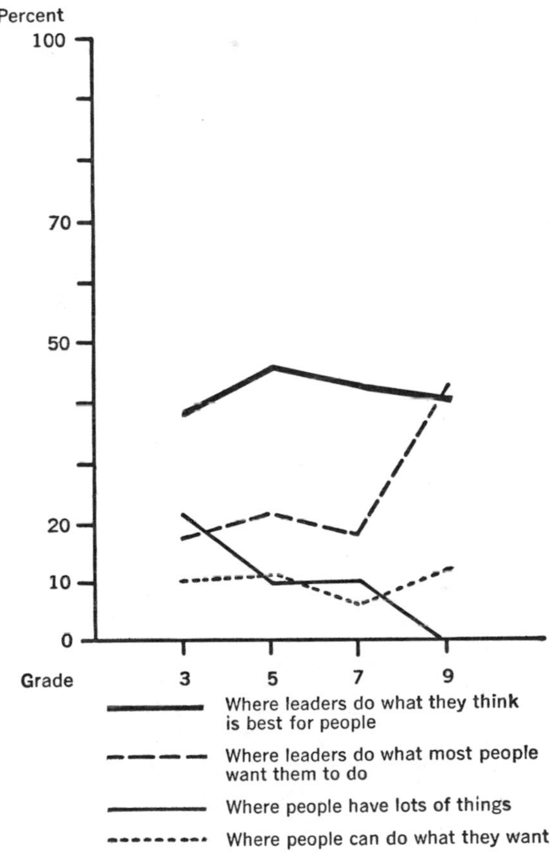

There is no reason to believe that attitudes toward government are different in any significant way. As in almost all other areas of their lives, government is seen as another institution beyond their immediate control, although sometimes helpful.

CONCLUSION

My concern in this paper has been the examination of the nature of the child's link to government. In light of the evidence presented, what conclusions might be drawn about these matters?

It is clear, in the first place, that black and white children in at least one

Figure 11 *White Children's Choice (by Grade) of Best Description of Democracy*

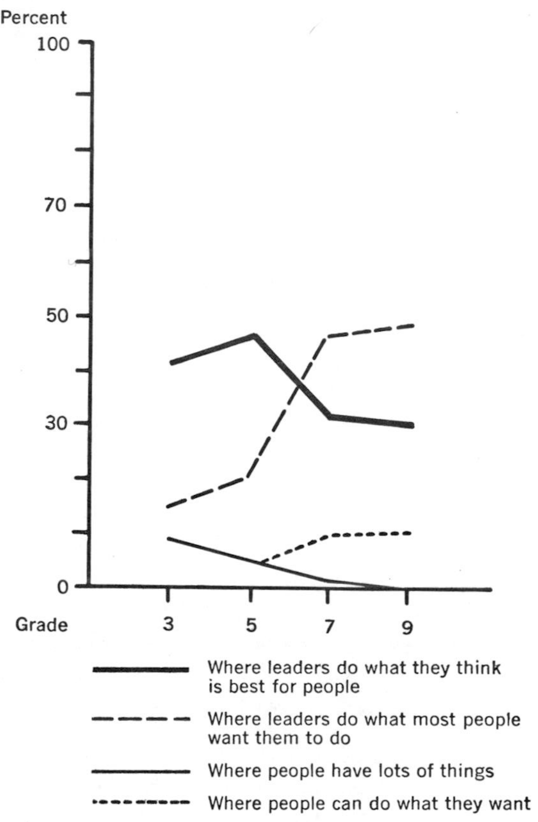

major urban area of the United States hold similar images of government with respect to some matters and diverge on others. There are great similarities to the extent that both groups fail to see government very clearly and accurately in the lower grades. All young children seem to hold a rather diffuse image of government, seeing it as uniformly powerful, protective and nurturant. Further, they hold similar images of government with respect to its functional competence and their own goodwill throughout the grade cycle.

Yet significant differences exist between whites and blacks in the general pattern of development of orientations toward government with respect to paternalism and benevolence. Black children manifest serious deterioration in confidence between the third and seventh grades, but dramatically recover

Table 4 *Children's Conceptions of What Democracy Is, Controlling for Race and Social Class*

Grade	N	Where Leaders Do What They Think is Best for People		Where Leaders Do What Most People Want		Where People Do What They Want		Where People Have Lots of Things		Don't Know	
		Middle Class	Lower Class	Middle Class	Lower Class	Middle Class	Lower Class	Middle Class	Lower Class	Middle Class	Lower Class
						Black Children					
3	52	39		23		12		8		19	
	56		38		13		7		23		20
5	53	49		25		11		4		11	
	72		42		18		11		13		17
7	40	45		30		13		3		10	
	29		38		7		3		14		38
9	43	33		37		16		0		14	
	54		39		43		11		0		7
						White Children					
3	55	36		20		11		4		29	
	56		45		13		9		13		21
5	70	47		21		9		3		20	
	44		39		21		7		11		23
7	85	28		51		15		0		6	
	34		41		32		6		0		21
9	81	31		56		9		0		5	
	36		31		33		17		2		17

during the junior high school years. Moreover, the strongest recovery is displayed by those black students who are best able to perceive inequality in race relations! Finally, this recovery of attachment seems to be directed primarily toward the national government.

This fits quite well with a simple exchange interpretation of socialization to support. In such an interpretation, children grant positive attitudes toward government in response to governmental activities that are perceived to be helpful. We would thus expect gaps between black children and white children to increase with age as black children become aware of the nature of life around them and the place assigned by society to their fellows. One would expect a recovery in confidence in the national government as black children become aware of efforts of that government in behalf of black people in general. One would also expect to see these patterns exaggerated among the most perceptive children, since they would be most aware of their deprivation, and as they grew older, of governmental efforts to alleviate problems. In fact, the data do conform to these expectations, increasing our confidence in an exchange intepretation.

Moreover, several strands of evidence seem to indicate that as the black child moves from a rather personalistic view of government in the lower grades to an institutional view in the upper grades, he tends to acquire a nascent "subject orientation" relative to the "participant" orientation of the white child. This adds evidence to the suggestion that the older black child comes to see the national government as a kind of benevolent protector.

An important question to be answered is whether this late rally to the national government by black children may best be described as specific or diffuse support.[27] In Easton's terms, specific support is that support offered by a citizen in return for the satisfaction of some specific attachment; attachment to a political object for its own sake. In light of the older major findings of this project (e.g., that black children demonstrate declining affect for the American political community, the President and police),[28] it would seem logical to suggest that the prominent late rebound in affect by black children may best be described as specific and not diffuse support.

A reasonable explanation for the reversal of affect for the national government and the continued decline for the other major elements of the political system among black children is the existence of highly visible civil rights activities by the former over the past two decades.

Apparently, black children come to realize that certain demands or wants of their community have been met by national government activities. Other sectors of the political system have not been as responsive. Most local jurisdictions have been notably lax in responding to the needs of the black community. The private sector has been even less flexible and beneficent. It does not seem unreasonable to suggest that the national government comes to be seen by these children as a general protector against the remainder of the political and social order. To retain this position, it would appear that government must continue to produce values for which children can trade sentiment.

ENDNOTES

1. This theme has gained a certain popularity in American political science. For the best statements on this theme see V. O. Key, *Public Opinion and American Democracy* (New York: Knopf, 1961); Robert Lane, *Political Ideology* (New York: The Free Press, 1962); and Lester Milbraith, *Political Participation* (New York: Rand-McNally, 1965).

2. See especially Robert Lane, *Political Life* (New York: The Free Press, 1959); Donald Matthews and James Prothro, *Negroes and the New Southern Politics* (New York: Harcourt, Brace and World, 1966); Milbraith, *Political Participation;* and James Q. Wilson, *Negro Politics* (Glencoe: The Free Press, 1960).

3. For useful summaries of this literature, see Richard Dawson, "Political Socialization," in James A. Robinson (ed.), *Political Science Annual,* Vol. I, 1966 (Indianapolis: Bobbs-Merrill Co., 1966); Richard Dawson and Kenneth Prewitt, *Political Socialization* (New York: Little, Brown & Co., 1969); and Fred Greenstein, "Political Socialization," *The International Encyclopedia of the Social Sciences* (New York: The Macmillan Co., and The Free Press, 1968).

4. This statement does not deny the importance of later changes, although the literature does suggest that except in extraordinary times, basic attachments, loyalties and identifications are made at a relatively tender age. For discussions of adult socialization, see Orville G. Brim, Jr. and Stanton Wheeler, *Socialization after Childhood* (New York: Wiley, 1965); Matilda W. Riley, *et al.*, "Socialization for the Middle and Later Years," in David A. Goslin (ed.), *Handbook of Socialization Theory and Research* (Chicago: Rand-McNally, 1969).

5. An excellent statement of this position may be found in Kenneth Clark, *Dark Ghetto* (New York: Harper and Row, 1965).

6. See note No. 3 for reviews of that research.

7. *Ibid.* A notable exception is Dean Jaros, *et al.*, "The Malevolent Leader: Political Socialization in an American Sub-Culture," *The American Political Science Review*, Vol. LXII (June 1968), 574–575.

8. The latter also involves a level of resources not available to the researcher.

9. For a number of excellent articles which highlight the relative economic positions of black and white see the following collections: Talcott Parsons and Kenneth Clark, *The Negro American* (Boston: Beacon Press, 1965); and Louis A. Ferman, *et al.*, Poverty in America (Ann Arbor: University of Michigan Press, 1965).

10. An excellent discussion of this phenomenon may be found in St. Clair Drake and Horace Cayton, *Black Metropolis: A Study of Negro Life in a Northern City* (New York: Harper and Row, 1945).

11. Census data reveal that the ratio between white collar and blue collar in metropolitan areas for whites is 1:1 and for blacks is 1:2.5. (Skilled labor was included in the white collar group for blacks given the different interpretation of the meaning of occupation in the black community discussed above.) Since approximately equal numbers of children were sampled in each group, the black lower class sample was weighted by a factor of 2.5 to allow for general statements about black children in Philadelphia. Failure to weight the sample would have seriously overrepresented the black middle class.

12. Louis McQuitty, "Elementary Factor Analysis," *Psychological Reports* IV (1961), 71–78.

13. The items are as follows:

		Factor Loadings
Goodwill	The government is/isn't very friendly	1.00
	The government almost never makes/makes a lot of mistakes	.44
	I'm often afraid of the government/I'm hardly ever afraid of the government	.27
Role Performance	The government knows/doesn't know a lot	1.00
	The government is/isn't very powerful	.46
Paternalism-Benevolence	The government cares/doesn't care about us	1.00
	The government is/isn't very helpful	.54
	The government can/can't be trusted	.50

14. In dealing with children and the development of political orientations, one faces certain intractable problems not faced in normal opinion research. That is, the problem of changing orientations with maturation makes the use of indices more precarious. In adult populations, it is usually the case that one finds consistent factors over most age groups and indices are easily built. With children, one has the case where a situation of no structure in world view evolves into a structured one as the child grows older. In short, one does not have the luxury of consistency. And yet, we still persist in the use of these indices. Why do we do so?

We do so because we face a similar problem using item analysis. The meaning of items changes for children with maturation, so as researchers we are always faced with inconsistency when dealing with children. Logically, the problem of consistency is not eliminated by moving from index analysis to item analysis.

Thus, indices are constructed with the full realization that they are based upon item clusters that do not appear until the upper grades. We must proceed on the assumption that latent structure exists in the lower grades and becomes apparent in the upper grades. This is not as farfetched as it sounds. If we compare the graphs of development of each item, items within clusters are almost identical to each other and differ significantly from items in the other clusters.

15. No social class differences are evident on this index, so that the data are not reported.

16. Key, *Public Opinion and American Democracy,* makes perhaps the most persuasive defense of this position.

17. This item, accuracy of perception, would seem to be a potentially powerful variable. In the first place, as mentioned in the text, political communities are stratified by levels of political information and sophistication, a phenomenon which is closely tied to significant differences in political behavior. Second, the various riot commission reports of recent years have all pointed out that riot participants tend to be more politically aware. That is, disaffection seems to be tied to knowledge. It would be interesting, therefore to examine at what point in the socialization process such a linkage is made.

While only a single item is used to assess accuracy of perception, it is highly correlated with other information items in the test instrument, thus reinforcing confidence in its use.

18. No social class differences are evident.

19. The reversal is even more striking with respect to two of the items in the index: government as helpful and caring.

20. Kenneth P. Langton and M. Kent Jennings, "Political Socialization and the High School Civics Curriculum in the United States," *American Political Science Review,* Vol. 62 (September, 1968), 852–867.

21. A number of sources are useful here. See William Brink and Louis Harris, *Black and White* (New York: Simon and Schuster, 1966); Detroit Urban League and The Detroit Free Press, "The People Beyond 12th Street: A Survey of Attitudes of Detroit Negroes After the Riot of 1967"; Report of the President's Advisory Commission on Civil Disorders (New York: Bantam, 1968).

22. Again, no social class differences are evident.

23. Langton and Jennings, "Political Socialization and The High School Civics Curriculum in the United States."

24. Gabriel Almond and Sidney Verba, *The Civic Culture* (Princeton: Princeton University Press, 1963), p. 19.

25. White lower class children tend to see government as least responsive. This is evident in the depressing frequency of comments such as "niggers get everything."

26. Statements of this position are too numerous to cite. For perhaps the most cogent argument see Warren Haggstrom, "The Power of the Poor," in Louis Fermin, *et al.* (eds.), *Poverty in America* (Ann Arbor: University of Michigan Press, 1965).

27. See the discussion of diffuse support in David Easton, *A Systems Analysis of Political Life* (New York: Wiley, 1965).

28. See Edward S. Greenberg, *Political Socialization to Support of the System: A Comparison of Black and White Children* (Unpublished Ph.D. dissertation. University of Wisconsin, 1969). Time and space limitations make the reporting of this data impossible. A few representative items from that larger study are instructive.

	Percent of black children by grade affirming the following propositions		
Grade	I like the President	I like the Policeman	The United States flag is best (out of a series of flags presented)
3	79	91	96
5	51	68	92
7	28	44	90
9	37	45	71

PART 4

SHAPING PUBLIC OPINION

PART 4

AN OVERVIEW

Public opinion can be influenced in a variety of ways ranging from subtle indirect persuasion to direct propaganda techniques. Much of socialization exemplifies the more indirect techniques of persuasion. Individuals are taught to conform to the values and goals of society by agents of socialization such as family, school, and church. The teaching of societal norms is often nondeliberate, and the agents are often unaware of their role in transmitting values. Individuals are introduced to these norms gradually, and they, in turn, are very often unaware that learning is taking place. Some of these indirect techniques of influencing public opinion have been treated in the preceding selections. In this section, instead, we address ourselves to the more deliberate efforts at molding public opinion. In general, such efforts take place over a short period of time and involve relatively specific goals on the part of those attempting to influence or manipulate opinion. Political and commercial public relations and advertising campaigns, propaganda, and censorship are all examples of direct attempts to influence public opinion. The following discussion is divided into categories relating to these questions: What is the more effective channel for influencing opinion—personal persuasion or mass media? How reliable are the mass media in terms of presenting unbiased information? What are the techniques for influencing public opinion?

METHODS OF INFLUENCE: PERSONAL PERSUASION VS. MASS COMMUNICATION

In general, personal persuasion has been found to be more effective than the mass media in influencing opinions and behavior. In the 1940 presidential election campaign, for example, persons who changed their vote intention cited personal influence as responsible more frequently than the mass media (Lazarsfeld, Berelson, and Gaudet, 1944). An analysis of opinion concerning movies, fashions, food, and public affairs revealed that personal communication was a more persuasive channel of influence than newspapers, radio, magazines, or books (Katz and Lazarsfeld, 1955).

It is not too surprising that personal communication is more effective than mass-media communication. There are several reasons why we might expect this to be so. For one thing, personal contacts are generally treated as nonpurposive. When people confront us, we are not expecting that they will attempt to persuade us, and in the course of the conversation we may find ourselves altering our opinions almost unknowingly. The mass media, on the other hand, confront people when they are, so to speak, on guard. There is an expectation that persuasion will be attempted. Second, personal interaction allows greater flexibility of communication. The persuader can tailor his message to the individual, as well as work around the listener's biases by responding directly to his objections. Third, personal communication can be followed by "rewards," such as expressions of personal approval. Individuals are more likely to give the desired response if rewarded. Fourth, there is frequently trust between people in interpersonal exchanges, which not only facilitates communication but makes persuasion more likely. Finally, people are more apt to be emotionally affected by interpersonal requests than by the more formal presentations of the media. All of these factors conspire to make personal communication more effective than mass communication in influencing opinion (Lazarsfeld, Berelson, and Gaudet, 1944).

Mass communication, by itself, is rarely an effective instrument of persuasion (Klapper, 1960). There are several reasons for this. First, there is a large group of persons who represent a "hard core of know nothings," as Hyman and Sheatsley point out in the article that follows *(see pp. 291–93)*. They do not tune to the media, therefore cannot be influenced by them. That relatively few follow public affairs in the media is confirmed in *The Civic Culture*—barely 50 per cent report following such matters in newspapers and magazines and on television and radio (Almond and Verba, 1965). Even during political campaigns, when interest peaks and information abounds, some people remain unexposed to political communication. During the 1972 presidential election, 57 percent indicated following the campaigns in newspapers, and 42 and 32 percent respectively on radio and in magazines. While 88 per cent reported following the campaigns on television, for many this was probably passive and inadvertent exposure. In short, one serious limitation of the mass media's effectiveness as a channel for influencing opinion is simply that it doesn't reach a significant portion of the population.

Certain psychological and sociological processes also limit the media's effectiveness as a channel for influencing opinion. It is a standing proposition among social scientists that attention to the media is selective. People tune in information that reinforces existing predispositions and tune out information that conflicts with such predispositions. In the 1940 and 1948 presidential elections, Lazarsfeld, Berelson, and others report that, in spite of a clear Republican bias in what was presented to the voters, both Republicans and Democrats were likely to hear information reinforcing their existing vote intention (Lazarsfeld, Berelson, and Gaudet, 1944; Berelson, Lazarsfeld, and McPhee, 1954). A need for consistency directs people to expose themselves to and perceive only that information which is congenial to their existing dispositions. Rarely does contrary or conflicting information filter through the psychological barriers. People do indeed have an extraordinary capacity to ignore what upsets them and to hear what they want to hear.

A further limitation on media effectiveness stems from the fact that only those interested in the subject are likely to pick up information. And it is the most interested who are the most rigid in their attitudes, and the least likely to be converted by what they read or hear in the media. Converse observes, for example, that those who are most likely to be exposed to political campaigns through the media are also those who are most extreme in their attitudes and the least likely to be swayed by outside influences. The fact that they are interested implies a store of information which insulates them from incoming information (Converse, 1960). It is something of a paradox that information campaigns have the greatest prospect of converting those persons who are the least likely to be exposed to them.

From the standpoint of sociological processes, it has been observed that so-called group forces also reduce the effectiveness of the media to persuade (Klapper, 1960). People receive most of their political orientation from groups to which they belong or to which they aspire. Opinions and attitudes are reinforced and made more intense by social contacts (which relates to personal persuasion, as discussed above). A notable finding from the 1948 presidential election was that Democrats who toyed with defecting at the start of the campaign returned to the Democratic Party following discussions with peers and coworkers who were voting for Truman. A vote for Truman was a group norm for members of the Democatic Party, and interaction with other group members reinforced that norm (Berelson, Lazarsfeld, and McPhee, 1954; Campbell, et al., 1960). On occasion a stimulus may be so strong that group members will violate group norms. Wholesale defections of partisans in the 1952, 1956, 1964, 1968, and 1972 elections testify to this. However, defections were more widespread among weak than strong partisans (Boyd, 1969).

One study has catalogued the conditions under which group forces are particularly strong in directing the political behavior of group members: 1. When there is an obvious and direct relationship between the group and political affairs—in other words, the group is tied in some way to politics. 2. When group standards are transmitted to group members— that is, group members are informed how "good" group members should behave. 3. When members feel that the group has a right to influence their judgment; that what the group asks it has a legitimate right to ask (Campbell, et al., 1964). The religious issue in the 1960 presidential election is illustrative. John Kennedy was a Roman Catholic. This was widely known among Catholics, and many perceived religion as a legitimate basis for deciding between the candidates. Strong group influences were set in motion and strong Catholics responded accordingly (Campbell, et al., 1964; Stokes, 1966).

It has been contended that the media work indirectly through interpersonal influence to persuade people. Much of what the mass media communicate reaches people via interpersonal communication. "Opinion leaders" may receive information from the mass media and then pass it along to personal acquaintances.[1] This is often referred to as the "two-step flow" of communications. In effect, the two-step flow of communication assures a double screening of information between media and mass public. The opinion leader himself, through the psychological process of selective exposure and perception described above, screens out uncongenial aspects of the communication, and screens again when he transmits the news to acquaintances. Opinion leaders not only unconsciously select out uncongenial aspects of communication, but they may consciously omit what may jeopardize their position vis-à-vis the group.

By way of summary, we can assert that mass communication is severely limited as an instrument of persuasion. Mass communication either fails to reach large segments of the population or serves primarily to reinforce what people already believe. Certain psychological processes direct persons to communication consistent with their existing dispositions. Certain social processes, such as group or opinion-leader influence, further dilute the effectiveness of the media as a channel for influencing opinion.

Conversions in response to media appeals do sometimes occur. When this happens, the processes discussed above are usually inoperative or work in the interest of opinion change rather than reinforcement (Klapper, 1960). The process of selective perception may not always be effective in insulating the individual from gaining information that conflicts with his opinions, for example. Also, group influence may be dormant at times as, for instance, when the group fails to communicate its expectations to its membership. Without such guidance, the group members are more susceptible to media (or other) influences. Also, members may feel the group has no right to influence their judgment in a particular area. For example, union members may feel that the union leaders should not give partisan political advice. In such a case, Converse and Campbell have shown that union members are less likely to vote Democratic (if the union leaders are making a Democratic appeal) than fellow union members who believe that it is quite proper for the union leadership to be involved in partisan political recommendations (1960).

In short, there are conditions in which media appeals can be effective, and knowledge of these conditions can be used to develop successful appeals and determine the appropriate medium for their transmission, as the following Mendelsohn reading indicates *(see pp. 304–15)*.

Despite the fact that the media have a limited capability for influencing opinion, they remain an important source of information. One important capability of television and radio is their ability to transmit information rapidly. News, almost regardless of where and when it occurs, can be transmitted virtually instantaneously. News of the assassination of President Kennedy reached the American people minutes after it occurred. Hours after the tragedy, millions were aware (Sheatsley and Feldman, 1964). Occasionally, television and radio transmit news as it happens—the shooting of President Kennedy's alleged assassin being a dramatic example. It is reasonable to assume that the live coverage of the Senate Watergate hearings had more dramatic impact and resulted in greater awareness of the scandal than would have been true if people learned of the scandal by word of mouth or through newspaper accounts.

The media have also been successful in transmitting relatively highly sophisticated information. Media coverage of space flights and man's landings on the moon succeeded in bringing dramatic images and highly technical information to many as the events were taking place. Evidence suggests that the media successfully impart general knowledge of public affairs, scientific and health information, as well. Television remains the chief information source regarding public affairs, while the print media are chief sources of scientific and health information (Wade and Schramm, 1969). By transmitting certain information, at times the media, particularly television and radio, have been capable of arousing people to action—at least toward those actions to which they were predisposed. An analysis of the 1967 riot in Detroit for example found that the media stimulated some people to participate (Singer, 1970). One may suppose that mass media not only inform people about the more routine political activities such as elections, but may very well encourage participation in such activities.

The media are also instrumental in setting the agenda of political campaigns. News stories and features seem to be quite effective in delineating the major issues of political campaigns and, though the media report the various positions of the candidates, voters appear to follow the news in determining what the major issues are (McCombs and Shaw, 1972). On the other hand, Stevenson et al., in the selection that follows *(pp. 325–26),* point out that, as far as television coverage of political campaigns is concerned, the emphasis tends to be on the conduct of the campaign, rather than on the substantive issues that define the compaign.

This "agenda setting" function occurs on a more general level as well. If the mass media give a good deal of attention to the Middle East situation, then people are more likely to be aware of that situation. "Poverty in America" existed long before journalists started discussing it, but the mass public only became aware of it after TV specials and news coverage. In conclusion, it is reasonable to say that the media have far greater impact in determining *what* people will think about, rather than *how* they will think about it.

BIAS IN THE MEDIA

Given that the media are important channels for transmitting information, it is appropriate to ask how reliable is the information that they transmit. Some background facts are relevant here. Newspapers are generally owned by wealthy businessmen, persons of rather conservative persuasion. Very often, this carries over to the editorial page of the newspaper. For example, most newspapers endorse conservative and Republican candidates. Further, owners and editors are sometimes reluctant to espouse policies contrary to the business interests of the community for fear of jeopardizing advertising revenue. Some contend that the recent growth of the monopoly newspaper has given added freedom to newspapers. With only one newspaper in a community, owners are naturally less fearful of losing advertising revenue as a result of taking positions contrary to the interests of local business. The business man simply has nowhere else to take his business. Practically, however, one might expect business people and the average newspaper owner to agree on most policies. Newspapers are money-making enterprises, and newspapers don't make money without advertising.

Offsetting the conservative bias of most editorial pages is the somewhat more liberal orientation of journalists, although the extent to which this influences news stories is problematic. Guarding against extreme bias is the professional orientation of most newsmen. A basic part of training for newsmen is learning to limit the extent to which they allow personal feelings to influence their reporting. Thus, while ownership and business concerns may influence editorial policy in one way, the liberal orientation of many news writers and, more importantly, their commitment to professional impartiality tends to offset this.

Where bias does exist, to what extent does it influence the public? The answer is that it can have some influence, particularly when other agents of influence are missing. In local controversies or elections, for example, newspapers may be the only source of cues concerning opinion for most people. Under such circumstances the press can play a forceful role. In primary elections where voters have relatively little information regarding the candidates, press endorsements can be decisive. Naturally a newspaper can be particularly influential where it is the sole paper in a community. Studies have shown that most cities under 100,000 population do have only one newspaper, although many of these cities have other media "voices" such as radio and TV (Nixon and Ward, 1966).

In other instances, press support is of little importance. In presidential elections, for example, the Republican candidate generally receives the overwhelming support of the nation's newspapers, but this has not resulted in a disproportionate number of Republican victories. In short, while newspapers have some potential for manipulating opinion, the structure of the press in the United States which tends to result in objectivity, coupled with the fact that Americans receive information from a variety of other sources, limits the extent to which newspapers can direct public opinion.

Television is subject to many of the same constraints as newspapers. As with newspapers, television is essentially a money-making business, and this, to a degree, influences what is presented. In television too, reporters and commentators are trained to present news impartially. Because television is licensed by the federal government, the material it presents comes under greater scrutiny and control than is generally exercised over newspapers. Since airwaves are deemed "public property," it is reasonable that steps be taken to ensure that television reporting is conducted with as much restraint and impartiality as possible. In the main, most researchers find that the networks do a respectable job of presenting the news in an unbiased and balanced way. For instance, in a study of bias in the news coverage of the Vietnam War, Russo (1972) found little bias over a two-year period against the Nixon Administration's policies. No more attention was given to those opposed to the war than to those supporting it. Other studies of coverage of the Vietnam War have shown that media statements casting the war in an unfavorable light followed rather than preceded shifts in public opinion against the war. In their analysis of the 1968 election campaign coverage by one major network, Stevenson et al. *(see pp. 324–25)* disclosed quite similar treatment of both major candidates. George Wallace, the third party candidate, was presented in a manner that did not significantly differ from that accorded Humphrey and Nixon. Current studies seem to indicate that most charges of bias in the media favoring a particular position or candidate are not borne out when tested rigorously.

The selection of what news stories are to be covered is perhaps more likely to reflect bias. It is in this area that journalists have the greatest discretion. Usually, however, there is great similarity across news networks in the stories that are presented (Pride and Warmsley, 1972). These basic similarities of presentation are not due to any conspiracy to air or suppress particular news items. The content of newscasts is dictated by the "newsworthiness" of certain stories and by certain production limitations. For example, stories are more likely to be covered if they occur in large cities where the networks have access to video equipment or if the news coverage can be scheduled in advance, as when the President calls a news conference or schedules a television address.

TECHNIQUES FOR INFLUENCING OPINION: PUBLIC RELATIONS AND POLITICAL CAMPAIGNS

The success of public relations campaigns—campaigns deliberately designed to promote a product, candidate, or cause—seems to be conditioned by a number of factors quite independent of the merit of the product or candidate being promoted. Public relations can be quite successful in influencing public reaction to relatively trivial matters, such as consumer behavior with respect to small store purchases. Most of us do not attach a great deal of significance to the kind of toothpaste we buy; we are open to influence. A public relation campaign on the merit of fluoridation can, for example, influence us to buy a particular brand or a particular product. Even when attitudes are firmly established, promotion may bring about a change.[2] Continuous exposure to promotion leads to perceptual change regarding some products. Purchase of the product leads to a change in attitude. The process characterizes situations where there are few connections or links between the individual's personal life and the object in question. Similarly, an extensive promotion campaign by one candidate for an obscure nonpartisan local political office may have some effect because people are generally uninvolved and uninformed about the office and candidate.

In other situations where patterns of behavior are more established—for example, in an important political election, public relation campaigns are less successful. The inefficacy of most political campaigns is revealed by the fact that in major partisan elections many people make up their minds whom to vote for even before a campaign begins. This is particularly true in presidential elections, where two-thirds or more decide how to vote before the campaign is under way. In 1972, for example, 62 per cent reported whom they would support for president before the campaign began. This left only one-third of the electorate to be influenced by the campaign. Characteristically, these late deciders are the least likely to be interested in politics (Lazarsfeld, Berelson, and Gaudet, 1944). Among this group are a large number of independents, persons who do not identify with a political party. Independents are generally less interested in politics and less concerned with the outcome of political contests than partisans. This lack of involvement means either that the independents are not particularly concerned with making a decision or that they have too little information, at the time, upon which to base a decision. Another characteristic of late deciders is that many are cross-pressured, i.e., they are rather ambivalent about candidates, issues, and parties and, as a consequence, they will either refrain from participating or will seek information which will allow them to decide.

It would be risky, however, to assert that political media campaigns have no influence. In a tight election, such as the 1960 Kennedy-Nixon one, late deciders may cast the deciding votes, and these are the people who may be influenced by media appeals.

The above comments on public relations campaigns apply as well to advertising compaigns where political groups buy media space or time to "sell" a candidate or their position on a political issue. Probably Mc Ginniss overstated the point when he attributed the victory of Richard Nixon in 1968 to his well-organized television campaign activity (Mc Ginniss, 1968). However, other findings have indicated that TV spot ads for candidates do have some impact on the uncommitted voter (Atkin, et al., 1973). Viewers find themselves inadvertently listening to spot advertisements. Many of the voters Atkin questioned indicated that political ads helped them make up their minds or reinforced their existing decision, although in several cases this was due more to their dislike for the ads of one candidate than to the effectiveness of the ads of another. In other words, TV spot ads "turned off" voters as well as stimulated positive feelings toward one candidate or another.

GOVERNMENT'S INFLUENCE ON PUBLIC OPINION

While most people are aware of overt government attempts to manipulate opinion in some contexts, few give much thought to the extent to which government influences our opinions and even our more basic attitudes and beliefs. Murray Edelman (1971), in a perceptive book dealing in part with this phenomenon notes that:

> Government affects behavior chiefly by shaping the cognitions of large numbers of people in ambiguous situations. It helps create their beliefs about what is proper; their perceptions of what is fact; and their expectations of what is to come.

The success of the government in shaping opinions, in Edelman's view, may be attributed to the fact that most of us have few cues that compete with those the government gives, particularly in terms of shaping future expectations. In the following selection *(pp. 329–35)*, Edelman notes that by and large, it is governmental cues that convince us that some group or nation is the enemy, that other nations or groups are friends, that the government is capable of handling the complex situations facing our nation, and that certain kinds of behavior are evil (prostitution, gambling, marijuana or liquor usage, for example) while other kinds of behavior, such as participating in a war declared by our nation, are acceptable or even commendable. Of course, as Edelman points out, our opinions and beliefs are shaped by many factors other than the government, but the impact of government influence on opinion is more apt to be overlooked or minimized.

In addition to this routine (but extensive) impact on our opinions, governments also have at their disposal other means of opinion manipulation and influence that range from censorship to outright lying. It has become increasingly clear that the American government, as well as other governments of both democratic and dictatorial varieties, engage in several of these more covert activities in an effort to mold and manipulate public opinion. While in the United States censorship has generally been used only in emergency situations, the growing practice of classifying as "secret" documents that tend to discredit governmental policies or actions is one form of censorship. A recent example of the attempt of government to "censor" information damaging to it was the Pentagon Papers case. In that case the government attempted to stop several major newspapers, most particularly the *New York Times,* from printing material concerning the history of U.S. policies toward Vietnam, justifying this attempt at censorship on the basis that the material came from governmental files that had been classified as secret. In a split decision, the Supreme Court ruled that government did not have the right to exercise this form of prior censorship on the newspapers. A good deal of justification for censorship currently rests with the proposition that the government has the right to withhold information damaging to national security. Clearly, the broader the definition of national security the greater the potential for this form of censorship.

Lying is another technique of opinion manipulation which seems to have been repeatedly used in recent American history, as Wise points out in the last selection of this section *(pp. 336–45)*. At times the government has sought to influence public opinion either by denying that certain unpopular activities have taken place or by falsely asserting that other activities have occurred which justified what would otherwise have been unacceptable governmental action. While the full facts regarding the Tonkin Gulf incident —the alleged firing of North Vietnamese ships on American crafts—and the invasion of Cambodia in 1970 with the later denial of bombing in Cambodia have not yet come to light, it seems naive to believe that deliberate lying to the public and Congress on the part of the Administration was not involved (Wise, 1973). Governmental attempts to "cover up" the Watergate break-in represent an even clearer example of deception in an effort to manipulate public opinion in order to avoid loss of popular support.

The line between the natural human tendency to want to place one's best face forward (which Presidents and bureaucrats share with the rest of us) and the deliberate distortion of facts in order to manipulate public opinion is, at times, a blurred one. Though our government's suppression and distortion of the news certainly is not on a level with that found in many other countries, these methods of manipulating opinion have been the source of increasing concern in recent years.

ENDNOTES

1. Opinion leaders are scattered throughout the population, and in some respects are much like the people they influence. Opinion leaders are usually leaders in only one sphere of activity—business or politics, for example—but not both. Aside from being more likely to hear and retain information from the media, opinion leaders, at least in public affairs, tend to be different from the rest of the public in that they are more highly educated and are engaged in more prestigious occupations. Further, they score higher on measures of political efficacy, political information, and political participation. They are also more likely to

split their tickets in elections and switch from one party to another in successive elections (Kingdon, 1970). In short, they seem to typify the well-informed citizen.

2. When brought about by advertising, Herbert Krugman labels the process "learning without involvement" (1965).

REFERENCES AND FURTHER READING

Almond, Gabriel A., and Verba, Sidney. *The Civic Culture: Political Attitudes and Democracy in Five Nations.* Boston: Little, Brown, & Co., 1965.

Atkin, Charles K., et al. "Quality versus Quantity in Televised Political Ads." *Public Opinion Quarterly* 37 (1973): 209–224.

Bagdikian, Ben H. *The Information Machines: Their Impact on Men and the Media.* New York: John Wiley & Sons, 1971.

Berelson, Bernard R.; Lazarsfeld, Paul F.; and McPhee, William N. *Voting: A Study of Opinion Formation in Presidential Campaigns.* Chicago: University of Chicago Press, 1954.

Boyd, Richard W. "Presidential Elections: An Explanation of Voting Defections," *American Political Science Review* 63 (1969): 498–514.

Campbell, Angus, et al. *The American Voter.* New York: John Wiley & Sons, 1964.

Converse, Philip E. "Information Flow and the Stability of Partisan Attitudes." In *Elections and the Political Order,* edited by Angus Campbell et al. New York: John Wiley & Sons, 1960.

Converse, Philip E., and Campbell, Angus. "Political Standards in Secondary Groups." In *Group Dynamics: Research and Theory,* edited by Dorwin Cartwright and Alvin Zander. New York: Harper & Row, 1960.

Edelman, Murray. *Politics as Symbolic Action: Mass Arousal and Quiescence.* Chicago: Marham Publishing, 1971.

Fedler, Fred. "The Media and Minority Groups: A Study of Adequacy of Access." *Journalism Quarterly* 50 (1973): 109–117.

Glaser, William A. "Television and Voting." *Public Opinion Quarterly* 29 (1965): 71–86.

Hyman, Herbert, and Sheatsley, Paul B. "Some Reasons Why Information Campaigns Succeed." *Public Opinion Quarterly* 11 (1947): 412–423.

Katz, Elihu. "The Two-Step Flow of Communication: An Up-to-Date Report on an Hypothesis." *Public Opinion Quarterly* 21 (1957): 61–78.

Katz, Elihu, and Lazarsfeld, Paul F. *Personal Influence: The Part Played by People in the Flow of Mass Communication.* New York: Free Press, 1955.

Kingdon, John W. "Opinion Leaders in the Electorate." *Public Opinion Quarterly* 34 (1970): 256–261.

Klapper, Joseph T. *The Effect of Mass Communication.* New York: Free Press, 1960.

Krugman, Herbert E. "The Impact of Television Advertising: Learning Without Involvement." *Public Opinion Quartely 29* (1965): 349–356.

Lazarsfeld, Paul F.; Berelson, Bernard R.; and Gaudet, Hazel. *The People's Choice: How the Voter Makes Up His Mind in a Presidential Campaign.* New York: Columbia University Press, 1944.

McCombs, Maxwell E., and Shaw, Donald L. "The Agenda-Setting Function of Mass Media." *Public Opinion Quarterly* 36 (1972): 176–187.

McGinniss, Joe. *The Selling of the President, 1968.* New York: Trident Press, 1969.

Mendelsohn, Harold. "Some Reasons Why Information Campaigns Can Succeed." *Public Opinion Quarterly* 37 (1973): 50–61.

Mendelsohn, Harold, and Crespi, Irving. *Polls, Television and the New Politics.* Scranton, Pa.: Chandler, 1970.

Nimmo, Dan. *The Political Persuaders: The Techniques of Modern Elections Campaigns.* Englewood Cliffs, N.J.: Prentice-Hall, 1970.

Nixon, Raymond B., and Ward, Jean. "Trends in Newspaper Ownership." In *Reader in Public Opinion and Communication*, edited by Bernard R. Berelson and Morris Janowitz. New York: Free Press, 1966.

Pride, Richard, and Warmsley, Gary "Symbol Analysis of Network Coverage of the Laos Invasion." *Journalism Quarterly* 49 (1972): 635–640.

Russo, Frank D. "A Study of Bias in TV Coverage of the Vietnam War: 1969-1970." *Public Opinion Quarterly* 35 (Winter 1971-1972): 539–543.

Sheatsley, Paul B., and Feldman, Jacob J. "The Assassination of President Kennedy: A Preliminary Report on Reactions and Behavior." *Public Opinion Quarterly* 26 (1964): 189–215.

Simon, Herbert A., and Stern, Frederick. "The Effect of Television on Voting Behavior in the 1952 Presidential Election." *American Political Science Review* 49 (1955): 10–13.

Singer, Benjamin D. "Mass Media and Communication Processes in the Detroit Riot of 1967." *Public Opinion Quarterly* 34 (1970): 236–245.

Stevenson, Robert L., et al. "Untwisting the News Twister: A Replication of Efron's Study." *Journalism Quarterly* 60 (1973): 211–219.

Stokes, Donald E. "Some Dynamic Elements of Contests for the Presidency." *American Political Science Review* 60 (1966): 19–28.

Swinehart, James W., and McLeod, Jack M. "Channels, Audiences, and Effects." *Public Opinion Quarterly* 24 (1960): 583–589.

Wade, Serena, and Schramm, William. "The Mass Media as a Source of Knowledge." *Public Opinion Quarterly* 33 (1969): 197–209.

Wells, Alan. *Mass Media and Society.* Palo Alto, Cal.: National Press Books, 1972.

Wise, David. *The Politics of Lying: Government Deception, Secrecy, and Power.* New York: Random House, 1973.

Reprinted from *The Public Opinion Quarterly,* 11 (1947), with permission of the publisher and authors.

Some Reasons Why Information Campaigns Fail

HERBERT H. HYMAN
and
PAUL B. SHEATSLEY

The Charter of the United Nations Educational, Scientific and Cultural Organization contains the following significant statement:

> . . . the States parties to this Constitution . . . are agreed and determined to develop and to increase the means of communication between their peoples and to employ these means for the purposes of mutual understanding and a truer and more perfect knowledge of each other's lives. To realize this purpose the Organization will . . . recommend such international agreements as may be necessary to promote the free flow of ideas by word and image.

As a preliminary step, the Preparatory Commission of UNESCO has instructed the Secretariat to survey the obstacles in the way of such a program.[1] These obstacles to be surveyed include such things as the breakdown and inadequacy of existing communication facilities in many parts of the world, and the political, commercial and economic restrictions which hamper the free exchange of information throughout the United Nations.

But even if all these *physical* barriers to communication were known and removed there would remain many *psychological* barriers to the free flow of ideas. It is the purpose of this paper to demonstrate some of these psychological factors that impede communication and thereby to formulate certain principles and guides which must be considered in mass information campaigns. Existence of these psychological factors will be demonstrated by a variety of data gathered in recent surveys of the American public by the National Opinion Research Center, and one general truth is implied throughout the discussion:

The physical barriers to communication merely impede the *supply* of information. In order to increase public knowledge, not only is it necessary to *present* more information, but it is essential that the mass audience *be exposed to* and that it *absorb* the information. And in order to insure such exposure and absorption, *the psychological characteristics of human beings must be taken into account.*

To assume a perfect correspondence between the nature and amount of material presented in an information campaign and its absorption by the public, is to take a naive view, for the very nature and degree of public exposure to the material is determined to a large extent by certain psychological characteristics of the people themselves.[2] A number of these psychological characteristics are discussed below under the following topics:

The Chronic "Know-Nothing's" in Relation to Information Campaigns
The Role of Interest in Increasing Exposure
Selective Interpretation Following Exposure
Differential Changes in Attitudes After Exposure

THERE EXISTS A HARD CORE OF CHRONIC "KNOW-NOTHINGS"

All persons do not offer equal targets for information campaigns. Surveys consistently find that a certain proportion of the population is not familiar with any particular event. Offhand, it might be thought that information concerning that event was not distributed broadly enough to reach them, but that this group would still have an equal chance of exposure to other information. Yet, when the knowledge of this same group is measured with respect to a second event, they tend also to have little information in that area. And similarly, they will have little or no information concerning a third event.

If all persons provided equal targets for exposure and the sole determinant of public knowledge were the magnitude of the given information, there would be no reason for the same individuals always to show a relative lack of knowledge. *Instead, there is something about the uninformed which makes them harder to reach, no matter what the level or nature of the information.*

Thus, in May 1946, NORC asked a question to determine public knowledge of the report of the Anglo-American Committee on Palestine which recommended the admission of 100,000 Jewish immigrants to that country. Only 28 percent of the national sample expressed any awareness of this report. It might be assumed that the remaining 72 percent were ready and willing to be exposed, but that there had been too little information about the report. Yet Table 1 shows that this unaware group consistently tended to have less awareness of other information about the international scene which had been much more widely reported.

The size of this generally uninformed group in the population may be indicated by computing an index of general knowledge based on all five information questions in the field of foreign affairs, which were asked on that particular survey. The five subjects covered by these questions were:

1. The Palestine report spoken of above [1][3]
2. The Acheson-Lilienthal report on atomic energy [2]
3. The Paris meeting of the Big Four Foreign Ministers, then in progress [3]
4. The proposed loan to England, then being debated in Congress [4]
5. The political status of Palestine, the fact that she is ruled by England [5]

Table 2 shows how the population divided in its awareness of these five items. As may be seen, roughly one person out of seven reported no aware-

Table 1

Per cent Aware of:	*Group Which is Not Aware of Palestine Report*	*Group Which is Aware of Palestine Report*
Acheson-Lillienthal report on atomic energy	32%	64%
Spring 1946 meeting of Foreign Ministers in Paris	39%	85%
Proposed loan to England	73%	96%
	N=931	N=358

Table 2

Aware of:	*Per cent of National Sample*
No items	14%
One item	18
Two items	20
Three items	17
Four items	19
Five items	12
Total sample	100%
	N=1292

ness of *any* of the five items, and approximately one person in three had knowledge of more than *one* of them. This generally uninformed group, therefore, is of considerable magnitude.[4] It is possible, of course, that the existence of this group may be related to external factors of accessibility to information media, and that if the information were somehow channelled into their vicinity, they would soon become exposed. For example, information on foreign affairs is probably less easily available to small-town residents than it is to city-dwellers, and we find a relationship, as shown in Table 3, between size of community and awareness of our five items. These differences, however, are relatively small, in comparison with the psychological differences to be shown later in Table 4 and elsewhere. The next section discusses the effect of certain psychological factors on level of knowledge.

Table 3

Size of Community	*Mean Score on Knowledge Index Number of Items Known*
Metropolitan Districts over one million	2.81
Metropolitan Districts under one million	2.45
Cities 2,500 to 50,000	2.38
Towns under 2,500	2.28
Farm	2.03

INTERESTED PEOPLE ACQUIRE THE MOST INFORMATION

The importance of *motivation* in achievement or learning, or in assimilating knowledge, has been consistently shown in academic studies. Yet this important factor is often ignored in information campaigns, amid all the talk of "increasing the flow of information." The widest possible dissemination of material may be ineffective if it is not geared to the public's interests.

It is well known that opinion polls can measure areas of knowledge and ignorance, but the complementary areas of apathy and interests have been more often overlooked. Yet they can be just as readily measured, and they are highly significant in understanding the factors behind a given level of knowledge.

NORC, in a poll taken in May 1946, measured the public's interest in eight different issues in the field of foreign affairs [6]. These issues were:

1. Our relations with Russia
2. The atomic bomb
3. Our policy toward Germany
4. The United Nations organization
5. The British loan
6. The meeting of Foreign Ministers in Paris
7. Our relations with Franco Spain
8. Our policy toward Palestine

Public interest varied widely in these eight issues, ranging from 77 percent of the national sample which reported "considerable" or "great" interest in our relations with Russia to 28 percent which reported "considerable" or "great" interest in our policy toward Palestine. Thus, it is clear that each specific information campaign does not start with the same handicap in terms of public apathy. Motivation is high on some issues, low on others.

Nevertheless, there is consistent evidence that interest in foreign affairs tends to be *generalized*. Some people are interested in many or all of the issues; another large group is apathetic toward most or all of them. Intercorrelations (based on approximately 1290 cases) between interest in one issue and interest in each of the other seven, definitely establish this point. The 28 tetrachoric correlation coefficients range from .40 to .82, with a median r of .58. Table 4 shows how the population divides in its interest in these eight issues.

Table 4

		Per cent of Total Sample Expressing Considerable or Great Interest
"High Interest"		37%
All eight issues	11%	
Seven issues	11	
Six issues	15	
"Medium Interest"		40
Five issues	15	
Four issues	14	
Three issues	11	
"Low Interest"		23
Two issues	7	
One issue	5	
None of them	11	
		100%
		N=1292

It will be noticed that 11 percent of the sample expressed little or no interest in any of the eight issues, and that another 12 percent were interested in only one or two of them. Almost one-quarter of the population, therefore, reported interest in no more than two of the eight issues—a state of apathy all the more significant when it is remembered that the list included such overpowering subjects as the atomic bomb and our relations with Germany and Russia, and that the respondent's own estimate of his degree of interest, doubtless subject to prestige considerations, was accepted without question.

The close relationship between apathy on the one hand, and ignorance of information materials on the other, is shown in Table 5. It is a likely assumption that both the contrasted groups in the table had equal *opportunity* to learn about the two reports. Yet the information reached approximately half of the interested group, and only about one-fifth of the disinterested.[5]

The relationship between interest and knowledge can be demonstrated in a different way, if we compare the scores of each of our interest groups on our knowledge index. As seen in Table 6, at each stage of increasing interest, knowledge rises correspondingly.

It can be argued, of course, that the exposed people became interested after they had been exposed to the information, and that the disinterested

Table 5

	Per cent Who Have Heard of Acheson Report on Atomic Energy	
Respondents with great or considerable interest in atomic bomb	48%	N=953
Respondents with little or no interest in atomic bomb	20	N=337
	Per cent Who Have Heard of Anglo-American Report on Palestine	
Respondents with great or considerable interest in Palestine policy	51%	N=365
Respondents with little or no interest in Palestine policy	19	N=921

Table 6

Interested in:	*Mean Score on Knowledge Index*
No items	.85
One item	1.42
Two items	1.12
Three items	1.89
Four items	2.37
Five items	2.64
Six items	3.15
Seven items	3.50
Eight items	3.81
	N=1292

persons are apathetic only because they were not exposed. It is probable that the two factors *are* interdependent; as people learn more, their interest increases, and as their interest increases, they are impelled to learn more. Nevertheless, from the point of view of initiating a *specific* campaign at some point in time, it remains true that in the case even of outstanding public issues, large groups in the population admit "little or no interest" in the problem.

This fact cannot be ignored by those in charge of information campaigns. Such groups constitute a special problem which cannot be solved simply by "increasing the flow of information." *Scientific surveys are needed to determine who these people are, why they lack interest, and what approach can best succeed in reaching them.*

PEOPLE SEEK INFORMATION CONGENIAL TO PRIOR ATTITUDES

Information campaigns, while they involve the presentation of *facts*, nevertheless present materials which may or may not be congenial with the attitudes of any given individual. Lazarsfeld,[6] in describing the exposure of a sample panel to political campaign propaganda, concludes that "People selected political material in accord with their own taste and bias. Even those who had not yet made a decision (on their vote) exposed themselves to propaganda which fit their not-yet-conscious political predispositions."

Our evidence from polling national samples in other information areas supports the view that people tend to expose themselves to information which is congenial with their prior attitudes, and to avoid exposure to information which is not congenial. Although it was not possible to administer before-and-after tests of attitudes, the following technique offers indirect evidence to support the argument of selective exposure.

National samples were asked if they had heard or read anything about a given piece of information. The entire sample was then given the gist of the information in one or two sentences. (In the case of those who had admitted familiarity with the material, the description was prefaced by some such phrase as, "Well, as you remember. . . .") Immediately following the description of the information, the entire sample was then asked some relevant attitude question.

We found in every case that the group who reported prior exposure to the information had a different attitudinal reaction from those without prior exposure. One could assume that this difference reflected the influence of the information on those previously exposed, except that, as described above, *both groups*, before being asked the attitude question, had been supplied with identical descriptions of the information in question.

Thus, in June 1946, a national sample of the adult population was asked whether they had heard or read about the Anglo-American Committee report on Palestine [1]. Every respondent was then either told or reminded of the essential provisions of the report, and was asked whether he favored United States assistance in keeping order in Palestine if 100,000 additional Jews were admitted to that country [7]. As seen in Table 7, those with prior knowledge of the report were significantly more favorable toward such assistance.

Similarly, in April 1946, a national sample was asked whether they had heard or read about the recent joint statement by England, France, and the United States which denounced the Franco government of Spain [8]. Included in the question was the gist of the statement: "the hope that General Franco's government in Spain would soon be followed by a more democratic one." The entire sample was then asked its attitude toward this country's Spanish policy [9]. Again, those who had prior knowledge of the three-power statement were significantly more hostile in their attitudes toward Franco. (See Table 7.)

Table 7

	Per cent of Those With Opinions Who Favor U.S. Aid in Keeping Order in Palestine	
Previous knowledge of Committee report	36%	N=339
No previous knowledge	30	N=805

	Per cent of Those With Opinions Who Favor Breaking Relations With Franco	
Previous knowledge of Three-Power statement	32%	N=657
No previous knowledge	21	N=268

It is true that those who learned about the report or statement for the first time during the interview were more inclined to offer no opinion when questioned on their attitudes, but the above table excludes the "No opinion" group, and comparisons are based only on those with definite opinions.

The differences reported, which are in all likelihood not due to chance, suggest the phenomenon of "selective exposure" to information. In both cases, every respondent was aware of the contents of the statement or report when he answered the question on policy. Yet in each case, those with *prior* knowledge of the information had significantly different attitudes. It would appear, therefore, that persons reached by the Palestine report were those who were more likely in the first place to favor United States assistance there, rather than that they favored U. S. assistance because they were familiar with the information contained in the report. Similarly, it would seem that the group which had prior knowledge of the statement on Spain was already more anti-Franco in their attitudes, rather than that they became more anti-Franco by virtue of exposure.

The fact that people tend to become exposed to information which is congenial with their prior attitudes is another factor which must be considered by those in charge of information campaigns. Merely "increasing the flow" is not enough, if the information continues to "flow" in the direction of those already on your side!

PEOPLE INTERPRET THE SAME INFORMATION DIFFERENTLY

It has been shown that it is false to assume a perfect correspondence between public exposure to information and the amount of material distributed. It is equally false to assume that exposure, once achieved, results in a uniform interpretation and retention of the material.

In a series of experimental studies beginning with the work of Bartlett,[7] and carried on by a host of other investigators such as Margolies, Clark, Nadel, and Murphy,[8] it has been consistently demonstrated that a person's perception and memory of materials shown to him are often distorted by his wishes, motives, and attitudes. One demonstration of these general psychological findings in the area of international affairs is available in a recent NORC survey.

In September 1946, a national survey was asked whether they thought that the newspapers *they read* made Russia out to look better than she really is, worse than she really is, or whether they presented accurate information about Russia [10]. The same survey also asked a question to determine where the respondent put the blame for Russian-American disagreements [11]. When the sample was classified into two groups—those who blamed Russia entirely and those who put the responsibility on both countries or on the United States alone—there were revealed striking differences in beliefs as to whether Russia was being presented fairly or unfairly in the newspapers they read (see Table 8). It is clear from this finding that people selectively discount the information they are exposed to, in the light of their prior attitudes.

The finding is all the more striking when one considers the fact that people tend to read the particular newspapers which are congenial to their own attitudes and beliefs. Thus, one would expect the anti-Russian group to be reading newspapers which, if studied by means of objective content analysis, would be found to slant their editorial content against Russia. Similarly, one would expect the pro-Russian group to read newspapers which, if measured objectively, would be found to emphasize favorable news about Russia. Despite this, the anti-Russian group is *less* likely to say *their* newspapers present Russia unfavorably, while the pro-Russian group is *more* likely to say *their* newspapers present Russia unfavorably.

Here, then, is another psychological problem that faces those responsible for information campaigns. Exposure in itself is not always sufficient. People will interpret the information in different ways, according to their prior attitudes.

INFORMATION DOES NOT NECESSARILY CHANGE ATTITUDES

The principle behind all information campaigns is that the disseminated information will alter attitudes or conduct. There is abundant evidence in all fields, of course, that informed people actually do react differently to a problem than uninformed people do. But it is naive to suppose that information always affects attitudes, or that it affects all attitudes equally. The general principle needs serious qualification.

There is evidence, based on investigations made with academic samples, that individuals, once they are exposed to information, change their views *differentially,* each in the light of his own *prior attitude.* Data gathered by NORC in recent national surveys show that these academic findings are equally applicable to the entire adult population.

In a continuing study of attitudes toward the proposed British loan, conducted between December 1945 and February 1946, it was found that a significant factor influencing attitudes toward the loan was the belief that this country would or would not get something out of it economically [12]. As shown by Table 9, those who were of the opinion that the loan held advantages to this country were strongly in favor, while those of a contrary opinion, or doubtful, were overwhelmingly opposed to the loan.

Furthermore, 39 percent of those who expressed approval of the loan mentioned some economic advantage as their reason, while 75 percent of

Table 8

	Per cent Who Say Their Newspapers Make Russia Look Worse Than She Really Is	
Blame Russia entirely for Russian-American disagreements	41%	N=458
Blame United States entirely or blame both countries	54	N=168

Table 9

	Per cent Who Approve Loan to England	
We will get advantages from the loan	66%	N=265
Don't know if advantages	29	N=291
We will not get advantages	20	N=294

those opposed listed an economic argument. Under these circumstances, it was logical to suppose that attitudes could be changed toward approval of the loan, by informing the public of its economic advantages to the United States. It was not possible to conduct a before-and-after test of this thesis, but some interesting findings were revealed by a study of two equivalent samples which were polled simultaneously.

One of these samples was given the appropriate information before being questioned on their attitude. They were told that England had agreed to pay the money back with interest over a period of years, and that England had further agreed to take definite steps to remove restrictions on their trade with us and to join us in promoting world trade in general.[9] They were then asked whether they approved or disapproved of lending England the specified amount [13]. This was the experimental sample. The control sample was specifically asked whether they approved or disapproved of the proposed loan, on the basis of what they had heard about it, with no additional information supplied them [4].

The experiment proved that the given information did materially change attitudes toward the loan. The experimental sample registered a 14 percent higher "Approve" vote than did the equivalent control sample which was not given the information. But this overall comparison obscured the *differential* effect of the information.

For example, there was no difference between the two samples in the proportion of "Disapprovers" who gave an economic argument for their disapproval. Fifty-one percent of those in the control group who were opposed gave as their reason that "England won't pay us back," and 50 percent of those in the experimental group who were opposed offered the same argument—in spite of the fact that they had been specifically informed of England's agreement to return the money with interest. It was apparent that a large group of those opposed to the loan were rooted in their belief that the money would not be repaid, and the mere information that England had *agreed* to repay the loan was of no effect in changing their attitudes.

Table 10 shows another significant differential effect of the information. Among those who were already favorably disposed toward England, the information given to the experimental group was sufficient to sway a large proportion toward approval of the loan [14]. Less than half of this group

Table 10

Per cent Approving Loan Among Those Who:	*Control Sample (Not exposed to Information)*		*Experimental Sample (Exposed to Information)*	
Trust England to cooperate with us	45%	N=619	70%	N=242
Do not trust England to cooperate	17	N=231	18	N=133

friendly to England favored the loan in the control sample, but in the experimental sample, which was given the information, the proportion rises to 70 percent. But among those with hostile or suspicious attitudes toward England, the information had *no effect whatever.* This group was overwhelmingly opposed to the loan without the information, and they remained overwhelmingly opposed to it even when they were exposed to the information.

CONCLUSIONS

The above findings indicate clearly that those responsible for information campaigns cannot simply rely on "increasing the flow" to spread their information effectively. The psychological barriers we have pointed out create real problems for those charged with the task of informing the public, and in many cases public opinion surveys offer the only means by which these problems can be recognized, and thereby overcome.

Surveys are already widely used to provide the information director with scientific knowledge of the quantitative distribution of his material. They can tell him how many people have been reached by his information, and more important, which particular groups have not been reached. Surveys, too, can quite easily measure public interest in information materials and areas, thus providing him with accurate knowledge of the handicaps his program faces within various population groups.

But on a different and higher level, surveys can inform the information director of the whole structure of attitudes on any public issue. They can tell him the major factors affecting public opinion on the issue, and the relative influence of these various factors in determining attitudes. They can tell us to what extent information has reached the public and how far it has changed existing opinions. They can also tell what information is still needed and what aspects of it must be stressed in order to reach the unexposed or unsympathetic groups.

Psychological barriers to information campaigns are readily admitted by those who stop to consider the point, but they seem often to be overlooked in the general eagerness simply to distribute *more* information. The data we have cited in this paper are merely those which happen to be available from recent NORC surveys, but the kinds of barriers we have mentioned apply eternally to all types of public information. By documenting the very real effect that these psychological barriers have on public exposure to and interpretation of information materials, we hope we will encourage a proportionately greater attention to these intangible factors on the part of those who plan and carry out programs involving mass communication.

NOTE: QUESTIONS REFERRED TO IN TEXT OF ARTICLE

1. Did you hear or read anything about the recent report by the Anglo-American Committee on Palestine?

2. Did you hear or read anything about the report on the control of atomic energy, which was published by the State Department a few weeks ago? It's sometimes called the Acheson report.

3. Have you heard or read anything about the recent meeting in Paris where Secretary of State Byrnes has been talking with the foreign ministers of England, France, and Russia?

4. Have you heard about the recent proposals for a United States loan to England, and for other economic and financial agreements between the two countries? (*If "Yes"*) In general, do you approve or disapprove of these proposals?

5. As far as you know, is Palestine an independent country, or is she ruled by someone else? (*If "Someone else"*) Do you happen to know what country does rule her?

6. We'd like to know how much interest the public takes in some of these questions. For instance, how much interest do you take in news about (*each item below*)—a great deal of interest, a considerable amount, only a little, or none at all? (The United Nations, Our policy toward Palestine, The proposed loan to England, Our policy toward Germany, Our relations with Franco Spain, The atomic bomb, The recent meeting of foreign ministers in Paris, Our relations with Russia.)

7. (As you remember) The report recommends that 100,000 more Jewish refugees be admitted to Palestine in spite of protests by the Arabs there. President Truman has said he thinks this ought to be done. Now England says that the United States ought to help her keep order in Palestine if trouble breaks out between the Jews and the Arabs. Do you think we *should* help keep order there, or should we keep out of it?

8. Now about Spain. Have you heard about the recent statement, in which the United States joined with England and France to express the hope that General Franco's government in Spain would soon be followed by a more democratic one?

9. Which one of these three statements comes closest to *your* opinion about our government's policy toward Spain? (*Card handed to respondent*)

A. We should go even further in opposing Franco, and should break diplomatic relations with his government.

B. It was a good thing to speak out against Franco, but we have gone far enough for the present.

C. We have already gone too far in working against Franco, and are interfering in Spain's internal affairs.

10. Do you think the newspapers you read generally make Russia look better or worse than she really is?

11. In the disagreements between Russia and the United States, do you think one of the countries is entirely to blame, or do you think both countries have something to do with the misunderstanding?

12. Aside from getting paid interest on the loan, do you know whether the United States would be getting anything else out of the deal—that is, would *we* be getting any advantages or concessions? (*If "Yes"*) What?

13. Under these proposals, we would lend England nearly four billion dollars, which they have agreed to pay back with interest during the next fifty years. England has also agreed to take definite steps to remove restrictions on our trade with them, and to join us in promoting world trade in general. President Truman has now asked Congress to approve this plan. Do you think Congress should or should not approve it? (*Unless "Don't know"*) Why do you think so?

14. In general, do you think England can be trusted to cooperate with us in the future, or don't you think so?

ENDNOTES

1. See "UNESCO's Program of Mass Communication: I," *Public Opinion Quarterly*, 10, No. 4 (1946).

2. For a theoretical discussion of the problem see Daniel Katz, "Psychological Barriers to Communications." *The Annals*, March, 1947.

3. Figures in brackets refer to actual question-wordings which are reported in the note at the end of this article.

4. If anything, the size of the group is underrepresented, for two reasons: (1) The respondent's claim to awareness was accepted at face value, wtihout any check on his actual knowledge; (2) Polls consistently tend to over-sample the more literate, higher socio-economic groups in the population.

5. Lazarsfeld reports a similar finding on the relationship of interest to exposure to political information. See Lazarsfeld, Berelson and Gaudet, *The People's Choice*, New York: Duell, Sloan and Pearce, 1944, p. 79.

6. *Op. cit*., p. 80.

7. F. C. Bartlett, *Remembering*, New York: Macmillan Co., 1932.

8. B. Margolies, unpublished M.A. thesis, Columbia University, New York City; K. Clark, "Some Factors Influencing the Remembering of Prose Material," *Archives of Psychology*, No. 253, 1940; S. F. Nadel, "A Field Experiment in Racial Psychology," *British Journal of Psychology*, 1937, Vol. 28, 195–211; and G. Murphy and J. M. Levine, "The Learning and Forgetting of Controversial Material," *Journal of Abnormal and Social Psychology*, 1943, Vol. 38, 507–518.

9. This sample was also informed that President Truman had asked Congress to approve the loan, an additional prestige factor probably having some persuasive effect.

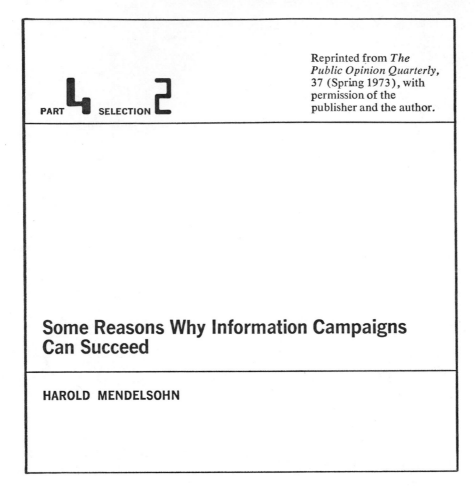

Reprinted from *The Public Opinion Quarterly,* 37 (Spring 1973), with permission of the publisher and the author.

Some Reasons Why Information Campaigns Can Succeed

HAROLD MENDELSOHN

Ever since Hyman and Sheatsley uncovered a substantial "know-nothing" (with regard to public issues) substratum in American society, it has become customary to rationalize away public information campaign failures with allusions to "public apathy."[1] As applied to the study of mass-mediated information effects, the concept of "apathy" is generally used to describe a nonreaction to information stimuli in terms which suggest that somehow the targets of given messages are at fault for the absence of effect, rather than the creators or the content of the messages, or the media through which they were disseminated. To put it another way, when the communications "hypodermic needle" fails, the patient is to blame.

An impressive fund of data gathered over the past thirty years indicates that the publics who are most apt to respond to mass-mediated information messages have a prior interest in the subject areas presented. As a consequence, information directed to this segment of a potential audience requires totally different communications strategies and tactics from information that is to be disseminated to an audience that is initially indifferent. At the very least, communicators who intend to use the mass media to produce information gain or attitude and behavior modification must realize that their targets do not represent a monolithic mass, although the media they may decide to utilize have the potential of reaching huge population aggregates. Delineating realistic targets along a continuum ranging from those whose initial interest in a given subject area may be extremely high to those who literally have no interest in what may be communicated becomes an essential step in developing effective public information campaigns.

Published research on the effects of mass-mediated information campaigns suffers from a serious flaw. Customarily, it reflects a consistent division of labor between the creators of messages and those who evaluate them. Most frequently, it reflects the *post hoc* efforts of researchers to evaluate information campaigns which were designed and implemented independently by anonymous communications practitioners without the active participation of the evaluators in the so-called creative process.

Evaluations of information-giving mass communications have focused more upon their *inability* to produce effects than upon their capabilities. Communications practitioners tend to eye these evaluations of their efforts with a great deal of suspicion and distrust. As a consequence, they often refuse stubbornly to incorporate the "findings" of mass communications research into their uniquely subjective repertory of communications assumptions and principles. Communicators and evaluators inhabit worlds apart quite literally. Essentially, past evaluation research suggests that practitioners who create content are guided mostly by subjectively derived principles of communications, and that information campaigns based on these subjectively derived principles alone are frequently ineffective. With rare exceptions, mass communications researchers have been documenting and redocumenting the by now obvious fact that when communicators fail to take into account fundamental principles derived from mass communications research, their efforts generally will be relatively unsuccessful. The implication of all this is that most evidence on the failures of information campaigns actually tells us more about flaws in the communicator—the originator of messages—than it does about shortcomings either in the content or in the audience. In short, very little of our mass communications research has really tested the effectiveness of the application of empirically grounded mass communications principles simply because most communications practitioners do not consciously utilize these principles.

An interesting question arises. What if information campaigns were designed to reflect empirically grounded mass communications orientations and principles?

Because the research-oriented mass communications practitioner is rare, it is necessary to set up teams of researchers and practitioners to work in tandem in the *development* of information-giving campaigns which are designed to incorporate principles derived from research. Additionally, such researcher-practitioner teams can *evaluate* the effectiveness of their own campaigns in terms of actual intent rather than in terms of assumed intent. A systematic effort to create just such a synergy has been made at the Communication Arts Center of the University of Denver over the past ten years.

What is required is literally a physical and social environment which is shared by writers, producers, film-makers, editors, and directors as well as social science researchers. As researchers and practitioners learn to work side by side, the interactive process becomes both routinized and commonplace. Over time practitioners began to interiorize social science percepts and principles, and researchers begin to appreciate both the realistic potentialities and the constraints that are inherent in working with the different media. The traditional compartmentalized structures of advertising agencies, major media complexes, and large-scale production organization which do both creative and research work in mass communications generally keep the two activities separate and apart from each other. I think this is a mistake. I also believe it is an error for independent academicians and applied mass communications researchers to keep themselves completely aloof from the pragmatic aspects of mass communications production.

Let us return to the question posed—what can we expect to learn about effective information campaigns by making conscious attempts to incorporate empirically grounded communications perspectives and principles into information messages from the start?

What little empirical experience we have accumulated from the past suggests that public information campaigns have relatively high success potentials:

1. If they are planned around the assumption that most of the publics to which they will be addressed will be either only mildly interested or not at all interested in what is communicated.

2. If middle-range goals which can be reasonably achieved as a consequence of exposure are set as specific objectives. Frequently it is equally important either to set up or to utilize environmental support systems to help sheer information-giving become effective in influencing behavior.

3. If, after middle-range objectives are set, careful consideration is given

to delineating specific targets in terms of their demographic and psychological attributes, their life-styles, value and belief systems, and mass media habits. Here, it is important not only to determine the scope of prior indifference, but to uncover its roots as well.

Given these perspectives on potential effectiveness inputs, let us examine three empirically based public information efforts which grew out of the work of the Communication Arts Center.

AN INFORMATIONAL CAMPAIGN DESIGNED TO GENERATE PUBLIC SELF-AWARENESS

If an information campaign starts with the assumption that large segments of its potential audience will be indifferent, it becomes essential to identify targets well before the campaign is actually implemented. However, before targets can be delineated, the objectives of the campaign must be spelled out explicitly, specifically, and realistically. For example, suppose a mass communications information campaign is to be launched for the purpose of effecting control over highway traffic accidents in which bad drivers are involved. The first targeting task is to pinpoint "bad drivers." Research accumulated over time has indicated that in at least eight out of ten cases operators of motor vehicles consider themselves to be either good or excellent drivers. Additionally, studies conducted by the Center showed that for the most part drivers tended to ignore the more than 300,000 persuasive traffic safety messages that appear annually in our print media alone.[2] How then should a mass media information campaign be directed to "bad drivers"—given the conditions that the great majority of vehicle operators consider themselves to be "good drivers," and that most people tend to ignore most traffic safety messages most of the time? Further, what can such an information campaign really expect to accomplish—the elimination of *all* highway accidents; the abolition of a small proportion of accidents? Indeed, is it feasible to believe that mass communications by themselves can do anything at all either to eliminate or to reduce such complex phenomena as highway traffic accidents?

Questions such as these immediately came to the fore when the Center was asked to participate in developing a television traffic safety program together with the Columbia Broadcasting System and the National Safety Council. It was clear from the beginning that if public indifference to traffic safety information was to be overcome, a completely innovative format designed to attract a high level of public attention must be developed. Second, it became obvious that the stereotyped didactic approach, which simply tries to inform people that they may be bad drivers, would be met with audience resistance. Consequently, it was considered vital to develop techniques whereby potential viewers of the proposed programming would be given some insights into their driving deficiencies without offending them. Finally, it was thought necessary to afford potential viewer-drivers the opportunity of actually doing something about correcting whatever deficiencies they were able to uncover. In short, it was decided that a television program directed to the driving public would be developed in pursuit of three middle-range objectives and no more: (1) to overcome public indifference to traffic hazards which may be caused by bad driving; (2) to make bad drivers cognizant of their deficiencies; (3) to direct viewers who become aware of their driving deficiencies into social mechanisms which had already been set up in the community to correct such deficiencies.

Note the specificity of these objectives. They are succinct, reasonable, and amenable to objective *post hoc* evaluation. Realizing that propaganda alone cannot alter the incidence of traffic accidents *per se*, it was decided to opt for a lower level effect manifestation.

Communications researchers, traffic safety experts, and television production personnel combined their expertise in implementing the objectives they themselves had promulgated. What resulted from this mix was "The CBS National Drivers Test."

Aired originally just prior to the 1965 Memorial Day holiday weekend, "The National Drivers Test" attempted to attract maximum public attention by publicizing the program in a massive promotional campaign. All in all, some 50 million official test answer forms were distributed via newspapers, magazines, and petroleum products dealers throughout the nation prior to air-time.

"The National Drivers Test" sought to overcome both prior public apathy and overconfidence in its ability to operate motor vehicles correctly by allowing drivers to measure their own abilities and then to decide for themselves whether or not they were sufficiently proficient. If drivers discovered themselves to be less well accomplished than they had expected, they were directed to enroll in driver improvement programs which were already available in their respective communities.

During the airing of the program and afterwards, evaluation research was carried out in order to determine the program's success in meeting the specific objectives it had set up for itself. In introducing his book, *The National Drivers Test* (Random House, New York, 1965), Warren V. Bush, the producer of the program, summed up the immediate effects of the presentation:

> The response was enormous, beyond all expectations. One of the highest public-affairs broadcasts of all time, "The National Drivers Test" was viewed by approximately 30 million Americans. Within days following the broadcast, CBS News had received mail responses from nearly a million and a half viewers.

> Most importantly, preliminary research indicated that nearly 40 per cent of the cross-section of *licensed* drivers who had participated in the broadcast had failed to pass The National Drivers Test. Perhaps it is this kind of individual self-discovery that is the necessary first step to genuine self-improvement. (pp. x-xi)

It should also be pointed out that according to the National Safety Council, some 35,000 drivers actually enrolled in driver improvement programs throughout the nation following the initial telecast of the "Test."

In terms of the specific goals set, the first airing of the program was judged to have been effective. In addition to the 30 million viewers who were made aware of certain high-risk traffic hazards, at least 600,000 individuals were made to realize their own driving deficiencies and presumably the need to correct them in some way. The 35,000 persons who actually enrolled in driver training and improvement courses immediately following the first airing of the program represented an estimated threefold increase in previous *total annual* voluntary enrollments in such courses. One need not go much beyond these gross figures to realize that the one-hour program was effective well beyond any prior expectations on the part of the planners.

The lessons learned from this exercise suggest that innovative information-giving formats, abetted by strong prior promotion, can overcome preexisting so-called public apathy to a great degree. Second, it is clear that reasonable middle-range goals, narrowly defined and explicitly stated, are amenable to successful accomplishment.

AN EFFORT TO DISSIPATE AUDIENCE ENNUI

When the Communication Arts Center undertook to create an information film on alcohol and traffic safety, it was aware of two preconditions: (1) if propaganda set out in its objectives to *eliminate* traffic accidents, it would undoubtedly fail; and (2) the stereotyped traffic safety messages to which all of us are exposed daily probably produce considerable ennui and surfeit among audiences. Additionally, the Center's researchers and practitioners were aware of the difficulties involved in persuading people to surrender such gratifying, solidly anchored attitudes and habits as those which pertain to drinking and driving. Exhortations to give up drinking were to be avoided as well, because such moralizing by the media rarely works, if at all.

Faced with a lack of consensus among experts about how moderate amounts of alcohol in the human system *always* affect *all* drivers, it was necessary first to develop accurate and reliable facts about the relationships between moderate alcohol intake and driving. As things turned out, we had to develop our own model from available data and theories. The model posited that (1) most traffic accidents result from subjective misperceptions of the actual risks present in any driving situation, and (2) the ingestion of even moderate amounts of alcohol directly affects the perception of risks. Consequently, the middle-range objective to be pursued by the projected film was to acquaint drivers with the idea that even moderate amounts of alcohol in the bloodstream cause drivers to underestimate dangers and to overestimate their skills in overcoming them, and that it is prudent not to drive after drinking, if at all possible. But how to implement this objective without being trite, hortatory, or boring?

Audience reaction tests which we had conducted on previous traffic safety films showed a heavy element of boomerang in the available blood-and-warped-steel-on-the-pavement treatments. What was sorely needed were messages which could overcome the ennui previous campaigns had produced and which, at the same time, would not immobilize audiences with screams in the night, nerve-bending police sirens, and varieties of human mayhem committed by colliding automobiles.

What we eventually came up with was a short six-minute "quiet" film which featured both live action and animated sequences drawn by the Pulitzer-prize winning cartoonist Pat Oliphant. The film, titled "A Snort History," demonstrates how alcohol affects perceptions of risk so that drinkers tend to become optimistic about surviving obvious dangers at those very instances when in fact prudent pessimism is called for. Of particular interest is the fact that not one single word is uttered throughout the entire film. The only sound emanating from "A Snort History" is the lively "blue-grass" musical background which accompanies the visual action. The film is serious in its live sequences and humorous in its animated ones.

To date reactions to "A Snort History" have been tested in audience reaction sessions among 905 subjects ranging from fourth-graders to alcoholic patients undergoing treatment at a state mental health institution. Although it was never explicitly stated nor visualized, 50 percent of the subjects reported that the major message they had received from the film was, "If you drink, don't drive"; 37 percent alluded to the idea that alcohol can cause misperceptions of risks as reflecting the major message of the film. Forty-three per cent reported that viewing "Snort History" left them feeling "concerned" about the problems of drinking and driving, and 48 per cent indicated that it had increased their interest in the problems of traffic safety generally. A surprising three out of ten subjects asserted that they will in fact consider changing some of their previously held ideas regarding safe driving as a consequence of viewing "A Snort History." (This was true of 53 of the 100 alcoholic patients under treatment at a state mental health facility whose reactions to the film were tested.)

As an addendum, worth noting is the fact that the quality of "Snort History" was so professional that it was exhibited in a local Denver first-run motion picture theatre as a short subject adjunct to a long-running box-office hit feature, "Dirty Harry." During this run "A Snort History" was seen by an estimated 50,000 adults under ideal conditions, in which audiences' defenses against being "educated" were down and in which there was a minimum of distraction in the viewing environment. We had rediscovered the tremendous potential information-giving power of films which can be shown to mass audiences via commercial motion picture exhibition facilities.

The public indifference which had to be tackled by "The National Drivers Test" and "A Snort History" represents just one specific type among many possibilities. In these two instances it appeared that prior public apathy stemmed less from a lack of interest in the subject matter *per se*—automobiles and their proper operation—than it apparently did from feelings of sheer surfeit with the overwhelming amount of information about traffic safety which the public encounters every day.

PUBLIC INFORMATION IN BEHALF OF SOCIAL AMELIORATION

In planning and developing a completely different type of televised information campaign, which was designed to ameliorate certain life-problems of Mexican-Americans in the Los Angeles area, researchers and practitioners at the University of Denver's Communication Arts Center encountered a quite different form of indifference among potential audiences. Primarily cultural in nature, prior so-called apathy among Mexican-American target groups had its roots in the indifference toward and distortions of Chicano subpopulations that the mass media have customarily shown. Since television's world was not the world that Chicanos knew, it was not surprising to find in our targeting research that members of this particular minority group exhibited a relatively tepid dependence upon television for either enlightenment or guidance. At the same time, preliminary research showed that formal instructional programing, of the sort that is usually seen on "educational television," would be met with a signal lack of enthusiasm. Previous experimental research which we had conducted—"Operation Gap-Stop"[3]—suggested strongly that information implanted in a nondidactic vehicle such as a drama had a much better chance of attracting and influencing subpopulations who were removed from the cognitive-pedagogic tradition. Furthermore, targeting research on the media behavior patterns of Mexican-Americans in Los Angeles indicated an uncommon amount of patronage of a local Spanish-language television channel which devoted large segments of its programing to "novellas"—a type of Mexican soap opera. Why not try to harness information-giving to the already established appeal of the soap opera? Out of this reasoning, engaged in by researchers and practitioners alike, grew the 65-installment Chicano information-giving soap opera series titled "Canción de la Raza—"Song of the People."

If the series was to reach Chicano audiences, it was essential that its ambience be thoroughly authentic. In order to accomplish authenticity and to establish credibility, Mexican-Americans were employed as writers, directors, producers, and actors. Dialogue was bilingual, in both Spanish and English. Sets and locations reflected reality as closely as possible. Story line, characterization, plot, and ameliorative information inputs were guided by eleven separate targeting studies of Chicanos residing in the Los Angeles area.

In effect two critical questions had to be resolved before production could begin: What shall we say, and to whom shall we say it? A considerable amount of exploratory research, the highlights of which follow, was of immeasurable help in resolving these problems.[4]

Although the evidence gathered in the targeting surveys of samples of Mexican-Americans showed very little dissatisfaction in general with such matters as health facilities, housing, local store prices, recreational facilities, police service, and the like, relatively high dissatisfaction was manifested by some 25 per cent of the sample. Women, middle-aged persons (35–49), and those earning at least $5,000 annually were most likely to be dissatisfied. Hence, it seemed reasonable to locate expressed dissatisfaction in the television series among these groups. At the same time, the elderly and the poor might serve as legitimate examples of complacency and self-satisfaction.

The relatively high level of dissatisfactions that respondents in the targeting sample voiced about youth (48 per cent) and the functioning of government (34 per cent) afforded additional insights that served to shape structure and direction.

On the matter of youth, it became evident that a major focus of the series would have to be placed on family affairs and the complex interrelationships that exist between parents who adhere to traditional ways of life and offspring who yearn desperately to adopt more modern life styles. A major target was delineated: parents, particularly of adolescents, who had a tendency to cling to dysfunctional traditional belief systems that clashed directly with the "new" aspirations of their children.

The observation that a full third of the targeting sample manifested dissatisfactions with the political processes through which they were governed, plus the fact that another third of the eligible voters contacted admitted that they were not even registered to vote, led to further communications decisions of importance. It was evident that "Canción de la Raza" would have to give special attention to that segment of the Mexican-American community which was *not* involved in the political process.

Target audiences were also tested for anomie (i.e. powerlessness). Highly anomic persons feel that as individuals they can do very little to control their everyday lives or their destinies. They feel overwhelmed by outside forces, and in general, they experience a debilitating sense of helplessness in coping with life directly. The mean anomic score for one targeting sample of Los Angeles Chicanos was 3.10, somewhat above the expected mean of 3.00. Most anomic within the sample were persons earning less than $4,000 annually (3.49); females (3.29); and the elderly (3.24). Least anomic were individuals earning $10,000 or more (2.78) and males (2.91).

It was decided that "Canción de la Raza" would not attempt to reduce anomie *per se*, but rather its symptomatic reflections. An effort would be made, first, to portray the high level of anomie that characterizes the Mexican-American population of Los Angeles; second, to generate concern with those aspects of Mexican-American life that serve to perpetuate high anomie (e.g. resignation, withdrawal, deviance); and third, to provide constructive sentiments by demonstrating the functional values of education, steady employment, joining with others in constructive communal efforts, and involvement in legitimate political activism. Special, though not exclusive, attention would be concentrated upon the most anomic segments of the target population—females, the elderly, and the poor.

Data derived from an application of Milton Rokeach's Terminal and Instrumental Value Scales[5] served as a final input for "Canción de la Raza." Two values were predominant among the target sample. One centered on the achievement of an untroubled, peaceful, and tranquil life (68 per cent). The other emphasized the desirability of a close, mutually interdependent, and warm family life (63 per cent). Less important were values relating to a sense of ethnic worth (50 percent), and self-esteem (42 per cent). Self-pride (51 per cent), ambition (51 per cent), and personal integrity (50 per cent) were seen by respondents as the major instrumental values through which major life-goals could be pursued and ultimately achieved.

By providing sentiments relating to self-esteem; by reinforcing the high valuations on the peaceful life, nurtured by strong family support; and by pointing out realistic problems and the legitimate mechanisms that were available for their alleviation, it was anticipated that the productions would reach targets with messages that would be both relevant and credible.

Evaluative research conducted after the initial airing of the "Canción de la Raza" series indicated that some 223,000 of the 1,500,000 Mexican-Americans in the Los Angeles area (15 per cent) had seen at least some of the programs that were telecast.[6] Major production concerns regarding the relevance and credibility of the programs were allayed when we found that 64 per cent of the viewers thought that "Canción de la Raza" presented issues and resolutions which had been of concern to their families and themselves, and that nine out of ten viewers found the programs to be credible.

Put succinctly, "Canción de la Raza" was designed to get its viewers to learn, to feel, and eventually to act by providing them with psychologically supportive material as well as with information *per se*.

Evaluative research conducted immediately after the series went off the air indicated that a moderate amount of success in each of these areas was achieved by the programs: (1) 66 per cent of the viewers queried reported they had learned something from watching "Canción de la Raza"; (2) 57 per cent claimed that watching the programs had provided them with ideas "about how Mexican-Americans in Los Angeles can improve their lives"; (3) 48 per cent of the viewers characterized the programs as "helpful" in a general sense, and 21 per cent reported the series to have been helpful to them specifically and personally; (4) one in every ten viewers asserted that the programs had stimulated them to rethink their own experiences as Mexican-Americans and to make changes in their lives, and 6 per cent reported that, as a direct consequence of having viewed "Canción de la Raza," they had undertaken activities which they ordinarily would not have considered; (5) most important; 39 percent of all the viewers surveyed reported that they had begun considering organizing or joining a community organization or club which either would be or was already dedicated to the improvement of life among Mexican-Americans; this was a prime objective of "Canción de la Raza." Indeed 6 per cent of the viewers (representing some 13,400 persons) reported that they had actually joined a community organization as a direct consequence of having seen "Canción de la Raza" in the short interval between the time the series was first taken off the air and the evaluation research began.

CONCLUSION

Our attempts to inject mass communications research principles and precepts into the creation of effective information campaigns have forced a considerable degree of humility upon all of us who wish to utilize the media for purposes of mass instruction and/or attitude-behavior modification. By themselves, the media are relatively powerless in effecting changes of consequence, primarily because there is considerable resistance among various publics against being moved away from their comfortable indifference to many public issues. The major task facing the communicator under such circumstances is to recognize, understand, and attempt to overcome much of this given "apathy." Here, solid social science research can be of immeasurable aid in determining appropriate targets, themes, appeals, and media vehicles. Without such prior research, it becomes impossible to evaluate information efforts realistically, and thus we learn very little from either our successes or our failures.

But researchers generally are not communicators. Rather than simply turning over their findings to communications practitioners (who generally ignore them), they have an obligation to work together with practitioners from the inception of information campaigns right on through to the evaluation of their effectiveness. Contrary to mass communications lore, the professional quality of information campaigns can be greatly enhanced in this process. Witness the fact that each of the campaigns I have described was accorded professional recognition for its technical excellence as well as for its content. "The National Drivers Test" won a basketful of prizes, citations, and awards, including an "Emmy." "A Snort History" placed first in the traffic category in the Industrial Film Festival Competition, and both "Operation Gap-Stop" and "Canción de la Raza" received regional "Emmys" for community programming from the National Academy of Television Arts and Sciences.

Finally, it should be noted that information campaigns can succeed if, in their evaluation, as much attention is paid to delineate specific elements of success as has previously been allotted to demonstrating failure. We should not lose sight of the fact that even when a considerable amount of social science input is in evidence, success in information-giving is a sometime thing. It therefore becomes doubly important to turn scholarly attention to discerning exactly what happens when it does occur—even in its most modest manifestations.

ENDNOTES

1. Herbert H. Hyman and Paul B. Sheatsley, "Some Reasons Why Information Campaigns Fail," *Public Opinion Quarterly*, Vol. 11, 1947, pp. 412–423.

2. See H. Mendelsohn, *Mass Communication for Safety: A Critical Review and a Proposed Theory*, Chicago, National Safety Council, 1963. Also, H. Mendelsohn, *The Dogmas of Safety*, Denver, Communication Arts Center, University of Denver, 1967 (offset).

3. H. Mendelsohn, T. Espie, and G. Rogers, "Operation Gap-Stop: A Study of the Application of Communication Techniques in Reaching the Unreachable Poor," *Television Quarterly*, Summer 1968, pp. 39–52.

4. A detailed discussion of the research that was conducted in developing targeting strategies appears in H. Mendelsohn, "What to Say to Whom in Social Amelioration Programming," *Educational Broadcasting Review*, December 1969, pp. 19–26.

5. M. Rokeach, "The Role of Values in Public Opinion Research," *Public Opinion Quarterly*, Vol. 32, 1968, pp. 547–559.

6. See H. Mendelsohn, "*Canción de la Raza* Evaluated," *Educational Broadcasting Review*, October, 1971, pp. 45–53, for additional data on audience reactions to the series.

Reprinted from *Journalism Quarterly* (Summer, 1973), with permission of the publisher.

Untwisting *The News Twisters*: A Replication of Efron's Study

ROBERT L. STEVENSON, RICHARD A. EISINGER, BARRY M. FEINBERG, and ALAN B. KOTOK

The News Twisters by Edith Efron,[1] purportedly a "documented analysis" of television network news coverage, created a modest stir when it was published in late 1971. It even appeared briefly on *Time* magazine's best-seller list.[2]

The book dealt with the performance of the three commercial networks during the seven weeks *prior* to the 1968 presidential election. Efron concluded that the campaign coverage "was massively slanted against Richard Nixon by all three major network news departments . . ."

But a comparison of actual scripts with Efron's summaries as reported in the book made it apparent that the examples of "bias" which she noted were at best questionable. Two examples illustrate the problem.

A story on October 17 was coded as anti-Nixon and summarized in the book as follows: "Reporter says Nixon, if elected, would be an obstacle to peace."[3] A reporter who called a presidential candidate an obstacle to peace might well be accused of bias, but did he?

The story concerned persistent rumors of a breakthrough at the Paris peace talks, Dan Rather reported from the White House. The scene then switched to Marvin Kalb at the State Department.

> KALB: The strong possibility of a bombing halt does not appear to be a political stunt, designed to win votes for Hubert Humphrey. It is the result, first, of an obvious softening in Hanoi's policy, and second, in the President's willingness to see it and act upon it. . . . High officials who have been wrapped up in the Vietnam agony for years are hopeful Hanoi will accept, because they believe *the North Vietnamese would prefer to deal with a lame duck Lyndon Johnson than with the current frontrunner, Richard Nixon.* (Emphasis added)

Furthermore, in a story aired a week earlier, Efron found a pro-Humphrey bias in a story which she summarized as follows: "Reporter elaborates poetically on public response to Humphrey."[4] Morton Dean had covered a visit by candidate Humphrey to a noon-hour Wall Street rally.

> DEAN: Hubert Humphrey, on his way to Wall Street, a must rallying place for any politician seeking this state's large bloc of electoral votes. If the advance men have done their jobs, Wall Street, piles of confetti and throngs of people will be ready and waiting. (He then interviewed a young lady who explained that Humphrey campaign workers had brought sacks of paper confetti to her office that morning for her to throw into the street when the candidate's procession approached.) On signal, paper snow, all chopped up into little bits, begins to fly from the skyscrapers. *From many floors below, it takes on the look of a spontaneous demonstration of affection as it drifts lazily onto the hair and into the eyes of the thousands who have given up their lunch hours to take a peek at Hubert Humphrey.* (A short excerpt of Humphrey's speech followed.) By coming to Wall Street, Mr. Humphrey may be more than just hinting at one big problem his campaign has been having—the raising of money, especially here in New York State, where some of the Humphrey for President workers say they've having great difficulty meeting the weekly payroll. (Emphasis added)

Pro-Humphrey bias? One wonders how the Humphrey campaign staff might have reacted to this report.

Efron's research method was simple and direct. From news broadcasts which she taped and transcribed, she coded material into one or more of 26 categories. The categories consisted of directional (pro and anti) references to 13 topics: Humphrey, Nixon, Wallace, US Policy on Vietnam War, US Policy on Bombing Halt, Viet Cong, Black Militants, White Middle Class Majority, Liberal, Conservative, Left, Demonstrators, Violent Radicals.

Then for each of the categories, she counted and tallied words which, in her view, were "biased." Word counts could include, presumably, an entire news item, or only a phrase. The words could come from a reporter, a crowd, a public figure, or the candidates themselves. Additionally, they could be multi-coded into as many categories as applied.

This technique has several basic shortcomings:[5]

1) *The categories are not all-inclusive.* The categories do not cover all newscast content, nor even all material related to the 13 topics, but only that defined to be pro or anti. Therefore, one cannot determine whether the 320 pro-Nixon words Efron attributes to CBS represent 1% or 50% of the total CBS coverage of candidate Nixon.

2) *The categories are not mutually exclusive.* By permitting multiple coding, one item or set of words will be counted as many times as it is coded. Results become a function of how many times the material was coded as well as how it was coded.[6]

3) *No rules are used for identifying material to be coded, or how to code it.* There is no evidence that different coders could replicate the study with comparable results.

The methodological weaknesses and the two "coding" examples are indicative of the techniques employed by Efron to produce her headline-grabbing conclusions. Yet few of the reviews of *The News Twisters* detected these errors or even questioned research techniques.

The following reports a partial replication of the Efron study.

METHOD

Transcripts of the newscasts used in the Efron study were requested from the three networks. CBS compiled immediately; the other two failed to respond to several inquiries.

It was decided to carry out the replication even though the absence of NBC and ABC data would preclude cross-network comparisons. With only the CBS transcripts, we believed we could produce a useful examination of portions of the Efron study and confirm, modify or refute some of its conclusions. More important, such a project might add evidence to the public debate on network news coverage. And finally, a rigorous analysis of the transcripts might develop some useful guidelines for other researchers and other campaigns.

Research questions

Three early decisions determined the thrust of the project. The first was to limit the category system to material directly related to the presidential campaign. This largely eliminated Efron's problem of overlapping categories (e.g., Liberal and Left) and spared us the impossible task of defining some of her categories, such as White Middle Class Majority.

We also agreed that no single analysis would provide us with a comprehensive picture of the CBS newscasts. Instead, we decided to use several levels of analysis, each directed at a different facet of the material and each employing a different research methodology.

Finally, we decided to conceptualize bias as imbalance or inequality of coverage rather than as a departure from truth. While the latter definition can be used in some circumstances, it did not seem possible or useful to try to develop a "true" picture of the campaign to compare with CBS' version.[8] And the definition of bias as imbalance had the advantage of being used both by Efron and the Federal Communications Commission in its "fairness doctrine."[9]

Three sets of research questions were developed, each set to be addressed by a different analysis:

Set 1: To what kinds of events do the network newscasts address themselves? How much attention is paid to the presidential campaign? To coverage of each of the major candidates?

Set 2: How much of the material related to the presidential campaign can be considered favorable to each of the candidates? How much unfavorable, neutral or mixed?

Set 3: With what activities, events and issues are candidates identified? Are particular issues or campaign elements associated with particular candidates?

Research technique. Set 1

The purpose of this analysis was to determine the proportion of coverage devoted to the presidential campaign and the major candidates. The news item was the analysis unit and was counted in two ways: by total number of news items coded into each of the categories and by item length.

For the latter count, we tallied the standard typewritten line (about 60 spaces) in the transcript, each measured to the nearest half line. While some distortion could result from counting transcriptions of action film coverage the same way as the newscaster's script (a minute of film might consist of only two or three lines in the transcript), we assumed that these distortions would apply about equally to all candidates and that the line count in the manuscript could serve as an accurate, if indirect, measure of air time.

The system of general news categories was based on that developed by Bush[10] with modifications to meet the peculiarities of the campaign and our special interests. For example, political aspects of the Vietnam war (rumors of settlement, foreign reaction, etc.) were separated from the military aspects (casualty reports, coverage of battlefield action, and the like). We established a separate category for each of the three major presidential candidates which also included their wives, vice-presidential running mates and national parties. A fourth category was provided for multi-candidate stories such as the CBS series on "The Candidates and the Issues" and minor candidates. This category was also used for items not directly related to the candidates but a part of the election—voting requirements, the polls and an occasional feature.

Eric Sevareid's analyses, while part of the CBS newscasts, and often concerned with the campaign, were not included in campaign coverage categories. They were clearly presented to the viewer as commentaries and thus would not qualify as news coverage *per se*. Instead, they were counted in a separate category.

Category boundaries were delineated more precisely as the coding progressed. It was decided, for example, that "international relations" news concerned the interactions of two or more nations while "foreign news" was that originating in a country other than the United States and confined to that country.

Because the categories were nominal and to some degree defined by the material assigned to them, we did not undertake a formal coder reliability check of this portion of the study. Instead, we adopted a procedure—continued in the other analyses—of coding while together as a group. Each of us coded one-fourth of the material; then each checked the work of one of the other coders. Discrepancies were discussed and resolved by the group.

Set 2

This exercise represented the most direct replication of the Efron book because it assigned direction (pro, anti, neutral, mixed) to the campaign material and counted the amount of such material in the coverage of the three candidates. After several sessions grouping unsuccessfully for adequate definitions of pro-candidate and anti-candidate material, we could appreciate and dispute Efron's comment that television news "presents invariably two stereotyped sets of slogans on both sides of everything."[11]

Our salvation was in heeding Berelson's admonition to deal with the manifest content rather than the probable intent of the speaker or likely perception by the viewer.[12]

Only material coded in Set 1 analysis as related to the campaign was examined. The analysis unit was defined as a sentence (or independent clause within a sentence), measured to the nearest half-line in the transcript.

Each candidate team was designated a category as in the Set 1 analysis. In addition, the material previously coded as "multi-candidate" was analyzed sentence by sentence and assigned to a "candidate team" category where possible. Single clauses which referred to more than one candidate or to a minor candidate or to no candidate were retained under a separate category. All other material related to the three candidates was coded, clause by clause, into one of the following sub-categories:

Campaign film—Film of the candidates and their wives themselves on the campaign trail.[13] We assumed (but did not test) that treatment of the three candidate teams was comparable. If the assumption was correct, differences in the way the candidates appeared in the newscasts would be a function of the differences in campaign style and tactics, not differences in treatment by CBS.

Favorable—Material which generally reflects favorably on the candidate, party or campaign; friendly crowd reaction, absence of hostile crowds; indications of gaining strength, winning or leading (including poll results); endorsement or support by another; summary of candidate's views by reporter; indications that candidate is getting attention or becoming known.

Unfavorable—Material which generally reflects unfavorably on the candidate, party or campaign; hostile crowd reaction; public apathy or coolness; loss of strength, losing, being behind (including poll results); attacks on candidate or his views by another person; candidate's refusal to state views or be interviewed; negative statements about candidate's personality or campaign style; references to campaign, organization, tactics and financing.

Mixed—Material which might be viewed favorably by some viewers and unfavorably by others; also clauses which contain both favorable and unfavorable references; candidate's appeal (or lack of appeal) to a specific geographic region, ethnic or social group; statements of the form "things aren't as bad as they were" ("Although he still trails in the polls, Vice President Humphrey has gained strength . . ."); statements about the candidate's relations with the President or the President's policies.

Neutral—Material which makes no evaluations of the candidate, party or campaign: statements of fact about the candidate ("Curtis LeMay is a retired Air Force general"); non-evaluative statements about the campaign ("A crowd of 5,000 greeted the candidate"; but note: "A crowd of only 5,000 . . ." is negative; "an enthusiastic crowd of 5,000 . . ." is positive.)

Multi-candidate—This category, not further subdivided, contains material originally coded in that classification which did not apply specifically to one candidate or which concerned a minor candidate or which made no reference to a candidate.

An occasional discrepancy did occur. For instance, it was agreed that favorable crowd reaction would be coded as favorable to the candidate. On one occasion during the campaign, a group of hirsute young people made their way to the podium at a Wallace rally and cheered everything he said including his denunciation of long-haired students. Their actions nearly broke up the rally and for a few minutes at least, the candidate himself was at a loss for words.

Pro-Wallace? By our definition, it was. One wonders, though, how it might have been perceived by an ardent Wallace supporter. We solved the problem of dealing with the likely perception by adhering to the coding rules despite an occasional difficulty.

As in the Set 1 analysis, coding was done by one person, then checked by another. Discrepancies were resolved by the group as a whole. In addition, all four coders independently coded a randomly selected segment of the material. At least three out of the four coders agreed on 90% of the coding decisions. Since all decisions were checked by at least one person beyond the original coder, we regarded the 90% figure as sufficient evidence of the adequacy of the coding rules.

Set 3

To address the questions about the kinds of events, issues, etc., with which each candidate is identified, a form of contingency analysis was employed.[14] The news item was the unit of analysis except when more than one candidate was mentioned directly in the item. In such cases—the series "The Candidates and the Issues," for example—each item was separated into sections dealing with each candidate mentioned in the story.

Each news item was multi-coded under a set of categories that encompassed both campaign activities (crowd response, poll results, for example) and major campaign issues. The categories were: winning—gaining endorsements; losing—being behind; favorable crowd response; hostile crowd response; Vietnam; law and order, economic issues; public welfare; civil rights; other issues; campaign staff—style—organization; appeals to specific regions or groups.

Our interest was in identifying the issues and campaign activities that were emphasized in the network coverage and also in observing if and how the issues and activities were linked to the three candidates. The actual linkages between each candidate and the campaign were compared with expected patterns to identify significant contingencies in the CBS campaign coverage.

RESULTS AND DISCUSSION

The campaign clearly and not surprisingly was a major concern of the CBS newscasts during the last seven weeks of the 1968 campaign. As shown in Table 1, more than one-third of the total news content dealt with the presidential election campaign.

Table 1 *Content Classification of the CBS Evening News: Sept. 16 to Nov. 4, 1968*

Content Category	Lines (n = 11,140)		Stories (n = 652)	
Presidential campaign	34.8%		25.7%	
Humphrey campaign		11.9%		8.7%
Nixon campaign		8.9		6.6
Wallace campaign		7.9		5.5
Multi-candidate, minor candidate		6.1		4.9
Vietnam war	13.8		17.5	
Military aspects		6.2		9.2
Political aspects		7.6		8.3
International relations	5.2		9.4	
Internal affairs of other nations	3.9		6.0	
Economics, labor, business	4.0		8.1	
Science, health, space, technology	7.6		5.8	
Activities of Congress	5.5		5.1	
Activities of Executive and Judicial branches	3.7		4.3	
Activities of state and local governments	1.7		0.9	
Violence, crime, disaster, accidents	2.6		3.5	
Human interest, prominent people	3.5		6.1	
Eric Sevareid's commentaries	9.6		4.1	
Protest *not related* to Vietnam	1.6		1.8	
Other	2.3		1.5	
Total	99.8%		99.8%	

Humphrey received more coverage (number of lines) than either of the two other major candidates. Wallace received only slightly less than Nixon but only two-thirds of the coverage given to Humphrey.

Over seven weeks the three percentage point advantage accorded to candidate Humphrey would total 20–30 minutes. The differences are shown more clearly in Table 2. In this table, the material originally coded as multi-candidate was added to the candidate categories where possible, and the table repercentaged to include only the material related to the campaign.

Tables 1 and 2 seem to offer little comfort to critics who charge CBS with massive favor to one candidate or party. Wallace's modest time disadvan-

Table 2 *Content Classification of 1968 Presidential Campaign News*

Candidate coverage	Lines (*n = 3,884.5*)
Humphrey	37.5%
Nixon	28.6
Wallace	24.8
Mixed or minor candidate	9.1
Total	100.0%

tage—even if deliberate—could be justified on the basis of his status as a third party candidate.

The data indicate, however, an advantage to the Democrats. While there is no evidence of intentional preference, the 20 to 30 minutes of extra exposure during the campaign could be an important advantage. And minor candidates, almost entirely overlooked by the network, might also be considered to have been at an unfair disadvantage to competing for the public's attention.

While amount of coverage is one part of the evaluation of television campaign coverage, the quality of coverage is more meaningful. Efron found a massive hostility toward Nixon (reflected by a 17:1 ration of anti-Nixon to pro-Nixon words on CBS), less hostility toward Wallace (1.2:1 ratio of anti-Wallace to pro-Wallace words) and a modest favorable ratio toward Humphrey (1.1:1 pro-Humphrey word count to anti-Humphrey). The two examples of Efron's categorization noted above may help explain how these ratios were derived.

Our replication of that portion of *The News Twisters*, shown in Table 3, indicates a far different pattern. The similarities in the treatment of Nixon and Humphrey are striking. Whether by design or happenstance, CBS' news team did not flagrantly favor one candidate over another during the 1968 campaign.

Table 3 *CBS Treatment of the 1968 Presidential Candidates*

		Candidate	
Type of Coverage	*Nixon (n = 1,113)*	*Humphrey (n = 1,459)*	*Wallace (n = 962)*
Favorable	24.5%	23.5%	17.8%
Neutral	17.7	16.8	16.9
Unfavorable	11.7	11.0	15.1
Mixed	8.8	9.0	8.6
Candidate before camera	37.3	39.7	41.6
Total	100.0%	100.0%	100.0%

Note: "n's" refer to number of typewritten lines in transcripts.

The coverage of Governor Wallace's campaign shows some differences: less emphasis on positive aspects than in coverage of the other two campaigns, more emphasis on negative aspects. But the differences are not large and to some degree are offset by greater attention to film coverage of the candidate himself. In the Nixon and Humphrey coverage, positive material outnumbered negative material two to one. Though the ratio was less (1.2:1), coverage of the Wallace campaign also gave more attention to positive material than to negative.

For all three candidates, a similar pattern was present: the most coverage was given to film of the candidates themselves. References favorable to the candidates were next most numerous, followed by neutral statements. Negative or anticandidate statements were (except in coverage of the Wallace campaign) much less frequent. In coverage of all three campaigns, mixed statements were found least frequently.

While Efron found a blatant anti-Nixon, pro-Humphrey bias on all networks (including CBS), the present study indicates a remarkably similar treatment of Nixon and Humphrey. Efron found CBS coverage of Wallace slightly more favorable than unfavorable.

Efron coded only those words which she considered "pro" or "anti" each candidate. We found that the time the candidates spent speaking before the camera overshadows the amount of reporter commentary. The major part of the network's coverage was to function as a common carrier of information about the candidates—information which they themselves largely determined by the content of their campaign appearances. Efron's study, emphasizing only part of the total network coverage, appears to lack the important context of total campaign coverage.

The final analysis—linking the candidates with campaign activities and issues—was expected to produce the greatest differences. But as Table 4 shows, the associations were most striking in their similarities, not in their differences.[15] Without major exception, the same campaign activities and the same campaign issues were associated with all three candidates to the same degree.

As a further test of association, category frequencies were converted to ranks and compared. The coefficient of concordance (W) among the three sets of ranks reinforced the earlier finding about the similarity of treatment ($W = +.85$). Spearman correlations computed between individual sets of ranks showed the greatest similarities between Humphrey and Wallace ($r_s = +.82$) and Humphrey and Nixon ($r_s = +.80$). The rank-order correlation between Nixon and Wallace was somewhat less ($r_s = +.66$) but still strong.

Yet a weakness of television coverage is evident from Table 4. The emphasis in coverage of all candidates tends to rest on the campaign itself, not

Table 4 *Associations Between the 1968 Presidential Candidates and Issues/activities*

		Candidate	
Issues/Activities	*Nixon (n = 81)*	*Humphrey (n = 91)*	*Wallace (n = 78)*
Winning, gaining, endorsements	30%	36%	15%
Losing, being behind, opposition	24	23	25
Favorable crowd response	9	9	11
Hostile crowd response	7	13	14
Campaign staff, style, organization, rhetoric	35	37	23
Appeals to specific groups or regions	16	9	9
Vietnam war	23	25	14
Law and order	12	5	10
Economic policy and issues	10	4	6
Public welfare	5	4	4
Civil rights	9	3	10
Other campaign issues	21	11	12

Note: "n's" refer to number of candidate references in CBS Evening News telecasts.

on the issues in the campaign. The most frequent associations of the candidates are with campaign organization and style, their standings in the polls and with crowds and the comments by other public figures. Except for the Vietnam war which was mentioned frequently, the issues which defined the great debate of 1968—economics, public welfare and safety, civil rights—received little attention.

The question arises whether the patterns of CBS coverage of the 1968 presidential campaign were significantly different from those of ABC and NBC. Without transcripts of the networks' newscasts, of course, we cannot be sure, but indirect evidence suggests that similarities are likely to be greater than differences. The Efron study itself argues that there were few differences among the three networks. And other studies have shown strong similarities among the networks.[16] Therefore, we would expect the results of this study to apply generally to the other networks.

SUMMARY

The campaign occupied about one-third of the total news content of the CBS Evening News during the period of the study. Humphrey received somewhat more coverage than Nixon or Wallace. The Humphrey advantage amounted to about three minutes per week more attention than that given to Nixon and about four minutes more than that accorded Wallace.

There was no evidence of any systematic evaluative bias for or against any of the three candidates. Coverage of all three candidates was remarkably similar. The most time on the air was given to film of the candidates themselves. The next largest category was material that could be considered favorable to the candidates and their campaigns. Negative references to the candidates and their campaigns were much less frequent.

Coverage of the three candidates was also strikingly similar in regard to the issues and campaign activities with which they were identified. For all three candidates, more attention was given to the conduct of the campaign itself, emphasizing the form and style of the campaign, than to substantive issues.

ENDNOTES

1. Los Angeles: Nash Publishing Co., 1971.

2. December 13, 1971.

3. Efron, *op. cit.*, p. 283.

4. *Ibid*, p. 261.

5. Our main reference on content analysis techniques was Richard W. Budd, Robert K. Thorp and Lewis Donohew, *Content Analysis of Communications*, New York: Macmillan, 1967.

6. We noted several instances in the CBS transcripts in which one news item was coded in three or more categories. A critique of the book commissioned by CBS notes one news story on ABC which was coded as seven separate "opinions," all in the same category. Charles Winick, "Critique of the Methodology of Edith Efron's *The News Twisters*," Oct. 7, 1971, available from CBS.

7. A notable exception was Ben H. Bagdikian's review in the Washington *Post*, Oct. 11, 1971. It was the only review we saw which compared the broadcast transcripts with the book's summaries of them. It convinced us to undertake the project.

8. Departure from truth can be used as a standard if an accurate record of the event—a trial transcript, for example—is available for comparison. Another possibility is to have the subject of a news story evaluate its accuracy. See Gary C. Lawrence and David L. Grey, "Subjective Inaccuracies in Local News Reporting," —JOURNALISM QUARTERLY, 46:753–7 (Winter 1969); William B. Blankenburg, "News Accuracy: Some Findings on the Meaning of Errors," *Journal of Communication*, 20:357–386 (1970); Philip J. Tichenor, *et al.*, "Mass Communication Systems and Communication Accuracy in Science News Reporting," JOURNALISM QUARTERLY, 47:673–83 (Winter 1970).

9. Efron claims that "Broadcast news is explicitly denied the First Amendment right to be biased" because of the FCC's fairness doctrine (p. 19). While the FCC has ruled that news is covered by the doctrine (32 Fed. Reg. 11531, Aug. 10,

1967), it has not used unfair news presentation as the sole criterion for action against a broadcaster.

10. Chilton R. Bush, "A System of Categories for General News Content," JOURNALISM QUARTERLY, 37:206–10 (1960).

11. The comment was made on William Buckly Jr., public broadcasting program "Firing Line," Oct. 24, 1971.

12. Bernard Berelson, *Content Analysis in Communication Research* (Glencoe: Free Press, 1952), p. 19.

13. This was established as a separate category for two reasons. First, it eliminated the problem of dealing with statements in which one candidate attacked another. Is a statement in the form, Candidate A attacks Candidate B, favorable to Candidate A because it represents his views (he could have spent his time supporting his own candidacy instead of attacking his opponent), or is it negative to Candidate B because it is an attack on him? This category also eliminates the problem of dealing with candidates' references to themselves. A second study commissioned by CBS concluded that coverage of Humphrey was more positive than that of Nixon but mainly because of differences in the ways Nixon and Humphrey referred to themselves. International Research Associates, Inc., "An Analysis of Thirty-Six Telecasts of 'The CBS Evening News with Walter Cronkite' Broadcast from September 16 to November 4, 1968," February, 1972, available from CBS.

14. The technique is described in Charles E. Osgood, "The Representational Model and Relevant Research Models," in Ithiel de Sola Pool, ed., *Trends in Content Analysis*, (Urbana: University of Illinois Press, 1959), pp. 33–88. The advantage of the method is that while categories are subjectively defined, contingencies—associations or linkages between categories—are objectively determined. Significant contingencies are determined by comparing the actual co-occurrence of two categories (Vietnam war and Nixon, for example) with an expected frequency of co-occurrences based on the total frequencies of the categories considered independently. If Nixon appears in 30% of all units and Vietnam war occurs in 20% of all units, then the expected frequency of the combination of Nixon and Vietnam war is 30% x 20% or 6% of all units. The significance of the difference between the actual and expected occurrence is measured by chi square test.

15. Neither the table as a whole nor any of the individual cells produced a significant contingency by chi square test at the .05 confidence level.

16. E.g., Frank D. Russo, "A Study of Bias in TV Coverage of the Vietnam War. 1969 and 1970," *Public Opinion Quarterly*, 35:539–43 (1971-1972).

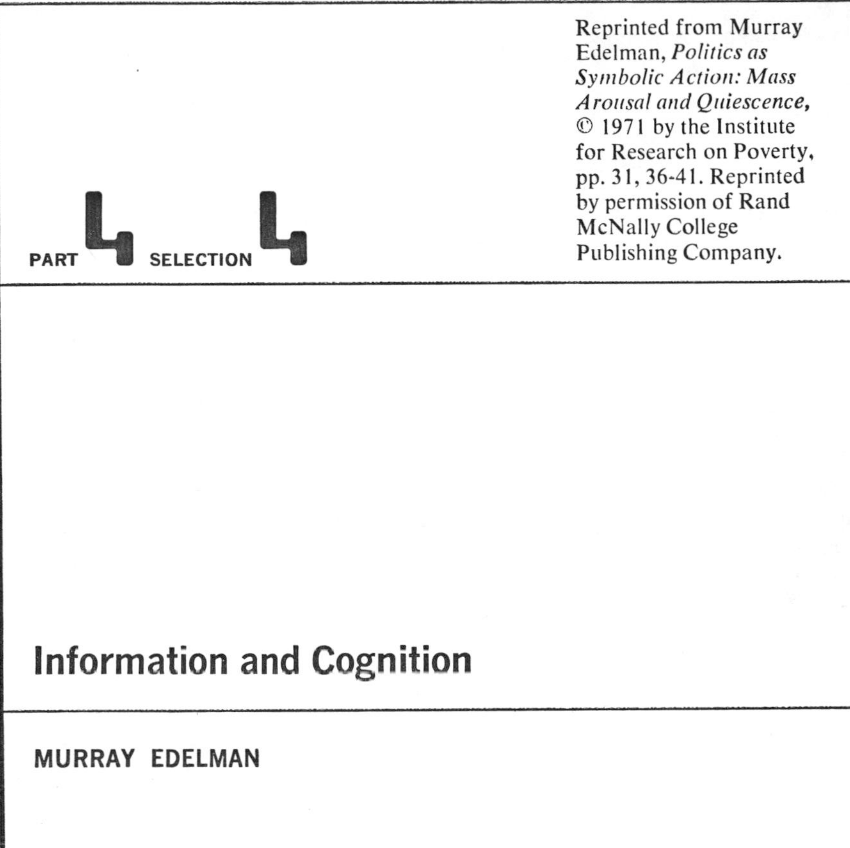

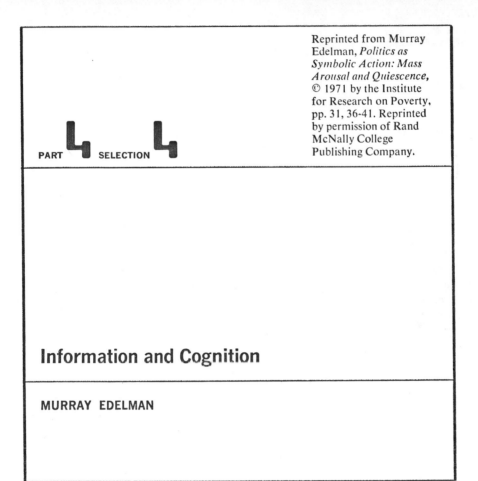

Reprinted from Murray Edelman, *Politics as Symbolic Action: Mass Arousal and Quiescence*, © 1971 by the Institute for Research on Poverty, pp. 31, 36-41. Reprinted by permission of Rand McNally College Publishing Company.

PART 4 SELECTION 4

Information and Cognition

MURRAY EDELMAN

Political beliefs and perceptions are very largely not based upon empirical observations or, indeed, upon "information" at all. More than that, non-empirically based cognitions are the most resistant to revision based upon observation of the world, and accordingly they have the most potent influence upon which empirical observations and social cues are taken into consideration and which ignored.

Neither of these two propositions is either self-evident or examined in political science literature, though a *prima facie* case for their validity will occur to any political scientist who considers the question. Yet, if they are valid, they bear fundamentally upon our understanding of political perceptions and expectations, for they deal with the dynamics of change in such cognitions and with the psychological conditions under which alternative cognitions emerge. . . .

. . . . Much of this [selection] is an effort to analyze the manner in which information not intended to prepare particular decisions or forms of action and not logical in its organization and mode of presentation nonetheless is perceived by receptors in ascertainable ways according to their diverse repertories of knowledge and prior cognitive structurings. Because the process is neither intentional nor logical, beliefs and perceptions created in this way are more resistant to debate and opposition, and especially to doubt and ambivalence within the individual who holds them, than are those based upon semantic information. Every message is bound to have both semantic and esthetic content; but the analytic distinction leads to some nonobvious observations.

GOVERNMENTAL GENERATION OF COGNITIONS

If esthetic information is a key element in the structure of political cognitions, it is clearly of crucial importance to learn as much as possible about the dynamics of their generation. What forms of political cues convey or reinforce which meanings in mass publics? The rationalist bias with which we are socialized to interpret political events makes a serious examination of this question difficult at first, but any observer of public affairs who can temporarily suspend his conventional assumptions is likely to recognize the following suggestions as conservative conclusions about the conditions under which large publics reach particular political beliefs and perceptions in ambiguous situations. Whether any particular cognition is valid is, of course, a separate question and must be ascertained by other kinds of research with which political scientists are more familiar, and which frequently cast doubt upon the validity of the cognitions in question. The issue here is how people come to hold particular cognitions, whether or not they are valid. Clearly, the beliefs and perceptions of mass publics and policymakers have more substantial political and social consequences than the conclusions of social scientists about their validity. The perceptions and beliefs examined here deal with the central issues affecting political consensus or dissensus, conformity or rebellion.

The following catalog lists forms of belief and perception generated chiefly by governmental actions or rhetoric.

A. Generation of the perception of popular participation and influence in policymaking.

   1. Voting. Both elections of candidates and referendums on issues are potent cues of this perception. The manifest attention is upon who

or what wins or loses, but a latent function of voting is to cue a belief in popular participation.

2. Hortatory language. That people are urged to take particular political positions conveys the signal that it matters what they think or do, regardless of the persuasiveness of the argument on a particular issue; though the manifest emphasis is upon the merits of particular positions.[1]
3. Legal language. In its popularly perceived form legal language purports to reflect in a highly precise, unambiguous way the will of the elected representatives of the people and to require administrators and judges to carry out this will rather than their personal predilections or values. The manifest emphasis is upon the content of particular legal provisions.[2]
4. The dramaturgy of publicized consultation of interest groups by public officials.
5. The dramaturgy involved in *expressing* opposition to established (or Establishment) policies. That minor parties exist and that dissent is expressed are taken as evidence that dissent can be influential; radical and dissenting groups therefore help bolster wide support for the regime. Sometimes a government takes pains to publicize its alleged incorporation of dissenting views within its own ranks, as when the Johnson Administration repeatedly referred to Undersecretary of State George Ball as a dove on Vietnam whose views were regularly taken into account.

B. Generation of the perception that particular groups are hostile and evil.

1. The publicized organization and subsequent escalation of defense pacts or police actions against them. Hostile speeches, gestures, arrests, and similar acts force political spectators either to perceive the targets of these actions as malevolent or to perceive the government as deceptive. In the absence of other cues the great majority will predictably resolve such dissonance in favor of the official regime, already bolstered by the cognition considered in (A). In the measure that it is formally defined as the object of "defensive" action, the perception is created that the target group is itself organizing for aggressing, conspiring and escalating.

   Actual attacks upon the target group are especially potent in creating a perception of their hostility and their guilt. The generation in bomber and FAC pilots in Vietnam of a belief that the people they were bombing were Viet Cong where the empirical evidence was either wholly lacking or contradictory exemplifies the phenomenon,[3] as does the conviction of policemen and of a majority of political spectators in the Chicago police riot of August 1968 that the demonstrators the police beat up and arrested were militant subversives.

2. Rituals of trials. That some people are arrested and formally tried while others are not itself evokes a presumption of guilt; psychologically, the formal insistence upon a presumption of innocence until the accused is found guilty very likely reflects an effort to repress or mask this phenomenon. The utility for regimes of show trials even where there is no question the accused will be found guilty is further evidence that trials play a major part in the bolstering of public perceptions that those the government accuses of vice are probably guilty.

C. The generation of the perception that political leaders can cope and will cope in the public interest with issues that concern and baffle mass publics.

1. A dramaturgy of self-assurance and confidence in attacking a personified enemy. People who are both anxious and uncertain how to cope with perceived threats want to believe that their leaders know what they are doing and so will accept a dramaturgical presentation of such ability on its own terms. This form of cuing is apparently especially effective if the issue is portrayed as an attack upon a personified enemy rather than as an effort to deal with complex economic trends or an unplanned incrementalization of small decisions, with nobody responsible for their cumulative effect.[4]
2. Artistry on the part of the leader in the employment of an accepted rhetorical style, especially when the rhetoric is banal in content. Where public anxiety is intense, rhetorical proficiency reinforces other dramaturgical signals that the incumbent of a high public office is an uncommon man who can cope. Unlike fresh or controversial *content* in speeches, the stylistic element does not raise questions of policy agreement or disagreement for debate and criticism. Where the content is banal, the very banality is taken as a signal of conformity to widely accepted values, further encouraging public support for the leader.

   By contrast, consider the modal response of audiences to political speeches that are highly innovative and unexpected in both style and content. Such speeches, by definition, contain both esthetic and semantic information. The information produces anxiety, for it conflicts with beliefs that order the world for the individual; and so it is resisted. The rhetoric of Black Panther leaders exemplifies this genre, and its impact upon most listeners is like a kick in the teeth. For those who already accept the vision of the future the Black Panther movement holds, the substance of these speeches is of course banal, and their impact no doubt like that of Roosevelt and Kennedy on the vast majority of *their* audiences, enlarging the charisma of the leader and solidifying his followers' support.

D. Generation of perceptions that particular groups are friendly and benevolent.

1. The publicized organization of alliances and joint action. An especially revealing example was American joint action and alliance with West Germany shortly after the bitter fighting of World War II and the revelation of the deliberate destruction by the Germans of six million people in extermination camps.
2. The metaphoric definition of the target groups as like "us" in values and modes of behavior.

For American military public relations officers to refer to hapless Vietnamese troops as "rangers" is to associate them with some romantic American military and western traditions rather than with a counterbelief in their sullen resistance to their own government and in their reluctance to fight for it.

Some less obvious examples are more revealing, though also more speculative. The talk and the emphasis over many years upon the desirability of Negro-white integration evokes in audiences a picture of group differences they are asked to ignore. In effect, the normative, ethical content of these speeches conflicts with the perceptions they generate, and that tension in turn contributes both to ambivalence and to group conflict. When avowed opponents, on the other hand, discuss each other's tactics and strategies, they are stressing a crucial respect in which they are alike. Military strategists thus come to respect their opposite numbers in a hostile foreign country, even while other information may lead the general public, including the military strategists in another role, to perceive them as aggressive and escalating. Many years of discussing Russian-American strategy after World War II has gradually led to increased perception of Russians as essentially engaged in the same game as we, and therefore more like us. To put it another way, we have come in some degree to perceive Russians and Russian policymakers as complex people subject to some of the same cross-pressures and interests as we, rather than perceiving them as embodiments of the malevolent conspiracy myth.

Recent developments in race relations in America have thus far exemplified a different pattern or, on an optimistic assumption, an early stage of the same pattern. In the talk among the most aroused whites about black militants, and vice versa, the emphasis is not upon similarities in strategies, but upon dark plot and escalation without limit. The meaning conveyed is therefore that the others are essentially alien and are simple embodiments of a myth of malevolent conspiracy.

Rhetorical suggestion, it appears, is a function neither of the conscious intent of the speakers nor of the particular phrases employed, but rather of an implication about future roles and future scenarios.

3. Elite status is itself accepted as evidence that those who enjoy it have the talents and perform the services that justify it. Very large subsidies to the affluent (as to the managements and stockholders of shipbuilding concerns, airlines, commercial farms, oil companies, etc.) generate and reinforce the perception that these companies are serving the national interest and so deserve some compensation for part of the alleged risks they are running. Far smaller subsidies to the poor are perceived as evidence that the latter are parasitic, wasteful, lazy, or immoral.

E. Generation of perceptions that particular kinds of actions are evil. The dynamics are essentially the same as those for generation of perceptions that particular people are malevolent. The most revealing cases are those in which a particular kind of behavior does not in itself necessarily harm others, but nonetheless comes to be widely perceived as immoral or threatening: prostitution, gambling, liquor or marijuana consumption, advocacy of unpopular policies or polities. To formally label them as illegal generates widespread perception of them as evil. People want to perceive them that way in order to conform to others' cues, and they perceive almost any ambiguous data as evidence of what they want to believe.

Language forms are relevant here too. Publicity to alleged bargaining among representives of groups with adversary interests may give rise to suspicions of elite plotting at the expense of the unrepresented masses.[5]

Governmental acts are not, of course, the only influences upon political cognitions; but they are the only type whose impact is systematically overlooked or undervalued. Because we are socialized to see governmental acts as reflections of people's cognitions and not as causes of them, and because it is not the official or deliberate intent of governmental acts to influence what people perceive and want, the influence of cues such as these is systematically overlooked. They constitute esthetic information.

Other social cues also shape cognitions: cues from family, school, and peers, as the socialization studies say. These studies also furnish evidence of the systematic tendency toward consonance and reinforcement among these various agents of socialization. If the socialization researchers were socialized to raise questions about the influence upon cognitions of the government itself, their data would establish the conclusion that the non-governmental influences serve chiefly to reinforce the governmental ones.[6] Dissonant cues apparently come from family or peers only where, as in the ghettos,[7] Appalachia,[8] or the communities of upper middle class college students in the late sixties, there is unambiguous evidence in everyday life that official policy hurts the group in question; protest movements and revolutionary parties can play on these cues. Even in these cases, the school continues to promote beliefs consonant with the governmentally cued cognitions.

ENDNOTES

1. Cf. Murray Edelman, *The Symbolic Uses of Politics* (Urbana: University of Illinois Press, 1964), pp. 134–38.

2. Ibid, pp., 138–42.

3. Jonathan Schell, *The Military Half* (New York: Knopf, 1968).

4. Edelman, *Symbolic Uses of Politics*, pp. 73–84.

5. Edelman, *Symbolic Uses of Politics*, pp. 145–49.

6. Fred I. Greenstein, *Children and Politics* (New Haven: Yale University Press, 1965); David Easton and Jack Dennis, *Children in the Political System* (New York: McGraw-Hill, 1969); David Easton and Robert Hess, "Youth and the Political System," in S. M. Lipset and Leo Lowenthal (eds.), *Culture and Social Character* (New York: Free Press, 1962); Robert Hess and Judith Torney, *The Political Development of Attitudes in Children* (Garden City, N.Y.: Anchor Books, 1967).

7. Edward S. Greenberg, "Children and Government: A Comparison across Racial Lines," *Midwest Journal of Political Science* 14 (May 1970), 249–75.

8. Dean Jaros, Herbert Hirsch, and Federic J. Fleron, Jr., "The Malevolent Leader: Political Socialization in an American Subculture," *American Political Science Review* 62 (June 1968), 564–75.

From *The Politics of Lying*, by David Wise. Copyright © 1973 by David Wise. Reprinted by permission of Random House, Inc.

The Anatomy of Deception

DAVID WISE

It is ironic that the United States first publicly acknowledged a lie during the Eisenhower Presidency. Although to many Americans, Eisenhower, as frequently noted, was a "father figure," his face never lost the ingenuous, open quality of a Kansas farm boy. His public personality was that of a Huckleberry Finn reluctantly and unexpectedly occuping the White House.[1]

Eisenhower often liked to emphasize that America's "moral" and "spiritual" power was the true source of its strength. Yet this man, who projected such a persuasive image of personal honesty, was hopelessly impaled on a lie and finally forced to admit it publicly to the nation and the world.

On May 1, 1960, high over Sverdlovsk, 1,200 miles inside the Soviet Union, a U-2 plane flown by CIA pilot Francis Gary Powers was downed by a SAM missile. Eisenhower had personally approved the secret development of the spy plane to gather photographic intelligence about Soviet strategic missiles, and U-2's had been overflying Russia for four years. Eisenhower knew this was risky, but he was not too worried when the May 1 flight failed to reach its destination in Norway; the U-2 carried a destructor unit containing enough cyclonite explosive to blow up the plane. In the event of trouble, the pilots were instructed to activate a timing device and bail out, after which, they were told, the explosion would occur. Some of the pilots, as CIA chief Allen Dulles knew, were concerned about the workings of this intriguing and delicate mechanism; they wondered just how much time they would have to bail out.[2] But as Eisenhower later wrote in his memoirs, the U-2 was extremely "fragile," and in the event of a "mishap," he had been assured, "the plane would virtually disintegrate." It would be impossible, the President had been told, for the Soviets to come into possession "of the equipment intact—or, unfortunately, of a live pilot."

On May 5 Soviet Premier Nikita S. Khrushchev disclosed that an American plane had been shot down inside Soviet territory. Washington announced that a NASA "weather research plane" on a flight inside Turkey had been missing since May 1 when the pilot reported oxygen trouble; perhaps it had drifted across the Soviet border by accident. The pilot was identified as Francis Gary Powers, a civilian employed by Lockheed Aircraft. In truth, of course, the plane belonged not to the space agency, but to CIA, and Powers was employed not by Lockheed, but by the intelligence agency, at a salary of $30,000 a year. On May 6 State Department Spokesman Lincoln White declared: "Now, our assumption is the man blacked out. There was absolutely no—N-O-no—deliberate attempt to violate Soviet air space. There never has been."

The next day Khrushchev triumphantly disclosed to the Supreme Soviet a fact he had carefully omitted mentioning two days earlier: the Russians had captured both the CIA pilot and the plane.[3] Powers did not blow up his U-2—he testified later to the U.S. Senate that he had been unable to reach the destruct switches—and he had parachuted to safety. At that, the State Department admitted the flight but said it had not been authorized in Washington. This was another lie, since Eisenhower had not only initiated the U-2 program, he had approved flight schedules for the missions. Furthermore, it had the disadvantage of sounding as though the United States had dispatched spy planes over Russia without the President's knowledge. So on May 9, by means of a State Department announcement, Eisenhower reversed himself, admitted the spy flights, took personal responsibility for them, and implied they would continue. Later that week he flew to Paris for a scheduled summit meeting with Khrushchev, President Charles de Gaulle of France, and Prime Minister Harold Macmillan of

Great Britain. In Paris, Khrushchev stormed over the U-2 affair and demanded an apology from Eisenhower. At the opening session Eisenhower announced he had suspended the spy flights for good, but it was too late; the summit meeting collapsed.

After he left office Eisenhower bitterly regretted his handling of the U-2 episode. In a filmed interview with CBS in 1961 he conceded that the initial U.S. denial of the spy flight had been a mistake. At the insistence of his son, Lieutenant Colonel John Eisenhower, this comment was snipped out of the film and not shown on the November 23, 1961, program *CBS Reports* in which Eisenhower discussed the U-2. Four years later, however, Eisenhower wrote in his memoirs: "The big error we made was, of course, in the issuance of a premature and erroneous cover story." Eisenhower put it even more candidly in 1962 when reporter David Kraslow interviewed him for the Knight newspapers at his Gettysburg farm. As Kraslow has recalled the scene, at the end of the interview he asked Eisenhower his "greatest regret" as Presidnt. "And he floored me when he said, 'The lie we told about the U-2. I didn't realize how high a price we were going to have to pay for that lie. And if I had to do it all over again, we would have kept our mouths shut.' "

Yet the U-2 episode was by no means the first time that the American public had been deliberately deceived by the Eisenhower administration. At least two other major intelligence operations led to high-level official lying; in both instances the CIA was seeking to overthrow another government. The difference was that in these earlier cases, unlike the U-2 affair, the public remained unaware that they were being lied to. . . .

But it was the Tonkin Gulf incident that emerged as the most crucial and disgraceful episode in the modern history of government lying. For Johnson used it to rally public support and to obtain the Congressional resolution that gave him a free hand to escalate the war in Vietnam, a war that had claimed more than 45,000 American lives by January, 1973, when the peace agreement was signed.

The incident began on August 2, 1964, when three North Vietnamese PT boats attacked two American destroyers, the *Maddox* and the *Turner Joy*. In fact, the *Maddox* fired the first shots, but claimed the boats were already closing toward her at high speeds. There were no U.S. casualties in this daylight engagement. One machine-gun bullet fired by a PT boat struck the *Maddox*.

On the dark, overcast night of August 4, patrolling in the middle of the gulf, the two destroyers, as previously noted, reported they were under "continuous torpedo attack." All of the twenty-one torpedo reports came from David E. Mallow, a twenty-three-year-old sonarman on the *Maddox* who had enlisted in the Navy two years earlier. The *Turner Joy* fired away in the darkness for four hours, but the *Maddox,* strangely, could find nothing on its fire-control radar to shoot at. And the *Turner Joy* sonar heard no torpedoes. In retrospect, both the captain of the *Maddox* and the commander in charge of both destroyers concluded that virtually all of the "torpedoes" reported by the *Maddox* were actually the sound of her own propellers.

In Washington, Johnson convened the National Security Council. But at 1:30 P.M. a cable reached the Pentagon from Commodore John J. Herrick, the task force commander on the bridge of the *Maddox.*

REVIEW OF ACTION MAKES MANY RECORDED CONTACTS AND TORPEDOES FIRED APPEAR DOUBTFUL. FREAK WEATHER EFFECTS AND OVEREAGER SONARMAN MAY HAVE ACCOUNTED FOR MANY REPORTS. NO ACTUAL SIGHTINGS BY MADDOX. SUGGEST COMPLETE EVALUATION BEFORE ANY FURTHER ACTION.

This cable, which was unearthed by Senate investigators four years later, was, of course, unknown to the public in August of 1964. Although he was there on the scene, and in command of both ships, Commodore Herrick clearly was not in the spirit of things; his warnings did not conform to the view of events in the Tonkin Gulf that Johnson and Robert McNamara wished to present to the American public.

There is no doubt that this cable was seen at the highest levels of the government; McNamara testified to the Senate Foreign Relations Committee four years later, on February 20, 1968, that *he* had seen it, and "Well, obviously, we were concerned. . . ." So McNamara telephoned Admiral Ulysses S. Grant Sharp, Jr., Commander in Chief, United States forces in the Pacific. Their conversation was taped, and McNamara offered a snippet, but only a snippet, of the transcript of that tape to the senators; he quoted himself as having told Admiral Sharp: "We obviously don't want to carry out the retaliatory strike unless we are damned sure what happened."[4]

But that night, even as planes began taking off from the aircraft carrier *Ticonderoga* to bomb North Vietnam, and as President Johnson waited in his Oval Office to speak to the nation on television, the Pentagon was still sending urgent messages to its Pacific commanders asking them to verify the attack.

For example, shortly after 11 P.M., when the bombers were already on their way, and the President was about to go on television, Vice-Admiral Roy L. Johnson sent an urgent cable to the *Turner Joy*: WHO WERE WITNESSES, WHAT IS WITNESS RELIABILITY? MOST IMPORTANT THAT PRESENT EVIDENCE SUBSTANTIATING TYPE AND NUMBER OF ATTACKING FORCES BE GATHERED AND DISSEMINATED.

In his 1968 testimony, McNamara leaned heavily, as proof of the attack, on classified intercepts by U.S. intelligence of alleged North Vietnamese radio traffic. He did not release the text of these messages, so there was no way for the Senate or the public really to judge. But he talked about and paraphrased them, and from what is known of the contents, the messages are far from conclusive proof of anything.

The controversy over the Tonkin Gulf incident has tended to focus on whether, or to what extent, American destroyers were in fact attacked on the night of August 4. Regardless of whether any attack took place, the messages between Washington and the Pacific that day demonstrate that *at the time* neither the President nor McNamara was certain that an attack had occurred.

There was an unseemly scramble for "evidence" to support the actions the President had determined to take. That evidence was still frantically being sought at 11:37 P.M., when Johnson stood before the cameras in the Fish Room and began: "My fellow Americans. . . ."

Three days later Congress passed the Tonkin Gulf resolution, authorizing the President to take "all necessary steps" in Southeast Asia.[5] And so America moved down the path to war, on the strength of "doubtful" torpedo reports by a twenty-three-year-old sonarman and a single bullet hole in a destroyer. Much later Senator Albert Gore, then a member of the Foreign Relations Committee, noted that McNamara and Pentagon official John McNaughton had retrieved the bullet that struck the *Maddox* and had displayed it to the committee. "Every time they came up here they waved that bullet around," Gore said. "One bullet and you went to war —Helen's face is insignificant by comparison."

But during the 1964 campaign, in the weeks after Tonkin Gulf, Lyndon Johnson appeared to promise the voters that there would be no war. Dedicating a dam at Eufaula, Oklahoma, on September 25, he declared: "There are those that say you ought to go north and drop bombs, to try to wipe out the supply lines. . . . We don't want our American boys to do the fighting for Asian boys. We don't want to get involved in a nation with seven hundred million people and get tied down in a land war in Asia."

At Akron, Ohio, on October 21, Johnson said: "But we are not about to send American boys nine or ten thousand miles away from home to do what Asian boys ought to be doing for themselves."

Eventually, of course, he sent 536,000 American boys to help the Asian boys in Vietnam, and a good many American voters later felt they had been misled.[6] Barry Goldwater, who left the impression that he favored using nuclear weapons in Vietnam, had sounded much too risky to most voters; they had overwhelmingly elected Johnson. Johnson's 1964 statements, were not unlike those of Wilson in 1916 or Roosevelt in 1940. His remarks could charitably be dismissed as campaign oratory, for which candidates are seldom held too closely to account. But taken together with all the other credibility incidents of the Johnson administration, there is no doubt that the 1964 campaign promises were highly damaging. A President whose reputation for veracity was otherwise impeccable might have been forgiven his campaign promises; Johnson was not.

Moreover, the Pentagon Papers revealed that even as Johnson was indicating in his campaign speeches that he would not "go north and drop bombs," he was secretly moving in that direction. On August 18, 1964, Ambassador Maxwell D. Taylor cabled from Saigon to propose "a carefully orchestrated bombing attack" on North Vietnam with "January 1, 1965, as a target D-Day." The Joint Chiefs were also pressing for air strikes against the North.

On September 9 Johnson approved NSAM 314, which authorized U.S. retaliation against the North in the event of any "special" attacks against American units by Hanoi or the Viet Cong. Left fuzzy was the degree to which the United States should, in the words of a memo by William P. Bundy, Assistant Secretary of State for the Far East, "deliberately . . . provoke" a reaction by Hanoi "and consequent relaliation by us." Bundy added: "Examples of actions to be considered would be running U.S. naval patrols increasingly close to the North Vietnamese coast and/or associating them with 34A operations.[7] We believe such deliberately provocative elements should not be added in the immediate future while the GVN [South Vietnam] is still struggling to its feet. By early October, however, we may recommend such actions. . . ."

A high-level committee headed by William Bundy, and appointed by Johnson to consider new moves against North Vietnam, held its first meeting on November 3, the day Johnson was reelected in a landslide. The group recommended bombing the North, and a month later Johnson, according to the Pentagon study, approved both this concept in "general outline" and the first part of a two-phase plan to bomb North Vietnam.

Britain's Prime Minister Harold Wilson, in Washington for a state visit December 7–9 was briefed on the President's plans.[8] After the enemy struck Pleiku on February 6, 1965, Johnson ordered U.S. bombers to attack, and on February 13 the sustained bombing of the North began.

But the bombing did not defeat North Vietnam, and on April 1, 1965, President Johnson secretly decided to commit American ground troops in South Vietnam. He specifically ordered that the decision be kept secret, and that it be disguised to look as though there had been no change in U.S. policy. Johnson's orders were contained in NSAM 328 of April 6, which must surely be one of the most shameful official documents of a shameful time in American history.

The memorandum was signed by McGeorge Bundy and addressed to Secretary of State Dean Rusk, Robert McNamara, and CIA director John A. McCone. It approved an eighteen-to-twenty-thousand man increase in

U.S. troops in Vietnam, the deployment of two more Marine battalions and an air squadron, and "a change of mission" for the Marines to permit their "more active use"—a euphemism for combat. With respect to these decisions, the NSC memo said, "the President desires that . . . premature publicity be avoided by all possible precautions. The actions themselves should be taken as rapidly as practicable, but in ways that should minimize any appearance of sudden changes in policy. . . . The President's desire is that these movements and changes should be understood as being gradual and wholly consistent with existing policy."

Did the President of the United States really believe that large numbers of American troops could be sent to fight a war halfway around the world, and that this could be kept secret, or falsified so that it did not seem to be happening? Apparently so, for that is what he ordered, and in writing. And it did remain secret for a time—until June 8, when State Department press spokesman Robert McCloskey let it be known that American forces in Vietnam would be available for "combat support" if needed. As might be imagined, his disclosure caused a tremendous storm, and the next day the White House issued a statement which began: "There has been no change in the mission of United States ground combat units in Vietnam in recent days or weeks."

Connoisseurs of government deception will note the artful insertion of the word "combat" in this sentence. The White House was attempting to admit almost incidentally the crucial fact that the United States had committed combat troops to a ground war, a fact that had been concealed for two months at the specific direction of the President. The words, technically accurate and totally misleading, proved to be symbolic of the Johnson administration's policy. By the time the President left office, in January, 1969, more than 30,000 Americans had died fighting in Vietnam.

President Nixon failed to bridge the credibility gap that had opened to such canyonlike proportions under Johnson. The prisoner raid at Son Tay, the Tydings affair, the Laos invasion have already been described there were many similar episodes. In May of 1970, for example, Nixon dispatched American troops into Cambodia for the purpose, he said, of cleaning out Communist sanctuaries and protecting American troops in Vietnam. Less than four months later Vice-President Agnew assured newsmen that "we're going to do everything we can to help the Lon Nol government" in Cambodia. As a result, the nature of the American commitment to Cambodia raised questions of candor.

Furthermore, on June 30, as American troops left Cambodia, Nixon himself told the nation in a televised address that while South Vietnam might continue operations inside Cambodia as necesssary, "there will be no U.S. air or logistics support." As the United States expanded the air war in Cambodia to include air support for South Vietnamese forces, newsmen thought it appropriate to ask Defense Secretary Laird, in January, 1971, whether this did not contradict the President's promise. The President, Laird replied, has said only that "air support would not be used . . . during the *termination* of those sanctuary operations . . ." [Emphasis added.] This was a novel and imaginative interpretation of the President's pledge, since Nixon had not said any such thing, and rather clearly was discussing "future policy," not the end of the Cambodia action, but Laird added quickly that he did not wish to get into "semantics."

Laird's celebrated fuel-pipe fiasco during the Laos invasion, while unimportant in itself, was symbolic of the larger problem. On February 24, 1971, Laird and General Vogt unveiled a three-foot section of pipe to Pentagon reporters. This, said Laird, was a segment of the gasoline pipeline running all the way down the Ho Chi Minh trail from North Vietnam, and used by the enemy to refuel his vehicles.

"It is four inches in diameter," said Laird. "It has a very clever, simple disconnect system with a gasket and a simple device to secure or unsecure, if you must, in a hurry." (Very clever, these North Vietnamese.) The United States had been bombing the pipelines, Laird said, but the disconnect feature "has made it possible for the North Vietnamese to take a ruptured section of the pipe out in a few minutes and insert a new section in, and the flow continues."

But, chimed in General Vogt, "in the last two days, ground forces have gotten to the pipeline at this point [indicates map] and they have torn up some three hundred meters of the pipeline. In other words, we have now severed the pipeline . . ."

A few days later, under pressure from newsmen, the Pentagon conceded that the pipe section displayed by Laird had been captured not during the current invasion, but in an earlier, clandestine raid into Laos on a date that the Pentagon would not reveal. Ironically, the pipeline gaffe had forced the Defense Department to confirm for the first time that South Vietnamese forces *had* been crossing the border into Laos.

And it was under Nixon that the disingenuous phrase "protective reaction" was coined by Secretary Laird to describe the resumption of U.S. bombing in North Vietnam.[9] As Nixon pulled the ground troops out of South Vietnam, he came to rely more and more heavily on U.S. air power over North Vietnam, Laos, and Cambodia. In the spring of 1972, after North Vietnam launched its massive ground offensive in the South, Nixon openly resumed intensive bombing of the North and mined Haiphong harbor and other North Vietnamese ports. Until then, for more than three years, the public, with its gaze riveted on the troop withdrawals and "Vietnamization," paid relatively little attention to the expanded air war. And it was hard for the news media to cover the air war during these years, since the Pentagon made news about it difficult to obtain.

The Pentagon's own figures on bombing tonnage indicated, however, that more bombs—almost 3,000,000 tons—were dropped in Indochina during Nixon's first three years as President than were dropped during the last three years of the Johnson Presidency. A Cornell University study published in 1971 concluded that by the end of that year, the U.S. had dropped 6,000,000 tons of bombs and other munitions in Indochina, three times the total tonnage used in World War II.

One of the most publicized credibility episodes of the Nixon administration began on December 7, 1971, when Henry Kissinger briefed reporters on the government's position in the India-Pakistan war. "You can attribute it to White House officials, but no direct quotations," said Ronald Ziegler, the President's press secretary. Senator Goldwater somehow obtained a copy of the transcript, however, and put it in the *Congressional Record* two days later, so Kissinger was identified as the source.

"First of all," Kissinger told the newsmen, "let's get a number of things straight. There have been some comments that the administration is anti-Indian. This is totally inaccurate." A position paper distributed to reporters at the briefing began: "The policy of this administration toward South Asia must be understood. It is neither anti-Indian nor pro-Pakistani."

On January 4, 1972, columnist Jack Anderson released the transcript of a meeting attended by Kissinger in the Situation Room of the White House on December 3, four days before he briefed the press. The document, stamped Secret Sensitive, contained verbatim dialogue of the high-level participants at a session of the Washington Special Action Group, an NSC subcommittee.

It contained this now-famous comment:

> KISSINGER: I am getting hell every half-hour from the President that we are not being tough enough on India. He has just called me again. He does not believe we are carrying out his wishes. He wants to tilt in favor of Pakistan.

The leak was highly embarrassing to the Nixon administration. Some commentators defended Kissinger on the grounds that he had said little more in the secret meeting in the White House basement than was already publicly known. Nevertheless, in his briefing for the newsmen, Kissinger had seemingly sought to leave the impression that Washington was even-handed in its attitude toward both India and Pakistan, which it was not.

Then in the 1972 Presidential campaign came the burglary and bugging of the Democrats' Watergate headquarters, and the indictment of seven men in the case, of whom three were either officials of the Committee to Re-elect the President or had served in the White House. The arrests were followed by the disclosure that Republican campaign funds, some "laundered" in Mexico City, had turned up in the bank account of one of the defendants, Bernard L. Barker. Later came widespread published reports of Republican political sabotage directed at the Democrats and financed from a huge secret fund. With each new disclosure, White House denials became more preposterous; it was as though the administration no longer even cared whether its explanations were remotely plausible; what was important was to deny everything.

Well before the Watergate controversy, however, Nixon was obliged to comment publicly on the credibility issue. In March of 1971 Howard K. Smith interviewed the President on ABC television. The broadcast took place as South Vietnamese forces were retreating in haste from Laos. Television, Nixon explained, had shown only the South Vietnamese troops "that were in trouble" and not the many other battalions that were doing fine. In covering the U.S. invasion of Cambodia, Nixon added, television had again failed to look at the bright side, but "I do not claim that this was deliberate or distorted or anything."

Smith also asked why American air power had been used to support South Vietnamese forces in Cambodia, although Nixon had explicitly said this would not be done. Well, the President replied, the "primary purpose" was to protect American forces, not to assist South Vietnamese forces.

Other Presidents, Nixon said, had been afflicted with a credibility gap, but the war was a key element, and once Americans were convinced that he was ending the war, "I think the credibility gap will rapidly disappear. It is events that cause the credibility gap," Nixon added, "not the fact that a President deliberately lies or misleads the people. That is my opinion."

ENDNOTES

1. Eisenhower's congenial public image did not always conform to his private personality. He had a sharp temper that flared easily, and his conversation, reflecting his Army career, tended to be punctuated by barracks-room language. One observer who has noted the gulf between the public and private Eisenhower is Richard Nixon, who served under him, although not always happily, as Vice-President. In an interview with reporters on March 13, 1971, President Nixon declared: ". . . you know, he was a great, gregarious, outgoing person, at least as far as his public image is concerned. As a matter of fact, individually, he was quite a man of dignity and reserve . . . I never called him Ike."

2. In a book published in 1970, Powers wrote that the destruct mechanism was arranged to allow the pilot "a small but supposedly sufficient margin of time to bail out before the explosion occurred." Powers denied that pilots were worried

that the timer was rigged by CIA to explode prematurely, thus destroying the pilot as well as the plane; he maintained that the cause of their concern was the fact that the timers were temperamental, sometimes as much as five seconds off. Ground crews always tested the timers before each flight, Powers noted, because "a few seconds could mean life or death."

3. Khrushchev, Eisenhower reported cryptically in his memoirs, had announced "what to me was unbelievable."

4. The business of the tape recording led to a curious, or perhaps not so curious, sequence of testimony during the hearing. The first time around, McNamara said: "I then called Admiral Sharp, and I have a transcript of that telephone conversation in which the specific words were 'We obviously don't want to carry out the retaliatory strike unless we are damned sure what happened.'" Tape recordings! This was the first mention of the existence of such transcripts, and Chairman Fulbright began asking McNamara whether the committee had received copies of these conversations. McNamara replied he would be "happy" to see that the chairman received them; but the more he thought about it, the less sure he was of how much was available "on such matters." As a matter of fact, McNamara added a few moments later, only conversations that were through "a very special channel, which is the channel of operational command" are recorded; he did not know "how much" of his conversation with Sharp had been recorded, he would have to see.

Fulbright then returned to the portion McNamara *had* quoted from the tape:

THE CHAIRMAN: What is the source of your statement there?

SECRETARY MCNAMARA: The source of my statement is my memory of what I myself said and did, since I am relying on my own conversations.

THE CHAIRMAN: I see.

5. Congress did not declare war; it simply expressed its overwhelming support for Johnson and wrote what amounted to a blanket endorsement of his future actions. Later the administration contended that the President could constitutionally wage war in Vietnam without the resolution. Quite aside from the legal aspect, however, there is no question that the Tonkin Gulf resolution mobilized public and Congressional support to a significant degree in 1964 and thereby paved the way for later escalation.

6. In *The Vantage Point*, Johnson, seeking to explain his 1964 campaign statements, wrote: "I did not mean that we were not going to do any fighting, for we had already lost many good men in Vietnam."

7. President Johnson approved Operation Plan 34A on February 1, 1964. The plan, drawn up by CIA, was a broad program of covert warfare against North Vietnam. It included naval raids by South Vietnam against North Vietnam, one of which took place on August 3, 1964, between the two Tonkin Gulf incidents. McNamara, testifying to the Senate Foreign Relations Committee about Tonkin Gulf on August 6, 1964, said that the U.S. Navy "played absolutely no part in, was not associated with, was not aware of, any South Vietnamese actions, if there were any." He specifically added that the *Maddox* "was not aware" of the South Vietnamese raid. Four years later the committee confronted McNamara with a

cable of instructions to the *Maddox*, telling the destroyer it would "possibly draw" North Vietnamese patrol boats "to northward away from the area of 34A operations."

"It is unusual," Senator Fulbright commented dryly, "that having received that cable . . . the *Maddox* did not know what 34A was."

McNamara, without batting an eyelash, replied: "They were not aware of the details is what I said . . ." which of course is not what McNamara had said.

8. On February 25, 1965, with a few other Washington correspondents, I attended a lunch for Lord Harlech, the departing British ambassador to the United States. Harlech said that the basic American policy decision to retaliate against Hanoi by bombing North Vietnam had been conveyed and explained to the British as far back as November, 1964, and that, therefore, the raids that began after Pleiku "came as no surprise."

While the record does not show that President Johnson had *decided* to bomb the North even while denying such intentions in his campaign speeches, a reasonable interpretation of the Pentagon Papers leads to the conclusion that both the President and the administration were moving steadily down that path during and after the 1964 campaign. Although the Pentagon Papers are somewhat ambiguous on the chronology of the development of the bombing policy, Harlech's comments would appear to shed interesting further light on the question.

9. Laird introduced the phrase at a news conference at the Pentagon on October 9, 1969. Euphemisms like "protective reaction," the tightening of information policies concerning the air war, and the administration's schedule of gradual troop withdrawals tended to divert public attention not only from the air war but from the overall casualty figures in Vietnam. During the Johnson administration more than 30,000 Americans died in combat in Vietnam and 192,000 were wounded. During the first four years of the Nixon administration more than 15,000 Americans died in combat in Vietnam and more than 111,000 were wounded. As a result, by the time of the peace agreement of January, 1973, combat deaths in Vietnam approached 46,000, and the number of wounded totaled more than 303,000.

PART 5

MEASURING PUBLIC OPINION

PART 5 AN OVERVIEW

The problems involved in obtaining an accurate picture of public opinion are so complex that there are some who question whether it will ever be possible. The technique of taking this picture is called polling or surveying. The accuracy of the picture depends on the techniques used—techniques that are the product of years of continuing research. In this section we touch on some of these techniques and discuss some of the major problems faced by pollsters and survey researchers.

SELECTING POLL SAMPLES—RANDOM AND QUOTA TECHNIQUES

The polls reported in newspapers, and which are cited in this reader, are based on interviews with a small number of people called respondents.

Even in polls to determine the presidential preferences of the electorate, most pollsters agree that they need to ask only 1200–1500 people.[1]

How can such a small number represent the opinion of the entire U.S. adult population? The answer lies in the way the 1200–1500 are selected. Asking the preferences of 1200 people we meet in a single shopping center is not going to give an accurate picture of the opinion of all adult citizens in the country. Why? Simply because all members of the population would not be represented. By sampling a shopping center, we would expect to find more women than men, more well-to-do than not well-off, and more young and middle-aged than elderly. Moreover, certainly the regional and probably the religious and ethnic groups within the national population would not be represented. The key to obtaining a sample that accurately reflects the opinions of the population at large is to ensure that every person in the population has an equal chance of being part of the sample. In a national sample, a rancher in Montana should have an equal chance of being included in the sample as a person who lives next to a polling headquarters in Chicago. In short, the accuracy of polls using a sample of 1200–1500 people rests in part with selecting the respondents at random.

Obtaining a random sample of respondents from small populations, such as the League of Women Voters or the faculty and student body of a university, is relatively easy. One could draw names from a hat, or if membership lists are available, one could pick every tenth or hundredth name from the list. However, when the population is large and there are no listings, the problems of obtaining a random sample become far more complex. Pollsters have developed some shortcuts to locate random samples. For example, most national survey research organizations divide the country into small geographical areas which contain nearly equal populations. These areas may be whole counties in rural regions or a few blocks in large cities. From these geographical areas small groups of sample areas are selected at random. Within these sample areas, respondents are also selected at random by a highly defined process. Interviewers are instructed to go to every 6th (or 5th or whatever the specified number is) house within the selected area. Once they locate the house and obtain a list of household members, the person within the household to be interviewed is found by consulting a table provided by the survey organization. The interviewer has no option whatsoever. He must interview the specific person in the specific household as designated (Bachstrom and Hursh, 1963; Roll and Cantril, 1972).

It is possible to estimate quite accurately the degree of error in the data that results from interviewing a sample selected in this way as compared with the data that would result from interviewing the entire population. For instance, 95 per cent of the time responses to questions obtained from a sample of 1500 will be within three percentage points of the same data obtained for the whole population.[2] A sample of 9500 would be necessary to reduce the error to one per cent, 95 per cent of the time. For most purposes, the added costs involved in increasing a sample by that much are not worth the small reduction in error. It should be emphasized that the error involved in sampling depends almost exclusively on the sample size and little on the size of the population being surveyed.[3] The error in data obtained from polling a sample of 1200-1500 is about the same whether the sample represents a population of one million or 200 million.

Some commercial polling agencies use quota sampling because it is less expensive than random sampling. Quota sampling attempts to obtain a sample that accurately represents groups within the population that are thought to hold opinions relevant to the questions being asked. For instance, quota sampling will try to get accurate representations of ethnic, religious, age, sex, and racial groups. This procedure has certain drawbacks. For one thing, the margin of error cannot be calculated. For another, there is no way to definitively establish which groups should be reflected in the sample. Furthermore, with quota sampling, interviewers are free to choose respondents as long as they fill their quota. Since there may be a tendency for interviewers to take the line of least resistence by opting for the friendly looking person rather than the unfriendly, the well-kept home rather than the run down, etc., this practice may result in the polling of a nonrepresentative sample.

THE TECHNIQUES AND EVALUATION OF ATTITUDE MEASURES

The questions asked in an interview are as important for obtaining a true measure of public opinion as the selection of the sample. How can we construct questions that really measure attitudes? As we have said elsewhere, an attitude may be defined as a tendency to respond to or act toward an object in a particular way. Two important properties of an attitude are direction and intensity. Direction generally refers to positive or negative feelings toward an object. Intensity refers to the degree of positive or negative feeling. To measure these properties one can either observe how a person behaves toward the object or simply ask him how he feels about it. The latter is the measure that survey researchers employ. Similarly, one can measure intensity either by observing behavior or by directly querying the person concerning the strength of his feelings.

Clearly, we cannot be perfectly sure that these methods give an accurate picture of a person's attitude. Attitude is a mental or psychological state. It cannot be observed directly. We infer its existence from something a person says or does, that is, from his behavior. By drawing inferences from behavior, we run the risk of error. A person may not effectively perceive an object or he may misperceive it. Further, he may not respond appropriately or his response may be misinterpreted. These are among the most serious difficulties facing opinion researchers. Comments that follow relate primarily to techniques of attitude measurements in surveys employed by political scientists.

Attitude measurement begins with the construction of a statement or statements designed to elicit responses that will identify (and measure) how a person feels about a certain object. The content of attitude statements can be drawn from a variety of sources containing information about the object, such as books, magazines, or newspapers; from the pollster's background knowledge, or even his intuition. To measure liberalism, for example, one might look to newspapers and books for statements regarding liberal beliefs or one might have to rely on one's own knowledge to come up with statements reflecting liberal ideology. Such statements should be both brief and simple. They should reflect single concepts and should not be complicated by awkward phrases or terminology. Loaded questions, those that cue persons how to respond, should also be avoided. For example, one would not ask: "Most people are horrified by recent events in the Middle East. Aren't you?" Rather, the researcher strives for neutrality in question wording: "Would you say the President is doing a good job, a fair job, or that he isn't doing a very good job in office." The importance of the way a question or statement is worded cannot be underestimated. In the selection that follows (*see pp. 391–98*), Schuman points out that "attitudes toward the same action show considerable variability depending on exactly how a question is phrased." The ability to write good statements comes with practice and a thorough understanding of the object concerning which an opinion is being sought.

Of course, a much simpler approach to attitude measurement is to employ an existing measure, one that has already been used in polls or surveys. A review of existing materials will generally reveal what measures are available. One might also consult the numerous attitude inventories which contain measures used by political and social scientists (Robinson, Rusk and Head, 1972). If appropriate, it is preferrable to use an existing measure rather than develop a new one. In addition to saving time, one has some data as to how the measure performs.

Scaling is a technique that combines several statements for more precise attitude measurement. A scale is composed of a series of questions or statements. Subjects are presented with one question or statement at a time. Responses are examined and aggregated to give each person a position or score on the scale vis-à-vis all others in the survey. For example, if we wanted to measure degree of liberalism, we would construct a series of statements relevant to liberalism and present them to the subjects of the study. We would score each response as more or less liberal than others in the survey. Clearly, a scale is superior to a single statement for measuring an attitude. The prospect of perceptual error is reduced by eliciting responses to several statements. A person may misperceive one or two statements, but it is not likely that he will misperceive eight or ten, particularly if one has been judicious in selecting the statements comprising the scale. As Schuman suggests in his article, the use of an attitude scale increases the likelihood that the attitude one is inferring is really present.

There are a variety of different scaling techniques employed in attitude research. The simplest is an additive scoring of items. For instance, if a person makes a "liberal" response to a total of eight out of ten liberal statements, he would be given a score of eight. If two of the responses are considered liberal, the respondent would be given a score of two. A respondent scoring eight would be among the most liberal; one scoring two would be among the least liberal. This is a simple scale, but it can give an accurate ordering of respondents. More sophisticated scaling techniques include the Thurstone, Likert, factoral, and semantic scales.[4]

Evaluating an attitude measure or scale is perhaps more difficult than developing one. A good measure should be constructed to measure one thing, and only one thing. In other words, to effectively measure political efficacy, for example, the measure must relate only to political efficacy and not be admixed with some other factor such as political trust. This property of the scale can be evaluated merely by intercorrelating the statements comprising the scale. If there is a low correlation, the statements probably are not measuring the same thing.

Reliability is another important attribute of an attitude measure. A reliable measure is one that gives the same result time after time. This means that if the same respondents are administered the same measure at two points in time, they would score the same. A problem in assessing reliability is, of course, that attitudes change. A person may be conservative while growing up, move away from his parents, begin to associate with persons of more liberal persuasion, and take on more liberal orientations. How can one distinguish between attitude unreliability and attitude change? Though it is impossible to distinguish between them perfectly, generally attitude changes take place only over long periods of time. Thus unreliability can generally be detected by examining the correlation between responses of the same subjects at different times within a short period.

Validity is also an important attribute of an attitude measure. A valid measure is one that measures only what it is supposed to, and nothing else. A valid measure of liberalism measures only liberalism. One might ask how a measure of liberalism can measure anything but liberalism. But recall, we infer attitude states from responses to statements in a questionnaire. We quite naturally make the assumption that statements designed to measure liberalism do in fact measure it. This need not be the case. Often, researchers believe that they are measuring one thing, only to find out later that they are measuring another.[5] There are ways of establishing the validity of an attitude measure. So-called face validity employs a group of judges to evaluate whether on its face a measure measures what it is supposed to. This technique has obvious limitations, but it can be employed with some degree of success if the judges have some expertise regarding the attitude being measured.

It is possible to establish convergent validity when some characteristic is known to correlate with the attitude to be measured. Of course, a problem here is finding a characteristic which is itself easy to measure and that correlates with the attitude. It is sometimes possible to isolate a group that possesses the attitude in question. For example, to validate a measure of liberalism, it may be that a liberal political party exists to which the measure can be administered. Presumably, members of a liberal political party should score high on a measure meaning liberalism. This is called criterion validity. Again, it is a problem to find a group that is known to possess the attitude being measured. Clearly, establishing the validity of a measure is not easy and, as a result, many measures in political and social research are not validated.

GATHERING INFORMATION

Attitude measurement does not end with the development of reliable and valid measures. Administration of a measure is another important stage in the measurement process that, if done improperly, may cause error. Most surveys are administered by interviewers and their behavior can be a source of error. For example, the expectations of an interviewer regarding an "appropriate" response may bias survey results, or the ideology of the interviewer may cause distortion (Hyman, 1954). The interviewer by voice inflection or by changing the wording of a question may suggest a response to the person being interviewed. Many people do not have firmly held attitudes about a wide variety of social and political issues and will look to the interviewer for some cue as to what they should answer.[6] These sources of potential error can be minimized by using professional interviewers.[7]

The face-to-face interview is one way to collect information and is generally considered the best, but attitudes can also be elicited through telephone interviews and self-administered questionnaires. As Wiseman points out in a following selection (*pp. 386–90*), these different techniques can influence survey responses, particularly where sensitive and controversial matters are concerned. People appear somewhat more willing to reveal their true feelings particularly in controversial areas, when they are not burdened by the social constraints of face-to-face interview. Of the three survey methods, the self-administered questionnaires pose the least threat and probably offer the respondent the greatest latitude in revealing his feelings.

The construction of the interview schedule—the order in which questions are posed—can be another source of bias. For example, questions concerning controversial issues should generally be asked toward the end of the interview. Questions on controversial issues are likely to strain relations between interviewer and respondent and if they are contained at the beginning of the interview they may affect responses to remaining questions or even jeopardize the chances of getting a completed interview. An interview generally opens with such uncontroversial questions as how long a person has resided at his present address, how long he has lived in a community, etc. These questions are good "ice breakers" and make it possible for the interviewer to develop some rapport with a respondent that will enable him to ask more controversial questions later.

Bias, and consequently errors in measuring opinions, may also stem from the type of questions employed in a survey. For example, some claim that so-called open-ended questions should be employed in attitude measurement. Open-ended questions allow the respondent to answer in his own words. He is not restricted to preselected alternatives characteristic of closed-ended questions. Some maintain that while closed-ended questions generally elicit responses, such responses do not necessarily reffect the presence of an attitude. People are asked to respond and do so, but it has been argued that such a response is not stable and is likely to change when the person is interviewed again (Converse, 1970). On the other hand, responses to open-ended questions more likely reflect a permanent reaction stemming from an attitude. Both techniques are useful if used properly. Open-ended questions should be employed when it is apparent that people know very little about a subject; close-ended questions, when the topics are familiar to the respondent; or the two may be asked in combination, with open-ended preceding the closed-ended questions. Closed-ended inquiries first may cue respondents how to answer open-ended questions.

POLLS AND POLLSTERS

Attitude measurement in surveys has evolved into a highly skilled art, and only the most astute practitioners can hope to pursue it successfully. Academic institutions, such as the Survey Research Center at the University of Michigan and the National Opinion Research Center at the University of Chicago do a commendable job. Commercial polling agencies are somewhat less successful. This disparity grows out of differences in methodology and research objectives. Commercial agencies generally have less complicated obectives, such as assessing the marketability of a product or candidate, or predicting the outcome of an election. Commercial polls, particularly the more reputable ones, such as Harris, Gallup, etc., are very capable in these limited areas. Academic institutes, on the other hand, are more skilled at uncovering factors and measuring attitudes that underline human behavior in general.

The commercial polls, at least those that engage in political prognostication, have become increasingly controversial. Poll accuracy has been a particular subject of concern, as Mendelsohn and Crespi discuss in the selection that follows (*see pp. 362–85*). Also there has been considerable controversy surrounding the question of poll influence on American politics. Alleged abuses have motivated calls for regulation of polls. The closing paragraphs of this section very briefly address themselves to two issues: the accuracy of the polls and their influence on certain aspects of American political life.

Since the debacle of the 1948 national election, when all the polls failed to predict Truman's victory—a debacle from which the polls never fully recovered—the accuracy of the major preelection presidential polls has been quite high. In 1960, both Gallup and Roper predicted the Kennedy-Nixon totals within one percentage point of the actual vote. Gallup and Harris were within two percentage points in their final preelection poll of the actual vote in Johnson's landslide in 1964. In 1968 Gallup predicted the actual vote in the presidential election and Harris was within two percentage points of the actual vote (*see pp. 362–85*). Most major polls predicted the Nixon landslide in 1972. Critics of the polls, however, still point to their failure to predict the outcome of the 1948 presidential election as evidence of unreliability. The failure of the polls in 1948 resulted from a last minute shift to Truman that escaped pollsters who quit polling two weeks prior to the election. More recently, the failure of the polls to predict the 1970 Conservative victory in Great Britain is used by critics who question the reliability of the polls, as Abrams states in the article contained in this section (*see pp. 399–406*). But in spite of these failures, evidence suggests that polls do a very respectable job in election forecasting.

One problem in evaluating the accuracy of polls is that there are many different kinds of polls. Only some of the many polls encountered by the layman have been conducted with rigorous application of sound survey methods. To judge the accuracy of a poll, a poll watcher should be concerned first of all with the sponsoring agency. Academic and the larger nationwide polling agencies adhere to sound research principles. Polls conducted by candidates for public office, so-called partisan polls, very often are more concerned with the results of the study than with its methodological soundness. The poll watcher should also be concerned with how a sample is drawn and the nature of the population from which the sample is taken. Larger samples are more accurate than smaller ones; random selection of respondents is more representative than nonrandom selection.

The date of a poll is also important in assessing its reliability. Data gathered two weeks prior to an election may not reflect the distribution of preferences on Election Day. The phenomenal shift of voters to Humphrey in the closing weeks of the 1968 elections suggests how rapidly patterns of preference can change.

Evaluating the influence of polls on politics is more problematic than assessing their accuracy. It is contended, for example, that published polls unduly influence election outcomes. The publishing of poll results prior to elections is claimed to influence turnout and candidate preference. For instance, polls showing a candidate in the lead are said to create a "bandwagon" effect for that candidate. There is however little evidence to support such claims. Indeed, the polls themselves indicate that differences in the voting strength of political candidates are reduced, if anything, during political campaigns. This has certainly been the case in most presidential elections. While there is little evidence to suggest that polls influence voters in any direct way, polls may exercise indirect influence. For example, presidential candidates very often are eliminated because of poor showings in preconvention public opinion polls. There is also some evidence that poll results may influence levels of campaign contributions for political candidates.

The influence of polls on political decision makers may be more significant. Political parties and political candidates, for instance, rely on polls to develop campaign strategies and tactics. Sometimes poll results are instrumental in the decision whether or not to run a candidate for public office. Public officials use polls to gather information from constituents as well as gauge public reaction, and this may well influence how they execute their office. Members of Congress, for example, followed with great interest the public opinion polls showing reaction to the Watergate affair. Finally, public opinion polls have made political candidates and public officials more concerned with the day-to-day reactions of the public. In this respect, polls may serve as a linkage mechanism between the public and elected officials.

ENDNOTES

1. The group whose opinions we are interested in is called a population. This "population" may be all adults in the United States 18 years and over, or it may be members of the local Young Republicans Club. The people selected to represent the "population" in a poll or survey are called a sample (Chein, 1951). A detailed description of the research methods employed by the Gallup Poll and

the Harris Survey to conduct preelection surveys (sample design, interviewing procedures, and analytical techniques) is contained in Mendelsohn and Crespi's selection *(pp. 362–85)*.

2. This means that if questions were presented to 100 different samples of the same population, in 95 out of 100 the result would be within 3 percent of what they would be for the population.

3. The exception to this rule is when we are dealing with small populations.

4. These techniques are discussed in most general references on scaling (Edwards, 1957; Oppenheim, 1966).

5. This is the case, for example, of a scale that tries to measure racial attitude and turns out instead to reflect economic opinion.

6. Obvious status differences between the interviewer and the respondent may represent another source of bias. If an interviewer appears to be of high social status, respondents, particularly those of lower socioeconomic status, may be reluctant to express their true feelings. Some may defer, while others may be put off and uneasy. It has been found, however, that class and racial differences between interviewer and respondent do not necessarily cause distortion. For example, while it may be unwise to use white interviewers to poll blacks and vice versa on racial issues, it appears that if the interview deals with topics other than race and civil rights, racial differences between interviewers and respondents make little difference in the outcome of the interview (Williams, 1964; Schuman and Converse, 1971; Welch, Comer, and Steinman, 1973).

7. Most interviewers used by reputable polling agencies are middle-aged, middle-class women. Such women are not very threatening to respondents who need to be reassured in order for the interview to take place. Students are sometimes used by academic survey researchers. After careful training, students may make good interviewers, but often their performance does not match that of professional interviewers.

REFERENCES AND FURTHER READING

Abrams, Mark. "The Opinion Polls and the 1970 British General Election." *Public Opinion Quarterly* 34 (1970): 317–324.

Bachstrom, Charles H., and Hursh, Gerald O. *Survey Research*. Evanston: Northwestern University Press, 1963.

Chein, Isidor. "An Introduction to Sampling." In *Research Methods in Social Relations,* edited by Claire Selltiz et al. New York: Holt, Rinehart, and Winston, 1951.

Converse, Philip E. "Attitudes and Non-Attitudes: Continuation of a Dialogue." In *The Quantitative Analysis of Social Problems,* edited by Edward R. Tufte. Reading, Mass.: Addison-Wesley, 1970.

Edwards, Allen L. *Techniques of Attitude Scale Construction*. New York: Appleton-Century-Crofts, 1957.

Hofstetter, C. Richard. "The Amateur Politician: A Problem in Construct Validation." *Midwest Journal of Political Science* 15 (1971): 31–56.

Hyman, Herbert H. et al. *Interviewing in Social Research.* Chicago: University of Chicago Press, 1954.

McClosky, Herbert. "Conservatism and Personality." *American Political Science Review* 52 (1958): 27–45.

Mendelsohn, Harold, and Crespi, Irving. *Polls, Television and the New Politics.* Scranton, Pa.: Chandler, 1970.

Oppenheim, Abraham N. *Questionnaire Design and Attitude Measurement.* New York: Basic Books, 1966.

Robinson, John P.; Rusk, Jerold G.; and Head, Kendra B. *Measures of Political Attitudes.* Ann Arbor, Mich.: Institute for Social Research, 1972.

Roll, Charles W. Jr., and Cantril, Albert H. *Polls.* New York: Basic Books, 1972.

Schuman, Howard. "Attitudes vs. Actions *versus* Attitudes vs. Attitudes." *Public Opinion Quarterly* 36 (1972): 347–354.

Schuman, Howard, and Converse, Jean. "The Effect of Black and White Interviewers on Black Responses in 1968." *Public Opinion Quarterly* 35 (1971): 44–68.

Welch, Susan; Comer, John; and Steinman, Michael. "Interviewing in a Mexican American Community: An Investigation of Some Potential Sources of Response Bias." *Public Opinion Quarterly* 37 (1973): 115–126.

Williams, J. A. "Interviewer-Respondent Interaction: A Study of Bias in the Information Interview." *Sociometry* 27 (1964): 338–352.

Wiseman, Frederick. "Methodological Bias in Public Opinion Surveys." *Public Opinion Quarterly* 36 (1972): 105–108.

PART 5 SELECTION 1

Copyright © 1970 by Chandler Publishing Company. Reprinted from *Polls, Television, and the New Politics* by Harold Mendelsohn and Irving Crespi by permission of Chandler Publishing Company.

The Credibility of Voter-Preference Surveys

HAROLD MENDELSOHN
and
IRVING CRESPI

Preprimary and preconvention surveys of voter preferences have not changed the bases upon which candidates are selected, but have added a new dimension to the process of selection. Parties still seek men who are believed to have the ability to become well known rapidly. They still seek men who have a particular appeal, or who have an affinity to important interest groups such as the business community, ethnic groups, and organized labor. With rare exceptions, they still seek men whose positions on issues are sufficiently congruent with the dominant trend in the electorate so as not to lead to widespread public disaffection. Particularly when a major office is at stake, they still prefer men with the political "sex appeal" known as charisma. In sum, they still seek candidates who they think can win, or if victory is out of the question, candidates they think will run the strongest possible race.

These criteria for selection antedate preelection polls and have not been outdated by them. The contribution of the sample-survey method has been to provide a new source of information to use in evaluating the credentials of potential candidates. Two questions that arise with respect to preelection polls as a source of information are (1) How much credibility does this new source have? and (2) How subject are the polls to behind-the-scenes manipulation? This [selection] is concerned with the first [of these] question[s] . . .

The credibility of preelection polls has been defended primarily on the basis of the record of accuracy of published polls in elections. The published record of such polls for elections, national as well as local, dating back to 1936 is usually cited as incontrovertible evidence of the fact that the survey method has developed to the point where it is now capable of accurately measuring voter preferences within a small margin of error. In opposition, it has been maintained by some critical observers that a form of statistical legerdemain has been used to create an exaggerated record of reliability.

PERCENTAGE POINT VERSUS PERCENT ERROR

Specifically, some critics of public-opinion polls have attacked the practice of evaluating the accuracy of preelection polls in terms of *percentage points*. Survey organizations, when they point with pride to how close their polls come to the actual election results, characteristically use this method. Illustrative are the final Gallup and Harris surveys in 1968. Gallup's final report, after allocation of the undecided, measured Nixon's strength at 43 percent,[1] while Harris reported him as having 41 percent of the vote.[2] In the official returns Nixon received 43.5 percent, considering only the vote for the three major-party candidates. In percentage points, Gallup's error margin is 0.5 points, while Harris' is 2.5 points. Critics such as Lindsay Rogers[3] and Senator Albert Gore[4] have in the past contended that the use of percentage points for evaluating error is a subterfuge in that it understates the true error. They maintain that the proper criterion is the *percent* error—for example, the percent that 0.5 is of 43.5 percent, or that 2.5 is of 43.5 percent. In these terms, Gallup's error in 1968 was about 1 percent and Harris' about 6 percent. (Complicating the issue is the fact that all too frequently the niceties of statistical usage are ignored by the less rigorous and uninformed who calculate the percentage-point error but then proceed to call it the "percent" error.)

The critics' contention is that the use of percentage points is a deliberate attempt to make preelection polls appear more accurate than they really are.

Thus the issue becomes not only the accuracy of these polls but also the integrity of the pollsters. Standard statistical practice and theory, however, indicate that the use of percentage points is proper and accurate. For example, consider the case in which a poll reports 80 percent for Candidate A and 20 percent for candidate B, but the election returns are 90 percent to 10 percent. Using the *percent* criterion the error for Candidate A would be 11 percent, but for Candidate B it would be 100 percent. The *percentage-point* criterion, in contrast, shows an error of ten percentage points no matter which candidate is considered. Clearly, the latter method is less subject to misinterpretation and confusion.

Second, and even more to the point, every statistical textbook deals with sampling error in terms of percentage points. Standard tests of statistical significance are calculated in terms of percentage points because this is the criterion that conforms to the appropriate mathematical theory. Thus, when evaluating what allowance should be made for the fact that a sample rather than the entire population was interviewed, the prescribed procedure is to calculate how many percentage points, plus or minus, should be allowed for a given sample size. Whatever vulnerability pollsters may have with respect to claims they make as to the accuracy of preelection polls, there is no doubt that they are on solid statistical ground in using the percentage-point criterion.

WHAT DO "THE POLLS" SHOW?

A major difficulty in assessing the credibility of preelection surveys is the widespread practice of referring to "the polls" and to what "they" are showing. There are many different types of "polls," ranging from carefully designed sample surveys based upon personal interviews to such devices as counting how many people send away for free copies of photographs of contending candidates. Other frequently encountered methods are mail surveys to telephone or newspaper subscribers, invitations to clip coupons out of newspapers and mail them in, requests for listeners to send a postal card to their local radio or television station, and interviews with "quotas" of men and women at supermarkets, factories, and other heavy-traffic locations. To treat all such methods, as comparable with personal interviews based on mathematically designed samples of the electorate can only becloud the issue. Unfortunately, as Elmo Roper has noted, "To too many members of the press, a poll is a poll is a poll."[5] Because of this "unwillingness to discriminate between the available polls," Roper continues, there is ". . . a general skepticism toward polls, which are often assumed to be as likely to miss as to hit election results on the nose."

In a pioneer effort to evaluate how well "the polls" did in 1960, Bernard C. and Erna R. Hennessy reviewed "26 separate measurements of electoral preference or voting intention. Of these, all except one were styled polls, straw votes, or opinion surveys."[6] The Hennessys used two criteria to measure the performance of these polls: (1) "error," that is, the percentage-point deviation from the election result; and (2) "accuracy," that is, whether the winner was predicted or not. In fourteen newspaper-conducted statewide polls, which used a conglomerate of methods ranging from postal cards mailed to subscribers to personal interviews with carefully drawn samples, thirteen correctly "predicted" the winner while one reported a 50-50 split. (The actual split in that case was 50.7-49.3.) In percentage points, one poll had an error of 16.8 points, four had errors between 3 and 6 points, four had errors between 2 and 3 points and five had errors of less than 2 points. Believing that "the critical question [is] who gets the most votes," the Hennessys maintain that the "errors were consistently errors which were irrelevant to picking the winner." They conclude that luck determines "accuracy," as they define it.[7]

They also reviewed "twelve" national polls, "three" of which were Gallup surveys. One of the Gallup surveys used, and the most accurate of all "twelve," was its final report of the 1960 election campaign. The other "two" Gallup surveys were results of a single national survey taken five weeks before the election and reported separately for the South and non-South. Since the *early* Gallup survey had "errors" of 1.8 points in the South and 2.7 points in the non-South, both in the wrong direction, they conclude that "luck again made Gallup a winner rather than a loser" in the *final* poll. The lesson the Hennessys draw from their analysis is that unsophisticated sampling such as loose quota samples and mail ballots may often be as satisfactory as rigorous adherence to the principles of scientific sampling, and that pollsters may, in close elections, have to rely to a considerable degree on hunch and luck.[8]

In a point-by-point critique of the Hennessys' analysis, Paul K. Perry made the following observations which are relevant to the issue of credibility:[9]

1. The Hennessys provide no specific information about sample sizes, without which it is impossible to compare the accuracy of any surveys. For example, all other things being equal, a sample of 5,000 interviews should be more accurate than one of 500 interviews. Reporting the size of "error" without relating this to sample size does not provide any basis for evaluating the accuracy of any survey.

2. The indiscriminate lumping of poll results regardless of proximity to Election Day, a practice which is reflective of the view that all results are equally "predictions," is not valid. The fact that a poll conducted more than

a month before an election deviates from the election results more than another conducted a few days before is no proof that the former's methodology is inferior. Some voters always change their minds in the final weeks of a campaign, so that an early poll, even though accurate as of when it was conducted, may deviate significantly from the election results.

3. Without an elucidation of the methods used in each poll and the care with which they were administered it is impossible to assess the role that luck played. Since the sample method has built into it random or "chance" fluctuations, in any single election a poorly designed and administered poll, through luck, could be as close to the election results as one that was carefully planned and executed. A single "chance" congruence of results is little reason for preferring the less expensive and less soundly conceived poll.

Perry concludes:

> . . . an evaluation of a poll or election survey result can be made only with reference to a number of factors. Some of the more important ones are: the length of time between the survey and the election, the sampling procedure, the method of obtaining a respondent's choice, the division of the vote, the method of selecting from among all the respondents those likely to vote, and the way in which the estimate is calculated.[10]

Unfortunately, since the Hennessys lacked detailed information about the methodology employed by the "polls" they reviewed, they had to proceed on the assumption that "a poll is a poll is a poll."

In addition, the Hennessys did not take into account a difficulty that arises in evaluating accuracy claims; namely, that even without a high degree of methodological sophistication the sample survey method has a basic validity in that a crude sampling can usually yield a rough approximation of the actual state of affairs. This makes it possible for many preelection "polls" which use crude methods to obtain measurements of voter preferences that often do not deviate excessively from actual election results. Thus, except in close elections, poorly designed polls may compile a seemingly impressive record of correctly "calling the winner" and consequently appear to be soundly conducted.

Illustrative of the inadequacy of the criterion of "calling the winner" is the case of the "*New York Daily News* Poll," acclaimed in the news media of 1966 as being "widely respected." In 1964, the *New York Daily News* had congratulated itself for its "bull's-eye accuracy" in correctly calling a landslide victory for Johnson in New York State.[11] Noted late in the story was their fairly large error of six percentage points. This was described as reflecting "one of the mysteries of polling . . . our concern has been with the people and how they want to vote, not with percentages, which are a statistical invention." An objective evaluation of the *News'* accuracy record and, therefore, its credibility, should be based on its percentage-point error. The actual performance of the *Daily News* Poll up through 1966 in terms of percentage-point error has been summarized by Roll:

> The average deviation between the winner's election percentage and his final *News* figure (in 26 elections) is 5.9 points . . . There are, furthermore, some drastically wide discrepancies between forecast and fact. Five Straw Polls gave results between 5.3 and 9.2 points from the winner's actual total . . . and six others, more than 10 points . . .[12]

A lack of awareness on the part of politicians and the news media of the size of error in earlier *Daily News* Polls in all likelihood led to the unwarranted weight given to it when, in the New York gubernatorial election, it incorrectly forecast an O'Connor victory over Rockefeller. For example, *The New York Times* noted a few days before Election Day:

> The News Poll in particular has made politicians cautious about predicting anything but an O'Connor victory. . . . It is the News Poll actually that is credited with producing much of the optimism that does exist in the O'Connor camp.[13]

Similarly, Rockefeller, despite his private polls which accurately measured his margin of victory, said after the election, "I didn't dare be optimistic in view of the *Daily News* Poll."[14]

If any methodological changes are made, however, as was done by the *Daily News* Poll for its 1968 operation, past performance may be a misleading guide. Changes in methodology undoubtedly account for the accuracy of the *Daily News* Poll in that year. Previously, the *News* had conducted its surveys as a single statewide operation based on 30,000 ballots accumulated over a 20-day period. In 1968, however, five statewide polls were conducted, each over a four-day period and each consisting of about 6,000 ballots. The *News* explained this methodological refinement in these terms:

> By comparing the results of one sample with those of another, it was possible to gauge shifts in opinion. . . . Because (in past years) early straws were combined with late straws . . . last minute opinion shifts were difficult to detect.[15]

The final *Daily News* Poll showed 43.5 percent for Nixon, 46.8 percent for Humphrey, 6.8 percent for Wallace, and 2.9 percent undecided in New York state. Allowing for some ambiguity due to the unallocated undecided vote, this breakdown compares quite favorably with the actual vote of 44.3 percent for Nixon, 49.8 percent for Humphrey, 5.3 percent for Wallace, and 0.6 percent for other candidates.

METHODOLOGICAL PROGRESS IN PREELECTION POLLING

One objective, statistical criterion for evaluating preelection polls—those surveys conducted close to Election Day—is the degree to which they *consistently* report final survey results that, in percentage points, are close approximations of the actual split in the election. Using the percentage-point criterion, a poll which "predicted" the winner with a six percentage-point error did very poorly as compared with one with a two percentage-point error but with the loser ahead. Using this criterion, there has been appreciable progress in the precision of preelection poll methodology, at least as practiced by some survey organizations.

The record of the Gallup Poll, which is the only organization that has published preelection survey results in every national election since 1936, provides a basis for assessing the degree to which methodological advances has been made since the beginnings of modern polling in that year. In the nine elections between 1936 and 1950, the average error of the final preelection Gallup Poll survey, as published the day before election, was 3.7 percentage points. In the eight elections from 1954 through 1968, the average error was reduced to 1.4 percentage points. Moreover, during these last eight elections the *largest* deviation was 2.8 percentage points, which is less than the average error in the previous nine elections.[16]

The research methods employed by the Gallup Poll since 1950 for its preelection surveys, which account for this reduction in error, have been described in considerable detail by Paul K. Perry, president of the Gallup Organization.[17] Perry, who has been in charge of preelection surveys since 1950, presents the most detailed description yet available of the actual methods employed by any public-opinion poll, which makes it possible to relate the Gallup Poll's accuracy record specifically to its methodology. As he describes them, these methods derive from no arcane techniques or subjectively derived insights, but rather from the meticulous application of statistical and social-science theory. The major features relate to the sample design, the identification of likely voters, the obtaining of valid expressions of voter preferences with a minimum "undecided" vote, and the measurement of shifts in voter preference during the campaign.

Sample

A sample of election precincts is drawn for the entire nation with probability of selection proportional to the size of the voting population. Interviewers are provided with maps of these areas; they follow a prescribed route and call at every *n'th* household, selecting those to be interviewed in accordance with a prescribed selection procedure. No sex, age, or socioeconomic "quotas" are used. Interviewing is conducted in the evening when both men and women are to be found at home. While a tight schedule of three days prevents calling back to interview people who are not at home when the interviewer calls, a statistical substitute for call-back is employed.[18]

This sample procedure takes the selection of those to be interviewed completely out of the hands of the interviewer; without this safeguard a sample bias could occur. While time schedules make necessary some deviation from the rules of probability sampling, this deviation is minimal. Thus, unlike hit-or-miss street-corner interviews, mail surveys with low response rates, or quota sampling, there is a reasonably sufficient mathematical basis for calculating what allowance should be made for sampling error, and the dangers of sample bias resulting from some kinds of people being systematically excluded from the sample is at a minimum. (Moreover, using election precincts as the areal sampling unit makes it possible to use the vote by precincts in a previous election as supplementary data to reduce the sampling variance [error] of the estimate of vote-preference formed from the survey data.)

Likely voters

A major source of error in election surveys, in addition to sampling error, is the fact that so many people do not vote. In 1968, about four out of every ten persons of voting age did not cast a ballot for any of the Presidential candidates. As Samuel Stouffer has pointed out, ". . . with the best of probability samples, if you get 85 percent of the people telling you whom they prefer, and only 50 percent are going to vote, you have a margin of error that is positively staggering. . . ."[19]

Perry, begining in 1950, developed for the Gallup Poll a method for identifying likely voters. First, to rank respondents by likelihood of voting the Gallup Poll in 1968 used a series of nine questions to construct a "turnout scale." (In earlier years, a shorter series was used.) This scale, first used in 1950 in its shorter form, has been validated in every election since then by checking registration books to find out *whether* respondents voted. The scoring system has been refined each year so that in 1968, of those identified as mostly likely to vote, 87 percent actually did so. Of those identified as least likely to vote, less than one percent voted.

Once respondents are ranked by likelihood of voting, it then becomes necessary to determine the "cutting point" on the scale; that is, the point that divides the sample into two groups—likely voters and unlikely voters. In 1956, a method was devised by Perry and Crespi using two of the items on the turnout scale to develop an indirect number which estimates the turnout in an election. In the four Presidential elections in which this method has been used, the estimated turnout ratio has been within less than two percentage points of the actual (Table 1). The reported Gallup

Poll preelection survey results are based on the preferences of likely voters as identified by this method.

Table 1 *Voter Turnout in Four Presidential Elections Compared with Gallup Poll Estimate*

	Actual Voter Turnout*	Gallup Poll Estimate**
	%	%
1956	62.8	62.9
1960	66.5	68.3
1964	65.3	65.5
1968	64.0	64.7

* Percentage who voted of total civilian resident population of voting age, excluding aliens and inmates of correctional and mental institutions.

** Previously unpublished estimates based on interviewing conducted five weeks before Election Day.

Expression of voter preference

A basic problem in obtaining valid expressions of voter preferences is the difficulty in minimizing the "undecided" vote and possible evasive or misleading answers. Three techniques are used to solve this problem: (1) wording the question in terms of voting preference "if the election were being held today," rather than asking how respondents say they intend to vote in the future; (2) using a forced-choice question which asks those who are undecided or refuse to voice a preference in which political direction they "lean"; and (3) using a paper "secret ballot" on which respondents mark their choice and which they then place in a sealed box. (The specific method in which the secret ballot is used was developed by the late Sidney Goldish, who at the time had been director of the Minnesota Poll.)

The combination of these methods, when applied to "likely voters," typically reduces the undecided vote to about 3 to 5 percent, and the closeness of the final survey results to the actual returns is indicative of the validity with which the questiton is answered.

Last-minute shifts

By asking for preferences as of "today," the Gallup Poll relates each measurement to a specific point in time. This makes it possible to measure trends in voter preference. The final preelection survey is taken during the week immediately preceding the election, and every effort is made to schedule the interviewing as close as possible to Election Day. In 1968 interviewing was conducted on Thursday and Friday evenings and Saturday mornings through noon. Immediately upon completion of their assignments, interviewers wired their results to Gallup headquarters in Princeton where data processing and analysis were completely by Saturday midnight. On Sunday afternoon the results were wired to subscribing newspapers for Monday publication.

To make possible such a time schedule, two identically designed surveys are conducted, one about a month before the election and the other the week previous, as just described. In each survey in 1968 about 4,500 individuals of voting age were personally interviewed. The data from the first survey were fully analyzed to determine the division of voter preferences *as of that time*. Then, by calculating the difference between a gross measurement on each of the two surveys, and applying this difference to the refined estimate based on the first survey, the "final figure" was reached.

The use of this full method, Perry reports, has reduced the average deviation of the final survey from the election to a point "which conforms closely to the theoretical expectation for samples of the sizes used drawn as random samples."[20]

The value of timing the final survey as close as possible to Election Day is threefold. First, and of greatest relevance to the question of credibility, is the fact that the final survey establishes a meaningful basis whereby the public evaluates the accuracy of the sample-survey method. It is true that the final survey is not, as such, a prediction of what will happen on Election Day, since intervening events could lead to a significant shift in opinion over the final weekend. Strictly speaking, using the final survey as a prediction requires projecting the survey result into the future; and this projection involves making assumptions that are not always warranted. But, in the absence of any particularly startling or dramatic occurrence in the last few days before election, it is reasonable to expect that the final survey results should correspond closely to the actual vote case. The record of these final surveys, consequently, is cited by the Gallup Poll as proof of the credibility of all its reports. Gallup has said:

> . . . I see no great social value in reporting twenty-four hours in advance of an election how the country is going to vote, or approximately how it is going to vote, but I do think that elections are valuable in providing an acid test for polling techniques.[21]

In the wake of the highly accurate 1968 results, Gallup made an even stronger claim as to the value of using preelection polls as a way of empirically validating the survey method:

> The Gallup Poll has developed a thoroughly scientific approach to election polling. Far more important than this, however, is that it has demonstrated that when a scientifiic method is used, instead of subjective judgment, human behavior in the aggregate can be predicted —the goal of social science. . . .
>
> Perhaps most important of all is the proof that reliable responses can be obtained from the public in sample surveys, and the employment of attitude measurements can be used to predict mass behavior with great accuracy.[22]

This function as been noted by the Social Science Research Council:

> Elections are useful for testing the adequacy of polling methods for estimating the percentages of the vote going to each candidate from various groups in the population. No better test is now known.[23]

Second, and of interest to politicians, political analysts, and social scientists, timing the final survey as close as possible to Election Day makes possible an analysis of the actual vote in terms of demographic and socioeconomics characteristics based on expressions of preferences voiced almost at the time when the votes are cast. Such analyses are regularly published after every election. Since actual votes are anonymous, they cannot be analyzed in terms of age, sex, income, or education, which makes the survey data extremely valuable to political analysts and scholars (Table 2).

The value of preelection polls to social scientists is also evident in Lazarsfeld's comment:

> I am very definitely in favor of political forecasts because only by trying and trying over again to make political forecasts will we finally learn to understand what really explains political behavior of people . . . forecasting and explaining are really the same. . . . If I understand something I can also predict what will happen, and if I cannot predict I cannot also understand . . . no one will seriously raise the question, "Should political behavior be understood?"[24]

Third, but of weight primarily to the financial security of the survey organization, is the preelection poll's journalistic value of being able to report a "final figure" the day before the election. If such a report were not available, it is likely that many newspapers would not support the published opinion polls. Gideon Seymour, Vice President and Executive Editor of *The Minneapolis Star and Tribune* which sponsors the Minneapolis Poll, in justifying the publication of preelection polls, has expressed the journalist's attitude in these terms:

> . . . in many respects . . . the most important point . . . [is] that opinion studies are eminently newsworthy. . . . Public opinion surveying . . . reflects the impact of ideas and prejudices and events and propaganda

Table 2 *Analysis of Presidential Vote by Demographic Characteristics, from 1952 to 1968*

Dem.–*D* Rep.–*R* Wallace–*W*	1952 *D* %	 *R* %	1956 *D* %	 *R* %	1960 *D* %	 *R* %	1964 *D* %	 *R* %	1968 *D* %	 *R* %	 *W* %
NATIONAL	44.6	55.4	42.2	57.8	50.1	49.9	61.3	38.7	43.0	43.4	13.6
Men	47	53	45	55	52	48	60	40	41	43	16
Women	42	58	39	61	49	51	62	38	45	43	12
White	43	57	41	59	49	51	59	41	38	47	15
Non-white	79	21	61	39	68	32	94	6	85	12	3
College	34	66	31	69	39	61	52	48	42	54	9
High School	45	55	42	58	52	48	62	38	42	43	15
Grade School	52	48	50	50	55	45	66	34	52	33	15
Prof. & Bus.	36	64	32	68	42	58	54	46	34	56	10
White Collar	40	60	37	63	48	52	57	43	41	47	12
Manual	55	45	50	50	60	40	71	29	50	35	15
Farmers	33	67	46	54	48	52	53	47	29	51	20
Under 30	51	49	43	57	54	46	64	36	47	38	15
30–49 years	47	53	45	55	54	46	63	37	44	41	15
50 years & older	39	61	39	61	46	54	59	41	41	47	12
Protestant	37	63	37	63	38	62	55	45	35	49	16
Catholic	56	44	51	49	78	22	76	24	59	33	8
Republicans	8	92	4	96	5	95	20	80	9	86	5
Democrats	77	23	85	15	84	16	87	13	74	12	14
Independents	35	65	30	70	43	57	56	44	31	44	25

Source: Gallup Poll release, December 8, 1968.

> upon the people themselves. It is simply news reporting in a new field, a field that has to be studied if a newspaper is to report fully the trend and patterns of the times and of the changing world.[25]

Gallup, in defending the publication of preelection polls, took essentially the same position when he said, ". . . as a matter of fact, I think the only justification for public opinion polls is to report the views of the people of this country on issues of the day."[26]

RECENT ACCURACY RECORD OF PUBLISHED POLLS

In the three most recent Presidential elections—1960, 1964, and 1968—as well as in the 1966 congressional elections, the final surveys of the leading published polls established the credibility of preelection polls for the general public, journalists, and politicians.

In 1960 all the major published polls indicated the closeness of the Kennedy-Nixon race. The two polls with the smallest deviations from the election results were those of Gallup and Roper. The final Gallup survey, published the day before election, reported a 51–49 lead for Kennedy, which was 0.9 percentage points from the actual vote. Roper's final survey, while it showed Nixon slightly ahead, was merely 1.1 percentage points off the mark.

In 1964 the final Gallup survey and the final Harris survey reported Johnson ahead in the popular vote by a 64–36 margin, which is quite close to the 61.7–38.3 percent split in the official returns. In the 1966 congressional elections the final Gallup Poll reported the Democrats ahead with a projected 52.5 percent of the total vote in all congressional races, indicative of a gain of 35 to 55 House seats for the Republicans. The final Harris Survey projected a 30–35 seat gain for the Republicans based upon a Democratic vote of 54 percent.[27] In the official tally of all votes, the Democrats received 51.9 percent of the vote and the Republicans gained 47 seats.

To evaluate the 1966 record fully, it should be noted that *The New York Times* had predicted that Republican gains were mostly likely to be limited to 29 seats.[28] In developing its forecast, *The Times* used the traditional journalistic method of having reporters interview leaders of both parties and other political "experts" in all states in order that an assessment of the outcome in each state's contests could be reached. Also reported by *The Times* was Richard Nixon's "optimistic," presumably partisan forecast of a Republican gain of about forty seats. The Gallup preelection report was given passing note, which would explain why on the day after election *The Times* headlined its report on the election results, "Republicans Stronger Than Expected In Off Year Vote." It is the increasing sophistication of the sample-survey method in accurately measuring trends in voter preferences, as compared with the methods of traditional journalism, that has made for the increasing credibility of preelection polls.

In 1968 the final Gallup Poll release reported 43 percent for Nixon, 42 percent for Humphrey, and 15 percent for Wallace, which results correctly presaged Nixon's narrow margin of victory over Humphrey—43.5 percent to 42.9 percent.[29] While the final Harris Survey had Humphrey in the lead, it was also very close to the actual election—Humphrey 45 percent, Nixon 41 percent, and Wallace 14 percent.[30]

VARIATIONS IN ACCURACY RESULTING FROM THE METHODS USED

To comprehend the significant improvements that have been made in sample surveys of voter preferences since 1936 and subsequent to 1948 it is necessary to recognize the extent to which different question-wordings and analytical procedures can produce varying results. The identification of how such factors affect survey results presents the pollster with the problem of determining which of the myriad methods that could be used will *consistently* produce accurate reflections of voter opinion.

For example, in 1952, before the efficacy of the Gallup Poll's new methodology had been validated, and in the wake of the 1948 experience, a very cautious way of reporting candidate strength was utilized. Two different questions were asked, one couched in terms of which *party* was preferred while the other measured the voter's preference of the *candidate's themselves*. Also, in the analysis of the undecided vote, weight was given to such factors as past voting behavior, basic party loyalties, position on issues, and socioeconomic characteristics. No objective basis for weighing these factors was available, making possible plausible alternate methods of allocating the "undecideds." The consequence of this method was the reporting of a series of alternatives as measurements of the comparative strength of Eisenhower and Stevenson. The final Gallup Poll report before election consequently presented the array of measurements shown in Table 3; the report indicated a possible range from a decisive Eisenhower victory to a narrow margin for Stevenson. The actual election returns gave Eisenhower 55.4 percent of the popular vote.

The data in Table 3 show, first of all, that the "party" question produced a measurement that overstated Stevenson's strength. Apparently there were enough Democrats willing to say they preferred Eisenhower, the man, but who were reluctant to say that they preferred the Republican party's candidate. Second, since one of Eisenhower's strengths was his appeal to Democrats, who tend to be of lower socioeconomic status than Republicans, assessing the undecided in terms of past preference and of socioecomonic characteristics also overstated Stevenson's position. A reanalysis of the same data, using only the candidate preference question and a "forced choice" follow-up to allocate the undecided vote, shows that if this method had been used, the final Gallup measurement of 1952 would have been within one percentage point of the actual vote.[31] This procedure for handling the "undecided," as already noted, is integral to the method now used by the Gallup Poll. This example demonstrates again the impossibility of evaluating the accuracy of polls as such. What must be assessed is the accuracy of a specific method, including sample design, interviewing procedures, and analytical techniques.

The importance and difficulty of fully and correctly assessing the reliability of preelection polls are further evidenced by the final Gallup and Harris reports in 1964. Both polls reported on the Monday before election a 64–36 margin for Johnson, after allocating the undecided votes. Their agreement, however, is not as complete as first reading might indicate. Throughout most of the campaign, the Gallup Poll measured Johnson's strength at a higher level than did the Harris Survey. Thus, in order for

Table 3 *Variations in Measured Voter Preferences as Reported in the Final 1952 Gallup Preelection Report*

	As Measured by Candidate Preference Question		As Measured by Party Preference Question	
		%		%
Before allocating "undecided":				
	Eisenhower	47	Republican	45
	Stevenson	40	Democratic	44
	Undecided	13	Undecided	11
		100		100
Allocating "undecided" 2–1 to Stevenson:				
	Eisenhower	51	Republican	49
	Stevenson	49	Democratic	51
		100		100
Allocating "undecided" 3–1 to Stevenson:				
	Eisenhower	50	Republican	48
	Stevenson	50	Democratic	52
		100		100

Source: Gallup Poll release, November 2, 1952.

the two surveys to be in agreement at the end, they had to be in disagreement as to what the trend was in the final weeks of the campaign. Judging from the Gallup Poll, there was a slight movement toward Goldwater, accounted for primarily by the return to the fold of some defecting Republicans. In contrast, the Harris Survey indicated that Goldwater lost some strength in the final weeks of the campaign, though by a slight margin.[32]

By the way of comparison, in a survey conducted in August 1964 for NBC, Roper reported 67 percent for Johnson, 28 percent for Goldwater, and 5 percent undecided.[33] At about that time, Gallup was reporting 65 percent for Johnson, 29 percent for Goldwater, and 6 percent undecided,[34] whereas the early August Harris Survey measurement was 59 percent for Johnson, 32 percent for Goldwater, and 9 percent undecided.[35]

Differences between the 1964 Harris and Gallup measurements may be the result of different methodologies rather than of sampling error. For example, early in the year, well before the conventions, Gallup and Harris issued reports that differed markedly as to how much stronger Johnson was than the three leading Republican contenders (Table 4). It is unlikely that sampling error could account for such a large divergence. In 1968 also, the somewhat divergent accuracy of the Gallup and Harris polls may have been the result of methodological differences as well as sampling error. The Gallup Poll had the smallest margin of error and indicated a Nixon victory by the narrowest of margins. While the Harris Survey indicated a Humphrey win, its error was within the "statistical margin of error of 3 to 4 points plus or minus" that Harris said should be allowed for his sample size.[36] This allowance for sampling error, Harris reported, made "the election too close to call in this highly volatile year."

In assessing the divergence of the Harris measurement, consideration must be given to the ways in which his methodology differs from that of the Gallup Poll. Harris has reported that three preference questions are asked in the course of an interview of one and one-half hours' duration—a direct

Table 4 *Comparison of Gallup Poll and Harris Poll "Trial Heats" Reported in January, 1964*

	Gallup %	Harris %
Johnson vs. Nixon		
Johnson	69	59
Nixon	24	41
Undecided	7	–
Johnson vs. Rockefeller		
Johnson	77	71
Rockefeller	16	29
Undecided	7	–
Johnson vs. Goldwater		
Johnson	75	67
Goldwater	18	33
Undecided	7	–

Source: *U.S. News & World Report,* February 10, 1964, p. 37.

question at the beginning of the interview, a secret question near the end, and another direct question at the end.[37] In contrast, the Gallup Poll asks one secret question relatively early in the interview. To measure last minute trends in 1968, the Harris Survey used a method very different from the Gallup Poll's. Surveys were conducted on the Friday, Saturday, and Sunday before the election, based on three independent, equal-sized samples, using a replicated sample design. In the Friday survey Nixon had a three-point lead over Humphrey, on Saturday Humphrey had achieved a one-point lead, and on Sunday Humphrey had a three-point lead. While a three-day average, Harris reports, would have shown Nixon and Humphrey in a dead heat, it was felt that the three surveys had measured a real trend, so the Sunday survey result was used by itself for the final Harris report.[38] This choice, apparently, is the basis for the last sentence in the report: "If the late trend continued, however, it would indicate a potential majority for Humphrey in the Electoral College."

A further differentiation between the two polls may lie in the area of identifying likely voters. The Gallup Poll samples all adults of voting age and then excludes likely nonvoters, as described earlier. The Harris Survey excludes from its sample persons who report they are not registered, and does not interview them at all. It then makes a further exclusion of likely nonvoters, but the specific manner in which this is done has not been published.

An incident in February, 1967 demonstrates the extent to which national political leaders who rely upon polls of voter preferences as they plan organization support for their candidates may be confused by methodological differences between surveys. On February 12, 1967, Warren Weaver reported in *The New York Times* that

> [a] Gallup Poll that would have shown Richard M. Nixon surging past George Romney as the presidential candidate preferred by most Republicans was ordered withdrawn today hours before its scheduled publication.
>
> A rough version of the poll figures, indicating an 11 point drop in Governor Romney's popularity in less than three months, had been circulating among politicians here for two days, causing consternation among supporters of the Governor and glee among his detractors.

Weaver also reported that it was "understood that the Harris poll will show Governor Romney with a lead of about 12 points over Mr. Nixon when all Republican candidates are considered," leading to speculation that political pressure had led to the suppression of the Gallup release.

The reason for the withdrawal of the release was given by the Gallup Poll in these terms:

> The Gallup Poll originally scheduled for Sunday, February 12, was withdrawn two days before the publication date because the results were incorrectly dealt with in terms of a trend since the November survey. A difference in question wording between the two surveys makes such a comparison invalid. Today's release gives the full findings for the latest survey.[39]

The release referred to in the statement was published on February 14, reporting the latest standings of Romney and Nixon. The difficulty was that in the survey reported on February 14 the question asked referred to which man was rated the "best" candidate, whereas in November the question was worded in terms of which man was "preferred." Since such a difference in question-wording could in itself cause a shift in standings, the reporting of a trend on the basis of two different question-wordings, as was mistakenly done in the withdrawn release, would be misleading. To determine whether the question-wording would, in fact, alter standings, both wordings were used in two subsequent surveys, both of which used a split-sample design. The full question-wordings were:

> *Best man:* Which one of the two men on this list do you think would make the best Presidential candidate for the Republican Party in 1968?

> *Like to See Nominated:* Here is a list of men who have been mentioned as possible Presidential candidates for the Republican Party in 1968. Which one would you like to see nominated as the Republican candidate for President in 1968?

The results for these questions as reported by the Gallup Poll on February 13 and March 19 are shown in Table 5. Comparing the two March figures, while the question-wording did not change the proportion that named Nixon, Romney fared somewhat better as the "best man" than as the man Republicans would "like to see nominated." While the difference is not large, reporting a "trend" based on the November and February surveys would have been incorrect.

Table 5 *Preferences of Republicans for 1964 Candidate*

	Best Man		Like to See Nominated	
	Feb. 1967	Mar. 1967	Mar. 1967	Nov. 1966
Nixon	39	39	39	31
Romney	28	34	30	39

Sources: Gallup Poll releases, February 13, 1967, and March 19, 1967.

The Harris Survey in February reported that 41 percent of Republicans named Romney as their first choice, while 28 percent named Nixon. These figures deviate significantly from the February Gallup Poll. However, since the exact wording of the Harris question was not given, since variations in question-wordings demonstrably can affect measurements of preferences, and since interviewing dates for the two surveys seem not to have been concurrent, it is difficult to evaluate the meaning of this deviation. In any case, this incident illustrates that party organizations, in their use of surveys of voter preferences, in order to interpret correctly exactly what a reported result means, must be informed about the specific methodology that was employed.

In the heat of a campaign, however, partisan allegiances make it very difficult for an objective assessment to be made of the effects of differing survey methodologies. During the 1968 Presidential campaign there were consistent differences between Gallup Poll and Harris Survey results that for a time seemed likely to form a political issue almost as important as some of those raised by the candidates themselves. Both survey organizations reported a dramatic surge in Humphrey's strength in the last weeks of the campaign. Nevertheless, they differed in that (1) the Gallup Poll trend showed Humphrey coming from further behind than did the Harris Survey; (2) the final Harris Survey indicated the probability that Humphrey had managed to move ahead of Nixon, whereas the final Gallup Poll indicated that Nixon appeared to have managed to hold on to a tenuous lead; and (3) the Gallup Poll showed Nixon picking up strength in July, which he mostly managed to retain up through Election Day, whereas the Harris Survey showed Nixon making a smaller gain in August, which he then held on to with little subsequent change (Table 6).

The press focused on this systematic difference between the two polls, and reported considerable speculation—some of which was obviously colored by political loyalties—as to the methodological reasons for it. Illustrative of the latter is a statement from a campaign speech by Senator Joseph D. Tydings about the credibility of the Gallup Poll:

> There is good reason to believe that the Gallup Poll is not properly weighted, is low on urban representation and minority group representation and is based on 1960 Census tracts, which are somewhat outdated. . . . I feel confident that the new Harris Poll . . . will show a dramatic spurt and that the election will be, in Mr. Harris's words, "too close to call." . . . Deficiencies [in Gallup's polling methods] . . . explain the discrepancy between the two polls.[40]

James M. Perry, writing in *The National Observer* a few days subsequent to Tydings' statement, also attempted to explain the difference

Table 6 *Comparison of Trends in Nixon-Humphrey-Wallace "Trial Heats" as Reported by Gallup Poll and Harris Survey*

Gallup Poll

Interviewing dates	Nixon	Humphrey	Wallace	Undecided
Oct. 31–Nov. 2	43	42	15	–
Oct. 17–21	44	36	15	5
Oct. 3–12	43	31	20	6
Sept. 27–30	44	29	20	7
Sept. 20–22	43	28	21	8
Sept. 3–7	43	31	17	7
Aug. 8–11	45	29	18	8
July 19–21	40	38	16	6
June 29–July 3	35	40	16	9
June 15–16	37	42	14	7

Sources: Gallup Poll releases, July 31 and November 4, 1968.

Harris Survey

Interviewing dates	Nixon	Humphrey	Wallace	Undecided
Nov. 4	41	45	13	–
Nov. 1–2	42	40	12	6
Oct. 27–28	40	37	16	7
Oct. 9–11	40	35	18	7
Sept. 11–13	39	31	21	9
Aug. 24	40	34	17	9
July 25–29	36	41	16	7
July 6–11	35	37	17	11
June 11–16	36	43	13	8

Sources: *New York Post*, November 4 and 5, 1968; *Philadelphia Inquirer*, November 1, 1968.

between the reported results of the two polls in terms of the sampling techniques used and methods for estimating turnout:

> It's not hard to determine where the problem lies. Both Mr. Gallup and Mr. Harris are in general agreement about voting intentions in the South, in the suburbs, in rural areas. But they are wildly at variance

> in the cities with populations of 1,000,000 or more. . . . Either Mr. Gallup or Mr. Harris is doing something very wrong in measuring the vote in these big cities. . . . [Other] polltakers believe that Mr. Harris tends to give more weight to the Negro vote than Mr. Gallup. Mr. Harris, they believe, assumes that 50 percent of the big city Negro electorate will actually go to the polls. Mr. Gallup, they believe, assumes a lower level of participation—perhaps on the order of 30 percent.[41]

Both of these attempts to account for the differences between the Gallup Poll and the Harris Survey focus on the methodologies used, but fail to pinpont the reasons for the differences because the attempts are based on hearsay and speculation rather than upon factual knowledge. For example, the Gallup Poll's method of identifying likely voters is applied to the entire sample and not to specific segments, such as Negroes. Rather than allowing the analyst to "assume" what the turnout of any ethnic group will be, the method makes it impossible to know the measured turnout level for any segment of the sample until after the analysis is completed. While it seems likely that differences in methods for estimating turnout were involved—the Gallup Polls measurement for its entire sample including likely and unlikely voters approximated the Harris Survey reports for likely voters (Table 7)—the speculations reported by James Perry provide little guidance for ascertaining with any precision how and why these

Table 7 *Preferences for President among All Adults of Voting Age and "Likely Voters"*

	Gallup Poll		Harris Survey
	Likely Voters, %	All Adults, %	Likely Voters, %
Nixon	44	41	40
Humphrey	36	35	37
Wallace	15	18	16
Undecided	5	6	7

Sources: Gallup Poll release, November 1, 1968, interviewing date October 17–21; The Harris Survey, *New York Post,* November 4, 1968, interviewing dates October 27–28.

methods may have produced conflicting measurements. Similarly, Senator Tydings' comments are the expressions of the needs of a political campaigner seeking to spur on his party's workers rather than the result of an empirical analysis of the sampling methods of the two polls in question.

On the other hand, a major methodological characteristic of the Harris Survey—the use of a panel technique in which persons are reinterviewed, contrasting with the reliance of the Gallup Poll on independent surveys—was ignored by the press.

Complicating further any attempt to assess objectively conflicting survey results is the possibility that the press may be misled when seeking guidance from presumably qualified experts. Illustrative of this danger is a report by Steven V. Roberts that appeared the day Senator Tydings made his above comments:

> A number of experts on public opinion polls agreed yesterday that the 7 point discrepancy between the current Harris and Gallup Polls on the Presidential race is too large to be caused by the normal imprecision of statistical surveys. . . . For example, (the experts) said, an accurate survey has to screen out eligible voters who will not cast ballots. Although the pollsters have developed some techniques for eliminating stay-at-homes, the experts generally believe their methods are not foolproof.[42]

While it can be taken for granted that no sampling method is foolproof, it nevertheless appears that at least some of the experts who were contacted were unfamiliar with the power of the advanced techniques such as those described above.

In the light of the skeptical concern expressed and reported by the press about the conflicting Gallup Poll and Harris Survey results in 1968, it is noteworthy that after the election there appeared an uncritical feeling that "the polls" did well. William V. Shannon, after noting that the final Gallup Poll report "turning out to be almost exactly right" continued by observing that "[t]he Harris poll was equally accurate."[43] Similarly, *The New York Times* commented editorially:

> Yet both the Gallup and Harris polls came extraordinarily close to mirroring the delicate balance of a final vote that gave both Richard M. Nixon and Hubert H. Humphrey almost exactly 43 percent of the popular ballots as against 13 percent for George Wallace. The discrepancy between these figures and those forecast by the two major polling organizations in their concluding surveys is readily explained by undecided voters and the margin of error inherent in any sampling process.[44]

Once the heat of the campaign had abated, the fact that in the final reports there was a continuance of the systematic difference between the two polls—with Humphrey's strength still at a higher level in the Harris Survey than in the Gallup Poll—was overlooked. Yet it would be plausible to hypothesize that the persistence of such a systematic difference is the result of methodology, and not only of sampling variance. In any event, the credibility of poll results, although contingent upon the attainment of a reasonable degree of accuracy, is also clearly colored by the observer's political involvement in a campaign.

ENDNOTES

1. *The New York Times*, November 4, 1968.
2. *Washington Post*, November 5, 1968.
3. Lindsay Rogers, *The Pollsters: Public Opinion, Politics, and Democratic Opinion* (New York: Alfred A. Knopf Co., 1949).
4. Senator Albert Gore, address to the Senate, February 11, 1960.
5. Elmo Roper, "Were the Polls Wrong?" *The Saturday Review* (December 10, 1966), p. 33.
6. Bernard C. Hennessy, and Erna R Hennessy, "The Prediction of Close Elections: Comments on Some 1960 Polls," *Public Opinion Quarterly* (Fall 1961), pp. 405–411.
7. *Ibid.*, p. 410.
8. *Ibid.*, p. 411.
9. Paul K. Perry, Letter to the Editor, *Public Opinion Quarterly* (Spring 1962), pp. 133–135.
10. *Ibid.*, p. 135.
11. *New York Daily News*, November 5, 1964.
12. Charles W. Roll, Jr., "Straws in the Wind: The Record of the Daily News Poll," *Public Opinion Quarterly* (Summer 1968), p. 25.
13. *The New York Times*, November 4, 1966.
14. *The New York Times*, November 11, 1966.
15. *New York Daily News*, November 4, 1968.
16. *Gallup Opinion Index*, no. 42 (December 1968), inside back cover.
17. Paul K. Perry, "Election Survey Procedures for the Gallup Poll," *Public Opinion Quarterly* (Fall 1960), pp. 531–542; "Gallup Poll Election Survey Experience 1950–1960," *Public Opinion Quarterly* (Summer 1962), pp. 272–279; "Election Survey Methods," *Gallup Political Index*, no. 7 (December 1965), pp. i–xii.
18. Alfred Politz and W. R. Simmons, "An attempt to get the 'Not-at-Homes' into the sample without call-backs," *Journal of the American Statistical Association*, vol. 44, pp. 9–31.
19. Samuel A. Stouffer, "The S.S.R.C. Committee Report" in *The Polls and Public Opinion*, Norman C. Meier and Harold W. Saunders, eds. (New York: Henry Holt and Company, 1949), p. 210.
20. Paul K. Perry, *loc. cit.*, *Public Opinion Quarterly* (1962), p. 279.
21. George Gallup, "Should Political Forecasts Be Made?" in Meier and Saunders, *op. cit.*, p. 286.
22. George Gallup, "Report on the 1968 Election" (mimeographed, undated).

23. Quoted by Gideon Seymour in Meier and Saunder, *op. cit.*, p. 272.
24. Paul F. Lazarsfeld in Meier and Saunders, *op. cit.*, p. 279.
25. Gideon Seymour in Meier and Saunders, *op. cit.*, p. 272.
26. George Gallup in Meier and Saunders, *op. cit.*, p. 286.
27. *Washington Post*, November 1, 1966.
28. Elmo Roper, *op. cit.*, p. 33.
29. *The New York Times*, November 4, 1968.
30. *Washington Post*, November 5, 1968.
31. Paul K. Perry, *op. cit.*, (1935), page v.
32. *Washington Post*, November 3, 1964.
33. *The New York Times*, August 25, 1964.
34. *Gallup Poll Report*, August 22, 1964.
35. *Washington Post*, October 12, 1964.
36. *Washington Post*, November 5, 1968.
37. Notes taken by Irving Crespi during talk given by Louis Harris on November 26, 1968, to the Princeton Chapter of the American Statistical Association.
38. *Ibid.*
39. *Gallup Poll Report*, February 9, 1967.
40. *Washington Post*, October 24, 1968.
41. *National Observer*, October 28, 1968.
42. *The New York Times*, October 23, 1968.
43. "The Week in Review," *The New York Times*, November 10, 1968.
44. *The New York Times*, November 8, 1968.

PART 5 SELECTION 2

Reprinted from *The Public Opinion Quarterly*, 36, 1 (Spring 1972), with permission of the publisher and the author.

Methodological Bias in Public Opinion Surveys

FREDERICK WISEMAN

Statistically designed sample surveys have enabled pollsters to gauge public opinion on a wide range of issues. In such surveys, selection of a data collection technique is generally based on four criteria: (1) cost; (2) completion time; (3) response rate; and (4) response bias. Typically, more weight is placed on the first three factors and, as a result, adequate attention has not been given to the latter consideration. The study described in this [selection] looks at one type of response bias—that which results from the use of a specific data collection method. More specifically, this research uses a controlled experimental design in order to determine whether responses given in a public opinion polling are influenced by the method used to collect data. Three methods are investigated: (1) mail questionnaire; (2) telephone interview; and (3) personal interview.

METHODS

Residents of a suburban Boston community were polled on nine current issues, both local and national. In order to determine the influence of the data collection technique, three experimental groups were formed and asked identical questions. Members of the first group received a mail questionnaire, while those in the second and third groups had telephone and personal interviews, respectively. If there were no technique bias, then one would expect identical results (except for random variation) in each of the three experimental groups.

Critical to the reasoning above is the assumption that the experimental groups are equivalent samples from a common population. A two-stage sampling process was used in an attempt to satisfy this requirement. In stage one, the population was divided into twelve mutually exclusive and collectively exhaustive clusters, and a random selection of a street within each cluster was made. In stage two, those residing on each of the selected streets were sequentially assigned to groups in the following order: mail—telephone—mail—personal. Approximately the same number of potential respondents was obtained for each of the twelve street listings.

As can be seen, there were twice as many potential mail respondents as potential telephone or personal interview respondents. This particular sample allocation was made because of (1) the belief that the response rate from the mail questionnaire would be significantly lower than that from the other two methods; and (2) the desire to obtain approximately the same number of completed interviews for each of the three data collection techniques. To improve upon the mail questionnaire response rate, a follow-up postcard was sent three days after the original mailing. In addition, on an experimental basis, approximately 25 percent of this group received a prior telephone notification. This brief notification informed potential respondents that they would be receiving a questionnaire in the mail within the next few days and that their cooperation in filling it out would be greatly appreciated.[1]

RESULTS

The response rates achieved for each of the three techniques are given in Table 1.[2]

As can be seen from Table 2, the number of completed interviews using the mail questionnaire was considerably larger than that for either the personal or the telephone interview. This particular result was unexpected and was primarily due to the relatively large number of questionnaires returned from those households which had received prior telephone notification.

Table 1 *Completion Rates for Each Data Collection Technique*

Data Collection Technique	*Attempts*	*Completions*
Mail questionnaire		
Prior notification[a]	75	50 (67%)
No prior notification	245	107 (47%)
Telephone interview	160[b]	102 (64%)
Personal interview	160	96 (60%)

[a] The position of the stamp on the self-addressed return envelope made it possible to identify all returns coming from households receiving prior notification.
[b] Not included are 56 households for which there was no telephone number.

Table 2 *Survey Results by Data Collection Technique*

	Percent Yes Answers[a]			
Issue	*Mail*	*Telephone*	*Personal*	X^2
1. In favor of Congress's decision to eliminate funds for the SST	74	73	75	.2
2. In favor of an all-volunteer army within two years	71	77	81	3.0
3. In favor of a reduction in the size of the Massachusetts House of Representatives	81	76	79	.7
4. In favor of legalizing marijuana	39	43	42	.8
5. In favor of making birth control devices readily available to unmarried people	83	67	72	8.0[b]
6. In favor of legalizing abortion	89	62	70	29.5[c]
7. In favor of the Court's decision in finding Lt. Calley guilty	64	58	53	2.6
8. In favor of giving state aid to Catholic schools	37	32	34	.6
9. In favor of lowering the legal drinking age to eighteen	60	62	67	1.7

[a] Excluding "Don't know" responses.
[b] Significant at the .05 level.
[c] Significant at the .01 level.

Sample validation

Socioeconomic and demographic data were obtained for each of the respondents. No statistically significant differences were found among the groups on any of the following characteristics: sex, marital status, age, occupation, income, and religion Thus, the previously described sampling process did, in fact, generate equivalent groupings of respondents. No differences in response patterns were found between those receiving and those not receiving prior notification in the mail questionnaire group.

Survey results

The results of the public opinion polling are shown in Table 2. Significant technique bias was present on only two of the nine questions: "Do you believe that birth control devices should be readily available to unmarried people?" and "Should abortion be legalized in Massachusetts?" These issues are both personal, and, in each instance, the largest percentage of socially undesirable responses was obtained in the mail questionnaire while the smallest percentage was obtained in the telephone interview.

Further analysis of the two significant questions revealed that the response bias was related to the religious preference of the respondent.

On the birth control issue, 75 percent of the Catholics who received a mail questionnaire were in favor of making birth control devices readily available to unmarried people, compared with only 44 percent of those Catholics receiving either a telephone or personal interview. On the abortion issue, Jewish members of the sample varied most depending on which method was used to collect the data. Ninety-eight percent of Jews receiving the mail questionnaire agreed with the proposition, compared with approximately 73 percent of those responding to one of the other data collection methods. Again, the largest percentage of socially undesirable responses was obtained with the mail questionnaire.

The problem of respondents not revealing socially undesirable traits or characteristics has been previously discussed by Edwards[3] and, more recently, by Dohrenwend.[4] The results of the present research suggest that research techniques affording greater privacy of response are more likely to reduce this problem than those affording less privacy.

A possible solution to the problem when personal interviews are used is to employ a data collection technique for which the probability of respondents' giving untruthful answers is relatively small. Such a technique is the randomized response model which was first proposed by Warner.[5] This promising technique, based on probability theory, has been empirically tested in a recently completed North Carolina abortion study. Results and discussion of this research, together with the methodological framework of the model itself, can be found in Greenberg *et al.*[6]

CONCLUSION

The major finding obtained from this research is that responses given in a public opinion polling are not always independent of the method used to collect the data. Response bias is likely to be a problem in telephone and personal interviews whenever the question being asked is one for which there exists a socially undesirable response. The significance of this result is twofold: (1) pollsters must be especially careful in designing sample surveys in which the objective is to measure public sentiment on sensitive issues; and (2) new data collection techniques, such as the randomized response model, must be developed so as to reduce the probability that respondents give socially desirable responses when, in fact, they do not hold such viewpoints.

ENDNOTES

1. Both these procedures have been found to have a positive effect on the response rate. See, for example, Morton L. Brown, "Use of a Postcard Query in Mail Surveys," *Public Opinion Quarterly*, Vol. 29, 1965, pp. 635–637; and James E. Stafford, "Influence of Preliminary Contact on Mail Returns," *Journal of Marketing Research*, Vol. 3, 1965, pp. 410–411.

2. Telephone and personal interviews were obtained by students in an advanced undergraduate marketing research course.

3. A. L. Edwards, *The Social Desirability Variable in Personality Assessment and Research*, New York, Dryden Press, 1957.

4. Barbara Snell Dohrenwend, "An Experimental Study of Directive Interviewing," *Public Opinion Quarterly*, Vol. 34, 1970, pp. 117–125.

5. S. L. Warner, "Randomized Response: A Survey Technique for Eliminating Evasive Answer Bias," *Journal of the American Statistical Association*, Vol. 60, 1965, pp. 63–69.

6. B. G. Greenberg, R. R. Kuebler, Jr., J. R. Abernathy, and D. G. Horvitz, "Application of the Randomized Response Technique in Obtaining Quantitative Data," *Journal of the American Statistical Association*, Vol. 66, 1971, pp. 243–250.

PART 5 SELECTION 3

Reprinted from *The Public Opinion Quarterly*, 36 (Fall 1972), with permission of the publisher and the author.

Attitudes vs. Actions *versus* Attitudes vs. Attitudes

HOWARD SCHUMAN

When attitudes as measured by survey interviews differ from actions as observed in "real life," a standard explanation is that the interview world and the non-interview world are quite different in the demands they place upon the individual. The former creates a special situation far removed from the social pressures of ordinary life, although containing the implicit social expectations of the interviewer, the questionnaire she administers, and the organization she represents. Especially on controversial issues, the gulf between the interview world and the real world is often seen as not only wide but unbridgeable.

While this point of view certainly contains some truth, it overestimates the gap between the interview world and the real world, and correspondingly underestimates the gap between one attitudinal response and another (or one action and another), holding context constant. That is, *within* the interview one can find—and interpret meaningfully—the same apparently sharp inconsistencies that are often given as instances of survey-nonsurvey differences. We shall not deny the logical inconsistency of such responses, but rather show that to respondents they make a certain sense in terms of reconciling two or more positively held values in conflict. As part of our general argument we assume, and partially demonstrate, that a set of survey questions can simulate some of the more familiar pressures of everyday life, and that respondents are able to imagine and deal openly with these pressures in giving responses.

Our first example comes from a survey done by the Detroit Area Study on white racial attitudes in 1969.[1] The following situation and three follow-up questions were included in the middle of the questionnaire exactly as presented here, except that codes and percentage distributions are added:[2]

> Suppose a good Negro engineer applied for a job as an engineering executive. The Personnel Director explained to him: "Personally I'd never given your race a thought, but the two men you would have to work with most closely—the plant manager and the chief engineer—both have strong feelings about Negroes. I *can* offer you a job as a regular engineer, but *not* at the executive level, because any serious friction at the top could ruin the organization."
>
> A. Was it all right for the personnel director in this case to refuse to hire the Negro engineer as an executive in order to avoid friction with the other employees?

1. Yes	39%
2. No.	56
9. Other, D.K., N.A.	5
	100(640)

> B. Should the personnel manager have asked the other men how they would feel about working with a Negro engineer and then made his decision on the basis of their wishes?

1. Yes	50%
2. No	45
9. Other, D.K., N.A.	5
	100(640)

> C. In general, do you think employees should hire men for top management without paying any attention to whether they are white or Negro?

1. Yes	85%
2. No	12
3. Other, D.K., N.A.	3
	100(640)

The story presents a clear case of employment discrimination, even though one that is not as crude as complete refusal to hire blacks at all. Each of the follow-up questions asks the respondent in a different way whether he is willing to condone such discrimination. Let us skip to Question C first, since it is the most general one. We can see that when the principle of nondiscrimination is proposed without qualification, it is supported by fully 85 per cent of the sample. In this survey, as in all recent surveys on white racial attitudes, we can say with some confidence that the American public is overwhelmingly against discrimination in the realm of employment.[3]

Or can we? If we turn back now to Question A, we find that when a "good reason" is given for job discrimination, the proportions change dramatically. If a straightforward policy of nondiscrimination is said to threaten the economic stability of the firm, some 39 percent of the respondents are willing to sacrifice the policy of equal treatment in favor of practices supposedly designed to make the firm prosper. Finally, with Question B we discover that when the principle of nondiscrimination is opposed to the principle of "democratic decision-making," 50 percent of the sample chooses the latter, thereby implicitly indicating willingness to support discrimination if it is the will of the (white) majority. To summarize, we find sharp variations in response to the three questions, as shown by the following percentages endorsing discrimination:[4]

C. Agrees to discrimination in principle	13%
A. Agrees to discrimination if necessary for the harmony of the firm	41%
B. Agrees to discrimination if majority of white favor it	52%

Thus, depending on the question examined, one could argue that employment discrimination is supported by only a small minority of the white metropolitan population, by two-fifths of that population, or by just over half.[5] This kind of difference, if demonstrated between survey and nonsurvey results, would probably be interpreted as an indication of the invalidity of attitude surveys in this sensitive area. In fact, however, these are divergencies between distributions for questions asked not only in the same survey but almost in the same breath. Respondents show themselves capable of taking quite different positions on the same basic action—with, according to our interviewers, very little sense of embarrassment.

Before attempting to explain these seeming inconsistencies, let us examine one additional example from a quite different study. The data are reported by Robin Williams to illustrate what he calls the "situational variability" of prejudice.[6] Among other things, the example shows that even the exact sequence of questions is probably not an important factor in increasing or reducing inconsistency. Williams asked his respondents to imagine themselves in a restaurant when a young, well-dressed Negro enters and is refused service. Some 90 percent of his white cross-section sample disapproved of such discrimination when the question of approval or disapproval was put in a simple fashion. Williams then continued the hypothetical story of having the manager explain to the Negro customer that he personally was without prejudice, but that if he provided service to a Negro his other customers would object. With this additional information, more than half the respondents who had previously opposed discrimination switched positions and supported the manager's discriminatory action. Finally, most of these changers switched back again when a third element was added to the story, namely, "a well-known doctor," overhearing the conversation, intervenes on the side of American values of equal treatment and threatens to take his own business elsewhere unless justice is done.

Let us now attempt to interpret both these patterns of results, moving from what appears to be fairly clear findings toward somewhat more speculative conclusions. First, attitudes toward the same action show considerable variability depending on exactly how a question is phrased. The variability hardly seems random or purposeless, however, nor are the alterations in wording that cause the changes either subtle or mysterious. On the contrary, it is clear that in both these studies (one done as long ago as 1949, the other as recently as 1969), respondents endorse nondiscrimination in principle, but easily depart from it when certain obstacles are raised. Moreover, they do so frankly and openly, not unconsciously, surreptitiously, or with obvious embarrassment.

Second, the changes we observe are remarkably similar to those one would anticipate in moving from the general survey attitude question to real life. (Williams terms this evidence of the "situational variability" of prejudice, but as he realizes it is all going on within the same survey interview.) It appears that many respondents are quite capable of entertaining mentally the various pressures of real life, and of answering accordingly. We have not demonstrated that the percentage changes within the survey are exactly those one would obtain in an experimentally created real-life situation, nor that exactly the same individuals would select themselves to make these switches in action. But at the gross level that we are able to examine here, it appears that the survey simulates quite well—and with remarkable ease—the kinds of shifts one expects in ordinary life.

Third, we must still explain what some might well consider the blatant inconsistency of respondents on this issue of racial discrimination. The placement of questions suggests that very little of this inconsistency is due to deception or self-deception of the respondent. The questions are simply too close together, yet the evidence of respondent concern over inconsistency too slight. Nor can the apparent inconsistency be treated as meaningless verbiage: it is all too obviously pregnant with meaning, and indeed reflects well, as we have noted, the inconsistencies one finds in ordinary life. Rather we must recognize that respondents see the questions as genuinely different from one another, and *intend* to give different responses to them.

At the same time, it is not possible to reconcile the various responses we have reported in a purely logical fashion. Levine[7] has recently reviewed data showing that most whites are willing to accept a small percentage of blacks in their neighborhoods, but are opposed to open-housing laws and probably also to the movement of *large* numbers of blacks into their neighborhoods. Levine argues, quite correctly, that these are not inconsistent patterns of response, even though they may be undesirable patterns from the standpoint of effective residential integration. But the contradictions revealed in our job and restaurant examples cannot be resolved so easily on a logical basis. We can agree fully with Levine that exact question wording is crucial, but we need a larger and less neatly logical scheme for reconciliation of these divergent responses—and probably of the ones he gives as well.

The following perspective seems compelling to this writer. For the survey investigator interested in measuring discriminatory attitudes—as to the strong black or white civil rights advocate—all of these questions can be conceptualized as "tests" of adherence to a single principle under various degrees of practical difficulty or counterpressure. Using Guttman or other assumptions, one notes a respondent's score for the desirable "aptitude" of nondiscrimination, much as one would on a vocabulary or arithmetic test where there are clearly right or wrong answers. But another way of looking at these items—and at similar situations in real life—is as clashes of abstract values in concrete form. The engineer question A and the second restaurant question both confront the value of nondiscrimination with the values of group harmony and economic success. The engineer question B confronts the principle of nondiscrimination with the principle of democratic rule. Probably *all* these principles would be endorsed by nearly 100 per cent of the sample if they were stated in isolation, as indeed was done in the engineer question C for the principle of nondiscrimination. Nor would such figures be meaningless, for they help identify the major abstract values of our society. (Other values, for example "free love," would not receive such unanimous approval, even if stated in the most positive way possible.) But only to a true believer will any one of these values win out in all situations regardless of the other values with which it competes. A few people will go to the stake for a single value, but history and common sense tell us that most people work out compromises depending upon the exact balance of positions. Almost everyone is opposed to killing another human being, for example, but only a few complete pacifists claim that they cannot imagine a situation where other values would lead to temporary sacrifice of that principle.

It is incorrect, or at least an oversimplification, to see this public shifting as merely subtle acquiescence to social pressure. If this were the case, our respondents would be less likely to make the shift so easily and with so little embarrassment in the survey interview testing. Such purely acquiescent shifting might well occur in real life, but the survey would more often lead to false consistency of expressed attitudes than we have found. The openness with which respondents change as we simulate situational changes strongly suggests that they perceive a genuine conflict of values in these questions, and not simply one answer that is *right* in value terms and another that is *wrong*. Depending upon the exact phrasing of the question—the values involved and how they are operationalized—a respondent chooses one side or the other, though he can very likely appreciate both to some extent.

The perspective we have described fits our intuition that a person who answers in a nondiscriminatory direction on *all* these questions believes very strongly in the value of nondiscrimination—that is, prefers it to almost any other value with which it conflicts. In our society a large proportion of the black population and a small proportion of the white population would be so classified. Leaving aside another small part of the white population that actively supports discrimination, most whites believe to one degree or another in nondiscrimination, but simply do not rate it very high on their scale of values.[8] Faced with issues that seem to call forth other values and goals—"a good education for their children," "business success," "paying attention to the opinions of one's neighbors," "keeping law and order in the city"—the principle of nondiscrimination often loses out. It does so in real life, and the carefully constructed attitude survey merely reflects this fact.

From a methodological standpoint our discussion suggests the continued need to write questions that reflect the genuine dilemmas in life between competing forces manifested or expressed in value terms. It is doubtful that there can be any single perfect item for a complex area such as job discrimination. Leaving aside problems of random error and misunderstanding, at least several questions are very likely required to provide the kinds of genuine conflicts that respondents need to think about and resolve in the form of their answers.[9] But our examples do suggest that an attitude survey can represent these conflicts with a good deal of success, provided only that we are willing to build into our questionnaires the problems and not merely the platitudes that life holds for most individuals.

ENDNOTES

1. The sample was an area probability cross-section of white adult heads and wives of heads of household in the metropolitan Detroit area. The response rate was 78 per cent, with a final *N* of 640 individuals. A sampling report is available on request. The overall study was designed by Irwin Katz and the present writer. My thanks to Robert Brannon, James Fields, and Mark Tannenbaum for their help at important points.

2. The questions essentially replicate a set administered in 1961 in an unpublished study carried out in Boston by John Harding and the present author. The only difference was that the person discriminated against was then described as Jewish, rather than as black. The internal *pattern* of results was quite similar, although the Boston sample was too haphazard in selection to allow comparability of actual marginals.

3. See, for example, Angus Campbell and Howard Schuman, *Racial Attitudes in Fifteen American Cities*, Ann Arbor, Michigan, Institute for Social Research, 1968, pp. 33–34.

4. Missing data are excluded from these calculations.

5. In terms of cumulative scaling, one might also expect discriminatory responses to C to imply discriminatory responses to A (or to B), but not necessarily the reverse. In fact, cross-tabulation of responses to C and A yields the following results (omitting missing data):

(1) Nondiscriminatory on both A and C	56%
(2) Discriminatory on A but not on C	31
(3) Discriminatory on both A and C	9
(4) Discriminatory on C but not on A	4
	100 (597)

In terms of the scheme being developed here, levels (1), (2), and (3) all "make sense," but the 4 per cent (23 cases) in the last category who agree with discrimination in principle but reject it in practice appear to be genuinely inconsistent. While a few such cases in a large survey sample are not surprising, it is instructive to understand their origin here. Examination of both the questions and the marginal comments in the interviews suggests two explanations: one an artifact of question construction, the other a more substantive point. The former is the rather complex, double-negative nature of the questions, especially Question A where the respondent answers "yes" to affirm a *refusal* to hire. In keeping with this point, we find that inconsistencies of this type are greater among the less educated. Second, and more substantively, marginal comments by three respondents indicated that while they opposed discrimination as described in A, they bridled at the idea in C of paying absolutely *no* attention to race. One said: "Look at qualifications first. Race should be one of the last things considered." In other words, they saw question C as more rather than less extreme than question A—the opposite of what we (and most respondents) assumed.

6. Robin M. Williams, Jr., *Strangers Next Door: Ethnic Relations in American Communities*, Englewood Cliffs, N.J., Prentice-Hall, 1964.

7. Robert A. Levine, "The Silent Majority: Neither Simple Nor Simple-Minded," *Public Opinion Quarterly*, Vol. 35, 1971, pp. 571–577.

8. Blacks are the main bearers in America of the norm of nondiscrimination, not only because it is in their interest to do so, but also because for over a hundred years these self-interests have been elaborated and socialized in terms of what Myrdal called the American Creed. Even today, after nearly a decade of emphasis on "Black Power" and "Black Nationalism," very few blacks are willing openly to support preferential hiring of blacks—that is, blacks are consistent and strong in their support of nondiscrimination. It is not inevitable for a group to support a value that is in its abstract interests: poll data show that American women have, at least until recently, approved of certain forms of discrimination against women (e.g., in politics). On the other hand, when one's perceived group interests do not support a value position, as in the case of whites with respect to racial discrimination, it is unlikely that the value will be adhered to very strongly when it conflicts with other value-interest combinations. There are always some exceptions to this general rule, exceptions which provide the white core to the civil rights movement.

9. It should be clear that the problem discussed here involves more than unreliability in the usual psychometric sense. Nor is the writer convinced that it is automatically handled by creating a multi-item scale of a Guttman or any other variety, even if this were practical for all the constructs used in a typical survey. Such scales doubtless provide a better measure of intensity of adherence to a value, but the problem requires close consideration of *what* we wish to measure, not simply how.

PART 5 SELECTION 4

Reprinted from *The Public Opinion Quarterly* 34, 3 (Fall 1970), with permission of the publisher and the author.

The Opinion Polls and the 1970 British General Election

MARK ABRAMS

After each British General Election the London *Times* publishes in book form its authoritative *Guide to the House of Commons.* Over the years the contents have been constant—the votes given to each candidate in the 630 constituencies, regionally aggregated figures of votes for the parties, a section on successful women candidates, occupational and educational background of the new House of Commons, etc., and a brief, straightforward, "for the record" account of how the parties conducted the three weeks of campaigning that precedes the voting.

The 1970 volume, however, has one break with tradition. Its section on the election campaign opens with a boisterous and obviously delighted account of the "failure" of the opinion polls (*The Times* itself had commissioned and prominently published and publicized its own Marplan Poll, which indicated a massive Labour victory). According to the opening words of the *Times Guide*:

> Long after the arguments are forgotten, the general election of June 18, 1970 will be remembered as the occasion when the people of the United Kingdom hurled the findings of the opinion polls back into the faces of the pollsters and at the voting booths proved them wrong—most of them badly wrong. In a way not experienced before, the campaign was dominated by the polls. Hardly a day went by without one newspaper or another recording the electorate's temperature. Mr. Heath had to fight the whole period of the campaign with the polls reporting the balance of opinion persistently against him and his party. To his credit, Mr. Heath refused to be bamboozled.

To some extent this forecast of the public's memory may well be colored by a newspaperman's understandable resentment at the prominence given during the campaign by both press and television to poll findings, and at their comparative neglect of the assessments and descriptive contributions from their established political commentators. (Though it is hard to find a single one of these commentators who did not start and stay with the assumption that the polls were right and that Labour would win. For example, the cautious *Economist*, in its issue of June 13, wrote: "The most rational Conservative hope for next Thursday night must be to keep Mr. Wilson to a majority of 30 or under . . . the Conservatives have managed to frighten too many people.") But it is certainly true that never before in an election has the British public been treated to so many election polls, never before have they been given so much prominence, and never before have they been so spectacularly wrong in giving guidance as to which party would win.

Inevitably and sensibly, the British Market Research Society (whose membership includes the managing directors of all the polling organizations) has set up a committee of inquiry to conduct a post-mortem. The committee's chairman is the Society's chairman-elect (Gerald de Groot, the research director of Lintas—Unilever's subsidiary advertising agency), and contains in addition a professor of statistics from the London School of Economics (Alan Stuart), a professor of political science from Newcastle University (Hugh Berrington), and two "elder statesmen" from the market research world (John Downham of Unilever and Norman Squirrell of Proctor and Gamble). It is unlikely that their report will emerge for some time, and meanwhile it seems useful to set out the known facts and take a look at some of the explanations that have already been aired.

We can start with the total and final voting figures for Great Britain (all the opinion polls, except one, excluded Northern Ireland from their surveys). It will be seen (Table 1) that the differences in votes for the two major parties was comparatively small—the Conservatives were ahead by no more than 2.4 percentage points, or a lead of less than 642,000 votes in a total turnout of over 27.5 million.

Table 1 *Great Britain Votes, June 18, 1970*

Party	%
Conservative	46.2
Labor	43.8
Liberal	7.6
Others[a]	2.4
Total	100.0

[a] Almost entirely Welsh and Scottish Nationalists, i.e. people who when forced to choose between the other parties usually vote Labor or Liberal.

In fact, in their final figures all but one of the published polls indicated a clear-cut Labour victory. It will be seen from Table 2 that some of them indicated a Labour lead of very substantial proportions.

The O.R.C. published figures call for some comment, since they represent survey findings modified in part by the polling director's decision to take a calculated risk and exercise his judgment. According to the *Sunday Times* of June 21 (i.e. after the voting results were known; the *Sunday Times* publishes O.R.C. polls):

Table 2 *The Opinion Poll's Final Figures*

Party	*Marplan*[a]	*Gallup*	*National Opinion Poll*	*Opinion Research Center*	*Louis Harris*
Conservative	41.5%	42.0%	44.1%	46.5%	46.0%
Labor	50.2	49.0	48.2	45.5	48.0
Liberal	7.0	7.5	6.4	6.5	5.0
Others	1.3	1.5	1.3	1.5	1.0
Total	100.0%	100.0%	100.0%	100.0%	100.0%
Labor lead	8.7	7.0	4.1	−1.0	2.0
Fieldwork dates	June 11–14	June 14–16	June 12–16	June 13–17	May 20–June 16
Sample size	2,267	2,190	1,562	1,583	4,841
Sample type	random	quota	random	quota	random

[a] Marplan's published figures related to the United Kingdom; when the Northern Ireland figures are excluded, the Marplan survey showed a 9.6% Labor lead.

> In their last poll but one of the campaign, O.R.C. stuck to measurement. . . . But their last poll was headed "final election forecast." In this the *unadjusted* intention to vote still gave Labour a 4.5 per cent lead. But when this figure was checked among "those most likely to turn out" it fell to 3 per cent. Then, to guard against late swing. O.R.C. reinterviewed a subsample of 300 voters. . . . The reinterviews showed that the Conservative vote had held firm, but that the Labour (and Liberal) vote had fallen off a little. This late swing reduced the unadjusted 4.5 per cent Labour lead to nothing. And when the turnout correction was applied to the new figure, O.R.C. concluded, "the final prediction emerged as a 1 per cent Conservative lead."

It will be seen from Table 2 that as indicators of voting behavior neither size of sample nor type of sample played a consistent part in determining the pattern of the findings; large samples were no more dependable than small samples, and quota samples were at least as reliable as random samples (although, of course, people differ in what they judge to be an effective random sample).

Before reviewing possible explanations it should be mentioned that at this election the pollsters had to cope with some unusual circumstances.

1. In 1969 the qualifying age for voting had been lowered from 21 to 18. At mid-1970 there were approximately 2.5 million people in this age group (equivalent to 6.5 per cent of the total population aged 18 and over). Various polls among these youngsters showed them to be more Labour-inclined than their elders, but spot checks carried out by the political parties showed that a large proportion of them had failed to register as electors and that therefore their political loyalties were irrelevant in any attempt to forecast how the electorate might behave. Estimates of the proportion which had failed to register ranged from 25 per cent to 33 per cent; the rate of self-disqualification was apparently highest among working-class youngsters —i.e. among those most likely to have voted Labour.

2. Midsummer general elections are very unusual in Britain. On June 18, 1970 approximately three-quarters of a million electors were away on vacation and therefore unable to vote; at least half of these, however, had been at home at the end of May and the beginning of June and were therefore actual or potential participants in the penultimate polling surveys.

3. For the first time the voting booths were kept open until 10 P.M. (previously 9 P.M.), and this provided active party workers with opportunities to bring to the booths more of the people with a normally poor turnout rate, e.g., women and old people.

4. In the past, Britain's main immigrant groups—West Indians, Pakistanis, Indians, and Irish Roman Catholics—have tended to have a high nonvoting rate; in part this has been the result of failure to register and in part because

of failure to vote even when registered. This time, however, they felt themselves to be very much involved in British politics: passionate minorities in both the major parties had gone out of their way to make colored immigrants self-conscious and alarmed, and the dispatch of British troops to Northern Ireland had aroused the Irish Catholics. According to the *Irish Post* (The Voice of the Irish in Britain) of July 11, a survey among 4,627 Irish people in Britain showed that "90 per cent of the Irish who were on the electoral register cast their votes (far higher than the national average), and (was) the biggest turnout ever on the part of the Irish community in Britain."

5. Finally, it must be remembered that never before had the pollsters and their findings received so much publicity in a British general election; almost all of them recorded unconditional certainty that Labour would win in a landslide. Typical banner headlines were "Tories Reeling," "12 per cent Swing to Labour," "Labour—by 100?" The *Sunday Times* published a "Poll of Polls" (i.e. an average of the findings of five separate polling organizations), and in its issue of the Sunday before the vote concluded that: "If people vote on Thursday as the opinion polls now say they will, Mr. Wilson will be returned to power with a lead of 100 seats over the Tories. . . . There are 19 chances in 20 that the Polls Index is within 2 per cent of a totally accurate reading."

It was almost impossible for the interviewers who worked for the polls to start the day's work ignorant of these assertions; if interviewer expectations played any part in affecting the survey findings, then the bias was undoubtedly in the direction of overstating intentions to vote Labour.

Before the election most political commentators considered that most of these innovations would favor Labour (the lowering of the voting age, the absence of middle-class voters on vacation, the extension of voting hours, the high turnout of immigrants). Clearly, any pollster who was going to be right this time was going to have to be both very competent and very lucky.

Within a couple of hours of the closing of the voting booths it was clear from the first results that the Conservatives would finish with a majority in the new Parliament. Almost simultaneously, those pollsters who had somewhat lightheartedly accepted invitations to appear on television and provide a running commentary on the results began to put forward explanations for this completely unexpected behavior on the part of the electorate. The two most favored explanations were concerned with the low turnout and a last-minute switch in party preferences.

Between the 1966 and 1970 general elections there was indeed a significant fall in the proportion of electors who voted. In Great Britain the decline was from 76.1 per cent to 71.9 per cent, i.e. a 5.5 per cent decline in the rate of turnout. (The statistical purist very properly would point out that with three-quarters of a million electors away from home on holiday the true 1970 turnout figure was 73.3 per cent.)

A higher rate of abstention, however, only upsets the predictive value of the polls if the rates are different among supporters of the various parties, and in this particular election only if the abstainers were predominantly people who would have voted Labour. (It is, of course, part of the conventional wisdom in all western democracies that a low poll always harms the parties of the Left.)

To test this "low turnout" explanation I arranged in alphabetical order the 511 English constituencies and then, starting at the top, picked the first 25 where the decline between 1966 and 1970 in the turnout rate was 3.0 per cent or less, and the first 25 where the decline was 9.0 per cent or more (for England as a whole—i.e. excluding Wales and Scotland—the fall in the turnout rate was 6.1 per cent). In the 25 constituencies where the decline in turnout was negligible, the 1966 to 1970 swing in votes from Labour to Conservative was 4.2 per cent. In the 25 seats where the fall in the turnout rate was abnormally high, the swing to the Conservatives was 5.2 per cent. These figures hardly support the contention that the pollsters were misled by unexpected abstentions that markedly raised the Conservative share of the votes cast.

Table 3 *England: Turnout and Swing*

	Decline in Turnout Rate 1966–1970	*Swing to Conservatives 1966–1970*
25 High-turnout constituencies	2.0%	4.2%
25 Low-turnout constituencies	10.6	5.2
All English constituencies	6.1	5.2

The second main explanation offered by the pollsters was that between their final surveys (taken approximately June 11 and June 16) and voting day (June 18) the electorate changed its mind to the extent that an anticipated Labour lead of 4 per cent turned into a Conservative lead of 2.8 per cent.

Marplan, for example, after the election reinterviewed 664 of its original respondents and found that "4 per cent of those who a few days before said that they would support Labour in fact voted Conservative" (and, of course, some earlier Conservatives also switched). Moreover, about a quarter of the 7.0 per cent who had said they would vote Liberal, "changed their allegiance, and from these the Conservative picked up almost twice as many votes as Labour." (However, the Liberals finished up with 7.6 per cent of all votes—more than in the Marplan poll.) Again, according to the Marplan inquest, "those who before June 18 said they were undecided how they would vote also made a contribution to the Conservative victory. . . . One in four of the voters in this category did not vote at all, but in the end 37 per cent voted Conservative compared with 27 per cent Labour. . . . (And finally) of those who before the election said they would vote Labour 10 per cent did not vote at all, compared with 8 per cent of potential Conservative voters. . . . Marplan and other opinion polls have vindicated their methods." (All quotations from the London *Times*—which published the Marplan poll—July 20, 1970.)

Gallup also checked back on 684 of their respondents (*Daily Telegraph*, July 10, 1970) and reported that of those who had said they were going to vote Labour, "only 77 per cent voted Labour, most of the rest did not vote, but 7 per cent voted Conservative." The usefulness of this and other post-election checks, however, is thrown into some doubt since Gallup found that "as many as 83 per cent claimed to have voted, compared with an actual turnout of 72 per cent." In spite of this the Gallup analysis carried the categorical readline "Tories won election in last two days."

One can only conclude from these inquests that, as usual, a handful of people switched parties, abstained rather than voted, or voted rather than abstained; and that this time the net effect of such cross-currents favored the Conservatives; but call-back inquests are not likely to prove this conclusively.

All one can do at this stage is to indicate some areas where error might have been generated in the polls and to suggest possible remedies. For example:

1. Most of the published polls either refrained completely from indicating the existence of uncommitted electors or else put their proportion at about 10 per cent of the electorate; in fact, nearly 30 per cent abstained. On historical grounds a figure of this order should have been expected. Much more effort should have gone into identifying the dimensions and composition of this minority. At the election the turnout rate varied from less than 50 per cent in London and some of the very big provincial cities (nearly all traditionally Labour strongholds) to over 80 per cent in many rural and suburban constituencies (traditional Conservative seats).

2. Much more effort should have been applied by the pollsters to a study of the considerable number of people who had been deviants in the 1966 election which Labour won so handsomely. The Party's 1966 gains came largely from young middle-class people, skilled manual workers, and women—groups which in 1966 voted Labour to an unexpectedly large extent. It was clear for some time (from more leisurely and deep-probing surveys) that

these groups were deeply resentful of what had happened under a Labour government (e.g. higher taxes and rising prices) and were fearful that another Labour victory would see more of the same. Resentment and fear are pretty powerful motivators of voting behavior.

3. The pollsters should have insisted that the text accompanying their figures be less newsworthy and more factual. They might have checked their present critics if there had been fewer headlines of the order, "Only a miracle can save the Tories," and more opening reminders that a Labour figure of 48 per cent should be interpreted as "anything between 46 per cent and 50 per cent"—and that if the former figure turned out to be right then Labour could lose the election. Apparently this lesson has been learned. "Opinion polls at the time of the General Election were overpublicized and badly editorialized. This was the view of Frank Teer, managing director of National Opinion Polls when he explained how the polls had gone wrong. He said his own company was negotiating to have a bigger say in how poll findings were subedited and headlined." (*Advertiser's Weekly*, July 17, 1970.)

4. The pollsters must find a way of solving the pressure on them to provide almost daily results during the last ten days of the campaigns. Reliable sampling under these circumstances is almost impossible unless very much more money is available. Interviewers who have to get each day's work back to London by the end of the afternoon are under a considerable strain. If they are working on a quota sample there is the unavoidable risk that their quota controls will become a little flexible; those on probability samples will have little time for call-backs on absentees. Both will be tempted to stay near the center of the very large urban centers where fast trains can deliver their work to London within two or three hours and where the post office can be depended upon to deliver packages to the head office within fifteen hours. This sort of clustering tends to give a sample in which working-class Labour supporters are overrepresented.

The more detailed review now under way will no doubt shed further light on the case of "the opinion polls and the 1970 British General Election."

PART 6

ASSESSING THE INFLUENCE OF PUBLIC OPINION

PART 6 AN OVERVIEW

Among the prerequisites for a democracy are the opportunity for citizens to make themselves heard and the right of citizens to have their preferences taken into account by those who are conducting the affairs of government (Dahl, 1971). From these basic rights comes the rationale for many of our political institutions and guarantees of civil liberties. The freedom to join organizations, the right to vote and run for office, the freedom of speech and press, the recognition of the legitimacy of opposition to those in power—all are attempts to guarantee citizens a climate in which they can formulate views on public policy, share these views with their fellow citizens, and transmit them to political policy makers. In other words, these civil liberties provide the means by which public opinion can have an impact on policy making. Most people in the United States believe in this process, at least in an abstract, general sense, and yet many feel, at one time or another, that the government is unresponsive to public demands and preferences (especially if they are their own demands and preferences). The purpose of this section is to discuss the means that citizens have to express their opinions to political leaders and the effectiveness of these means. This section also treats the question of whether the government is responsive to public opinion and, if so, in what way.

SOME LINKAGE MECHANISMS

In the following discussion we shall first address ourselves to the relationship between the elected representative and his constituency, and then turn to reviewing the means by which public opinion is transmitted to governmental officials—elections, political parties, organized interest groups, and protest activities.

The representative

The effect of public opinion on political decision makers depends to a certain extent on how the elected official views his role. The elected representative and his function have been the subject of considerable discussion among political scientists. Wahlke and his associates (1959) have outlined three distinct views a representative might hold concerning his or her role. First the representative might see his role as a "trustee." A trustee is a free agent, elected by his constituents bcause he is a person of responsibility and good judgment and, consequently, is entrusted with the responsibility of using his independent best judgment in the decisions facing him. The trustee, therefore, does not see himself as necessarily bound by the public opinion of his constituency, but rather as an informed person who can make independent judgments about important issues. He is willing to let the voters have their say at the polls about his overall performance, but does not feel bound to vote as the majority of his constituents want on every issue.

A second conception of the representative's role is that of a delegate—a person sent to represent the wishes of his constituents, not to make his own decisions. A delegate sees himself as being bound by what his constituents favor, rather than by his own personal predilections. A third conception is a combination of the first two, called a politico. The politico is one who sometimes sees himself as a trustee, at other times as a delegate.

Clearly, a representative who sees himself as a trustee is likely to be unresponsive to public opinion on any given issue, and probably can only be rewarded or punished at the polls every two, four, or six years for his overall performance. This kind of representative is not apt to be swayed by public opinion polls if he feels that the views expressed by the polls are wrong. Most representatives studied by Wahlke et al. viewed themselves as trustees (63 per cent); of the remainder, 23 per cent viewed themselves as politicos, and only 14 per cent as delegates.[1] Thus less than one in seven saw themselves as bound to go along with their constituents' opinion.

Even if a representative wished to assume the role of delegate on all issues facing him, it would be very difficult for him to do so. For one thing, unanimity of public opinion on any issue is generally lacking and on many issues there is not even a majority opinion. So whose views is a representative to reflect? Secondly, representatives are not particularly well informed about opinion in their own districts (Miller and Stokes, 1963; see further data from Miller and Stokes reported in Erickson and Luttbeg, 1973).[2] Even community leaders supposedly close to "grass-roots opinion" have been found to be ignorant of opinion in their own communities. This ignorance is most pronounced where community leaders and the public differ (Sigel and Friesema, 1965). Thus, if the representative turns to these leaders for information, he ends up with a misconception concerning the dominant viewpoint in his own district, although this is less likely to occur on salient issues than on issues of less immediate interest to his constituents.

The assumption by the representative that his views are those of his constituents can be a reason for the climate of ignorance or misperception in which many representatives work. Another reason is simply the lack of accurate information on just what the constituents do think. Congressmen and other representatives tend to rely on individual contacts, mail, hometown newspaper editorials, and the like to judge public opinion. Yet analyses of this sort of opinion have shown it to be unrepresentative of the way the mass public feels about a given issue. For example, voters who claim to have written letters to the editor during the 1964 presidential campaign were found to support Goldwater and to be conservative to a much greater extent than members of the public at large (Converse, et al., 1965). Studies of letter writers on the Vietnam issue revealed a similar distortion, with "hawks" greatly overrepresented, "doves" slightly overrepresented, and middle-opinion holders underrepresented (Verba and Brody, 1970). The community leaders and personal acquaintances that congressmen and other representatives talk to in their home districts are also likely to be unrepresentative, since they generally belong to higher socioeconomic strata and tend to be better informed and more interested in issues than the public at large (Boynton et al., 1969). Commissioning public opinion polls just to tap opinion in their own districts is too expensive for most congressmen or state representatives. While some representatives attempt their own public opinion surveys by sending out mail questionnaires to voters in their districts, those who return such questionnaires are again likely to be unrepresentative. Generally they have above average income and education and hold stronger opinions concerning political issues.

Thus, even if a representative wishes to be a delegate—to reflect his constituents' opinion—there are many constraints on his doing so. Conceivably, a representative might reflect his constituents' opinion for a reason other than accurate perception of their views. It is plausible to assume that voters elect a person to be their representative because his views, in a general way, coincide with their own. However, the available empirical evidence suggests that the opinions of representatives only imperfectly match those of their constituents. The pattern is similar to that cited above: except on a matter of extreme salience (e.g., civil rights), representative opinion and constituent opinion are little related (Miller and Stokes, 1963).

In sum, there is evidence that most representatives do not see themselves as bound to represent public opinion, do not in fact know what opinion in their districts is on many issues, and do not have personal views that coincide with those of their constituents. Moreover, while representatives pay lip service to doing what their constituents want, in actuality even this reflection of public opinion is probably not necessary. In many districts, congressmen need not worry about serious electoral competition; the district is so one-sided with regard to party competition that effective challenge is rarely mounted. Most representatives, then, seem to go their own way, taking care not to offend their constituents' sensibilities too strikingly. Should they do so, the mechanism that voters have to force responsiveness on the part of their elected representatives is elections. It is to this topic we now turn.

Elections

One way that democratic government is made responsive to the will of the people in a large society is through the mechanism of fair and free elections (Downs, 1957; Dahl, 1971; Ranney and Kendall, 1956). Through elections citizens may reward representatives who make decisions that the voters perceive to be in their interest and punish those whose decisions are perceived to be against their interests. Elections assure that government will stay responsive to the public (or so it is assumed) because in order to be reelected leaders will be continually trying to fulfill citizen interests. However rational this simplified description of the electoral process seems, its practical validity rests on several assumptions about both the citizen and the candidate for office.

First it assumes that voters will be aware of the various policy stands of candidates and that citizens will vote on the basis of policy differences among the candidates. That is, the voter must be aware of whether a candidate's policy is in the voter's interest or not[3] and must vote on this basis rather than on other considerations, such as personality, popular name, and so on. Further, the efficacy of elections as a mechanism to insure governmental responsiveness assumes that candidates will have different policy positions, and that once elected the winning candidate will maintain and act on his policies as stated in the election campaign (otherwise the choice made by the voter will be vitiated).

Much has been written about the voter's ignorance and lack of interest in politics. Most citizens have little knowledge concerning their representatives, let alone the positions of their representatives on current issues (Stokes and Miller, 1962). Many citizens indicate little interest in politics. There is some recent evidence, however, that many voters do pay some attention to policy matters when casting their votes (Key, 1966); and in addition it appears that a very small number of voters are quite well informed, do vote on policy matters, and in some cases have decisive effects on the outcome of elections (Erickson, 1971). In sum, though, the average voter is not particularly knowledgeable. However, some argue that citizen shortcomings at the individual level may make a contribution at the system level. Lack of interest and awareness among the citizenry may, as Berelson, Lazarsfeld, and McPhee suggest in their selection (*see pp. 427–43*), provide the system with the flexibility it needs to survive.

Sometimes even reasonably well-informed voters cannot vote to reward candidates with whom they agree and punish candidates with whom they disagree because the candidates' records, qualifications, or positions on salient issues do not offer a real choice. A certain number of potential voters say they do not vote because, as George Wallace has often stated, "there's not a dime's worth of difference" between the parties (or candidates). For voter rationality to have any impact, the candidates have to offer contrasting positions. Do they? In the Page and Brody article that follows (*see pp. 444–69*), voters in the 1968 Presidential elections who were well informed and had strong views on Vietnam could not translate their concerns into votes because the candidates' stated positions on the problem were nearly identical. Another study, however, found that in the 1966 congressional election campaign voters were offered a considerable choice in candidates for Congress (Sullivan and O'Connor, 1972). Had all the more "liberal" candidates won seats across the nation, the resulting Congress would have been quite different from the Congress that would have resulted from the election of all the more conservative candidates. The differences in terms of stated policy positions were quite substantial: one potential Congress would have passed all the pending liberal socioeconomic legislation, while the other extreme would have resulted in a Congress where most of this legislation would have been blocked. Here was an instance where the national voting public had a choice between effectively contrasting sets of candidates (though in any one particular district the two competitors may not have been much different).

Another equally important finding, in terms of responsiveness, emerged from Sullivan and O'Connor's study: the winning candidates did implement their preelection positions after the election. Related to this, Pomper (1968) finds that a substantial number of the campaign pledges made by political parties are in fact carried out after the election.

Thus we can see that the conditions necessary for making elections an effective mechanism for translating public opinion into political action are present only from time to time. Sometimes voters are offered clear choices; at other times not. Even when they are offered choices, only some voters will perceive and act upon the choice. Although candidates tend to behave "responsibly" when elected—they generally vote in accordance with their campaign positions—there are roadblocks to carrying out election promises. Key (1956) has shown incisively the institutional barriers which impede elected officials from carrying out electoral mandates. These include overlapping terms of office, separation of powers, and, in many state governments, the division of the executive power among many independent officers. Each of these mechanisms, by standing in the way of the implementation of the electoral mandate, insures the existence of decision makers unaffected by such mandate.

In sum, in order for elections alone to be an effective mechanism for translating public opinion into public policy, there are many obstacles to be overcome. Under existing conditions, elections at best seem to give only general indications of public mood—indications which in turn either encourage or discourage those elected from pursuing policy positions taken before the elections.[4] On the other hand, there is some evidence that politicians believe that voters make choices on policy positions (Kingdon, 1966). Thus elected officials are receptive to the demands of a variety of voter groups in the belief that any one group might make the crucial difference in an election. Overall, however, while indications are that policy voting is on the increase (at least in the sixties as contrasted with the more apolitical fifties), elections as a procedure for making elected officials responsive to public opinion on major issues is a far cry from the civics books model.

Political parties

A variant of viewing the electoral process per se as a means of making elected officials responsive to public opinion is to see the political parties themselves as links between the electorate and the decision makers.[5] By viewing the political parties as the linkage mechanisms, the voters can rationally exercise their franchise without being aware of the specific policy positions of incumbents and their opponents. All voters have to know are the broad differences between the political parties, and with that general knowledge they can make a reasonably informed decision. The political parties mediate between the citizens and the decision makers: by knowing the rough outlines of the party positions, voters can decide which party best serves their interest and vote on that basis. Party voting, then, is seen not as a detriment to democracy and responsiveness, but as a distinct aid.[6]

The conditions necessary for parties to serve as effective mechanisms for translating public opinion into public policy are somewhat easier to meet than those necessary for elections to serve as such linkages. The advantage is primarily that voters need only be aware of the differences between the parties, not among a whole series of candidates. The basic assumptions, however, are similar: like the candidates, the parties must present a clear set of proposals that offer the voter a real choice, and once in office the party must strive to carry out these proposals and have the institutional means to do so. These assumptions define what is often called the "responsible party model."

Are these assumptions met in American politics? Contrary to popular judgment, the leaders of the two major political parties do differ in their opinions about important issues (see McClosky, Hoffman, and O'Hara, 1960). Pomper (1968) has also found significant differences between the two parties' platforms—statements of purpose drawn up at party conventions where presidential candidates are nominated. Republicans tend to place more emphasis on defense and government issues (i.e. making the government more efficient, reorganizing it, making it less corrupt, and so on), whereas Democrats stress labor and welfare issues. Further, again contrary to popular impression, Pomper found that party platforms do contain matters of substance as well as rhetoric; that platforms provide evaluations of past party performance and some indications of future directions.[7]

Moreover, Democrats do behave differently from Republicans once in office. Both in Congress and in state legislatures, party differences are more effective than individual differences in predicting how a representative will vote on a roll-call vote. The percentage of votes that might be called party votes (where most members of one party vote one way, most members of the opposition vote another) differs from legislative body to legislative body, but in most states voters can find significant party differences in terms of voting behavior (LeBlanc, 1969; Shannon, 1968; Turner, 1970; McRae, 1970).

Thus an informed voter who studies party voting behavior can discern differences between the parties on a variety of issues at any given point in time, although perhaps not on any one specific issue he is interested in. Party differences are not clear-cut, however, and only the most interested and informed voter may accurately perceive them. Further, not all members of the two major parties act in accord with these differences. The political parties themselves, then, meet in only a minimal way some of the conditions required to make political parties an effective channel of public opinion. On the other side, it should be noted that the voters themselves fail to meet some of these conditions. Campbell and his associates (1964) find that only a small proportion of voters are aware of any ideological or policy differences between the political parties. The party differences that most voters do perceive are expressed in terms of the groups that one party is seen as helping or hurting (Democrats are no good for the farmer; or, Democrats help the working person) or in terms of "nature of the times" differences (the Republicans keep us out of war; there are higher wages when Democrats are in). Relatively few people evaluate the parties in terms of ideology (such as the Republicans are more conservative than the Democrats) although the number of those making this sort of comparison increased from 1956 to 1964 (Pierce, 1970). Even people who are avid partisans do not connect specific ideological or policy stands with specific parties, even when such an association could reasonably be made (Stokes and Miller, 1962). The failure of voters to discern differences between the parties in terms of ideology and policy is an important limitation of the effectiveness of parties as a linkage mechanism.

A second limitation stems from the fact that the voter cannot be sure that his representative is going to vote with the party leadership. On any particular set of issues, a given party member may, and often does, defect from his party's position. A third limitation is that neither voters nor elected representatives are perfectly consistent in their policy stands. Both might be quite liberal on foreign policy, conservative on domestic policy or vice versa. A final problem relates to the fact that the party leadership does not always have the resources to carry out the party platform. Though a Republican president may have the loyal support of most Republican congressmen to carry out the Republican platform, unless the Republicans have a majority in Congress, the president's proposals may be blocked. In order for parties to serve as effective linkage mechanisms, they must operate along the lines of what is termed the "responsible party model" and as we have seen, this model is quite limited when applied to U.S. politics.

Interest groups

In recent decades attention has turned from structured mechanisms of linkage between public opinion and policy formation to more informal ones. The possibility of interest groups representing public opinion has been widely explored by political scientists. Many believe that interest groups provide a more informal, continuous, and personal avenue for citizens to express their views to governmental decision makers than do elections and political parties (see Truman, 1951). The premise that interest groups can adequately represent public opinion to policy makers rests on certain assumptions: first, that citizens with views on any given public issue will organize into groups of like-minded persons who are concerned about that issue; second, that leaders of these groups will then effectively represent group interests to governmental decision makers; finally, that decision makers will actually heed the voices of these groups in their policy-making process.

An analysis of membership in interest groups raises a question about the first assumption—that citizens concerned about specific issues organize themselves into groups of like-minded persons. First, not all citizens belong to groups of any sort, politically active or not. In fact, almost 40 percent do not belong to any organization. For these 40 percent, representation of their interests by a group is purely fortuitous as Verba and Nie point out in the selection that follows (*see pp. 470–77*). Verba and Nie's findings also reveal that only about one-third of U.S. citizens belong to groups that they perceive as having any political interests whatever. Thus, for two-thirds of the population, there is no group membership, or such membership is concentrated in nonpolitical clubs such as bowling leagues, garden clubs, or church groups. Even though these groups could occasionally become politically involved (for example, a garden club might participate in a local conservation campaign), probably the two-thirds estimation of nonpolitical group activity is reasonably accurate. At any rate, it is clear that many citizens, probably a great majority, do not belong to any groups having political relevance.

Further, those who do belong to groups are not typical of the entire U.S. population. Higher-income people, those with more education, and those who are white and male are overrepresented in groups. Persons of lower income or education, minority groups, and women are underrepresented. As noted by Verba and Nie, since higher-status people tend to be the greatest participants in groups, and groups in turn tend to stimulate political participation of other kinds, the group membership process tends to promote inequality in participation. Rather than finding group participation distributed over the entire range of socioeconomic classes, we find that upper-class people participate more and hence have some edge in having their views heard by decision makers.

In order for a group to effectively promote its interests, it naturally must have access to those decision makers relevant to the groups' interests. But access to decision makers depends, at least in part, on the socioeconomic status of the group. Groups with the most financial resources, the most prestigious membership and the best organization are likely to have the greatest access to decision makers.[8] It takes a substantial amount of money to maintain lobbyists in Washington, D.C. and throughout state capitals. Decision makers, too, on the local as well as higher levels, may be more sympathetic to groups that represent interests of the middle and upper classes rather than to groups representing poor people, welfare mothers, and the like. Further, groups with "mainstream" views, seeking only small changes in the status quo, may be given more sympathetic hearing than those advocating radical changes.[9] The most active groups in terms of number of lobbyists and amount spent seem to be business groups, with labor groups next, then a variety of citizens and governmental organizations and a scattering of other professional, farm, and miscellaneous groups (Jewell and Patterson, 1966). As a result, the distribution of groups is quite unlike the occupational and social characteristics of the population at large.

Another assumption made when one posits that interest groups are an effective linkage mechanism is that group members have common interests and that group leaders effectively represent group interests. Some evidence indicates that many group leaders do not really know the opinion of group members, and hence can hardly effectively represent them. Luttbeg and Zeigler (1966), for example, find large differences in leader and follower attitudes in a state educational association. Further, there are indications that group members themselves are not usually homogeneous in their own attitudes. Erickson and Luttbeg (1973) found that knowing the groups to which an individual belongs does not aid in predicting that individual's position on issues; hence group membership does not necessarily mean that unanimity, or near unanimity, of opinion exists on issue positions.

In sum, the group model does not seem to reflect more than a limited portion of the public opinion spectrum. Many citizens are not members of groups, and most are not members of politically active groups. Groups do not always consist of "like minded" people, and leaders are often unaware of the beliefs and opinions of group members. Further, group membership is skewed toward people of upper social and economic status. Those groups that do exist are unequal in strength and in financial, organizational, and other resources; and these inequalities may be quite unrelated to the number of people the groups represent. Finally, the influence of groups on decision makers is uncertain, and such influence as may be exerted is possibly not in accordance with the wishes of the public at large. Therefore, while interest groups may serve many functions for the individual and for the society as a whole, accurately representing public opinion to decision makers probably occurs only infrequently and accidentally.

Protest activities

Protest activities represent another channel through which individuals and groups seek to make their opinions heard. By protest activities we mean political action whose major purpose is to focus attention in a very dramatic way on a group's grievances or demands. Lipsky, in the selection that follows (*pp. 478–503*), describe protest behavior as being characterized by "showmanship or display of an unconventional nature, and undertaken to obtain rewards for political or economic systems while working within the system." Others include in their definition of protest activities such as riots and violent demonstrations, and we shall use this broader definition. While violent riots of the type that occurred in U.S. urban areas in the middle and late sixties had different characteristics than demonstrations, rallies, and sit-ins, many of the riot participants were, in their own way, also voicing opinions about the system (Fogelson, 1968; Caplan and Paige, 1968).[10]

The last two decades have seen many different groups in U.S. society engaged in protest activities—massive demonstrations for and against the administration's Vietnam war policies were characteristic of the period from 1966 to 1969. The civil rights movement utilized nonviolent demonstrations such as picketing, sit-ins, marches, and the like throughout the late fifties and early sixties culminating in a huge "March on Washington" in 1963. Protest activities by labor unions, Chicanos, antibusing advocates, women's rights supporters, antiabortion groups, and a host of other groups are further indication that large numbers of people feel that organized protest is one way to make their voices heard by those in positions of power.

The urban riots can also be viewed as a means of voicing public opinion. The riots of the sixties of course, generally were not attended by presentation of a set of group demands by leaders of the protest; in fact, most, if not all, were apparently unplanned and leaderless. Although some of those who participated in the riots may have had no specific political grievance, and although in most cases no grievances were articulated at the time, the riots were interpreted by many in both the black and white communities as expressions of political protest. (Report of the National Advisory Commission on Civil Disorders, 1968; Aberbach and Walker, 1973).

An enormous amount of research has focused on protest behavior of both a peaceful and a violent nature, but almost all of it is concerned with such questions as who participated and why (Caplan and Paige, 1968; Caplan, 1970; McPhail, 1971), and what kinds of environments promote rioting and other, similar forms of protest (Spilerman, 1970, 1971; Downes, 1970; Eisinger, 1973). Amazingly little is known about the effects of protest in bringing about the changes wanted by the protesters. In other words, we know little, except on an intuitive level, about the effectiveness of protest as a linkage mechanism. For example, though many attribute the passage of civil rights legislation in 1964, 1965, and 1966 to the many civil rights demonstrations of the early sixties, few attribute much impact to the later, more violent demonstrations and urban riots of the middle and late sixties. These latter protests seemed to have created an immediate aftermath of concern and attention, but little long-range change.[11] The effects of the antiwar protests have also been debated. Some felt that they played a relevant role in President Lyndon Johnson's decision not to run for reelection in 1968 and in the eventual withdrawal of the United States from Vietnam short of a clearcut "victory." Others would deny that the effects were that great, but certainly vociferous and intense expression of antiwar feeling on the part of large numbers of people was a salient feature of the political landscape throughout the late sixties.

Do protest activities serve as a linkage mechanism between masses and decision makers? As illustrated in the above examples, our knowledge is equivocal and far from well established. At least, as Lipsky points out, protest activities appear to be channels whereby group without substantial resources can make themselves heard by decision makers. Their actual impact on policy making is much less clear. However, we would not expect their impact to be substantial since most groups that resort to protest activities are forced to do so because of lack of other resources, such as money and prestige. Also, it would seem from recent history that those who might be reasonably considered potential participants, have come to feel that violent protest is not a good way to express opinions to and about the government. Reasons for this change are unclear. It may be the result of fear of reprisal or a belief that violence is not a good way to solve problems, or simply the belief that the appropriate circumstances have not arisen to justify or support a mass violent protest. It remains to be seen whether this diminution of violent protest is a good omen (that people believe that their problems can be solved through democratic processes) or a bad one (that problems are festering and a belief is building that democratic processes are incapable of solving social problems).

THE PLURALISTS AND ANTIPLURALISTS

An issue of continuing debate among political scientists in the past two decades has been how well the linkage methods we have just discussed work. Does the American system provide means whereby all major segments of public opinion can be heard and taken into account in the making of governmental policy on the national, state, and local levels?

A number of political scientists have expressed the strong belief that the American system is a pluralist system—one where the leadership stratum is not united or monolithic and one that provides reasonably effective ways whereby all people with an interest in a particular issue can have access to those making the decision. Dahl, for example, in the following selection (*see pp. 518–31*), notes that in pluralist systems the political stratum—those active in politics—is not a closed group but a highly porous one, divided by many cleavages. As a result, political leadership is fragmented and lacks unity in both orientation and strategy (see also Dahl, 1971; Polsby, 1963; and Wolfinger, 1972). More generally, pluralists portray the American system as one of overlapping social, religious, economic, and ethnic groupings, each with a voice in decisions relevant to it. Through peaceable conflict over issues, compromises emerge, resulting in a workable, if not optimal, public policy, that assures the rights of all. Pluralists assert that all existing linkage mechanisms discussed above work together to ensure people an opportunity to organize and be heard on issues they consider to be relevant to them (Dahl, 1958). They argue that the most likely reason for people's lack of participation stems from a general feeling of satisfaction with the way issues are being handled, or at least sufficient satisfaction so that they do not feel it is worth the effort to try to effect a change. The pluralists' overall view of the system is one of conflict, but conflict whereby all potentially interested parties have a fair chance at influencing those making the decisions.

Other voices argue that linkage mechanisms in the United States work very poorly in representing all shades of opinion. One of the most influential of these voices is that of C. Wright Mills. In his classic work *The Power Elite* (1956), Mills argued that important decisions are made by a relatively small group of people in top military, government, and business positions without any reference to public wishes. He acknowledged that interest groups were free to organize, lobby and petition, but stated that by and large they influenced only the "middle range" of decisions, not those decisions that have a major impact on society at large—"war or peace," "boom or bust," and the like. While Mills did not allege that there was a conspiracy of top leaders to have things their own way, he did argue that community of interests, similarity of socialization patterns, and interchangeability of elites from business to government and the reverse led to their common "status quo preserving" outlook.

Other analysts have pointed to a different kind of elite control. Lowi (1967) sees national politics, and indeed government in general, as a product of interest group manipulation. Organized groups, he asserts, run the government, producing policies that primarily satisfy group interests, but pay little attention to generating policies favorable to the unorganized majority of the public. Lowi argues that logrolling among powerful interest groups (i.e., "you support our position on this issue, we'll support your position on the next") has taken control of public policy out of the hands of the public.

Other antipluralists, such as Bachrach and Baratz (1962), argue that the mass public is prevented from having an impact on many governmental acts because those in power simply define some issues as "nonissues," that is, not subject to public debate. Influentials, they argue, can keep potentially troublesome issues from arising, by threatening sanctions against those who raise them, denying the legitimacy of new demands (for example, by calling them "socialistic" or "Communistic") or by erecting or enforcing barriers against change. Bachrach and Baratz argue that the pluralists find conflict and balance in the American system simply because they look only at issues surrounded by conflict. They believe that one should look at the areas in which there are no public conflicts—where the status quo is jealously guarded—for a clue as to who holds the real power in America.

Still other antipluralists point to the advantages held by people of upper status in terms of group organization and involvement and in terms of access to decision makers as evidence that the linkage mechanisms fail to represent the full spectrum of public opinion. They state that one has to be organized to be heard, and that organization, by and large, favors the upper status.

The arguments between the pluralists and the various antipluralists are complex and cannot be satisfactorily summarized in a few lines. However, we can highlight their respective positions by saying that although both the pluralists and the antipluralists see conflict in the American system, the pluralists see the important decisions arising from the resolution of this conflict, while the antipluralists, by and large, view conflict among various groups as camouflaging the fact that the important decisions are being made elsewhere. Pluralists argue that over the long run (though perhaps not on any specific issue) all segments of the population with politically active opinions will have an opportunity to be heard. Antipluralists believe that significant segments of this population lack the political power or expertise necessary to make themselves heard.

At present, the pluralists seem to be on the defensive (see Margolis, 1973), and current conditions in American society have perhaps made it more difficult to argue the pluralist position. Indeed, it is difficult to deny, from the empirical evidence as well as from policy outcomes, that the financial resources and societal prestige associated with upper-class status, do provide a better guarantee that one's opinions will be at least listened to than those held by the lower and middle strata of society.

ENDNOTES

1. Curiously, no one has ever shown that trustees do in fact vote differently than delegates or politicos. The influence of role conception on actual behavior has only been inferred.

2. Miller and Stokes (1963) found that in case of members of the House of Representatives, their perceptions of constituencies' feelings were most accurate in the area of civil rights, and far less accurate in socioeconomic matters and foreign policy. It would seem that even on issues that are regularly discussed in Congress and in the press, the ability to accurately perceive constituents' attitudes is far from high among congressmen. State legislators, too, have been found to have inaccurate

perceptions of constituency opinion, especially on matters that do not attract wide public attention (Hedlund and Friesema, 1972).

3. This ignores the more complex questions of the rationality involved when the voter sees no difference, or little difference, between the candidates. In this situation, the voter may feel that the benefits gained by voting for one candidate over another are not worth the effort involved in voting.

4. It should be noted that interpretations of the public mood can be a risky undertaking. What may seem like an overwhelming endorsement of "retrenchment" in public programs, or expansion of such programs, for example, may in reality be public reaction to a particular personality or the feeling that one party has been in control long enough, rather than a policy-oriented vote.

5. For an extensive discussion of this point, see Luttbeg, 1968.

6. In the real world, the choice is not between the informed voter who votes on the basis of issues and policies and the straight-line party voter but, rather, between the totally ignorant voter and the straight-line voter.

7. This is not to say that much of platform content is not rhetoric designed less for its policy implications than as concessions to various party factions.

8. For a good discussion of means and requisites of access, see Truman, 1951.

9. While some information is available on the number of groups represented in various state legislatures and in Congress, much less is known about the relative strength of each group and about the reliance legislators place on the information they receive from lobbyists of various groups. Zeigler and Baer (1969) find that over 200 lobbyists are registered in an average state, and the *Congressional Quarterly* reports a substantially larger number for Congress. The various groups registered are quite disproportional to their representation in the larger society.

10. This is not to deny that many participants in urban riots had nonpolitical goals as well as, or instead of, political ones. The possibility of economic gain through looting and the lure of "being where the action is" must be seen as powerful stimulants to participation.

11. Some contemporary political commentators feared that the riots would bring about a backlash against the demonstrators and their demands, though little evidence of this was found.

REFERENCES AND FURTHER READINGS

Aberbach, Joel D., and Walker, Jack L. *Race in the City: Political Trust and Public Policy in the New Urban System.* Boston: Little, Brown & Co., 1973.

Bachrach, Peter, and Baratz, Morton S. "Two Faces of Power." *American Political Science Review* 56 (1962): 947–962.

Bachrach, Peter, and Baratz, Morton S. *Power and Poverty: Theory and Practice.* New York: Oxford University Press, 1970.

Berelson, Bernard R.; Lazarsfeld, Paul F.; and McPhee, William N. *Voting.* Chicago: University if Chicago Press, 1954.

Berelson, Bernard R., et al. "The Missing Links in Legislative Politics." *Journal of Politics* 31 (1969): 700-721.

Campbell, Angus, et al. *The American Voter*. New York: John Wiley & Sons, 1964.

Caplan, Nathan S. "The Consolidation of Black Consciousness." *Journal of Social Issues* 26 (1970): 59–73.

Caplan, Nathan S., and Paige, Jeffrey M. A "Study of Ghetto Rioters." *Scientific American* 219 (August 1968): 15–21.

Converse, Philip E. "The Nature of Belief Systems in Mass Publics." In *Ideology and Discontent*, edited by David E. Apter. New York: Free Press of Glencoe, 1964.

Dahl, Robert A. *A Preface to Democratic Theory*. Chicago: University of Chicago Press, 1958.

Dahl, Robert A. *Polyarchy: Participation and Opposition*. New Haven, Conn.: Yale University Press, 1971.

Dahl, Robert A. *Who Governs? Democracy and Power in an American City*. New Haven, Conn.: Yale University Press, 1961.

Downes, Bryan. "A Critical Reexamination of the Social and Political Characteristics of Riot Cities." *Social Science Quarterly* 51 (1970): 349–360.

Downs, Anthony. *An Economic Theory of Democracy*. New York: Harper & Bros., 1957.

Eisinger, Peter K. "The Conditions of Protest Behavior in American Cities." *American Political Science Review* 63 (1973): 11–28.

Erickson, Robert. "The Electoral Impact of Congressional Roll Call Voting." *American Political Science Review* 65 (1971): 1018–1032.

Erickson, Robert, and Luttbeg, Norman. *American Public Opinion: Its Origins, Content, and Impact*. New York: John Wiley & Sons, 1973.

Fogelson, Robert M. "Violence as Protest." In *Urban Riots: Violence and Social Change,* edited by Robert H. Connery. New York: Random House, 1968.

Frey, Frederick W. "On Issues and Non-Issues in the Study of Power." *American Political Science Review* 65 (1971): 1081–1101.

Hedlund, Ronald D., and Friesema, H. Paul. "Representatives' Perceptions of Constituency Opinion." *Journal of Politics* 34 (1972): 730–752.

Jewell, Malcolm E., and Patterson, Samuel C. *The Legislative Process in the United States*. New York: Random House, 1966.

Key, V. O., Jr. *American State Politics: An Introduction*. New York: Alfred A. Knopf, 1956.

Key, V. O., Jr., and Cummings, M. C. *The Responsible Electorate: Rationality in Presidential Voting*. Cambridge, Mass.: Harvard University Press, 1966.

Kingdon, John W. *Candidates for Office: Beliefs and Strategies*. New York: Random House, 1966.

LeBlanc, Hugh. "Voting in State Senates: Party and Constituency Influences." *Midwest Journal of Political Science* 13 (1969): 33–57.

Lipsky, Michael. "Protest as a Political Resource." *American Political Science Review* 62 (1968): 1144–1158.

Lowi, Theodore. "The Public Philosophy: Interest Group Liberalism." *American Political Science Review* 61 (1967): 15–74.

Luttbeg, Norman R. *Public Opinions and Public Policy: Models of Political Linkage.* Homewood, Ill.: Dorsey Press, 1968.

Luttbeg, Norman R., and Zeigler, Harmon. "Attitude Consensus and Conflict in an Interest Group." *American Political Science Review* 60 (1966): 655–667.

McClosky, Herbert; Hoffman, Paul J.; and O'Hara, Rosemary. "Issue Conflict and Consensus among Party Leaders and Followers." *American Political Science Review* 54 (1960): 406–427.

McPhail, Clark. "Civil Disorder Participation: A Critical Examination of Recent Research." *American Sociological Review* 36 (1971): 1058–1073.

McRae, Duncan, Jr. *Issues and Parties in Legislative Voting: Methods in Statistical Analysis.* New York: Harper and Row, 1970.

Margolis, Michael. "The New American Government Textbooks." *American Journal of Political Science* 17 (1973): 457–463.

Miller, Warren, and Stokes, Donald. "Constituency Influence in Congress." *American Political Science Review* 57 (1963): 45–46.

Mills, C. Wright. *The Power Elite.* New York: Oxford University Press, 1956.

National Advisory Commission on Civil Disorders. *Report.* New York: Bantam, 1968.

Page, Benjamin I., and Brody, Richard A. "Policy Voting and the Electoral Process: The Vietnam War Issue." *American Political Science Review* 66 (1972): 979–995

Pierce, John C. "Party Identification and the Changing Role of Ideology in American Politics." *Midwest Journal of Political Science* 14 (1970): 25–42.

Polsby, Nelson W. *Community Power and Political Theory.* New Haven, Conn.: Yale University Press, 1963.

Pomper, Gerald. *Elections in America: Control and Influence in Democratic Politics.* New York: Dodd, Mead & Co., 1968.

Ranney, Austin, and Kendall, Willmoore. *Democracy and the American Party System.* New York: Harcourt, Brace & Co., 1956.

Shannon, W. Wayne. *Party, Constituency and Congressional Voting: A Study of Legislative Behavior in the United States House of Representatives.* Baton Rouge: Louisiana State Press, 1968.

Sigel, Roberta, and Friesema, H. Paul. "Urban Community Leaders' Knowledge of Public Opinion." *Western Political Quarterly* 18 (1965): 881–895.

Spilerman, Seymour. "The Causes of Racial Disturbances: A Comparison of Alternative Explanations." *American Sociological Review* 35 (1970): 627–649.

Spilerman, Seymour. "The Causes of Racial Disturbances: Tests of an Explanation." *American Sociological Review* 36 (1971): 427–442.

Stokes, Donald E., and Miller, Warren. "Party Government and the Saliency of Congress." *Public Opinion Quarterly* 26 (1962): 531–546.

Sullivan, John L., and O'Connor, Robert. "Electoral Choice and Popular Control of Public Policy: The Case of the 1966 House Elections." *American Political Science Review* 66 (1972): 1256–1268.

Truman, David B. *The Governmental Process: Political Interests and Public Opinion.* New York: Alfred A. Knopf, 1951.

Turner, Julius. *Party and Constituency: Pressures on Congress.* Revised edition by Edward V. Schneier, Jr. Baltimore: Johns Hopkins Press, 1970.

Verba, Sidney, and Brody, Richard A. "Participation, Policy Preferences and the War in Vietnam." *Public Opinion Quarterly* 34 (1970): 325–332.

Verba, Sidney, and Nie, Norman. *Participation in America: Political Democracy and Social Equality*. New York: Harper and Row, 1972.

Wahlke, John C., et al. *The Legislative System: Explorations in Legislative Behavior*. New York: John Wiley & Sons, 1962.

Walker, Jack. "A Critique of the Elitist Theory of Democracy." *American Political Science Review* 60 (1966): 285–295.

Weinbaum, Marvin, and Judd, Dennis. "In Search of a Mandated Congress." *Midwest Journal of Political Science* 14 (1970): 276–302.

Wolfinger, Raymond. "Nondecisions in the Study of Local Politics." *American Political Science Review* 65 (1971): 1063–1080.

Zeigler, Harmon, and Baer, Michael. *Lobbying: Interaction and Influence in American State Legislatures*. Belmont, Calif.: Wadsworth Publishing Co., 1969.

Reprinted from *Voting* by Bernard Berelson *et al.* by permission of the senior author and The University of Chicago Press. Copyright 1954 by The University of Chicago.

Democratic Practice and Democratic Theory

BERNARD R. BERELSON, PAUL F. LAZARSFELD, and WILLIAM N. McPHEE

There is always a terrible gulf between the fine and elevating theories about democracy which we read in books on political theory and the actual facts of politics.

LORD LINDSAY

I

What does all this mean for the political theory of democracy?* For we have been studying not how people come to make choices in general but how they make a political choice, and the political content of the study has broad ramifications beyond the technical interests. In the end, of course, we must

*Here and throughout this selection, the authors refer to the findings of their study of the voters in Elmira, New York, in the 1948 presidential election. Among other things, this study revealed—as the reader will gather from the remainder of

leave such theoretical questions to the political theorists and the political philosophers. But the fact that they would not be at home in our empirical material has encouraged us to speak at least briefly to their concerns. Both theory and facts are needed. As Schumpeter says in *Capitalism, Socialism and Democracy:* "The question whether [certain] conditions are fulfilled to the extent required in order to make democracy work should not be answered by reckless assertion or equally reckless denial. It can be answered only by a laborious appraisal of a maze of conflicting evidence."

With respect to politics, empirical-analytic theory and normative theory have only recently become truly separated—and often to their mutual disadvantage and impoverishment. In a recent essay a British scholar comments on "The Decline of Political Theory." That there has been and is now a "decline" seems to be generally accepted. Why? Because, says Alfred Cobban, the theory of the great political thinkers of the past was written "with a practical purpose in mind. Their object was to influence actual political behavior. They wrote to condemn or support existing institutions, to justify a political system or persuade their fellow citizens to change it: because, in the last resort, they were concerned with the aims, the purposes of political society." He points out that John Stuart Mill tried to reconcile the demands for state action with established ideals of individual liberty, Bentham to establish a theoretical basis for the legislative and administrative reforms that were then urgently needed, Burke to provide an alternative to the new democratic principle of the sovereignty of the people, Locke to provide a political theory for a generation that had overthrown divine right and established parliamentary government, Hobbs to maintain the primacy of sovereignty in an age of civil wars, etc. From being "formerly the work of men intently concerned with practical issues," the study of political theory

> has become instead an academic discipline written in various esoteric jargons almost as though for the purpose of preventing it from being understood by those who, if they did understand it, might try to put it into practice. . . . Political theory has in this way become disengaged from political facts. Even worse, it has become disengaged on principle, as it has seldom if ever been in the past.

Here, it seems to us, lies one potential use of our data. If the political theorists do not engage directly in politics, they might explore the relevance, the implications, and the meaning of such empirical facts as are contained in this and similar studies. Political theory written with reference to practice

---

the article—that voters were not as interested and informed as one might hope in a democracy, and that instead of listening to reasoned and informative arguments for and against each party or candidate, voters tended to make up their minds early on the basis of standing party loyalties, group preferences, and the like.—ED.

has the advantage that its categories are the categories in which political life really occurs. And, in turn, relating research to problems of normative theory would make such research more realistic and more pertinent to the problems of policy. At the same time, empirical research can help to clarify the standards and correct the empirical presuppositions of normative theory. As a modest illustration, this [selection] turns to some of the broad normative and evaluative questions implied in this empirical study.

REQUIREMENTS FOR THE INDIVIDUAL

Perhaps the main impact of realistic research on contemporary politics has been to temper some of the requirements set by our traditional normative theory for the typical citizen. "Out of all this literature of political observation and analysis, which is relatively new," says Max Beloff, "there has come to exist a picture in our minds of the political scene which differs very considerably from that familiar to us from the classical texts of democratic politics."

Experienced observers have long known, of course, that the individual voter was not all that the theory of democracy requires of him. As Bryce put it:

> How little solidity and substance there is in the political or social beliefs of nineteen persons out of every twenty. These beliefs, when examined, mostly resolve themselves into two or three prejudices and aversions, two or three prepossessions for a particular party or section of a party, two or three phrases or catch-words suggesting or embodying arguments which the man who repeats them has not analyzed.

While our data do not support such an extreme statement, they do reveal that certain requirements commonly assumed for the successful operation of democracy are not met by the behavior of the "average" citizen. The requirements, and our conclusions concerning them, are quickly reviewed.[1]

Interest, discussion, motivation. The democratic citizen is expected to be interested and to participate in political affairs. His interest and participation can take such various forms as reading and listening to campaign materials, working for the candidate or the party, arguing politics, donating money, and voting. In Elmira the majority of the people vote, but in general they do not give evidence of sustained interest. Many vote without real involvement in the election, and even the party workers are not typically motivated by ideological concerns or plain civic duty.

If there is one characteristic for a democratic system (besides the ballot itself) that is theoretically required, it is the capacity for and the practice of discussion. "It is as true of the large as of the small society," says Lindsay, "that its health depends on the mutual understanding which discussion makes possible; and that discussion is the only possible instrument of its democratic government." . . . In [Elmira] there was little true discussion between the candidates, little in the newspaper commentary, little between the voters and the official party representatives, some within the electorate. On the grass-roots level there was more talk than debate, and, at least inferentially, the talk had important effects upon voting, in reinforcing or activating the partisans if not in converting the opposition.

An assumption underlying the theory of democracy is that the citizenry has a strong motivation for participation in political life. But it is a curious quality of voting behavior that for large numbers of people motivation is weak if not almost absent. It is assumed that this motivation would gain its strength from the citizen's perception of the difference that alternative decisions made to him. Now when a person buys something or makes other decisions of daily life, there are direct and immediate consequences for him. But for the bulk of the American people the voting decision is not followed by any direct, immediate, visible personal consequences. Most voters, organized or unorganized, are not in a position to foresee the distant and indirect consequences for themselves, let alone the society. The ballot is cast, and for most people that is the end of it. If their side is defeated, "it doesn't really matter."

Knowledge. The democratic citizen is expected to be well informed about political affairs. He is supposed to know what the issues are, what their history is, what the relevant facts are, what alternatives are proposed, what the party stands for, what the likely consequences are. By such standards the voter falls short. Even when he has the motivation, he finds it difficult to make decisions on the basis of full information when the subject is relatively simple and proximate; how can he do so when it is complex and remote? The citizen is not highly informed on details of the campaign, nor does he avoid a certain misperception of the political situation when it is to his psychological advantage to do so. The electorate's perception of what goes on in the campaign is colored by emotional feeling toward one or the other issue, candidate, party, or social group.

Principle. The democratic citizen is supposed to cast his vote on the basis of principle—not fortuitously or frivolously or impulsively or habitually, but with reference to standards not only of his own interest but of the common good as well. Here, again, if this requirement is pushed at all strongly, it becomes an impossible demand on the democratic electorate.

Many voters vote not for principle in the usual sense but "for" a group to which they are attached—their group. The Catholic vote or the hereditary vote* is explainable less as principle than as traditional social allegiance. The ordinary voter, bewildered by the complexity of modern political problems, unable to determine clearly what the consequences are of alternative lines of action, remote from the arena, and incapable of bringing information to bear on principle, votes the way trusted people around him are voting. A British scholar, Max Beloff, takes as the "chief lesson to be derived" from such studies:

> Election campaigns and the programmes of the different parties have little to do with the ultimate result which is predetermined by influences acting upon groups of voters over a longer period. . . . This view has now become a working hypothesis with which all future thinking on this matter will have to concern itself. But if this is admitted, then obviously the picture of the voter as a person exercising conscious choice between alternative persons and alternative programmes tends to disappear.

On the issues of the campaign there is a considerable amount of "don't know"—sometimes reflecting genuine indecision, more often meaning "don't care." Among those with opinions the partisans *agree* on most issues, criteria, expectations, and rules of the game. The supporters of the different sides disagree on only a few issues. Nor, for that matter, do the candidates themselves always join the issue sharply and clearly. The partisans do not agree overwhelmingly with their own party's position, or, rather, only the small minority of highly partisan do; the rest take a rather moderate position on the political considerations involved in an election.

Rationality.—The democratic citizen is expected to exercise rational judgment in coming to his voting decision. He is expected to have arrived at his principles by reason and to have considered rationally the implications and alleged consequences of the alternative proposals of the contending parties. Political theorists and commentators have always exclaimed over the seeming contrast here between requirement and fulfilment. Even as sensible and hard-minded an observer as Schumpeter was extreme in his view:

> Even if there were no political groups trying to influence him, the typical citizen would in political matters tend to yield to extra-rational or irrational prejudice and impulse. The weakness of the rational processes he applies to politics and the absence of effective logical control over the results he arrives at would in themselves suffice to account for that. Moreover, simply because he is not "all there," he will relax his usual

*Here the authors are referring to the phenomena discussed in the introduction to Section III of this reader under the heading "Political Socialization," namely, the process by which the child, and later the adult, acquires and modifies his political beliefs, and the agencies responsible for such process.—ED.

> moral standards as well and occasionally give in to dark urges which the conditions of private life help him to repress.

Here the problem is first to see just what is meant by rationality. The term, as a recent writer noted, "has enjoyed a long history which has bequeathed to it a legacy of ambiguity and confusion. . . . Any man may be excused when he is puzzled by the question of how he ought to use the word and particularly how he ought to use it in relation to human conducts and politics." Several meanings can be differentiated.

It is not for us to certify a meaning. But even without a single meaning—with only the aura of the term—we can make some observations on the basis of our material. In any rigorous or narrow sense the voters are not highly rational; that is, most of them do not ratiocinate on the matter, e.g., to the extent that they do on the purchase of a car or a home. Nor do voters act rationally whose "principles" are held so tenaciously as to blind them to information and persuasion. Nor do they attach efficient means to explicit ends.

The fact that some people change their minds during a political campaign shows the existence of that open-mindedness usually considered as a component of rationality. But among whom? Primarily among those who can "afford" a change of mind, in the sense that they have ties or attractions on both sides—the cross-pressured voters in the middle where rationality is supposed to take over from the extremes of partisan feeling. But it would hardly be proper to designate the unstable, uninterested, uncaring middle as the sole or the major possessor of rationality among the electorate. As Beloff points out: "It is likely that the marginal voter is someone who is so inadequately identified with one major set of interests or another and so remote, therefore, from the group-thinking out of which political attitudes arise, that his voting record is an illustration, not of superior wisdom, but of greater frivolity."

The upshot of this is that the usual analogy between the voting "decision" and the more or less carefully calculated decisions of consumers or businessmen or courts, incidentally, may be quite incorrect. For many voters political preferences may better be considered analogous to cultural tastes—in music, literature, recreational activities, dress, ethics, speech, social behavior. Consider the parallels between political preferences and general cultural tastes. Both have their origin in ethnic, sectional, class, and family traditions. Both exhibit stability and resistance to change for individuals but flexibility and adjustment over generations for the society as a whole. preferences." While both are responsive to changed conditions and unusual stimuli, they are relatively invulnerable to direct argumentation and vulnerable to indirect social influences. Both are characterized more by faith than by conviction and by wishful expectation rather than careful prediction of consequences. The preference for one party rather than another must be highly similar to the preference for one kind of literature or music rather than another, and the choice of the same political party every four years may be parallel to the choice of the same standards of conduct in new social situations. In short, it appears that a sense of fitness is a more striking feature of political preference than reason and calculation.

II

If the democratic system depended solely on the qualifications of the individual voter, then it seems remarkable that democracies have survived through the centuries. After examining the detailed data on how individuals misperceive political reality or respond to irrelevant social influences, one wonders how a democracy ever solves its political problems. But when one considers the data in a broader perspective—how huge segments of the society adapt to political conditions affecting them or how the political system adjusts itself to changing conditions over long periods of time—he cannot fail to be impressed with the total result. Where the rational citizen seems to abdicate, nevertheless angels seem to tread.

The eminent judge, Learned Hand, in a delightful essay on "Democracy: Its Presumptions and Reality," comes to essentially this conclusion:

> I do not know how it is with you, but for myself I generally give up at the outset. The simplest problems which come up from day to day seem to me quite unanswerable as soon as I try to get below the surface. . . . My vote is one of the most unimportant acts of my life; if I were to acquaint myself with the matters on which it ought really to depend, if I were to try to get a judgment on which I was willing to risk affairs of even the smallest moment, I should be doing nothing else, and that seems a fatuous conclusion to a fatuous undertaking.

Yet he recognizes the paradox—somehow the system not only works on the most difficult and complex questions but often works with distinction. "For, abuse it as you will, it gives a bloodless measure of social forces—bloodless, have you thought of that?—a means of continuity, a principle of stability, a relief from the paralyzing terror of revolution."

Justice Hand concludes that we have "outgrown" the conditions assumed in traditional democratic theory and that "the theory has ceased
Both seem to be matters of sentiment and disposition rather than "reasoned
to work." And yet, the system that has grown out of classic democratic theory, and in this country, out of quite different and even elementary social conditions, does continue to work—perhaps even more vigorously and effectively than ever.

That is the paradox. *Individual voters* today seem unable to satisfy the requirements for a democratic system of government outlined by political theorists. But the *system of democracy* does meet certain requirements for a going political organization. The individual members may not meet all the standards, but the whole nevertheless survives and grows. This suggests that where the classic theory is defective is in its concentration on the *individual citizen.* What are undervalued are certain collective properties that reside in the electorate as a whole and in the political and social system in which it functions.

The political philosophy we have inherited, then, has given more consideration to the virtues of the typical citizen of the democracy than to the working of the *system* as a whole. Moreover, when it dealt with the system, it mainly considered the single constitutive institutions of the system, not those general features necessary if the institutions are to work as required. For example, the rule of law, representative government, periodic elections, the party system, and the several freedoms of discussion, press, association, and assembly have all been examined by political philosophers seeking to clarify and to justify the idea of political democracy. But liberal democracy is more than a political system in which individual voters and political institutions operate. For political democracy to survive, other features are required: the intensity of conflict must be limited, the rate of change must be restrained, stability in the social and economic structure must be maintained, a pluralistic social organization must exist, and a basic consensus must bind together the contending parties.

Such features of the system of political democracy belong neither to the constitutive institutions nor to the individual voter. It might be said that they form the atmosphere or the environment in which both operate. In any case, such features have not been carefully considered by political philosophers, and it is on these broader properties of the democratic political system that more reflection and study by political theory is called for. In the most tentative fashion let us explore the values of the political system, as they involve the electorate, in the light of the foregoing considerations.

REQUIREMENTS FOR THE SYSTEM

Underlying the paradox is an assumption that the population is homogeneous socially and should be homogeneous politically; that everybody is about the same in relevant social characteristics; that, if something is a political virtue (like interest in the election), then everyone should have it; that there is such a thing as "the" typical citizen on whom uniform requirements can be imposed. The tendency of classic democratic literature to work with an image of "the" voter was never justified. For, as we will attempt to illustrate here, some of the most important requirements that democratic values impose on a system require a voting population that is not homogeneous but heterogeneous in its political qualities.

The need for heterogeneity arises from the contradictory functions we expect our voting system to serve. We expect the political system to adjust itself and our affairs to changing conditions; yet we demand too that it display a high degree of stability. We expect the contending interests and parties to pursue their ends vigorously and the voters to care; yet, after the election is over, we expect reconciliation. We expect the voting outcome to serve what is best for the community; yet we do not want disinterested voting unattached to the purposes and interests of different segments of that community. We want voters to express their own free and self-determined choices; yet, for the good of the community, we would like voters to avail themselves of the best information and guidance available from the groups and leaders around them. We expect a high degree of rationality to prevail in the decision; but were all irrationality and mythology absent, and all ends pursued by the most coldly rational selection of political means, it is doubtful if the system could hold together.

In short, our electoral system calls for apparently incompatible properties —which, although they cannot all reside in each individual voter, can (and do) reside in the heterogeneous electorate. What seems to be required of the electorate as a whole is a *distribution of qualities* along important dimensions. We need some people who are active in a certain respect, others in the middle, and still others passive. The contradictory things we want from the total require that the parts be different. This can be illustrated by taking up a number of important dimensions by which an electorate might be characterized.

Involvement and indifference

How could a mass democracy work if all the people were deeply involved in politics? Lack of interest by some people is not without its benefits, too. True, the highly interested voters vote more, and know more about the campaign, and read and listen more, and participate more; however, they are also less open to persuasion and less likely to change. Extreme interest goes with extreme partisanship and might culminate in rigid fanaticism that could destroy democratic processes if generalized throughout the community. Low affect toward the election—not caring much—underlies the resolution of many political problems; votes can be resolved into a two-party split instead of fragmented into many parties (the splinter parties of the left, for example, splinter because their advocates are *too* interested in politics). Low interest provides maneuvering room for political shifts necessary for a complex society in a period of rapid change. Compromise might be based upon sophisticated awareness of costs and returns—perhaps impossible to demand of a mass society—but it is more often induced by indifference. Some people are and should be highly interested in politics, but not everyone is or needs to be. Only the doctrinaire would deprecate the moderate indifference that facilitates compromise.

Hence, an important balance between action motivated by strong sentiments and action with little passion behind it is obtained by heterogeneity within the electorate. Balance of this sort is, in practice, met by a distribution of voters rather than by a homogeneous collection of "ideal" citizens.

Stability and flexibility

A similar dimension along which an electorate might be characterized is stability-flexibility. The need for change and adaptation is clear, and the need for stability ought equally to be (especially from observation of current democratic practice in, say, certain Latin-American countries).

How is political stability achieved? There are a number of social sources of political stability: the training of the younger generation before it is old enough to care much about the matter, the natural selection that surrounds the individual voter with families and friends who reinforce his own inclinations, the tendency to adjust in favor of the majority of the group, the self-perpetuating tendency of political traditions among ethnic and regional strata where like-minded people find themselves socially together. Political stability is based upon social stability. Family traditions, personal associations, status-related organizational memberships, ethnic affiliations, socioeconomic strata—such ties for the individual do not change rapidly or sharply, and since his vote is so importantly a product of them, neither does it. In effect, a large part of the study of voting deals not with why votes change but rather with why they do not.

In addition, the varying conditions favoring the country, the varying political appeals made to the electorate, and the varying dispositions of the voters activated by these stimuli—these, combined with the long-lasting nature of the political loyalties they instil, produce an important cohesion within the system. For example, the tendencies operating in 1948 electoral decisions not only were built up in the New Deal and Fair Deal era but also dated back to parental and grandparental loyalties, to religious and ethnic cleavages of a past era, and to moribund sectional and community conflicts. Thus, in a very real sense any particular election is a composite of various elections and various political and social events. People vote for a President on a given November day, but their choice is made not simply on the basis of what has happened in the preceding months or even four years; in 1948 some people were in effect voting on the internationalism isssue of 1940, others on the depression issues of 1932, and some, indeed, on the slavery issues of 1860.

The vote is thus a kind of "moving average" of reactions to the political past. Voters carry over to each new election remnants of issues raised in previous elections—and so there is always an overlapping of old and new decisions that give a cohesion in time to the political system. Hence the composite decision "smooths out" political change. The people vote *in* the same election, but not all of them vote *on* it.

What of flexibility? Curiously, the voters least admirable when measured against individual requirements contribute most when measured against the aggregate requirement for flexibility. For those who change political preferences most readily are those who are least interested, who are subject to conflicting social pressures, who have inconsistent beliefs and erratic voting histories. Without them—if the decision were left only to the deeply concerned, well-integrated, consistently-principled ideal citizens—the political system might easily prove too rigid to adapt to changing domestic and international conditions.

In fact, it may be that the very people who are most sensitive to changing social conditions are those most susceptible to political change. For, in either case, the people exposed to membership in overlapping strata, those whose former life-patterns are being broken up, those who are moving about socially or physically, those who are forming new families and new friendships—it is they who are open to adjustments of attitudes and tastes. They may be the least partisan and the least interested voters, but they perform a valuable function for the entire system. Here again is an instance in which an individual "inadequacy" provides a positive service for the society: The campaign can be a reaffirming force for the settled majority and a creative force for the unsettled minority. There is stability on both sides and flexibility in the middle.

Progress and conservation

Closely related to the question of stability is the question of past versus future orientation of the system. In America a progressive outlook is highly valued, but, at the same time, so is a conservative one. Here a balance between the two is easily found in the party system and in the distribution of voters themselves from extreme conservatives to extreme liberals. But a balance between the two is also achieved by a distribution of political dispositions through time. There are periods of great political agitation (i.e., campaigns) alternating with periods of political dormancy. Paradoxically, the former—the campaign period—is likely to be an instrument of conservatism, often even of historical regression.

Many contemporary campaigns (not, however, 1952) must be stabilizing forces that activated past tendencies in individuals and reasserted past patterns of group voting. In 1948, for example, the middle-class Protestants reaffirmed their traditional Republican position, the working-class Protestants reverted toward their position of the 1930's and the working-class Catholics toward their position not only of the 1930's but of a generation or more earlier. In this sense the campaign was a retreat away from new issues back toward old positions.

Political campaigns tend to make people more consistent both socially and psychologically; they vote more with their social groups and agree more with their own prior ideas on the issues. But new ideas and new alignments are in their infancy manifested by inconsistency psychologically and heterogeneity socially; they are almost by definition deviant and minority points of view. To the extent that they are inhibited by pressure or simply by knowledge of what is the proper (i.e., majority) point of view in a particular group, then the campaign period is not a time to look for the growth of important new trends.

This "regressive tendency" may appear as a reaction to intense propaganda during decisive times. The term "regressive" need not imply a reversion to less-developed, less-adaptive behavior; in fact, one might argue that the revival of a Democratic vote among workers was functional for their interests. What it refers to is simply the reactivation of prior dispositions—dispositions in politics that date back years and decades, often to a prior political era.

Its counterpart, of course, is what we believe to be an important potential for progress during the periods of relaxed tension and low-pressure political and social stimuli that are especially characteristic of America between political campaigns. The very tendency for Americans to neglect their political system most of the time—to be "campaign citizens" in the sense that many are "Sunday churchgoers"—is not without its values. Change may come best from relaxation.

Again, then, a balance (between preservation of the past and receptivity to the future) seems to be required of a democratic electorate. The heterogeneous electorate in itself provides a balance between liberalism and conservatism; and so does the sequence of political events from periods of drifting change to abrupt rallies back to the loyalties of earlier years.

Consensus and cleavage

We have talked much in the text, and perhaps implied more, about consensus and cleavage.* Although there were certain clusters of political opin-

*See Editor's note on p. 427.

ion in Elmira, at the same time there were a number of opinions that did not break along class or party lines. American opinion on public issues is much too complex to be designated by such simple, single-minded labels as *the* housewife opinion or *the* young people's opinion or even *the* workers' opinion. If one uses as a base the central Republican-Democratic cleavage, then one finds numerous "contradictions" within individuals, within strata and groups, and within party supporters themselves. There are many issues presented, cafeteria-style, for the voter to choose from, and there are overlaps in opinion in every direction.

Similarly there are required *social* consensus and cleavage—in effect, pluralism—in politics. Such pluralism makes for enough consensus to hold the system together and enough cleavage to make it move. Too much consensus would be deadening and restrictive of liberty; too much cleavage would be destructive of the society as a whole.

Consider the pictures of the hypothetical relationships between political preference (e.g., party support) and a social characteristic as presented in this chart:

PERCENTAGE FOR PARTY Y, BY CHARACTERISTIC X

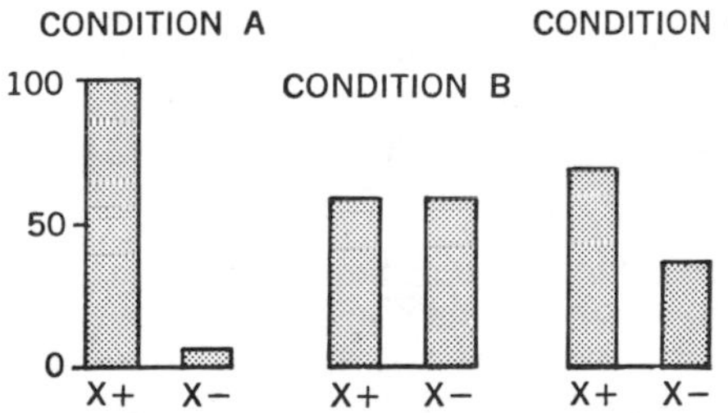

In Condition A there is virtual identity between the characteristic and political preference; all the people of type $X+$ vote one way, and all the people of $X-$ vote the other way. In Condition B the opposite is the case, and there is no relationship between vote and the characteristic; both parties are supported equally by people of the two types. In Condition C there is neither a complete relationship nor a complete absence; more $X+$'s than $X-$'s are partisans of a given side, but there are some members of each type in each political camp.

Now a democratic society in which Condition A was intensified would probably be in danger of its existence. The issues of politics would cut so deeply, be so keenly felt, and, especially, be so fully reinforced by other social identifications of the electorate as to threaten the basic consensus itself. This might be called "total politics"—a conception of politics, incidentally, advanced by such leading theorists of National Socialism and communism as Carl Schmitt and Lenin. This involves the mutual reinforcement of political differences and other social distinctions meaningful to the citizen. The multiplication of Condition B, on the other hand, would suggest a community in which politics was of no "real" importance to the community, in which it was not associated with special interests. Condition C is a combination of Conditions A and B—that is, a situation in which special interests are of some but not of overriding importance. It portrays neither the extremist or fanatical community like A nor the "pure" or utopian community like B.

There is nothing in Elmira that represents Condition A; the closest approximation would be the relationship between vote and religion or minority ethnic status, and even here there are group overlaps in vote amounting to form a quarter to a third of the members. The nearest approximation to Condition B is the relationship between vote and sex, which is another way of saying that there is little relevance of this characteristic to political matters, at least so far as party preference is concerned. The relationships between vote and socioeconomic status or vote and occupation are examples of Condition C.

The social and political correlations we find in places like Elmira (that are not a priori meaningless) are of the C type to a greater or less extent. What this means is that there is a good deal of cross-group and cross-party identification and affiliation within the community. The political lines are drawn in meaningful ways but are not identical with the lines of social groupings. The same social heterogeneity that produces self-interest also produces a cross-cutting and harmonious community interest.

Thus again a requirement we might place on an electoral system—balance between total political war between segments of the society and total political indifference to group interests of that society—translates into varied requirements for diffierent individuals. With respect to group or bloc voting, as with other aspects of political behavior, it is perhaps not unfortunate that "some do and some do not."

Individualism and collectivism

Lord Bryce pointed out the difficulties in a theory of democracy that assumes that each citizen must himself be capable of voting intelligently:

> Orthodox democratic theory assumes that every citizen has, or ought to have, thought out for himself certain opinions, i.e., ought to have a definite view, defensible by argument, of what the country needs, of what principles ought to be applied in governing it, of the man to whose hands the government ought to be entrusted. There are persons who talk, though certainly very few who act, as if they believed this theory, which may be compared to the theory of some ultra-Protestants that every good

> Christian has or ought to have . . . worked out for himself from the Bible a system of theology.

In the first place, however, the information available to the individual voter is not limited to that directly possessed by him. True, the individual casts his own personal ballot. But . . . that is perhaps the most individualized action he takes in an election. His vote is formed in the midst of his fellows in a sort of group decision—if, indeed, it may be called a decision at all—and the total information and knowledge possessed in the group's present and past generations can be made available for the group's choice. Here is where opinion-leading relationships, for example, play an active role.

Second, and probably more important, the individual voter may not have a great deal of detailed information, but he usually has picked up the crucial *general* information as part of his social learning itself. He may not know the parties' positions on the tariff, or who is for reciprocal trade treaties, or what are the differences on Asiatic policy, or how the parties split on civil rights, or how many security risks were exposed by whom. But he cannot live in an American community without knowing broadly where the parties stand. He has learned that the Republicans are more conservative and the Democrats more liberal—and he can locate his own sentiments and cast his vote accordingly. After all, he must vote for one or the other party, and, if he knows the big thing about the parties, he does not need to know all the little things. The basic role a party plays as an institution in American life is more important to his voting than a particular stand on a particular issue.

It would be unthinkable to try to maintain our present economic style of life without a complex system of delegating to others what we are not competent to do ourselves, without accepting and giving training to each other about what each is expected to do, without accepting our dependence on others in many spheres and taking responsibility for their dependence on us in some spheres. And, like it or not, to maintain our present political style of life, we may have to accept much the same interdependence with others in collective behavior. We have learned slowly in economic life that it is useful not to have everyone a butcher or a baker, any more than it is useful to have no one skilled in such activities. The same kind of division of labor—as repugnant as it may be in some respects to our individualistic tradition—is serving us well today in mass politics. There is an implicit division of political labor within the electorate.

III

In short, when we turn from requirements for "average" citizens to requirements for the survival of the total democratic system, we find it unnecessary for the individual voter to be an "average citizen" cast in the classic or any other single mold. With our increasingly complex and differentiated citizenry has grown up an equally complex political system, and it is perhaps not simply a fortunate accident that they have grown and prospered together.

But it is a dangerous act of mental complacency to assume that conditions found surviving together are, therefore, positively "functional" for each other. The apathetic segment of America probably has helped to hold the system together and cushioned the shocks of disagreement, adjustment, and change. But that is not to say that we can stand apathy without limit. Similarly, there must be some limit to the degree of stability or nonadaptation that a political society can maintain and still survive in a changing world. And surely the quality and amount of conformity that is necessary and desirable can be exceeded, as it has been in times of war, . . . to the damage of the society itself and of the other societies with which it must survive in the world.

How can our analysis be reconciled with the classical theory of liberal political democracy? Is the theory "wrong"? Must it be discarded in favor of empirical political sociology? Must its ethical or normative content be dismissed as incompatible with the nature of modern man or of mass society? That is not our view. Rather, it seems to us that modern political theory of democracy stands in need of revision and not replacement by empirical sociology. The classical political philosophers were right in the direction of their assessment of the virtues of the citizen. But they demanded those virtues in too extreme or doctrinal a form. The voter does have some principles, he does have information and rationality, he does have interest—but he does not have them in the extreme, elaborate, comprehensive, or detailed form in which they were uniformly recommended by political philosophers. Like Justice Hand, the typical citizen has other interests in life, and it is good, even for the political system, that he pursues them. The classical requirements are more appropriate for the opinion leaders in the society, but even they do not meet them directly. Happily for the system, voters distribute themselves along a continuum:

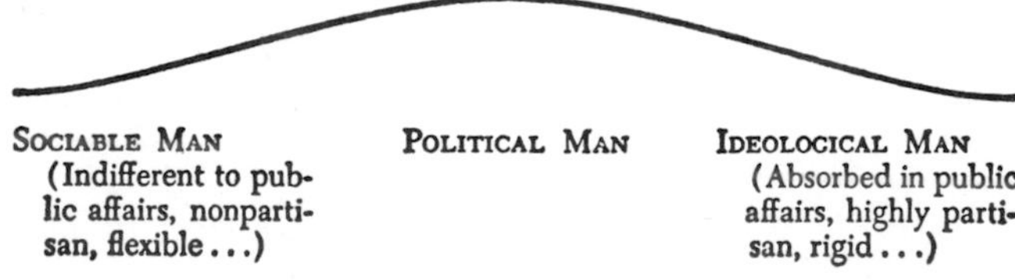

And it turns out that this distribution itself, with its internal checks and balances, can perform the functions and incorporate the same values ascribed by some theorists to each individual in the system as well as to the constitutive political institutions!

Twentieth-century political theory—both analytic and normative—will arise only from hard and long observation of the actual world of politics, closely identified with the deeper problems of practical politics. Values and the behavior they are meant to guide are not distinctly separate or separable parts of life as it is lived; and how Elmirans choose their government is not completely unrelated to the considerations of how they are *supposed* to choose them. We disagree equally with those who believe that normative theory about the proper health of a democracy has nothing to gain from analytic studies like ours; with those who believe that the whole political tradition from Mill to Locke is irrelevant to our realistic understanding and assessment of modern democracy; or with those like Harold Laski who believe that "the decisions of men, when they come to choose their governors, are influenced by considerations which escape all scientific analysis."

We agree with Cobban: "For a century and a half Western democracies have been living on the stock of basic political ideas that were restated toward the end of the eighteenth century. That is a long time. . . . The gap thus formed between political facts and political ideas has steadily widened. It has taken a long time for the results to become evident; but now that we have seen what politics devoid of a contemporary moral and political theory means, it is possible that something may be done about it."

To that end we hope this [selection] will contribute.

Reprinted from the *American Political Science Review,* 66 (September 1972), 979–995, with the permission of the American Political Science Association and the authors. Copyright 1972 by the American Political Science Association.

Policy Voting and the Electoral Process: The Vietnam War Issue

BENJAMIN I. PAGE
and
RICHARD A. BRODY

Most theories which hold that the preferences of the public affect policy making are predicated on the assumption that elections link opinions with policies. Electoral links, in turn, are thought to depend upon the ability of citizens to take account of their policy preferences when deciding how to vote. For that reason "issue voting" has been a focus of research by scholars concerned with empirical democratic theory.

Previous research on voting behavior in America has not, on the whole, been kind to democratic theory. It has supported two main propositions: first, that policy voting is quite rare; and second, that the infrequency of policy voting results from the shortcomings of citizens. Voters' lack of attention, information, and involvement with the issues saps their ability to choose candidates on the basis of policy preferences.[1] In short, voters are incapable of policy rationality.

Before final judgment is passed upon the capacities of the American voter, however, several challenges to one or both of these propositions ought to be tested.

One challenge alters the grounds of discussion. V. O. Key has argued that however little prospective *policy* voting may occur, the requirements of some democratic theories may be met if retrospective evaluations of governmental *performance* takes place. He claimed that such evaluations are common.[2]

A second challenge points out that different members of the population are concerned with, and have strong opinions about, different policy areas; policy voting may be widespread, but the relevant area of policy may vary from one voter to the next.[3]

A third challenge notes that much of the strongest evidence against issue voting derives from the politically tame 1950s; perhaps citizens have subsequently become more aware of the political world around them, more assertive in their reactions to it, and more willing to act on the basis of their opinions.

Finally, a fourth challenge is suggested by such diverse observers as Anthony Downs and George Wallace: perhaps there isn't "a dime's worth of difference" between Democratic and Republican candidates.[4] If rational campaigning dictates a side-by-side position for the candidates on the issues, then voters do not have the option of choosing between them on policy grounds—even if, given a real choice, they would be perfectly capable of doing so. Further, if candidates equivocate and hedge their position on the issues, voters should not be blamed for failing to perceive their positions clearly, or failing to vote on policy grounds.[5]

At present we are concerned only with the third and fourth challenges.[6] In the context of a single, highly salient issue we will consider these questions: First, was there a strong relationship between policy preferences and the vote? A positive answer to this question would impeach the generality of findings from studies which were carried out in the 1950s.

Second, were citizens able to vote their preferences? Did they have opinions; could they perceive what policy positions candidates took; could they take their opinions and perceptions into account in deciding how to vote? Positive answers to these questions would tend to overturn the proposition of incapacity, but not necessarily the proposition that policy voting is rare.

Finally, if we find that citizens were able to vote their preferences but did not do so, we will inquire into candidate behavior to see whether it depressed the extent of policy voting.

THE STUDY

The 1968 presidential election, coming at the height of the war in Vietnam, offered an opportunity to examine these questions. At the outset of 1968, nearly 500,000 American troops were in Vietnam; at least 20 billion dollars per year were being spent on the war; and each week about 100 Americans—and countless Vietnamese—were being killed. The war had a direct impact upon the lives of servicemen, their families, and friends. It affected many others indirectly, through rampant inflation and curtailment of domestic governmental spending.

Most Americans were thoroughly sick of the war. By late March, 1968, nearly two-thirds of the people disapproved of the way President Johnson was handling Vietnam, and a plurality thought it had been a mistake to send U.S. troops to fight there.[7] Dissent was loud on university campuses, in the U.S. Senate and even on Wall Street. A political candidate, Eugene McCarthy—followed by Robert Kennedy—offered a serious challenge to the incumbent President for the nomination of his own Democratic Party. To most observers it seemed that if Americans ever voted on the basis of policy preferences, they would vote their opinions on Vietnam in 1968.

Beginning in February 1968, we commissioned a series of nationwide opinion surveys, designed primarily to discover how Vietnam entered into public perceptions and evaluations of presidential candidates, and into the final voting decision.[8] In addition, the Survey Research Center of the University of Michigan, carrying out its usual election study for the Inter-University Consortium for Political Research, agreed to include some of our key items in its questionnaire. The November 1968 findings reported in this paper come from our analysis of the SRC data: findings concerning previous months are drawn from the ORC/IEP surveys.

In each survey, respondents were asked to indicate what Vietnam policy they preferred, on a seven-point rating scale. The scale was introduced by a prologue in which it was stated that opinions about Vietnam differed; some people favored all necessary measures to achieve a complete military victory; others favored immediate American withdrawal from Vietnam; and others, of course, had opinions somewhere in between. The interviewer then displayed a printed card with the numbers 1 through 7 arrayed at equal intervals along a line. Point number 1 was labeled "immediate withdrawal," and point number 7 "complete military victory." Other points were designated only by numbers. Respondents were then asked where on this scale they would place themselves, or whether they had no opinion.

Evidence from previous research indicated that the Vietnam preferences of most of the population were jointly single-peaked. That is, policy options concerning the level of American troops in Vietnam, bombing of North

Vietnam, coalition government and the like could be arrayed along a single dimension running from de-escalation to escalation.[9] When a respondent chose a single point as his most preferred policy, one could infer that alternative policies would be progressively less favored by him as they were located farther from his position. Examination of attitudes in 1968 has confirmed that Vietnam policy preferences continued to be unidimensional, and that our rating scale measured them satisfactorily.[10]

In addition to expressing their own opinions on the seven-point scale, respondents in each survey were asked to locate each presidential candidate's stand on the same scale. They also gave their evaluations of each candidate, on a scale ranging from "very unfavorable," and "not very favorable," through neutral, to "fairly favorable" and "very favorable."[11]

CANDIDATE SIMILARITY AND POLICY VOTING

It is quite difficult to assess precisely how much effect policy preferences have upon voting. In order to do so, it is probably necessary to calculate citizens' perceptions of similarity or dissimilarity between their own opinions and candidates' stands on an issue; to ascertain the relationship between these "perceived issue differences" and the vote; to estimate the extent of issue-oriented evaluation, disentangling that process from the confounding effects of rationalization (perceiving a favored candidate's position as being the same as one's own, or shifting one's opinion to conform with the position of a favored candidate); and, finally, to calculate net impact on the electoral outcome in terms of the average amount of issue difference from the candidates which is perceived by the population, and the average effect of a single unit of difference. It is probably correct to say, therefore, that the impact of issue voting has never been adequately measured.[12]

It is rather easy, on the other hand, to discover when a given issue has little or no impact. The more traditional mode of analysis, a simple cross-tabulation of vote by policy preferences, reveals whether those who held one opinion voted differently, on the average, from those who held a contrary opinion. If there is little or no relationship between opinion and vote, one can conclude that there is little policy voting.[13]

Using this method, we examined the relationship between votes for Richard Nixon and Hubert Humphrey in 1968, and Vietnam policy preferences, as measured on our seven-point scale and by a similar three-alternative item. It is apparent that Vietnam policy preferences did not have a great effect on voting for the major party candidates in 1968.[14] (See Table 1.)

"Hawks" tended to vote for Nixon in somewhat greater proportion than "doves" did. This tendency was statistically significant, and was larger than such relationships for many other issues in this and other elections. Yet,

Table 1 *Vietnam Policy Preferences and the Major Party Vote, 1968*

Vote	Opinion on Vietnam: Pull Out Entirely	Keep Soldiers, Try to End Fighting	Take Stronger Stand, Even if it Means Invading North Vietnam
Nixon	51% (88)	47% (174)	62% (180)
Humphrey	49 (86)	53 (194)	38 (109)
	100 (174)	100 (368)	100 (289)

Note: Tau b = .10 Correlation ratio (eta) = .018.
Pearson correlation (r) = .10 r^2 = .010.

Vote	Opinion on Vietnam: Immediate Withdrawal 1	2	3	4	5	6	Complete Military Victory 7
Nixon	42% (46)	51 (38)	51 (39)	52 (139)	59 (60)	64 (47)	59 (83)
Humphrey	58 (63)	49 (36)	49 (37)	48 (130)	41 (42)	36 (26)	41 (57)
	100 (109)	100 (74)	100 (76)	100 (269)	100 (102)	100 (73)	100 (140)

Note: Tau b = .10 Correlation ratio (eta) = .015.
Pearson correlation (r) = .11 r^2 = .012.

considering the enormous impact of the war on American society, a difference of 10 to 15 per cent in candidate choices by extreme hawks and extreme doves does not seem very impressive. Even less impressive is the fact that Vietnam opinions could account for only a minuscule fraction—between 1 and 2 per cent—of the variation in voting behavior.[15]

We are not able, then, to challenge as time-bound the established finding of little issue voting. Times may have changed between the apathetic 1950s and the militant 1960s and 1970s, but if so, this change was not reflected in Vietnam policy voting. Voters did not treat the 1968 election as a referendum on Vietnam policy.[16]

We are left, however, with the question of why such a potent issue had so little effect on voting. One possibility—that Americans simply didn't have opinions about the war—can be rejected at the outset. Only 7 per cent failed to express an opinion in response to the three-alternative item, and only 5 per cent failed to locate themselves on the seven-point Vietnam scale.

Further, we can reject the explanation that people failed to attach some minimal level of intensity to their opinions. When asked what they felt was the most important problem the government in Washington should try to take care of, nearly half the people spontaneously mentioned Vietnam—far more than mentioned any other issue or cluster of issues. Most of those who cited Vietnam said they were "extremely" concerned about the problem. This was not a case of "nonattitudes," or weakly held opinions.

Instead, the explanation seems to lie with public perceptions of where the candidates stood on Vietnam.

The average American perceived Nixon and Humphrey as standing very close together on the escalation/de-escalation dimension. With seven distinct points to choose from, in fact, the average perceptions of Nixon's and Humphrey's positions on the Vietnam scale were only one-third of one point apart.[17] (See Figure 1.) The perceived similarity between Nixon and Humphrey is underscored by the fact that George Wallace was seen, on the average, as fully two points more hawkish than Nixon.

Figure 1 *Average Perceptions of Candidates' Vietnam Positions, November 1968*

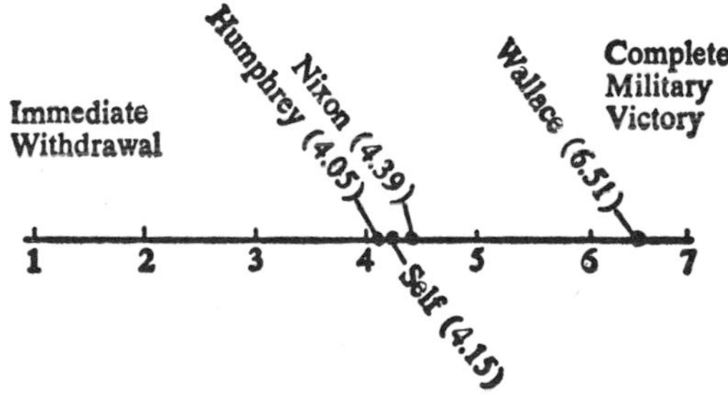

Entries are the median ratings of respondents' own opinions and their perceptions of candidates' positions on the seven-point Vietnam scale.

Average perceptions like those displayed in Figure 1 smooth over the considerable variations in perceptions by individuals. An examination of perceptions at the individual level buttresses this finding, however. Of those who assigned both Nixon and Humphrey to positions on the seven-point scale, well over half saw no difference at all, or only a difference of one point, between the two.[18] For these citizens, there was little to choose between Nixon and Humphrey in terms of Vietnam policy. As they saw it, either candidate would act about equally in accord with—or equally contrary to—their wishes on Vietnam; even if Vietnam policy was extremely important to them, they had to ignore the issue and vote on other grounds.[19]

In order to explain the widespread failure to perceive a difference between the candidates, it is not necessary—at least in this case—to postulate that people were unable to perceive clearly. The candidates' campaign speeches reveal that there was, in fact, rather little difference between Nixon's and Humphrey's stated positions on Vietnam policy.[20]

We examined the texts of some 156 speeches and statements by Nixon, and of 120 by Humphrey, including all of their major addresses.[21] Neither candidate devoted much attention to the specifics of Vietnam policy, but in each case it was possible to find a few fairly extensive statements on the subject. Humphrey's most detailed pronouncements were made in his nationally televised address from Salt Lake City on September 30.[22] Nixon's came at the Republican convention,[23] and on October 7, in a question and answer session for United Press International editors and publishers.[24] These statements, together with comments made on other occasions, formed reasonably coherent positions; both candidates remained consistent throughout the rest of the campaign.[25]

. . . Taken as a whole, the Vietnam positions of both candidates amounted to advocacy of war as usual, with a rather gradual de-escalation of American effort if and when certain conditions were met. Members of the public were entirely justified in seeing Nixon and Humphrey as standing close together near the center of the Vietnam policy scale, far from the extremes of immediate withdrawal or escalation for complete military victory. One major explanation for the absence of Vietnam policy voting, therefore, is not that the public failed to perceive reality, but that in reality there was little difference between the candidates.

Pushing the inquiry one step further, we may ask why the two major party candidates took such similar positions on Vietnam. Plainly such a finding is consistent with the predictions of many spatial models of electoral competition.[26] But a judgment about the general validity of those theories should not rest on evidence concerning a single issue in a single election; it requires a broader data base. If study of candidates' behavior shows that major party nominees tend to take highly similar positions on all issues, then we will be able to conclude that the two-party electoral system itself inhibits policy voting. If candidates tend to converge under certain conditions but not under others—if, for example the degree of issue salience, or opinion polarization, or party cleavage on the issue affects the extent to which candidates converge—then these same factors may account for variations in the extent of issue voting.[27]

CANDIDATE AMBIGUITY AND POLICY VOTING

The similarity between Humphrey's and Nixon's Vietnam positions can account for an absence of Vietnam voting among more than half of the voters—those who didn't see much difference between the two. But what of the large minority of voters who did perceive a difference of two or more points on the seven-point scale? Did they vote their Vietnam preferences? If so, why didn't they bring about a strong relationship between opinion and vote in the population as a whole?

Part of the answer is apparent when we look at the full distribution of perceptions. Those who saw a big difference between the candidates' positions were quite unable to agree which candidate was more of a hawk, and which more of a dove. To be sure, the majority considered Nixon more hawklike, but over one third thought that Humphrey was more of a hawk than Nixon. (See Table 2.)

Among those who thought Humphrey more hawklike than Nixon, the tendency of Table 1 was reversed: hawks voted strongly for Humphrey, and doves for Nixon. These people of course counterbalance some of the doves who voted for Humphrey and hawks who voted for Nixon. Their effect was to decrease the relationship found in Table 1. It does not follow, however, that Americans voted their Vietnam preferences to a greater extent than Table 1 indicates. On the contrary, most people's perceptions were too confused to play a part in voting decisions.[28]

Those who saw a big difference between Humphrey and Nixon—a difference in either direction—were generally perceiving each candidate as standing wherever they wanted him to stand. They projected their own opinions onto their favored candidate. Among Republicans, who mostly favored Nixon, extreme hawks thought that Nixon was an extreme hawk; extreme doves thought he was an extreme dove; and those in the middle thought that Nixon stood in the middle! The relationship between opinion and perception was quite strong. (See Table 3.) Similarly, among Democrats, extreme hawks tended to think Humphrey was an extreme hawk; extreme doves thought Humphrey an extreme dove; and those in the middle thought he stood in the middle.[29] (See Table 4.) Moreover, Republicans tended to perceive Humphrey as taking a position quite different from their own opinion.[30]

Many of those who saw a big difference between Nixon and Humphrey, in other words, were responding to their own wishes. Their perceptions were the result of intended vote, not the cause. These people were not engaged in policy voting.

This finding does not, on its face, cast great credit upon the American voter: it seems to support the view that voters are ignorant and incapable

Table 2 *Perceptions of Differences Between the Vietnam Positions of the Major Party Candidates, November 1968*

			Amount and Direction of Difference
Humphrey more hawkish 17% (152)	1.0% (8)	6	Humphrey much more hawkish
	0. (2)	5	
	1. (13)	4	
	6. (52)	3	
	9. (77)	2	
Difference slight or nonexistent 57% (523)	11. (104)	1	
	29. (260)	0	No difference
	18. (159)	−1	
Nixon more hawkish 26% (236)	14. (128)	−2	
	9. (79)	−3	
	2. (18)	−4	
	0. (4)	−5	
	1. (7)	−6	Nixon much more hawkish

Entries are percentages of those voters locating both candidates on the 7-point Vietnam scale who saw a given amount of difference between the two. The amount and direction of difference in perceptions is the arithmetic difference between the scale scores given the two candidates.

Table 3 *Projection of Nixon's Vietnam Position by Republicans Who Saw a Substantial Difference Between Nixon and Humphrey**

	Policy Preference on Vietnam					
Perception of Nixon's Stand	Immediate Withdrawal				Complete Military Victory	
Immediate Withdrawal	20% (4)	0 (0)	0 (0)	0 (0)	0 (0)	3 (4)
	55 (11)	42 (10)	19 (5)	4 (1)	14 (3)	25 (30)
	20 (4)	25 (6)	54 (14)	7 (2)	9 (2)	23 (28)
	0 (0)	33 (8)	23 (6)	89 (25)	55 (12)	43 (51)
Complete Military Victory	5 (1)	0 (0)	4 (1)	0 (0)	23 (5)	6 (7)
	17 (20)	20 (24)	22 (26)	23 (28)	18 (22)	100 (120)

Note: Tau b=.50 Correlation ratio (eta)=.376.
* This table is based on Republicans who voted and who perceived a difference of more than one point on the Vietnam scale between Nixon's position and Humphrey's. Scores of "2" and "3" and of "5" and "6" on the seven-point scale have been combined.

of rational political decisions. Again, however, it is not necessary to rely entirely upon an explanation based on voters' deficiencies. Further examination of the candidates' behavior shows that Nixon and Humphrey both made it quite easy to misperceive their Vietnam positions, and quite hard to vote on the basis of the slight differences which actually existed. Both candidates were very vague and ambiguous.

. . . Again we must push the inquiry one step further, and ask why Nixon and Humphrey were both so ambiguous. The case of Vietnam is consistent with theories which suggest that ambiguity may be the rule in candidates' rhetoric. Vagueness defuses issues. If a candidate is vague, he fails to gain new support which might come from those who would agree with his posi-

Table 4 *Projection of Humphrey's Vietnam Position by Democrats Who Saw a Substantial Difference Between Nixon and Humphrey**

Perception of Humphrey's Stand	Policy Preference on Vietnam: Immediate Withdrawal				Complete Military Victory	
Immediate Withdrawal	28% (11)	17 (4)	2 (1)	4 (1)	2 (1)	9 (18)
	23 (9)	46 (11)	20 (12)	36 (10)	12 (5)	24 (47)
	21 (8)	21 (5)	53 (32)	18 (5)	17 (7)	30 (57)
	18 (7)	13 (3)	18 (11)	36 (10)	19 (8)	20 (39)
Complete Military Victory	10 (4)	4 (1)	7 (4)	7 (2)	50 (21)	17 (32)
	20 (39)	12 (24)	31 (60)	15 (28)	22 (42)	100 (193)

Note: Tau b=.33 Correlation ratio (eta)=.211.
* This table is based on Democrats who voted and who perceived a difference of more than 1 point on the Vietnam scale between Nixon's position and Humphrey's. For clarity in presentation, scores of "2" and "3" and scores of "5" and "6" have been combined. This collapsing does not materially affect the form or strength of the relationship.

tion, if he took one; but he also avoids alienating the many who would not agree with his position, whatever it was. In many cases, or even all cases, ambiguity might profit a candidate more than any single specific position could.[31]

Still, evidence from the study of a single issue does not permit generalizations about the electoral process. The question of candidates' ambiguity, like that of convergent issue positions, might be answered in the context of a cross-section of issues. If it is the case that candidates are always ambiguous, that would constitute a way in which candidates' behavior and the electoral process itself regularly inhibited issue voting.[32]

THE ABILITY TO VOTE POLICY PREFERENCE

We have shown that the candidates' behavior was such that it could explain the general absence of Vietnam policy voting in 1968, without recourse to arguments about the ignorance or incapacity of voters. Yet we have not refuted the ordinary explanation for low issue voting, since we have not yet shown that, under more favorable circumstances, citizens can or do perceive objective differences between the candidates' policy stands, and vote on the basis of those differences.

In 1968, several candidates other than Nixon and Humphrey took somewhat clearer positions on Vietnam, and stood somewhat farther apart from each other on the issue. Examination of the public's perceptions of those candidates' issue positions, and of public evaluations of those candidates, permits us to put citizens' capacities for issue voting to a fairer test. The evidence shows that Americans *were able,* to a substantial extent to vote their policy preferences.

Eugene McCarthy, in challenging President Johnson for the Democratic nomination, campaigned heavily on the Vietnam issue. McCarthy talked much about the past—the morality of the war, misrepresentations by the administration, usurpations of Senatorial power, and the like; his proposals for future policy were surprisingly few, and not free from ambiguity.[33] Still, he said enough to make clear that he favored de-escalation of the war.

Early in the year, McCarthy urged that the bombing of North Vietnam be stopped, in order to bring about negotiations.[34] He also criticized the use of napalm and antipersonnel bombs on the Vietnamese.[35] After the March 31 bombing limitations, he ceased to emphasize the matter of bombing, and even said it had become part of general tactics; he would leave it to the military to decide if it was necessary to bomb in order to prevent supply and infiltration.[36] In August, however, he proposed that the bombing of North Vietnam, as well as naval and artillery bombardment, be stopped immediately.[37]

McCarthy, like all other candidates, disavowed any desire for "immediate" or "unilateral" withdrawal of U.S. troops from Vietnam.[38] He did, however, endorse a pull-back of American troops to enclaves, rather than trying to hold all of South Vietnam[39] he urged that "search and destroy" missions be cut back.[40] If the South Vietnamese were unwilling to negotiate a settlement with the N.L.F., he suggested that the U.S. should carry out some "phased withdrawals" of troops until they did so.[41] In August, he advocated a cease-fire and complete withdrawal after an interim coalition government was agreed to.[42]

Coalition government was the key element in McCarthy's position on Vietnam. Repeatedly he advocated a coalition government and said that if the present South Vietnamese government did not agree, they ought to be told to carry on the war by themselves.[43] He stressed that since we had failed to destroy the N.L.F. on the field of battle, we must be prepared to allow it to be a force in the future government of South Vietnam.[44] He warned that the U.S. must accept the possibility of an eventual reunification of North and South Vietnam.[45]

McCarthy's most definitive—and best publicized—proposals about Vietnam came in late August, with the controversy over the Democratic platform. He advocated a two-stage plan for settlement. First, the U.S. would stop bombing North Vietnam, reduce the level of conflict, and negotiate a new interim government for South Vietnam with substantial participation by the N.L.F. Second, the coalition government would prepare for elections with international supervision and guarantees. Before the election, the U.S. would withdraw its troops and a cease-fire would be maintained. The new, freely elected government would then deal with North Vietnam as it chose.[46]

Thus, McCarthy was a fairly clear—though not extreme—dove. He put forth a program which involved de-escalation of the fighting and a conciliatory settlement. It is not so easy, however, to find a hawkish candidate. After the fortunes of war appeared to turn against the U.S. with the Tet offensive of early 1968, no presidential candidate very forcefully advocated military escalation.

Ronald Reagan, for example, had hawkish inclinations. He urged in early 1968 that the U.S. resist any communist proposals for a coalition government.[47] He favored escalation: the U.S. should stop the entrance of supplies to Haiphong harbor, and should invade North Vietnam or pose the threat of doing so.[48] In May, he suggested that if the Communists stalled in the Paris Peace talks, the U.S. should serve notice and then "kick the devil out of them."[49] If it proved desirable to invade North Vietnam, South Vietnamese troops should be used and should be supported logistically by the U.S.[50] At hearings on the Republican platform, Reagan urged that the U.S. stand firm and fight to win.[51]

Reagan's comments about Vietnam were infrequent, however, and received very little national publicity.[52] Until the eve of the convention Reagan disavowed presidential ambitions and did not enter any primaries or conduct a national campaign. To most citizens, he was just another governor who was occasionally mentioned as a dark-horse candidate. It would not be a fair test of public abilities, therefore, to ask that citizens perceive his inconspicuously hawkish position, or that they judge him on the basis of Vietnam.

The nearest thing to a hawk among active presidential candidates in 1968 was George Wallace. Even Wallace was not an absolutely clear case, since Vietnam concerned him much less than civil rights and urban disorders, and he said relatively little about it.[53] When Wallace did discuss Vietnam, he emphasized peripheral issues: he wanted to "crack down" on people who asked for a communist victory in Vietnam, and on allies who traded with North Vietnam or otherwise failed to support the U.S. effort.[54] In his standard speech he declared that if he became President:

> I'm going to ask my Attorney General to seek an indictment against every professor in this country who calls for a communist victory (voice rising) and see if I can't put them under a good jail somewhere. (Loud cheers.) I'm sick and tired of seeing these few college students raise money, blood, and clothes for the Communists and fly the Vietcong flag; they ought to be dragged by the hair of their heads and stuck under a good jail also.[55]

Wallace's tone was certainly belligerent, but his specific policy proposals were only mildly hawkish. In his standard speech he expressed hope for success of the Paris talks; if they failed he would ask the Joint Chiefs of Staff for a plan to attain military victory, with conventional weapons only.[56] In September Wallace declared he was not "advocating invading anybody at the moment," nor did he favor using nuclear weapons.[57] He opposed a declaration of war and denied that any large number of troops would be needed to win.[58] He did not even totally oppose a bomb halt, but insisted only that North Vietnam be required to make concessions: stop attacks on South Vietnamese cities, de-escalate in the South, and stop infiltration of South Vietnam.[59] Wallace was not an extreme hawk unless perhaps by inference from his aggressive rhetoric about war protesters, and from his choice of General Curtis LeMay, the tough and outspoken former head of the Strategic Air Command, as his vice-presidential running mate.[60]

Despite the qualifications we have made about their tendencies to be moderate and ambiguous McCarthy and Wallace represented much more clear and sharply different Vietnam policy options than Nixon and Humphrey did. How did the public react to these stimuli? How clearly did they perceive what Wallace's and McCarthy's positions were, and to what extent did they take Vietnam into account in evaluating the candidates?

Public perceptions of Wallace's and McCarthy's Vietnam positions were fairly accurate. In August, people saw the two as standing at far different points on the seven-point scale: McCarthy near the dovish end, between points two and three, and Wallace near the hawkish end, between points five and six. (See Figure 2.) Such ratings would seem to be faithful reflections of the positions which the candidates had actually taken in their

Figure 2 *Average Perceptions of Candidates' Vietnam Positions, August 1968*

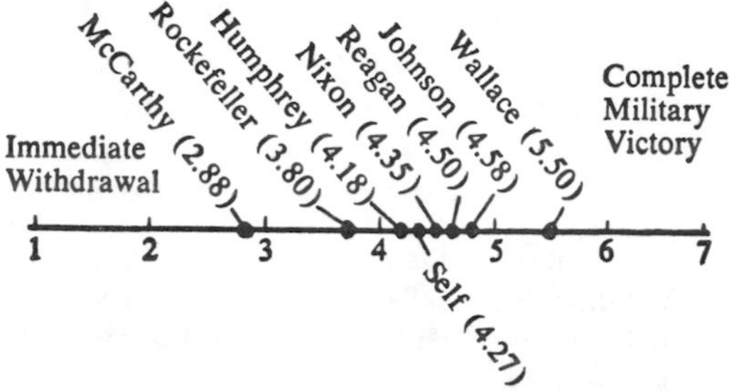

Entries are the median ratings of respondents' own opinions and their perceptions of candidates' positions on the seven-point Vietnam scale.

speeches. A panel of well-informed judges, who rated the candidates' positions at approximately the same time the public did, came to quite similar conclusions.[61]

We should not understate the extent to which perceptions of the two candidates were scattered over the scale. A few people, in fact, misperceived Wallace's or McCarthy's position so drastically that they placed one of them at the extreme point on the wrong end of the scale.[62] These individuals were distinctly in the minority, however. In mid-August, before McCarthy had made his clearest Vietnam statements, 59 per cent were able to place him at one of the three positions on the dovish side of the scale; only 21 percent saw him on the hawkish side of the midpoint. Similarly, 61 per cent saw Wallace as a hawk, and only 22 per cent thought him a dove. In November, after Wallace had received more media exposure and had picked LeMay as his running mate, perceptions were still more clear: 75 per cent saw him as a hawk, and only 16 per cent as a dove.[63]

We cannot ascertain how much difference individuals saw between Wallace's and McCarthy's positions in November, as we did for Nixon and Humphrey, because we lack November data on McCarthy.[64] Even in mid-August, however, before the public had received the full input of information about either candidate's position, four times as many people thought Wallace more hawkish than McCarthy as thought the opposite.[65]

We can conclude, then, that the public displayed a reasonable ability to perceive candidates' issue positions, when those positions were fairly clear.

Next we must inquire whether people took those perceptions and their own Vietnam preferences into account when they evaluated the candidates.

In order to answer this question, we conducted what might be called a "mock election" between McCarthy and Wallace. Using November data on respondents' evaluations of each candidate,[66] we calculated which of the two each respondent favored more. Such comparative evaluations can be taken as closely resembling votes.[67] We cross-tabulated respondents' hypothetical votes for McCarthy or Wallace by their Vietnam policy preferences, just as we had done with actual votes for Humphrey and Nixon in Table 1.

The results are unmistakable: in evaluating McCarthy and Wallace, Americans took their Vietnam preferences strongly into account. McCarthy was more popular than Wallace among holders of all shades of opinion, but his share of the "vote" varied greatly: doves supported McCarthy at a far higher rate than hawks did.[68] (See Table 5.). Vietnam opinions, in fact correlated with comparative evaluations at the high level of .29; they accounted for more than 8 per cent of the variance, many times as much as in the case of Humphrey and Nixon.

Considering the other factors which were relevant to choices between McCarthy and Wallace—their personal styles and abilities, for example, and their positions on civil rights—the impact of Vietnam preferences was very great indeed.

To be sure, the idea of a presidential election between McCarthy and Wallace is somewhat fanciful, since Wallace did not seek a major party nomination. Our point does not really require any speculation about the outcome of a hypothetical vote; it is made sufficiently well by the outcome of actual comparative evaluations.

The same point can be made, if it seems more convincing, with a pair of candidates who might conceivably have been nominated in 1968; McCarthy and Reagan. As we have indicated, Reagan's Vietnam position had low visibility, and perceptions of it were blurred. Yet in a mock election between McCarthy and Reagan, Vietnam preferences had a sizable impact —much greater than in the actual Humphrey-Nixon election.[69] We can conclude that, when the American people are presented with a clear choice, they are able and willing to bring their policy preferences to bear on it.

CONCLUSION

Despite the unusually high salience of the Vietnam war in 1968, the conventional wisdom about American electoral politics remained true; policy preferences had little effect on the major-party vote. The reason for this

Table 5 *Vietnam Policy Preferences and Comparative Evaluations of McCarthy and Wallace, November 1698*

Preferred Candidate	Opinion on Vietnam: Pull Out Entirely	Keep Soldiers, Try to End Fighting	Take Stronger Stand, Even if it Means Invading North Vietnam
Wallace	15% (23)	13 (42)	40 (125)
McCarthy	85% (135)	87 (292)	60 (187)
	100 (158)	100 (334)	100 (312)

Note: Tau b = .26 Correlation ratio (eta) = .095.
Pearson correlation (r) = .26 r^2 = .068.

Preferred Candidate	Opinion on Vietnam: Immediate Withdrawal 1	2	3	4	5	6	Complete Military Victory 7
Wallace	15% (16)	11 (8)	4 (3)	15 (39)	27 (26)	45 (38)	45 (68)
McCarthy	85 (90)	89 (68)	96 (66)	85 (222)	73 (71)	55 (46)	55 (82)
	100 (106)	100 (76)	100 (69)	100 (261)	100 (97)	100 (84)	100 (150)

Note: Tau b = .27 Correlation ratio (eta) = .117.
Pearson correlation (r) = .29 r^2 = .084.
The preferred candidate is the one given a higher rating on the 100 point "thermometer" of candidate evaluations. Those who rated the two candidates equally are omitted.
In order to ensure comparability with Table 1, only those who voted are included in the table.

slight impact of a great issue lay in voters' perceptions of where the candidates stood on Vietnam. Most people saw little or no difference between Nixon's position and Humphrey's. Further, those who saw a difference did not have firmly grounded perceptions, but tended to imagine the candidates as standing wherever they wanted them to stand.

The widespread failure to see any difference between the candidates, and general confusion over where they stood, did not result from inability on the part of the public to perceive correctly. Most people were able to perceive that George Wallace favored a hard line in Vietnam and that Eugene McCarthy wanted to de-escalate the war. Indeed, people's comparative evaluations of Wallace and McCarthy were very strongly influenced by their preferences about Vietnam. Americans seem to have had the capacity to vote their policy preferences.

In fact, those who saw little difference between Nixon and Humphrey on Vietnam were responding to reality. There was only a slight difference between them, as evidenced by their campaign speeches. Those who misperceived the candidates' positions were given ample opportunity by the candidates ambiguity. Nixon and Humphrey rarely discussed specific Vietnam policies, and avoided the issue of Vietnam altogether when they could.

The similarity of the Vietnam positions of the major party candidates was consistent with—though it would in itself confirm—theories of electoral competitions which predict that vote-maximizing candidates in a two-party system adopt similar issue positions. The ambiguity of Humphrey and Nixon was likewise consistent with theories which suggest that ambiguity is frequently advantageous.

In this case, at least, the behavior of candidates seems to have inhibited the occurrence of policy voting. If similar candidates and ambiguous rhetoric are the rule in American elections, they may well have depressed voting on other issues, and in other elections as well. Our picture of the ignorant voter may be, as V. O. Key, Jr. has suggested, largely a reflection of the choices which he is offered.[70] Even if policy voting is regularly inhibited by the electoral process, however, the implications of this finding for democratic theory are not straightforward. Those who rejoice in the opportunity to vote for a candidate they like, regardless of the outcome of the election, may well regret excessive similarity between major party candidates. Those who seek a democratic outcome from elections, however, may reply that similarity of candidates is not at all to be disdained, so long as both of them stand for the policies most preferred by the public. The proponents of convergence could point out that, as is indicated in our Figure 1, the American public (for better or worse) got about the Vietnam positions it wanted from both candidates in 1968. Whichever one had been elected would, if he had kept his campaign promises, have pursued a Vietnam policy quite close to the midpoint of public opinion.[71]

If the implications of candidate similarity are controversial, the consequences of ambiguity are rather obvious. Vague candidates cannot contribute much to the education of the public, and cannot facilitate the casting of policy-oriented votes when there *is* a real difference between candidates. Murkiness in political rhetoric is almost universally deplored. But if candidates have a real incentive to be vague, and ambiguity is rooted in the electoral process itself, it may be quite resistant to reform.

ENDNOTES

1. The literature bearing on these points is extensive. It includes Paul F. Lazarsfeld, Bernard Berelson, and Hazel Gaudet, *The People's Choice: How the Voter Makes Up His Mind in a Presidential Campaign* (New York: Columbia University Press, 1944), which emphasizes social factors in voting; Bernard Berelson, Paul F. Lazarsfeld, and William N. McPhee, *Voting: A Study of Opinion Formulation in a Presidential Campaign* (Chicago: University of Chicago Press, 1954), which explores social influences on the vote, and misperceptions of candidates' issue positions; Angus Campbell, Philip E. Converse, Warren E. Miller, and Donald E. Stokes, *The American Voter* (New York: Wiley, 1960), which establishes the primacy of party identification, and shows the weakness of opinion and perceptions about issues; Philip E. Converse, "The Nature of Belief Systems in Mass Publics," in *Ideology and Discontent* ed. David E. Apter (New York: Free Press, 1964), pp. 206–261, which demonstrates that opinions on policy lacked any simple ideological structure, and were unstable over a four-year period; and Donald E. Stokes, "Some Dynamic Elements of Contests for the Presidency," *American Political Science Review*, 60 (March 1966), 19–28, which shows that issues have been less important than candidate images as "short term forces" affecting electoral outcomes.

The late V. O. Key manfully tried to find evidence of an issue-oriented "responsible electorate" among those who switched their votes from one election to the next, but his effort was beset by methodological difficulties. Respondents' recollections of their votes four years previously, which Key used to identify switchers, are not very reliable; the issues upon which he found agreement between opinions and direction of switch were broadly phrased judgments about governmental performance, which are particularly subject to rationalization by voters who switch for other reasons. V. O. Key, Jr., *The Responsible Electorate* (Cambridge, Mass.: Harvard University Press, 1966).

2. V. O. Keys, Jr., *Public Opinion and American Democracy* (New York: Knopf, 1961), pp. 458–480. Gerald H. Kramer, "Short-Term Fluctuations in U.S. Voting Behavior, 1896–1964," *American Political Science Review*, 65 (March 1971), 131–143, provides some evidence of electoral punishment in response to bad economic conditions.

3. The existence of "issue publics" is demonstrated in Converse, "Belief Systems," pp. 245–246. David E. RePass, "Issue Salience and Party Choice," *American Political Science Review*, 65 (June 1971), 389–400, finds a strong correspondence between voting choices and the party whose stand is preferred on salient issues; as he points out, however (p. 395), some of this correspondence may result from rationalization.

4. Electoral competition models which predict party convergence are set forth in Harold Hotelling, "Stability in Competition," *Economic Journal*, 39 (March 1929), 41–57; Anthony Downs, *An Economic Theory of Democracy* (New York: Harper, 1957), pp. 114–141; and Otto A. Davis, Melvin J. Hinich, and Peter C. Ordeshook, "An Expository Development of a Mathematical Model of the Electoral Process," *American Political Science Review*, 64 (June 1970), 426–448.

5. Stanley Kelley, *Political Campaigning* (Washington, D.C.: Brookings, 1960) finds considerable evidence of candidate ambiguity. Theoretical arguments predicting ambiguity are given in Downs, pp. 135–137; and in Kenneth A. Shepsle, "The Strategy of Ambiguity: Uncertainty and Electoral Competition," *American Political Science Review*, 66 (June, 1972), pp. 555–569.

6. In the IEP project as a whole, we are studying a variety of questions about the issue-related behavior of citizens and candidates, including the other challenges mentioned above.

7. *Gallup Opinion Index*, April 1968, p. 3, 14.

8. The surveys were conducted in February, June, August, and November 1968 by the Opinion Research Corporation (Princeton, New Jersey) for the IEP project. In addition to the present authors, the project includes Jerome Laulicht and Sidney Verba.

9. In 1967, specific Vietnam items formed a satisfactory Guttman scale, with CR = .88 and CS = .66. Richard A. Brody and Sidney Verba, "Hawk and Dove: The Search for an Explanation of Vietnam Policy Preferences," *Acta Politica*, forthcoming. In an earlier paper, based on data from 1966, it was reported that opinions fell into *two* imperfectly related scales, one expressing attitudes toward escalation, and the other attitudes toward de-escalation. Sidney Verba, Richard A. Brody, Edwin B. Parker, Norman H. Nie, Nelson W. Polsby, Paul Ekman, and Gordon S. Black, "Public Opinion and the War in Vietnam," *American Political Science Review*, 61 (June 1967), 317–333, material cited is on pp. 320–321. Reinterpretation of those data suggests that a single escalation/de-escalation dimension might have existed even as early as 1966.

10. In 1968 we did not have enough policy items to replicate the Guttman scaling analyses of 1966 and 1967. We found, however, that opinions on the Vietnam rating scale correlated quite highly with opinions concerning bombing, troop levels, and three general policy alternatives.

11. In the SRC survey, evaluations were measured on a 100-point "thermometer" which yielded almost precisely the same levels of evaluation and the same relationship with other variables as the five-point ORC/IEP favorability scale. Benjamin I. Page, "Party Loyalty and the Popularity of Presidential Candidates" (unpublished ditto, Feb., 1972). For a discussion of the candidate thermometer, and some findings based on it, see Herbert F. Weisberg and Jerold G. Rusk, "Dimensions of Candidate Evaluation," *American Political Science Review*, 64 (December 1970), 1167–1185.

12. The approach to policy voting which is sketched here would blend two theoretical and two methodological traditions. A formal model of issue voting drawn from the electoral competition literature (see Davis et al.) would be supplemented by psychologists' understanding of the processes of projection and persuasion. Simultaneous equation techniques from econometrics would be combined with Donald Stokes's method of computing net effects from means and estimated slopes. (See Stokes, "Some Dynamic Elements of Contests for the Presidency," pp. 27–28.) See Richard A. Brody and Benjamin I. Page, "Comment: The

Assessment of Policy Voting," *American Political Science Review*, 66 (June, 1972), pp. 450–459.

Our early efforts to perform such an analysis with respect to the Vietnam issue are reported in Brody et al., "Vietnam, the Urban Crisis and the 1968 Presidential Election" and in Brody and Page, "Issues in an Election." It will not be possible to reach a precise conclusion about the impact of the issue without completing estimation of a nonlinear three-equation model. As is argued below, however, such a degree of precision is not needed for our present purpose.

Empirical work with perceived issue differences (or "distances," or "proximities"), in addition to our own, includes Michael J. Shapiro, "Rational Political Man: A Synthesis of Economic and Social-Psychological Perspectives," *American Political Science Review*, 63 (December 1969), 1106–1119; and papers by David M. Kovenock and James W. Prothro of the Comparative State Elections project.

13. The traditional technique has one great advantage over an analysis which uses perceived issue differences: the opinion-vote relationship is not inflated by projection, in which respondents tend to imagine that the positions of favored candidates are the same as their own opinions. It has two major defects, however: (1) it may *understate* the importance of policy voting as a psychological process among individuals. Two people with the same policy preferences can receive different information (even different but *correct* information) about the stands of candidates; even if they both vote in accord with their opinions and their information about candidates' positions, they may vote for different candidates and thereby reduce the apparent relationship between opinion and vote. As we argue above, precise assessment of policy voting requires explicit consideration of perceptions. (2) It may *overstate* the amount of policy voting: some people whose opinions and votes correspond may have brought opinions into line with intended vote, rather than vice versa.

In most cases the second defect is probably the more serious. Since it inflates the relationship found in the table, however, it cannot impeach a finding of little or no relationship. The first defect, which can lead to an underestimate of policy voting, requires that even a claim of no relationship be qualified, or that it be supported by additional evidence.

14. This claim requires evidence that the weak relationship in the table does not conceal policy voting by those with differing preceptions. In previous work, employing the concept of issue distance, we also found the effects of Vietnam policy preferences to be relatively small. Brody et al., "Vietnam, the Urban Crisis, and the 1968 Presidential Election;" Brody and Page, "Issues in an Election." Since those findings inflated the apparent impact of Vietnam, by accepting all opinions and perceptions as causally prior to the vote, they support the present finding *a fortiori*. Further evidence is presented in the next section.

15. According to the coefficients of determination (r^2), in a linear regression, variations in opinion could account for only 1.0 per cent or 1.2 per cent of the variance in voting. According to the correlation ratio (eta), which better reflects the nonlinear relationship, variations in preference could account for 1.5 per cent of the 1.8 per cent of the variance in the vote.

16. This conclusion must be distinguished sharply from the assertion that Vietnam opinions had little effect upon the 1968 election. We are concerned here only with preferences about future policy, not with evaluations of past performance in Vietnam. Further, we are concerned only with the effects of these attitudes on voting choices between Humphrey and Nixon: we do not consider their effects on voting for Wallace, abstentions from voting, or decisions whether or not to give time and money to the campaign, to say nothing of effects on the launching and subsequent fate of the prenomination candidacies of Eugene McCarthy and Robert Kennedy, or the withdrawal from candidacy of President Johnson. From this broader perspective the impact of Vietnam opinions seems to have been profound.

17. This difference is statistically significant, according to a one tailed *t*-test of the means, but substantively it is quite small.

18. Fifty-seven per cent saw little or no difference. Thirty per cent saw no difference at all: they placed Nixon and Humphrey at exactly the same point on the scale. Similarly, in response to another SRC item, 33 per cent replied that they saw no difference between the two *parties* with respect to three general Vietnam policy alternatives.

19. These people did not in fact vote their Vietnam preferences. Among them, the relationship between opinion and vote was irregular.

20. We do not assume that the candidates' speeches reflected their true beliefs or intentions. They did, however, represent the best information about those intentions which was available to the public.

21. Humphrey's speeches were kindly provided by Raymond Wolfinger, John Stewart, and the Democratic National Committee; Nixon's were provided by Representative Charles Gubser and the Republican National Committee. The texts of some of Nixon's speeches are reprinted in *Nixon Speaks Out* (New York: Nixon-Agnew Campaign Committee, 1968).

We have also used the *New York Times* (hereafter *NYT*) to find comments which candidates made in interviews, question and answer sessions, and the like.

22. A transcript of this speech is printed in *NYT*, October 1, 1968, p. 33. Our citations refer to the press release.

23. "Vietnam," Statement to the Committee on Resolutions, August 1, 1968.

24. Portions of Nixon's answers are given in *Nixon on the Issues* (New York: Nixon-Agnew Campaign Committee, 1968), pp. 6–12.

25. Humphrey was consistent after September 30; prior to his Salt Lake City speech he had vacillated, with a tendency to be more hawkish.

26. Hotelling, "Stability in Competition"; Downs, *An Economic Theory of Democracy*; Davis, "Mathematical Model of the Electoral Process."

27. Arthur Smithies, "Optimum Location in Spatial Competition," *Journal of Political Economy*, 49 (June 1941), 423–439, hypothesizes, on the basis of certain assumptions about turnout, that polarization of opinions could prevent convergence. Otto A. Davis and Melvin Hinich, "A Mathematical Model of Policy Formation in a Democratic Society," in *Mathematical Applications in Political*

Science, ed. Joseph L. Bernd (Dallas: S.M.U. Press, 1966), pp. 175–208, suggests that the need to win nomination could lead to divergent policies on party-related issues.

We are presently completing a study of the positions which presidential candidates have taken on a number of policy issues. Our preliminary findings indicate that it is possible to specify conditions under which Republican and Democratic nominees do and do not tend to take similar positions.

28. We are defining policy voting as a process in which an individual's policy preference, together with his perception of the candidates' stands on the issue, influences his vote. Under this definition it is impossible for citizens with varying perceptions—even misperceptions—to engage in policy voting. (See footnote 13, above). The crucial question is whether opinions and perceptions are causally prior to the vote.

We present evidence, below, that although those who saw a big difference between Nixon and Humphrey tended to have congruent opinions, perceptions, and votes, much of the congruence resulted from projection rather than policy voting: vote intentions (as determined by party identification) were causally prior to perceptions.

29. The greater strength of the relationship for Nixon may in part reflect his greater ambiguity on Vietnam, which made projection easier; but it also results from the fact that Republicans tended to like Nixon more than Democrats liked Humphrey. Republicans therefore felt a greater need to make their perceptions of Nixon's position congruent with their own opinions.

30. Negative projection of the opposing candidate's position was more marked among Republicans than Democrats. Only 5 per cent of these Republicans saw Humphrey standing at exactly the same point as themselves, compared to the 14 per cent which would have been expected on the basis of the marginals. The overall negative relationship was significant at better than $p = .001$, by a chi-square test. The corresponding relationship for Democrats' perceptions of Nixon was not significant at the $p = .10$ level, however. The reason for this difference appears to be that Republicans felt negative toward Humphrey, but Democrats were merely neutral about Nixon and had less reason to project his position away.

All these tables are based only on voters who saw a large difference between the candidates. Projection was also widespread among other groups, such as non-voters, but it was much less common among voters who saw little difference between Nixon and Humphrey. We are grateful to Sue Bessmer for assistance in the analysis of perceptions.

31. Similar reasoning is given in Downs, *An Economic Theory of Democracy,* pp. 135–137. Candidate ambiguity is predicted under special circumstances in Shepsle, "The Strategy of Ambiguity."

32. Stanley Kelley, *Political Campaigning,* pp. 50–84, found that Eisenhower and Stevenson were vague concerning practically all issues in 1956. The televised debates of 1960 compelled Nixon and Kennedy to be somewhat more specific. Stanley Kelley, Jr., "The Presidential Campaign," in Paul T. David, ed., *The*

Presidential Election and Transition 1960–61 (Washington, D.C.: Brookings, 1961), p. 87.

We have found that Humphrey and Nixon took ambiguous positions on most policies in 1968. Nixon, especially, was quite ingenious at appearing to say much while actually saying little.

33. A complete set of McCarthy's speeches was generously made available to us by Robert Axelrod and John D. Shilling. Sally Soth has helped greatly in analyzing these speeches.

34. Television interview on "Issues and Answers," January 7, 1968, p. 14. This and subsequent page numbers refer—unless otherwise noted—to official press releases and transcripts.

35. Remarks, Stanford University, January 15, 1968, p. 4.

36. Televised news conference, June 2, 1968, p. 6.

37. Vietnam platform proposal, *NYT*, August 18, 1968, p. 66.

38. Press conference, Indiana University, April 18, 1968, p. 4; televised interview on "Meet the Press," July 7, 1968, p. 2.

39. Press conference, Washington, D.C., June 12, 1968, p. 7.

40. Remarks, San Francisco, May 29, 1968, p. 5.

41. Response to question, Stanford University, January 15, 1968, pp. 3–4.

42. Vietnam platform proposal, p. 66.

43. Response to question, Wisconsin State University at Eau Claire, February 21, 1968, p. 12; press conference, Indiana University, April 18, 1968, p. 3.

44. Remarks, San Francisco, May 29, 1968, p. 5.

45. Response to question, University of Oregon, May 24, 1968.

46. Vietnam platform proposal, p. 66.

47. *NYT*, January 24, 1968, p. 55.

48. *NYT*, March 4, 1968, p. 16.

49. *NYT*, May 24, 1968, p. 20.

50. *NYT*, May 27, 1968, p. 30.

51. *NYT*, August 1, 1968, p. 20.

52. In the seven months from January to the Republican convention, for example, the *New York Times* reported Reagan's comments on Vietnam only nine times. All of these reports were very brief and none were prominently featured.

53. Wallace, even more than other candidates, relied upon a single basic speech, which he modified only slightly as the campaign progressed. We have transcribed a tape recording distributed by the American Independent Party of a typical speech which Wallace delivered in Charlotte, North Carolina, in mid-June, 1968. We have relied upon the *New York Times* for reports of deviations from the basic speech.

54. *NYT*, July 5, 1968, p. 14; July 27, 1968, p. 10; July 30, 1968, p. 27.

55. Remarks, Charlotte, North Carolina, June 1968.

56. Remarks, Charlotte, N.C.

57. *NYT*, September 2, 1968, p. 17.

58. *NYT*, September 26, 1968, p. 53.

59. *NYT*, October 21, 1968, p. 38.

60. The choice of LeMay was very likely a mistake, which undercut Wallace's careful effort to be acceptable to those who opposed the war. LeMay disclaimed any intention of using nuclear weapons in Vietnam, *NYT*, October 4, 1968, pp. 50 ff.; but his hawkish image persisted.

61. The judges were 22 journalists, international relations specialists, and economists, from a variety of geographical areas. They gave McCarthy a median rating of approximately 2.0, and Wallace a rating of 6.6. They located Humphrey and Nixon much closer together and nearer the middle of the scale, at 4.0 and 5.0, respectively.

62. In August, 4 per cent rated McCarthy as an extreme hawk, and 6 per cent rated Wallace as an extreme dove. The percentages are based on those respondents, some 70 per cent of the sample, who made a rating.

63. Slightly more than half the respondents placed him at the most extremely hawkish position on the scale.

64. In both the SRC and ORC/IEP November surveys, respondents were asked to rate the positions only of the active candidates and President Johnson.

65. The percentages, of those who had rated both candidates, were 47 per cent and 11 per cent, respectively. Forty-two per cent saw no differences between the two, however, and in addition a large number of respondents failed to assign one or both candidates to any position on the scale.

As we have seen, public perceptions of Wallace's position were clearer in November. Indirect evidence suggests that perception of McCarthy improved as well, after the Democratic convention.

66. These evaluations were measured on the 100-point SRC thermometer. See Weisberg and Rusk, "Dimensions of Candidate Evaluation."

67. Actual votes for Humphrey and Nixon correspond almost perfectly with comparative evaluations of the candidates. Brody et al., "Vietnam, the Urban Crisis and the 1968 Presidential Election," pp. 7–8.

68. The slight nonlinearity in Table 5 suggests that a few respondents who placed themselves at the "immediate withdrawal" end of the scale may actually have favored a policy of "win or get out," and supported Wallace.

69. Vietnam preferences can account for approximately 4 per cent of the variance. The resemblance between the McCarthy-Reagan mock election and a real election is still not perfect, of course. If McCarthy and Reagan had been nominated, party identification might have affected evaluations of them more strongly, and might have blunted the impact of Vietnam opinion somewhat. On the other hand, nomination would have increased public exposure to the candidates' positions on Vietnam, and might on balance have increased the effect of Veitnam preferences.

70. V. O. Key, Jr., *The Responsible Electorate*, pp. 2, 7.

71. When we consider a single issue, upon which preferences are jointly single-peaked, a policy at the median of public opinion is the only policy which would not be defeated by any other in a series of two-way votes. The median may therefore be said to represent what "the public wants."

As Figure 1 shows, the public generally perceived both Nixon and Humphrey as standing very close to the median of public opinion on the seven-point Vietnam scale. Commercial poll data and the candidates' speeches confirm that both candidates stood close to the median of public opinion on specific aspects of Vietnam policy.

Reprinted from pp. 174–181 in *Participation in America: Political Democracy and Social Equality,* by Sidney Verba and Norman H. Nie.
Copyright © 1972 by Sidney Verba and Norman H. Nie. By permission of Harper & Row, Publishers, Inc.

The Organizational Context of Political Participation

SIDNEY VERBA
and
NORMAN NIE

[Political] participation is fully comprehensible only if one takes into account the individual's institutional context. . . . In this [selection] we consider the role of organizations . . . in relation to political participation. . . .

Voluntary associations have figured in many theoretical speculations about the social bases of democracy and, in particular, about some special features of American democracy. A rich associational life has been considered the hallmark of American democracy. Such associations provide an intermediary level of organization between the individual and the government. And this, it is claimed (sometimes supported by data, other times not), prevents the development of mass political movements in this society, mediates conflict, and increases citizen efficacy, participation, and influence. Our interest is in the latter function of organizations and their role in relation to the political participation of American citizens.

Do organizations increase the potency of the citizenry *vis-à-vis* the government? Organizations could play such a role in a number of ways. Voluntary associations and other organizations can themselves, through the activities of their officers and other paid officials, participate in the political process. In this way the organization participates *for* its members. Or the citizen who is a member of an organization may use that affiliation as a channel to gain access to the government: either the organization itself (through its officers or representatives) may transmit the grievances of the individual to the government, or the individual may use connections made within the organization to further his acts of participation. Here the member participates *through* the organization. Last, organizations may have an impact on political life in a society through the influence they have on the participatory activities of their members. Citizens may participate directly *because of* their affiliation with an organization. In studies in a variety of countries, organizational affiliation has been shown to be one of the most powerful predictors of citizen activity, a predictor of political activity that remains strong over and above the social class of the individual. A rich political participant life, these data suggest, may rest on a rich associational life. . . .

To begin with, we will sketch out the facts of organization participation in the United States, asking what kinds of individuals participate in what ways in what kinds of organizations. This . . . sketch will present some descriptive information about participation in organizations and its distribution in the population. In addition, it introduces the various aspects of organizational membership in which we are interested. These characteristics include: (1) the number of organizations to which an individual belongs; (2) the type of organization to which he belongs; (3) the degree to which he is active in them; (4) the degree to which he is exposed to politically relevant stimuli, in particular, to discussions about politics within the organizations; and (5) the degree to which the organizations themselves are actively involved in community and civic affairs.

These characteristics are the raw materials of an analysis of the process of political mobilization that takes place within organizations. . . .

ORGANIZATIONAL MEMBERSHIP: AN OVERVIEW

The data on the amount and character of organization membership in the United States are reported in Table 1.* The basic data are quite consistent

*This selection is an excerpt from a larger study of participation, based on a random sample of the nation's adult population.—ED.

Table 1 *Organizational Involvement of American Population*

Percentage of sample reporting:	
That they belong to an organization	62
That they belong to more than one organization	39
That they are active in an organization	40
That they belong to an organization in which political discussion takes place	31
That they belong to an organization active in community affairs	44

with a number of other studies of organizational affiliations in the United States. The overall amount of organizational membership found by one study or another will vary somewhat with the question asked and with whether one includes membership in unions (as we do) as part of one's overall indicator of organizational membership. But most studies have found a figure for membership usually close to the figure of 62 percent that we report in Table 1.

Is this figure high or low? The question is unanswerable, unless one first asks "compared to what?" Those who have heard the United States described as a nation of joiners may be somewhat disappointed to find that roughly four out of ten Americans belong to no organization. But such characterizations are usually based on broad tendencies and ought never to be taken to imply that an entire nation—something close to 100 percent of all Americans—are involved in organizations. In fact, the figure of 62 percent is roughly equivalent to that found in other industrialized societies.[2]

As the data in Table 1 also indicate, four out of ten Americans (or two out of three organizational members) are members of more than one organization. A more important figure, perhaps, is the proportion [of those] who are active members in some organization. Most theories that relate organizational affiliation to participation in democratic politics suggest that the private voluntary association offers more opportunities for individual activity than does the larger political system. Our data indicate that some 40 percent of our sample, or about half the organizational members, are in some way active within the organizations to which they belong. In this particular respect, the data for the United States do differ from those for other industrial societies. Though the United States appears quite similar to such societies as Britain, Germany, and Japan in terms of the overall membership rate, American organizational members seem to be much more likely to be active within their organizations when they are members.[3]

In our study we included two other characteristics of organizational membership that may help us understand the way in which affiliation operates to increase the participation potential of the average citizen. We asked whether individuals were exposed to political discussion at the meetings of the organizations to which they belonged. These might be formal discussions initiated by the organizational leadership or informal political conversations. In either case, the organization would be acting as a channel of political communication or as a potential means of arousing political interest in the citizen. As the data on Table 1 indicate, 31 percent of our sample (about one out of two of all organizational members) belong to organizations within which political discussions take place. Last, we were interested in whether the organizations to which individuals belong were themselves active in the kind of community-oriented activities about which we asked our individual respondents. Forty-four percent of our sample (a little more than two out of three organizational members) indicate that they belong to organizations that take some active role in dealing with general community problems.

Table 2 contains the data on the specific kinds of organizations to which our respondents belong. The range of organizations to which individuals belong is wide. The most frequently reported memberships are in such groups as trade unions, school-service clubs, fraternal groups, and sports clubs. In addition, respondents report membership in a wide range of other kinds of associations, some connected with their work, such as professional associations; some involved in political or communal activities, such as service groups and political clubs; and some purely recreational, such as hobby clubs or art and literary groups.

The data in the next two columns give us a better understanding of the nature of some of these organizations, at least in terms of the two characteristics of involvement in community affairs and political discussions that we have been stressing. The data in the second column indicate the proportion of members of each kind of organization who report that it is involved in community affairs and the data in the third column present the proportion who report that political discussions take place in their organizations. Where 70 percent or more report either community involvement or political discussion we have enclosed that figure in a solid line; where between 50 and 70 percent report such involvement the figure is enclosed in a dashed line; and where less than 50 percent report such involvement the figure is unshaded. Thus a quick glance at the columns of figures indicates that we have several kinds of organizations. Political clubs are frequently involved in dealing with general community problems, and as one would expect, they are almost universally the site of political discussions. A number of other organizations are highly involved in communal affairs, though political discussions are

Table 2 *The Types of Organizations to Which Individuals Belong*

Type of organization	Percentage of the *population* who report membership	Percentage of *members* who report the organizations involved in community affairs	Percentage of *members* who report that political discussion take place in the organization
Political groups such as Democratic or Republican clubs, and political action groups such as voter's leagues	8	85	97
School service groups such as PTA or school alumni groups	17	82	54
Service clubs, such as Lions, Rotary, Zonta, Jr. Chamber of Commerce	6	81	64
Youth groups such as Boy Scouts, Girl Scouts	7	77	36
Veterans' groups such as American Legion	7	77	56
Farm organizations such as Farmer's Union, Farm Bureau, Grange	4	74	61
Nationality groups such as Sons of Norway, Hibernian Society	2	73	57
Church-related groups such as Bible Study Group or Holy Name Society	6	73	40
Fraternal groups such as Elks, Eagles, Masons, and their women's auxiliaries	15	69	33
Professional or academic societies such as American Dental Association, Phi Beta Kappa	7	60	57
Trade unions	17	59	44

Table 2 *(Continued)*

Type of organization	Percentage of the *population* who report membership	Percentage of *members* who report the organizations involved in community affairs	Percentage of *members* who report that political discussion take place in the organization
School fraternities and sororities such as Sigma Chi, Delta Gamma	3	[53]	37
Literary, art, discussion, or study clubs such as book-review clubs, theater groups	4	40	[56]
Hobby or garden clubs such as stamp or coin clubs, flower clubs, pet clubs	5	40	35
Sports clubs, bowling leagues, etc.	12	28	20

somewhat less frequent than in the political clubs. This is the case with school-service organizations, service clubs, veterans' groups, farm associations, and nationality associations.

In several types of organizations there appears to be a heavy stress on communal activities with a relatively low frequency of reporting of political conversation. This includes youth groups, religious associations, and fraternal groups. The disparity between the amount of communal involvement and infrequency of political discussions suggest—as does the character of these groups more generally—that these may be organizations within which political discussions are generally avoided. Among professional associations, trade unions, and school fraternities or sororities, one finds a moderate amount of involvement in community problems coupled with, in the case of professional associations, a moderate frequency of political discussion and, in the case of unions and fraternities, relatively infrequent political discussions. Because political discussions represent something that may go on informally at organization meetings, the high rate of these discussions in professional associations may simply reflect the higher social-class composition of such groups.

Three kinds of groups seem decidedly less involved in political or communal affairs. These are art and literary groups, hobby clubs, and sports clubs. There is a moderate amount of political discussion in the first kind of group, which is a likely reflection of the social-class compositions of such groups.

One further point should be made about the organizations listed on Table 2. When one looks at the groups near the bottom of the table, one finds quite a bit less involvement in general community problems and quite a bit less political discussion compared with some of the groups near the top. However, when one considers the manifest character of these organizations, such as the three recreational organizations at the bottom of the list, the amount of communal and political discussion activity may seem much larger. Even among sports clubs, which are the least likely to become involved in community problems and the least likely settings for political discussion, 28 percent of the members report that their club has been involved in some general communal activity, and 20 percent report political discussions. Much of the speculation about the role played by voluntary associations in relation to democratic participation has been based on the assumption that these organizations have an impact on the political attitudes and activities of their members even when the explicit purpose of the organization is totally nonpolitical. The data suggest that such may indeed be the case. . . .

Who belongs to organizations?

. . . The rates of organizational membership and of organizational activity for a few select groups in the population are presented in Table 3. They can be briefly described. Men are somewhat more likely to be organizational members than women, though the difference is not very great. The higher level of education one has, the more likely one is to be a member of an organization, and here the difference is somewhat more substantial. About one in two of those who have not graduated from high school belong to some organization while over three out of four of those with some college education are organizational members. Whites are far more likely to be organizational members than blacks, and again the difference is fairly great. With age one finds a curved pattern. Organizational affiliation seems greatest among those in the middle group, between 30 and 49. The younger group is the least active in organizations and those over 50 also fall off.

The same patterns apply to active membership in organizations. If one's education is higher, if one is white rather than black, and middle-aged rather than old or young, one is more likely to be an active member in organizations. The one variation on this theme is the difference between men and women. Women are as likely to be active in organizations as are men. When this is coupled with a somewhat lower rate of organizational membership among women, it becomes clear that the average female member is

Table 3 *Some Demographic Differences in Organizational Membership and Activity*

	Percentage reporting	
	Belonging to at least one organization	Active in at least one organization
Total sample	62	40
Men	65	41
Women	57	39
Not high-school graduate	49	27
High-school graduate	67	43
Some college	78	59
White	66	41
Black	52	30
Age 17-29	52	31
Age 30-49	70	47
Age 50 and above	57	37

more likely to be an active member of that organization than is the average malc member. A great deal of this difference derives from the higher rate of male membership in trade unions, organizations in which the average level of activity tends to be quite low.

ENDNOTES

1. Nie, Powell, and Prewitt, "Social Structure and Political Participation;" Almond and Verba, *The Civic Culture*, Chapter 12.
2. Almond and Verba, *The Civic Culture*, Chapter 12.
3. Ibid.

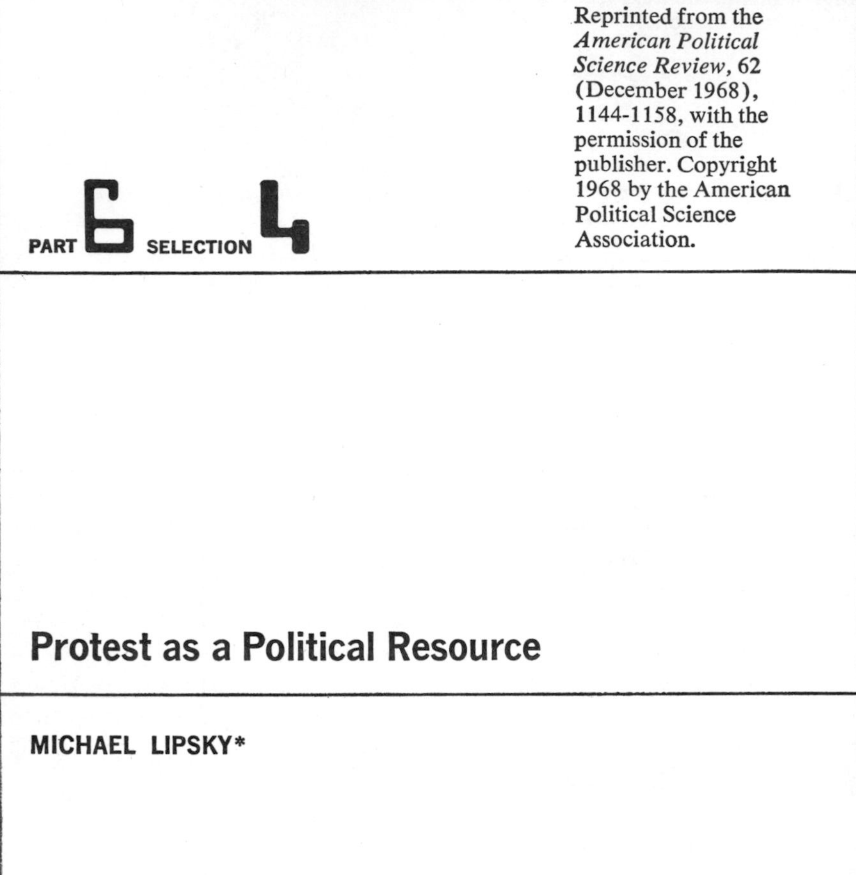

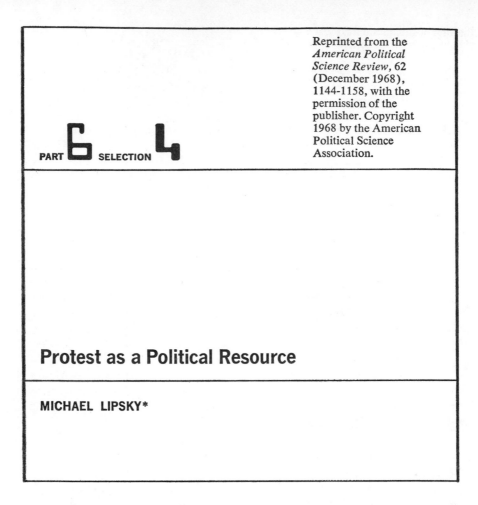

Reprinted from the *American Political Science Review,* 62 (December 1968), 1144-1158, with the permission of the publisher. Copyright 1968 by the American Political Science Association.

PART 6 SELECTION 4

Protest as a Political Resource

MICHAEL LIPSKY*

The frequent resort to protest activity by relatively powerless groups in recent American politics suggests that protest represents an important aspect of minority group and low income group politics.[1] At the same time that Negro civil rights strategists have recognized the problem of using protest as a meaningful political instrument,[2] groups associated with the "war on poverty" have increasingly received publicity for protest activity. Saul Alinsky's Industrial Areas Foundation, for example, continues to

*This article is an attempt to develop and explore the implications of a conceptual scheme for analyzing protest activity. It is based upon my studies of protest organizations in New York City, Washington, D.C., Chicago, San Francisco, and Mississippi, as well as extensive examination of written accounts of protest among low-income and Negro civil rights groups.

receive invitations to help organize low income communities because of its ability to mobilize poor people around the tactic of protest.[3] The riots which dominated urban affairs in the summer of 1967 appear not to have diminished the dependence of some groups on protest as a mode of political activity.

This article provides a theoretical perspective on protest activity as a political resource. The discussion is concentrated on the limitations inherent in protest which occur because of the need of protest leaders to appeal to four constituencies at the same time. As the concept of protest is developed here, it will be argued that protest leaders must nurture and sustain an organization comprised of people with whom they may or may not share common values. They must articulate goals and choose strategies so as to maximize their public exposure through communications media. They must maximize the impact of third parties in the political conflict. Finally, they must try to maximize chances of success among those capable of granting goals. The tensions inherent in manipulating these four constituencies at the same time form the basis of this discussion of protest as a political process. It is intended to place aspects of the civil rights movement in a framework which suggests links between protest organizations and the general political processes in which such organizations operate.

"PROTEST" CONCEPTUALIZED

Protest activity as it has been adopted by elements of the civil rights movement and others has not been studied extensively by social scientists. Some of the most suggestive writings have been done as case studies of protest movements in single southern cities.[4] These works generally lack a framework or theoretical focus which would encourage generalization from the cases. More systematic efforts have been attempted in approaching the dynamics of biracial communities in the South,[5] and comprehensively assessing the efficacy of Negro political involvement in Durham, N.C., and Philadelphia, Pa.[6] In their excellent assessment of Negro politics in the South, Matthews and Prothro have presented a thorough profile of Southern Negro students and their participation in civil rights activities.[7] Protest is also discussed in passing in recent explorations of the social-psychological dimensions of Negro ghetto politics[8] and the still highly suggestive, although pre-1960's, work on Negro political leadership by James Q. Wilson.[9] These and other less systematic works on contemporary Negro politics,[10] for all of their intuitive insights and valuable documentation, offer no theoretical formulations which encourage conceptualization about the interaction between recent Negro political activity and the political process.

Heretofore the best attempt to place Negro protest activity in a framework which would generate additional insights has been that of James Q. Wilson.[11] Wilson has suggested that protest activity be conceived as a problem of bargaining in which the basic problem is that Negro groups lack political resources to exchange. Wilson called this "the problem of the powerless."[12]

While many of Wilson's insights remain valid, his approach is limited in applicability because it defines protest in terms of mass action or response and as utilizing exclusively negative inducements in the bargaining process. Negative inducements are defined as inducements which are not absolutely preferred but are preferred over alternative possibilities.[13] Yet it might be argued that protest designed to appeal to groups which oppose suffering and exploitation, for example, might be offering positive inducements in bargaining. A few Negro students sitting at a lunch counter might be engaged in what would be called protest, and by their actions might be trying to appeal to other groups in the system with positive inducements. Additionally, Wilson's concentration on Negro civic action, and his exclusive interest in exploring the protest process to explain Negro civic action, tend to obscure comparison with protest activity which does not necessarily arise within the Negro community.

Assuming a somewhat different focus, protest activity is defined as a mode of political action oriented toward objection to one or more policies or conditions, characterized by showmanship or display of an unconventional nature, and undertaken to obtain rewards from political or economic systems while working within the systems. The "problem of the powerless" in protest activity is to activate "third parties" to enter the implicit or explicit bargaining arena in ways favorable to the protesters. This is one of the few ways in which they can "create" bargaining resources. It is intuitively unconvincing to suggest that fifteen people sitting uninvited in the Mayor's office have the power to move City Hall. A better formulation would suggest that the people sitting in may be able to appeal to a wider public to which the city administration is sensitive. Thus in successful protest activity the *reference publics* of protest *targets* may be conceived as explicitly or implicitly reacting to protest in such a way that target groups or individuals respond in ways favorable to the protesters.[14]

It should be emphasized that the focus here is on protest by relatively powerless groups. Illustrations can be summoned, for example, of activity designated as "protest" involving high status pressure groups or hundreds of thousands of people. While such instances may share some of the characteristics of protest activity, they may not represent examples of developing political resources by relatively powerless groups because the protesting groups may already command political resources by virtue of status, numbers or cohesion.

It is appropriate also to distinguish between the relatively restricted use of the concept of protest adopted here and closely related political strategies which are often designated as "protest" in popular usage. Where groups already possess sufficient resources with which to bargain, as in the case of some economic boycotts and labor strikes, they may be said to engage in "direct confrontation."[15] Similarly, protest which represents efforts to "activate reference publics" should be distinguished from "alliance formation," where third parties are induced to join the conflict, but where the value orientations of third parties are sufficiently similar to those of the protesting group that concerted or coordinated action is possible. Alliance formation is particularly desirable for relatively powerless groups if they seek to join the decision-making process as participants.

The distinction between activating reference publics and alliance formation is made on the assumption that where goal orientations among protest groups and the reference publics of target groups are similar, the political dynamics of petitioning target groups are different than when such goal orientations are relatively divergent. Clearly the more similar the goal orientations, the greater the likelihood of protest success, other things being equal. This discussion is intended to highlight, however, those instances where goal orientations of reference publics depart significantly, in direction or intensity, from the goals of protest groups.

Say that to protest some situation, A would like to enter a bargaining situation with B. But A has nothing B wants, and thus cannot bargain. A then attempts to create political resources by activating other groups to enter the conflict. A then organizes to take action against B with respect to certain goals. *Information concerning these goals must be conveyed through communications media* (C, D, and E) to F, G, and H, which are B's *reference publics*. In response to the reactions of F, G, and H, or in anticipation of their reactions, B responds, *in some way*, to the protesters' demands. This formulation requires the conceptualization of protest activity when undertaken to create bargaining resources as a political process which requires communication and is characterized by a multiplicity of constituencies for protest leadership.

A schematic representation of the process of protest as utilized by relatively powerless groups is presented in Figure 1. In contrast to a simplistic pressure group model which would posit a direct relationship between pressure group and pressured, the following discussion is guided by the assumption (derived from observation) that protest is a highly indirect process in which communications media and the reference publics of protest targets play critical roles. It is also a process characterized by reciprocal relations, in which protest leaders frame strategies according to their perception of the needs of (many) other actors.

Figure 1 *Schematic Representation of the Process of Protest by Relatively Powerless Groups*

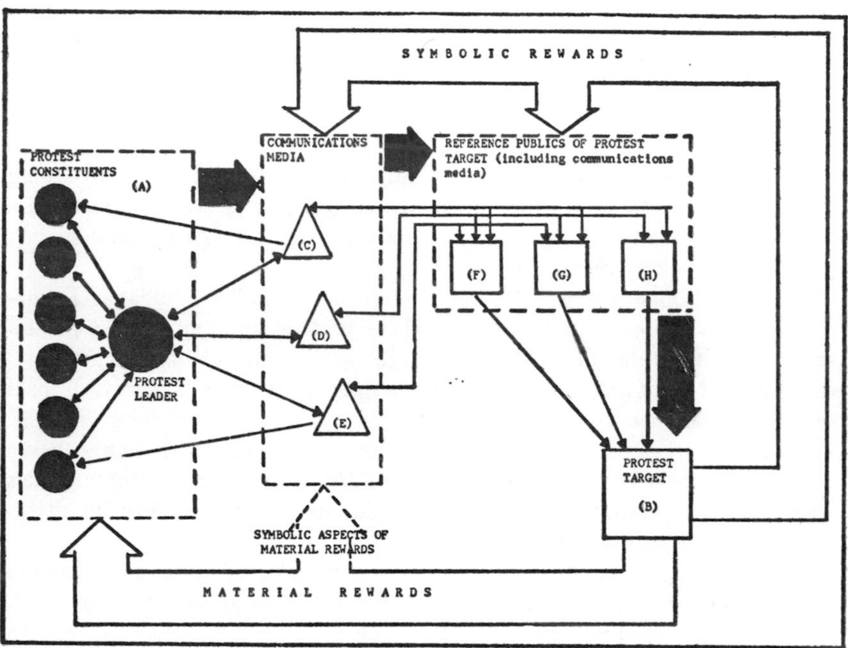

In this view protest constituents limit the options of protest leaders at the same time that the protest leader influences their perception of the strategies and rhetoric which they will support. Protest activity is filtered through the communications media in influencing the perceptions of the reference publics of protest targets. To the extent that the influence of reference publics is supportive of protest goals, target groups will dispense symbolic or material rewards. Material rewards are communicated directly to protest constituents. Symbolic rewards are communicated in part to protest constituents, but primarily are communicated to the reference publics of target groups, who provide the major stimuli for public policy pronouncements.

The study of protest as adopted by relatively powerless groups should provide insights into the structure and behavior of groups involved in civil rights politics and associated with the "war on poverty." It should direct attention toward the ways in which administrative agencies respond to "crises." Additionally, the study of protest as a political resource should influence some general conceptualizations of American political pluralism.

Robert Dahl, for example, describes the "normal American political process" as

> one in which there is a high probability that an active and legitimate group in the population can make itself heard effectively at some crucial stage in the process of decision.[16]

Although he agrees that control over decisions is unevenly divided in the population, Dahl writes:

> When I say that a group is heard "effectively" I mean more than the simple fact that it makes a noise; I mean that one or more officials are not only ready to listen to the noise, but expect to suffer in some significant way if they do not placate the group, its leaders, or its most vociferous members. To satisfy the group may require one or more of a great variety of actions by the responsive leader: pressure for substantive policies, appointments, graft, respect, expression of the appropriate emotions, or the right combination of reciprocal noises.[17]

These statements, which in some ways resemble David Truman's discussion of the power of "potential groups,"[18] can be illuminated by the study of protest activity in three ways. First, what are the probabilities that relatively powerless groups can make themselves heard effectively? In what ways will such groups be heard or "steadily appeased"?[19] Concentration on the process of protest activity may reveal the extent to which, and the conditions under which, relatively powerless groups are likely to prove effective. Protest undertaken to obstruct policy decisions, for example, may enjoy greater success probabilities than protest undertaken in an effort to evoke constructive policy innovations.[20]

Second, does it make sense to suggest that all groups which make noises will receive responses from public officials? Perhaps the groups which make noises do not have to be satisfied at all, but it is other groups which receive assurances or recognition. Third, what are the probabilities that groups which make noises will receive tangible rewards, rather than symbolic assurances?[21] Dahl lumps these rewards together in the same paragraph, but dispensation of tangible rewards clearly has a different impact upon groups than the dispensation of symbolic rewards. Dahl is undoubtedly correct when he suggests that the relative fluidity of American politics is a critical characteristic of the American political system.[22] But he is less precise and less convincing when it comes to analyzing the extent to which the system is indeed responsive to the relatively powerless groups of the "average citizen."[23]

The following sections are an attempt to demonstrate the utility of the conceptualization of the protest process presented above. This will be done by exploring the problems encountered and the strains generated by protest leaders in interacting with four constituencies. It will be useful to concentrate attention on the maintenance and enhancement needs not only of the large formal organizations which dominate city politics,[24] but also of the ad hoc protest groups which engage them in civic controversy. It will also prove rewarding to examine the role requirements of individuals in leadership positions as they perceive the problems of constituency manipulation. In concluding remarks some implications of the study of protest for the pluralist description of American politics will be suggested.[25]

PROTEST LEADERSHIP AND ORGANIZATIONAL BASE

The organizational maintenance needs of relatively powerless, low income, ad hoc protest groups center around the tension generated by the need for leadership to offer symbolic and intangible inducements to protest participation when immediate, material rewards cannot be anticipated, and the need to provide at least the promise of material rewards. Protest leaders must try to evoke responses from other actors in the political process, at the same time that they pay attention to participant organizational needs. Thus relatively deprived groups in the political system not only receive symbolic reassurance while material rewards from the system are withheld,[26] but protest leaders have a stake in perpetuating the notion that relatively powerless groups retain political efficiency despite what in many cases is obvious evidence to the contrary.

The tension embraced by protest leaders over the nature of inducements toward protest participation accounts in part for the style adopted and goals selected by protest leaders. Groups which seek psychological gratification from politics, but cannot or do not anticipate material political rewards, may be attracted to militant protest leaders. To these groups, angry rhetoric may prove a desirable quality in the short run. Where groups depend upon the political system for tangible benefits, or where participation in the system provides intangible benefits, moderate leadership is likely to prevail. Wilson has observed similar tendencies among Negro leaders of large, formal organizations.[27] It is no less true for leadership of protest groups. Groups whose members derive tangible satisfactions from political participation will not condone leaders who are stubborn in compromise or appear to question the foundations of the system. This coincides with Truman's observation:

> Violation of the "rules of the game" normally will weaken a group's cohesion, reduce its status in the community, and expose it to the claims of other groups.[28]

On the other hand, the cohesion of relatively powerless groups may be strengthened by militant, ideological leadership which questions the rules of the game and challenges their legitimacy.

Cohesion is particularly important when protest leaders bargain directly with target groups. In that situation, leaders' ability to control protest constituents and guarantee their behavior represents a bargaining strength.[29] For this reason Wilson stressed the bargaining difficulties of Negro leaders who cannot guarantee constituent behavior, and pointed out the significance of the strategy of projecting the image of group solidarity when the reality of cohesion is a fiction.[30] Cohesion is less significant at other times. Divided leadership may prove productive by bargaining in tandem,[31] or by minimizing strain among groups in the protest process. Further, community divisions may prove less detrimental to protest aims when strong third parties have entered the dispute originally generated by protest organizations.

The intangible rewards of assuming certain postures toward the political system may not be sufficient to sustain an organizational base. It may be necessary to renew constantly the intangible rewards of participation. And to the extent that people participate in order to achieve tangible benefits, their interest in a protest organization may depend upon the organization's relative material success. Protest leaders may have to tailor their style to present participants with tangible successes, or with the appearance of success. Leaders may have to define the issues with concern for increasing their ability to sustain organizations. The potential for protest among protest group members may have to be manipulated by leadership if the group is to be sustained.[32]

The participants in protest organizations limit the flexibility of protest leadership. This obtains for two reasons. They restrict public actions by leaders who must continue to solicit active participant support, and they place restraints on the kinds of activities which can be considered appropriate for protest purposes. Poor participants cannot commonly be asked to engage in protest requiring air transportation. Participants may have anxieties related to their environment or historical situation which discourages engagement in some activities. They may be afraid of job losses, beatings by the police, or summary evictions. Negro protest in the Deep South has been inhibited by realistic expectations of retribution.[33] Protests over slum housing conditions are undermined by tenants who expect landlord retaliation for engaging in tenant organizing activity.[34] Political or ethical mores may conflict with a proposed course of action, diminishing participation.[35]

On the other hand, to the extent that fears are real, or that the larger community perceives protest participants as subject to these fears, protest may actually be strengthened. Communications media and potential allies will consider more soberly the complaints of people who are understood to be placing themselves in jeopardy. When young children and their parents made the arduous bus trip from Mississippi to Washington, D.C. to protest the jeopardizing of Head Start funds, the courage and expense represented by their effort created a respect and visibility for their position which might not have been achieved by local protest efforts.[36]

Protest activity may be undertaken by organizations with established relationship patterns, behavior norms, and role expectations. These organizations are likely to have greater access to other groups in the political system, and a demonstrated capacity to maintain themselves. Other protest groups, however, may be ad hoc arrangements without demonstrated internal or external relationship patterns. These groups will have different organizational problems, in response to which it is necessary to engage in different kinds of protest activity.

The scarcity of organizational resources also places limits upon the ability of relatively powerless groups to maintain the foundations upon which protest organizations develop. Relatively powerless groups, to engage in political activity of any kind, must command at least some resources. This is not tautological. Referring again to a continuum on which political groups are placed according to their relative command of resources, one may draw a line somewhere along the continuum representing a "threshold of civic group political participation." Clearly some groups along the continuum will possess some political resources (enough, say, to emerge for inspection) but not enough to exercise influence in civic affairs. Relatively powerless groups, to be influential, must cross the "threshold" to engage in politics. Although the availability of group resources is a critical consideration at all stages of the protest process, it is particularly important in explaining why some groups seem to "surface" with sufficient strength to command attention. The following discussion of some critical organizational resources should illuminate this point.

Skilled professionals frequently must be available to protest organizations. Lawyers, for example, play extremely important roles in enabling protest groups to utilize the judicial process and avail themselves of adequate preparation of court cases. Organizational reputation may depend upon a combination of ability to threaten the conventional political system and of exercising statutory rights in court. Availability of lawyers depends upon ability to pay fees and/or the attractiveness to lawyers of participation in protest group activity. Volunteer professional assistance may not prove adequate. One night a week volunteered by an aspiring politician in a housing clinic cannot satisfy the needs of a chaotic political movement.[37] The need for skilled professionals is not restricted to lawyers. For example, a group seeking to protest an urban renewal policy might require the services of architects and city planners in order to present a viable alternative to a city proposal.

Financial resources not only purchase legal assistance, but enable relatively powerless groups to conduct minimum programs of political activities. To the extent that constituents are unable or unwilling to pay even small membership dues, then financing the cost of mimeographing flyers, purchasing supplies, maintaining telephone service, paying rent, and meeting a modest payroll become major organizational problems. And to the extent that group finances are supplied by outside individual contributions or government or foundation grants, the long-term options of the group are sharply constrained by the necessity of orienting group goals and tactics to anticipate the potential objections of financial supporters.

Some dependence upon even minimal financial resources can be waived if organizations evoke passionate support from constituents. Secretarial help and block organizers will come forward to work without compensation if they support the cause of neighborhood organizations or gain intangible benefits based upon association with the group. Protest organizations may also depend upon skilled non-professionals, such as college students, whose access to people and political and economic institutions often assist protest groups in cutting across income lines to seek support. Experience with ad hoc political groups, however, suggests that this assistance is sporadic and undependable. Transient assistance is particularly typical of skilled, educated, and employable volunteers whose abilities can be applied widely. The die-hards of ad hoc political groups are often those people who have no place else to go, nothing else to do.

Constituent support will be affected by the nature of the protest target and whether protest activity is directed toward defensive or assertive goals. Obstructing specific public policies may be easier than successfully recommending constructive policy changes. Orientations toward defensive goals may require less constituent energy, and less command over resources of money, expertise and status.[38]

PROTEST LEADERSHIP AND COMMUNICATIONS MEDIA

The communications media are extremely powerful in city politics. In granting or withholding publicity, in determining what information most people will have on most issues, and what alternatives they will consider in response to issues, the media truly, as Norton Long has put it, "set . . . the civic agenda."[39] To the extent that successful protest activity depends upon appealing to and/or threatening, other groups in the community, the communications media set the limits of protest action. If protest tactics are not considered significant by the media, or if newspapers and television reporters or editors decide to overlook protest tactics, protest organizations will not succeed. Like the tree falling unheard in the forest, there is no protest unless protest is perceived and projected.

A number of writers have noticed that the success of protest activity seems directly related to the amount of publicity it receives outside the immediate arena in which protest takes place. This view has not been stated systematically, but hints can be found in many sources. In the literature on civil rights politics, the relevance of publicity represents one of the few hypotheses available concerning the dynamics of successful protest activity.[40]

When protest tactics do receive coverage in the communications media, the way in which they are presented will influence all other actors in the system, including the protesters themselves. Conformity to standards of newsworthiness in political style, and knowledge of the prejudices and desires of the individuals who determine media coverage in political skills, represent crucial determinants of leadership effectiveness.

The organizational behavior of newspapers can partly be understood by examining the maintenance and enhancement needs which direct them toward projects of civic betterment and impressions of accomplishment.[41] But insight may also be gained by analyzing the role requirements of reporters, editors, and others who determine newspaper policy. Reporters, for example, are frequently motivated by the desire to contribute to civic affairs by their "objective" reporting of significant events; by the premium they place on accuracy; and by the credit which they receive for sensationalism and "scoops."

These requirements may be difficult to accommodate at the same time. Reporters demand newsworthiness of their subjects in the short run, but also require reliability and verifiability in the longer run. Factual accuracy may dampen newsworthiness. Sensationalism, attractive to some newspaper editors, may be inconsistent with reliable, verifiable narration of events. Newspapers at first may be attracted to sensationalism, and later demand verifiability in the interests of community harmony (and adherence to professional journalistic standards).

Most big city newspapers have reporters whose assignments permit them to cover aspects of city politics with some regularity. These reporters, whose "beats" may consist of "civil rights" or "poverty," sometimes develop close relationships with their news subjects. These relationships may develop symbiotic overtones because of the mutuality of interest between the reporter and the news subject. Reporters require fresh information on protest developments, while protest leaders have a vital interest in obtaining as much press coverage as possible.

Inflated reports of protest success may be understood in part by examining this relationship between reporter and protest leader. Both have role-oriented interests in projecting images of protest strength and threat. In circumstances of great excitement, when competition from other news media representatives is high, a reporter may find that he is less governed by the role requirement of verification and reliability than he is by his editor's demand for "scoops" and news with high audience appeal.[42]

On the other hand, the demands of the media may conflict with the needs of protest group maintenance. Consider the leader whose constituents are attracted solely by pragmatic statements not exceeding what they consider political "good taste." He is constrained from making militant demands which would isolate him from constituents. This constraint may cost him appeal in the press.[43] However, the leader whose organizing appeal requires militant rhetoric may obtain eager press coverage only to find that his inflamatory statements lead to alienation of potential allies and exclusion from the explicit bargaining process.[44]

News media do not report events in the same way. Television may select for broadcast only thirty seconds of a half-hour news conference. This coverage will probably focus on immediate events, without background or explanatory material. Newspapers may give more complete accounts of the same event. The most complete account may appear in the weekly edition of a neighborhood or ethnic newspaper. Differential coverage by news media, and differential news media habits in the general population,[45] are significant factors in permitting protest leaders to judge conflicting demands of groups in the protest process.

Similar tensions exist in the leader's relationships with protest targets. Ideological postures may gain press coverage and constituency approval, but may alienate target groups with whom it would be desirable to bargain explicitly. Exclusion from the councils of decision-making may have important consequences, since the results of target group deliberations may satisfy activated reference publics without responding to protest goals. If activated reference publics are required to increase the bargaining position of the protest group, protest efforts thereafter will have diminished chances of success.

PROTEST LEADERSHIP AND "THIRD PARTIES"

I have argued that the essence of political protest consists of activating third parties to participate in controversy in ways favorable to protest goals. In previous sections I have attempted to analyze some of the tensions which result from protest leaders' attempts to activate reference publics of protest targets at the same time that they must retain the interest and support of protest organization participants. This phenomenon is in evidence when Negro leaders, recognized as such by public officials, find their support eroded in the Negro community because they have engaged in explicit bargaining situations with politicians. Negro leaders are thus faced with the dilemma that when they behave like other ethnic group representatives, they are faced with loss of support from those whose intense activism has been aroused in the Negro community, yet whose support is vital if they are to remain credible as leaders to public officials.

The tensions resulting from conflicting maintenance needs of protest organizations and activated third parties present difficulties for protest leaders. One way in which these tensions can be minimized is by dividing leadership responsibilities. If more than one group is engaged in protest activity, protest leaders can, in effect, divide up public roles so as to reduce as much as possible the gap between the implicit demands of different groups for appropriate rhetoric, and what in fact is said. Thus divided leadership may perform the latent function of minimizing tensions among elements in the protest process by permitting different groups to listen selectively to protest spokesmen.[46]

Another way in which strain among different groups can be minimized is through successful public relations. Minimization of strain may depend upon ambiguity of action or statement, deception, or upon effective intergroup communication. Failure to clarify meaning, or falsification, may increase protest effectiveness. Effective intragroup communication may increase the likelihood that protest constituents will "understand" that ambiguous or false public statements have "special meaning" and need not be taken seriously. The Machiavellian circle is complete when we observe that although lying may be prudent, the appearance of integrity and forthrightness is desirable for public relations, since these values are widely shared.

It has been observed that "[t]he militant displays an unwillingness to perform those administrative tasks which are necessary to operate an organization. Probably the skills of the agitator and the skills of the administrator . . . are not incompatible, but few men can do both well."[47] These skills may or may not be incompatible as personality traits, but they indeed represent conflicting role demands on protest leadership. When a protest leader exhausts time and energy conducting frequent press conferences, arranging for politicians and celebrities to appear at rallies, delivering speeches to sympathetic local groups, college symposia and other forums, constantly picketing for publicity and generally making "contacts," he is unable to pursue the direction of office routine, clerical tasks, research and analysis, and other chores.

The difficulties of delegating routine tasks are probably directly related to the skill levels and previous administrative experiences of group members. In addition, to the extent that involvement in protest organizations is a function of rewards received or expected by individuals because of the excitement or entertainment value of participation, then the difficulties of delegating routine, relatively uninteresting chores to group members will be increased. Yet attention to such details affects the perception of protest groups by organizations whose support or assistance may be desired in the future. These considerations add to the protest leader's problem of risking alienation of protest participants because of potentially unpopular cooperation with the "power structure."

In the protest paradigm developed here, "third parties" refers both to the reference publics of target groups and, more narrowly, to the interest groups whose regular interaction with protest targets tends to develop into patterns of influence.[48] We have already discussed some of the problems associated with activating the reference publics of target groups. In discussing the constraints placed upon protest, attention may be focused upon the likelihood that groups seeking to create political resources through protest will be included in the explicit bargaining process with other pressure groups. For protest groups, these constraints are those which occur because of class and political style, status, and organizational resources.

The established civic groups most likely to be concerned with the problems raised by relatively powerless groups are those devoted to service in the public welfare and those "liberally" oriented groups whose potential constituents are either drawn from the same class as the protest groups (such as some trade unions), or whose potential constituents are attracted to policies which appear to serve the interest of the lower class or minority groups (such as some reform political clubs).[49] These civic groups have frequently cultivated clientele relationships with city agencies over long periods. Their efforts have been reciprocated by agency officials anxious to develop constituencies to support and defend agency administrative and budgetary policies. In addition, clientele groups are expected to endorse and legitimize agency aggrandizement. These relationships have been developed by agency officials and civic groups for mutual benefit, and cannot be destroyed, abridged or avoided without cost.

Protest groups may well be able to raise the saliency of issues on the civic agenda through utilization of communications media and successful appeals or threats to wider publics, but admission to policy-making councils is frequently barred because of the angry, militant rhetorical style adopted by protest leaders. People in power do not like to sit down with rogues. Protest leaders are likely to have phrased demands in ways unacceptable to lawyers and other civic activists whose cautious attitude toward public policy may reflect not only their good intentions but their concern for property rights, due process, pragmatic legislating or judicial precedent.

Relatively powerless groups lack participation of individuals with high status whose endorsement of specific proposals lend them increased legitimacy. Good causes may always attract the support of high status individuals.

But such individuals' willingness to devote time to the promotion of specific proposals is less likely than the one-shot endorsements which these people distribute more readily.

Similarly, protest organizations often lack the resources on which entry into the policy-making process depends. These resources include maintenance of a staff with expertise and experience in the policy area. This expertise may be in the areas of the law, planning and architecture, proposal writing, accounting, educational policy, federal grantsmanship or publicity. Combining experience with expertise is one way to create status in issue areas. The dispensing of information by interest groups has been widely noted as a major source of influence. Over time the experts develop status in their areas of competence somewhat independent of the influence which adheres to them as information-providers. Groups which cannot or do not engage lawyers to assist in proposing legislation, and do not engage in collecting reliable data, cannot participate in policy deliberations or consult in these matters. Protest oriented groups, whose primary talents are in dramatizing issues, cannot credibly attempt to present data considered "objective" or suggestions considered "responsible" by public officials. Few can be convincing as both advocate and arbiter at the same time.

PROTEST LEADERSHIP AND TARGET GROUPS

The probability of protest success may be approached by examining the maintenance needs of organizations likely to be designated as target groups.[50] For the sake of clarity, and because protest activity increasingly is directed toward government, I shall refer in the following paragraphs exclusively to government agencies at the municipal level. The assumption is retained, however, that the following generalizations are applicable to other potential target groups.

Some of the constraints placed on protest leadership in influencing target groups have already been mentioned in preceding sections. The lack of status and resources that inhibit protest groups from participating in policy-making conferences, for example, also helps prevent explicit bargaining between protest leaders and city officials. The strain between rhetoric which appeals to protest participants and public statements to which communications media and "third parties" respond favorably also exists with reference to target groups.

Yet there is a distinguishing feature of the maintenance needs and strategies of city agencies which specifically constrains protest organizations. This is the agency director's need to protect "the jurisdiction and income of his organization [by] . . . [m]anipulation of the external environment."[51] In so doing he may satisfy his reference groups without responding to protest

Kinds of outputs

group demands. At least six tactics are available to protest targets who are motivated to respond in some way to protest activity but seek primarily to satisfy their reference publics. These tactics may be employed whether or not target groups are "sincere" in responding to protest demands.

1. Target groups may dispense symbolic satisfactions. Appearances of activity and commitment to problems substitute for, or supplement, resource allocation and policy innovations which would constitute tangible responses to protest activity. If symbolic responses supplement tangible pay-offs, they are frequently coincidental, rather than intimately linked, to projection of response by protest targets. Typical in city politics of the symbolic response is the ribbon cutting, street corner ceremony or the walking tour press conference. These occasions are utilized not only to build agency constituencies,[52] but to satisfy agency reference publics that attention is being directed to problems of civic concern. In this sense publicist tactics may be seen as defensive maneuvers. Symbolic aspects of the actions of public officials can also be recognized in the commissioning of expensive studies and the rhetorical flourishes with which "massive attacks," "comprehensive programs," and "coordinated planning" are frequently promoted. 1

City agencies establish distinct apparatus and procedures for dealing with crises which may be provoked by protest groups. Housing-related departments in New York City may be cited for illustration. It is usually the case in the agencies that the Commissioner or a chief deputy, a press secretary and one or two other officials devote whatever time is necessary to collect information, determine policy and respond quickly to reports of "crises." This is functional for tenants, who, if they can generate enough concern, may be able to obtain shortcuts through lengthy agency procedures. It is also functional for officials who want to project images of action rather than merely receiving complaints. Concentrating attention on the maintenance needs of city politicians during protest crises suggests that pronouncements of public officials serve purposes independent of their dedication to alleviation of slum conditions.[53]

Independent of dispensation of tangible benefits to protest groups, public officials continue to respond primarily to their own reference publics. Murray Edelman has suggested that:

> Tangible resources and benefits are frequently not distributed to unorganized political group interests as promised in regulatory statutes and the propaganda attending their enactment.[54]

His analysis may be supplemented by suggesting that symbolic dispensations may not only serve to reassure unorganized political group interests, but may also contribute to reducing the anxiety level of organized interests and wider publics which are only tangentially involved in the issues.

2. Target groups may dispense token material satisfactions. When city agencies respond, with much publicity, to cases brought to their attention representing examples of the needs dramatized by protest organizations, they may appear to respond to protest demands while in fact only responding on a case basis, instead of a general basis. For the protesters served by agencies in this fashion it is of considerable advantage that agencies can be influenced by protest action. Yet it should not be ignored that in handling the "crisis" cases, public officials give the appearance of response to their reference publics, while mitigating demands for an expensive, complex *general* assault on problems represented by the case to which responses are given. Token responses, whether or not accompanied by more general responses, are particularly attractive to reporters and television news directors, who are able to dramatize individual cases convincingly, but who may be unable to "capture" the essence of general deprivation or of general efforts to alleviate conditions of deprivation.

3. Target groups may organize and innovate internally in order to blunt the impetus of protest efforts. This tactic is closely related to No. 2 (above). If target groups can act constructively in the worst cases, they will then be able to pre-empt protest efforts by responding to the cases which best dramatize protest demands. Alternatively, they may designate all efforts which jeopardize agency reputations as "worst" cases, and devote extensive resources to these cases. In some ways extraordinary city efforts are precisely consistent with protest goals. At the same time extraordinary efforts in the most heavily dramatized cases or the most extreme cases effectively wear down the "cutting-edges" of protest efforts.

Many New York City agencies develop informal "crisis" arrangements not only to project publicity, as previously indicated, but to mobilize energies toward solving "crisis" cases. They may also develop policy innovations which allow them to respond more quickly to "crisis" stiuations. These innovations may be important to some city residents, for whom the problems of dealing with city bureaucracies can prove insurmountable. It might be said, indeed, that the goals of protest are to influence city agencies to handle every case with the same resources that characterize their dispatch of "crisis" cases.[55]

But such policies would demand major revenue inputs. This kind of qualitative policy change is difficult to achieve. Meanwhile, internal reallocation of resources only means that routine services must be neglected so that the "crisis" programs can be enhanced. If all cases are expedited, as in a typical "crisis" response, then none can be. Thus for purposes of general solutions, "crisis" resolving can be self-defeating unless accompanied by significantly greater resource allocation. It is not self-defeating, however, to the extent that the organizational goals of city agencies are to serve a clientele while minimizing negative publicity concerning agency vigilance and responsiveness.

4. Target groups may appear to be constrained in their ability to grant protest goals.[56] This may be directed toward making the protesters appear to be unreasonable in their demands, or to be well-meaning individuals who "just don't understand how complex running a city really is." Target groups may extend sympathy but claim that they lack resources, a mandate from constituents, and/or authority to respond to protest demands. Target groups may also evade protest demands by arguing that "If-I-give-it-to-you-I-have-to-give-it-to-everyone."

The tactic of appearing constrained is particularly effective with established civic groups because there is an undeniable element of truth to it. Everyone knows that cities are financially undernourished. Established civic groups expend great energies lobbying for higher levels of funding for their pet city agencies. Thus they recognize the validity of this constraint when posed by city officials. But it is not inconsistent to point out that funds for specific, relatively inexpensive programs, or for the expansion of existing programs, can often be found if pressure is increased. While constraints on city government flexibility may be extensive, they are not absolute. Protest targets nonetheless attempt to diminish the impact of protest demands by claiming relative impotence.

5. Target groups may use their extensive resources to discredit protest leaders and organizations. Utilizing their excellent access to the press, public officials may state or imply that leaders are unreliable, ineffective as leaders ("they don't really have the people behind them"), guilty of criminal behavior, potentially guilty of such behavior, or are some shade of "left-wing." Any of these allegations may serve to diminish the appeal of protest groups to potentially sympathetic third parties. City officials, in their frequent social and informal business interaction with leaders of established civic groups, may also communicate derogatory information concerning protest groups. Discrediting of protest groups may be undertaken by some city officials while others appear (perhaps authentically) to remain sympathetic to protest demands. These tactics may be engaged in by public officials whether or not there is any validity to the allegations.

6. Target groups may postpone action. The effect of postponement, if accompanied by symbolic assurances, is to remove immediate pressure and delay specific commitments to a future date. This familiar tactic is particularly effective in dealing with protest groups because of their inherent instability. Protest groups are usually comprised of individuals whose intense

political activity cannot be sustained except in rare circumstances. Further, to the extent that protest depends upon activating reference publics through strategies which have some "shock" value, it becomes increasingly difficult to activate these groups. Additionally, protest activity is inherently unstable because of the strains placed upon protest leaders who must attempt to manage four constituencies (as described herein).

The most frequent method of postponing action is to commit a subject to "study." For the many reasons elaborated in these paragraphs, it is not likely that ad hoc protest groups will be around to review the recommendations which emerge from study. The greater the expertise and the greater the status of the group making the study, the less will protest groups be able to influence whatever policy emerges. Protest groups lack the skills and resource personnel to challenge expert recommendations effectively.

Sometimes surveys and special research are undertaken in part to evade immediate pressures. Sometimes not. Research efforts are particularly necessary to secure the support of established civic groups, which place high priority on orderly procedure and policy emerging from independent analysis. Yet it must be recognized that postponing policy commitments has a distinct impact on the nature of the pressure focused on policy-makers.

CONCLUSION

In this analysis I have agreed with James Q. Wilson that protest is correctly conceived as a strategy utilized by relatively powerless groups in order to increase their bargaining ability. As such, I have agreed, it is successful to the extent that the reference publics of protest targets can be activated to enter the conflict in ways favorable to protest goals. I have suggested a model of the protest process which may assist in ordering data and indicating the salience for research of a number of aspects of protest. These include the critical role of communications media, the differential impact of material and symbolic rewards on "feedback" in protest activity, and the reciprocal relationships of actors in the protest process.

An estimation of the limits to protest efficacy, I have argued further, can be gained by recognizing the problems encountered by protest leaders who somehow must balance the conflicting maintenence needs of four groups in the protest process. This approach transcends a focus devoted primarily to characterization of group goals and targets, by suggesting that even in an environment which is relatively favorable to specific protest goals, the tensions which must be embraced by protest leadership may ultimately overwhelm protest activity.

At the outset of this essay, it was held that conceptualizing the American political system as "slack" or "fluid," in the manner of Robert Dahl, appears inadequate because of (1) a vagueness centering on the likelihood that any group can make itself heard; (2) a possible confusion as to which groups tend to receive satisfaction from the rewards dispensed by public officials; and (3) a lumping together as equally relevant rewards which are tangible and those which are symbolic. To the extent that protest is engaged in by relatively powerless groups which must create resources with which to bargain, the analysis here suggests a number of reservations concerning the pluralist conceptualization of the "fluidity" of the American political system.

Relatively powerless groups cannot use protest with a high probability of success. They lack organizational resources, by definition. But even to create bargaining resources through activating third parties, some resources are necessary to sustain organization. More importantly, relatively powerless protest groups are constrained by the unresolvable conflicts which are forced upon protest leaders who must appeal simultaneously to four constituencies which place upon them antithetical demands.

When public officials recognize the legitimacy of protest activity, they may not direct public policy toward protest groups at all. Rather, public officials are likely to aim responses at the reference publics from which they originally take their cues. Edelman has suggested that regulatory policy in practice often consists of reassuring mass publics while at the same time dispensing specific, tangible values to narrow interest groups. It is suggested here that symbolic reassurances are dispensed as much to wide, potentially concerned publics which are not directly affected by regulatory policy, as they are to wide publics comprised of the downtrodden and the deprived, in whose name policy is often written.

Complementing Edelman, it is proposed here that in the process of protest symbolic reassurances are dispensed in large measure because these are the public policy outcomes and actions desired by the constituencies to which public officials are most responsive. Satisfying these wider publics, city officials can avoid pressures toward other policies placed upon them by protest organizations.

Not only should there be some doubt as to which groups receive the symbolic recognitions which Dahl describes, but in failing to distinguish between the kinds of rewards dispensed to groups in the political system, Dahl avoids a fundamental question. It is literally fundamental because the kinds of rewards which can be obtained from politics, one might hypothesize, will have an impact upon the realistic appraisal of the efficacy of political activity. If among the groups least capable of organizing for political activity there is a history of organizing for protest, and if that activity, once engaged in, is rewarded primarily by the dispensation of symbolic gestures without perceptible changes in material conditions, then rational behavior might lead to expressions of apathy and lack of interest in politics or a rejection of conventional political channels as a meaningful arena of activity. In this sense this discussion of protest politics is consistent with Kenneth Clark's observations that the image of power, unaccompanied by material and observable rewards, leads to impressions of helplessness and reinforces political activity in the ghetto.[57]

Recent commentary by political scientists and others regarding riots in American cities seems to focus in part on the extent to which relatively deprived groups may seek redress of legitimate grievances. Future research should continue assessment of the relationship between riots and the conditions under which access to the political system has been limited. In such research assessment of the ways in which access to public officials is obtained by relatively powerless groups through the protest process might be one important research focus.

The instability of protest activity outlined in this article also should inform contemporary political strategies. If the arguments presented here are persuasive, civil rights leaders who insist that protest activity is a shallow foundation on which to seek long-term, concrete gains may be judged essentially correct. But the arguments concerning the fickleness of the white liberal, or the ease of changing discriminatory laws relative to changing discriminatory institutions, only in part explain the instability of protest movements. An explanation which derives its strength from analysis of the political process suggests concentration on the problems of managing protest constituencies. Accordingly, Alinsky is probably on the soundest ground when he prescribes protest for the purpose of building organization. Ultimately, relatively powerless groups in most instances cannot depend upon activating other actors in the political process. Long-run success will depend upon the acquisition of stable political resources which do not rely for their use on third parties.

ENDNOTES

1. "Relatively powerless groups" may be defined as those groups which, relatively speaking, are lacking in conventional political resources. For the purposes of community studies, Robert Dahl has compiled a useful comprehensive list. See Dahl, "The Analysis of Influence in Local Communities," *Social Science and Community Action,* Charles R. Adrian, ed. (East Lansing, Michigan, 1960), p. 32. The difficulty in studying such groups is that relative powerlessness only becomes apparent under certain conditions. Extremely powerless groups not only lack political resources, but are also characterized by a minimal sense of political efficacy, upon which in part successful political organization depends. For reviews of the literature linking orientations of political efficacy to socioeconomic status, see Robert Lane, *Political Life* (New York, 1959), ch. 16; and Lester Millbrath, *Political Participation* (Chicago, 1965), ch. 5. Further, to the extent that group

cohesion is recognized as a necessary requisite for organized political action, then extremely powerless groups, lacking cohesion, will not even appear for observation. Hence the necessity of selecting for intensive study a protest movement where there can be some confidence that observable processes and results can be analyzed. Thus, if one conceives of a continuum on which political groups are placed according to their relative command of resources, the focus of this essay is on those groups which are near, but not at, the pole of powerlessness.

2. See, e.g., Bayard Rustin, "From Protest to Politics: The Future of the Civil Rights Movement," *Commentary* (February, 1965), 25–31; and Stokely Carmichael, "Toward Black Liberation," *The Massachusetts Review* (Autumn, 1966.)

3. On Alinsky's philosophy of community organization, see his *Reveille for Radicals* (Chicago, 1945); and Charles Silberman, *Crisis in Black and White* (New York, 1964), ch. 10.

4. See, e.g., Jack L. Walker, "Protest and Negotiation: A Study of Negro Leadership in Atlanta, Georgia," *Midwest Journal of Political Science*, 7 (May, 1963), 99–124; Jack L. Walker, *Sit-Ins in Atlanta: A Study in the Negro Protest*, Eagleton Institute Case Studies, No. 31 (New York, 1964); John Ehle, *The Free Men* (New York, 1965) [Chapel Hill]; Daniel C. Thompson, *The Negro Leadership Class* (Englewood Cliffs, N.J., 1963) [New Orleans]; M. Elaine Burgess, *Negro Leadership in a Southern City* (Chapel Hill, N.C., 1962) [Durham].

5. Lewis Killian and Charles Grigg, *Racial Crisis in America: Leadership in Conflict* (Englewood Cliffs, N.J., 1964).

6. William Keech, "The Negro Vote as a Political Resource: The Case of Durham," (unpublished Ph.D. Dissertation, University of Wisconsin, 1966); John H. Strange, "The Negro in Philadelphia Politics 1963-65," (unpublished Ph.D. Dissertation, Princeton University, 1966).

7. Donald Matthews and James Prothro, *Negroes and the New Southern Politics* (New York, 1966). Considerable insight on these data is provided in John Orbell, "Protest Participation among Southern Negro College Students," *The American Political Science Review*, 61 (June, 1967), 446–456.

8. Kenneth Clark, *Dark Ghetto* (New York, 1965).

9. *Negro Politics* (New York, 1960).

10. A complete list would be voluminous. See, e.g., Nat Hentoff, *The New Equality* (New York, 1964); Arthur Waskow, *From Race Riot to Sit-in* (New York, 1966).

11. "The Strategy of Protest: Problems of Negro Civic Action," *Journal of Conflict Resolution*, 3 (September, 1961), 291–303. The reader will recognize the author's debt to this highly suggestive article, not least Wilson's recognition of the utility of the bargaining framework for examining protest activity.

12. *Ibid.*, p. 291.

13. *Ibid.*, pp. 291–292.

14. See E. E. Schattschneider's discussion of expanding the scope of the conflict, *The Semisovereign People* (New York, 1960). Another way in which bargaining resources may be "created" is to increase the relative cohesion of groups, or to increase the perception of group solidarity as a precondition to greater cohesion. This appears to be the primary goal of political activity which is generally designated "community organization." Negro activists appear to recognize the utility of this strategy in their advocacy of "black power." In some instances protest activity may be designed in part to accomplish this goal in addition to activating reference publics.

15. For an example of "direct confrontation," one might study the three-month Negro boycott of white merchants in Natchez, Miss., which resulted in capitulation to boycott demands by city government leaders. See *The New York Times*, December 4, 1965, p. 1.

16. *A Preface to Democratic Theory* (Chicago, 1956), pp. 145–146.

17. *Ibid.*

18. *The Government Process* (New York, 1951), p. 104.

19. See Dahl, *A Preface to Democratic Theory*, p. 146.

20. Observations that all groups can influence public policy at some stage of the political process are frequently made about the role of "veto groups" in American politics. See *Ibid.*, pp. 104 ff. See also David Reisman, *The Lonely Crowd* (New Haven, 1950), pp. 211 ff., for an earlier discussion of veto-group politics. Yet protest should be evaluated when it is adopted to obtain assertive as well as defensive goals.

21. See Murray Edelman, *The Symbolic Uses of Politics* (Urbana, Ill., 1964), ch. 2.

22. See Dahl, *Who Governs?* (New Haven, 1961), pp. 305 ff.

23. In a recent formulation, Dahl reiterates the theme of wide dispersion of influence. "More than other systems, [democracies] . . . try to disperse influence widely to their citizens by means of the suffrage, elections, freedom of speech, press, and assembly, the right of opponents to criticize the conduct of government, the right to organize political parties, and in other ways." *Pluralist Democracy in the United States* (Chicago, 1967), p. 373. Here, however, he concentrates more on the availability of options to all groups in the system, rather than on the relative probabilities that all groups in fact have access to the political process. See pp. 372 ff.

24. See Edward Banfield, *Political Influence* (New York, 1961), p. 263. The analysis of organizational incentive structure which heavily influences Banfield's formulation is Chester Barnard, *The Functions of the Executive* (Cambridge, Mass., 1938).

25. In the following attempt to develop the implications of this conceptualization of protest activity, I have drawn upon extensive field observations and bibliographical research. Undoubtedly, however, individual assertions, while representing my best judgment concerning the available evidence, in the future may require modification as the result of further empirical research.

26. As Edelman suggests, cited previously.

27. *Negro Politics*, p. 290.

28. *The Governmental Process*, p. 513.

29. But cf. Thomas Schelling's discussion of "blinding oneself," *The Strategy of Conflict* (Cambridge, Mass., 1960), pp. 22 ff.

30. "The Strategy of Protest," p. 297.

31. This is suggested by Wilson, "The Strategy of Protest," p. 298; St. Clair Drake and Horace Cayton, *Black Metropolis* (New York, 1962, rev. ed.), p. 731; Walker, "Protest and Negotiation," p. 122. Authors who argue that divided leadership is dysfunctional have been Clark, p. 156; and Tilman Cothran, "The Negro Protest Against Segregation in the South," *The Annals,* 357 (January, 1965), p. 72.

32. This observation is confirmed by a student of the Southern civil rights movement:

> Negroes demand of protest leaders constant progress. The combination of long-standing discontent and a new-found belief in the possibility of change produces a constant state of tension and aggressiveness in the Negro community. But this discontent is vague and diffuse, not specific; the masses do not define the issues around which action shall revolve. This the leader must do.

Lewis Killian, "Leadership in the Desegregation Crises: An Institutional Analysis," in Muzafer Sherif (ed.), *Intergroup Relations and Leadership* (New York; 1962), p. 159.

33. Significantly, southern Negro students who actively participated in the early phases of the sit-in movement "tended to be unusually optimistic about race relations and tolerant of whites [when compared with inactive Negro students]. They not only *were* better off, objectively speaking, than other Negroes but *felt* better off." Matthews and Prothro, *op. cit.*, p. 424.

34. This is particularly the case in cities such as Washington, D.C., where landlord-tenant laws offer little protection against retaliatory eviction. See, e.g., Robert Schoshinski, "Remedies of the Indigent Tenant: Proposal for Change," *Georgetown Law Journal*, 54 (Winter, 1966), 541 ff.

35. Wilson regarded this as a chief reason for lack of protest activity in 1961. He wrote: "... some of the goals now being sought by Negroes are least applicable to those groups of Negroes most suited to protest action. Protest action involving such tactics as mass meetings, picketing, boycotts, and strikes rarely find enthusiastic participants among upper-income and higher status individuals": "The Strategy of Protest," p. 296.

36. See *The New York Times*, February 12, 1966, p. 56.

37. On housing clinic services provided by political clubs, see James Q. Wilson, *The Amateur Democrat: Club Politics in Three Cities* (Chicago, 1962), pp. 63–64, 176. On the need for lawyers among low income people, see e.g., *The Extension of Legal Services to the Poor, Conference Proceedings* (Washington, D.C., n.d.), esp. pp. 51–60; and "Neighborhood Law Offices: The New Wave in Legal Services for the Poor," *Harvard Law Review*, 80 (February, 1967), 805–850.

38. An illustration of low income group protest organization mobilized for veto purposes is provided by Dahl in "The Case of the Metal Houses." See *Who Governs?*, pp. 192 ff.

39. Norton Long, "The Local Community as an Ecology of Games," in Long, *The Polity,* Charles Press, ed. (Chicago, 1962), p. 153. See pp. 152–154. See also Roscoe C. Martin, Frank J. Munger, *et al., Decisions in Syracuse: A Metropolitan Action Study* (Garden City, N.Y., 1965) (originally published: 1961), pp. 326–327.

40. See, e.g., Thompson, *op. cit.*, p. 134, and *passim*; Martin Oppenheimer, "The Southern Student Movement: Year I," *Journal of Negro Education*, 33 (Fall, 1964), p. 397; Cothran, *op. cit.*, p. 72; Pauli Murray, "Protest Against the Legal Status of the Negro," *The Annals*, 357 (January, 1965), p. 63; Allan P. Sindler, "Protest Against the Political Status of the Negroes," *The Annals*, 357 (January, 1965), p. 50.

41. See Banfield, *op. cit.*, p. 275.

42. For a case study of the interaction between protest leaders and newspaper reporters, see Michael Lipsky, "Rent Strikes in New York City: Protest Politics and the Power of the Poor," (unpublished Ph.D. dissertation, Princeton University, 1967), pp. 139–49. Bernard Cohen has analyzed the impact of the press on foreign policy from the perspective of reporters' role requirements: see his *The Press and Foreign Policy* (Princeton, N.J., 1963), esp. chs. 2–3.

43. An example of a protest conducted by middle-class women engaged in pragmatic protest over salvaging park space is provided in John B. Keeley, *Moses on the Green*, Inter-University Case Program, No. 45 (University, Ala., 1959).

44. This was the complaint of Floyd McKissick, National Director of the Congress of Racial Equality, when he charged that ". . . there are only two kinds of statements a black man can make and expect that the white press will report. . . . First . . . is an attack on another black man. . . . The second is a statement that sounds radical, violent, extreme—the verbal equivalent of a riot. . . . [T]he Negro is being rewarded by the public media only if he turns on another Negro and uses his tongue as a switchblade, or only if he sounds outlandish, extremist or psychotic." Statement at the Convention of the American Society of Newspaper Editors, April 20, 1967, Washington, D.C., as reported in *The New York Times*, April 21, 1967, p. 22. See also the remarks of journalist Ted Poston, *ibid.*, April 26, 1965, p. 26.

45. Matthews and Prothro found, for example, that in their south-wide Negro population sample, 38 percent read Negro-oriented magazines and 17 percent read newspapers written for Negroes. These media treat news of interest to Negroes more completely and sympathetically than do the general media. See pp. 248 ff.

46. See footnote 31 above.

47. Wilson, *Negro Politics,* p. 225.

48. See Wallace Sayre and Herbert Kaufman, *Governing New York City* (New York, 1960), pp. 275 ff. Also see Banfield, *op. cit.*, p. 267.

49. See Wilson, *The Amateur Democrats*, previously cited. These groups are most likely to be characterized by broad scope of political interest and frequent intervention in politics. See Sayre and Kaufman, *op. cit.*, p. 79.

50. Another approach, persuasively presented by Wilson, concentrates on protest success as a function of the relative unity and vulnerability of targets. See "The Strategy of Protest," pp. 293 ff. This insight helps explain, for example, why protest against housing segregation commonly takes the form of action directed against government (a unified target) rather than against individual homeowners (who present a dispersed target). One problem with this approach is that it tends to obscure the possibility that targets, as collections of individuals, may be divided in evaluation of and sympathy for protest demands. Indeed, city agency administrators under some circumstances act as partisans in protest conflicts. As such, they frequently appear ambivalent toward protest goals: sympathetic to the ends while concerned that the means employed in protest reflect negatively on their agencies.

51. Sayre and Kaufman, *op. cit.*, p. 253.

52. See *ibid.*, pp. 253 ff.

53. See Lipsky, *op. cit.*, chs. 5–6. The appearance of responsiveness may be given by city officials *in anticipation* of protest activity. This seems to have been the strategy of Mayor Richard Daley in his reaction to the announcement of Martin Luther King's plans to focus civil rights efforts on Chicago. See *The New York Times*, February 1, 1966, p. 11.

54. See Edelman, *op. cit.*, p. 23.

55. See Lipsky, *op. cit.*, pp. 156, 249 ff.

56. On the strategy of appearing constrained, see Schelling, *op. cit.*, pp. 22 ff.

57. Clark, *op. cit.*, pp. 154 ff.

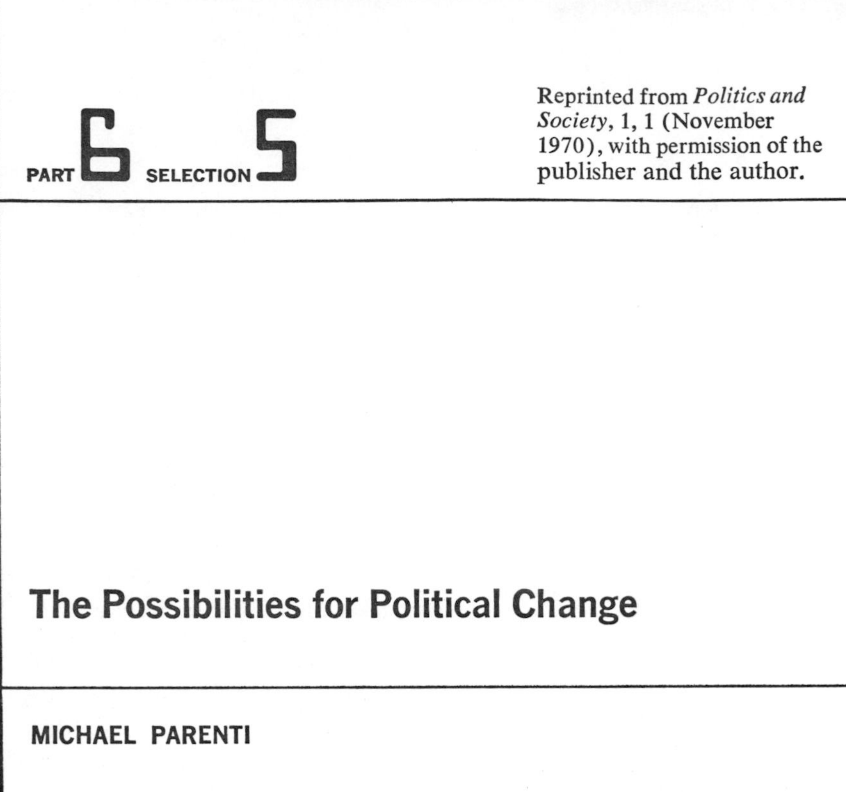

PART 6 SELECTION 5

Reprinted from *Politics and Society*, 1, 1 (November 1970), with permission of the publisher and the author.

The Possibilities for Political Change

MICHAEL PARENTI

A question pressing upon us with increasing urgency is, what are the possibilities for political change in America? More specifically, can the political system serve as a means of effecting the substantive reallocations needed to solve the enormous problems created within and by our economic system? What can we hope will be done about the continued plunder and pollution of our natural resources, the growth of a titanic military-industrial establishment, the massive concentration of corporate wealth and all its ensuing abuses, and the widespread infestations of rural and urban poverty? What kinds of solutions are in the offing, and, indeed, what kinds of definitions do we bring to the idea of "solution"?

I

Before considering the possibilities for political change, let us give some critical attention to the usual ways of approaching social problems. Social scientists and lay commentators alike have commonly assumed that solutions are arrived at by a process of systematic investigation. By identifying all the salient variables and then constructing paradigms which unravel the complex interactions of these variables, we can equip ourselves with inventories of causes and resources and develop strategies for solution. The remaining task would be to convince the decision makers to push the buttons provided by the social scientists. It is expected that the human stupidity and inertia of political actors would deter the implementation of certain proposals, but decision makers are thought to be as hungry as anyone else for viable programs and sooner or later would not be unresponsive to the promises of science.

This scientistic, technocratic view of social problems presumes that decision makers are as immune to the pressures of power and interest as scientists are, or as scientists think they are. What is missing from this scientism is the essence of politics itself, an appreciation of the inescapability of interest and power in determining what solutions will be deemed suitable, what allocations will be thought supportable, and, indeed, what variables will even be considered as interrelating and salient. The presumption that there is a scientifically discoverable "correct" solution to problems overlooks the fact that social problems involve conflicting ends and often irreconcilable value distributions; thus one man's "solution" is often another man's disaster. A "correct" proposal for some political actors may be one which resolves the threat of an opposing interest without causing any loss of profit or status to oneself. Hence the first instinct of established interest is so often toward halfhearted reform and wholehearted repression ("law and order"). For other advocates, a "correct" program is one calling for nothing less than momentous reallocations in the substance and process of the entire productive system (a remedy which offers the kind of paradigm that usually escapes the serious attentions of most liberal middle-class social scientists).

Unlike mathematical problems which might be resolved by procedures exogenous to the life subjectivities of various mathematicians, the solutions to social problems cannot be treated except in the context of vested and conflicting interests which give vested and conflicting definitions to the problem. This is true whether the question is rebuilding the ghettos or withdrawing our troops from Vietnam: the solutions are potentially "at hand" or "nowhere in sight," depending on the ideological priorities and commitments of various proponents.

The scientistic approach presumes that problems exist because of the prevailing ignorance of the would-be problem solvers rather than because of the prevailing conditions of power among social groups. But, again, unlike mathematical problems which begin and end on paper, it goes without saying that social problems are never resolved by study but by action. Many of the social ills we live with have been studied repeatedly, but since they have not yet been resolved it is assumed by the proponents of scientism that they need further study. Here we have an uncharacteristic instance of social scientists pretending to an *ignorance* they do not really possess. For the last thing some of our problems need is further study. Witness the hundreds of studies, reports, surveys and exposés done on Appalachia by a variety of commissions, committees, economists, and journalists, extending back more than half a century.[1] Neither history nor the historians have "bypassed" or "neglected" the people of Appalachia. The material forces of history, in this case the timber and mining companies that swindled the Appalachians of their lands, exploited their labor, and wreaked havoc with their lives, were all too attentive to the destinies of that region even though they were never held accountable for the social costs of their actions. The plunder and profit which is the history of the region has been duly documented; yet Appalachia is still treated today as a kind of historical mishap, an impersonal and presumably innocent development of "changing times," a "complex situation" needing our concerted attention.

Similarly, the plight of the urban poor in various Western industrial societies has been documented by official and unofficial sources for more than a century, and in recent decades we have traced the web of interests, the private and public forces, North and South, at the national and local levels, which have contributed to, and perpetuated, the black ghettos. The story is well known to us, but our discoveries have brought forth no solutions.

To be sure, the first step toward remedy is to investigate reality. But, eventually, if no second step is taken, no move toward action, then the call for "a study of the problem" is justifiably treated as nothing more than a symbolic response, an "appropriate reciprocal noise," designed to convey the impression that decision makers are fulfilling their responsibilities.[2] The commissioned "study" becomes an act which violates its own professed purpose; rather than inducing change, it is designed to mitigate the demands for change. Appearing before the Kerner Commission, the psychologist Kenneth B. Clark noted:

> I read that report . . . of the 1919 riot in Chicago, and it is as if I were reading the report of the investigating committee on the Harlem riot of '35, the report of the investigating committee on the Harlem riot of '43, the report of the McCone Commission on the Watts riot.

> I must again in candor say to you members of this Commission—it is a kind of Alice in Wonderland—with the same moving picture reshown over and over again, the same analysis, the same recommendations, and the same inaction.[3]

By incorporating Clark's admonition into its pages, the Kerner Report may have achieved the ultimate in co-optation, for it, itself, is a prime example of that kind of official evasion and obfuscation designed to justify the very status quo about which Clark was complaining. The Kerner Report demands no changes in the way power and wealth are distributed among the classes; it never gets beyond its indictment of "white racism" to specify the forces in the political economy which brought the black man to riot; it treats the obviously abominable ghetto living conditions as "causes" of disturbance but never really inquires into the causes of the "causes." It does not deal, for instance, with the ruthless enclosure of Southern sharecroppers by big corporate farming interests, the subsequent mistreatment of the black migrant by Northern rent-gouging landlords, price-gouging merchants, urban "redevelopers," discriminating employers, insufficient schools, hospitals, and welfare, brutal police, hostile political machines and state legislators, and, finally, the whole system of values, material interests, and public power distributions from the state to the federal capitols which gives greater priority to "haves" than to "have-nots," servicing and subsidizing the interests of private corporations while neglecting the often desperate needs of the municipalities. The Kerner Report reflects the ideological cast of its sponsor, the Johnson administration, and in that sense is not better than the interests it served.[4]

To treat the *symptoms* of social dislocation (e.g., slum conditions) as the *causes* of social ills is an inversion not peculiar to the Kerner Report. Unable or unwilling to pursue the implications of our own data, we tend to see the effects of a problem as the problem itself. The victims, rather than the victimizers, are defined as "the poverty problem." This is what might be described as the "VISTA approach" to economic maladies: a haphazard variety of public programs are initiated, focusing on the poor and ignoring the system of power, privilege, and profit which makes them poor. It is a little like blaming the corpse for the murder.

II

In looking to the political system as a means of certifying the abuses and inequities of the socio-economic system we are confronted with the inescapable fact that any political system, including one which observes democratic forms, is a system of power. As such, it best serves those who have the wherewithal to make it serviceable to their interests—those who own and control the resources of money, property, organization, jobs, social prestige, legitimacy, time and expertise, and who thereby command the attentive responses of political decision makers. Indeed, our political system works well for those large producer and corporate interests that control the various loci of power in the state and federal legislatures and bureaucracies. One can find no end to the instances in which public agencies have become captives of private business interests.[5] Economic power is to political powers as fuel is to fire, but in this instance the "fire" actually feeds back and adds to the fuel; for political power when properly harnessed becomes a valuable resource in expanding the prerogatives of those economic interests which control it. To think of government as nothing more than a broker or referee amidst a vast array of competing groups (the latter presumably representing all the important and "countervailing" interests of the populace) is to forget that government best serves those who can best serve themselves.

But the material advantages of the owning classes are supposedly offset by the representative forms of a democratic system which makes explicit and institutionalized provision for the power of numbers and if the non-elites have nothing else they at least have their numbers. But numbers are not power unless they are organized and mobilized into forms of political action which can deliver some reward to or punishment upon decision makers. And the mobilization of potential numerical strength requires the use of antecedent resources. Just as one needs the capital to make capital, so one needs the power to use power. This is especially true of the power of numbers, which, to be even sporadically effective, requires large outputs of time, manpower, publicity, organization, knowledgeability, legitimacy, and—the ingredient that often can determine the availability of these other resources —money. The power of numbers, then, like the power of our representative institutions, is highly qualified by material and class considerations.

Consider those agencies which are specifically intended to mobilize and register the power of numbers, the political parties. The image of the political party as an organization inclusive of and responsive to the interests of rank and file voters does not find ready confirmation in the experiences of dissenters who have sought entry into the party system. To be sure, new voters in both rural and urban counties are usually welcomed onto the party rolls especially if they are white and if their loyalties promise to fit into the established spectrum of political choices, but new ideas and issues, new and potentially disruptive interests, are treated most unsympathetically by the county bosses and district captains whose overriding concern is to maintain their own position in the ongoing "equilibrium," more often than not, the instinct of the local clubhouse, that "cogwheel of democracy," is to operate with exclusive rather than inclusive intent.[6]

In general, the two-party system throughout the local and national levels *avoids* rather than confronts many of the basic social problems of our society, or, when confrontation materializes, the electoral stances are usually reiterations of conventional formulas rather than invitations to heterodox ideas and choices. One need only recall how liberals and conservatives, Democrats and Republicans, spent twenty-five postwar years demonstrating their anti-Communist militancy on almost all domestic and foreign policy issues, thereby driving public debate on the question of "America's role in the world" to new levels of impoverishment. In an earlier work, I suggested: "The American political system has rarely been able to confront fundamental images, or serve as an instrument of creative discourse, or even engage in public discussion of heterodox alternatives. The two-party competition which supposedly is to provide for democratic heterodoxy, in fact, has generated a competition for orthodoxy [on most important questions]. In politics, as in economics, competition is rarely a certain safeguard against monopoly and seldom a guarantee that the competitors will produce commodities which offer the consumer a substantive choice."[7]

Offering itself as the choice of the people, as a measure of the polyarchic will, the representative system becomes one of the greatest legitimating forces for the ongoing social order and all its class abuses. A closer study of the "eras of reform" seems to support rather than refute this view. If the political system has done anything in the nineteenth and twentieth centuries, it has kept the populace busy with symbolic struggles while manfully servicing the formidable appetites of the business community. To take one instance among countless ones: the legislation of 1887 marking Congress's "great" reform effort in transportation gave the people their railroad regulation law and gave the business magnates their railroads complete with risk-free investment capital (compliments of the U.S. taxpayer), free land, and many millions of dollars in profits.[8] Similarly, the history of who got what during the New Deal has still to be written. There yet may emerge an American historian who will spare us his description of the inspirational rhetoric, the colorful personalities, the electoral ballyhoo, the hundred days of legislative flurry, the Brain Trust, the court-packing fight, etc., and get down to a systematic and, I suspect, startling study of the New Deal's dealings with the political economy, revealing what classes carried the burdens of public finance, what ideologies prevailed at the operational level, what interests were left out and what interests actually got what magnitude of material outputs.[9] *Symbolic allocations to public sentiment and substantive allocations to private interests—such has been the overall performance of our political system even in times of so-called social reform.*

Speaking about the late nineteenth-century American political life, Matthew Josephson refers to the "contradictions between ideology and interest, between 'eternal principles of truth and right' and class-economic necessities . . . between the mask and parade—the theatrical duelings of prejudice, associations of thought, patriotic sentiment, illusions—and the naked clash of different conditions of existence, different forms of property and economy. . . . Behind the marching songs and slogans of the Ins and Outs . . . we must grasp at the pecuniary objects, the genuine, concrete interests, the real stakes being played for, as in every historic social conflict."[10] For Josephson, the captains of industry were the "men who spoke little and did much" in determining the shape of our society and the quality of our lives, while the political leaders were "men who, in effect, did as little as possible and spoke all too much."[11] Together, the "robber barons" and the "politicos" represented the difference between substantive and symbolic politics.

Indeed, one might better think of ours as a dual political system: first, there is the *symbolic* input-output system centering around electoral and representative activities including party conflicts, voter turnout, political personalities, public pronouncements, official role-playing and certain ambiguous presentations of some of the public issues which bestir presidents, governors, mayors and their respective legislatures.[12] Then there is the *substantive* input-output system, involving multibillion dollar contracts, tax write-offs, protections, rebates, grants, loss compensations, subsidies, leases, giveaways and the whole vast process of budgeting, legislating, allocating, "regulating," protecting, and servicing major producer interests, now bending or ignoring the law on behalf of the powerful, now applying it with full punitive vigor against heretics and "troublemakers." The symbolic system is highly visible, taught in the schools, dissected by academicians, gossiped about by newsmen. The substantive system is seldom heard of or accounted for.

The have-nots who hope to win substantive outputs by working their way through the symbolic input-output system seldom see the light at the end of the tunnel. The crucial function of the electoral-representative process is to make people believe there is a closer connection between the symbolic and the substantive than actually exists. But those dissidents and protestors who decide to make the long march through primaries, fund-raising, voter registration, rallies, canvassing, and campaigning soon discover the bottomless, endless qualities of electoral politics. They find out that the political system, or that visible portion of it they experience, absorbs large quantities of their time, money, and energy while usually leaving them no closer to the forces which make the important substantive allocations of this society. On those infrequent occasions when reform candidates do win elections, they discover still other absorbent, deflective, and dilatory forces lying in wait. They find themselves relegated to obscure legislative tasks; they receive little cooperation from party leaders or from bureaucratic agencies. To achieve some degree of effectiveness in an institution whose dominant forces can easily outflank him, the newly arrived dissenter frequently decides that "for now" he must make his peace with the powers that be, holding his fire until some future day when he might attack from higher ground; thus begins that insidious process which lets a man believe he is fighting the ongoing arrangements when in fact he has become a functional part of them. Many of the accounts of life in Congress are studies in the methods of co-optation, the ways would-be dissenters are socialized to the goals and priorities of a conservative leadership.[13]

There are, of course, less subtle instances of co-optation: reformers have been bought off with promotions and favors from those who hold the key to their advancement. Having tasted the spoils of victory, they may reverse their stance on essential issues and openly make common cause with the powers that be, much to the shock of their supporters.[14] Well-meaning electoral crusaders who promise to get things moving again by exercising executive leadership, upon accession to federal, state, or local executive office soon discover that most of the important options involving jobs, property, money, and taxes are dependent upon resources controlled by large corporations capable of exercising an influence extending well beyond the political realm as it is usually defined. When local, state, and federal officials contend that the problems they confront are of a magnitude far greater than the resources they command, we might suspect them of telling the truth, for in fact the major decisions about how the vast resources of our society are used are made by the private sector of the economy and the economic institutions of a capitalist society are rarely, if ever, held accountable for the enormous social costs of their profit system.

III

Contrary to the gradualistic vision of America, things are getting worse, not better. As opposed to a decade ago, there are more, not less, people living in poverty today, more substandard housing, more environmental pollution and devastation, more deficiencies in our schools, hospitals, and systems of public transportation, more military dictatorships throughout the world feeding on the largesse and power of the Pentagon, more people from Thailand to Brazil to Greece to Chicago suffering the social oppression and political repression of an American-backed status quo. The long march through the American electoral-representative process has not saved the Vietnamese; it has not even saved the redwoods; nor, if our ecologists are correct, will it save the environment. Nor has it put a stop to the aggrandizements of American imperialism and its military-industrial complex. Nor has it brought us any closer to a real "war on poverty." Nor has

there been any revision of priorities, any reallocations of resources away from the glut of a private commodity market and toward essential public needs and services. It is a small wonder that as social dissenters become increasingly aware of the limitations of debate, petition, and election for purposes of effecting substantive changes, they become less dedicated to election rituals and less attentive to the standard public dialogues heard within and without representative assemblies. For the same reason, those who *oppose* change become *more* dedicated to dialogue and symbolic politics, urging protestors to place their faith in reason, in free, open (and endless) discussion, and in the candidate of their choice.

In a system that responds only to power, what do the powerless do? Consider, once more, the problem of poverty: the people most needful of sociopolitical change, in this case, the poor, are by that very fact most deprived of the resources needed to mobilize political influence and least able to make effective use of whatever limited resources they do possess. If the poor controlled the values and goods needed to win substantive payoffs, they would not be poor and have less need to struggle for outputs which the economic and political systems readily allocate to more favored groups. This is the dilemma of lower strata groups: their deprivation leaves them at the lower end of any index of power and their relative powerlessness seems to ensure their continued deprivation.

Lacking control of the things that would make decision makers readily responsive to them, and, therefore, lacking the specialized, organized, persistent, and well-financed forces of influence needed to function successfully in the *substantive* area of our dual political system, the dispossessed are left with the only resources they have: their voices, their bodies, their buying power and their labor; denunciations and demonstrations, sit-ins and scuffles, boycotts and strikes, the threat of disruption and actual disruption. The effectiveness of their protest actions, of course, is handicapped by the same scarcity of resources and consequent instability of organization that limits their opportunities for standard political influences. Nevertheless, the last decade has witnessed a growing tendency among aggrieved groups to heed the old Populist dictum to "raise less corn and more hell," to embark upon actions which inconvenience the normal arrangements of middle-class life and often upset middle-class sensibilities.

That is the idea—to inconvenience and upset. By increasing their nuisance value, the protestors hope to achieve a greater visibility for themselves and a greater sense of urgency in the public mind for the problems at hand. The nuisance and disruption caused by direct actions also become a leverage for those of little power, the withdrawal of the disruption being used as a negotiable resource. Thereby do dispossessed groups such as workers, blacks, students, and the poor attempt to induce through crude means, a responsiveness from officialdom which the business community accomplishes through more effective and less strenuous channels.

But many of the demands put forth by protestors might be described as "transitional revolution." That is, they are essentially reformist and non-revolutionary in appearance *yet they are impossible to effect within the present system if that system is to maintain itself.* Students demand, for instance, that the university cease performing indispensable services for the corporate-military economy, including various kinds of vital research and personnel training, and that it withdraws its investments in giant corporations and devote a substantial portion of its resources to the needs of the impoverished, many of whom live within a stone's throw of its ivy-covered walls. And they demand that the multimillion dollar system of domestic and international service and armed protection given to the corporate elites be ceased on behalf of the multibillion dollar public investment against domestic and international poverty (one that would preempt some important private producer interests at home and abroad). While sounding enough like the reformist, peaceful-change-within-the-system policies of the gradualist, these demands are essentially revolutionary in their effect in that they presuppose a dedication to interests which deny the essential interests and power of the prevailing elites.

It becomes understandable, then, why appeals to reason and good will do not bring reforms: quite simply, the problem of change is no easier for the haves than for the have-nots. Contrary to the admonitions of liberal critics, it is neither stupidity nor opaqueness which prevents those who own and control the property and institutions of this society from satisfying the demand for change. To be sure, the established elites suffer from their share of self-righteous stubborness, but more often than not, meaningful changes are not embarked upon because they would literally undercut the security and survival of privileged interests, and it is in the nature of social elites that they show little inclination to commit class suicide.

In the early stages of particular social conflicts neither the haves nor the have-nots are fully appreciative of the systemic contradictions and limited options they face. An "Upward Bound" plan here, a "Head Start" program there, and an outpouring of rhetoric everywhere—such are the responses of the ruling interests, believing as they do that an abundance of symbolic outputs should sufficiently placate the malcontents. America was not built in a day, they remind us, and only time and patience will—through unspecified means—rectify our "remaining" social ills.

At the onset, protestors operate under somewhat similar assumptions about the basic viability of the system. There are "pockets" of poverty, "discrimination" against blacks and a "senseless" war in Southeast Asia social problems are seen as aberrant offshoots of a basically good, if not great, society, rather than as endemic manifestations of the prevailing forms of social privilege, power, and property. The first soundings of dissent are accompanied by anticipations of change. There is often a kind of exhilaration when people, finally moved by that combination of anger and hope which is the stuff of protest, take to the streets: the handclapping, slogan shouting, the signs, the crowd are all encouraging evidence that many others share one's grievances. But, as time passes, as the symbolic dramatizations of protest produce little more than the symbolic responses of politicians (along with the free-swinging clubs, mace, tear gas, and guns of the police) dissent begins to escalate in tactics—from petitioning one's congressman to marching in the streets to "trashing" stores to the burning and bombing of draft boards, banks, and corporation offices, to sporadic armed encounters.

Just as significantly, dissent begins to escalate in the scope and level of its indictment. Increasingly convinced that the political system is not endowed with the responsible, responsive, creative, and inclusive virtues its supporters ascribe to it, dissenters begin to shift from incrementalist pleas to challenges against the fundamental legitimacy of the established economic and political elites. There is evidence of a growing militancy among deprived racial minorities, of a consciousness which begins with pleas for equal treatment in the ongoing society and soon evolves into a sweeping condemnation of white America's "power structure." A visible number of blacks, Mexican-Americans, Puerto Ricans, Indians, Orientals, and others have made the journey from civil rights "moderation" to radical militancy, from Thurgood Marshall and Roy Wilkins to Malcolm X and Eldridge Cleaver.

The white student movement has undergone similar transitions in both tactics and ideology. Many of those who pleaded for a cessation of the bombing in North Vietnam in 1966 were urging that we "bring the war home" in 1970; the V-sign of peace has been replaced by the clenched fist of resistance; "staying clean with Gene" has less appeal today than more direct and more radical forms of action. And in May 1970, the sporadic peace parades were replaced by a national student strike, the first of its kind in American history, affecting over four hundred college campuses and at least an equal number of high schools.

Even among those who are described as "the silent majority" one finds some signs of a leftward discontent. White workers suffering the deprivations of their class as laborers, taxpayers, and consumers have experienced the contagion of protest. More often than not, the experiences of their own oppression are expressed in resentment toward "pampered" and "subversive" students and an almost obsessive animosity toward blacks who are seen as "getting everything" while they, themselves, must bear the costs. Yet there are indications that this picture is oversimplified. Labor has not reacted toward the protestors with one voice. The Vietnam war, the tax burden, inflation, and other such things could not be blamed on students and blacks. Discontent with "the establishment" can be found among small but growing numbers of working whites and there is clear indication that important elements in the labor movement, especially the ALA, look upon the national student strike and upon student militancy in general with something other than disfavor. There are indications, in places like Detroit with its "Black-Polish Alliance" and Chicago with its "Unity Coalition," that blacks and whites are beginning to join forces in protest action.[15] With increasing frequency students have been moving off campus, both individually and in organized moves, to join picket lines and to draw bonds of common action and interest with workers. Meanwhile, there has begun to emerge among the more literate segments of professional, middle-class America a spirit of protest which began as an antiwar expression and has since become an indictment against the whole quality of life in America. Finally, one should not overlook the increasingly widespread problems of morale and disaffection found in that most crucial of all power institutions, the U.S. Army, problems which, if they continue at the present rate may have real revolutionary potential.

Yet neither should we overestimate the potential strength of radical protest nor underestimate the coercive, repressive, and preemptive capacities of the established politico-economic powers. From election laws to property laws, from city hall to federal bureaucracy, from taxation to welfare, government helps those who can best help themselves and this does not mean those wanting and needing fundamental changes in the class structure and in the ways in which the wealth of this nation is produced, distributed, controlled, and used. To deal with the protestors, the elites still have a variety of symbolic outputs as close at hand as the next election or the next press conference. Along with this they have the ability to discredit, obfuscate, delay and "study" (what Richard Neustadt calls the "almost unlimited resources of the enormous power of standing still").[16] Furthermore, elites are rarely hesitant to use the systemic rewards and punishments, the jobs, wealth, and institutions they control for the purpose of encouraging political conformity. And should all else fail, they have at their command the most decisive of political resources—the one the pluralists rarely talk about—the forces of obedient and violent repression: the clubbing, gassing, beating, shooting, arresting, imprisoning, rampaging forces of "law and order."

In sum, it is no longer a certainty that we will be able to solve our social ills by working with the same operational values and within the same systematic structures that have helped to create them. It does seem that we have seldom appreciated the extent to which the political system responds to, and indeed, represents, the dominant interests of the socioeconomic system, and also how frequently political structures are simply bypassed by a corporate economy which significantly shapes the quality of our lives while in most respects remaining answerable to no one. A more realistic notion of how power is allocated and used in the United States should leave us less sanguine about the possibilities for political change. As of now we have no reason to hope that the "guardians of the public trust" will stop behaving like the servants of the dominant private interests, and no reason to presume that our political institutions will prove viable in treating the immense problems of this unhappy society.

Protest of a radical or potentially radical nature has arisen in a great many sectors of the American public. But the growth in protest has not brought forth a commensurate move toward needed changes from the powers that be, and the reason for this unresponsiveness, I have suggested, lies not in the technical nature of the problems but in the political nature of the conflicting interests, specifically in *the inability of the dominant politico-economic elites to satisfy the demands for structural changes while maximizing and maintaining their own interests.* Radical protest, then, is both a cause of and a response to the increasingly evident contradictions of the social system. Given the "Three R's" of politics—reform, repression, and revolution—it can no longer be taken as an article of faith that we are moving toward the first.

ENDNOTES

1. See Harry M. Caudill, *Night Comes to the Cumberlands* (Boston: Little, Brown, 1962), for the best recent study of Appalachia.

2. Murray Edelman, *The Symbolic Uses of Politics* (Urbana, Ill.: University of Illinois Press, 1964), offers a most provocative discussion of the ritualistic and control functions of political acts.

3. Clark's testimony is quoted in the *Report of the National Advisory Commission on Civil Disorders* (The Kerner Report) (New York: Bantam Books, 1968), p. 29.

4. See Andrew Kopkind's excellent critique of The Kerner Commission "White on Black: The Riot Commission and the Rhetoric of Reform," *Hard Times*, 44, September 15-22, 1969, pp. 1–4.

5. See Grant McConnell, *Private Power and American Democracy* (New York: Alfred A. Knopf, 1966), for a good discussion of the public powers of private interest groups.

6. For two studies of the ways local political parties work to defeat and exclude the dissident poor, see Philip Meranto, "Black Majorities and Political Power: The Defeat of an All-Black Ticket in East St. Louis," in Herbert Hill, ed. *The Revolt of the Powerless* (New York: Random House, 1970), and Michael

Parenti, "Power and Pluralism, A View from the Bottom," in Marvin Surkin and Alan Wolfe, eds., *The Caucus Papers* (New York: Basic Books, 1970).

7. Michael Parenti, *The Anti-Communist Impulse* (New York: Random House, 1969), p. 101.

8. Many of the rail lines built were overextended and of dubious use to American communities, but pecuniary gain rather than public service was the primary consideration. See Matthew Josephson, *The Robber Barons* (New York: Harcourt, Brace & World, 1934), pp. 306–307.

9. At least one American historian, in a very brief study, does note how the New Deal serviced the corporate owning class while devoting its best rhetoric to the common man: see Paul K. Conkin, *The New Deal* (New York: Thos. Y. Crowell, 1967). See Gabriel Kolko, *Wealth and Power in America* (New York: Frederick Praeger, 1962), pp. 30 ff. for a discussion of New Deal taxation policy.

10. Matthew Josephson, *The Politics, 1865–1896* (New York: Harcourt, Brace, & World, 1938), pp. 8–9.

11. Ibid., p. *v*.

12. See Edelman, *The Symbolic Uses of Politics*, for the best discussion of these components of the political system.

13. See Donald R. Matthews, *U.S. Senators and Their World* (Chapel Hill: University of North Carolina Press, 1960). For a discussion of how protest organizations and left-wing parties become co-opted into established parliamentary system, see Ralph Millband, *The State in Capitalist Society*, (New York: Basic Books, 1969), Chapter Seven.

14. This is a common enough occurrence in local politics but also not unknown at the national level where the symbolic appearances developed during the campaign soon collide with the substantive interests of the powers that be. Within four years, the American people elected two presidents who promised to end the war in Vietnam and who, once in office, continued to pursue that conflict with full force.

15. See William Greider, "Poles, Blacks Join Forces in Detroit," *Chicago Sun-Times*, 12 October 1969, p. 10.

16. Richard Neustadt, *Presidential Power* (New York: John Wiley, 1960), p. 42.

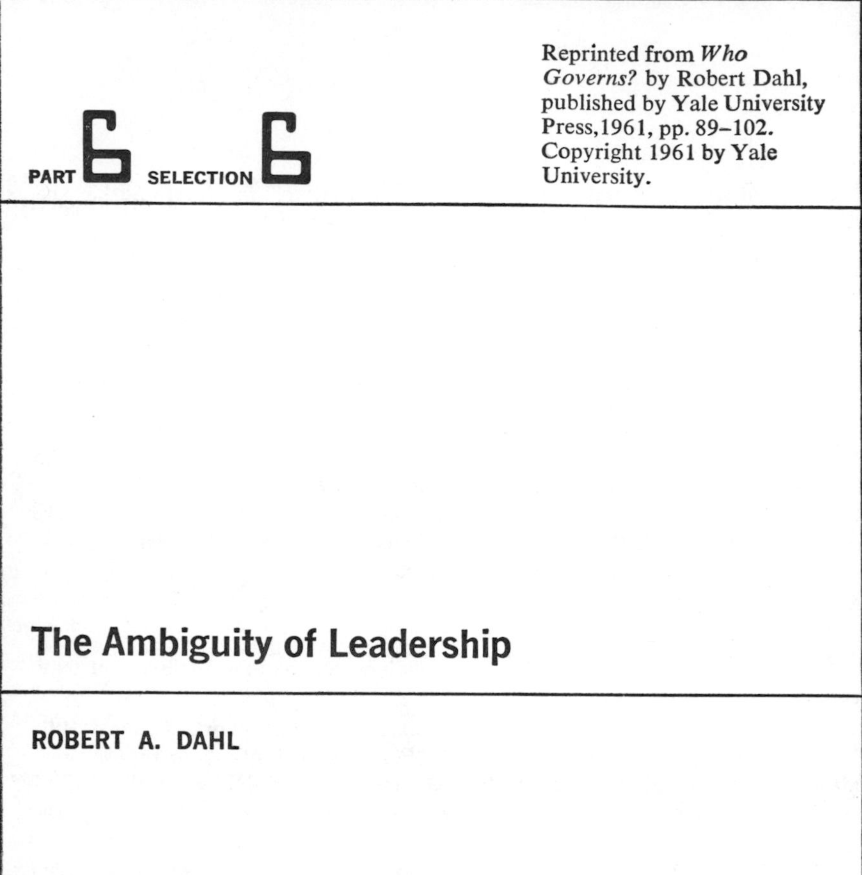

PART 6 SELECTION 6

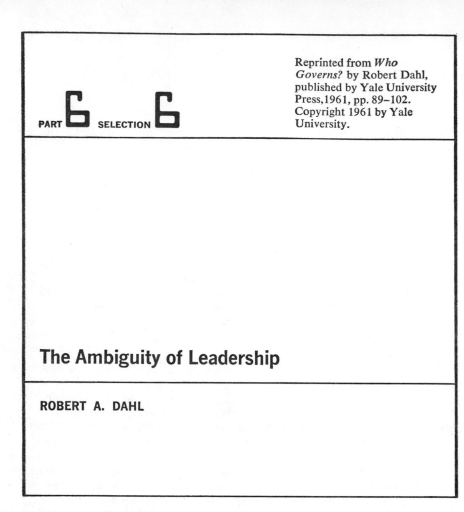

Reprinted from *Who Governs?* by Robert Dahl, published by Yale University Press, 1961, pp. 89–102.
Copyright 1961 by Yale University.

The Ambiguity of Leadership

ROBERT A. DAHL

One of the difficulties that confronts anyone who attempts to answer the question "Who rules in a pluralist democracy?" is the ambiguous relationship of leaders to citizens.

Viewed from one position, leaders are enormously influential—so influential that if they are seen only in this perspective they might well be considered a kind of ruling elite. Viewed from another position, however, many influential leaders seems to be captives of their constituents. Like the blind men with the elephant, different analysts have meticulously examined different aspects of the body politic and arrived at radically different conclusions. To some, a pluralistic democracy with dispersed inequalities is all head and no body; to others it is all body and no head.

Ambiguity in the relations of leaders and constituents is generated by several closely connected obstacles both to observation and to clear conceptualization. To begin with, the American creed of democracy and equality prescribes many forms and procedures from which the actual practices of leaders diverge. Consequently, to gain legitimacy for their actions leaders frequently surround their covert behavior with democratic rituals. These rituals not only serve to disguise reality and thus to complicate the task of observation and analysis, but—more important—in complex ways the very existence of democratic rituals, norms, and requirements of legitimacy based on a widely shared creed actually influences the behavior of both leaders and constituents even when democratic norms are violated. Thus the distinction between the rituals of power and the realities of power is frequently obscure.

Two additional factors help to account for this obscurity. First, among all the persons who influence a decision, some do so more directly than others in the sense that they are closer to the stage where concrete alternatives are initiated or vetoed in an explicit and immediate way. Indirect influence might be very great but comparatively difficult to observe and weigh. Yet to ignore indirect influence in analysis of the distribution of influence would be to exclude what might well prove to be a highly significant process of control in a pluralistic democracy.

Second, the relationship between leaders and citizens in a pluralistic democracy is frequently reciprocal: leaders influence the decisions of constituents, but the decisions of leaders are also determined in part by what they think are, will be, or have been the preferences of their constituents. Ordinarily it is much easier to observe and describe the distribution of influence in a political system where the flow of influence is strongly in one direction (an asymmetrical or unilateral system, as it is sometimes called) than in a system marked by strong reciprocal relations. In a political system with competitive elections, such as New Haven's, it is not unreasonable to expect that relationships between leaders and constituents would normally be reciprocal.

One who sets out to observe, analyze, and describe the distribution of influence in a pluralistic democracy will therefore encounter formidable problems. It will, I believe, simplify the task of understanding New Haven if I now spell out some of the theory and assumptions that guided our study of the distribution of influence.*

*This is one chapter of a larger study of decision making in politics in New Haven, Connecticut. The distribution of influence in New Haven was dispersed among many people. While elites had direct influence over proposals, they operated with constraints set up by the citizens of New Haven. These contraints operated through political parties and elections.—ED.

THE POLITICAL STRATUM

In New Haven, as in other political systems, a small stratum of individuals is much more highly involved in political thought, discussion, and action than the rest of the population. These citizens constitute the political stratum.

Members of this stratum live in a political subculture that is partly but not wholly shared by the great majority of citizens. Just as artists and intellectuals are the principal bearers of the artistic, literary and scientific skills of society, so the members of the political stratum are the main bearers of political skills. If intellectuals were to vanish overnight, a society would be reduced to artistic, literary, and scientific poverty. If the political stratum were destroyed, the previous political institutions of the society would temporarily stop functioning. In both cases, the speed with which the loss could be overcome would depend on the extent to which the elementary knowledge and basic attitudes of the elite had been diffused. In an open society with widespread education and training in civic attitudes, many citizens hitherto in the apolitical strata could doubtless step into roles that had been filled by members of the political stratum. However, sharp discontinuities and important changes in the operation of the political system almost certainly would occur.

In New Haven, as in the United States, and indeed perhaps in all pluralistic democracies, differences in the subcultures of the political and the apolitical strata are marked, particularly at the extremes. In the political stratum, politics is highly salient; among the apolitical strata, it is remote. In the political stratum, individuals tend to be rather calculating in their choice of strategies; members of the political stratum are, in a sense, relatively rational political beings. In the apolitical strata, people are notably less calculating; their political choices are more strongly influenced by inertia, habit, unexamined loyalties, personal attachments, emotions, transient impulses. In the political stratum, an individual's political beliefs tend to fall into patterns that have a relatively high degree of coherence and internal consistency; in the apolitical strata, political orientations are disorganized, disconnected, and unideological. In the political stratum, information about politics and the issues of the day is extensive; the apolitical strata are poorly informed. Individuals in the political stratum tend to participate rather actively in politics; in the apolitical strata citizens rarely go beyond voting and many do not even vote. Individuals in the political stratum exert a good deal of steady, direct, and active influence on government policy; in fact some individuals have a quite extraordinary amount of influence. Individuals in the apolitical strata, on the other hand, have much less direct or active influence on policies.

Communication within the political stratum tends to be rapid and extensive. Members of the stratum read many of the same newspapers and magazines; in New Haven, for example, they are likely to read the *New York Times* or the *Herald Tribune*, and *Time* or *Newsweek*. Much information also passes by word of mouth. The political strata of different communities and regions are linked in a national network of communications. Even in small towns, one or two members of the local political stratum usually are in touch with members of a state organization, and certain members of the political stratum of a state or any large city maintain relations with members of organizations in other states and cities, or with national figures. Moreover, many channels of communication not designed specifically for political purposes—trade associations, professional associations, and labor organizations, for example—serve as a part of the network of the political stratum.

In many pluralistic systems, however, the political stratum is far from being a closed or static group. In the United States the political stratum does not constitute a homogeneous class with well-defined class interests. In New Haven, in fact, the political stratum is easily penetrated by anyone whose interests and concerns attract him to the distinctive political culture of the stratum. It is easily penetrated because (among other reasons) elections and competitive parties give politicians a powerful motive for expanding their coalitions and increasing their electoral followings.

In an open pluralistic system, where movement into the political stratum is easy, the stratum embodies many of the most widely shared values and goals in the society. If popular values are strongly pragmatic, then the political stratum is likely to be pragmatic; if popular values prescribe reverence toward the past, then the political stratum probably shares that reverence; if popular values are oriented toward material gain and personal advancement, then the political stratum probably reflects these values; if popular values are particularly favorable to political, social, or economic equality, then the political stratum is likely to emphasize equality. The apolitical strata can be said to "govern" as much through the sharing of common values and goals with members of the political stratum as by other means. However, if it were not for elections and competitive parties, this sharing would—other things remaining the same—rapidly decline.

Not only is the political stratum in New Haven not a closed group, but its "members" are far from united in their orientations and strategies. There are many lines of cleavage. The most apparent and probably the most durable are symbolized by affiliations with different political parties. Political parties are rival coalitions of leaders and subleaders drawn from the members of the political stratum. Leaders in a party coalition seek to win elections, capture the chief elective offices of government, and insure that government officials will legalize and enforce policies on which the coalition leaders can agree.

In any given period of time, various issues are salient within the political stratum. Indeed, a political issue can hardly be said to exist unless and until it commands the attention of a significant segment of the political stratum. Out of all the manifold possibilities, members of the political stratum seize upon some issues as important or profitable; these then become the subject of attention within the political stratum. To be sure, all the members of the political stratum may not initially agree that a particular issue is worthy of attention. But whenever a sizable minority of the legitimate elements in the political stratum is determined to bring some question to the fore, the chances are high that the rest of the political stratum will soon begin to pay attention.

Although political issues are sometimes generated by individuals in the apolitical strata who begin to articulate demands for government action, this occurs only rarely. Citizens in the apolitical strata are usually aware of problems or difficulties in their own circle; through word of mouth or the mass media they may become aware of problems faced by people in other circles. But to be aware of a problem is by no means equivalent to perceiving a political solution or even formulating a political demand. These acts are ordinarily performed only by members of the political stratum. Within the political stratum, issues and alternatives are often formulated by intellectuals, experts, and reformers, whose views then attract the support of professionals. This is how questions as abstract and difficult as the proper rate of growth in the Gross National Product are injected into national politics; and, as we shall see, this is roughly the route by which urban redevelopment came into the politics of New Haven.

However, in gaining attention for issues, members of the political stratum operate under constraints set by party politicians with an eye on the next election. Despite the stereotype, party politicians are not necessarily concerned *only* with winning elections, for the man who is a party politician in one role may, in another, be a member of a particular interest group, social stratum, neighborhood, race, ethnic group, occupation, or profession. In this role he may himself help to generate issues. However, simply qua party politician, he not only has a powerful incentive to search for politically profitable issues, but he has an equally strong motive for staying clear of issues he thinks will not produce a net gain in his votes in the next election.

Because of the ease with which the political stratum can be penetrated, whenever dissatisfaction builds up in some segment of the electorate party politicians will probably learn of the discontent and calculate whether it might be converted into a political issue with an electoral payoff. If a party politician sees no payoff, his interest is likely to be small; if he foresees an adverse effect, he will avoid the issue if he can. As a result, there is usually some conflict in the political stratum between intellectuals, experts, and others who formulate issues, and the party politicians themselves, for the first group often demands attention to issues in which the politicians see no profit and possibly even electoral damage.

The independence, penetrability, and heterogeneity of the various segments of the political stratum all but guarantee that any dissatisfied group will find spokesmen in the political stratum, but to have a spokesman does not insure that the group's problems will be solved by political action. Politicians may not see how they can gain by taking a position on an issue; action by government may seem to be wholly inappropriate; policies intended to cope with dissatisfaction may be blocked; solutions may be improperly designed; indeed, politicians may even find it politically profitable to maintain a shaky coalition by keeping tension and discontent alive and deflecting attention to irrelevant "solutions" or alternative issues.

In his search for profitable issues, the party politician needs to estimate the probable effects various actions he might take will have on the future votes of his constituents. Although he is generally unaware of it, he necessarily operates with theory, a set of hypotheses as to the factors that influence the decisions of various categories of voters and the rough weights to assign to these factors.

The subculture of the political stratum provides him with the relevant categories—businessmen, Italians, wage earners, and the like. It also furnishes him with information as to the voting tendencies of these groups, e.g., their predisposition to vote Democratic or Republican. Given a category and its voting tendency, the party politician typically operates on the simple but sound assumption that human responses can be influenced by rewards and deprivations, both past and prospective. His task then is to choose a course of action that will either reinforce the voting tendency of categories predisposed in favor of him or his party, or weaken the voting tendency of categories predisposed to vote against him or his party. This he does by actions that provide individuals in these categories with rewards or the expectation of rewards.

SOME POLITICAL AXIOMS

Most of the people in the political stratum at any given moment take for granted a number of assumptions so commonplace in the political culture of the time and so little subject to dispute that they function as "self-evident" axioms. The axioms include both factual and normative postulates. In New Haven, the most relevant current axioms among the political stratum would appear to be the following:

1. To build an effective political coalition, rewards must be conferred on (or at least promised to) individuals, groups, and various categories of citizens.

2. In devising strategies for building coalitions and allocating rewards, one must take into account a large number of different categories of citizens. It would be dangerous to formulate strategies on the assumption that most or all citizens can be divided into two or three categories, for a successful political coalition necessarily rests upon a multiplicity of groups and categories. (In the early decades of the century a minority in the political stratum, leaders of the Social Democratic and Socialist Labor parties, pursued a strategy that reflected a confident belief in the existence of a bipolar socioeconomic structure in which political beliefs and actions were almost wholly determined by working-class or white-collar ways of making a living. But because this strategy failed to win elections, it has never been widely approved in the political stratum, least of all among the party politicians in the two major parties.)

3. Although a variety of attributes are relevant to political strategy, many different attributes can either be subsumed under or are sometimes overridden by ethnic, racial, and religious affiliations.

4. In allocating rewards to individuals and groups, the existing socioeconomic structure must be taken as given, except for minor details. (The local political stratum has not been strongly reformist, certainly not on social and economic matters. Except perhaps for socialists, local reform movements have concentrated on defects in the political system, not the socioeconomic structure of the society. And except for a few men who dreamed and spoke of changing the face of the city, until recently the political stratum has assumed that the physical and economic features of the city are determined by forces beyond their control.)

5. Although a certain amount of legal chicanery is tolerable, legality and constitutionality are highly prized. The pursuit of illegal practices on a sizable scale is difficult to conceal; illegal actions by public officials ordinarily lead, when known, to loss of public office; unconstitutional action is almost certain to become entangled in a complex network of judicial processes. The use of violence as a political weapon must be avoided; if it were used it would probably arouse widespread alarm and hostility.

6. The American creed of democracy and equality must always be given vigorous and vociferous support. No one who denies the validity of this creed has much chance of winning political office or otherwise gaining influence on the local scene. Among other things, the creed assumes that democracy is the best form of government, public officials must be chosen by majority vote, and people in the minority must have the right to seek majority support for their beliefs.[1]

7. In practice, of course, universalistic propositions in the American creed need to be qualified. Adherence to the creed as a general goal and a set of criteria for a good government and a good society does not mean that the creed is, or as a practical matter can be, fully applied in practice. (Some elements in the political stratum are deeply disturbed by the gap between ideal and reality. Most people in the political stratum, however, are probably either unaware of any sharp conflict between ideal and reality, or are indifferent to it, or take the gap for granted in much the same spirit that they accept the fact that religious behavior falls short of religious belief.)

LEADERS AND SUBLEADERS

In any durable association of more than a handful of individuals, typically a relatively small proportion of the people exercises relatively great direct influence over all the important choices bearing on the life of the association—its survival, for example, or its share in such community resources as wealth, power, and esteem, or the way these resources are shared within the association, or changes in the structure, activities, and dominant goals of the association, and so on. These persons are, by definition, the leaders. . . .

The goals and motives that animate leaders are evidently as varied as the dreams of men. They include greater income, wealth, economic security, power, social standing, fame, respect, affection, love, knowledge, curiosity, fun, the pleasure of exercising skill, delight in winning, esthetic satisfaction, morality, salvation, heroism, self-sacrifice, envy, jealousy, revenge, hate—whatever the whole wide range may be. Popular beliefs and folklore to the contrary, there is no convincing evidence at present that any single common denominator of motives can be singled out in leaders of associations. We are not compelled, therefore, to accept the simple view that Moses, Jesus, Caligula, Savanarola, St. Ignatius, Abraham Lincoln, Boss Tweed, Mahatma Ghandi, Carrie Chapman Catt, Huey Long, and Joseph Stalin all acted from essentially the same motives.

To achieve their goals, leaders develop plans of action, or strategies. But actions take place in a universe of change and uncertainty; goals themselves emerge, take shape, and shift with new experiences. Hence a choice among strategies is necessarily based more on hunch, guesswork, impulse, and the assessment of imponderables than on scientific predictions. Adopting a strategy, is a little bit like deciding how to look for a fuse box in a strange house on a dark night after all the lights have blown.

Ordinarily the goals and strategies of leaders require services from other individuals. (Both Christ and Lenin needed disciples to increase and rally their followers.) To perform these services more or less regularly, reliably, and skillfully, auxiliaries or subleaders are needed. The tasks of subleaders include aid in formulating strategies and policies; carrying out the dull, routine, time-consuming or highly specialized work of the eternal spear bearers, the doorbell ringers, the file clerks; recruiting and mobilizing the following; and, in a country like the United States where there exists a strong democratic ethos, helping by their very existence to furnish legitimacy to the actions of the leaders by providing a democratic façade.

To secure the services of subleaders, leaders must reward them in some fashion. Here too the range of rewards seems to be as broad as the spectrum of human motives. However, some kinds of rewards are easier to manipulate than others. In business organizations, the rewards are mainly financial ones, which are probably the easiest of all to manipulate. In many other kinds of associations—and evidently to some extent even in business—either financial rewards are too low to attract and hold subleaders capable of performing the tasks at the minimum levels required by the leaders, or within a certain range other kinds of rewards are more important to the auxiliaries than financial ones. Leaders may therefore contrive to pay off their auxiliaries with nonfinancial rewards like social standing, prestige, fun, conviviality, the hope of salvation, and so on.

Thus the survival of an association of leaders and subleaders depends on frequent transactions between the two groups in which the leaders pay off the subleaders in return for their services. To pay off the subleaders, leaders usually have to draw on resources available only outside the association. Sometimes leaders can obtain these resources from outside by coercion, particularly if they happen to control the single most effective institution for coercion: the government. This is one reason—but by no means the only one—why government is always such an important pawn in struggles among leaders. Ordinarily, however, the association must produce something that will appeal to outsiders, who then contribute resources that serve, directly or indirectly, to maintain the association. Probably the most important direct contribution of these outsiders—let us call them constituents—is money; their most important indirect contribution is votes, which can be converted into office and thus into various other resources.

In some associations, subleaders themselves may be put to work on tasks that produce a surplus available, directly or indirectly, for allocation by the leaders. Political party leaders in New Haven, for example, appoint as many of their subleaders as they can to municipal jobs. The income from these jobs is a payoff to the subleaders for their party work. Subleaders in city jobs are in turn assessed at election time for campaign contributions; these contributions provide a "surplus" that may be spent to pay off subleaders who don't have city jobs.

Because every person's time is to some extent limited, every activity competes with every other. Therefore it is not enough for leaders merely to provide *some* rewards for subleaders; they must furnish rewards big enough to attract subleaders they want from other associations or from individual, family, friendly, neighborly pastimes like watching television, mowing the lawn, taking the family to the beach, playing cards, drinking beer in a tavern, reading the newspaper, and so on.

In a rough way, associations can be classified as either vocational or avocational. In vocational associations the subleaders have full-time jobs for which they are paid; in avocational associations they do not. To the extent that an association can produce services for which others will pay, as in the case of a business organization, auxiliaries can be given full-time employment. But many associations cannot or do not sell their services for money because to do so would be inconsistent with the leaders' goals or the loyalty of auxiliaries and followings. (The sale of indulgences, for example, helped generate the Reformation that split Protestantism from the Roman Catholic Church.) If an association also lacks other means of securing a large income, such as levying assessments on followings, it must necessarily remain avocational. Because it cannot lure subleaders away from other activities by paying them adequately, an avocational association often resorts to other kinds of rewards, such as prestige, social status, and conviviality.

POLICIES

To achieve their own goals, secure the services of subleaders, and obtain outside support from constituents, leaders usually find it a useful strategy to commit themselves (or appear to commit themselves) to certain choices they will make under some specified conditions. These commitments represent their policies—or at any rate their *promises* as to policy. For many reasons, not the least being the general uncertainty and constant flux of events, leaders frequently do not live up to their promises. But their proposed or actual policies often contain a direct or indirect, actual or expected payoff *of some kind* to subleaders and constituents. The attempt to satisfy the preferences of both subleaders and constituents by policies is one of the commonest sources of conflict that leaders of political associations encounter.

Despite some general theories of considerable persuasiveness, the precise reasons why an individual prefers one alternative to another are not so well understood that any general and comprehensive explanation for all preferences can be offered with confidence. (Part of the uncertainty arises because of persistent doubts that a white rat in a maze is exactly equivalent to a human being in a quandary.) Whatever the reasons may be, individuals do have preferences on matters of policy. Sometimes these preferences are extraordinarily strong, sometimes weak. Sometimes one's preferences can be explained by one's hopes that a policy will produce concrete benefits to oneself or to the people nearest one's center of life. In other cases (though I take it as axiomatic that any policy one approves of is expected to be rewarding in *some* sense) the benefits may be general or, if specific, may be conferred on individuals remote from oneself. I do not mean to suggest that what would ordinarily be called altruism plays anything like a dominant role in politics, but it would be misleading to exclude it altogether. Not everyone ceases to be interested in good public schools when his own children grow up; advocates of public housing usually turn out to be middle-class people who have no need for it themselves; individuals have pressed for compulsory smallpox vaccination even though they and their families were already immunized; dentists have generally supported the fluoridation of public water supplies. One could multiply the examples.

Policies are an important means, though not the only means, by which leaders attract the support they need from constituents. In fact, policies sometimes win over constituents who then identify themselves with the association more or less permanently and can be regularly counted on to support the association even when some of its leaders and policies change. These constituents make up the *following* of the association.

The policies that leaders promise to constituents and followings—I shall call them *overt* policies—are not always identical to, or indeed even consistent with, the covert commitments they make to their subleaders. From the point of view of a leader concerned with the task of building his following, it would be ideal if his subleaders were indifferent to his overt policies, for this would give him freedom to develop overt policies exclusively adapted to the desires of constituents and followings. But this kind of complete independence from the desired subleaders is almost impossible for a leader to attain. It could exist only where the flow of rewards for which subleaders gave their services did not depend at all on the overt policies of leaders. For example, such a situation might exist where a group of subleaders needed an excuse to justify the convivial activities generated by their service in the association and therefore happily contributed their services without regard to any policies of the leaders simply in order to maintain the camaraderie they experienced in the association.

By providing jobs, certain kinds of vocational associations may also come close to liberating the overt policies of leaders from the demands of subleaders, particularly if the role of the subleader as it is defined in the culture is confined simply to doing his job and receiving his wage or salary without caring about or having a right to participate in the shaping of the overt policies of the association. In business organizations, rank-and-file employees are usually assumed to have only slight interest in the overt policies of the business other than those touching on their own wages, hours, and working conditions.

However, political associations, at least in the United States and certainly in New Haven, are more nearly avocational than vocational. (For the leaders, to be sure, they are often vocational—although paradoxically, the virtues of amateurism are so highly regarded that leaders whoe major occupation and source of income is politics often try to disguise the fact in order to avoid the epithet "professional politician.") Political associations, unlike business firms, do not produce services or commodities that can be openly sold for a price. Indeed the laws of the state of Connecticut as of other states flatly prohibit transactions of this kind. In New Haven, the amount of income legally or illegally secured by an association engaged in politics is tiny compared with that of a business firm with an equivalent number of full-time and part-time workers. Nor are nonfinancial rewards easily obtainable. The esteem among persons of high social standing that political officials seem to have enjoyed in New Haven in the nineteenth century has probably declined. Even the amount of influence open to a subleader is usually slight. (One minor subleader encountered in New Haven in the course of our study displayed his influence by "fixing" parking tickets for his friends. On investigation, it turned out that he fixed the tickets by paying the fines out of his own pocket.)

Despite the avocational character of political associations in New Haven, two processes help to reduce conflicts between the overt and covert policies of political leaders and to produce a loyal corps of subleaders who, while concerned with covert policies, are often indifferent to overt policies.

First, a prerequisite to success for both the overt and covert policies of political leaders ordinarily is to win elections and thereby attain the rights and powers of office. Office is necessary if jobs, contracts, and other favors are to be dispensed to subleaders; office is also necessary if overt policies are to be executed. Hence subleaders are motivated to win elections and to support whatever overt policies are needed to win, as long as these do not threaten covert postelection commitments.

Secondly, even if a subleader is initially attracted into an association because of the overt policies of the leaders, participation generates new rewards. Because an association provides opportunities for conviviality, it can come to fill a normal human need for friendliness, comradeship, respect, and social intercourse. And a subleader who participates in an association may strengthen his identification with it so that it becomes an extension of his own personality; the victories and defeats of the association are then equivalent to victories and defeats for the subleader himself.

These two processes, however, do not always eliminate conflict between the overt and covert policies of political leaders. Conflict is likely to arise, for example, whenever large elements of the political stratum are developing stricter standards of political morality. In particular, if the middle- and upper-class segments of the political stratum increase in size, then demands for extending civil service requirements, professionalism, public review, fixed procedures, and neutrality are likely to become more widespread and more insistent. Bureaucratization and middle-class influence in local policies are likely to go together. Conflicts may also arise if overt policies with seemingly great popularity among constituents require structural changes in the organization of government that would make it more difficult to honor traditional kinds of covert policies. In New Haven, . . . an attempt to reform the city charter produced such a conflict.

In these and many other similar cases, political leaders face a painful dilemma, for they must either fight the "organization" or lose the support of some of their constituents and perhaps even hitherto reliable followings. Either choice may involve electoral defeat and possibly the end of a political career.

DEMOCRACY, LEADERSHIP, AND MINORITY CONTROL

It is easy to see why observers have often pessimistically concluded that the internal dynamics of political associations create forces alien to popular control and hence to democratic institutions. Yet the characteristics I have described are not necessarily dysfunctional to a pluralistic democracy in which there exists a considerable measure of popular control over the policies of leaders, for minority control by leaders within associations is not necessarily inconsistent with popular control over leaders through electoral processes.

For example, suppose that (1) a leader of a political association feels a strong incentive for winning an election; (2) his constituents comprise most of the adult population of the community; (3) nearly all of his constituents are expected to vote; (4) voters cast their ballot without receiving covert rewards or punishments as a direct consequence of the way they vote; (5) voters give heavy weight to the overt policies of a candidate in making their decision as to how they will vote; (6) there are rival candidates offering alternative policies; and (7) voters have a good deal of information about the policies of the candidates. In these circumstances, it is almost certain that leaders of political associations would tend to choose overt policies they believed most likely to win the support of a majority of adults in the community. Even if the policies of political associations were usually controlled by a tiny minority of leaders in each association, the policies of the leaders who won elections to the chief executive offices in local government would tend to reflect the preferences of the populace. I do not mean to suggest that any political system actually fulfills all these conditions, but to the extent that it does the leaders who directly control the decisions of political associations are themselves influenced in their own choices of policies by their assumptions as to what the voting populace wants.

. . . In each of a number of key sectors of public policy, a few persons have great *direct* influence on the choices that are made; most citizens, by contrast, seem to have rather little direct influence. Yet it would be unwise to underestimate the extent to which voters may exert *indirect* influence on the decisions of leaders by means of elections.

In a political system where key offices are won by elections, where legality and constitutionality are highly valued in the political culture, and where nearly everyone in the political stratum publicly adheres to a doctrine of democracy, it is likely that the political culture, the prevailing attitudes of the political stratum, and the operation of the political system itself will be shaped by the role of elections. Leaders who in one context are enormously influential and even rather free from demands by their constituents may reveal themselves in another context to be involved in tireless efforts to adapt their policies to what they think their constituents want.

To be sure, in a pluralistic system wih dispersed inequalities, the direct influence of leaders on policies extends well beyond the norms implied in the classical models of democracy developed by political philosophers. But if the leaders lead, they are also led. Thus the relations between leaders, subleaders, and constituents produce in the distribution of influence a stubborn and pervasive ambiguity that permeates the entire political system.

ENDNOTES

1. On the extent of belief in this creed in two cities (Ann Arbor, Michigan, and Tallahassee, Florida) see James W. Prothro and Charles M. Grigg, "Fundamental Principles of Democracy: Bases of Agreement and Disagreement," *Journal of Politics*, *22* (1960), 276–94.

CONTRIBUTORS

Mark Abrams Survey Unit, Social Science Research Council, London

Lance Bennett Professor of Political Science, University of Washington

Bernard Berelson President, Population Council, New York City

Richard Brody Professor of Political Science, Stanford University

Walter Dean Burnham Professor of Political Science, Massachusetts Institute of Technology

Angus Campbell Professor of Sociology and Psychology and Director, Institute for Social Research, University of Michigan

Irving Crespi The Gallup Organization

Hadley Cantril Chairman of the Board, Institute for International Social Research and Research Associate, Department of Psychology, Princeton University

Philip Converse Professor of Sociology and Poltical Science and Program Director, Institute for Social Research, University of Michigan

Robert Dahl Professor of Political Science, Yale University

Murray Edelman Professor of Political Science, University of Wisconsin-Madison

Lloyd Free Director, Institute of International Social Research, Princeton University

Andrew Greeley Program Director, National Opinion Research Center, University of Chicago

Fred Greenstein Professor of Political Science, Princeton University

Edward Greenberg Associate Professor of Political Science, University of Colorado

Charles Grigg Director, Institute for Social Research, Florida State University

Herbert Hyman Professor of Sociology, Wesleyan University

V. O. Key formerly Jonathan Trumbull Professor of American History and Government, Harvard University, died 1963

Robert Lane Professor of Political Science, Yale University

Paul Lazarsfeld Emeritus Quitelet Professor of Social Science, Columbia University and Professor of Sociology, University of Pittsburg

Michael Lipsky Professor of Political Science, Massachusetts Institute of Technology

William McPhee Professor of Sociology, University of Colorado

Harold Mendelsohn Professor of Communications, University of Denver

Warren Miller Director, Center for Political Studies and Professor of Political Science, University of Michigan

Norman Nie Associate Professor of Political Science, University of Chicago

Benjamin Page Associate Professor of Political Science, University of Chicago

Michael Parenti Associate Professor of Political Science, State University of New York at Albany

John Pierce Associate Professor of Political Science, Washington State University

James Prothro Professor of Political Science, University of North Carolina

Howard Schuman Professor of Sociology, University of Michigan

David Sears Professor of Psychology and Political Science, University of California, Los Angeles

Paul Sheatsley Director, National Opinion Research Center, University of Chicago

Robert Stevenson Media Research Division, Research Service, United States Information Agency

Donald Stokes Dean, Woodrow Wilson School of Public and International Affairs, Princeton University

John Sullivan Associate Professor of Political Science, Indiana University

Sidney Verba Professor of Political Science, Harvard University

David Wise Author and Journalist

Frederick Wiseman Associate Professor of Marketing and Quantitative Methods, Northeastern University

SUBJECT INDEX

NAME INDEX